SWAT

Through the Millennia

From Prehistory to the Early Twentieth Century

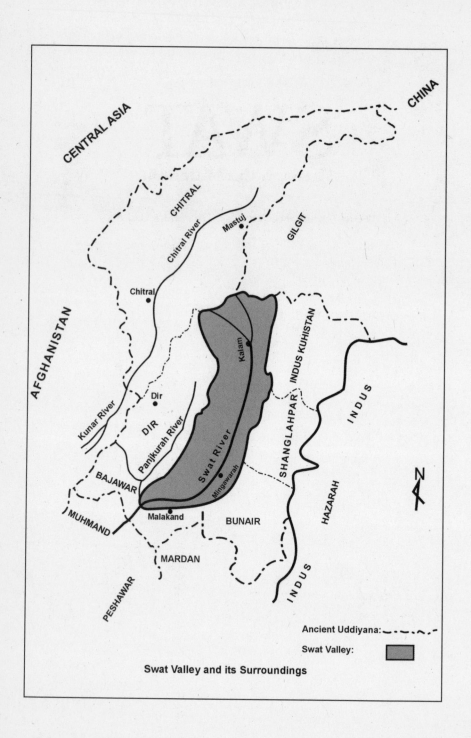

CENTRAL ASIA

CHINA

CHITRAL

Chitral River

Mastuj

GILGIT

AFGHANISTAN

Chitral

Kalam

INDUS KUHISTAN

Kunar River

Dir

DIR

Panjkurah River

Swat River

INDUS

BAJAWAR

Mingawarah

SHANGLAHPAR

HAZARAH

MUHMAND

Malakand

BUNAIR

INDUS

MARDAN

PESHAWAR

N

Ancient Uddiyana: ⋅—⋅—⋅—⋅

Swat Valley:

Swat Valley and its Surroundings

SWAT

Through the Millennia

From Prehistory to the Early Twentieth Century

SULTAN-I-ROME

OXFORD

UNIVERSITY PRESS

OXFORD
UNIVERSITY PRESS

Oxford University Press is a department of the University of Oxford.
It furthers the University's objective of excellence in research, scholarship,
and education by publishing worldwide. Oxford is a registered trade mark of
Oxford University Press in the UK and in certain other countries

Published in Pakistan by
Oxford University Press
No. 38, Sector 15, Korangi Industrial Area,
PO Box 8214, Karachi-74900, Pakistan

ISBN 978-0-19-070422-3

Typeset in Times New Roman
Printed on 55gsm Book Paper

Printed by Mas Printers, Karachi

To my Wife

CONTENTS

Author's Note   vii

Acknowledgements   viii

Abbreviations and Acronyms   xi

Introduction   xiii

1. Geographical Perspective   1

2. Prehistoric and Protohistoric   14

3. The Greeks and Swat   24

4. Mauryas to Shahis   49

5. Religious Perspective   74

6. Pre-Yusufzi Muslim Period   100

7. Yusufzi Occupation, Social System, and Mode of Ruling   123

8. The Mughals and Swat   161

9. Khushal Khan Khattak and Swat   178

10. 1707–1857 CE   200

11. 1857–1915 CE   233

12. Kuhistan   271

Glossary   277

Selected Bibliography   281

Index   299

AUTHOR'S NOTE

I have tried to write the local names and non-English words and terms to their greater conformity with their local pronunciation and rendering, and also to the transliteration rules. Therefore, in many cases the spellings of such names and terms, and titles of books, etcetera, in this work are different from those generally written. For example:

Mula	instead of *mulla* and *mullah*
Jargah	instead of *jarga/jirga/jirgah*
Dalah	instead of *dalla*
Malak	instead of *malik*
Waish	instead of *wesh*
Sirai	instead of *serai*
Mingawarah	instead of Mingora and Mingawara
Landakay	instead of Landakai
Yusufzi	instead of Yusufzai/Yusufzais

In general, diacritical marks are not used, but in the direct quotes, the spellings and the diacritical marks have been given as in the sources quoted. The inconsistency in the diacritical marks is because, as stated, they are reproduced as they appear in the sources quoted. In cases of non-availability of the same diacritical marks in the symbols or marks in the computer software, the nearest rendering of the symbols or diacritical marks have been given. Any omission may be an error or typo.

ACKNOWLEDGEMENTS

Research on subjects like this is always a difficult, painstaking undertaking. It took me years to bring this work to completion. A major hurdle and problem faced while working on this study was the scarcity and lack of availability of source material, especially primary sources. And this was also because of my being based and working in Swat—that too in the uncertain situation of the crisis that had prevailed in Swat since 2007 and could not be termed as fully normalised till date in 2020. The problem of the scarcity of source material was sharper in the case of the periods covered in Chapters 4 and 6.

With this background, work of such a nature could not be carried out and completed without the cooperation of others. A number of persons cooperated with me. They are mentioned as follows.

When working on my PhD dissertation, the cooperation I received from Saifur Rahman (Librarian, Department of History, University of Peshawar); Naheed Jahan (Librarian, Liaquat Memorial Library, Karachi); Tanveer Sajjad (Librarian, Department of Archaeology, Government of Pakistan, Karachi); Muqarab Khan, Akram Khan Marwat and others (at the Provincial Archives at Peshawar); Abdul Hamid (Librarian, Islamia College, Peshawar); Nasrullah Khan (Librarian, Pakistan Study Centre, University of Peshawar); Muhammad Sayyal (Librarian, Department of Archaeology, University of Peshawar); Sarfaraz Khan Marwat (Librarian, Pashto Academy, University of Peshawar); and the other staff members at these places and also at Dr Mahmood Husain Library (University of Karachi) proved useful also in this work.

The cooperation I received from Rustam Ali Qazalbash, Irfanullah Khan, and Liaqat Ali (at the Tribal Affairs Research Cell at Peshawar); Ali Akbar (Librarian), Shah Wazir Khan, and Khwajah Samiullah aka Tuta (at the Library of Govt. Jahanzeb College, Saidu Sharif, Swat); Prof. Subhani Gul; Shah Salam Khan (advocate); and Muhammad Islam also proved fruitful and productive.

Dr Tahira Tanweer, and Gauhar Ali helped in providing the source material especially relevant to the first chapters. Dr Luca M. Olivieri,

Dr Muhammad Farooq Swati, Dr Altaf Qadir, and Dr Ishtiaq Ahmad also helped by providing some source material.

Dr Tahira Tanweer, Dr Mohammad Usman FRCS, Shaukat Ali Sharar (architect), Dr Luca M. Olivieri, and Prof. Khurshid went through the earlier drafts of some of the chapters. Their critical evaluations and suggestions are a significant contribution.

Dr Rafiullah Khan deserves special mention as he provided source material, went through the earlier drafts of some of the chapters and gave valuable comments, discussed a number of points, and greatly assisted in the Glossary.

This work would have not been possible without the support of my elder brothers, Alamzeb Bacha and Sultan Mahmud, and my nephews Irfanullah Khan and Dr Abdullah. They shared the burden of some of my domestic responsibilities and facilitated me in continuing this work. My dear children and wife no doubt suffered on several occasions as I was unable to give them enough time while busy in this work; my wife also shouldered numerous responsibilities.

I am grateful to all the above mentioned and also to those who have shown interest in this work and helped me in many ways but whose names remained un-mentioned.

* * * *

While working on this study, I would give earlier drafts of some of the chapters to my students, because of non-availability of relevant material for some of the topics of the course entitled 'History of Swat (327 BCE–2013 CE)'. To be on the safe side, and ensure that the drafts given to my students were not pirated and published by someone else, I also sent these versions to research journals to be published under my name, and the risk of piracy was thus minimized. Therefore, earlier versions of some chapters and sections of this book have been published as research articles as follows:

Chapters 3 and 8	*Journal of the Pakistan Historical Society* (Karachi)
Chapter 5	*Journal of Ancient Civilizations* (Islamabad)
Chapter 7	*Hamdard Islamicus* (Karachi)
Chapter 9	*Journal of the Research Society of Pakistan* (Lahore)

Chapter 10   *Proceedings of the Two Day International
                              Conference on 150th Anniversary of the War
                              of Independence* (Peshawar); also in *Mutiny at
                              the Margins: New Perspectives on the Indian
                              Uprising of 1857* (New Delhi)

However, where necessary, new material has been added and
modifications made. Hence, wherever there is a difference in the
versions published as research articles and this book, the version in this
volume should be considered as authoritative. Some portions of the last
chapter are mainly a modified form of some sections of chapter 3 of my
book *Swat State (1915–1969): From Genesis to Merger*, conformed to
the context of this book.

ABBREVIATIONS
and
ACRONYMS

AC	Assistant Commissioner
BCE	Before Common Era, also called BC
BN	Bundle Number
c/c./ca.	about
CC	Chief Commissioner
CE	Common Era, also called AD
cf.	compare
CNWFPD	Confidential, North-West Frontier Provincial [Political] Diary
comp.	compiler; compiled by
COP	*Files of the Commissioner Office, Peshawar, at the Provincial Archives at Peshawar*
CPD	Commissioner Peshawar Division
CS	Chief Secretary
CSPD	Commissioner and Superintendent, Peshawar Division
DC	Deputy Commissioner
DCOP	*Files of the Deputy Commissioner Office, Peshawar, at the Provincial Archives at Peshawar*
DS	Deputy Secretary
DSC	Dir, Swat, and Chitral
ed.	editor; edited by (one person)
edn.	edition
eds.	editors; edited by (more than one person)
et al.	*et alii*, and others
FD	Foreign Department
ff.	and the following pages
FN	File Number
FO	Foreign Office
GI	Government of India
Govt.	Government
ibid.	*ibidem*, in the same place

MS/MS.	Manuscript
n.	note
NWFP	North-West Frontier Province
PA	Political Agent
passim	here and there
PD	Punjab and its Dependencies
RA	Raziyallahu Anha/Raziyallahu Anhu
repr.	reprint
rev.	revised, revised by, revision
SAW	Sallalahu Alaihi wa Alihi wa Sallam
Secy.	Secretary
SN	Serial Number
TARC	*Tribal Affairs Research Cell, Home and Tribal Affairs Department, Khyber Pukhtunkhwa, at Peshawar*
trans.	translation
TRCA	*Files of the Tribal Research Cell, Agencies, at the Provincial Archives at Peshawar*
viz.	that is to say
vol.	volume
vs.	versus

INTRODUCTION

The historic Valley of Swat is renowned for its picturesque landscape and scenic beauty. Inhabited for millennia, as is evident from the richness of the archaeological remains, sites, and graveyards excavated, it has been one of the centres of the Gandhara civilization. It has remained independent or semi-independent for most of its known history. Situated in a geo-strategic area of the world it has been invaded periodically by formidable armies, of which the huge deployment of the Pakistani armed forces in 2007 CE is a living example.

In the eleventh century CE it was occupied by Muslims and Muslim rule was established. In the sixteenth century, it was occupied by the Yusufzi Afghans, who emerged as the dominant segment of society. The Yusufzi, however, did not establish a state or government and lived in a tribal welter, divided into two opposite blocks. Although the Muslims occupied Swat in the eleventh century CE and the door for the spread of Islam was opened, the non-Muslims still formed a significant portion of the population. It was with the Yusufzi occupation that Islam became the dominant religion in Swat.

When I was working on my PhD dissertation, it was felt that the history of the Swat State (1915–1969 CE) could not be properly comprehended and evaluated without a proper understanding of the pre-state history. Therefore, although it did not fall within the period of my PhD dissertation, I dealt in detail with the pre-state history of Swat in two chapters. But one of the external examiners of the dissertation suggested that, not being the core period of the study, the detail about the pre-Swat State period should be condensed into ten or fifteen pages.

Thus, with an account of pre-state Swat history thus abridged, the need for a detailed study of the period remained greatly felt. This is the point of departure for this study. Therefore, I took it in earnest to conduct the required study and produce a separate work on the history of the earlier period.

Dealing with the Swat Valley, the objective of the study was to cover in detail the period from prehistory to the early twentieth century. This includes more specifically the following issues:

- Geographical perspective: This deals with the etymology of Swat, ancient political geography, Uddiyana vs. Gandhara, and the capital.
- Prehistoric and protohistoric: This deals with the periods mainly on the basis of the archaeological sources or the works of the archaeologists.
- The Greeks and Swat: mainly deals with Alexander's invasion of Swat and the related issues.
- Mauryas to Shahis: deals with and cover the Maurya, Indo-Greek, Indo-Scythian, Kushana, Turki Shahi and Hindu Shahi periods, in respect of Swat Valley.
- Religious Perspective: deals with the theme from prehistoric period.
- Pre-Yusufzi Muslim Period: deals with the period from the occupation of Swat by the Muslims in the eleventh century CE till its occupation by the Yusufzi in the sixteenth century.
- Yusufzi occupation, Social System, and Mode of Ruling: deals with the Yusufzi's occupation of Swat, the social system they evolved and their mode of ruling till the formation of Swat State in 1915.
- The Mughals and Swat: deals with the theme from the Mughal ruler Babur till Aurangzeb's time.
- Khushal Khan Khattak and Swat: deals with Khushal Khan Khattak's visit to Swat, and his contentions about Swat and the Yusufzi of Swat.
- 1707–1857 CE: deals with the period with special reference to Sayyad Ahmad Barailwi's visit to Swat, Sayyad Akbar Shah's rulership and rule (1849/1850–1857), the role of Swat in the War of Independence 1857 and its repercussions for Swat, the Akhund of Swat, and relations between the colonial Britons and Swat during the period.
- 1857–1915 CE: deals with the period with special reference of Swat and the British, the Malakand war of 1895 with reference to the Chitral crisis (1892–1895) and Umara Khan of Jandul, the Malakand war of 1897, and post-Malakand war years, with special reference to the internal power game and political dimension, British entrance in the local power game and the formation of Swat State in 1915.
- Kuhistan: deals with the Swat Kuhistan (a significant part of the Swat Valley), although in brief because of the scarcity of the source material, so the study should cover and encompass the entire Swat Valley.

Thus, beginning with details of its nomenclature and geography, the study continues with covering and thoroughly examining and discussing the prehistory and protohistoric periods of Swat, different aspects of Alexander of Macedonia's invasion, the period from the Mauryas to the Hindu Shahis, religious perspective of Swat, Muslims' occupation and pre-Yusufzi's period, the Yusufzi's occupation, their social system and mode of ruling, the Mughals and Swat, Khushal Khan Khattak and Swat, the period from 1707 till 1915 CE, and the Kuhistan.

The study is comprehensive, and systematic. Rich in factual information, it is heavily based on primary source material; but respected secondary sources are also utilized.

The study details the above topics and themes in the regional, international, geopolitical, and strategic contexts of the periods concerned. It enables the reader to gain the kind of knowledge that might have required the reading of a number of separate books. Each topic and theme discussed has been fully researched and presented with a knowledgeable and learned commentary.

Although falling in the scope of this study, the Gandhara civilization of Swat has not been covered, as I have no background knowledge of the theme, not being a student of archaeology and ancient civilizations.

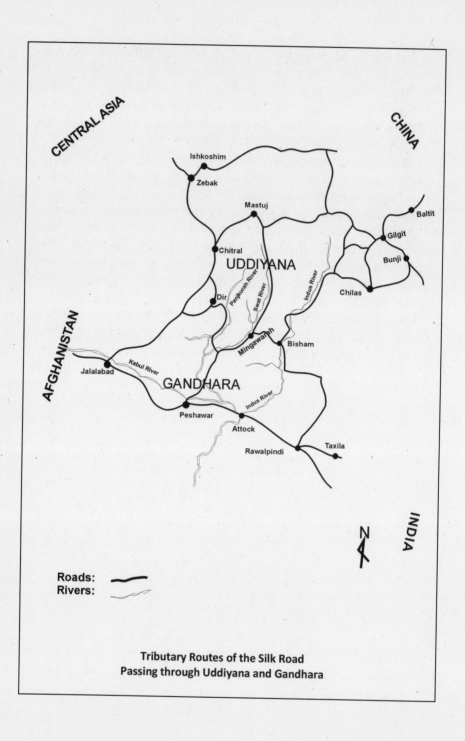

Tributary Routes of the Silk Road
Passing through Uddiyana and Gandhara

1

GEOGRAPHICAL PERSPECTIVE

ETYMOLOGY

Various theories have been put forward regarding the etymology of the word (noun) 'Swat'. The names found in ancient sources for the region of Swat are Uddiyana and Suvastu, with some variations in the spellings in ancient Sanskrit and Greek literatures, reflecting the scenic beauty of the valley and the name of the river, respectively. Additionally, 'Suvāstu', mentioned in the *Vedas* and also by Panini, means 'having good dwelling'.[1] Hiuen Tsiang (now spelled as Xuanzang; also Xuan Zang) has mentioned the Swat River as Su-po-fa-su-tu,[2] which is the. 'Subhavastu, the Swat river of the present day', which Arrian has termed as '*Soastos*'.[3] According to Samuel Beal 'Udyana (Prakrit, Ujjana), the *U-chang* of Fa-hian…is so called because of its garden-like appearance'.[4] It has also been contended:

> *The kingdom of Ou chhang.*—This name signifies *a garden*; in Sanskrit 'Udyana'; the country was so named because the park of a 'king of the wheel' (*Chakravarti raja*) was formerly there. Fa hian is the first Chinese by whom it is spoken of: according to his orthography, the name is 'Ou chang'; Soung yun writes it 'Ou chhang', and Hiouan thsang 'Ou chang na'. The last mentioned traveller preserves two other spellings, 'Ou san chhang' and 'Ou chha'. That which he has himself adopted is the most exact transcription the Chinese admits of, Oudyana, the *tch* or *dj* almost always being substituted for the soft dental in the transcription of Indian words.[5]

James Legge has given the spelling as 'Woo-chang';[6] and of Hiuen Tsiang's (Xuanzang's) is 'U-chang-na'.[7]

However, in a later study, Dr Abdur Rahman has disagreed/differed with the contentions of Samuel Beal and other authorities about the etymology of Uddiyana, in which it was asserted that Uddiyana was called so 'because of its garden-like appearance'. He has contended that the area got the name 'Uḍiyāna' because of the then tribe called 'Oḍis' which ruled at Gandhara.

> Oḍis have been a ruling tribe in Gandhāra and their history goes back to at least the fourth century B.C. [BCE] when they are first referred to by Alexander's historians under the name Oṛa correctly identified by Stein with Oḍigrām/Uḍigrām in Swāt.... The Oḍis, it seems, had been so dominant in Swāt that the whole valley came to be known as Uḍiyāna, that is, "the Land of Oḍis".[8]

He, moreover, has contended that 'at the time of Beal's interpretation of the word, the Oḍis were not known'.[9]

While dealing with the name Udegram/Udigram, Aurel Stein has stated that 'the second part is the term grām (Sanskrit grāma), "village".' As far 'the first part Uḍe-, also heard as Uḍi-' is concerned, after dealing with its different pronunciations, he has asserted: 'Thus the temptation is great to recognize in Arrian's...the Greek rendering of an earlier form of this name Uḍe-, and to derive this name itself from the ancient Sanskrit name of Swāt, Uḍḍiyana.'[10] Giuseppe Tucci also has analyzed Urdi, Aurddi, Uḍi and Wu ch'a, Yü ti yen and has contended that 'Udi, Urḍi, Udri, Uḍe is the name of another tribe which confederated with the Assakenói and probably represents an ethnic group related to them, but quite separate'.[11] And 'as regards the Urdi (inhabitants of Ora).... the change of a dental d into ḍ can be explained considering that Uḍḍi may be a local pronunciation which accounts for the Ora of the Greek historians influenced by the frication characteristic of those dialects'.[12] He, moreover, at another place has contended that the name 'Urdi (Ora)....cannot be separated from Oḍḍiyāna < Aurdiyāna, Audriyāna', which became the capital of the federation after Alexander's destruction of Massaga, 'thus giving its name to the country'.[13]

Taking the contentions of Aurel Stein, Giuseppe Tucci, and Dr Abdur Rahman, it can be said that it was from Odis/Udis that Odigram/ Udigram/Udegram took its name referring to the village or headquarter or capital of the Odis/Udis and Swat as Odiyana/Udiyana, that is the land of the Odis/Udis. It is to be noted that 'the real name of Swāt was not Udyāna but Uḍḍiyāna'.[14]

Akhun Darwizah has given interesting background of the etymology of Swat. According to him, Sultan Bahram and Sultan Fakhal were two brothers among the Sultans of Panj. When the line of rulers reached these two brothers, Sultan Fakhal proceeded to the hills of Bajawar,

Swat, and Kashmir, and brought the people of these areas under his suzerainty. After his death, his sons disputed in the State of Swat and fought a great war against each other. When the news of the war reached their mother, and she inquired about the affair, she cursed this state with the imprecation that the Almighty should not bring normalcy and peace to this state for long years. And this state was named 'Swat' in the meaning of 'one where cries or tumult are raised' (غوغا کردہ شدہ).[15]

Although not ancient ones, it would not be out of place to mention the theories of etymologies of the other names of Swat. One states that it is derived from 'Suvastu'[16] or 'Suastus',[17] the name given to the river traversing the Swat Valley, in ancient Sanskrit and Greek literature respectively. Another claim that it is derived from the word 'Sweta' (سویتا),[18] meaning 'white', which describes the lucid and crystal clear water of the Swat River. Yet another claim that the plain valley was a lake and shone owing to the rays of the sun. It was consequently called 'Suadat' (سُوادت), meaning 'shiny place', which eventually became 'Swat'.[19]

Some believe that, as it was forested with a fertile black soil, the valley seemed black and the Muslim invaders called it 'Aswad' (اَسوَد), an Arabic word meaning black, and with the passage of time it became 'Sawad' (سَوَاد).[20] Babur and historians of the Mughal period call it 'Sawād'[21] which later became 'Swat' (سوات).[22] Local contemporary writers of the Mughal period such as Khushal Khan Khattak, refer to it as 'Swat' and not 'Sawad'.[23]

Yet another contention is that 'Swat' is derived from the Arabic word 'Sawt' (صوت) meaning sound and echo, as the surrounding high mountains reverberate and sounds echo in the valley.[24] In support of this contention, it can be said that in the villages situated near the banks of the river, and also the streams, the echo of the noise of the water is heard at night especially in spring and summer, when the water rises.[25] Whatever the origin, the name has been written as 'Swat' (صوات) in local writings before[26] and after[27] the emergence of Swat State.

However, the Muslim invaders of Swat were neither Arabs nor was their language Arabic. They were from Afghanistan with their own languages. Therefore, when they had no command over Arabic nor did they speak it in daily life, it is unlikely that an Arabic name would have been given to the land they conquered. The Arabic etymology to the words 'Sawt' (صوت) and 'Aswad' (اَسوَد) has been attributed later.

Still another theory, mentioned by Abdul Halim Asar, is that the word 'Swat' is made up of two components, i.e. 'Su' (سُ) meaning sun, pronounced in the ancient Syriac way, and 'At' (اَتْ) meaning 'earth'. Thus, the word 'Suat' (سُوَاتْ) means the land attributed to the sun. This meaning has been put forward because in ancient times the sun god was worshiped here, or the valley was open and bright with the light of the sun.[28]

However, as stated earlier, the names found in ancient sources for the region of Swat are 'Uddiyana'[29] and 'Suvastu', with some variations in the spellings.

It must be noted and highlighted here that, in the context of the discussion in this section, or the preceding text, 'Swat' applies to or means not the present-day Swat District or the former Swat State's (1915–1969 CE) area, but the Swat Valley.

ANCIENT POLITICAL GEOGRAPHY

One of the sources has stated that Uddiyana 'lay to the north of Peshawar on the Swat river, but from the extent assigned to it by Hiuen Tsiang the name probably covered the whole hill-region south of the Hindu Kush and the Dard country from Chitral to the Indus'.[30] Although the geographical boundaries of Uddiyana have been stated differently by different writers, according to Dr Muhammad Farooq Swati: 'It is, no doubt, to be identified with the region situated adjacent and to the north of Gandhāra as a separate state.'[31] He, moreover, has asserted:

> Uḍḍiyāna, thus, was comprised of the modern districts of Swāt, Dīr, Chitral and, the Bājaur [Bajawar] and Malakaṇḍ Agencies. It also included the Swāt and Indus *kōhistāns*, in the north and east respectively. It was bounded by the offshoots of the Hindu-Kush—separating it from Central Asia, Afghanistan and ancient Gandhāra—in the north-west, west and south respectively. The Indus in the east separated it from the rest of the South Asian sub-continent.[32]

This means that the present-day (2020 CE) Malakand Division and the area reaching in the east up to the right bank of the Indus was in fact Uddiyana. Dr Muhammad Farooq Swati's further contention is that Uddiyana and Suvastu were names of two different geographical units; the former denoted an ancient province and comprised the whole of the territory of the present-day Malakand Division extending down to the

Malakand mountains, which separated it from another ancient province Gandhara in the south, while the latter, being one of the several valleys or a smaller geographical unit, occupied the heart of Uddiyana.[33]

According to this viewpoint, Swat is a portion of Uddiyana while some others take Uddiyana for Swat alone. For example Woo-Chang, or Udyâna;[34] and that 'Udyâna meaning "the park"; just north of the Punjâb, the country along the Subhavastu, now called the Swat'.[35] Alexander Cunningham has given the heading Udyâna, or Swât and has stated:

> Hwen Thsang travelled...to *U-chang-na*, or *Udyâna*, which was situated on the river *Su-po-fa-su-tu*, the *Subhavastu* and *Suvastu* of Sanskrit, the *Suastus* of Arrian, and the *Swât* or Süât river of the present day. It is called *U-chang* by the earlier pilgrims Fa-Hian and Sung-yun, which is a close transcript of *Ujjâna*, the Pali form of Udyâna.[36]

Alexander Cunningham and other authorities, however, have also included territories outside Swat or beyond the boundaries of the valley of the Swat River and its tributaries, in Uddiyana, because the political boundaries of the Kingdom of Uddiyana were extended to the territories beyond the geographical limits of Uddiyana proper or 'Suvastus'. Aurel Stein has also referred to this change by stating that he 'was fortunately able to give' the ruler of Swat State in 1926 'a piece of information.... that the union of Swât and Bunēr accomplished under his rule had already been duly recorded by the early Chinese pilgrims'.[37] H.A. Deane has considered 'the Swat valley, and neighbourhood' as 'the principal portion of the old province of Udyāna'.[38]

Besides, Thomas Holdich has stated about Fa-Hein (now spelled as Faxian and also Fa Xian) that fifteen day journey from Darel 'took him to Wuchung (Udyana), where he remained during the rains. Thence he went to "south" to Sin-ho-to (Swat) and finally "descended" into Gandhara, or the Upper Punjab'.[39] This, in other words, means, Fa-Hein (Faxian) has stated and considered Uddiyana and Swat different entities. At another place, Holdich, however, has stated that 'crossing the Indus, Fa Hian came to Wuchung, which is identified with Udyana, or Upper Swat, and there he remained during the rains'.[40]

Significantly, Hiuen Tsiang (Xuanzang) has stated that 'the country of U-chang-na' is 'about 5000 li in circuit',[41] that is approximately 833 miles in circuit.[42] But the Swat Valley by itself has no such extent. This means that Oddiyana/Uddiyana/Udyana was not only the Swat Valley but also encompassed and contained the neighbouring areas. That was why this assertion that 'from the extent assigned to it by Hiuen Tsiang the name probably covered the whole hill-region south of Hindu Kush and the Dard country from Chitral to the Indus'[43] seems correct and justifiable.

'As a matter of fact, Udyana…never' remained 'a political unit throughout its history except for brief periods'[44] and its political geography changed, that was why the capitals and territory, or units, of the Kingdom of Uddiyana varied at different periods of history. So, these alien territories became its political units and have been mentioned its parts and parcels. That was why some writers take Uddiyana only for Swat, namely Swat Valley, and some also include in it the adjoining territories.

It can be inferred from the sources that Udyana, originally Uḍḍiyana[45] and Ujjana[46] of Prakrit, was the name and territory of the Swat Valley, namely the valley of the Swat River: which is the 'Su-po-fa-su-tu'[47] of Hiuen Tsiang (Xuanzang), the Subhavastu[48] and Suvastu[49] of Sanskrit, the Souastos,[50] Suastus,[51] Soastos[52] and Souastênê[53] of the Greeks and the Swat Valley of the present-day. Thus 'Uddiyana' and 'Suvastu' were basically names of the same geographical unit, but with the passage of time, both differed due to political developments or changes in the political geography.

Uddiyana vs. Gandhara

A misconception found in certain quarters is that Swat had been part of Gandhara. It needs to be clarified that though Swat, the ancient Uddiyana, had commonalities in artistic and cultural progress with Gandhara, spread over centuries, it had been 'considered as a separate entity geographically and ethnically'.[54] Giuseppe Tucci has aptly contended that 'Uḍḍiyāna was not included in Gandhāra, though the chiefs of Gandhāra may have kept under control Uḍḍiyāna or both countries may have been ruled over by other kings like the Shāhis of Kabul or the kings of Ohind; but Uḍḍiyāna was a well-defined province with its own geographical features and the peculiarities of its people'.[55] Therefore, Swat or Uddiyana may have been subservient to Gandhara or Gandhara may have had held sway over it as well, but Swat or Uddiyana has neither been integral part of Gandhara geographically nor has remained its part politically at all times.

Swat did not remain a geographical part of Gandhara. The misconception, it seems, is created mainly by the art commonly called and referred to as 'Gandhara art' having prevailed in Swat, the remains of which abound throughout the country. Although Swat was one of the cradles or centres of the civilization called 'Gandhara civilization', it never means that Swat was part of Gandhara geographically. K.M. Verma also has stated: 'It is however, inferred that this art (Gandhara Art) begins not in ancient Gandhara country, which apparently corresponds to the present Peshawar valley and its surrounding tracts, but in Swat Valley, which is known in ancient times as Udyana (or Uddiyana or even Oddiyana).'[56]

It is noteworthy that the map of the Asokan Empire given by V.A. Smith, on the last page of his book: *Asoka: The Buddhist Emperor of India*,[57] has shown Uddiyana and Gandhara separately. Similarly, in map-II of 'Northern India and Adjacent countries in the period of Menander or mid-second century B.C.', given by A.K. Narain on the second last page of his book, *The Indo-Greeks*,[58] Uddiyana and Gandhara have also been shown as separate identities.

THE CAPITAL

Hiuen Tsiang (Xuanzang) has stated that Mungali (Mung-kie-li) a town of 'about 16 or 17 li in circuit and thickly populated', was the capital of the Kingdom[59] of Uddiyana. Vivien de St. Martin and Stein have identified it as Manglawar;[60] and according to Alexander Cunningham it 'is probably the Mangora of Wilford's surveyor, Mogal Beg, and the *Manglora* of General Court's map'.[61] Whereas Harold Deane too has stated that the capital of the old province of Uddiyana in Hiuen Tsiang time was Mungali, or Mung Kie-li. Deane says that according to Cunningham's assertion it 'could be identified with Minglaur'. Cunningham however 'also thought Mingaur, or Mingora [Mingawarah] of Wilford's Surveyor, to be the same place'. Deane, however, has asserted that 'the identity of Minglaur with Mungali is undoubted'.[62]

Giuseppe Tucci—who has stated that Darel was 'the first capital of Swāt according to the local tradition…, or possibly capital for a certain time of Swāt'[63]—has contended that Mingawarah, not Manglawar, was the capital of Uddiyana. While dealing with the previous identification of 'Mēng chie li' with Manglawar, he has stated that 'it seemed that this identification…suggested by Vivien de Saint Martin and then universally accepted, could not be rejected. But in rereading carefully Hsüan tsang, I began to feel some doubts about the correspondence of the Chinese transcription with the name of Mangalaor.' After elaborating about the Chinese transcription, he has asserted: 'My doubt of the accuracy of the identification of Mêng chie li with Mangalaor [Manglawar] was only strengthened by a careful examination of the ground around Mangalaor, bare as it is of ruins and archaeologically very poor compared to the many places in Swat.'[64] He has given the supposed grounds for his identification of or terming Meng chie li as Mingawarah.[65]

According to Dr Muhammad Farooq Swati, in the northern territory Darel 'is another place mentioned as the capital of ancient Uḍḍiyāna. It seems, however, that the capital of Swāt kept shifting from one place to another in the past.'[66] This supports the proposition that, as the political geography of Uddiyana did not remain static, its capital also changed from time to time due to the shift in political hegemony from one part or portion or locality to another. D.H. Muncherji seems justified in claiming, in 1959, 'To begin with, it is almost certain that Udegram was the capital of the country or principality to which it gave its name.'[67]

Muncherji's contention is augmented by Giuseppe Tucci, who, as stated earlier, has contended that Udi, 'is the name of another tribe which confederated with the Assakenói and probably represents an ethnic group related to them, but quite separate';[68] and that, 'There is reason to believe that the northern neighbours of them were the Aurdi… whose chief town was Urdi, Ora. No reference in Arrian authorizes the conclusion that the people of Bazira and Ora were the same as the Assakenoi.'[69] Dr Abdur Rahman too, in a later study, has contended that, 'Oḍis have been a ruling tribe in Gandhāra and their history goes back to at least the fourth century B.C. [BCE] when they are first referred to by Alexander's historians under the name Oṛa correctly identified by Stein with Oḍigrām/Uḍigrām in Swāt'. And that, 'the Oḍis, it seems, had been so dominant in Swāt that the whole valley came to be known as Uḍiyāna, that is, "the Land of Oḍis".'[70]

Keeping in view full accounts of the relevant sources, Stein's and Martin's contentions do not seem sound; and Mungali is certainly Mingawarah. In support of this contention, I give Muncherji's observation, in which he has asserted:

Till now the ancient Mang-chi-Li [Meng-chi-li] of Yuan Chwang was identified with Mangalor [Manglawar], but a careful study of the account of the Chinese pilgrim led Prof. Tucci to doubt this identification drawn by Stein and others. This doubt was confirmed by the study of the actual ground at Mangalor. The site seemed to be archaeologically very poor and no trace of the pottery of different colours, as mentioned by Chinese pilgrims, was to be found. There were no walls or remains of large monuments to give an impression that this place was once the capital of Udyana.

The situation at Mingora [Mingawarah]....make it quite clear that Mingora and not Mangalor [Manglawar] is the site of the ancient Meng-chi-Li.[71]

Above all, the distance between Meng-chi-li and the *stupa* that is near Ghaligay or the one above Naway Kalay (neighbouring Abuhah and Kutah) do not correspond with Manglawar but corresponds with Mingawarah. 'The identification of Manglawar as Mêṅg-ch'ieh-li, especially after the discovery of Butkara I (T'o-lo), is completely baseless (like the identification of mount Aornos in the present-day Pir-sar for instance; Olivieri personal communication)'.[72]

The discovery of urban layers and their excavation at Barama I, 'indicate that Barama-I and Butkara-I were parts of a larger ancient settlement, or urban area, approximately coinciding with the nowadays Mingora [Mingawarah] city area'.[73] This too suggests that the ancient Mungali and Meng-chi-li was the present-day Mingawarah, not the Manglawar.

NOTES

1. Giuseppe Tucci, 'On Swāt. The Dards and Connected Problems', *East and West* (Rome), 27/1–4 (December 1977), 39.
2. [Hiuen Tsiang], *Chinese Accounts of India: Translated from the Chinese of Hiuen Tsiang*, trans. and annotated by Samuel Beal, Vol. 2 (new edn., Calcutta: Susil Gupta (India) Limited, 1958), 167.
3. Ibid., n. 4.
4. Ibid., 166 n. 1.
5. [Fa Hian], *The Pilgrimage of Fa Hian, from the French edition of the Foe Koue Ki of MM. Remusat, Klaproth, and Landresse with additional notes and illustrations*, trans. and ed. by anonymous (Calcutta: The "Bangabasi" Office, 1912), 50 n. 1. Also see Tucci, 'On Swāt. The Dards and Connected Problems', 65.
6. Fa-Hein, *A Record of Buddhistic Kingdoms*, trans. and annotated by James Legge (repr., New Delhi: Munshiram Manoharlal Publishers Pvt. Ltd., 1991), 28.
7. [Tsiang], *Chinese Accounts of India: Translated from the Chinese of Hiuen Tsiang*, Vol. 2, 166. Also see Aurel Stein, *On Alexander's Track to the Indus: Personal*

Narrative of Explorations on the North-West Frontier of India (repr., Karachi: Indus Publications, 1995), 57.

8. Abdur Rahman, 'Ethnicity of the Hindu Shahīs', *Journal of the Pakistan Historical Society* (Karachi), 51/3 (July–September 2003), 9.

9. Ibid., 10 n. 23. Dr Muhammad Farooq Swati also stated that some of the scholars have now started thinking that Uddiyana means the place or land of Uddiyan, a tribe or race (Dr Muhammad Farooq Swati, personal communication with the author, at the Department of Archaeology, University of Peshawar, 20 November 2000).

10. Stein, *On Alexander's Track to the Indus*, 60; Aurel Stein, *An Archaeological tour in Upper Swāt and Adjacent Hill Tracts* (Calcutta: Government of India, Central Publication Branch, 1930), 40.

11. Tucci, 'On Swāt. The Dards and Connected Problems', 39.

12. Ibid.

13. Giuseppe Tucci, 'The Tombs of the Asvakayana-Assakenoi', in Giuseppe Tucci, *On Swāt. Historical and Archaeological Notes*, with introduction by Domenico Faccenna, eds. P. Callieri and A. Filigenzi, reprint of the original 1997 edition, with preface by M. Ashraf Khan (Islamabad: Taxila Institute of Asian Civilizations, 2013), 117–18.

14. Tucci, 'On Swāt. The Dards and Connected Problems', 65 n. 89a.

15. See Akhun Darwizah, *Tazkiratul Abrar-i wal Ashrar* (Persian) (Peshawar: Islami Kutub Khanah, n.d.), 107–8.

16. The Swat River has been mentioned as 'Suvastu' also in *Rigveda*. See *The Hymns of the Rigveda*, Eng. trans. Ralph T.H. Griffith (2nd edn., Kotagiri (Nilgiri), 1896), Hymn XIX, Agni, verse 37 (p. 314) downloaded in pdf form from http://www.sanskritweb.net; accessed also on http://www.hinduwebsite.com/sacredscripts/rigintro.htm on 20/8/2019.

17. [Alexander Cunningham], *Cunningham's Ancient Geography of India*, ed. with introduction and notes by Surendranath Majumdar Sastri (Calcutta: Chuckervertty, Chatterjee & Co., Ltd., 1924), 93–5.

18. Allah Bakhsh Yusufi, *Yusufzai* (Urdu) (Karachi: Muhammad Ali Educational Society, 1960), 457; *Malakand, 1958–68: A Decade of Progress*, with foreword by Mohammad Humayun Khan (n.p., n.d.), 4; *Population Census of Pakistan 1961: Census Report of Tribal Agencies*, Parts 1–3, *General Description, Population Tables and Village Statistics* (Karachi: Manager of Publications, Government of Pakistan, n.d.), I–33; *Population Census of Pakistan 1972: District Census Report, Swat* (Karachi: Manager of Publications, Government of Pakistan, 1975), 3.

19. Saranzeb Swati, *Tarikh Riyasat-i Swat* (Pashto) (Peshawar: Azeem Publishing House, 1984), 64.

20. Oral tradition. Also see Mahmud Danishwar, *Kafiristan aur Chitral-Dir-Swat ki Sayahat* (Urdu), trans. Khalil Ahmad (2nd revised edn., Lahore: West Pak Publishing Company Limited, October 1953), 299; Muhammad Asif Khan, *Tarikh-i Riyasat-i Swat wa Sawanih-i Hayat Baniy-i Riyasat-i Swat Hazrat Miangul Gul Shahzadah Abdul Wadud Khan Bacha Sahib* (Pashto), with *dibachah*, *hisah awal*, *saluramah hisah* and *hisah pinzamah* by Muhammad Asif Khan] (Printed by Ferozsons Ltd., Peshawar, [1958]), 37; Swati, *Tarikh Riyasat-i Swat*, 64.

21. See Zahirud-din Muhammad Babur, *Babur-Nama*, trans. from the original Turki text by Annette S. Beveridge (repr., Lahore: Sang-e-Meel Publications, 1987), 372–3, 375–6; Abū 'l-Fazl ᵉAllāmī, *The Āᵉīn-i Akbarī*, trans. from the original Persian by H.S. Jarrett, 2nd edn. corrected and further annotated by Jadunath Sarkar, Vol. 2, *A Gazetteer and Administrative Manual of Akbar's Empire and Past History of India* (3rd edn. repr. from 2nd edn. of 1949, New Delhi: Oriental Books Reprint Corporation, 1978), 397; Mahomed Kasim [Muhammad Qasim] Ferishta, *History of the Rise of the Mahomedan [Muhammadan] Power in India, till the Year A.D. 1612*, trans. from the original Persian of Mahomed Kasim Ferishta by John Briggs, Vol. 2 (repr., Lahore: Sang-e-Meel Publications, 1977), 35, 259.

22. Oral tradition. Also see Khan, *Tarikh Riyasat-i Swat wa Sawanih-i Hayat Baniy-i Riyasat-i Swat Hazrat Miangul Gul Shahzadah Abdul Wadud Khan Bacha Sahib*, 37; Muhammad Asif Khan, *The Story of Swat as told by the Founder Miangul Abdul Wadud Badshah Sahib to Muhammad Asif Khan*, preface, introduction and appendices by Muhammad Asif Khan, and trans. preface and trans. by Ashruf Altaf Husain (Printed by Ferozsons Ltd., Peshawar, 1963), xxiv.

23. See Khushal Khan Khattak, *Swat Nama of Khushal Khan Khattak*, edited and trans. in to English by Shakeel Ahmad, with preface by Raj Wali Shah Khattak (Peshawar: Pashto Academy, n.d.), passim; Khushal Khan Khattak, *Swat Namah da Khushal Khan Khattak* (Pukhtu) with *muqadimah, tahqiq aw samun* by Hamesh Khalil (Akurah Khattak: Markazi Khushal Adabi wa Saqafati Jargah Regd., 1986), passim. Nevertheless, MS of the *Swat Namah* bears once, the 'Swad' for 'Swat.' See MS No. ق [Qaaf]-569, *Swat Namah da Khushal Khan Khattak* (Library of the Pashto Academy, University of Peshawar), 3.

24. This contention can be augmented by the narration of Hiuen Tsiang (Xuanzang) who has stated: 'There are high crags and deep caverns, and placid streams winding through the valleys: sometimes are heard the sounds of people's voices, sometimes the reverberation of musical notes.' [Tsiang], *Chinese Accounts of India: Translated from the Chinese of Hiuen Tsiang*, Vol. 2, 169.

25. My personal observation, having hailed from both the river and a stream side village. Although the stream usually remain dry now, previously it was not so.

26. For instance, see letter from various *khan*s of Swat to Mr Udney, Commissioner Peshawar Division, 22 Jamadi-ul-Awal, AH 1310/13 December 1892, *Files of the Commissioner Office Peshawar, at the Provincial Archives at Peshawar*, Bundle No. 74, Serial No. 2118; Applications of Latif Khan, Aladand, to Lieut. Governor, Punjab, 20, 27 and 28 May 1886, *Files of the Frontier Foreign Department, at the Provincial Archives at Peshawar*, Bundle No. 18, Serial No. 128; Darwizah, *Tazkiratul Abrar-i wal Ashrar*, 93, ff; MS, *Jang Namah* (Persian, verse), scribed by Mirza Abdul Haq, date torn. *Personal Collection of Ziaullah Khan, Gulkadah, Swat*, 39 and back pages of pages 66, 69, 71, 115, passim (its photo-state copy also is in my, Sultan-i-Rome's, personal collection). MS of the *Swat Namah* also bears once along with its title the name such. See MS No. ق [Qaaf]–569 (Library of the Pashto Academy, University of Peshawar), title, 10.

27. For instance, see Muhammad Ali Qasuri, *Mushahidat Kabul wa Yaghistan* (Karachi: Anjuman Taraqi Urdu, n.d.), passim; Taj Muhammad Khan Zaibsar, *Uruj-i Afghan* (Pashto verse), Vol. 2 (Riyasat-i Swat, 1361 AH), 1, 2, 85; 'Kitab No. 55: Mashir Kuz Swat', Iqrar Namah No. nil, 20 October 1945, p. nil, *District*

Record Room, at Gulkadah, Swat; Muhammad Yusuf Hazrawi, *Sir-i Swat: Hisah Awal* (Urdu) (Calcutta: Manager Aksirat-i Hind Dawa Khanah, [1945]), passim; Letters to Habibullah Khan aka Miandam Khan, *Personal Collection of Bahadar Khan, Fatihpur, Swat*; W.W. Hunter, *Hamaray Hindustani Musalman*, Urdu trans. Sadiq Husain (Lahore: Qaumi Kutub Khanah, n.d.), 49 n. 1, 60, 65 n. 1.

28. See Abdul Halim Asar, *Swat da Tarikh pah Ranra kay* (Pashto) (Bajawar: Darul Ishaat Bajawar, n.d.), 9–25 cf. Khan, *The Story of Swat as told by the Founder Miangul Abdul Wadud Badshah Sahib to Muhammad Asif Khan*, xxiv.

29. For details about Uddiyana being Swat and not Orissa, as it is asserted by some Indian scholars that Uddiyana is Orrisa, see Luca Maria Olivieri, 'Guru Padmasambhava in Context: Archaeological and Historical Evidence from Swat/ Uddiyana (c. 8th century CE)', *Journal of Bhutan Studies* (Thimphu), 34 (Summer 2016), 20–42.

30. [Tsiang], *Chinese Accounts of India: Translated from the Chinese of Hiuen Tsiang*, Vol. 2, 166 n. 1.

31. Muhammad Farooq Swati, *Gandhara Art in the Swat Valley, Pakistan: A Study Based on the Peshawar University Collection*, Vol. 1, (*Text*) (Unpublished PhD Dissertation, Faculty of Oriental Studies, University of Cambridge, 1996), 11.

32. Ibid., 12.

33. Dr Muhammad Farooq Swati, personal communication with the author, at the Department of Archaeology, University of Peshawar, 8 February 1999.

34. Fa-Hein, *A Record of Buddhistic Kingdoms*, 28.

35. Ibid., n. 5.

36. [Cunningham], *Cunningham's Ancient Geography of India*, 93–4.

37. Stein, *On Alexander's Track to the Indus*, 67.

38. H.A. Deane, 'Note on Udyāna and Gandhāra', *Journal of the Royal Asiatic Society of Great Britain and Ireland* (October 1896), 655 (Stable URL: http://www.jstor.org/stable/25207806; accessed: 16/05/2011).

39. Thomas Holdich, *The Gates of India: Being an Historical Narrative* (1st edn. published in Pakistan, Quetta: Gosha-e-Adab, 1977), 179.

40. Ibid., 184.

41. [Tsiang], *Chinese Accounts of India: Translated from the Chinese of Hiuen Tsiang*, Vol. 2, 166.

42. [Cunningham], *Cunningham's Ancient Geography of India*, 94; Yusufi, *Yusufzai*, 457.

43. [Tsiang], *Chinese Accounts of India: Translated from the Chinese of Hiuen Tsiang*, Vol. 2, 166 n. 1.

44. D.H. Muncherji, 'Swat: The Garden of Asoka', *Pakistan Quarterly* (Karachi), 9/3 (1959), 43.

45. Stein, *On Alexander's Track to the Indus*, 13.

46. [Tsiang], *Chinese Accounts of India: Translated from the Chinese of Hiuen Tsiang*, Vol. 2, 166 n. 1.

47. Ibid., 167.

48. Ibid., n. 4; [Cunningham], *Cunningham's Ancient Geography of India*, 93.

49. [Cunningham], *Cunningham's Ancient Geography of India*, 93.

50. J.W. M'crindle, *The Invasion of India by Alexander the Great: As Described by Arrian, Q Curtius, Diodoros, Plutarch and Justin*, with introduction by J.W. M'crindle (repr., Karachi: Indus Publications, 1992), 61 n. 1.

51. [Cunningham], *Cunningham's Ancient Geography of India*, 93.
52. [Tsiang], *Chinese Accounts of India: Translated from the Chinese of Hiuen Tsiang*, Vol. 2, 167 n. 4.
53. M'crindle, *The Invasion of India by Alexander the Great*, 59 n. 5.
54. Giuseppe Tucci, 'Preliminary Report on an Archaeological Survey in Swat', *East and West* (Rome), 9/4 (December 1958), 324 n. 1.
55. Ibid.; Giuseppe Tucci, 'Preliminary Report on an Archaeological Survey in Swat', in Tucci, *On Swāt. Historical and Archaeological Notes*, with introduction by Domenico Faccenna, eds. P. Callieri and A. Filigenzi, 62 n. 1.
56. Quoted in Muhammad Habibullah Khan Khattak, *Buner: The Forgotten Part of Ancient Uddiyana* (Karachi: By the Author, Department of Archaeology and Museums, Government of Pakistan, 1997), 4.
57. See Vincent A. Smith, *Asoka: The Buddhist Emperor of India* (repr., Delhi: S. Chand & Co., 1957).
58. See A.K. Narain, *The Indo-Greeks* (repr., Oxford: At the Clarendon Press, 1962).
59. [Tsiang], *Chinese Accounts of India: Translated from the Chinese of Hiuen Tsiang*, Vol. 2, 167–8.
60. See ibid., n. 9; Stein, *On Alexander's Track to the Indus*, 76.
61. [Cunningham], *Cunningham's Ancient Geography of India*, 95.
62. Deane, 'Note on Udyāna and Gandhāra', 655–6.
63. Tucci, 'On Swāt. The Dards and Connected Problems', 61.
64. Tucci, 'Preliminary Report on an Archaeological Survey in Swat', 286.
65. For his contention, see ibid., 286–8, 292, 312.
66. Muhammad Farooq Swāti, 'Recent Discovery of Buddhist Sites in the Swāt Valley', *Āthāriyyāt* (Peshawar), 1 (1997), 154.
67. Muncherji, 'Swat: The Garden of Asoka', 43.
68. Tucci, 'On Swāt. The Dards and Connected Problems', 39.
69. Tucci, 'Preliminary Report on an Archaeological Survey in Swat', in Tucci, *On Swāt. Historical and Archaeological Notes*, with introduction by Domenico Faccenna, eds. P. Callieri and A. Filigenzi, 62 n. 1.
70. Rahman, 'Ethnicity of the Hindu Shahīs', 9.
71. Muncherji, 'Swat: The Garden of Asoka', 42. Also see Swāti, 'Recent Discovery of Buddhist Sites in the Swāt Valley', 154.
72. Rafiullah Khan, 'Visual iconicity along the ancient routes: Buddhist heritage of the Malam-jabba valley (Swat)', *Journal of Asian Civilizations* (Islamabad), 34/1 (July 2011), 217 n. 14.
73. Elisa Iori, 'The Early-Historic Urban Area at Mingora in the light of Domenico Faccenna's Excavations at Barama – I (Swat)', with note by Luca M. Olivieri, *Frontier Archaeology* (Peshawar), 7 (2016), 101.

2

PREHISTORIC AND PROTOHISTORIC

The historical record and information about the background and ancient history of Swat are very scanty. However, the excavations carried out in Swat by various archaeological missions since 1956 CE,[1] have not only exposed many remains to careful study but also added valuable information to the ancient history of the region and enhanced the understanding of scholars concerning the region's art and architecture, customs and traditions, social life and religious beliefs. The archaeological excavations carried out at various places in the Swat Valley unveiled several aspects of the prehistoric and protohistoric periods of the history of Swat. To connect the links for producing an authentic and critical account, one has to strive painstakingly.

With the archaeological excavations, pieces of evidence regarding the distant past have emerged. The excavation near Ghaligay has provided proof of 'a succession of varied and well-differentiated culture phases,[2] a practically uninterrupted sequence from the second half of the 3rd millennium B.C. to historical times'.[3]

The earliest cultural/archaeological material from the Ghaligay cave, ca. 2970–2920 BCE, consists of 'coarse handmade pottery'. The use of metal is found lacking during the period. The subsequent occupation showing painted pottery exhibits the early Indus character, a culture which precedes the developments of the mature Indus period. In Period III, at Ghaligay cave, cultural material of a different character pertaining to the Northern Neolithic are found. This cultural tradition,[4] as shown by radiocarbon dates from Loebanr, Aligrama (Aligramah), etcetera, did continue in the early centuries of the second millennium BCE. Comparison of cultural material from these early sites of Swat relates the culture of the time to the cultural patterns of Burzahom (Kashmir) and Sarai Khola I (Taxila).[5]

The archaeological excavations in the rock shelter near Ghaligay have revealed four main occupation periods. On the basis of the typology of pottery and other findings collected from Period I and Period II, the site is chronologically dated 3000 BCE. On the other hand, findings from the two subsequent periods fall in protohistoric times.[6]

On the basis of the excavations of the prehistoric and protohistoric graveyards, it has been contended that various migrations had taken place into the area, generally representing different cultures, 'which continued up to periods more recent than those testified by the early settlement of Loebanr 1700 B.C.'.[7]

Giorgio Stacul has opined, on the basis of the excavations, that Swat was exposed, during the prehistoric period, from about 2400 to about 400 BCE,[8] 'to a prolonged renewal of cultural waves coming from without, accompanied by sudden upheavals with their relative widespread phenomena of immigration on a large scale',[9] especially from Central Asian peoples and 'from Iran or from the zone between the Caspian Sea and the Lake of Aral'.[10]

This was because of the Swat location 'near the main passes that link the sub-continent with Central Asia, placed as well near the important traffic routes between East and West, it has been exceptionally exposed to the influence of currents from various sources, and to repeated cultural influxes'.[11] Besides, favourable 'climatic and environmental conditions of the Valley' have, in the past, also played a role in this respect.[12]

The archaeological excavations at Aligrama (Aligramah) unveil different strata or phases of settlements on the same site/place, the older ones, however, have been badly damaged or even razed to the ground at the time of a succeeding phase.[13]

The 'cultural Period V in the Swāt Valley seems to show the contemporary presence of two distinct tribal groups, one of which probably had relations with the peoples to whom the Iranian cemeteries of Iron-Age Period I refer'.[14]

It is pertinent to mention that the new archaeological excavations in Swat, carried out by the same Italian Archaeological Mission, at Saidu Sharif, Gugdarah (Gogdara), Udigram and Barikut, has unveiled and provided more evidences and fresh data that deconstruct the above mentioned contentions of Giorgio Stacul, based on the earlier excavations. In light of the new data, Stacul was wrong on the upper chronological limit as the graveyards explored are ca. 1200–800 BCE.[15] In 400 BCE, there were other peoples with other customs and funerary customs.[16] And the Barikut early-historic (now protohistoric) sequence starts from 800 to 150 BCE (arrival of Indo-Greeks).[17]

It is probable that the Indo-Aryans remained settled in Swat. The mention of 'Suvastu, the modern Swat', in the *Rigveda* 'signifies "fair dwellings" and may therefore indicate Aryan settlements in this beautiful valley'.[18] It, however, is worth mentioning that the theory of the Aryan migration to India is now seriously under question in some circles.[19]

The *Imperial Gazetteer of India* asserts that, during the Persian domination of the whole Indus Valley, Darius Hystaspes sent a Greek seaman, Skylax, at some date later than 516 BCE 'to explore the course of the river'. With the subsequent subjugation of the ethnicities 'dwelling west of the Indus and north' of the Kabul rivers, the territory of Gandhara was incorporated in a Persian satrapy while the Assakenoi, the 'tribes further north on the Indus, formed a special satrapy, that of the Indians'. Both of them sent their 'troops for Xerxes' invasion of Greece'.[20] The Assakenoi were the inhabitants of Swat in those days (see the next chapter).

This assertion of the formation of the separate or special satrapy of Gandhara is attested by the account of Thomas Holdich, but not that of the Assakenoi, who were the people of Swat (see the next chapter). However, stating about 'the eleventh satrapy', he has written:

> The eleventh satrapy is also probably a district of the Indian trans-frontier, although Bunbury associates the name Kaspioi with the Caspian Sea. It is far more likely that the Kaspioi of Herodotus are to be recognized as the people of the ancient Kaspira or Kasmira, and the Daritæ as the Daraddesa (Dards) of the contiguous mountains. All Kashmir, even to the borders of Tibet (whence came to the story of the gold-digging ants), was well enough known to the Persians and through them to Herodotus.[21]

This account is based on analogy and conjecture and not on sound grounds and proofs.

Dr Luca M. Olivieri, however, has asserted that this region 'was politically integrated at least from the end of the 6th century B.C. as part of the Achaemenid Empire'.[22] Although the influence of the Persian, or Achaemenid, political hegemony in the region on 'the material culture of Swat has been hotly debate[d] in the recent past' and there are some historical evidence and puzzling archaeological data, 'the material cultural context seems to have been little affected by its integration into the Achaemenid Empire'.[23] However, in a later study Dr Luca M. Olivieri and Elisa Iori have asserted, 'On the basis of the data presented, we can conclude that the marginality of the Swat area during the second half of the first millennium BCE was only presumed.'[24]

As far 'the political-administrative point of view', is concerned, 'it is certain that this area, which probably formed part of the satrapy of Gadara (Gandhara), was included in the Empire between the reigns of Darius I and of Xerxes II', that is, between the end of the sixth and the middle of the fourth centuries BCE. It can be maintained that at the time of Alexander's arrival in India the Achaemenid domination had ended here some half a century earlier.[25] Hence, 'Alexander found some kingdoms or well-organised autonomous federations, and chiefdoms'.[26]

Dr Muhammad Farooq Swati, however, has contended: 'We do not have any historical reference whether the Achaemenians of Iran ruled Uḍḍiyāna or not, although, their cultural influence is seen in the sculptures from the Swāt Valley'.[27] Whatever it was, 'under the last weak Achaemenidian [Achaemenian] "kings of kings",' the sovereignty of the Persian Empire 'had probably become very shadowy in the mountainous tracts to the north'[28] of which Swat or Uddiyana was a part.

Giuseppe Tucci has raised a question: 'Are we really in a condition to state that Swāt was subject to the Achaemenian administration, either as a district within the Satrapies or as a separate ethnic group?'[29] After discussing some points, Tucci has contended:

> Thus, we may conclude that Swāt had a position by itself, as a particular ethnic group of the Dadíkai, separate from Gandhāra; the people had only to pay some tributes and to send contingents of troops, as agreed upon, in case of war. We must therefore refer to the division into districts on the basis of the tributes due (*Steuer–Berzirke*) or of their ethnic identity rather than on that of Satrapies.[30]

In spite of various migrations, it can safely be affirmed that 'in Swāt we are confronted with a series of homologous cultures; notwithstanding the evident differences, in…details…of the artefacts'.[31]

The logical result of these migrations was that Swat did not remain a country inhabited by a homogeneous population and people of one origin. Giuseppe Tucci, who had tried to prove that the prehistoric and protohistoric people of Swat were 'Dards', has also admitted:

> This does not imply that we have to suppose that from the beginning to the end, Swāt was the habitat, as well as older settlements, of the Dardic

tribes only; other related groups might have joined or followed them coming down from the Central Asian reservoir, through the same or parallel routes.[32]

Tucci has opined that 'any hypothesis on the organizations of these groups once they settled down, on account of the scanty material we possess, can be only a mere guessing'.[33] He, however, has asserted at another place that the tribes who confronted Alexander 'shared a common culture and...were most probably allied, recognizing in case of necessity the chief of one tribe as their leader'. At the time of Alexander's attack, the chief of Massaga was the recognized leader among them. At the fall of Massaga 'the supremacy passed over to the Urdi, the inhabitants of Ora of Arrian (the Nora of Curtius Rufus is evidently a mistake), who then gave the name to the country: Urdi, Udri, Uḍī, Uḍḍiyāna'. However, despite having a 'common culture', they have 'peculiarities among them'.[34] He, moreover, has asserted:

> That they were divided into tribes composed of different clans seems to me the most probable; they must have had a kind of a council of elders for the solution of any problem involving the interests of the community; delimitation of pasture grounds and such like eventual disputes. In case of necessity the tribes united their forces and selected a most able man to be the leader. It is possible that a tribe like that of the Assakenói, asserted its supremacy over the others and assumed a kind of hegemony. They fought because their independence was at stake. As soon as Mássaga fell and Áornos was captured the confederation collapsed.[35]

At another place, he has asserted that 'the Aurdāyana', Urdi, Odi, 'superseded in power, or prestige, at a certain time, the other tribes.... especially the Āśvakāyana, or at least, that after the destruction of Massaga, the capital of the federation became Ora'. And that: 'All of these people, if we are to judge from the material found in Chakdarra, Swat, Chitral, Darel, Buner, were most probably ethnically, or at least for a certain time, culturally related.'[36]

The 'ethnic components' of Swat, 'in the era before the penetration of the Pashtu populations, were varied. Over an older stratum which is still difficult to establish but about which we have some information thanks to archaeological finds at Uḍegram....a population was rapidly superposed which, from the linguistic point of view, is partly related to the Dardic group and partly to a third branch of ancient Aryan.'[37]

Moreover, 'there was probably a second migration, perhaps coming from the north, and it is not unlikely that it left traces in the tradition of the country, if what the Chinese monk Hsüan tsang said is to be believed'.[38]

Socio-Cultural Dimension

The peculiar pottery ware that was found in layers 19 and 18 of the rock-shelter near Ghaligay, 'strongly suggests that Swat, in the 3rd Millennium BCE, had some permanent settlement practicing agriculture, interacting with the trade networks of the lower basin, and developing its own complex craft traditions, but such settlements were destroyed or are not yet discovered'.[39]

The pottery, implements, sculptures, and tools got by the archaeological excavations and the information gained through their analysis show that Swat had links and relations with as well as had been influenced by the developments, migrations, and movements in the surrounding areas in the subcontinent, Iran, Central Asia, and China— both culturally and ethnically—even in the third and second millennium BCE.[40] Besides, 'the inclusion in a commercial network connecting Swat Valley with Indus plain as well as Kashmir and trans-Himalayan territories allowed a economic development during this period'.[41] It, therefore, can be said that 'the high civil development of Swāt in protohistorical times has been ascertained'.[42]

The excavated necropolises unveil digging of tombs above tombs and also the custom of double burial or the burial of another person in the same grave in later period.[43] Even an 'instance of triple burial' has been found.[44] 'The finding of a skeleton without its skull which had been buried in a small hole at the bottom of the lower cavity' of the tomb, although, is 'a wholly exceptional phenomenon',[45] indicate that beheading the body of the murdered person had been practiced in prehistoric times and the practice survives till this time in the twenty-first century CE.

Various elements emerging in the excavation of 'multiple-burial tombs', confirmed 'that the site was used in successive stages'.[46] Some tombs, containing single disconnected skeletons, confirm the hypothesis of the custom of secondary burial—the custom of a particular form of ritual found in protohistoric cultures: 'the burial of a corpse in two stages'.[47] Besides, 'inhumation' was 'far more common than cremation'.[48] According to Giuseppe Tucci, in Swat different types of burials coexisted, in respect of 'the disposal of the dead': 'inhumation in bent position, combustion, secondary burials etc.'.[49] Proofs of the burial of horses have also been found.[50]

A significant point is the presence of utensils, vases, and weapons (spear-heads, knife-blades, axes and arrow-heads), earrings, etcetera, in the tombs.[51] Interestingly, locals popularly interpret these material from the tombs as meant for the angels Munkir and Nakir, as 'bribe', so that the angels agree not to punish them, and, in case they do not agree by means of bribes, and are bent upon meting out the punishment, they may be struck with the weapons so that the buried person is saved from the would be punishment: a strange perception, without sound proof or authority, prevailing in the twentieth century CE about the beliefs of the millennia back people. According to Dr Rafiullah Khan, this may be called the people's perception or interpretation in light of the archaeological excavation but without any solid knowledge or knowhow on its back. This can or may be called popular or folk archaeology or is a sort of popular folk archaeology.[52]

The new data, made and in the process of being made available, by the explorations and excavations by the Italian Archaeological Mission, at different places in Swat, especially, in the last decade of the twentieth century and the early twenty-first century, in the suburbs of Mingawarah, Udigram, Gugdarah, Barikut, and in the side valleys, has provided and provides new venues and dimensions for analysis of the protohistoric and early historic periods of Swat. This has radically changed the perspective and leads to modify, re-mould and re-interpret some of the hitherto known facts and conclusions drawn on the basis of the previous explorations and excavations in Swat. Hence, Dr Luca M. Olivieri has aptly stated, 'Our understanding of ancient Swat is in a continuous flux.'[53]

NOTES

1. Although formal archaeological excavations started in Swat in 1956, by Italian Archaeological Mission, in the summer of 1938, Evert Barger and Philip Wright carried out the first excavation in Swat.

2. A 'Phase' in archaeology is understood as: 'An archaeological unit defined by characteristic groupings of culture traits that can be identified precisely in time and space. It lasts for a relatively short time and is found at one or more sites in a locality or region. Its culture traits are clear enough to distinguish it from other

phases.' Brian M. Fagan, *Archaeology: A Brief Introduction* (4th edn., New York: HarperCollins Publishers, 1991), 233.

3. Giorgio Stacul, 'The Gray Pottery in the Swāt Valley and the Indo-Iranian Connections (ca. 1500–300 B.C.)', *East and West* (Rome), 20/1–2 (March–June 1970), 92. For detail, see Giorgio Stacul, 'Excavation near Ghālīgai (1968) and Chronological Sequence of Protohistorical Cultures in the Swāt Valley', *East and West* (Rome), 19/1–2 (March–June 1969), 44–91.

4. 'In archaeology, [cultural tradition is] a distinctive toolkit or technology that lasts a long time, longer than the duration of one culture, at one locality or several localities.' Fagan, *Archaeology: A Brief Introduction*, 228.

5. Bridget and Raymond Allchin, *The Rise of Civilization in India and Pakistan* (repr., New Delhi: Cambridge University Press India Pvt. Ltd., 2008), 113–16.

6. See Massimo Vidale, Roberto Micheli, and Luca Olivieri, 'Iconography of Protohistoric Swat and the Agricultural Intensification of Period IV (2nd Millennium BCE)', *Journal of Asian Civilizations* (Islamabad), 34/1 (July 2011), 94–100; 'Italian Archaeological Activities in Swat: An Introduction', *Journal of Asian Civilizations* (Islamabad), 34/1 (July 2011), 51–2.

7. Giuseppe Tucci, 'On Swāt. The Dards and Connected Problems', *East and West* (Rome), 27/1–4 (December 1977), 35.

8. It is to be noted that elsewhere in Pakistan and India this long period could not be solely associated with prehistoric times (Dr Rafiullah Khan's note to the point on an earlier draft of this chapter).

9. Stacul, 'Excavation near Ghālīgai (1968) and Chronological Sequence of Protohistorical Cultures in the Swāt Valley', 64.

10. Chiara Silvi Antonini, 'Swāt and Central Asia', *East and West* (Rome), 19/1–2 (March–June 1969), 113–14. Although this contention makes sense, the contentions of the old scholars need not to be correct. Diffusion is not a strong model of explanation/investigation nowadays; thus, scholars associated with such views need to be studied between the lines with great care (Dr Rafiullah Khan's note to the point on an earlier draft of this chapter).

11. Stacul, 'Excavation near Ghālīgai (1968) and Chronological Sequence of Protohistorical Cultures in the Swāt Valley', 86.

12. Ibid. Also see Stacul, 'The Gray Pottery in the Swāt Valley and the Indo-Iranian Connections (ca. 1500–300 B.C.)', 92–102.

13. See Giorgio Stacul and Sebastiano Tusa, 'Report on the Excavations at Aligrāma (Swāt, Pakistan), 1974', *East and West* (Rome), 27/1–4 (December 1977), 151, 184–5.

14. Stacul, 'The Gray Pottery in the Swāt Valley and the Indo-Iranian Connections (ca. 1500–300 B.C.)', 98–9.

15. For detail, see Massimo Vidale and Roberto Micheli, 'Protohistoric graveyards of the Swat Valley, Pakistan: new light on funerary practices and absolute chronology', *Antiquity* (Cambridge), 91/356 (2017), 389–405; Massimo Vidale, Roberto Micheli and Luca M. Olivieri, eds., *Excavations at the Protohistoric Graveyards of Gogdara and Udegram* (Lahore: Sang-e-Meel Publications, 2016).

16. See Luca M. Olivieri, 'The Graveyard and the Buddhist Shrine at Saidu Sharif I (Swat, Pakistan): Fresh Chronological and Stratigraphic Evidence', with Contributions by Filippo Terrasi, Fabio Marzaioli, Isabella Passariello, and

Manuela Capano, and notes by Aatif Iqbal, *Journal of Ancient History* (Moscow), 76/3 (2016), 559–78.

17. See Luca M. Olivieri and Elisa Iori, 'Early-historic Data from the 2016 Excavation Campaigns at the Urban Site of Barikot, Swat (Pakistan): A Shifting Perspective' in A. Hardy and L. Greaves, eds., *South Asian Art and Archaeology* (New Delhi: Dev Publishers & Distributers, 2016), 19–43.

18. Bridget and Raymond Allchin, *The Rise of Civilization in India and Pakistan*, 306.

19. Dr Rafiullah Khan also asserts that the Aryan theory is no more maintainable (Dr Rafiullah Khan's note on an earlier draft of this chapter).

20. *Imperial Gazetteer of India: Provincial Series; North-West Frontier Province* (repr., Lahore: Sang-e-Meel Publications, 1991), 13.

21. Thomas Holdich, *The Gates of India: Being an Historical Narrative* (1st edn. published in Pakistan, Quetta: Gosha-e-Adab, 1977), 31.

22. Luca M. Olivieri, 'Notes on the Problematical Sequence of Alexander's Itinerary in Swat: A Geo-Historical Approach', *East and West* (Rome), 46/1–2 (June 1996), 66 (Stable URL: http://www.jstor.org/stable/29757254; accessed: 30/10/2011).

23. Ibid.

24. Olivieri and Elisa Iori, 'Early-historic Data from the 2016 Excavation Campaigns at the Urban Site of Barikot, Swat (Pakistan): A Shifting Perspective', 35.

25. Olivieri, 'Notes on the Problematical Sequence of Alexander's Itinerary in Swat: A Geo-Historical Approach', 66.

26. Ibid.

27. Muhammad Farooq Swāti, 'Recent Discovery of Buddhist Sites in the Swāt Valley', *Āthāriyyāt* (Peshawar), 1 (1997), 154. Also see Muhammad Farooq Swāti, 'Special Features of the Buddhist Art in the Swāt Valley', *Ancient Pakistan* (Peshawar), 18 (2007), 106.

28. Aurel Stein, *On Alexander's Track to the Indus: Personal Narrative of Explorations on the North-West Frontier of India* (repr., Karachi: Indus Publications, 1995), 41.

29. Tucci, 'On Swāt. The Dards and Connected Problems', 10.

30. Ibid., 11.

31. Ibid., 36.

32. Ibid., 37.

33. Ibid., 38.

34. Giuseppe Tucci, 'Oriental Notes, II: An Image of a Devi Discovered in Swat and Some Connected Problems', in Giuseppe Tucci, *On Swāt. Historical and Archaeological Notes*, with introduction by Domenico Faccenna, eds. P. Callieri and A. Filigenzi, reprint of the original 1997 edition, with preface by M. Ashraf Khan (Islamabad: Taxila Institute of Asian Civilizations, 2013), 131.

35. Tucci, 'On Swāt. The Dards and Connected Problems', 38.

36. Giuseppe Tucci, 'The Tombs of the Asvakayana-Assakenoi', in Tucci, *On Swāt. Historical and Archaeological Notes*, 118.

37. Giuseppe Tucci, 'Recent Explorations in Swat', in Tucci, *On Swāt. Historical and Archaeological Notes*, 300–1.

38. Ibid., 302.

39. Vidale, Roberto Micheli, and Luca Olivieri, 'Iconography of Protohistoric Swat and the Agricultural Intensification of Period IV (2nd Millennium BCE)', 97.

40. For some detail, see Giorgio Stacul, 'Excavations in a Rock Shelter near Ghālīgai (Swāt W. Pakistan). Preliminary Report', *East and West* (Rome), 17/3–4 (September–December 1967), 185–219; Stacul, 'Excavation near Ghālīgai (1968) and Chronological Sequence of Protohistorical Cultures in the Swāt Valley', 44–91; Antonini, 'Swāt and Central Asia', 100–115; Stacul, 'The Gray Pottery in the Swāt Valley and the Indo-Iranian Connections (ca. 1500–300 B.C.)', 92–102; Giorgio Stacul, 'An Archaeological Survey near Kālām (Swāt Kohistān)', *East and West* (Rome), 20/1–2 (March–June 1970), 87–91; Giorgio Stacul, 'Dwelling- and Storage-Pits at Loebanr III (Swāt, Pakistan), 1976 Excavation Report', *East and West* (Rome), 27/1–4 (December 1977), 227–53.

41. 'Italian Archaeological Activities in Swat: An Introduction', 56.

42. Stacul, 'An Archaeological Survey near Kālām (Swāt Kohistān)', 91.

43. See Giorgio Stacul, 'Preliminary Report on the Pre-Buddhist Necropolises in Swat (W. Pakistan), *East and West* (Rome), 16/1–2 (March–June 1966), 40–7.

44. Ibid., 47.

45. Ibid., 40

46. Ibid., 48.

47. Ibid., 49.

48. Ibid., 47.

49. Tucci, 'On Swāt. The Dards and Connected Problems', 21. For detail in this respect, see ibid., 21–6.

50. See ibid., 29.

51. See Stacul, 'Preliminary Report on the Pre-Buddhist Necropolises in Swat (W. Pakistan)', 37–79.

52. Dr Rafiullah Khan's personal communication with the author: August 2016.

53. Luca M. Olivieri, 'The Last Phases at Barikot: Urban Cults and Preliminary Chronology: Data from the 2012 Excavation Campaign in Swat', *Journal of Inner Asian Art and Archaeology* (New York), 6/2011, 12.

3

THE GREEKS AND SWAT

History bears evidence that wars and struggle between the West and the East have continued over the millennia. One such case is of the struggle between the Persians and the Greeks in the centuries before Jesus.

In the wars between the Persians and the Greeks, Alexander of Macedonia defeated the Persian ruler in 333 and 331 BCE; and became undisputed master of the realm with the death of the Persian king in 330 BCE. After his conquest of Persia and some parts of modern Afghan territories he continued his march towards India in order to take revenge for the help the area had provided to the Persians against the Greeks. In this arduous Campaign of the East, Alexander invaded Swat in person in 327 BCE.

ALEXANDER'S INVASION

Crossing the mountains to the east, after the conquest of the areas of modern Afghanistan, Alexander of Macedonia 'began the invasion of the country of the powerful nation of the Assakēnoi, and reference to the map shows that this could be no other than Swāt, as has also been long since recognized'.[1] It, however, should be mentioned, as agreed to by Giuseppe Tucci, that Assakenoi did not inhabit the entire Swat Valley and there were certainly other tribes as well, whether related to the Assakenoi or not. 'The Assakenói were settled chiefly in the lower part of Swāt (Chakdarra), then Bājaur [Bajawar], Bunēr. Their capital was Mássaga'.[2] The 'geographical considerations' show 'that the several fortified towns which Alexander successively besieged and captured were probably situated in the main Swāt valley; for this at all times must, as now, have been the most fertile and populous portion of the territory'.[3]

George Woodcock has claimed that, when Alexander 'crossed the Hindu Kush into the Swat valley, now in Pakistan, he encountered the inhabitants of a town called Nysa'. These Nysans 'claimed to be

24

descended from the soldiers of Dionysus, the divine conqueror of India' and, moreover, 'to be a "free and independent people".' They 'welcomed Alexander as a fellow Greek, and provided a force of three hundred cavalry for his army'.[4] Woodcock has termed the story of the presence of the Greeks in the region prior to Alexander's invasion and their provision of a force to Alexander as true by stating that 'the story of Nysa, repeated in so many of the accounts of Alexander's expedition, has the ring of truth' and that 'there is little doubt that the people of Nysa were a group of islanded Greeks living among the Kafir tribesmen who then inhabited the region of Swat'.[5]

The location of Nysa, however, has its own complications to be established and so has not been agreed upon by the available sources. Q. Curtius Rufus, Plutarch, and Justin have mentioned the affair/ capitulation of Nysa before Alexander's campaign and exploits of Massaga, Ora, and Bazira, but Arrian has given the details of the Nysan affairs after Alexander's exploits of Massaga, Ora, Bazira, and Aornos.[6] Giuseppe Tucci has dealt with the point and location of Nysa and has opined that 'Nysa is here out of place'. He has, moreover, stated that 'it is known that a town or a mountain of this name has been connected with the myth of Dionysos and that in fact there have been many Nysa', but the place 'has remained a mythic place' and a 'city of a mythic geography which has no relation with the physical geography'.[7]

When Alexander crossed Panjkurah River[8] towards Swat, Arrian has recorded that instead of encountering him in the open field with their collective forces the natives went to their cities, which they resolved to defend to the end. He marched first to attack Massaga, the greatest city of the area.[9] These natives were called 'Assakenians' (Assakenoi), who reportedly had 'an army of 20,000 cavalry and more than 30,000 infantry, besides 30 elephants'.[10] Assisted by a body of about 7000 Indian[11] soldiers, or mercenaries as they have been termed by the Greeks, the natives sallied out against the Macedonians when they were encamping. Alexander ordered his soldiers, as a strategy, to fallback to a nearby little hill. This gave the natives 'fresh courage' and they charged the Macedonians 'at a running pace and without any observance of order'.[12] By this strategy, Alexander succeeded to draw the natives into the open field. After a skirmish in the open, the natives once more 'gave way' and retreated 'to the city'. Therefore, 'Alexander brought up the phalanx against the fortifications, but was wounded in the ankle, though not severely, by an arrow shot from the battlements'.[13] In Agnes

Savill's words, 'Probably it was on this occasion that he jested ruefully: "They call me a son of Zeus! But this is not the ichor of the gods; it is mortal blood".'[14] Whereas, according to Q. Qurtius Rufus, Alexander 'is reported to have said that though he was called, as all knew, the son of Jupiter, he felt notwithstanding all the defects of the weak body'.[15]

'The next day', Alexander 'brought up the military engines' and succeeded to batter 'down a part of the wall', but the Macedonians' attempt to force their way into the city was repelled 'with so much spirit' that Alexander was compelled to 'draw off his forces' for that day.[16] The Macedonians' assault on the morrow, with might and main, was also foiled; despite their using advanced technology. On the third day, Alexander made a more determined assault, using engines, but it was a failure. The fourth day proved fruitful for Alexander and fateful for the natives. Although the Indians and the natives stood firm, the chief 'was struck by a missile from an engine and was killed by the blow'.[17]

At this, the Indians, who sustained great casualties, 'sent a herald to treat with Alexander'. Alexander entered into 'an agreement with the Indian mercenaries to the effect that they should change' sides 'and take service in his ranks'. Thereupon, they left the city and encamped on a nearby hill but, not being ready to fight 'against their own countrymen, they resolved to arise by night and make off with all speed to their homes'. On knowing this, Alexander 'surrounded the hill that same night with all his troops', 'intercepted the Indians in the midst of their flight', and 'cut them to pieces'. In the wake of thus being 'stripped of its defenders', Alexander took the city 'by storm, and captured the mother and daughter of Assakênos'.[18]

Significantly, it took Alexander nine days before making an assault on the city to complete all the strategic arrangements required for the conquest of such a formidable fortification.[19] Interestingly, Qurtius Rufus had stated that 'Assacanus', the 'previous sovereign' of Massaga, 'had lately died, and his mother Cleophis now ruled the city and the realm'.[20] Giuseppe Tucci, however, has contended that 'the name, Assacános (of the dead king of Mássaga) is not only a proper name but chiefly an ethnic name'.[21]

The defenders at Massaga showed heroic courage and gave a tough time to the invaders. They foiled the attempts on the city and defended their possession 'with the greatest vigour'. They, at last, 'concluded a treaty of peace'[22] with Alexander because of the death of their king, who was hit by the enemy, and owing to the introduction and use of advanced and unfamiliar techniques and strategies by the Macedonians.[23]

After the fall of Massaga, Alexander 'despatched Koinos to Bazira'. He was 'convinced that the inhabitants would capitulate on learning that Massaga had been captured' by the Macedonians. Moreover, he 'sent Attalos, Alketas, and Dêmêtrios, the captain of cavalry, to another city, Ora, instructing them to draw a rampart round [around] it, and to invest it until his own arrival'. The inhabitants of Ora 'sallied out against' the invading forces but the invaders drove 'them back within the walls of the city'.[24]

Both the places (Ora and Bazira) were situated eastward in Upper Swat. Due to the strong fortifications and standing 'on a very lofty eminence' of Bazira, its inhabitants stood firm and matters did not go well with the Macedonians. On learning this, Alexander directed his own march for Bazira, but changed his plan because some of the neighbouring country people, 'sent by Abisares', 'were going to steal unobserved into the city of Ora' and therefore he personally proceeded directly against Ora. He sent directions to Koinos at Bazira 'to fortify some strong position as a basis of operations against the city of the Bazirians, and to leave in it a sufficient garrison to prevent the inhabitants from going into the country around for provisions without fear of danger' and then to join him 'with the remainder of his troops'.[25]

When Koinos departed, the Bazirians came out of the city and attacked the Macedonians but suffered a casualty of 500 dead and more than 70 taken as prisoners in a fearful battle. Resultantly, the rest retreated to the city and 'debarred all access to the country by the garrison of the fort'. After its siege, Alexander captured Ora 'at the first assault',[26] but only after the arrival of 'Coenus' reinforcements' and 'the contingent from Massaga'.[27] Determined to defend their position and possession, on reaching the news of the fall of Ora, the Bazirians 'regarded their case as desperate'. Therefore, 'at the dead of night', they 'fled from their city to the Rock'.[28] Regarding the capture of Ora, as reported by the Greek writers, Dr Abdur Rahman and Shah Nazar Khan have commented:

> The siege of Ora did not cost Alexander much Labour [labour], for he is said to have captured the place at the first assault and got possession of all the elephants which were left there. It is very strange, although the classical writers would like us to believe, that in spite of the reinforcements from neighbouring princes, which must have enormously

augmented the defence capability of Ora and bolstered the courage of its inhabitants as effectively as they did at Massaga, and also of the natural strength of its fortification wall, it fell an easy prey to the Macedonians.[29]

As a result of protracted and arduous siege, both Ora and Bazira fell to the Macedonians despite gallant resistance. After the fall of the cities, Alexander 'made Ora and Massaga strongholds for bridling the districts around them, and at the same time strengthened the defences of Bazira'[30] and left Swat for the cis-Indus areas.

ANALYSIS OF SOME POINTS

The Queen's Affair

Two important issues interlinked with and inseparable from the events and capitulation of Massaga are the affair of the queen and the Indian soldiers or mercenaries (so termed by the Greek writers). The Greek writers of the events have presented the affair of the queen in different versions. Arrian, whose description is the most detailed and, according to Aurel Stein, is 'the most reliable and avowedly based on contemporary records',[31] has stated only this much about the queen: 'The city [Massaga] now stripped of its defenders he [Alexander] took by storm, and captured the mother and daughter of Assakênos.'[32] M'crindle has aptly remarked in a note to this: 'The attack upon the city after it had capitulated on terms admits of no justification.'[33] Arrian's account has clearly stated that the ruler of Massaga 'was struck by a missile from an engine and was killed by the blow'[34] in the course of the Macedonians' siege of and operation against the city.

But, as stated earlier, Q. Curtius Rufus has stated that 'Assacanus', Massaga's 'previous sovereign, had lately died, and his mother Cleophis now ruled the city and the realm'.[35] After dealing with Alexander's preparation of the siege and the initial encounters, Rufus has stated that, hopeless before the Macedonians' war tools and techniques and seeing no other option but the surrender, the Massagans 'sent down envoys' to Alexander 'to sue for pardon'.[36]

> This being granted, the queen came with a great train of noble ladies who poured out libations of wine from golden bowls. The queen herself, having placed her son, still a child, at Alexander's knees, obtained not only pardon, but permission to retain her former dignity, for she was styled queen, and some have believed that this indulgent treatment

was accorded rather to the charms of her person than to pity for her misfortunes. At all events she afterwards gave birth to a son who received the name of Alexander, whoever his father may have been.[37]

Whereas, Diodoros Siculus has stated this much: 'When the capitulation on those terms had been ratified by oaths, the Queen [of Massaga], to show her admiration of Alexander's magnanimity, sent out to him most valuable presents, with an intimation that she would fulfil all the stipulations.'[38] While Plutarch is silent on the point,[39] Justin, although giving no detail of the siege and fall of Massaga, has stated:

> Thence he marched to the Daedali mountains…[40] and the dominions of Queen Cleophis…, who, after surrendering her kingdom, purchased its restoration by permitting the conqueror to share her bed, thus gaining by her fascinations what she had not gained by her valour. The offspring of this intercourse was a son, whom she called Alexander, the same who afterwards reigned as an Indian king. Queen Cleophis, because she had prostituted her chastity, was therefore called by the Indians *the royal harlot*.[41]

This is all that the Greek writers have stated. Although 'Curtius Rufus' version', contends Dr Luca M. Olivieri, 'proves to be more reliable than Arrian's' in respect of the 'local topography and the strategy chosen',[42] Frederic Pincott has asserted that 'Curtius, it is generally admitted, was not very accurate as to details'.[43] A close analysis of the text of the aforesaid Greek writers reveals that Rufus' and Justin's accounts suffer from rhetoric and romanticism. In dealing with the queen's aforesaid story, Giuseppe Tucci also has asserted: 'All this seems a mixture of historical facts and romantic stories.'[44] While dealing with the question of Aornos, Thomas Holdich has remarked: 'The story told by Arrian (and possibly maltreated by translators) is doubtless full of inaccuracies and exaggerations, but we decline to believe that it is pure invention.'[45] However, compared to the other Greek writers, Arrian's account of the events at Massaga seems sounder, which, according to Aurel Stein, as stated earlier, is 'the most reliable'. He had dealt in detail with all the events and, instead of romanticism, has made it clear that Alexander captured the queen by storming the city after weakening the defence of the city and entering into agreement, after the death of the ruler of Massaga, with the Indian soldiers or mercenaries, an agreement he did not keep.

V.A. Smith did not recognize that the queen was the mother of the chief who was killed in the course of the war and has contended that she was his wife, as he has termed 'Kleophis, the consort of the slain chieftain'[46] and has said that 'apparently, Kleophis must have been the widow of the chief who was killed in the siege'.[47] All the aforesaid, about the queen, are not unanimous, are confused, and suffer from romanticism.

The Indian Soldiers' Affair

The second significant point is the affair of the Indian soldiers or mercenaries (as termed by the Greek writers), and their families. We are told that there were 7000 Indians who were in the garrison of Massaga as mercenaries against Alexander. After the death of the ruler at Massaga, they made a peace deal with Alexander, as a result of which they were spared by him. However, sensing that they were not ready to fight their fellow countrymen on his side, and were going to desert him, Alexander attacked them.[48] They 'at first loudly protested that they were attacked in violation of sworn obligations' but to no avail. Therefore, they fought bravely and were also joined in this by their women. They, 'however, after fighting desperately along with their wives, were at last overpowered by superior numbers, and met a glorious death which they would have disdained to exchange for a life with dishonour'.[49]

Discussing the affairs of Alexander and the Indian soldiers at Massaga, V.A. Smith has contended, about the incident of the slaughter of the Indian soldiers, 'which has been severely condemned by various writers, ancient and modern, as a disgraceful breach of faith by Alexander':

> While the accession of seven thousand brave and disciplined troops would have been a welcome addition to Alexander's small army, the addition of such a force to the enemy in the plains would have been a serious impediment to his advance; and he was, I think, justified in protecting himself against such a formidable increase of the enemy's strength.[50]

Agnes Savill's account has given a somewhat different sense. She, however, too has tried to justify the killing of the Indians by asserting:

> Alexander's Intelligence was rarely at fault; if he had knowledge of a plot to circumvent the surrender terms, his precaution to prevent the

flight of the mercenaries was correct. The tragic slaughter could not have been foreseen; in the darkness the army was beyond normal control. As Alexander was always a strict observer of his promises and had greatly admired the prowess of the Massagan defence, it is difficult to believe that he would have committed a grave breach of an agreement which he had himself drawn up.[51]

Compared to the other Greek writers, Diodoros Siculus has dealt in detail with the affair of the Indian soldiers.[52] It is pertinent to reproduce the following extract from his account, for making the position clearer.

> Then the mercenaries at once, in accordance with the terms of the agreement, evacuated the city, and after retiring to a distance of eighty stadia, pitched their camp unmolested without thought of what was to happen. But Alexander, who was actuated by an implacable enmity against the mercenaries [the Indian soldiers at Massaga], and had kept his troops under arms ready for action, pursued the barbarians, and falling suddenly upon them, made a great slaughter of their ranks. The barbarians at first loudly protested that they were attacked in violation of sworn obligations, and invoked the gods whom he had desecrated by taking false oaths in their name[s]. But Alexander with loud voice retorted that his covenant merely bound him to let them depart from the city, and was by no means a league of perpetual amity between them and the Macedonians.[53]

Diodoros Siculus has thus removed the mess and has made it clearer that it was not the desertion of the Indian soldiers that prompted Alexander's strict action against them, but it was Alexander's 'implacable enmity against' them that he 'kept his troops under arms ready for action' and 'suddenly' attacked them. And when, upon his such action, the Indian soldiers protested and reminded him of his 'sworn obligations' in this respect, he 'with loud voice retorted that his covenant merely bound him to let them depart from the city, and was by no means a league of perpetual amity between them and the Macedonians'. If 'his covenant merely bound' Alexander 'to let' the Indian soldiers 'depart from the city' and he was not bound not to harm or take action against them, this in other words means that he deceived them by making a false promise or peace treaty with them, just to get them out of the fortified city and isolate them. Therefore, whatever justification may be put forward for Alexander's action against the Indian soldiers and for their massacre, the fact is that he did not abide by terms of the 'treaty of peace', concluded with the Indian soldiers. Plutarch has justly admitted that 'this rests as a foul blot on his martial fame'.[54]

ALEXANDER'S COMING ABOVE UDIGRAM

Some of the Swat and Pukhtunkhwa modern-day writers have contended that, during his campaign in Swat, Alexander of Macedonia came to Manglawar and defeated the Raja Arans.[55] Keeping in view the general flow of the accounts of the Greek writers and other authorities, it appears that Alexander did not come beyond Udigram in the Swat Valley. He proceeded south-westward to the Peshawar Valley or southward via the Karakar Pass through Bunair (Buner), joined his second contingent, and crossed the Indus. Details of the battle attributed at Manglawar are those of the battle of Assakenoi somewhere in Lower Swat. In Aurel Stein's words:

> In the Swāt valley itself, it is clear that the capture of Ora had brought Alexander's operations to a triumphant conclusion; for Arrian's narrative shows us that, after establishing Macedonian posts at Ora and Massaga, as well as at Bazira, to guard the country, the conqueror turned south to the Peshawar valley. There he was to establish his junction with the division of the army that had preceded him down the Kābul river and then to carry his campaign farther east to the Indus.[56]

Whereas, according to Giuseppe Tucci: 'When Alexander had reached Peukelāoitis, Puskālavatī, his campaign in Swāt had come to an end.'[57] A.H. Dani, too, has contended that Udigram was 'the last place occupied by Alexander the Great in Swat'.[58]

Alexander's Motives

Motives behind Alexander's exploits in Swat were not its occupation or revenge[59] but the need to secure his chain of communications, to safeguard his rear and flanks, and to restrain the inhabitants of Swat from helping and supporting the cis-Indus people against whom 'he advanced...to avenge, he said, the help given by the Indians nearly two centuries before to the Persians in their attack on Greece'.[60] In V.A. Smith words: 'With this force he undertook a flanking movement through the difficult hill country north of the Kābul river, in order to subdue the fierce tribes which inhabited, as they still inhabit, that region;

and thus to secure his communications, and protect his army from attacks on the flank and rear.'[61] And in Powell-Price words: 'He could not let his communications be threatened by these robber [sic] tribes, and so he dealt with them as the frontier tribes have never been dealt with before or since.'[62] And according to Aurel Stein, besides asserting his authority in the area west of the Indus, previously part of the Persian Empire to which Alexander laid his claim, 'together with the obvious need of securing the flank of his main line of communication, explains why Alexander, on arriving in the upper valley of the Kābul river, led one corps of his army into the hill country to the north, while the rest was to move down into the present Peshawar district and secure the passage across the Indus'.[63] Thomas Holdich has also accepted this interpretation of Alexander's exploits in Swat, by stating:

> On the northern flank of the Khaibar route, however, there had been large tribal settlements from the very beginning of things, and it was most important that these outliers should feel the weight of Alexander's mailed fist *if the road between the Kabul and the Indus were ever to be made secure* [my italics]. He accordingly directed his attention to a more northerly route to India which would bring him into contact with the Aspasians, Gauraians, and Assakenians.[64]

Dr Luca M. Olivieri also agrees with this viewpoint by stating:

> The historical episode under examination shows of what great strategic importance Swat was to Alexander. As the main body of troops marched through the Kabul Valley towards India "true and proper" it becomes evident that the purpose of the expedition in Swat was to establish a strong salient in the north to serve, at least for a time, as a dynamic advanced system of defence…to defend a vital territory that was not Swat but the Peukelaotis Plain watered by the River Kabul.[65]

Alliance of the king of the Abhisara country, beyond the Indus, with the Assakenois, the consequent presence of the Indian soldiers at Massaga and Ora, and Alexander's arrangements at Massaga, Ora, and Bazira—before leaving Swat for India or the cis-Indus territories—are testaments to the view that Alexander's invasion of Swat was not an act of revenge but a defensive measure in relation to his campaigns in the Peshawar Valley and beyond into the cis-Indus areas.

The measures taken and the strategy adopted by Alexander, in respect of the sieges of Bazira and Ora, explains the positions and importance of these places and also that 'Ōra lay beyond' Barikut. 'The importance of Ōra', moreover, is also evident from the fact that Alexander personally 'felt prompted to secure it quickly, in view of the reported move to reinforce the defenders'.[66]

Location of Massaga, Bazira, Ora, and Aornos

Neither do the sources give clear locations for the cities of Massaga, Bazira, and Ora, and the mountain Aornos, connected with Alexander's exploits in Swat, nor do the authorities agree upon them.[67] Aurel Stein has contended that Arrian's and Curtius' 'accounts contain details of the places besieged and taken by Alexander; but it had not been possible to fix their position with any assurance so long as by far the greater portion of that extensive area remained inaccessible to antiquarian research'.[68] He, however, seems justified in writing that 'on general grounds I believe that the site of Massaga may probably have to be looked for in Lower Swāt'[69] and 'in tracing the further course of Alexander's operations in Swāt we are fortunately helped by definite archaeological and topographical indications'.[70] Stein's contention of locating Massaga in Lower Swat gets support from the description of Arrian about Alexander's course beyond Bajawar. S.M. Sastri also has opined that it was 'probably situated not very far to the north of the Malakand Pass but not yet precisely identified'.[71] Tracing Alexander's route, Dr Abdur Rahman and Shah Nazar Khan are inclined to locate Massaga at the present-day 'Gumbatūna' in the Talash Valley.[72] Stein identifies Bazira at the ruins on the Bir-Kut (Barikut; Barikot) Hill, Ora at Ude-gram (Udigram), and Aornos as Pir-sar.[73]

Dr Luca M. Olivieri, however, has quoted a passage from Stein's letter written in the 1930s to B.J. Gould, British colonial political agent at Malakand, stating:

> The site of Massaga, if it can be identified at all, has to be looked for either in the protected area north of the Malakand or else not far from the northern bank of the river in the Wali's [Swat State's ruler] territory. If only Curtius' topographical details could be relied upon there ought to be a fair chance of locating the site.[74]

On the basis of this passage from Stein, Dr Luca has asserted: 'This passage by Stein is particularly significant because it demonstrates that Stein's idea about the whereabouts of the ancient capital of Massaga, besieged by Alexander the Great, had been modified.'[75]

Dr Abdur Rahman and Shah Nazar Khan have asserted that 'most scholars…in the past believed' that from Bajawar Alexander went to the Peshawar Valley through the Muhmand (Mohmand) area and 'therefore the sites for the towns such as Massaga, Bazira and Ora….were looked for in the Peshawar valley. But Sir Aurel Stein, who picks up the story at this point, is in favour' of the 'longer but more well-frequented road running through the fertile valleys of Panjkora [Panjkurah] and Swat'. He 'in this regard closely follows Arrian'.[76] In elaborating on the route Alexander followed, they have stated:

> Leaving the Aspasians of Kunar and Bajaur [Bajawar], and the Guraeans of Panjkhora [Panjkurah] behind, Alexander now entered the territory of the Assakenians as Aśvakas whose chief cities were Massaga, Bazira, and Ora. Stein therefore attempted to identify the sites of these cities in the Swāt rather than the Peshawar valley.[77]

Interestingly, Giuseppe Tucci 'fifteen years later' modified his opinion and stated, on the basis of Curtius Rufus' version, that Massaga was located in the Swat Valley beyond Bazira, viz. upstream from the site of Barikut Ghwandai.[78] 'The whereabouts of Massaga should be sought in the area of Nipkhi-khel [Nikpi Khail/Khel], close to Aligrama [Aligramah], where excavations were revealing interesting particulars.'[79] Elaborating on this hypothesis, Dr Luca M. Olivieri has opined that 'Curtius Rufus' description of the position of Massaga fits the site of Aligrama rather well, since it is situated to the west of the River Swat like Massaga was'.[80] Besides: 'It likewise corresponds to the information given by the Latin historian in that it shows signs of the usual levelling work and hewing into the rock, preparatory to any building, which is supported by the archaeological evidence, and lastly, as shown above, by the type of building method employed.'[81] To further augment his hypothesis, Dr Luca has taken the name of the torrent Mahak, at a distance from Aligramah which, according to Giuseppe Tucci, derive from that of Massaka (Massaga) and has contended:

> In this case the Massaga of Alexander's time must surely have been situated upstream from Barikot, higher up the Swat Valley, almost

certainly in the wide, fertile alluvial plain, formed by the confluence of the rivers Jambil, Saidu and Swat, seen to the north-west from Aligrama hill.[82]

It must be noted that 'the wide, fertile alluvial plain, formed by the confluence' of the Jambil and Saidu [Marghuzar] streams and then their confluence with the Swat River are not 'seen to the north-west from Aligrama hill', but to its southeast and southwest respectively. Besides, although in the end Dr Luca has attempted to derive the same conclusion, he has nevertheless admitted that 'to lay siege to which [Aligramah] it would have been necessary to cross the Swat River a second time, a fact, however, of which there is no record in the sources'.[83]

Dr Luca M. Olivieri's reconstruction of locating Massaga 'perhaps near the modern Aligrama....or in any case somewhere in that fertile and important area where the Saidu, Jambil and Swat Rivers meet',[84] is based on conjectures and analogies which need to be established by solid proofs. For locating Massaga near Aligramah, Alexander was to cross the Swat River a second time which, as quoted above, Dr Luca has admitted is not supported by the sources. And as far its location in the 'fertile and important area where the Saidu, Jambil and Swat Rivers meet' is concerned, although the Jambil and Saidu (or Marghuzar) streams meet in Mingawarah-Amankut (formerly Katilai), to the southeast of Aligramah Hill, its confluence with the Swat River is near Udigram, which is to the southwest of Aligramah Hill and which is identified as Ora. Hence, if Dr Luca's hypothesis is accepted, there remain no other option but for Massaga and Ora to be recognized one and the same place, which certainly they were not.

Although the succeeding researches about the area are more authentic, and although his article has been published much earlier in 1894, it needs to be mentioned for the readers' information that, following Arrian's account, which he has termed as 'the careful statements',[85] Frederic Pincott has given Alexander's route into and from Swat quite differently. He has identified the 'Daedala' of Curtius Rufus as the village 'Daiolai' (Deolai/Diwlai) and 'Acadira' as 'Azara'[86] (Hazara/Hazarah), in the Nikpi Khail or present-day Kabal *tahsil* area. He has endeavoured to prove that Aornos was not situated 'on the bank of the Indus'.[87] But Giuseppe Tucci has tried to prove that Curtius' Daedalae was an ethnic group, Daradas or Dards, in which 'Swāt was included'.[88]

Arrian has stated that the Bazirians (the inhabitants of Bazira) 'at the dead of night fled from their city to the Rock, as all the other barbarians were doing, for, having left their cities, they were fleeing to the rock in that land called Aornos;…for this is a mighty mass of rock in that part of the country'.[89] If Bazira was the present-day Barikut, the Bazirians must have fled to a rock situated nearby, which they attain in the dead of night. That could not be but Mount Ilam. If Aornos was the Pir-sar (as asserted by Aurel Stein), it would have been difficult or well-nigh impossible to flee from Barikut there 'at the dead of night', because for this a journey of days was required. Flight to Aornos, in such a manner, if it was Pir-sar, was possible only if Bazira was situated in eastern Bunair.

Therefore, Giuseppe Tucci—who has asserted that Stein's identification of 'Bazira' as 'Bari-kot, Bir-kot is beyond any doubt'[90]—has rightly questioned Stein's identification of the rock of Aornos as Pir-sar. Tucci's indication to the rock where the Bazirians at last fled and took shelter, after their protracted and gallant defence of Bazira, as the rock Ilam,[91] near Barikut, is appealing. Giuseppe Tucci has asserted at another place as well that 'because of its sacredness, Ilam was the refuge for the vanquished from Bazira'.[92]

While dealing with this point and the identification of Aornos as Una-sar on Pir-sar by Aurel Stein, Dr Abdur Rahman and Shah Nazar Khan have stated that Olaf Caroe 'considers this identification as Stein's most fascinating work. But it may be noted, philologically at least, the identification has no' legs 'to stand' on.[93] Stein too himself has stated in this respect: 'In view of these local observations the suggestion appears to me justified that the place of safety sought by the fugitives from Bazira was much more likely to have been Mount Ilam than the distant Aornos by the Indus.'[94] And that 'the text does not necessarily imply that they [the Bazirians] too fled to the "rock" of Aornos'.[95] Stein has clarified that it was not the Bazirians who fled to Aornos but the inhabitants of the areas above Ora, up the valley, who because of the fear of the Macedonians' advance, and having no option to flee to the west or to the south, fled to the east to Aornos.[96] It is worth noting that 'Una' or 'Unra' is the name of a place not only on Pir-sar in Chakisar or Shanglahpar area but places with this name are found in the Swat Valley proper as well. One place with such name is found in the Nikpi Khail, or present-day Kabal *tahsil* area, and one in the present-day Matta *tahsil* area.

From Arrian's detailed account of Aornos and its campaign and
Alexander's other campaigns mentioned just after his exploits in Swat,
it can be easily inferred that Aornos was situated outside Swat proper;
whether it be the 'Mahaban' identified by James Abbott,[97] or the 'Ranigat'
of Alexander Cunningham,[98] or Aurel Stein's 'Pir-sar'. However, dealing
with '*The Problem of Aornos*', Dr Luca M. Olivieri has analyzed the
accounts of the Greek writers and, keeping them in view, the possible
routes of Alexander. He has contended that 'Arrian's conception of the
geography of the region was rather confused even though he had fuller
information'; and that: 'By contrast, the identification of Aornos with
Mount Ilam is plausible and logical.'[99] He has endeavoured to prove that
Aornos is Mount Ilam.[100] In concluding his analysis, he had mentioned:

> However, by accepting the alterative hypothesis that sees Aornos in
> Mount Ilam, and crediting Curtius Rufus' account, it is plausible that
> Alexander, after having captured the stronghold, would have gone
> through the Karakar Pass on his way to the Indus via Buner and passed
> the site known to Alexander's historians as Embolima or Ecbolima....
> before joining the bulk of the army near the Indus.[101]

Gallantry of the People of Swat

A critical analysis of the accounts of the Greek writers shows that,
although Arrian had given a detailed account of Alexander's campaign
and exploits in Swat, he is not simply biased, which is natural,[102] but
prejudiced. For instance he has contended: 'When the *barbarians* [the
Assakenoi or the people of Swat] saw Alexander approaching they had
not the *courage* to encounter him in the open field with their collective
forces, but dispersed to their several cities, *which they resolved to defend
to the last extremity* [my italics].'[103] Arrian himself terms the retreat
of the natives to their cities as a defensive measure and, as for lack of
courage, he has admitted in the same sentence that they resolved to
defend their cities 'to the last extremity'.

Arrian's own succeeding narration has itself fully endorsed the valour,
dauntless courage, gallantry, and bravery of the Assakenoi. It was not their
cowardice, which took them to their cities against Alexander but their
policy and strategy of 'passive defence'. Aurel Stein has aptly observed:

> From this and the account of the several sieges which followed it seems
> safe to infer that the Assakēnoi, *though a brave race*, could not have been

addicted to those fierce ways of fighting which make the present Pathān tribes such formidable opponents on their own ground. This conclusion is fully supported by what I have already noted regarding the character of the fortified residences found scattered on the hill-sides of Swāt and the reliance that *the ancient inhabitants of Swāt were evidently accustomed to place upon such means of passive defence* [my italics].[104]

Furthermore, although the city of Massaga was taken by storm, it was after a brave and sustained defence and due to the use of unfamiliar battering engines by the Macedonians and then only after the king of the Assakenois was killed and Alexander entered into a peace agreement with the natives, which he then proceeded to violate.[105] Similarly, although Alexander expected that the inhabitants of Bazira would capitulate, when they would learn that Massaga had fallen,[106] they, and those in Ora too, stood firm and tried to gallantly defend their position and possession till the last. It was only after the arrival of 'Coenus' reinforcements' and of 'the contingent from Massaga' that 'Alexander was able to occupy Ora without difficulty'.[107] And the Bazirians, already continuously besieged and hard pressed, left their city only after the fall of Ora, because now all the Macedonian forces in the area under Alexander, having advanced technology and means of war, were concentrating on Bazira. The protracted and arduous siege of both the places worked in bringing about their occupation by or fall to the Macedonians, as has also been asserted by Aurel Stein that 'the hill of Bīr-kōṭ was a place very difficult to take by anything less than a protracted and arduous siege'.[108]

   The inhabitants of Swat of that time were so determined in their defence that their ruler, the Assakenois, employed a large contingent of 7000 Indians from outside. This 'clearly indicates conditions of organized defence wholly different from those with which a modern invader of tribal territories on the North-West Frontier would have to reckon'.[109] This ruler even made an alliance, for the defence of his country, 'with the king of the Abhisāra country beyond the Indus, who sent contingents to his support'.[110] The main reasons and factors responsible for the defeat or capitulation of the natives in Swat was their reliance on Indians, or outsiders, for their defence; their 'reliance', as pointed out by Aurel Stein, 'upon...means of passive defence';[111] and the use of advanced scientific means of war[112] and better strategy by Alexander and the Macedonians.

POST-ALEXANDER

The inhabitants of Swat of that time, who dwelled in their rock citadels, 'were unschooled to recognise an overlord, and as prepared to give trouble to anyone who tried to incorporate them in an imperial system as their Pathān successors of a later day'.[113] They so detested alien rule that 'whilst Alexander was encamped among the rivers of the Punjab' they 'threw off fear and renounced allegiance'.[114]

After his exploits in Swat, Alexander established Macedonian posts at Ora, Bazira, and Massaga, to guard the country, and personally 'turned south to the Peshawar valley' to carry his campaign into the trans-Indus country to the east.[115] Alexander made arrangements for administering the country west of the Indus by appointing a Macedonian, Nicanor, a satrap of the country in 327 BCE before proceeding on his campaign to the east of the Indus. Nicanor held the position 'from the Autumn of 327 B.C. to an unknown time in 326 [BCE] when Sisicottus (Sandracottus), Commander of the Aornos stronghold, informed Alexander that the former had been assassinated by Assacenian rebels'.[116] Olga Tribulato and Dr Luca M. Olivieri have asserted: 'We know that the Swat rebelled as early as 326 BCE (Arr. *An.* V 20, 7), and that probably by 324–323 [BCE] it had been abandoned by the Macedonians.'[117]

Nicanor was succeeded by other Macedonian satraps till the Macedonian power totally collapsed on the Indian borderland when Porus, the reigning Macedonian satrap, was murdered by a Macedonian General Eudamos in 317 BCE.[118] Dr Luca M. Olivieri has contended: 'We may suppose that after a series of complicated events…by 324–323, at the latest, Macedonian control of the region was reduced to the fluvial corridor of the Kabul River dominated by Peukelaotis… and that the Swat Valley was definitively lost'.[119] And that: 'Even if one does not wish to exclude the presence of a Macedonian garrison at Bazira, this could have lasted at most for no more than three or four years (always supposing that Nicanor's successors regained control and enforced Macedonian rule in Swat) or else but a few months (in the opposite case).'[120]

It, therefore, can be said that though Macedonian satraps were appointed for the territories west of the Indus, the people of Swat threw off Macedonian yoke once for all, after Alexander's departure and resumed their independent and sovereign status.

NOTES

1. Aurel Stein, *On Alexander's Track to the Indus: Personal Narrative of Explorations on the North-West Frontier of India* (repr., Karachi: Indus Publications, 1995), 42. Also see Aurel Stein, 'Alexander's Campaign on the Indian North-West Frontier: Notes from Explorations between Upper Swāt and the Indus', *The Geographical Journal* (London), 70/5 (November 1927), 423–4 (Stable URL: http://www.jstor.org/stable/1783476; accessed: 30/10/2011).

2. Giuseppe Tucci, 'On Swāt. The Dards and Connected Problems', *East and West* (Rome), 27/1–4 (December 1977), 14.

3. Stein, *On Alexander's Track to the Indus*, 43.

4. George Woodcock, *The Greeks in India* (London: Faber and Faber Ltd., 1966), 21. Also see Thomas Holdich, *The Gates of India: Being an Historical Narrative* (1st edn. published in Pakistan, Quetta: Gosha-e-Adab, 1977), 16, 19–22, 128.

5. Woodcock, *The Greeks in India*, 21.

6. See Rufus, Plutarch, Justin, and Arrians' accounts in J.W. M'crindle, *The Invasion of India by Alexander the Great: As Described by Arrian, Q Curtius, Diodoros, Plutarch and Justin*, with introduction by J.W. M'crindle (repr., Karachi: Indus Publications, 1992), 191–4, 305, 321, 79–82 respectively.

7. Giuseppe Tucci, 'Oriental Notes, II: An Image of a Devi Discovered in Swat and Some Connected Problems', in Giuseppe Tucci, *On Swāt. Historical and Archaeological Notes*, with introduction by Domenico Faccenna, eds. P. Callieri and A. Filigenzi, reprint of the original 1997 edition, with preface by M. Ashraf Khan (Islamabad: Taxila Institute of Asian Civilizations, 2013), 131–2.

8. For discerning confusion in the names of the rivers and passages Alexander crossed and passed through in the region, see Abdur Rahman and Shah Nazar Khan, 'Alexander's Route and Stein: Massaga to Ora', *Ancient Pakistan* (Peshawar), 19 (2008), 49–54; Luca M. Olivieri, 'Notes on the Problematical Sequence of Alexander's Itinerary in Swat: A Geo-Historical Approach', *East and West* (Rome), 46/1–2 (June 1996), 58–61 (Stable URL: http://www.jstor.org/stable/29757254; accessed: 30/10/2011).

9. Arrian, Fourth Book, *Chapters XXV–XXVI*, in M'crindle, *The Invasion of India by Alexander the Great*, 66.

10. Ibid., 65–6; Vincent A. Smith, *The Early History of India: From 600 B.C. to the Muhammadan Conquest, Including the Invasion of Alexander the Great*, 4th edn., revised by S.M. Edwardes (repr., Oxford: At the Clarendon Press, 1957), 57.

11. India at that time was not one political entity but divided into numerous petty kingdoms or principalities, ruled by local rulers. As the political geography changes throughout the history, the unified India, as a political entity, came into being later. Therefore, India, during Alexander's time, may not be construed for a political unified India but for the geographical region generally or commonly called and referred to India, and the Indians for the inhabitants of that area.

12. Arrian, Fourth Book, *Chapter XXVI*, in M'crindle, *The Invasion of India by Alexander the Great*, 66–7.

13. Ibid., 67. Also see Q. Curtius Rufus, Eighth Book, *Chapter X*, in M'crindle, *The Invasion of India by Alexander the Great*, 195.

14. Agnes Savill, *Alexander the Great and His Time* (3rd edn., London: Barrie and Rockliff, 1959), 95–6.

15. Rufus, Eighth Book, *Chapter X*, in M'crindle, *The Invasion of India by Alexander the Great*, 195.

16. Arrian, Fourth Book, *Chapter XXVI*, in M'crindle, *The Invasion of India by Alexander the Great*, 67.

17. Ibid., *Chapters XXVI–XXVII*, 67–8.

18. Ibid., *Chapter XXVII*, 68–9.

19. See Rufus, Eighth Book, *Chapter X*, in M'crindle, *The Invasion of India by Alexander the Great*, 195–6.

20. Ibid., 194.

21. Tucci, 'On Swāt. The Dards and Connected Problems', 15.

22. Plutarch, *Chapter LIX*, in M'crindle, *The Invasion of India by Alexander the Great*, 306.

23. For Alexander's strategy and war techniques, he used against the locals at Massaga, see Smith, *The Early History of India*, 58; Savill, *Alexander the Great and His Time*, 95–6; Rufus, Eighth Book, *Chapter X*, in M'crindle, *The Invasion of India by Alexander the Great*, 195–6.

24. Arrian, Fourth Book, *Chapter XXVII*, in M'crindle, *The Invasion of India by Alexander the Great*, 69.

25. Ibid., 69–70.

26. Ibid., 70.

27. Olivieri, 'Notes on the Problematical Sequence of Alexander's Itinerary in Swat: A Geo-Historical Approach', 57.

28. Arrian, Fourth Book, *Chapter XXVIII*, in M'crindle, *The Invasion of India by Alexander the Great*, 70.

29. Rahman and Shah Nazar Khan, 'Alexander's Route and Stein: Massaga to Ora', 53.

30. Arrian, Fourth Book, *Chapter XXVIII*, in M'crindle, *The Invasion of India by Alexander the Great*, 71.

31. Stein, *On Alexander's Track to the Indus*, 43. Also see Aurel Stein, *An Archaeological tour in Upper Swāt and Adjacent Hill Tracts* (Calcutta: Government of India, Central Publication Branch, 1930), 25; Aurel Stein, 'Alexander's Campaign on the Indian North-West Frontier: Notes from Explorations between Upper Swāt and the Indus', *The Geographical Journal* (London), 70/6 (December 1927), 515 (Stable URL: http://www.jstor.org/stable/1782915); accessed: 30/10/2011). It is worth noting, however, that Luca M. Olivieri has contended that Arrian's account is 'actually somewhat confused if the *Anabasis* and the *Indica* are compared' (Olivieri, 'Notes on the Problematical Sequence of Alexander's Itinerary in Swat: A Geo-Historical Approach', 61). Aurel Stein, however, at another place, while referring to the inaccuracy of Arrian's statement of the lying of Pushkalavati, close to the present Charsada, 'not far from the Indus', has cautioned that 'the error must warn us as to possible geographical mistakes even in the most reliable of the narratives dealing with Alexander's Indian campaign' (Stein, 'Alexander's Campaign on the Indian North-West Frontier: Notes from Explorations between Upper Swāt and the Indus', No. 5, November 1927, 437).

32. Arrian, Fourth Book, *Chapter XXVII*, in M'crindle, *The Invasion of India by Alexander the Great*, 69.

33. Ibid., n. 1.

34. Arrian, Fourth Book, *Chapter XXVII*, in M'crindle, *The Invasion of India by Alexander the Great*, 68.
35. Rufus, Eighth Book, *Chapter X*, in M'crindle, *The Invasion of India by Alexander the Great*, 194.
36. Ibid., 196.
37. Ibid., 196–7.
38. Diodoros Siculus, Seventeenth Book, *Chapter LXXXIV*, in M'crindle, *The Invasion of India by Alexander the Great*, 269.
39. See Plutarch, *Chapter LIX*, in M'crindle, *The Invasion of India by Alexander the Great*, 305–6.
40. For a note about the Daedali mountains, see M'crindle, *The Invasion of India by Alexander the Great*, 194 n. 1.
41. Justin, Twelfth Book, *Chapter VII*, in M'crindle, *The Invasion of India by Alexander the Great*, 322.
42. Olivieri, 'Notes on the Problematical Sequence of Alexander's Itinerary in Swat: A Geo-Historical Approach', 70–1.
43. Frederic Pincott, 'The Route by which Alexander entered India', *Journal of the Royal Asiatic Society of Great Britain and Ireland* (October 1894), 686 (Stable URL: http://www.jstor.org/stable/25197226; accessed: 30/10/2011).
44. Tucci, 'On Swāt. The Dards and Connected Problems', 49.
45. Holdich, *The Gates of India: Being an Historical Narrative*, 119–20.
46. Smith, *The Early History of India*, 58.
47. Ibid., n. 1.
48. See Arrian, Fourth Book, *Chapters XXVI–XXVII*, in M'crindle, *The Invasion of India by Alexander the Great*, 66–9.
49. Siculus, Seventeenth Book, *Chapter LXXXIV*, in M'crindle, *The Invasion of India by Alexander the Great*, 269–70. Also see Smith, *The Early History of India*, 58–9.
50. Smith, *The Early History of India*, 59.
51. Savill, *Alexander the Great and His Time*, 96.
52. See Siculus, Seventeenth Book, *Chapter LXXXIV*, in M'crindle, *The Invasion of India by Alexander the Great*, 269–70.
53. Ibid., 269.
54. Plutarch, *Chapter LIX*, in M'crindle, *The Invasion of India by Alexander the Great*, 306.
55. See Muhammad Asif Khan, *Tarikh-i Riyasat-i Swat wa Sawanih-i Hayat Baniy-i Riyasat-i Swat Hazrat Miangul Gul Shahzadah Abdul Wadud Khan Badshah Sahib*, with *dibachah*, *hisah awal*, *saluramah hisah*, and *hisah pinzamah* by Muhammad Asif Khan (Pashto) (Printed by Ferozsons Ltd., Peshawar [1958]), 25; Muhammad Asif Khan, *Tarikh Riyasat-i Swat wa Sawanih-i Hayat Bani Riyasat-i Swat Miangul Abdul Wadud* (Urdu) (2nd edn., Mingawarah, Swat: Shoaib Sons Publishers and Booksellers, 2001), 22–3; Muhammad Asif Khan, *The Story of Swat as told by the Founder Miangul Abdul Wadud Badshah Sahib to Muhammad Asif Khan*, with preface, introduction and appendices by Muhammad Asif Khan, and trans. preface and trans. by Ashruf Altaf Husain (Printed by Ferozsons Ltd., Peshawar, 1963), xix; Sayyed Abdul Ghafoor Qasmay, *Tarikh-i Riyasat-i Swat* (Pashto) (Printed by Hamidia Press, Peshawar, n.d.), 17; Sayyed Mohd. Abdul Ghafoor Qasmi, *The History of Swat* (Printed by D.C. Anand & Sons, Peshawar,

1940), 2; Sayyed Abdul Ghafoor Qasmi, *Hidyah Wadudiyah yani Sawanih Hayat Ala Hazrat Badshah Abdul Wadud Khan Khuldullah Mulkahu Hukamran Riyasat-i Yusufzai Swat wa Mutaliqat* (Urdu) (Printed by Sawdagar Press, Baraili, n.d.), 10; Abdul Halim Asar, *Swat da Tarikh pah Ranra kay* (Pashto) (Bajawar: Darul Ishaat Bajawar, n.d.), 29; Fazle Rabbi Rahi, *Swat Tarikh kay Ayiynay mayn* (Urdu) (2nd edn., Mingawarah, Swat: Shoaib Sons Publishers, Booksellers, 1997), 23–4; Fazle Rabbi Rahi, *Riyasat-i Swat: Tarikh ka Aik Warq* (Urdu) (Mingawarah, Swat: Shoaib Sons Publishers and Booksellers, 2000), 18–19; Fazle Rabbi Rahi, *Swat: Sayahu ki Jannat* (Urdu) (Mingawarah, Swat: Shoaib Sons Publishers and Booksellers, 2000), 15; Muhammad Parwaish Shaheen, *Da Swat Gwalunah* (Pashto) (Mingawarah, Swat: Shoaib Sons Publishers, Booksellers, 1988), 55–8; Nur Muhammad Shah Ghubah Jan, *Manzum Tarikh-i Swat* (Pashto, verse) (Printed by Ahmad Printing Press, Mingawarah, Swat, n.d.), 2–3; Abdul Qayum Balala, *The Charming Swat* (Lahore: Maqsood Publishers, [2000]), 9; Abdul Qayum Balala, *Dastan-i Swat* (Urdu) (Kabal, Swat: Jan Kitab Koor, 2010), 3. Strange enough, Muhammad Parwaish Shaheen has termed 'Massaga' as Manglawar (see Shaheen, *Da Swat Gwalunah*, 55).

56. Stein, *On Alexander's Track to the Indus*, 61. Also see ibid., 120; Stein, *An Archaeological tour in Upper Swāt and Adjacent Hill Tracts*, 41.

57. Tucci, 'On Swāt. The Dards and Connected Problems', 16, 55.

58. Ahmad Hasan Dani, *Peshawar: Historic City of the Frontier* (2nd edn., Lahore: Sang-e-Meel Publications, 1995), 256.

59. Muhammad Parwaish Shaheen has claimed that Alexander wished to take revenge in Swat for the burning Athens by the Swati forces who took part in the war against the Greeks on the Persian side (see Shaheen, *Da Swat Gwalunah*, 54–5). However, Dr Rafiullah Khan asserts: 'But this view also seems to have sound ground, to some extent at least, though of secondary importance in the overall dominating preoccupation with defence. If I am not wrong it is also written by some scholars, though it is difficult to remind the sources at the moment. At least it was an act of laying a claim to the legacy of Persian empire' (Dr Rafiullah Khan's note to this point on an earlier draft of this chapter). It is pertinent to mention that Swat's remaining part of the Persian Empire is not historically tested and agreed upon contention. And 'laying a claim to the legacy of Persian empire' is quite different from invasion in revenge.

60. J.C. Powell-Price, *A History of India* (London: Thomas Nelson and Sons Ltd., 1955), 31.

61. Smith, *The Early History of India*, 54.

62. Powell-Price, *A History of India*, 31.

63. Stein, *On Alexander's Track to the Indus*, 41. Also see Stein, *An Archaeological tour in Upper Swāt and Adjacent Hill Tracts*, 23.

64. Holdich, *The Gates of India: Being an Historical Narrative*, 95–6.

65. Olivieri, 'Notes on the Problematical Sequence of Alexander's Itinerary in Swat: A Geo-Historical Approach', 72.

66. Stein, *An Archaeological tour in Upper Swāt and Adjacent Hill Tracts*, 40.

67. For details, see M'crindle, *The Invasion of India by Alexander the Great*, 334–8; [Alexander Cunningham], *Cunningham's Ancient Geography of India*,

edited with introduction and notes by Surendranath Majumdar Sastri (Calcutta: Chuckervertty, Chatterjee & Co., Ltd., 1924), 67–90; Olaf Caroe, *The Pathans: 550 B.C.–A.D. 1957* (repr., Karachi: Oxford University Press, 1976), 49–57; Tucci, 'On Swāt. The Dards and Connected Problems', 9–103.

68. Stein, *On Alexander's Track to the Indus*, 43.

69. Ibid., 44. Also see Stein, *An Archaeological tour in Upper Swāt and Adjacent Hill Tracts*, 26.

70. Stein, *On Alexander's Track to the Indus*, 45. Also see Stein, *An Archaeological tour in Upper Swāt and Adjacent Hill Tracts*, 26–7.

71. [Cunningham], *Cunningham's Ancient Geography of India*, 667 n. (i) 3.

72. See Rahman and Shah Nazar Khan, 'Alexander's Route and Stein: Massaga to Ora', 51.

73. For Aurel Stein's details about Massaga, Bazira, Ora, and Aornos, see Stein, *On Alexander's Track to the Indus*, 43–8, 53–61, 113–48; Stein, *An Archaeological tour in Upper Swāt and Adjacent Hill Tracts*, 25–6 (for Massaga), 28–9 (for Bazira), 38–41 (for Ora), 66–94 (for Aornos); Stein, 'Alexander's Campaign on the Indian North-West Frontier: Notes from Explorations between Upper Swāt and the Indus', No. 5, November 1927, 425–6 (for Massaga), 426–33 (for Bazira), 433–7 (for Ora), 438–40 (and No. 6, December 1927), 515–40 (for Aornos). Muhammad Habibullah Khan Khattak has said that in his 'opinion Bazdara in the Malakand Agency is very close to the ancient name Bazira' (Muhammad Habibullah Khan Khattak, *Buner: The Forgotten Part of Ancient Uddiyana* (Karachi: By the Author, Department of Archaeology and Museums, Government of Pakistan, 1997), 37). It, however, is noteworthy that it was much earlier that Frederic Pincott has tried to identify Bazira as the present-day Bazdira (Bazdarah) (see Pincott, 'The Route by which Alexander entered India', 685–8). Whereas, much earlier than Fredric Pincott, M. Court, in 1837, has, although not with certainty, hypothetically identified Bajawar as the Bazira of the Greeks (see M. Court, 'Conjectures on the March of Alexander', *The Asiatic Journal and Monthly Register for British and Foreign India, China, and Australia* (London), New Series, 23/89 (May–August 1937), 50). Thomas Holdich, has located Massaga near 'Matkanai, close to the Malakand Pass', in Lower Swat Valley (see Holdich, *The Gates of India: Being an Historical Narrative*, 105, 128). He, moreover, is inclined to recognize Bazira at Rustam and Ora at Bazar (see ibid., 106. For details about Thomas Holdich's contentions about Massaga, Bazira, Ora, and Nysa, see ibid., 94–134). It should be mentioned that his study, first published in 1910, precedes that of Aurel Stein's; about whose former work he has asserted: 'Dr. Stein's methods are thorough. He leaves nothing to speculation, and indulges in no romance, whatever may be the temptation' (ibid., 109). Later authorities, however, did not agree with these contentions or identifications.

74. Luca M. Olivieri, '"Frontier Archaeology": Sir Aurel Stein, Swat, and the Indian Aornos', *South Asian Studies* (London), 31/1 (2015), 63.

75. Ibid.

76. Rahman and Shah Nazar Khan, 'Alexander's Route and Stein: Massaga to Ora', 50.

77. Ibid., 51.

78. Quoted in Olivieri, 'Notes on the Problematical Sequence of Alexander's Itinerary in Swat: A Geo-Historical Approach', 62; Olivieri, '"Frontier Archaeology": Sir Aurel Stein, Swat, and the Indian Aornos', 70 n. 26, 63.

79. Quoted in Olivieri, '"Frontier Archaeology": Sir Aurel Stein, Swat, and the Indian Aornos', 70 n. 26, 63.

80. Olivieri, 'Notes on the Problematical Sequence of Alexander's Itinerary in Swat: A Geo-Historical Approach', 62.

81. Ibid., 62–4.

82. Ibid., 64.

83. Ibid., 71.

84. Ibid.

85. Pincott, 'The Route by which Alexander entered India', 688, 686.

86. Ibid., 684.

87. See ibid., 686–7. For his detailed analysis of Alexander's route and the identification of the places Massaga, Ora, Bazira, and Aornos, see ibid., 677–89.

88. See Tucci, 'On Swat. The Dards and Connected Problems', 17–18.

89. Arrian, Fourth Book, *Chapter XXVIII*, in M'crindle, *The Invasion of India by Alexander the Great*, 70.

90. Giuseppe Tucci, 'Preliminary report on an archaeological survey in Swat', *East and West* (Rome), 9/4 (December 1958), 327 n. 28. For the confirmation of Bazira, being Barikut, also see Luca M. Olivieri and Elisa Iori, 'Early-historic Data from the 2016 Excavation Campaigns at the Urban Site of Barikot, Swat (Pakistan): A Shifting Perspective' in A. Hardy and L. Greaves, eds., *South Asian Art and Archaeology* (New Delhi: Dev Publishers & Distributers, 2016), 35.

91. See Tucci, 'On Swat. The Dards and Connected Problems', 52–5.

92. Giuseppe Tucci, 'Recent Explorations in Swat', in Tucci, *On Swāt. Historical and Archaeological Notes*, with introduction by Domenico Faccenna, eds. P. Callieri and A. Filigenzi, 306.

93. Rahman and Shah Nazar Khan, 'Alexander's Route and Stein: Massaga to Ora', 53.

94. Stein, *An Archaeological tour in Upper Swāt and Adjacent Hill Tracts*, 30; Stein, 'Alexander's Campaign on the Indian North-West Frontier: Notes from Explorations between Upper Swāt and the Indus', No. 5, November 1927, 433.

95. Stein, 'Alexander's Campaign on the Indian North-West Frontier: Notes from Explorations between Upper Swāt and the Indus', No. 5, November 1927, 432; Stein, *An Archaeological tour in Upper Swāt and Adjacent Hill Tracts*, 29. For Dr Luca M. Olivieri's observation on the point, see Olivieri, '"Frontier Archaeology": Sir Aurel Stein, Swat, and the Indian Aornos', 58–70.

96. See Stein, 'Alexander's Campaign on the Indian North-West Frontier: Notes from Explorations between Upper Swāt and the Indus', No. 5, November 1927, 437–9; Stein, *On Alexander's Track to the Indus*, 120–3; Stein, *An Archaeological tour in Upper Swāt and Adjacent Hill Tracts*, 67–8.

97. See [Cunningham], *Cunningham's Ancient Geography of India*, 68.

98. See ibid., 67–90.

99. Olivieri, 'Notes on the Problematical Sequence of Alexander's Itinerary in Swat: A Geo-Historical Approach', 65.

100. See ibid., 64–70.

101. Ibid., 72.

102. Because: 'To be biased in favour of our own community or the communities which are of the same religion or race, or which are allied with us against our enemies, is not something that is within our own will' (Zia Gökalp, *Turkish Nationalism and Western Civilization: Selected Essays of Zia Gökalp*, trans. and ed. with introduction by Niyazi Berkes (London: George Allen and Unwin Ltd, 1959), 113). And the stone 'is the only thing that may be described truthfully as unbiased' (Ghani Khan, *The Pathans: A Sketch* (repr., Islamabad: Pushto Adabi Society (Regd), 1990), 50).

103. Arrian, Fourth Book, *Chapter XXV*, in M'crindle, *The Invasion of India by Alexander the Great*, 66.

104. Stein, *On Alexander's Track to the Indus*, 42. Also see Stein, 'Alexander's Campaign on the Indian North-West Frontier: Notes from Explorations between Upper Swāt and the Indus', No. 5, November 1927, 424; Stein, *An Archaeological tour in Upper Swāt and Adjacent Hill Tracts*, 24.

105. To discern several prejudiced accounts, that also ignore Alexander's highhandedness and weaknesses—e.g. even fierce fighting by the local women along with their men against the invaders, Alexander's breach of the terms of capitulation and massacre of those who capitulated, and his violation of the chastity of their women, and the account of his wound and his remarks at its pain—cf. Arrian accounts with those of the Curtius Rufus, Diodoros Siculus, Plutarch, and Justin in M'crindle, *The Invasion of India by Alexander the Great*.

106. Arrian, Fourth Book, *Chapter XXVII*, in M'crindle, *The Invasion of India by Alexander the Great*, 69.

107. Olivieri, 'Notes on the Problematical Sequence of Alexander's Itinerary in Swat: A Geo-Historical Approach', 57.

108. Stein, 'Alexander's Campaign on the Indian North-West Frontier: Notes from Explorations between Upper Swāt and the Indus', No. 5, November 1927, 430. Also see Stein, *An Archaeological tour in Upper Swāt and Adjacent Hill Tracts*, 27.

109. Stein, *An Archaeological tour in Upper Swāt and Adjacent Hill Tracts*, 26.

110. See *The Cambridge History of India*, Vol. 1, *Ancient India*, ed. E.J. Rapson (1st Indian repr., Delhi: S. Chand & Co., 1955), 316, 323.

111. Stein, *On Alexander's Track to the Indus*, 42.

112. Also see ibid., 45; Stein, 'Alexander's Campaign on the Indian North-West Frontier: Notes from Explorations between Upper Swāt and the Indus', No. 5, November 1927, 426; Stein, *An Archaeological tour in Upper Swāt and Adjacent Hill Tracts*, 26.

113. *The Cambridge History of India*, Vol. 1, *Ancient India*, 315.

114. Ibid., 331.

115. Stein, *On Alexander's Track to the Indus*, 61.

116. Olivieri, 'Notes on the Problematical Sequence of Alexander's Itinerary in Swat: A Geo-Historical Approach', 51.

117. Olga Tribulato and Luca Maria Olivieri, 'Writing Greek in the Swat Region: A New Graffito from Barikot (Pakistan)', *Zeitschriftfür Papyrologie und Epigraphik* (Köln), 204 (2017), 133.

118. *Imperial Gazetteer of India: Provincial Series; North-West Frontier Province* (repr., Lahore: Sang-e-Meel Publications, 1991), 13. Also see R.C. Majumdar,

H.C. Raychaudhuri, and Kalikinkar Datta, *An Advanced History of India* (repr., Lahore: Famous Books, 1992), 97–101.

119. Olivieri, 'Notes on the Problematical Sequence of Alexander's Itinerary in Swat: A Geo-Historical Approach', 51.
120. Ibid., 52.

4

MAURYAS TO SHAHIS

MAURYA PERIOD

With the decline of the Macedonian power in the region and Chandragupta Maurya's acquisition of power, the new dynasty came on the scene about 321 BCE.[1] Chandragupta Maurya ruled 'for 24 eventful years, from 322 to 298 B.C.'.[2] The Mauryas expanded their domain and brought most of the South Asian subcontinent and the territory beyond it, as far as the area of Afghanistan, under their rule. It is unclear when the Mauryas—about whom Mohammad Yunus has said that originally they 'belonged to Swat'[3] and that it was due to their dwelling in and connection with the Mount Mora (Murah) that they got the epithet of Maurya[4]—brought Swat under their control and how far they maintained their sway here. V.A. Smith has contended:

> There is no reason to suppose that the trans-Indus provinces were lost by Bindusara, and it is reasonable to assume that they continued under the sway of Asoka [Ashoka, ca. 269–232 BCE], who refers to Antiochos, King of Syria, in terms which suggest that the Syrian and Indian empires were conterminous.... The Swat valley also contained evidences of Asoka's passion for building.[5]

He has further stated: 'Asoka's [Ashoka's] empire, therefore, comprised the countries now known as Afghanistan, as far as the Hindu Kush, Baluchistan, Makran, Sind, Kachh (Cutch), the Swat Valley, with the adjoining regions.'[6]

Hiuen Tsiang (now spelled as Xuanzang; also Xuan Zang) reports 'a *stupa* called Lu-hi-ta-kia (Rohitaka)' built by Ashoka-raja at a distance of 50 li or so, in the west, from the town Mungali.[7] This points to Ashoka's authority or at least influence in the area. Radhakumud Mookerji's version that 'Yuan Chwang saw Asokan topes in Kapis (Kafiristan), Nagar (Jelalabad), and Udyāna in the north-west',[8] too have been taken as proof of Uddiyana's being part of Ashokan Empire.

The contention of Giuseppe Tucci that the Cakravartin Raja mentioned by Hiuen Tsiang (Xuanzang) is 'evidently Aśoka',[9] also suggests that, when Swat was Ashoka's park, it would logically have been under his suzerainty. However, according to Dr Rafiullah Khan, scholars have recently contended that the number of *stupa*s (84,000) assigned to Ashoka is an exaggerated number and is the result of his legend-making process. Thus, we should be careful in attributing *stupa*s in Swat to Ashoka, because recently, even the well-known *stupa* of Dharmarajika (Taxila) has been questioned as hardly belonging to Ashoka's period.[10]

Beni Madhab Barua considers Swat part of the Ashokan Empire by stating: 'Similarly Udyāna or Oḍḍiyāna, the city of Siṃhapura, the town of Sākala, Chīnapati, Kuluta, Śatadru and Parvata, which were honoured with the stūpas of Aśoka, were all places in the Uttarāpatha division within Aśoka's empire.'[11] But the author has contended this as well:

> In Aśoka's time, however, the major portion, if not the whole, of the trans-
> Indus territory of the Gāndhāras and the southern portion of their hinter-
> Indus territory were under his direct rule, and only the northern portion
> of both above Shahbazgarhi and Mansehra formed the semi- independent
> tribal state of the Gāndhāras.[12]

This assertion impliedly states that Uddiyana, or Swat, was though to be a part of Ashoka's Empire but with semi-independent status.

V.A. Smith's contention is also of the same nature when he writes: 'The secluded valleys of Suwāt (Swat) and Bājaur [Bajawar] *probably were more or less* [my italics] thoroughly controlled by the imperial officers.'[13]

With the death of Ashoka, the collapse of the mighty Mauryan Empire began.[14] The archaeological excavation in Swat has brought to light pottery, tools and settlements etcetera, that correspond to the Mauryan period at later and later periods.[15]

Indo-Greeks and Indo-Scythians

The Indo-Greek and Indo-Scythian coins found in Swat indicate that Swat had either directly been under the Indo-Greeks—those Greek rulers who occupied the seats in India after the down fall of the Mauryas—and of the Scythians, or had retained close relations and economic ties. It was the downfall of the Mauryas that 'paved the way for the Bactrian Greeks to extend their authority in the south to [the] Kābul valley and

in the south-east to Gandhāra, Uḍḍiyāna, and the west Punjāb'.[16] On
the basis of the newly acquired materials in the process of excavation
at Barikut Ghwandai, it has been stated: 'These data may confirm the
hypothesis that the Swat valley was military [militarily] annexed and
fortified *ex Qriente*, in a mature phase of the Indo-Greek kingdoms.'[17]

In his division of 'the Indo-Greek kingdom as it existed in
c. 130 B.C....into seven regions', A.K. Narain has given the 5th one as
'The Swat valley, or Udyāna'.[18] And in the chart of the '*Groups of kings*'
he has given for 'The Swat valley', names of the kings: Apollodotus,
Antimachus II, and Zoilus I for groups I, II and III respectively, but
no name is given for the Swat Valley in the columns of the IV and
V groups.[19]

W.W. Tarn has contended: 'Gandhāra,...the country between the
Kunar river and the Indus, comprising the modern Bajaur [Bajawar],
Swat, Buner, the Yusufzai country, and the country south of the Kabul
river about Peshawur [Peshawar], was to be one of the strongholds of
Greek power; it has been called a kind of new Hellas.'[20] W.W. Tarn,
however, was overly obsessed by the Greeks. His works need to be
studied carefully and a number of recent studies have presented new
perspectives. The now classical counter narrative has been produced
by Narain.[21]

The Swat Valley was occupied by Menander of the Indo-Greeks.
Two hundred drachms (drachmas) of his reign have been found in Swat
in mint condition. It is quite certain from the discovery of the Bajawar
casket inscription of Menander's reign that 'the Swat valley was included
within his kingdom and was under the governorship of Viyakamitra,
who, as the name shows, must have been a prince of Indian origin'.[22]
'Menander evidently controlled Udyāna'[23] and the vast numbers of his
coins found 'as far north as the Swat valley show that he reigned for
many years in this region; he must therefore have recovered it almost
immediately after he assumed the diadem'.[24]

Tarn argues that from the coins found in mint condition here,
'showing little signs of circulation', it appears that this area 'was part
of Menander's realm' as 'coins in this condition have nothing to do with
trade'.[25] He has elaborated, on the authority of Ptolemy's list:

The second fragment of the list (VII, I, 42) gives two names of provinces
in the Gandhāra kingdom, Souastene (Swat) and Goruaia.... Souastene
must be Lower and perhaps Middle Swat; how far up the river Greek rule

extended cannot be said,...for though Ptolemy describes Souastene as below the sources of the Swat river, it does not follow that anyone knew where those sources were.[26]

He has explained in the note that 'Sir A. Stein, *On Alexander's track to the Indus* 1929, found Graeco-Buddhist art motives still freely employed in wood carvings, not only in Middle Swat (p. 64) but as far north as Branial (p. 93). *But this does not mean that Greeks ever ruled there* [my italics].'[27] And that 'we know then three of the Greek provinces: Goruaia (Bajaur), Souastene (Swat), and Peucelaïtis (between Swat and the Kabul river)'.[28]

Swat was included in Menander's kingdom, but it was later handed over to a sub-king Antimachus II, as it is evident 'from the distribution of his coins that Antimachus II governed the Swat valley and northern Arachosia, each for some time'.[29] Because, due to 'his busy career and wide dominions', it is very likely that Menander 'appointed a few sub-kings'. It is, generally, thought that Antimachus II was one of them.[30] A.K. Narain has argued: 'Tarn called him a sub-king of Gandhāra, but Gandhāra is a large region, and we prefer to confine him first to Swat valley and later to northern Arachosia, to which province he may have been transferred towards the end of his career.'[31]

Of Menander's sub-kings the most important was Antimachus II, who not only ruled the Swat Valley but being 'a military king, bearing the title Nikepheros—the Victorious', he 'actively defended' it.[32] Inscription of the casket found in the Swat Valley 'tells how Theodorus the Meridarch preserved a relic of the Buddha for the good of the people'. Dated to the middle of the second century BCE, the casket shows 'that Theodorus also was a local ruler under Menander'.[33] But Jairazbhoy has stated: 'We know of a man by the same name in a Kharoshṭhī inscription from the Swat Valley, dated in the year 113 of an uncertain era. The inscription states that this Theodorus son of Datia caused a tank to be made "in honour of all beings".'[34]

Interestingly, a coin of Apollodotus I (160 BCE) has been discovered in Period IV of the Barikut Ghwandai (Barikut, Swat) excavated by the Italian Archaeological Mission.[35] 'The urban site of Barikot....was founded in the second half of the 2nd [sic] century BCE by the Indo-Greeks, as proved by numismatic evidence and 14C data';[36] and it was fortified by them and the number of Indo-Greek coins found in the excavations at Barikut Ghwandai is extremely high-plus. Besides, there has Hellenistic (and Bactrian) pottery, and Greek inscriptions.[37]

After the death of Apollodotus, the last phase of the Indo-Greek reign begins. A.K. Narain suggests that Menander, Antimachus II, Zoilus I, and Apollodotus ruled in the Swat Valley in the given order, and that:

> It is possible that Zoilus I was appointed sub-king of the Swat valley after Agathocleia in the period of her regency had transferred Antimachus II to Arachosia... Zoilus I may have been related to Agathocleia, for both used Heracles on their coins,...and it is generally believed that the latter type belonged to the family of Demetrius I,...so naturally she may have had confidence in Zoilus I in that unsettled period to which we have already referred... It is likely that Zoilus I was a sub-king first of Arachosia[38] and later of the Swat valley, which will explain the presence of his coins in the Mir Zakah Treasure.[39]

At the death of Menander, 'his wife Agathocleia first ruled in her own right as the daughter of Agathocles' and later 'jointly with her son until, on reaching manhood, he reigned alone as Strato I'. In order to counterbalance the influence of Antimachus II—who assumed independence at Arachosia (around Ghazni)—and other descendants of Diodotus, she appointed Zoilus I, a member of her family, 'as a sub-king in the Swat valley'. 'Zoilus ruled briefly in Swat' for he was, it appears, sent to Arachosia on the death of Antimachus II, to regain it.[40]

After Zoilus I, the known sub-king of Swat is Apollodotus. He 'seems to have begun his career at....about 115 B.C.; on the basis of his coinage he may be assigned a reign of at least twenty years, including his career as joint-king; thus, he ruled until c. 95 B.C., and outlived Antialcidas. He must have started on his career in the Swat valley'.[41] The 'Hellenistic traditions in speech and material culture' brought by the 'Bactrian-Greek chiefs' to Swat, even 'held sway' in the upper reaches of Swat or Swat Kuhistan, as was observed by Aurel Stein.[42]

Another Scythian tribe, 'the Sai of the Upper Ili', different from 'the Scythians of the Jaxartes valley or other areas west of them', also came to the region and occupied Swat and the adjoining area. It is difficult to determine how they reached the Swat region from the Hanging Pass. Nevertheless, their dominion included the Swat Valley and the adjoining areas.[43] It was soon after 100 BCE that Maues, 'the first-known Śaka king in India, followed the Indo-Greek rulers in the Swat valley and Gandhāra' by occupying some territories of Apollodotus.[44] Nevertheless, 'the existence of a copper coin of Apollodotus overstruck on a coin of Maues...suggests that the former was able to recover at least a part of his kingdom lost to the latter; this recovery must have been of very brief duration, for obviously Maues soon occupied Taxila'.[45]

It is argued that Maues did not want to disturb the cultural and political systems he had inherited from his predecessors. He purposely continued with them.[46] Obviously, reigns of both the 'Apollodotus and Maues overlapped and mints changed hands from one to another' which is clear from the overstrike coin and the use of similar monograms on the square copper coins of both of them.[47]

> The only square silver issue of the Śakas and the Pahlavas in India is that struck by Maues,…which indicates that he was not far removed in time from Apollodotus and Philoxenus, the king of the preceding generation, who were the only Indo-Greeks to strike square silver money; and this square money has been noticed in the Swat valley.[48]

It was after occupying Swat Valley and the Hazarah region that 'Maues occupied Taxila'.[49] 'Sāgala, where King Milinda is said to have ruled, has been identified with Sialkot' by J.F. Fleet, but 'the archaeological evidence would, in our opinion', contends A.K. Narain, 'favour Udyāna as the right place'.[50]

Aurel Stein, in his Swat tour of 1926, found a lot of the specimens of the minted coins of the Indo-Greeks, Indo-Parthians, and Indo-Scythians or Kushanas down to the Hindu Shahis in and around Barikut and the side valleys. Of these specimens, the 'most numerous' were 'issued by Azes, Azilises, and other Indo-Scythian kings who exercised extensive rule on the north-western confines of India during the first century B.C., as well as specimens of the copper coinage of the Kushana Emperors who succeeded them'.[51]

The new archaeological excavations at Barikut Ghwandai have revealed that, although 'the town was founded as a fortified settlement at the time when the Indo-Greek rulers were extending their control over the Swat valley', it 'was maintained as a fortified settlement in Saka-Parthian times' and was 'demilitarized only in Kushan times, possibly during the 2nd [sic] century CE'.[52]

Interestingly, observing and analysing Muslim graves of the 'Lesser Traditions', John Burton-Page has observed 'on one grave only, near Mankyāl' a shape, although rough but recognized 'horse's head, more like a chess knight than a real horse'. To this, he has asserted, temptingly following Tod, 'a specifically Scythian origin' may be ascribed.[53]

KUSHANA PERIOD

Kadphises I—leader of the Kushanas, who were from a nomadic race of Central Asia—seized vast territories extended to the south of the Kabul River and established his rule. His successors extended the boundaries of the domain. In Kanishka's reign, it comprised the territories of the Kabul Valley, Bactria, and in the south and east, in India, as far as Malwa and Benares (Banaras), respectively. The exact dates of their rule have been disputed. However, it was early in the Common Era (CE).

During the reign of the Kushana dynasty, in the west and south of Swat, the factual position on whether Swat became an integral part of the Kushana Empire or retained its own independent status is unclear. Giuseppe Tucci, however, has contended:

> Most probably Swāt (or its petty chiefs) had been a tributary of the Kuṣāṇa [Kushana]: nevertheless under the Kuṣāṇa period Uḍḍiyāna reached the apex of its culture and wealth...; the best testimonials of such a welfare are the *stūpas*, the monasteries then built, the ability of the craftsmen and artists, masons and sculptors, or the learning of his monks too: famous monks and artisans were invited to China. There were also in Swāt occasional local mints.[54]

On the basis of 'the archaeological data from the excavation of the ancient city of Bazira or Vajirasthana', it has been asserted that 'this new city pattern therefore suggested that the city was under the political control of local Kushan vassal chiefs'.[55]

Although not coming under the direct rule of the Kushanas, Uddiyana enjoyed the greatest of prosperity during the rule of Kanishka and his successors. As it was situated on the edge of the roads that connected Afghanistan, Central Asia, and India, it 'profited greatly by the trade that the Kuṣāṇa Empire, astride between Central Asia and the Indian ports, favored and monopolised'.[56] As it was 'for the first time in history' that 'all regions of the three big rivers, Indus, Oxus and Ganges, were united under the rule of the Early Kuṣāṇa dynasty, c 60–240 AD', and this led to 'cultural admixture in these regions' which 'also affected' Swat 'to a great extent'.[57]

On the basis of the new archaeological evidences at Barikut Ghwandai, it has been, as 'a preliminary conclusion', stated that 'in the second half of the 3rd century CE, certainly Kushan power was in great crisis in Swat, and their local allies lost their political force'.[58]

The rule of the Kushana dynasty came to an end at the hands of Shapur I, the Sassanian ruler of Persia, in 241 CE.[59] During this period, 'though sharing a common artistic and cultural tradition with Gandhara and dominated by its powerful neighbours', Swat 'enjoyed a separate entity both geographically and ethnically'.[60]

In dealing with the coins and chronology at Barikut Ghwandai, Dr Luca M. Olivieri has opined, as 'a preliminary conclusion', that:

> It doesn't seem that Swat was directly under the rule of the first Sasanian [Sassanian] governors, as the scarce number of coins indicates. Certainly, after defeating the Kushans, the Sasanians [Sassanians] should have found new local allies. In this regard, I found it very interesting that the sub-Kushan coins started possibly being minted already in the second half of the 3rd century by these new ruling groups, as an issue convertible with both the new and previous currencies.[61]

However:

> After the *pax kushanica*....urban centres along the main trade routes were largely abandoned; new invasions ravaged the country, and the population retired again on top of the hills, and rebuilt fortified villages on the remains of the old ones....there are heaps of ruins and the highest one was partially excavated by Dr. Faccenna. The upper parts of those ruins go back to the time of the Hindu Śāhi: when the excavations reached the rocky soil, fragments of the same pottery as that of the graveyards were discovered, and can still be found all along the slopes of the hill mixed with postherds of the Kuṣāṇa period.[62]

According to Ahmad Nabi Khan: 'In 460 A.D., however, the valley received a set-back and the incessant plunder by the White Huns destroyed many a splendid and imposing building throughout the valley.'[63] The destruction attributed to the White Huns in Swat, however, has been debated by some writers. For instance, Giuseppe Tucci has asserted: 'I believe that the ravages attributed to the Ephtalites [Ephthalites] have been somehow exaggerated. Another problem to be deeply investigated.'[64] And that 'as far as Swat is concerned we must be cautious before attributing all the ruins to invaders, especially as we have ample and visible documents of natural causes of destruction'.[65] Besides, seeking help against the White Huns, by the Swati Prince, has been stated by D.H. Muncherji in 502, 511 and 521 CE,[66] i.e. some forty to sixty years later.

However, Giuseppe Tucci has raised a question: 'Are we really in a condition to state that Swat was subject to the Achaemenian administration either as a district within the Satrapies or as a separate ethnic group?'[67] In the course of his discussion, he has contended:

Swāt has no doubt been under the influence of Gandhāran culture, especially during the Buddhist period; even in later times, Uḍḍiyāna-Swāt presents itself, in the different periods of its history, with its own petty rulers (perhaps many of them), or under the domination of the Kuṣāṇas, but it should not be considered as being identical with or included in Gandhāra or in Kapiśa, Afghanistan....though later it lost its independence to Turki Śāhi.[68]

THE TURKI SHAHI AND HINDU SHAHI PERIOD

Swat held its independent position, till the time, when the boundaries of the Turki Shahi (also Sahi) kingdom of Kabul were extended from the borders of Sistan to northern Punjab, in the middle of the seventh century CE, and Swat was annexed in the process in about 745 CE.[69] The Turki Shahi kingdom of Kabul was overthrown by Yaqub bin Lais in 870 CE.

Giuseppe Tucci has referred to the Tibetan and Chinese sources of the eighth century which has described Swat split into two political entities: Sambola (or Kampala) and Lankapuri. The former was ruled by the Buddhist King Indrabhuti and the latter by Jalendra. Lankapuri is said to be in the Laghman area.[70] This, in other words, indicates that the Turki Shahi's did not annex the entire Swat but some portion of it, may be the lower portion of the valley, which at that time may have been unified with the Laghman or Jalalabad area.

The Hindu Shahi (also written as Hindu Sahi) dynasty established itself at Hund, after the downfall of the Turki Shahis and, with the passage of time, extended the boundaries of its kingdom.[71] The Hindu Shahis gained control of the entire North-West Frontier region of India and some parts of Afghanistan in the tenth century CE. An inscription belonging to the Hindu Shahi ruler Raja Jaipal's (Jayapala's) reign has been found near Barikut.

Information about Swat for the Hindu Shahi reign is scanty and hence detailed account about Swat, its society, the masses, and so forth, for this period could not be produced. Nevertheless:

The Bari Kot inscription of the reign of Jayapaladeva...found on a hill to the north of Bari Kot in Upper Swat and now preserved in the

Lahore Museum (No. 119) mentions the name of the reigning king as *Sri-Jayapaladeva* in line 2 with the following epithets that precede it:

(i)   *Paramabhattaraka* (…)
(ii) *Maharajadhiraja* (…), and
(iii) *Paramesvara* (…).[72]

This means 'in the reign of the supreme sovereign, the superior king of great kings and the supreme lord the illustrious Jayapaladeva'.[73]

The question whether Swat remained an integral part of the Hindu Shahi kingdom is debatable and is not easy to be clarified in light of the available source material.

Habibullah Khan Khattak has asserted that Swat remained under local rulers for the most part of the ninth and tenth centuries CE.[74] Yogendra Mishra has opined on the basis of the inscription found in Barikut that 'the document must have been inscribed when Waziristan and Swat formed part of the kingdom of Jayapala'[75] and 'because the Bari Kot (Upper Swat) inscription…of Sri Jayapaladeva issued much earlier seems to imply that Upper Swat (and for that reason, Swat itself), being the region of the findspot of the inscription, was in the dominions of that king'.[76] Whereas Deambi has asserted that 'the record gives no details about Jayapāla but points to the extension of his dominions up to the Swat valley'.[77]

Moti Chandra has stated that the Hindu Shahi kingdom extended from Laghman to the Beas River, and from the frontier of Kashmir to Multan; and 'the Chinese sources inform us that Swat was also under the control of the Śāhīs but the mountainous territory in the south-west was independent'.[78] Whereas, Dr Muhammad Farooq Swati has asserted that 'the archaeological remains suggest that the Hindu Śāhīs of Hund in Gandhāra….dominated the Swāt Valley as well for about two centuries. It is evident from a number of building remains of this period.'[79]

It was in the years 1001–02, during Mahmud of Ghazna's reign, that the Muslim invasion of Swat started[80] and was completed in the years to come (detailed in chapter 6 hereinafter). The oral traditions and the books written locally in Swat (secondary sources) state that the last Hindu Shahi ruler of Swat was Raja Gira (Gira Kafir), with his capital at Udigram.[81] But neither can Raja Gira be found among the Hindu Shahi *rajas*, at the time of Mahmud's exploits, nor was Udigram a capital of

the Hindu Shahi dynasty. It seems that a 'local Hindu *rājā*'[82] ruled Swat
at that time. Dr Abdur Rahman has asserted that Rajagira is not the name
of the reigning *raja* but is 'correctly Rājagṛha, i.e. seat of government',[83]
that was 'situated on the mountain top at Ūḍigrām'.[84]

Giorgio Gullini has observed about the ruins of the aforesaid fortress
or castle of Raja Gira: 'It is easy to see that it must have been the seat
of successive stages in historical development as, owing to the position
it occupies, it could be used as a citadel by those who ruled the city and
the surrounding territory, and this probability accounts for the important
architectural features to which the ruins bear witness.'[85] This observation
also supports the assertion of Dr Abdur Rahman.

After inspecting the ruins of the place in 1926, Aurel Stein has
asserted that the remains 'clearly pointed to "Raja Gira's fortress"
having sheltered at times a fairly large population'.[86] He however has
contended:

> In view of the extreme steepness of the slopes over which the remains of
> ruined dwellings within the walled area are scattered and the consequent
> inconvenience of approach and communication between them it is hard
> to believe that these quarters were regularly occupied except at times of
> danger. On the other hand the construction of massive defences on these
> difficult slopes must have implied such exceptionally great efforts that it
> is not likely to have been undertaken except for the purpose of assuring
> a safe retreat for the inhabitants of an important locality.[87]

The traditions locating one of the many exploits of Mahmud of Ghazna
at 'King Girā's Castle' will 'suffice to prove the high antiquity that local
popular belief ascribes to the site'.[88]

D.H. Muncherji has aptly summed up the political position and status
of Uddiyana through the centuries in the following words:

> As a matter of fact, Udyana was never a political unit throughout its
> history except for brief periods. It was divided amongst different princes
> who ruled from their hilly fortresses. Yuan Chwang speaks of nearly
> four to five such fortresses. This impression of lack of political unity
> is strengthened by the total absence of a local coinage. In other words
> this proves that Udyana was always a dependency of its neighbours—
> Indo-Greeks, Sakas, Parthians, Kushans and others. It is only when these
> states became weak that some local prince or the other was able to assert
> his authority over the rest.[89]

After dealing with in some detail the points given in summarized form by Muncherji, Giuseppe Tucci has asserted: 'So with the exceptions above recorded we may conclude in a general way that the country was always under a feudal regime.'[90] And in the words of Dr Luca M. Olivieri: 'Certainly between the 1st century BCE and the 4th century CE, the territories in question were under the political control of local aristocrats linked first to the Indo-Greeks, then to the Saka, Parthians, followed by the power of the Kushans and their successors.'[91]

Praising the rich archaeological past of Swat, Khushal Khan Khattak has stated that it has great ancient minarets (may be referring to the *stupas*) and monasteries, and remains of palatial houses and forts of great antiquity.[92]

SOCIO-CULTURAL DIMENSION

In his analysis of the 'Special Features of the Buddhist Art in the Swāt Valley', on the basis of the 'sculptures from different localities in the Swāt Valley...excavated by the Department of Archaeology, University of Peshawar',[93] Dr Muhammad Farooq Swati has provided valuable information and review about a long period, namely from the second century BCE to 800 CE. On the basis of his discourse and historical sequence, he has opined that 'it is likely that Swāt in ancient times was the home of a series of multi-national or tribal-units'.[94] He has, moreover, observed:

> Throughout the historical context (3rd century BC to the eight century (AD) the Swāt Valley remained strictly Buddhist which means that all the invaders and emigrants that settled in there during this period were also absorbed into Buddhism in the course of time. Nonetheless, the new settlers always contributed some of their traditions to the Buddhist pantheon and are observed in sculpture of various zones... This normally happens after mixing up of two or more different cultures....there existed distinct cultural traditions in the sub-valleys of Swāt.[95]

The analysis of and the information provided by Dr Farooq Swati has shown that during this period, third century BCE to 800 CE, rather 1000 CE, the culture and traditions of Swat received and absorbed influences, from different aspects, from the Greeks, the Persians, and different Central Asian groups, and also from India.[96] It is to be mentioned that, according to Dr Rafiullah Khan, diffusionary explanations have seriously been criticized and challenged. All of Indian history has been revisited from new theoretical standpoints. Because there was also local or indigenous potential of development, that too has provided sources for the development of culture and traditions.[97]

Another later study of similar nature, but covering a somewhat different area and offering a different sort of perspective also shows somewhat different cultural traits, 'difference of the local traditions', the changing mode of living, emergence of fortified cities and abandoning of the cities, crafts activities, complex social organizations, changing means of livelihood, following of different Buddhist cults in different localities in Swat, through the course of time.[98]

All these speaks of and are testimony of the Swat being a dynamic, not a stagnant, society throughout, that has not only absorbed and accepted foreign influences and influences from the surrounding areas and elements, but on its part has influenced and transmitted changes to the other areas. The evident proof of which is the spread of Buddhism from here to Tibet and China, and the origin and spread from here of the civilization commonly called and known as the 'Gandhara civilization'.

The art and sculpture that developed here was influenced by both Greek and Buddhist patterns and thoughts and hence has been defined and called 'the "Graeco-Buddhist art of Gandhara".'[99] Dr Luca M. Olivieri and others have spoken of a sea change in the human landscape in Swat from the sixth century CE onward. During this phase, the large cities like Barikut Ghwandai and Udigram 'began to decline; their inhabitants withdrew to more protected dwellings in the mountains. The cities emptied and were gradually abandoned.'[100] 'This phase saw the beginning of the process of fortification typical of late ancient Swat.'[101] They have stated that 'in the present-day Kafir villages there are buildings similar to our tower-houses, known as *kot*';[102] and has asserted: 'In accordance with an old and consolidated thesis, on which numerous researchers agree....Swat can thus perhaps be included in the area of diffusion of Kafir culture ("Peristan" better than "Greater Kafiristan") before the latter was reduced to the present enclaves in upper Chitral.'[103] It, however, is important to note that the new data from Barikut, evaluated by Dr Luca, proves that the crisis started earlier in the third century CE.[104]

Dr Luca has highlighted, besides other points, the production of wine from the grapes and also grape juice. Although the grapes, it seems, were harvested in the mountains, they 'could have been pressed inside the cultivation/harvest areas and the juice transported to the Buddhist foundations' where it was fermented 'in complex work stations', which 'were composed of a multiple series of tanks, or surfaces with tanks posts utilized to set-up tripods to suspend filtering pots'.[105] The consumption of alcoholic beverages in Swat as late as the seventeenth century CE, in a population in which elements of Kafir culture may be discerned, is evident from the evidence provided by the Tibetan pilgrim sTag ts'an ras pa.[106]

Interestingly, Akhun Darwizah has reported that Mir Sayyad Ali Hamdani, a renowned saint of the age (in the fourteenth century CE), thrice toured the areas from the East till the West. When he left Kashmir for these areas and placed his steps on the Shahkut Pass and reached the top of the pass, he turned back because of the smell of alcoholic beverages that reached him at this place.[107] This, if it be accepted or taken as authentic, also speaks of and testifies to the fact that alcoholic beverages were hugely prepared and consumed in Swat.

On the basis of analysis of some aspects of the information obtained from the field work in some areas on the left bank of the Swat River, Dr Luca has asserted that 'the consideration of these factors would seem to lead toward an early form of the otherway [other way] defined as "Kafir"-Dardic environment'. The existence of the cultures called 'the "Kafir"-Dardic cultures', in Swat 'is positively attested in late antiquity (around 12th century), and, in their "Dardic" form, are still recorded in modern times (until the 20th centuries [century]) in different areas of Middle and Upper Swat'.[108]

Similarly, the Chinese pilgrims have informed us not only of the religious life but they have also keenly observed other dimensions of the land and society. It will be of great interest to give, here, brief passages from the accounts of these Chinese pilgrims and visitors, which throw light not only on the nature, behaviour and trends of the people and society but also on the aspects and practices that were influenced by religion and beliefs. Fa-Hein (now spelled as Faxian; also Fa Xian) has stated, in about 403 CE, that all the people 'use the language of Central India' and that 'the food and clothes of the common people are the same' like that of the people of Central India.[109]

Giuseppe Tucci has considered it an erroneous contention on the part of Fa-Hein (Faxian) that the people of Swat used the language of Central India:

A mistake probably due to the fact that he used to meet chiefly monks or people coming from the plains; Hsüan-tsang, on the contrary, makes two very important statements a) that their language was different, but similar to a certain extent to that of India and b) that the "rules of their written language was in a rather unsettled state".[110]

It, however, is noteworthy that there lapsed a period of more than two centuries between the visits and writings of both the Chinese pilgrims; so the versions of both Fa-Hein (Faxian) and Hiuen Tsiang (Xuanzang) are likely to be correct in their own place and the noted changes might have taken place in the course of the time that lapsed between the two. Even Hiuen Tsiang's (Xuanzang's) version is: 'Their language, though different in some points, *yet greatly resembles that of India* [my italics].'[111]

Sung Yun's account of the country and the people, after he spent a whole winter and summer in Swat, is enthusiastic. He has described:

Although in former times their manners were far from perfect, nevertheless, following the example of the king, the people had made some advance in purity; they observed the fasts, lived on vegetables, and honored Foe [Buddha] morning and night: they beat the drum, sounded the conch, played on the guitar, the flute, and other wind instruments; and it was not till half the day had been so employed that they engaged in the affairs of the state. They never punished criminals with death, but exposed them on a barren mountain and there left them to seek their own means of sustenance. When any matter was involved in doubt, they appealed to drugs, and decided upon the evidence of these.

The soil is good and fertile; the inhabitants live amidst abundance. All the cereals flourish there; and the five principal fruits, as well as many others, come to perfection. At night you hear the noise of bells which fills the air (literally, the world) on all sides. The richness of the soil gives birth to extraordinary flowers, which succeed in summer as well as in winter. The priests collect these as offerings to Foe [Buddha].[112]

Whereas Hiuen Tsiang (Xuanzang) has stated:

The people are soft and effeminate, and in disposition are somewhat sly and crafty. They love learning yet have no application. They practise the art of using charms (*religious sentences as charms*)... Their clothing is white cotton, and they wear little else. Their language, though different in some points, yet greatly resembles that of India. Their written characters and their rules of etiquette are also of a mixed character as before. They greatly reverence the law of Buddha and are believers in the Great Vehicle.[113]

Interestingly, O rgyan pa's (thirteenth century CE) and sTag ts'an ras pa's (seventeenth century CE) diaries also possess fantastic and fascinating accounts about the beliefs, way of life and manners of the people of the area.[114]

Regarding the progress and achievements in various fields, through the centuries in ancient Uddiyana, Muncherji has asserted:

> That all round progress took place at this great cultural centre, can hardly be doubted. Its economic prosperity, based upon a thriving agriculture and prosperous international trade, provided all the necessary resources for development. To add to this was the sound planning of the defensive system of Udyana. By virtue of its relations with the neighbouring states and its own defences, Udyana had all protection that it required for the growth of an orderly and progressive life. The long periods of peace which sometimes extended over centuries is a proof of that fact. But more than anything else, the achievements of Udyana in the field of religion— the inner development of 'Man'—are worthy of the highest praise.[115]

Aurel Stein's observations, during his visit in 1926, of the higher degree of civilization in the pre- and post-Alexander's period in Swat are worth noting. He has recorded:

> From the superior type of the abundant structural remains still extant in Swāt from early Buddhist times, and from what we know through the Chinese pilgrims' account of the character of its inhabitants at a later period, it may, in fact, be safely concluded that the material civilization and culture prevailing in that region in Alexander's time and for centuries after was far higher than those to be met with there now, or among the semi-barbarous [sic] Pathān tribes holding the barren hills from the Mohmand country down to Wazīristān. Nor should it be forgotten that the possession of lands so fertile as those of Swāt, combined with the enfeebling effect of the rice cultivation preponderant in its valleys, tends to have a debilitating influence on the inhabitants. This is apparent even among the present Pathān population, and must have asserted itself also in the case of its earlier occupants.[116]

RELATIONS WITH NEIGHBOURING POWERS

Swat remained under the overlordship of its strong neighbouring rulers on occasions but it can be inferred from the scanty available information that it retained its separate entity from the three powerful and large neighbouring states of South Asia, Persia/Central Asia, and China. In the course of its history, after Alexander's invasion and departure, its position on the whole remained the same as it was before. Relations with the neighbouring powers were established. The Chinese and the Kingdom of Uddiyana had political intercourse and relations for centuries.[117]

The mentions of tributes from the Kingdom of Uddiyana to China and the account that 'in the sixteenth year *Chhing kouan* (642), the king "Tha mo in tho po sse", sent ambassadors bearing "camphor." An imperial rescript conveyed to him the satisfaction produced by his conduct'[118] is striking and speaks of a sort of political dominance on the part of China over the Kingdom of Uddiyana. Nevertheless, the historical existence of Uddiyana in about 403 CE, when visited by Fa-Hein (Faxian), and in the year 642 CE, 'when its king addressed a letter to the Emperor of China' cannot be doubted.[119]

The rulers of Uddiyana sent missions to China 'in the years 502, 511, 518, 521 when the White Huns were threatening the country'.[120] Not only ambassadors from Uddiyana went to the Imperial Court of China, in 665 CE, but Uddiyana indirectly remained 'involved in the fights against the Arabs' in the Pamir area.[121] When the Arabs 'were renewing their attacks' under Qutaybah bin Muslim, they 'also approached the eastern borders of Uḍḍiyāna' but 'the local ruler' supported 'the policy of the Shāhi, being under the same impending danger' and refused 'to accept the offers of the Arabs'.[122] Although the Chinese did not intervene in Uddiyana at the moment, they sent some ambassadors in 720 CE to confer upon its king and other neighbouring states the investiture, as a reward for opposing the Arabs.[123]

During the Chinese–Tibetan collision, especially from 745 to 755 CE, the Tibetans tried to find allies in the region for cutting off the Gilgit–India routes. The easiest route of these was the one which passed through Chitral *via* Kalam and Swat to Gandhara.[124] In this troubled situation, Swat might have had sided with the Tibetans. So China conferred 'the investiture of King of "Ki-pin and Uḍḍiyāna",' in 745 CE, 'upon the king of Ki-pin'; and in about 748 CE 'the king of Ki-pin sent tributes to China….which mean that Swāt had lost its independence to Kapiśa'.[125]

This also implies that 'impressed by the power of the Tibetans reaching Baltistan', Swat changed its policy towards China.[126] Giuseppe Tucci has asserted:

> Now that we have seen how Swāt was in the very middle of the Chinese-Tibetan quarrels for the control of the main routes connecting Central Asia with Kashmir and Northern India, in a general way, it is clear that *we have to look to Swāt with other eyes. A region, by its very geographical situation open to all sorts of trade and cultural influences* [my italics]; a fact which explains its wealth documented by the immense number of religious settlements and its high culture testified by the archaeological discoveries; these documents will certainly greatly increase when the orthogonal town laying underneath the fields near the present play-ground of Mingora will be excavated.[127]

Interestingly, the same is the situation of the strategic significance of Swat even now, after about more than twelve and a half centuries, in the twenty-first century in the Sino-American-Central Asian scene; and vested interests of a number of international state and non-state actors, including Pakistan, become one of the major causes of the Swat crisis and destruction of 2007–2009. Giuseppe Tucci, moreover, has asserted:

> Thus, we may conclude that Swāt had already come in contact with China, since the 6th century; this explains how at the times of Sung Yün there was in Uḍḍiyāna a Chinese interpreter; there must have been at that time not only an increasing number of pilgrims, but also a more consistent bulk of trade between Swāt, Gilgit and Central Asia. The fact itself that Uḍḍiyāna had sent missions to China from the beginning of the 7th century shows that the pilgrims coming and going to and from China gave the first news of the great empire and its power: its conquests had brought China near to its frontiers; when the Tibetans advanced, and the Chinese lost to them some parts of Central Asia, Swāt could not help sharing the apprehensions resulting from the fact that the Pamir had become a meeting-point of the three rival powers: Swāt opposed itself to the Arabs and was rewarded by the Chinese.[128]

H.A. Deane has taken the extensive fortification of Uddiyana on the south as proof of 'the supposed peaceable nature of' its 'people or their cordial relations with their neighbours in Gandhāra'.[129]

It is to be mentioned that certain periods/dynasties/rulers that fall in the scope of this chapter are not mentioned. The reason is, I did not find authentic material especially about Swat in respect of those periods/ dynasties/rulers. The material available in some secondary sources in their respect is, in my opinion, neither authentic nor relevant to Swat.

As stated at the end of chapter 2, the researches and new data made available, and in the process of being made available, by the Italian Archaeological Mission, and also by the Pakistani archaeologists, enrich the source material and provide fresh information regarding different aspects of the period covered in this chapter (Mauryas to Shahis), which may add, in future, new dimensions to the early period of the history of Swat.

NOTES

1. A.H. Dani, *Book One: Pre-Muslim Period*, in I.H. Qureshi, ed., *A Short History of Pakistan* (2nd edn., Karachi: University of Karachi, 1984), 99. The year of the acquisition of power by Chandragupta Maurya is not agreed upon. For detail, see R.C. Majumdar, H.C. Raychaudhuri, and Kalikinkar Datta, *An Advanced History of India* (repr., Lahore: Famous Books, 1992), 97–101.
2. B.G. Gokhale, *Ancient India: History and Culture* (4th edn., Bombay: Asia Publishing House, 1959), 38.
3. Mohammad Yunus, *Frontier Speaks*, with foreword by Jawahar Lal [Jawaharlal] Nehru, preface by Khan Abdul Ghaffar Khan, and maps by Sardar Abdur Rauf (Lahore: Minerva Book Shop, Anarkali, n.d.), 12. However, Dr Rafiullah Khan opines that it was Laurence A. Waddell who visited the area in 1895 and suggested the possibility of the association of the Mauryas with Mora. (Dr Rafiullah Khan's comment on an earlier draft of this chapter.)
4. For other etymologies of the term Maurya, see Radhakumud Mookerji, *Chandragupta Maurya and His Times* (Facts of publication have been torn out), 9–15.
5. Vincent A. Smith, *Asoka: The Buddhist Emperor of India* (repr., Delhi: S. Chand & Co., 1957), 76.
6. Ibid., 80–1.
7. [Hiuen Tsiang], *Chinese Accounts of India: Translated from the Chinese of Hiuen Tsiang*, trans. and annotated by Samuel Beal, Vol. 2 (new edn., Calcutta: Susil Gupta (India) Limited, 1958), 172.
8. Radhakumud Mookerji, *Asoka* (repr., Delhi: Motilal Banarsidass, 1986), 15.
9. Giuseppe Tucci, 'On Swāt. The Dards and Connected Problems', *East and West* (Rome), 27/1–4 (December 1977), 65.
10. Dr Rafiullah Khan's note to the point on an earlier draft of this chapter.
11. Beni Madhab Barua, *Asoka and His Inscriptions* (2nd edn., Calcutta: New Age Publishers Ltd., 1955), 105.
12. Ibid., 93.

13. Vincent A. Smith, *The Early History of India: From 600 B.C. to the Muhammadan Conquest, Including the Invasion of Alexander the Great*, 4th edn., revised by S.M. Edwardes (repr., Oxford: At the Clarendon Press, 1957), 170.

14. Gokhale, *Ancient India: History and Culture*, 45.

15. See Georgio Stacul and Sebastiano Tusa, 'Report on the Excavations at Aligrāma (Swāt, Pakistan), 1974', *East and West* (Rome), 27/1–4 (December 1977), 151–205.

16. Muhammad Farooq Swāti, 'Recent Discovery of Buddhist Sites in the Swāt Valley', *Āthāriyyāt* (Peshawar), 1 (1997), 155. Also see, Muhammad Farooq Swāti, 'Special Features of the Buddhist Art in the Swāt Valley', *Ancient Pakistan* (Peshawar), 18 (2007), 106.

17. Olga Tribulato and Luca Maria Olivieri, 'Writing Greek in the Swat Region: A New Graffito from Barikot (Pakistan)', *Zeitschrift für Papyrologie und Epigraphik* (Köln), 204 (2017), 130.

18. A.K. Narain, *The Indo-Greeks* (repr., Oxford: At the Clarendon Press, 1962), 103.

19. See ibid., 104.

20. W.W. Tarn, *The Greeks in Bactria & India* (repr., Cambridge: At the University Press, 1966), 135.

21. Dr Rafiullah Khan's personal communication with the author: August 2016.

22. Narain, *The Indo-Greeks*, 79.

23. Ibid., 80.

24. George Woodcock, *The Greeks in India* (London: Faber and Faber Ltd, 1966), 97.

25. Tarn, *The Greeks in Bactria & India*, 229.

26. Ibid., 237.

27. Ibid., n. 1.

28. Ibid., 238.

29. Narain, *The Indo-Greeks*, 96.

30. Ibid., 95.

31. Ibid., 96.

32. Woodcock, *The Greeks in India*, 105.

33. Ibid., 106.

34. R.A. Jairazbhoy, *Foreign Influence in Ancient India* (Bombay: Asia Publishing House, 1963), 125. Also see Woodcock, *The Greeks in India*, 134.

35. See Luca Colliva, 'The Excavation of the Archaeological Site of Barikot (Bīr-koṭ-ghwaṇḍai) and its Chronological Sequence', *Journal of Asian Civilizations* (Islamabad), 34/1 (July 2011), 155.

36. Elisa Iori, 'The Early-Historic Urban Area at Mingora in the light of Domenico Faccenna's Excavations at Barama – I (Swat)', with note by Luca M. Olivieri, *Frontier Archaeology* (Peshawar), 7 (2016), 102; Elisa Iori, Luca M. Olivieri, and Amanullah Afridi, 'Urban Defenses at Bīr-koṭ-ghwaṇḍai, Swat (Pakistan). The Saka-Partian Phases: Data from the 2015 Excavation Campaign', *Pakistan Heritage* (Mansehra), 7 (2015), 73.

37. For detail, see Luca M. Olivieri, 'The Last Phases at Barikot: Urban Cults and Preliminary Chronology: Data from the 2012 Excavation Campaign in Swat', *Journal of Inner Asian Art and Archaeology* (New York), 6/2011, 7–40; Luca M. Olivieri, 'Urban Defenses at Bīr-koṭ-ghwaṇḍai, Swat (Pakistan): *New Data from the 2014 Excavation Campaign*', *Ancient Civilizations from Scythia to*

Siberia (Leiden), 21 (2015), 183–99; Iori, Luca M. Olivieri, and Amanullah Afridi, 'Urban Defenses at Bīr-koṭ-ghwaṇḍai, Swat (Pakistan). The Saka-Partian Phases: Data from the 2015 Excavation Campaign', 73–94; Tribulato and Luca Maria Olivieri, 'Writing Greek in the Swat Region: A New Graffito from Barikot (Pakistan)', 128–35; Luca M. Oliveri and Elisa Iori, 'Early-historic Data from the 2016 Excavation Campaigns at the Urban Site of Barikot, Swat (Pakistan): A Shifting Perspective' in A. Hardy and L. Greaves, eds., *South Asian Art and Archaeology* (New Delhi: Dev Publishers & Distributers, 2016), 19–43.

38. For importance of Arachosia, and its gaining significance from some counts, in those times, see Paul Bernard, 'Hellenistic Arachosia: A Greek Melting Pot in Action', *East and West* (Rome), 55/1–4 (December 2005), 13–34 (Stable URL:http://www.jstor.org/stable/29757633; accessed: 04/11/2013).

39. Narain, *The Indo-Greeks*, 115.

40. Woodcock, *The Greeks in India*, 116.

41. Narain, *The Indo-Greeks*, 126.

42. See Aurel Stein, *On Alexander's Track to the Indus: Personal Narrative of Explorations on the North-West Frontier of India* (repr., Karachi: Indus Publications, 1995), 92–3. Also see Colliva, 'The Excavation of the Archaeological Site of Barikot (Bīr-koṭ-ghwaṇḍai) and its Chronological Sequence', 162.

43. See Narain, *The Indo-Greeks*, 134–6.

44. Ibid., 142–5.

45. Ibid., 145.

46. For details about this point as well as of Maues occupation of Taxila, see François Widemann, 'Maues King of Taxila: An Indo-Greek Kingdom with a Saka King', *East and West* (Rome), 53/1–4 (December 2003), 95–125 (Stable URL:http://www.jstor.org/stable/29757574); accessed: 12/11/2013).

47. Narain, *The Indo-Greeks*, 145. Also see Muhammad Farooq Swāti, 'Pre-Kuṣāṇa Reliquaries from Pātaka, Swāt', *Journal of the Royal Asiatic Society*, 7/2 (July 1997), 251–4 (Stable URL:http://www.jstor.org/stable/25183351; accessed: 30/10/2011).

48. Narain, *The Indo-Greeks*, 145. Also see Swāti, 'Pre-Kuṣāṇa Reliquaries from Pātaka, Swāt', 251–4.

49. Narain, *The Indo-Greeks*, 146.

50. Ibid., 172–3. For an interesting study about Sakala (Pali: Sagala), its identification as Sialkot, and its remaining seat of government or capital for long, see Bimala Churn Law, 'Śākala: an Ancient Indian City', *East and West* (Rome), 19/3–4 (September–December 1969), 401–9 (Stable URL:http://www.jstor.org/stable/29755450); accessed: 08/11/2013).

51. Aurel Stein, 'Alexander's Campaign on the Indian North-West Frontier: Notes from Explorations between Upper Swāt and the Indus', *The Geographical Journal* (London), 70/5 (November 1927), 430 (Stable URL: http://www.jstor.org/stable/1783476); accessed: 30/10/2011). Also see Aurel Stein, *An Archaeological tour in Upper Swāt and Adjacent Hill Tracts* (Calcutta: Government of India, Central Publication Branch, 1930), 22, 28; Stein, *On Alexander's Track to the Indus*, 32, 34, 40, 57.

52. Iori, Luca M. Olivieri, and Amanullah Afridi, 'Urban Defenses at Bīr-koṭ-ghwaṇḍai, Swat (Pakistan). The Saka-Partian Phases: Data from the 2015

Excavation Campaign', 73–4; Olivieri, 'Urban Defenses at Bīr-koṭ-ghwaṇḍai, Swat (Pakistan): *New Data from the 2014 Excavation Campaign*', 184.

53. John Burton-Page, 'Muslim Graves of the "Lesser Traditions": Gilgit, Puniāl, Swāt, Yūsufzai', *Journal of the Royal Asiatic Society of Great Britain and Ireland*, No. 2 (1986), 251 (Stable URL: http://www.jstor.org/stable/25211996, accessed: 30/10/2011).

54. Tucci, 'On Swāt. The Dards and Connected Problems', 67.

55. Luca Maria Olivieri, 'Guru Padmasambhava in Context: Archaeological and Historical Evidence from Swat/Uddiyana (c. 8th Century CE)', *Journal of Bhutan Studies* (Thimphu), 34 (Summer 2016), 22–3.

56. Giuseppe Tucci, 'Preliminary report on an archaeological survey in Swat', *East and West* (Rome), 9/4 (December 1958), 282.

57. Swāti, 'Special Features of the Buddhist Art in the Swāt Valley', 113.

58. Luca M. Olivieri, 'When and why the ancient town of Barikot was abandoned?: A preliminary note based on the last archaeological data', *Pakistan Heritage* (Mansehra), 4 (2012), 167.

59. Swāti, 'Special Features of the Buddhist Art in the Swāt Valley', 106.

60. M. Ashraf Khan, *Buddhist Shrines in Swat* (Saidu Sharif: By the Author, Archaeological Museum, Saidu Sharif, Swat, 1993), 7.

61. Olivieri, 'When and why the ancient town of Barikot was abandoned?: A preliminary note based on the last archaeological data', 167.

62. Tucci, 'On Swāt. The Dards and Connected Problems', 49–50.

63. Ahmad Nabi Khan, *Buddhist Art and Architecture in Pakistan* (Islamabad: Ministry of Information and Broadcasting, Directorate of Research, Reference and Publications, Government of Pakistan, n.d.), 63.

64. Tucci, 'On Swāt. The Dards and Connected Problems', 67 n. 91b.

65. Tucci, 'Preliminary report on an archaeological survey in Swat', 282.

66. D.H. Muncherji, 'Swat: The Garden of Asoka', *Pakistan Quarterly* (Karachi), 9/3 (1959), 43.

67. Tucci, 'On Swāt. The Dards and Connected Problems', 10.

68. Ibid., 11.

69. Abdur Rehman, *The Last Two Dynasties of the Śāhis: (An analysis of their history, archaeology, coinage and palaeography)* (Islamabad: Director Centre for the Study of the Civilizations of Central Asia, Quaid-i-Azam University, 1979), 3–4. Also see Tucci, 'On Swāt. The Dards and Connected Problems', 11.

70. See Tucci, 'Preliminary report on an archaeological survey in Swat', 324 n. 1.

71. For detail about the Hindu Shahi period, see Yogendra Mishra, *The Hindu Sahis of Afghanistan and the Punjab, A.D. 865–1026* (Patna: Vaishali Bhavan, 1972); Rehman, *The Last Two Dynasties of the Śāhis*.

72. Mishra, *The Hindu Sahis of Afghanistan and the Punjab, A.D. 865–1026*, 89.

73. Ibid., 98.

74. See Muhammad Habibullah Khan Khattak, *Buner: The Forgotten Part of Ancient Uddiyana* (Karachi: By the Author, Department of Archaeology and Museums, Government of Pakistan, 1997), 43.

75. Mishra, *The Hindu Sahis of Afghanistan and the Punjab, A.D. 865–1026*, 99.

76. Ibid., 124.

77. B.K. Koul Deambi, *History and Culture of Ancient Gandhāra and Western Himalayas from Sāradā Epigraphic Sources* (New Delhi: Ariana Publishing House, 1985), 17.

78. Moti Chandra, *Trade and Trade Routes in Ancient India* (New Delhi: Abhinav Publications, 1977), 189.

79. Swāti, 'Special Features of the Buddhist Art in the Swāt Valley', 106.

80. See Abdur Rehman, 'The Zalamkot Bilingual Inscription', *Lahore Museum Bulletin* (Lahore), 10–11/1–2 (1997–1998), 38; Abdur Rahman, 'Arslān Jādhib, Governor of Ṭūs: the First Muslim Conqueror of Swat', *Ancient Pakistan* (Peshawar), 15 (2002), 14; Mishra, *The Hindu Sahis of Afghanistan and the Punjab, A.D. 865–1026*, 124.

81. See Sayyed Abdul Ghafoor Qasmay, *Tarikh-i Riyasat-i Swat* (Pashto) (Printed by Hamidia Press, Peshawar, n.d.), 19; Sayyed Mohd. Abdul Ghafoor Qasmi, *The History of Swat* (Printed by D.C. Anand & Sons, Peshawar, 1940), 3; Muhammad Asif Khan, *Tarikh-i Riyasat-i Swat wa Sawanih-i Hayat Baniy-i Riyasat-i Swat Hazrat Miangul Gul Shahzadah Abdul Wadud Khan Badshah Sahib*, with *dibachah, hisah awal, saluramah hisah,* and *hisah pinzamah* by Muhammad Asif Khan (Pashto) (Printed by Ferozsons Ltd., Peshawar [1958]), 30–1; Muhammad Asif Khan, *Tarikh Riyasat-i Swat wa Sawanih-i Hayat Bani Riyasat-i Swat Miangul Abdul Wadud* (Urdu) (2nd edn., Mingawarah, Swat: Shoaib Sons Publishers and Booksellers, 2001), 26; Muhammad Asif Khan, *The Story of Swat as told by the Founder Miangul Abdul Wadud Badshah Sahib to Muhammad Asif Khan*, with preface, introduction and appendices by Muhammad Asif Khan, trans. preface and trans. by Ashruf Altaf Husain (Printed by Ferozsons Ltd., Peshawar, 1963), xx; Saranzeb Swati, *Tarikh Riyasat-i Swat* (Pashto) (Peshawar: Azeem Publishing House, 1984), 29, 31. Also see Stein, *On Alexander's Track to the Indus*, 57–8. Muhammad Asif Khan, and Saranzeb Swati, however, has mentioned him as the Buddhist Raja.

82. Swāti, 'Recent Discovery of Buddhist Sites in the Swāt Valley', 155.

83. Rehman, 'The Zalamkot Bilingual Inscription', 39 n. 11; Swāti, 'Recent Discovery of Buddhist Sites in the Swāt Valley', 155.

84. Swāti, 'Recent Discovery of Buddhist Sites in the Swāt Valley', 155.

85. Giorgio Gullini, 'Marginal note on the excavations at the Castle of Udegram: restoration problems', *East and West* (Rome), 9/4 (December 1958), 331–2.

86. Stein, *An Archaeological tour in Upper Swāt and Adjacent Hill Tracts*, 37.

87. Ibid.

88. Ibid., 38.

89. Muncherji, 'Swat: The Garden of Asoka', 43.

90. Tucci, 'Preliminary report on an archaeological survey in Swat', 290. For some detail, see ibid., 288–90.

91. Luca M. Olivieri, 'Behind the Buddhist Communities: Subalternity and Dominancy in Ancient Swat', *Journal of Asian Civilizations* (Islamabad), 34/1 (July 2011), 133.

92. Khushal Khan Khattak, *Swat Nama of Khushal Khan Khattak*, ed. and trans in to English by Shakeel Ahmad, with preface by Raj Wali Shah Khattak (Peshawar: Pashto Academy, n.d.), 4; Khushal Khan Khattak, *Swat Namah da Khushal Khan Khattak*, with *muqadimah, tahqiq aw samun* by Hamesh Khalil (Akurah Khattak:

Markazi Khushal Adabi wa Saqafati Jargah (Regd.), 1986), 49; Afzal Khan Khattak, *Tarikh Murasa: Muqabilah, tashih aw nutunah lah* Dost Muhammad Khan Kamil Momand (Peshawar: University Book Agency, 2006), 378.

93. Swāti, 'Special Features of the Buddhist Art in the Swāt Valley', 105.

94. Ibid., 120.

95. Ibid., 119. Dr Rafiullah Khan has contended that recent studies in the context of Taxila have expressed doubts about the phenomenal amplification of views of major/codified religions. Possibilities—as new interpretations suggest—of existence of minor cults and folk belief systems have always been there. Swat's ancient history and archaeology direly need revisits and I think Anna Filigenzi has done some work in this direction (Dr Rafiullah Khan's note to the point on an earlier draft of this chapter).

96. For detail, see Swāti, 'Special Features of the Buddhist Art in the Swāt Valley', 105–57.

97. Dr Rafiullah Khan's note to the point on an earlier draft of this chapter and personal communication: August 2016.

98. For detail, see Luca M. Olivieri et al., 'Archaeology and Settlement History in a Test Area of the Swat Valley: Preliminary Report on the AMSV Project (1st Phase)', *East and West* (Rome), 56/1–3 (September 2006), 73–150 (Stable URL:http://www.jstor.org/stable/29757683); accessed: 12/11/2013).

99. A. Bagnera et al., 'Italian Archaeological Activities in Swat: An Introduction', *Journal of Asian Civilization* (Islamabad), 34/1 (July 2011), 65.

100. Olivieri et al., 'Archaeology and Settlement History in a Test Area of the Swat Valley: Preliminary Report on the AMSV Project (1st Phase)', 138.

101. Ibid.

102. Ibid., 139.

103. Ibid., 141–2.

104. For detail, see Olivieri, 'When and why the ancient town of Barikot was abandoned?: A preliminary note based on the last archaeological data', 157–69.

105. Olivieri, 'Behind the Buddhist Communities: Subalternity and Dominancy in Ancient Swat', 135–6. Also see Olivieri et al., 'Archaeology and Settlement History in a Test Area of the Swat Valley: Preliminary Report on the AMSV Project (1st Phase)', 142–5.

106. See G. Tucci, *Travels of Tibetan Pilgrims in the Swat Valley* (Calcutta: The Greater Indian Society) in G. Tucci, *On Swāt. Historical and Archaeological Notes*, eds. P. Callieri and A. Filigenzi (Rome: 1997), 43–45; Olivieri et al., 'Archaeology and Settlement History in a Test Area of the Swat Valley: Preliminary Report on the AMSV Project (1st Phase)', 145.

107. See Akhun Darwizah, *Tazkiratul Abrar-i wal Ashrar* (Persian) (Peshawar: Islami Kutub Khanah, n.d.), 108.

108. Olivieri, 'Behind the Buddhist Communities: Subalternity and Dominancy in Ancient Swat', 140–1. Also see Olivieri et al., 'Archaeology and Settlement History in a Test Area of the Swat Valley: Preliminary Report on the AMSV Project (1st Phase)', 138–42.

109. Fa-Hein, *A Record of Buddhistic Kingdoms*, trans. and annotated by James Legge (repr., New Delhi: Munshiram Manoharlal Publishers Pvt. Ltd, 1991), 28. See also, [Fa Hian], *The Pilgrimage of Fa Hian: From the French Edition of the Foe*

Koue Ki of MM. Remusat, Klaproth, and Landresse with Additional Notes and Illustrations, trans. and ed. by anonymous (Calcutta: The 'Bangabasi' Office, 1912), 49.

110. Tucci, 'On Swāt. The Dards and Connected Problems', 65. For Tucci's detailed discussion, see ibid.

111. [Tsiang], *Chinese Accounts of India: Translated from the Chinese of Hiuen Tsiang*, Vol. 2, 167.

112. [Fa Hian], *The Pilgrimage of Fa Hian: From the French Edition of the Foe Koue Ki of MM. Remusat, Klaproth, and Landresse with Additional Notes and Illustrations*, 53–4.

113. [Tsiang], *Chinese Accounts of India: Translated from the Chinese of Hiuen Tsiang*, Vol. 2, 167.

114. See Tucci, *Travels of Tibetan Pilgrims in the Swat Valley*, 28–31, 41–4.

115. Muncherji, 'Swat: The Garden of Asoka', 40.

116. Stein, *An Archaeological tour in Upper Swāt and Adjacent Hill Tracts*, 24–5.

117. For detail, see [Fa Hian], *The Pilgrimage of Fa Hian: From the French Edition of the Foe Koue Ki of MM. Remusat, Klaproth, and Landresse with Additional Notes and Illustrations*, 50–63 n. 1.

118. Ibid., 57.

119. Ibid., 50 n. 1.

120. Tucci, 'Preliminary report on an archaeological survey in Swat', 289–90. Also see Muncherji, 'Swat: The Garden of Asoka', 43; [Fa Hian], *The Pilgrimage of Fa Hian: From the French Edition of the Foe Koue Ki of MM. Remusat, Klaproth, and Landresse with Additional Notes and Illustrations*, 50 n. 1.

121. Tucci, 'On Swāt. The Dards and Connected Problems', 75.

122. Tucci, 'Preliminary report on an archaeological survey in Swat', 290.

123. Tucci, 'On Swāt. The Dards and Connected Problems', 75. Also see Tucci, 'Preliminary report on an archaeological survey in Swat', 290.

124. Tucci, 'On Swāt. The Dards and Connected Problems', 79.

125. Ibid., 75.

126. Ibid., 85.

127. Ibid.

128. Ibid., 84.

129. H.A. Deane, 'Note on Udyāna and Gandhāra', *Journal of the Royal Asiatic Society of Great Britain and Ireland* (October 1896), 663 (Stable URL: http://www.jstor.org/stable/25207806; accessed: 16/05/2011).

5

RELIGIOUS PERSPECTIVE

Religion, in whatever manner, has played a pivotal role in guiding the norms, values and beliefs of human beings. Its importance in history cannot be ignored. About the religious perspective of pre-Muslim Swat, information is scanty. An attempt is made here to connect the dots and produce a sketch on the basis of the available primary and secondary sources.

About the religion of the prehistoric and protohistoric residents of Swat, Giuseppe Tucci has put a question: 'Can we say anything about the religion of those ancient Swātis of whom, so far, only the graveyards and a few habitations have been found?' And answering the question he has said: 'Very little indeed, and this also cannot but be largely hypothetical.'[1]

HINDUISM

Although 'the presence of Hinduism in Swāt is certain',[2] traces of a great diffusion of Hinduism here are not so many. Hiuen Tsiang (now spelled as Xuanzang; also Xuan Zang) has spoken (in about 630 CE) of 'about ten temples of Devas [Hindus], and a mixed number of unbelievers who dwell in them'.[3] It, however, has rightly been pointed to that Yuan Chwang (Hiuen Tsiang; Xuanzang), however, has not mentioned the location of these temples.[4] H.A. Deane, however, has written in 1896 of the presence of 'a fine Deva temple' near the *stupa* situated between Shingardar (Shinkardar) and Ghaligay.[5] Not only have Hindu temples reportedly been found in Swat, 'but a very important Śaiva school, the *Kramasaṃpradāya*, was originated or had some of its most famous authors in Swāt'.[6]

Besides, the legend goes that Ram Chandar Ji (Rama; Ramachandara), a demi-god of the Hindus, spent some (six to seven years) of his *ban-bas* time (*vanavasa*: forest-dwelling; banishment; life passed in the forest) in the forest of Mount Ilam on the southern side of Swat at Jugyanu Sar (Yogis' Peak)—at the altitude of about 9200 feet from the sea level—where situates Ram Takht (Ram Throne), which Hindus venerate.[7] According to the Hindu belief, Rama spent time at Jugyanu Sar 'with his beloved wife Sita to meditate and cogitate'.[8] Therefore, Hindus used to hold Sawan Sangran, a sacred festival, here, each year. To participate in the congregation, pilgrims of both sexes used to travel from far-off areas and reach Jugyanu Sar, three or four days before the congregation day—first day of Sawan—with great 'ordeals and tribulations'.[9] In the changed religious-political situation, the festival has ceased to be congregated. There were sheds for the Hindu pilgrims at Jugyanu Sar but these were removed by the ruler of Swat State, Miangul Abdul Wadud, who ruled from 1917 till 1949. He, moreover, used a number of tactics to discourage pilgrims from going to Jugyanu Sar.

After the Amar Nath Cave in Kashmir, Ram Takht at Jugyanu Sar in Mount Ilam is considered a second sacred place for the Hindus thanks to Rama spending some of his *ban-bas* time here.[10] Swat, therefore, features a Hindu sacred place. Although Walmiki's *Ramayan* (Valmiki's *Ramayana*) is silent about Rama's *ban-bas* time in Mount Ilam[11] and it is hard to infer such a clue from the *Ramayan*'s text, Hindus believe in his coming and spending some of his *ban-bas* time here.

Under the heading 'religion', Giuseppe Tucci has dealt with 'a common belief of the Proto-Indo-Aryans' about the sacred mountains. He has termed it 'the mountain patron of the tribe' which is considered 'the seat of the ancestor, the place upon which the ancestor or a patron god had descended' and hence has been regarded 'the centre of the Universe'; which is 'the Meru of Indian cosmology'. He has said that 'the Meru of Swāt was the Ilam (Chinese I-lo, Tibetan Hilo)'.[12]

Giuseppe Tucci, moreover, has stated that 'the Hilo mountain of the Chinese, the Ilo parvata of the Tibetans, the Ilam of today, is a holy mountain, the seat of a god'. Personally visiting the peak in 1955, he has said, 'Nowadays on the highest spot there is written on a rock the name of Śrī Rām (Rāma, incarnation of Viṣṇu). Hindus, Sikhs and even Muslims go there.' He has elaborated that 'just in front of Barīkot one can admire the peak of the Ilam, abode of gods from the oldest times up to now'; which 'continued to be a holy place till our times'. Ilam has been sacred for the Buddhists too, because, 'It was here that the Buddha once, in a former birth, gave up his life for the hearing of a half "stanza of the Doctrine".' The sacredness of the Ilam, therefore, not only 'goes back to prehistoric times' but 'has survived the changes of religions'.[13] Besides, Murundaka was 'another holy mountain of Swāt' which was 'hard to ascend and famous because it was the theatre of a magical contestation between Kambala and Kukkuripā'.[14]

Alberuni also has pointed to the sacredness of the area to Hindus on another count. On the authority of Jîvaśarman, he has stated that 'in the country of Svât [Swat], opposite the district of *Kîrî* (?), there is a valley in which fifty-three streams unite. It is called *Tranjâi* (cf. Sindhi *trêvanjâha*). In those two days [26th–27th Bhâdrupadâ (Bhadu)] the water of this valley becomes white, in consequence of Mahâdeva's washing in it, as people believe.'[15] And 'according to *Devīpurāṇa*, Uḍḍiyāna is one of the places where the Devī always remains'.[16]

BUDDHISM

Prof. A.R. Burn has claimed that at the time of Alexander's invasion 'there is no evidence that Buddhism had yet reached the Punjab'.[17] If it had not yet reached Punjab, it may not have reached Swat either; but this is not necessary because the religion could have reached Swat through traders or missionaries even before it had reached Punjab. The *Imperial Gazetteer of India* has claimed that at the time of Alexander's invasion of Swat, in 327 BCE, Buddhism was 'the prevailing religion'.[18] Some modern-day writers from Swat have also written that at the time of Alexander's invasion Buddhism was prevalent in Swat.[19] Buddhism, however, achieve greater prominence in Swat during the reign of Ashoka. Habibullah Khan Khattak has contended that the entry of Buddhism in Swat 'does not go back beyond the middle of the 3rd century B.C.'.[20] This gets support from H.W. Bellew's contention in which he has stated that 'from the religious emblems found on' the coins dugout of the ruins of the ancient dwellings in Swat 'it would appear that Budhism [Buddhism] was not known in the time of the Greeks'.[21] Hiuen Tsiang (Xuanzang) has reported a *stupa* called Lu-hi-ta-kia (Rohitaka), some 50 feet high, built by Ashoka-raja at a distance of fifty li or so in the west of the town Mungali. He, moreover, has stated that when Tathagata (Buddha) was king of a great country and 'was practising the life of a Bodhisattva', it was 'in this place' that 'he pierced his body, and with his blood fed the five Yakshas'.[22] About the introduction of Buddhism in Swat, Giuseppe Tucci has observed, 'We may safely assume that the missionary work in Swāt coincides with the building of the big stūpa which has been excavated by the Italian archaeological mission...; the construction was most probably begun about the middle of the third century B.C. enclosing a nucleus housing the relics.'[23]

Quoting Tucci, Dr Muhammad Farooq Swati has contended that 'Buddhism was well established in Uḍḍiyāna' by the time of Ashoka the Great (ca. 273–232 BCE).[24] He has noted, 'However, some scholars think that introduction of Buddhism in the Valley occurred much before Aśoka, that is at the end of fourth century B.C.'[25] During the Mauryas' heyday, the tenets of the Hinayana school were predominantly followed, which were brought here just after the time of Ashoka.[26] Importantly, Giuseppe Tucci has pointed to the absence of a bulk of Buddhist monuments and archaeological sites on the western part or right bank of Swat River—compared to the eastern part or left bank—and has asserted:

> Only excavations and further researches can lead us to a definite conclusion, but I am inclined to think that the different proportion of peculiarly Buddhist monuments between the Eastern and Western parts of Swat, may be indicative of a very important fact, that is that Buddhism did not completely dominate the country and that in some parts and side valleys, non-Buddhist beliefs, which we may designate for convenience sake as Hinduism (because Hinduism covers a very large variety of religious experiences) survived. In fact, Hsüan-tsang tells us of the existence in Swat of some Buddhist [Hindu] temples (about ten) though he does not say where he found them.[27]

Buddhism was firmly established in Swat during Kanishka's time, 'who so favored the community that he became the subject of a prophecy contained in the *Vinaya* of the Mūlasarvāstivādins'.[28] In Tucci's words:

> With the progressive advance of Buddhism towards the North West, the law spread so widely in Uḍḍiyāna, and the monasteries there were so prosperous that the *Bhaiṣajyavastu* of the *Vinaya* of the Mūlasarvāstivādins includes several Swat localities in the peregrination to the North-West made by the Buddha, who flew there in the company of Vajrapāṇi. This celebrated passage which Przyluski[29]...first made known in full, confirms the desire felt to confer nobility on a region where Buddhism must have been in full expansion. The passage tells how the Buddha sanctified the region by his presence, and subdued the *nāga* Apalāla..., of whom the canonical writings in the pāli [Pāli] language make no mention.[30]

Of the sacred sites, sanctified by the Jataka stories, special mention is to be made of the 'Buddha's foot-prints left on a stone', which survived at Tirat and 'within a few miles' of which was 'the clothes-drying rock' where Buddha, it is believed, 'dried his clothes after washing them and which miraculously retained impressions of them',[31] which has been on the right side of the Swat River opposite village Jaray.

The stone bearing Buddha's footprints was shifted to the Swat Museum a few days before the Museum's inauguration on 10 November 1963 by President Ayub Khan. It was brought by the village people to the road, for which they were paid by the Museum staff, and was then transported in a vehicle by the Museum staff. It is on display in the Museum. There was also a *stupa* near the site, which was washed away by the floodwaters of Swat River, on 28–29 July 2010. And 'the clothes-drying rock', that 'miraculously retained impressions' of Gautama Buddha's clothes, was blasted with explosive in 1993 by unknown treasure hunters; or the owners of the neighbouring fields so that the government should not occupy the place as an archaeological site resulting in loss of ownership of the land. The site and the broken stone blocks were washed away by the floodwaters of the Swat River, on 28–29 July 2010. Hence, now there is no trace left of the site and the clothes-drying rock as the Swat River flows over the place.

The fertile land of Swat proved fertile for Buddhism and emerged as its great centre. Buddhism flourished here, the attractive remains of which abound throughout the region. Swat was regarded 'throughout the world as the holy land of Buddhist learning and piety' and 'during the early centuries' CE 'it was imperative upon every Buddhist pilgrim to visit this enchanting land'.[32]

Fa-Hien (Faxian), the first known Chinese pilgrim to the region, recorded in about 403 CE that the Law of Buddha was vigorously flourishing here. The places where the monks stayed for a time or resided permanently were called Sangharamas (monasteries), which were 500[33] in number. All the monks were students of the Hinayana school of Buddhism. Stranger *bhikshu*s were supplied, for three days, their wants after their arrival at one of the Sangharamas. They were then 'told to find a resting-place for themselves'.[34] Aurel Stein's observations are also worth mentioning. He has stated:

Fertile as Swāt still is, and thickly populated as it once was, the whole of the great valley must have been crowded with Buddhist sanctuaries and religious establishments in the centuries immediately before and after Christ. This explains the care taken by the old Chinese pilgrims to visit Swāt on their way from the Hindukush to the sacred sites of India, and the glowing account that they have left us of the land. No doubt, they and other pious visitors knew also how to appreciate the material attractions of Swāt, the abundance and variety of its produce, its temperate climate, and the beauty of its scenery.

These attractions are significantly reflected in the popular etymology that has transformed the ancient name of the country, *Uḍḍiyana*, into Sanskrit *Udyāna*, the 'Garden', as it meets us in the narrative of old Hsüan-tsang, the most famous of those old Chinese travellers.[35]

The civilization that developed in the region not only received momentum and inspiration from Buddhism and its art and literature, but also from outside influences. However, the role played by the local people themselves has been equally, or perhaps more, important 'in receiving these inspirations with an open mind; tempering and refining them and stamping them with the marks of Gandharan or Uddiyanian genius'.[36]

The next Chinese pilgrim, Sung Yun 'found Buddhism still very flourishing' in Swat in 519 CE and that the king strictly followed 'the rules of the Buddha's Law'.[37] Sung Yun has stated that, following the king, 'the people had made some advance in purity; they observed the fasts, lived on vegetables, and honored Foe [Buddha] morning and night'.[38] He, moreover, has talked of about 6000 gold images in the monastery at T'a lo (most probably Butkara) in the southeast of the modern Mingawarah. This was confirmed by a multitude of stone or stucco images, some with traces of gold-wash that 'once covered them', found in the excavation at Butkara I.[39] All these 'prove the wealth and religious fervour of the people'.[40]

There have been sacred lakes in Swat with which a number of rituals and sacred stories are connected. The excavations carried out in Swat also reveal that the horse had been considered sacred and was worshiped. Besides, cults of female deities were also found.[41]

With the passage of time, Buddhism declined in Swat. When the next Chinese pilgrim Hiuen Tsiang (Xuanzang) arrived in Swat, about 630 CE, he found Buddhism in a state of decline and desperation. He has recorded:

On both sides of the river Su-po-fa-su-tu,...there are some 1400 old *sangharamas* [monasteries]. They are now generally waste and desolate;

formerly there were some 18,000 priests in them, but gradually they have become less, till now there are very few. They study the Great Vehicle; they practise the duty of quiet meditation, and have pleasure in reciting texts relating to this subject, but have no great understanding as to them. The (*priests who*) practise the rules of morality lead a pure life and purposely prohibit the use of charms... The schools...of the *Vinaya* traditionally known amongst them are the Sarvastivadins, the Dharmaguptas, the Mahisasakas, the Kasyapiyas,...and the Mahasanghikas: these five...

There are about ten temples of Devas [Hindus], and a mixed number of unbelievers who dwell in them.[42]

Old schools of Buddhism were represented in Uddiyana at the time of the visit of Fa-Hein (Faxian), in spite of the later inclination towards the Mahayana rather than the Hinayana. Hiuen Tsiang (Xuanzang) has stated, as quoted above, that some ancient Vinayas have been preserved.[43]

Most writers have held the White Huns (Ephthalites) responsible, on the assumption of John Marshall, for the decline of Buddhism and the destruction of its establishments in the region. The archaeological evidence, however, show that, while there might have been destruction by the White Huns in the Peshawar plains, but Buddhism still flourished in the hilly areas, viz. Swat, Dir, and Buner.[44] Dr M. Ashraf Khan has contended: 'According to Fa-Hien, Swat had already been overrun by the White Huns, who had destroyed everything that came in their way and they levelled to [the] ground most of the Buddhist establishments.'[45] Fa-Hien (Faxian), however, has not mentioned any such thing in his account of Swat. To the contrary, he has spoken of the flourishing condition of Buddhism and its establishments in Swat.[46] Moreover, Fa-Hein (Faxian) visited Swat in about 403 CE, but the White Huns' inroads occurred later in the second half of the fifth century CE, evidently after his visit to the country.

Giuseppe Tucci has contended that 'the ravages attributed to the Ephtalites [Ephthalites] have been somehow exaggerated' and hence need deep investigation.[47] He has opined: 'The Sasanians [Sassanians] had passed there before Sung Yün, and perhaps took control of Swāt for a certain period; the Ephtalites [Ephthalites] followed and might have caused other damages...; Buddhism was still prosperous at the times of Sung Yün; something had, then, happened between the visit of Sung Yün and that of Hsüan-tsang.'[48] He, therefore, has supposed:

The cause may be attributed to natural calamities and social unrest: earthquakes and floods documented by the excavations, at Butkara and elsewhere, greatly impoverished the country, then the decrease of trade with the plains and with Central Asia, *via* Gilgit, the probable attempts by the Turki Śāhis to control Swāt, a fact which was realized in the year 747, the division of the country among different petty vassals chiefs.[49]

And dealing with the point in an earlier report, he has opined: 'I therefore think that as far as Swat is concerned we must be cautious before attributing all the ruins to invaders, especially as we have ample and visible documents of natural causes of destruction.'[50] Dr Abdur Rahman has argued, even about Gandhara: 'There is no reason to assume, as is generally believed, that Buddhism disappeared altogether with the Ephthalite invasion of Gandhāra in A.D. 455, in spite of the depredations of Mihira Kula. The Turk Śāhis were decidedly Buddhists.'[51]

The last known Chinese visitor to Swat, Wu Kung, reached here in the year 752 CE, settled down in a monastery and resided here for about thirty years. 'During his long residence in the country he is said to have "visited all the holy vestiges". But his laconic record has little more to tell us than that he found "not the slightest difference between what he saw and that which Hsuan-tsang's narrative says".'[52]

Although Sung Yun has praised 'the piety of the Swāti monks' and has spoken 'of their austerity', Hiuen Tsiang (Xuanzang) 'does not seem to have a high opinion' of them. In spite of their piety, the Swati monks have had 'their inborn inclination to magic', which increased with the passage of time. That was why 'the country seems to be then dominated by Vajrayāna, opening the way to the revival of the aboriginal, cruel presences and of the magic rituals for which Swāt had been famous from its origin'.[53] Although, the situation is 'well documented by literary tradition', Giuseppe Tucci has asserted, 'it is a fact that during the excavation no image or symbol belonging to Vajrayāna schools has so far been discovered in Swāt'.[54]

Recent researches, however, unearthed statutes and rock carvings, which shed light on many facets of the Buddhist art and beliefs, etcetera. Dealing with the point of the presence of Vajrayanic themes in the rock sculptures found in Swat, Dr Anna Filigenzi has contended: 'This approximate chronological correspondence is in fact the single superficial link between the rock sculptures and Vajrayāna.'[55] Elaborating on the point, she has argued: 'Vague as it may be, it allows us to associate the history of this artistic phenomenon with the documentation concerning two important personalities of the period: Xuanzang and Padmasambhava.'[56] Detailing the features of the rock sculptures, she has stated:

> Nevertheless, the latter do show the occasional fleeting pointer to the new ideological horizon. In them we find features distinctly associated with a view of the religious path, and even with rituals, typical of the Tantric doctrines…
>
> Among these there is an interesting relief which, if my interpretation is correct, is able to illustrate this Vajrayanic "presence" in the rock sculpture in a particularly direct and eloquent manner.[57]

At the time of Fa-Hien's (Faxian's) visit, the Hinayana School of Buddhism was flourishing in Swat, which was later on superseded by the Mahayana School. With the passage of time, a third school, known as Vajrayana or Tantric Buddhism, developed in Swat in the seventh–eighth centuries and Swat gained fame for legends of spirits and demons, and for magic and mystery. Even Indrabhuti, the King of Swat, it is believed, was a great magician and he wrote the Tantric commentaries. The Kingdom of Swat became a famous centre of esoteric doctrines, of magic and the leading one among 'the four most famous Tantric centres of all India, the Uḍḍiyāna-pīṭha'.[58]

The traditions say that, in the end, the aspirations of the people were no more being satisfied by traditional Buddhism, so Tantric books were recovered and handed over to the Nagas by Vajrapani. The King of Swat, Indrabhuti, 'wrote them down, changing the Nāgas either in "heroes"… or in flying entities'. 'Uḍḍiyāna was therefore considered one of the most famous Tantric places in India': being 'one of the pīṭhas, holy centres of Tantrism, the Uḍḍiyānapīṭha and it turned into a kind of Mecca [Makkah] for the Tibetans, as the birthplace of Padmasaṃbhava, and the home of the ḍākinīs…(in Tibetan: mk'a' agro ma "sky-flying" [fairies or female spirits, witches, and wizards])'.[59]

It was from Swat that Tantric Buddhism was brought to Tibet and all over the Himalayas. According to Tibetan traditions, 'Buddha Sakyamuni made a prophecy…that a much wiser and a more powerful Buddha would be born in a lotus in the Dhanakosha lake of Urgyan'. Therefore, Guru Rimpoche Padmasambhava, preacher of Tantric Buddhism 'all over the Himalayas and in Tibet…is admitted to be the same incarnation'.[60] It, however, has been asserted that 'Padmasambhava was the son of Indrabhuti, king of Swat in the early eighth century AD',[61] and was invited by the Tibetan 'king Khri-droṅ-lda-btsan' to Tibet.[62] Accepting the invitation and 'escorted by' the king's 'messengers' he 'came to Tibet in 747 A.D.'.[63]

D.H. Muncherji has spoken not only of the presence of Buddhism in Swat but also of the followers of Manichaeism and Nestorianism by contending that 'no less important was the location of Udyana (linking central Asia with India) which resulted in the convergence of ideas. Buddhism, Manichaenism [Manichaeism], Nestorianism, all had their followers at this place'.[64] But, although traces of the cultural influence of Persia can be found, no details are available about the presence and followers of Manichaeism and Nestorianism. Giuseppe Tucci too has spoken of 'the conditions prevailing in Swat' being 'very favorable to the convergence of ideas'. Therefore, here met 'the most active religions of those times: Buddhism, Manichaeism, Nestorianism, each laden with the spiritual and intellectual traditions of its country of origin and of adoption'.[65] Tucci has asserted that 'according to reliable evidence, several sects [of Buddhism] were represented in Swat: the Sarvāstivādin, the Mahāsāṅghika, the Mahīsāsaka, the Dharmaguptaka, the Kāśyapīya'.[66]

Swat not only remained a centre of Buddhism for a long period but Buddhist philosophy and metaphysics also developed here. Many interesting traditions are found which make Swat a sanctuary of the Buddhists. For instance, Fa-Hein (Faxian) has stated:

> There is a tradition that when Buddha came to North India, he came at once to this country, and that here he left a print of his foot [feet], which is long or short according to the ideas of the beholder (on the subject). It exists, and the same thing is true about it, at the present day [about 403 CE]. Here also are still to be seen the rock on which he dried his clothes, and the place where he converted the wicked dragon... The rock is fourteen cubits high, and more than twenty broad, with one side of it smooth.[67]

The lake where the miracle-working Nagaraja lived has been stated was to the west of the river and has been identified by H.A. Deane, as the Saidgai Lake.[68] And according to Hiuen Tsiang (Xuanzang), who came here in about 630 CE:

> To the south-west of the fountain of the dragon Apalala ('O-po-lo-lo), about 30 li on the north side of the river, there is a foot [feet] trace of

Buddha on a great rock. According to the religious merit of persons, this impression appears long or short. This is the trace left by Buddha after having subdued the dragon. Afterwards men built up a stone residence (*over the impression*). Men came here from a distance to offer incense and flowers.[69]

Besides the traditions of Buddha's visit to Swat, his footprints and the marks of his clothes on the rock, as well as his conversion of a wicked dragon, Swat has got 'of the relics of the Buddha's body' according to Buddha's 'own command preceding Nirvāṇa' for covering which the then King of Swat, Uttarasena, built a *stupa*—according to the local tradition recorded by Hiuen Tsiang (Xuanzang).[70] Aurel Stein has identified Uttarasena's built *stupa* near village Ghaligay,[71] but Giuseppe Tucci does not agree with this and has asserted, after evaluating the issue and the marks of the surroundings mentioned by Hiuen Tsiang (Xuanzang), that it was most probably situated at the hamlet of Naway Kalay about 500 meters from Kutah near Landakay.[72]

Moreover, according to Hiuen Tsiang, the Buddha in his Swat visit told the mother of the Uttarasena-raja that he was going about to die and the *raja* should 'come for a share of the relics to honour them'. The *raja* went to the stated spot 'where Buddha had already died'. The other kings 'treated him scornfully' and were not giving 'him a share of the much-prized relics they were taking to their own countries'. However, 'a great assembly of Devas acquainted them with Buddha's wishes' on the point and thence 'the king[s] divided the relics equally beginning with him'.[73] He, moreover, has stated that 'four or five li to the east' of the town Mungali is the 'great *stupa*, where very many spiritual portents are seen'; and 'this is the spot where Buddha, when he lived in old time,... was the Rishi who practised patience (Kshanti-rishi), and for the sake of Kaliraja endured the dismemberment of his body'.[74]

O rgyan pa's (thirteenth century CE) and sTag ts'an ras pa's (seventeenth century CE) diaries have also provided mythical, fantastic and fascinating accounts about the beliefs of the people of the area.[75]

One of the subtle changes that Buddhism brought to Swat was that it made the people peaceable. H.A. Deane has opined: 'The extensive manner in which the Udyāna is fortified on the south speaks of anything but the supposed peaceable nature of the people, or their cordial relations with their neighbours in Gandhāra.'[76] D.H. Muncherji has observed:

Whatever may be the final opinion of the authorities on the life led by the people in ancient Udyana, it is already clear that the beautiful and fertile valley of Swat was selected by the Buddhist[s] as a haven of refuge from the endless wars and disorders of the country. The propitious surroundings proved very helpful in the development of Buddhism, and made it one of the great centres of the religion. Through the course of many centuries great scholars, priests, and saints of that religion tried to lead the masses of men on the path of truth and righteousness. This effort for the achievement of the higher values of life affected almost every activity of the people of Udyana. Besides their religion, it found its greatest fulfilment in their art, which for its spiritual quality and aesthetic refinement is worthy of all admiration.[77]

In Dr Muhammad Farooq Swati's words: 'Since the advent of Buddhism in the third century B.C. until the resurgence of Brāhmanism at the end of the eighth century A.D., Swāt remained the main centre of Buddhist culture.'[78] Interestingly, recent excavations and researches has unearthed remains that open new venues and vistas even from the religious perspective of Swat. Basing his arguments on such new information, Dr Luca M. Olivieri has contended:

We believe that we can say that Buddhism, inasmuch as it had a popular character, did not have universalist ambitions: at least in contexts such as these, its main target would have been to have on its side the political elites, merchants and craftsmen: in other words, the residents of the cities. But if even in the cities, as the evidence at Barikot shows, forms of popular religion persisted, we can imagine that the communities of mountains or forests, although involved in the activities of the monasteries, were not converted.[79]

Dr Luca's contention is supportive of or a continuation of an earlier contention of Giuseppe Tucci, made in 1963, which runs thus:

Buddhism developed along the main routes, in the trade centres and in the towns: but in the villages, in the far-off places and in the mountain hamlets the older ideas were not driven out by its impact. This holds true chiefly for the mountainous parts of Swat, where its population, half-nomad, half agricultural (because some of it attempted, in the hot season, the cultivation of the terraces set up with great toil along the slopes of the hills, like the Gurjars [Gujars] of present days) was but scarcely or superficially influenced by the agricultural and trade-centers of the valley. This does not mean that the farmers and the shepherd-nomad-semi-agricultural groups did not intercomunicate [intercommunicate], or were definitely living apart or isolated.[80]

Aurel Stein has spoken of the 'Buddhist relievos' in Swat, almost all of whom 'represented Bodhisattvas, in the *varamudrā* or "pose of largess".' He has said that 'probably most of these figures were meant to represent Avalokiteśvara, pre-eminently the dispenser of mercy and help in the northern Buddhist Patheon'.[81] However, according to Dr Anna Filigenzi: 'In proportion to the total number of reliefs and the frequency of the various subjects, the figure of Avalokiteśvara/Padmapāṇi ("the lotus bearer") occupies a position of absolute predominance.' And that 'in fact at a modest estimate half the reliefs portray the isolated figures of this Bodhisattva, and yet this calculation excludes occurrences within groups of divinities, where the figure is often the main subject of the composition'.[82] At another place, Stein has observed: 'Of all the Buddhist relievos found on the rocks near Manglawar and miles up the valley...the colossal image of a seated Buddha some thirteen feet in height is certainly the most striking.'[83]

RESURRECTION OF HINDUISM

V.V.S. Sarma has asserted: 'After the decline of Buddhism, Hinduism reasserted itself and Swat was wholly Hindu till the 11th century attacks of Muhammad [Mahmud] of Ghazni.'[84] And H.W. Bellew has asserted that when the Hindu Shahis established their rule, Hinduism had already started replacing Buddhism.[85]

In spite of starting its decline in Swat, 'a quantity of rock reliefs (on walls, isolated blocks or steles showing minimal shaping) datable roughly between the seventh and eighth century AD, which burgeoned about the ancient sacred areas by then probably in ruins' testify to 'the persistence of Buddhism—or, it might be said, its resistance to generally less favourable conditions'.[86] According to Giuseppe Tucci, in spite of 'general decay of Buddhism, except for the unique image of a goddess... and even an image of Śiva, there are not many traces of a great diffusion of Hinduism in Swāt'.[87] Interestingly and significantly, however, in an earlier Oriental Note II, he has said:

Be that as it may, the stele confirms, it appears, what I anticipated in *PR.* [Preliminary Reports and Studies on the Italian Excavations in Swat

(Pakistan)] that Buddhism did not succeed in completely overthrowing the original belief of the inhabitants of Swat and surrounding countries; on the contrary, the ḍākinīs and the ḍākas..., now known under the name of shisha, peri, hapiḍei, rū-ī or daiyals (when male) are but the last remnants of old, prebuddhistic [pre-Buddhistic] cults which resisted what I should call traditional Buddhism to such an extent that, when it began to collapse, they took again the upper hand and found their way into Vajrayāna.[88]

And that:

We know for certain that Hindu communities had their temples in Uḍḍiyāna; these shrines may have well contained images of more dignified and carefully executed images like those exemplified by a good number of pieces belonging to the Turki and Hindu Shahi periods.[89]

Commenting on 'a beautiful stone relief from the Swat valley', illustrated by G. Gnoli, R.C. Agrawala has opined that 'this Swat valley relief may present the blending of Viṣṇu, Śiva and Indra in one form'.[90] He later on has stated that this 'relief, then has an important bearing on the cult of composite icons in Ghandaran art of the Swat region'.[91] And that 'the idea of a composite figure may, indeed, be traced back to as early as the Kuṣāṇa period'.[92] And in a note on the note of A.G. Agrawala, Maurizio Taddei has spoken 'of the possibility of iconographic exchanges between Buddhism and Hinduism'.[93] He, however, while dealing with the point of 'religiously «Indian» explanation of the Gandharan images', has pointed out an important issue of representation from the Roman age, in the Gandharan art images, and 'so Buddhist Gandhāra gave a western form to its religious concepts' and 'we must understand that these imported representations carry with them at least a part of their original meaning'.[94]

The artistic production of the sculptures that developed in Swat during the seventh–eighth century CE, although mainly Buddhist, in some cases represents 'Surya, Ganesha and Shiva'.[95] A statue has even been found in Barikut that by 'iconographic comparisons indicate' it as being 'part of a triad composed by *Viṣṇu* and his two āyudhapuruṣa: *Gadādevī* and *Cakrapuruṣa*'.[96] Basing arguments on the Hindu temple excavated on the top of the hill at Barikut and the 'beautiful Gadādevī figure', unearthed therefrom, it has been asserted that 'the temple of Barikot, placed in such a prominent position, is the first, important witness to non-buddhist [non-Buddhist] cults during the period that we can label as Śāhi or, more precisely, judging from the archaeological context, Turki Śāhi'.[97] And that:

> Time is perhaps not yet ripe to further speculations, but what is undisputable is the coexistence, within the same chronological, geographic and artistic frame, of two different religious systems, as the odd mixture of the Tindo Dag reliefs clearly witnesses to. Whether this coexistence was marginal or ample, friendly or bellicose, temporary or lasting, we are still unable to affirm, but these two places, Tindo Dag-Manyar and Barikot, that look at each other from their prominent position open a new chapter of the history of Swat and, more in general, of the cultural and political trends which were running at that time within the Hindukush areas.[98]

Whereas, while dealing with 'the religious identity' of a new unearthed building, termed as the 'Sacred Building', in the course of excavations at Barikut Ghwandai, the excavators have said that they 'are far from a clear understanding' of it. However, it seems to them 'more likely that the monument is a temple or a *caitya*'. And 'in the late date to which the building seems to belong…Buddhism and Hinduism were closely intermingled'. After dealing with the point of intermingling and coexistence of Buddhism and Hinduism, they have said that 'if the Sacred Building belongs to the period of the Hindu Shahis, then it is likely to have been a Hindu temple'.[99]

All the aforementioned testify to the presence and coexistence of both Hinduism and Buddhism in the area, despite the decay of the Buddhist dominance.

THE ADVENT OF ISLAM

H.W. Bellew has claimed that Brahmanism (Hinduism), which steadily increased and soon entirely suppressed Buddhism and flourished for centuries, 'was suddenly swept away by the flood of Islam under Mahmud' of Ghazna, because:

> Mahmud's ruthless soldiery only spared the lives of their victims on an immediate and unconditional adoption of Islam, whilst, with untiring exertions, they strove to wipe out every trace of heathenism from the country by a general sacking, burning, and razing of the temples and

monasteries, and a complete destruction, or, where this was impracticable, the disfigurement of the idols and implements of worship. Not a temple, tope, or monastery escaped the keen scrutiny of these barbarians [sic], and much less the dwellings of the people. Fire appears to have been the chief means of destruction; for most of the ruins that have been excavated bear marks of its action, and shew signs of the hasty flight of their former inhabitants.[100]

Giuseppe Tucci, too, has stated: 'In the 10th [11th] century Swāt was plundered by Mahmud of Ghazni and then by his successors. They inflicted a great blow on Buddhism and Hinduism.'[101] And that:

While at the time of Orgyan pa it seem that small Buddhist or Hindu islands still survived, all traces of them had disappeared at the times of sTag Ts'aṅ ras pa (first half of the seventeenth century).

During the invasions by the Ghaznavides [Ghaznavids] and their successors many inhabitants of Swat fled to Hazara (so the tradition goes); others were converted to Islam.[102]

Prof. Mohammad Habib has contended that Mahmud of Ghazna started in 1021 CE

from Ghaznin with "a large number of carpenters, blacksmiths and stone-cutters" with the definite intention of establishing a regular government over the Punjab. The first objective were [was] the frontier tribes of Swat, Bajaur and Kafiristan, who had "not yet put the yoke of Islam round their necks" and worshipped the Buddha in the form of the lion (Sakya Sinha). The inhabitants were subdued and converted, and a fort was built in their territory.[103]

Prof. Habib has mentioned Swat in the account; but Dr Muhammad Nazim has, on the authority of Alberuni, identified the valleys of the rivers Nur and Qirat (taken for Swat by some writers[104]) in 'Kāfiristān to the north of Lamaghān [Laghman]'.[105] Prof. Habib's note to the text and the sentence: 'Doubtless the frontier tribes are meant',[106] never testify and prove that the said expedition of Mahmud of Ghazna was led to Swat.

Similarly, in V.V.S. Sarma's words: 'The vagaries of time have taken its [their] toll and destroyed the places of worship today but some people say that all the monasteries were razed to the ground by the first Muslim ruler of Swat.'[107]

Bellew's contention of the destruction at the hands of Mahmud's soldiery, and Sarma's of razing all the monasteries to the ground by the first Muslim ruler of Swat as well as Prof. Habib's of the conversion of the people to Islam does not stand, at least as far as Swat is concerned, as *stupa*s and Buddha's and Bodhisattvas' statues are found in Swat in great numbers till this time in 2020 CE, despite the passage of about one thousand years since then.

Similarly, Giuseppe Tucci's above contention also does not stand as the diaries of the Tibetan pilgrims O rgyan pa (1230–1293 CE), who visited Swat after 1260 CE, and sTag ts'an ras pa, also known as O rgyan pa Nag dban rgya mts'o, who came here in about the middle of the seventeenth century CE, have evidence that suggests Buddhists existed in the area as late as the seventeenth century.[108] Tucci himself has contended elsewhere: 'We can gather from O rgyan pa that at the time of his travels some Hindu principalities had survived in Swat.'[109] And when sTag ts'an ras pa arrived at Uddiyana (Udigram), 'it was a big holiday corresponding to the tenth of the third month of the Buddhist calendar. All people were assembled and singing and dancing, they drank all kinds of liquors without restriction. This place is the very core of O rgyan [Swat].'[110] Tucci, moreover, has elaborated:

> The only thing worth remembering, as I said before, is that we find both in O rgyan pa and in sTag ts'an ras pa the reflex of a different historical situation, that the habits of the people were not yet completely islamized [Islamized], that there were survivals both of Buddhism and Hinduism, and that the ancient monuments were in a far better condition than they are today, though it is a matter of regret that the Tibetan pilgrims did not think it worth while to write a more detailed description of them.[111]

Tawarikh Hafiz Rahmat Khani also has spoken of the presence, in the first quarter of the sixteenth century CE, of numerous idols in But Bat (بت بت) since the days of *kufar* (infidels). When the Yusufzi occupied that place, they broke them. That place is at a mile distance from village Ambuh [Abuhah; Aboha?].[112] The book also has spoken of the presence of the Dihgan *kafir*s (infidels), inhabiting the Lower Talash area (adjacent to Adinzi, Lower Swat) at the time of the Yusufzi's occupation of the areas in the early years of the sixteenth century.[113] This, too, testifies that Islam was not yet the dominant religion in the area, or all the population of the area was not Muslim till that time.

Although the Muslims invaded Swat Valley in the beginning of eleventh century (during Mahmud of Ghazna's rule[114]) and the foundation of a general spread of Islam here was laid, Buddhism and Hinduism prevailed here for centuries to come, as discussed above, which negates Bellew's contention that Hinduism completely overtook Buddhism and that Mahmud of Ghazna's soldiery destroyed all the sacred places of Hinduism and Buddhism and spared only the life of those who embraced Islam unconditionally. It also negates Mohammad Habib's contention that the inhabitants of Swat were converted to Islam by Mahmud of Ghazna, and Tucci's contention of inflicting a great blow on Buddhism and Hinduism by Mahmud of Ghazna and of his successors' plundering Swat. It also negates the contention that the people either fled from Swat or converted to Islam.

In fact, 'it was with the Yusufzais's conquest', in the sixteenth century CE, 'that Islam became the dominant religion of Swat as it is these days'.[115] But, despite this, namely Islam's becoming the dominant religion in Swat, the pre-Buddhist and Buddhist beliefs in *dakinis* and *dakas* and the likes, under the names of *shishakah*, *piray/pirai* (pl. *piryan*), *khapiray/khapirai* (pl. *khapiri*) etcetera, have survived till this time in 2020 CE.[116]

With the Yusufzi's occupation of Swat, Islam became the dominant religion in the plain Swat Valley, but non-Muslims still existed, especially in the hilly areas and Kuhistan. Later, *jihad* was proclaimed against or invasion over the Kuhistan areas was undertaken under some religious figures.[117] Resultantly, the inhabitants of the Kuhistan area, too, gradually embraced Islam. Hence, Islam became dominant both in the plain and hilly areas of the valley.

The Sunni sect and Hanafi School of *fiqah* (jurisprudence) were followed by the people of Swat. Shias and the followers of other schools of Sunnis did not exist here till recent times. Khushal Khan Khattak, who visited Swat in the second half of the seventeenth century, also has talked of the non-existence of Shias in Swat, by stating:

دا دوه نشته په سوات کښے څوک چه وائي یا علی

اَلصّالِحُــــوْنَ لِلّٰهِ وَالطّالِحُـــوْنَ لِـــئ 118

Meaning: These two are non-existent in Swat: those who call Ali (i.e. Shia) and those who attribute all the good things to Allah and the bad to themselves (probably referring to some sect or religion).

The overwhelming majority of the population have had the beliefs and performed the rituals which are now attributed to and are performed by the Barailwi School of thought, followers of Ahmad Raza Khan Barailwi of Bans Baraili,[119] of the Sunnis in the subcontinent.

It is worth mentioning that, although not Buddhists, Hindu and Sikh non-Muslims have inhabited Swat till this time in 2020 CE: although as small minorities. They live in peace, honour, and amity with the Muslim majority: with no threat to their person and property from the Muslims.

NOTES

1. Giuseppe Tucci, 'On Swāt. The Dards and Connected Problems', *East and West* (Rome), 27/1–4 (December 1977), 26.
2. Ibid., 38.
3. [Hiuen Tsiang], *Chinese Accounts of India: Translated from the Chinese of Hiuen Tsiang*, trans. and annotated by Samuel Beal, Vol. 2 (new edn., Calcutta: Susil Gupta (India) Limited, 1958), 167.
4. See D.H. Muncherji, 'Swat: The Garden of Asoka', *Pakistan Quarterly* (Karachi), 9/3 (1959), 41; Giuseppe Tucci, 'Preliminary report on an archaeological survey in Swat', *East and West* (Rome), 9/4 (December 1958), 283.
5. H.A. Deane, 'Note on Udyāna and Gandhāra', *Journal of the Royal Asiatic Society of Great Britain and Ireland* (October 1896), 660 (Stable URL: http://www.jstor.org/stable/25207806; accessed: 16/05/2011).
6. Tucci, 'On Swāt. The Dards and Connected Problems', 68. Importantly, 'one of the first revealers of this school was *Khagendra* "the lord of those flying in the air", the Śaiva match of the Ḍāka, masculine form of the Ḍākinīs'. Ibid.
7. See also, Sadullah Jan Barq, *Da Pukhtanu Asal Nasal* (Pashto), Vol. 3 (Peshawar: University Book Agency, 2010), 13–15; V.V.S. Sarma, 'From Udyana, the Seat of Rig-Veda, to the Present Swat Valley in Pakistan under Taliban Control', *Hindu Heritage of Swat Valley*, 3 May 2009, 11:07 am (Website: http://indianrealist.wordpress.com/2009/05/03/hindu-heritage-of-swat-valley; accessed: 10/06/2010). Aurel Stein, *On Alexander's Track to the Indus: Personal Narrative of Explorations on the North-West Frontier of India* (repr., Karachi: Indus Publications, 1995), 168–9. For some detail about Rama and his banishment etcetera, see A.L. Basham, *The Wonder that Was India: A survey of the history and culture of the Indian sub-continent before the coming of the Muslims* (3rd revised edn., 1st paperback edn., London: Sidgwick & Jackson, 1985), 303, 412–13.
8. Naveed Hussain, 'Sawan Sangran' (Website: www.valleyswat.net; accessed: 20/09/2010). Also see Stein, *On Alexander's Track to the Indus*, 170–1; Aurel Stein, *An Archaeological tour in Upper Swāt and Adjacent Hill Tracts* (Calcutta: Government of India, Central Publication Branch, 1930), 103–4.
9. Congregating Sawan Sangran, Hindus would festoon the Ram Takht with golden and silver cloth and colourful papers and place incense sticks along the way to and around the Ram Takht. They participated in this ritual with extraordinary

dedication and sincerity and would engage in worship and recite their holy book for the whole of the first night of Sawan. At dawn, headed by their religious leader or Pundit, all the pilgrims were required to climb up the Ram Takht. The leader had to perform several religious rituals after which *prashad* (blessed confectionary) was to be distributed among all the pilgrims. They would perambulate around the Ram Takht for heavenly blessing and fasten holy threads and bracelets around their wrists and bring some for their near and dears. With this, the festival was to end (Hussain, 'Sawan Sangran'). While dealing with the track from Mingawarah to Ilam, the holy mountain for the Hindus and the Sikhs, Giuseppe Tucci has contended, in his account of 1955 tour: 'This is certainly the easiest way to the holy mountain and it was followed up to some years ago by the Sikhs or the Hindus going on pilgrimage to Ilam every year.' (Tucci, 'Preliminary report on an archaeological survey in Swat', 312).

10. Sarma, 'From Udyana, the Seat of Rig-Veda, to the Present Swat Valley in Pakistan under Taliban Control'.

11. See *Walmiki Urdu Ramayan ba Taswir wa Mukammal*, Urdu trans. Babu Munawwar Sahib, Khalf-ur-Rashid Munshi Dwarka Prashad Sahib, Ufaq Lakhnawi, Hasb-i Farmaish J.S. Sanat Singh and Sons, Publishers wa Tajiran-i Kutub, Chawak Mati Lahore (Lahore: Printed by Hindustan Press, Haspatal Road, n.d.).

12. Tucci, 'On Swāt. The Dards and Connected Problems', 26–7; Stein, *On Alexander's Track to the Indus*, 171.

13. Tucci, 'On Swāt. The Dards and Connected Problems', 54. In the account of his Swat visit, made in 1926, Aurel Stein has observed about Mount Ilam: 'I now began to understand why legends of all sorts, some manifestly of very early origin, cluster around this peak and cause it to be reverenced not merely by the few local Hindus, hardy survivals, as it were, from pre-Muhammadan times, but also by Pathāns and Gujars' (Stein, *On Alexander's Track to the Indus*, 72).

14. Tucci, 'On Swāt. The Dards and Connected Problems', 28.

15. [Abu Rehan Alberuni], *Alberuni's India: An Account of the Religion, Philosophy, Literature, Geography, Chronology, Astronomy, Customs, Laws and Astrology of India about A.D. 1030*, edited with notes and indices by Edward C. Sachau, two vols. in one, Popular edn., 1st Indian reprint, Vol. 2 (Delhi: S. Chand & Co., 1964), 182. See also, Abu Rehan Alberuni, *Hindu Dharam: Hazar Bars Pihlay* (Urdu trans.) (Lahore: Nigarishat, 2000), 183; Alberuni, *Kitabul Hind*, Urdu trans. Sayyad Asghar Ali, revised by Sayyad Atta Hussain (Lahore: Al-Faisal Nashiran, 2008), 209–10. In Swat Valley, at present, there is no evidence of this juncture of fifty-three streams of which Alberuni speaks. It might have been outside the valley proper but part of the then Swat State as the political geography of Swat has changed from time to time.

16. R. Ch. Hazra, *Studies in the Upapuraṇas*, Calcutta, 1963, 50 quoted in Giuseppe Tucci, 'Oriental Notes, II: An Image of a Devi Discovered in Swat and some Connected Problems', in Giuseppe Tucci, *On Swāt. Historical and Archaeological Notes*, with introduction by Domenico Faccenna, eds. P. Callieri and A. Filigenzi, reprint of the original 1997 edition, with preface by M. Ashraf Khan (Islamabad: Taxila Institute of Asian Civilizations, 2013), 123 n. 5a.

17. A.R. Burn, *Alexander the Great and the Hellenistic Empire* (2nd edn., London: English Universities Press, Ltd., 1951), 208.

18. *Imperial Gazetteer of India: Provincial Series; North-West Frontier Province* (repr., Lahore: Sang-e-Meel Publications, 1991), 217.

19. See Muhammad Asif Khan, *Tarikh-i Riyasat-i Swat wa Sawanih-i Hayat Baniy-i Riyasat-i Swat Hazrat Miangul Gul Shahzadah Abdul Wadud Khan Badshah Sahib* (Pashto), with *dibachah, hisah awal, saluramah hisah* and *hisah pinzamah* by Muhammad Asif Khan (Printed by Ferozsons Ltd., Peshawar, [1958]), 25; Muhammad Asif Khan, *Tarikh Riyasat-i Swat wa Sawanih-i Hayat Bani Riyasat-i Swat Miangul Abdul Wadud* (Urdu) (2nd edn., Mingawarah, Swat: Shoaib Sons Publishers and Booksellers, 2001), 22; Saranzeb Swati, *Tarikh Riyasat-i Swat* (Pashto) (Peshawar: Azeem Publishing House, 1984), 27; Fazle Rabbi Rahi, *Swat Tarikh kay Ayinay mayn* (Urdu) (2nd edn., Mingawarah, Swat: Shoaib Sons Publishers, Booksellers, 1997), 24; Fazle Rabbi Rahi, *Riyasat-i Swat: Tarikh ka Aik Warq* (Urdu) (Mingawarah, Swat: Shoaib Sons Publishers and Booksellers, 2000), 17; Fazle Rabbi Rahi, *Swat: Sayahu ki Jannat* (Urdu) (Mingawarah, Swat: Shoaib Sons Publishers and Booksellers, 2000), 15; Abdul Qayum Balala, *The Charming Swat* (Lahore: Maqsood Publishers, [2000]), 9; Nur Muhammad Shah Ghubah Jan, *Manzum Tarikh-i Swat* (Pashto, verse) (Printed by Ahmad Printing Press, Mingawarah, Swat, n.d.), 2.

20. Muhammad Habibullah Khan Khattak, *Buner: The Forgotten Part of Ancient Uddiyana* (Karachi: By the Author, Department of Archaeology and Museums, Government of Pakistan, 1997), 5.

21. H.W. Bellew, *A General Report on the Yusufzais* (3rd edn., Lahore: Sang-e-Meel Publications, 1994), 57.

22. [Tsiang], *Chinese Accounts of India: Translated from the Chinese of Hiuen Tsiang*, Vol. 2, 172.

23. Tucci, 'On Swāt. The Dards and Connected Problems', 58.

24. Muhammad Farooq Swāti, 'Recent Discovery of Buddhist Sites in the Swāt Valley', *Āthāriyyāt* (Peshawar), 1 (1997), 155.

25. Ibid., 169 n. 42.

26. Ahmad Nabi Khan, *Buddhist Art and Architecture in Pakistan* (Islamabad: Ministry of Information and Broadcasting, Directorate of Research, Reference and Publication, Government of Pakistan, n.d.), 62; Tucci, 'Preliminary report on an archaeological survey in Swat', 281.

27. Tucci, 'Preliminary report on an archaeological survey in Swat', 283.

28. Ibid., 281.

29. Jean Przyluski: A French linguist and scholar of Buddhism.

30. Tucci, 'Preliminary report on an archaeological survey in Swat', 281.

31. Aurel Stein, *An Archaeological tour in Upper Swāt and Adjacent Hill Tracts* (Calcutta: Government of India, Central Publication Branch, 1930), 56. For details about Buddha's footprints and the place where, as it is believed, he dried his clothes, see Fa-Hein, *A Record of Buddhistic Kingdoms*, trans. and annotated by James Legge (repr., New Delhi: Munshiram Manoharlal Publishers Pvt. Ltd., 1991), 29; [Fa Hian], *The Pilgrimage of Fa Hian: From the French Edition of the Foe Koue Ki of MM. Remusat, Klaproth, and Landresse with Additional Notes and Illustrations*, trans. and ed. by anonymous (Calcutta: The 'Bangabasi' Office,

1912), 49; [Tsiang], *Chinese Accounts of India: Translated from the Chinese of Hiuen Tsiang*, Vol. 2, 169; Stein, *An Archaeological tour in Upper Swāt and Adjacent Hill Tracts*, 56–61; Stein, *On Alexander's Track to the Indus*, 86–8. Aurel Stein, however, at another place has stated: 'But of the holy markings left by the Buddha's garments no trace remained—except the place which they had once occupied' (Stein, *On Alexander's Track to the Indus*, 87).

32. Khan, *Buddhist Art and Architecture in Pakistan*, 62.

33. Dr Farzand Ali Durrani, former Professor of Archaeology and former Vice-Chancellor, University of Peshawar, has stated: 'Indeed the fifth century AD Chinese pilgrim, Fa Hiun, recorded that there were 600 monasteries in the valley' [Farzand Ali Durrani, 'Foreward [Foreword]' to Makin Khan, *Archaeological Museum Saidu Sharif, Swat: A Guide* (Saidu Sharif: By the Author, Archaeological Museum, Saidu Sharif, Swat, 1997), 1]. Dr M. Ashraf Khan too has stated: 'According to Fa-Hien who came to Swat in 4th century [5th century] A.D[.], there flourished about 600 monasteries in the area' (M. Ashraf Khan, *Buddhist Shrines in Swat* (Saidu Sharif: By the Author, Archaeological Museum, Saidu Sharif, Swat, 1993), 15). Fa-Hein, however, has recorded the number of the monasteries as '500' only (see Fa-Hein, *A Record of Buddhistic Kingdoms*, 28; [Fa Hian], *The Pilgrimage of Fa Hian: From the French Edition of the Foe Koue Ki of MM. Remusat, Klaproth, and Landresse with Additional Notes and Illustrations*, 49.

34. Fa-Hein, *A Record of Buddhistic Kingdoms*, 28–9; [Fa Hian], *The Pilgrimage of Fa Hian: From the French Edition of the Foe Koue Ki of MM. Remusat, Klaproth, and Landresse with Additional Notes and Illustrations*, 49.

35. Stein, *On Alexander's Track to the Indus*, 13.

36. Khattak, *Buner: The Forgotten Part of Ancient Uddiyana*, 20.

37. Stein, *On Alexander's Track to the Indus*, 14.

38. [Fa Hian], *The Pilgrimage of Fa Hian: From the French Edition of the Foe Koue Ki of MM. Remusat, Klaproth, and Landresse with Additional Notes and Illustrations*, 53.

39. Tucci, 'Preliminary report on an archaeological survey in Swat', 280, 288. For details about the excavation and the images etcetera found at Butkara I, see Domenico Faccenna, '*Mingora: Site of Butkara I*' in Domenico Faccena and Giorgio Gullini, *Reports on the Campaigns 1956–1958 in Swat (Pakistan)* (Roma: Istituto Italiano per il Medio ed Estremo Oriente, 1962), 3–169.

40. Muncherji, 'Swat: The Garden of Asoka', 40.

41. For some detail, see Tucci, 'On Swāt. The Dards and Connected Problems', 28–30.

42. [Tsiang], *Chinese Accounts of India: Translated from the Chinese of Hiuen Tsiang*, Vol. 2, 167.

43. Tucci, 'On Swāt. The Dards and Connected Problems', 58.

44. Khattak, *Buner: The Forgotten Part of Ancient Uddiyana*, 20.

45. Khan, *Buddhist Shrines in Swat*, 8.

46. For Fa-Hein version, see Fa-Hein, *A Record of Buddhistic Kingdoms*, 28–9; [Fa Hian], *The Pilgrimage of Fa Hian: From the French Edition of the Foe Koue Ki of MM. Remusat, Klaproth, and Landresse with Additional Notes and Illustrations*, 49.

47. Tucci, 'On Swāt. The Dards and Connected Problems', 67 n. 91b.

48. Ibid., 67. See also Tucci, 'Preliminary report on an archaeological survey in Swat', 282.
49. Tucci, 'On Swāt. The Dards and Connected Problems', 67–8.
50. Tucci, 'Preliminary report on an archaeological survey in Swat', 282.
51. Abdur Rehman, *The Last Two Dynasties of the Śāhis: (An analysis of their history, archaeology, coinage and palaeography)* (Islamabad: Director Centre for the Study of the Civilizations of Central Asia, Quaid-i-Azam University, 1979), 285.
52. Stein, *On Alexander's Track to the Indus*, 15–16.
53. Tucci, 'On Swāt. The Dards and Connected Problems', 68.
54. Ibid., 69.
55. Anna Filigenzi, 'A Vajrayanic Theme in the Rock Sculpture of Swat' in Giovanni Verardi and Silvio Vita, eds., *Buddhist Asia 1: Papers from the First Conference of Buddhist Studies Held in Naples in May 2001* (Kyoto: Italian School of East Asian Studies, 2003), 40–1.
56. Ibid., 41.
57. Ibid., 43–4. See also, Anna Filigenzi, 'Wisdom and Compassion: Concept and Iconography of Avalokiteśvara/Padmapāṇi', *Annali* (Napoli), 60–61 (2000–2001), 247–64.
58. Tucci, 'Preliminary report on an archaeological survey in Swat', 280. Dr M. Ashraf Khan has stated that it was during the Kushana dynasty that 'Swat became an important centre of exoteric doctorine [doctrine] of Buddhism' (Khan, *Buddhist Shrines in Swat*, 7). But the two periods have a lapse of centuries in between, and Dr Ashraf Khan's contention appears contradictory.
59. Tucci, 'On Swāt. The Dards and Connected Problems', 68–9.
60. Nirmal C. Sinha, 'Gilgit (and Swat)', 50 (URL: http://himalaya.socanth.cam.ac.uk. collections/journals/bot/pdf/bot_08_01_03.pdf; accessed: 03/05/2010).
61. Sarma, 'From Udyana, the Seat of Rig-Veda, to the Present Swat Valley in Pakistan under Taliban Control'.
62. Anukul Chandra Banerjee, 'Expansion of Buddhism in Tibet', *Journal of the Asiatic Society of Pakistan* (Dacca), 10/2 (December 1965), 23.
63. Ibid.
64. Muncherji, 'Swat: The Garden of Asoka', 41.
65. Tucci, 'Preliminary report on an archaeological survey in Swat', 282.
66. Giuseppe Tucci, 'Recent Explorations in Swat', in Tucci, *On Swāt. Historical and Archaeological Notes*, with introduction by Domenico Faccenna, eds. P. Callieri and A. Filigenzi, 304.
67. Fa-Hein, *A Record of Buddhistic Kingdoms*, 29. See also, [Fa Hian], *The Pilgrimage of Fa Hian: From the French Edition of the Foe Koue Ki of MM. Remusat, Klaproth, and Landresse with Additional Notes and Illustrations*, 49; [Shui-ching-chu], *Northern India According to the Shui-ching-chu*, trans. L. Petech, Rome Oriental Series 2 (Roma: Istituto Italiano per il Medio ed Estremo Oriente, 1950), 19, 61–2.
68. See Deane, 'Note on Udyāna and Gandhāra', 661; Stein, *An Archaeological tour in Upper Swāt and Adjacent Hill Tracts*, 57.
69. [Tsiang], *Chinese Accounts of India: Translated from the Chinese of Hiuen Tsiang*, Vol. 2, 169.
70. Stein, *On Alexander's Track to the Indus*, 50.

71. See ibid.

72. See Tucci, 'Preliminary report on an archaeological survey in Swat', 299–302.

73. [Tsiang], *Chinese Accounts of India: Translated from the Chinese of Hiuen Tsiang*, Vol. 2, 176–7.

74. Ibid., 168.

75. See G. Tucci, *Travels of Tibetan Pilgrims in the Swat Valley* (Calcutta: The Greater Indian Society) in G. Tucci, *On Swāt. Historical and Archaeological Notes*, eds. P. Callieri and A. Filigenzi (Rome: 1997), 28–31, 41–4.

76. Deane, 'Note on Udyāna and Gandhāra', 663.

77. Muncherji, 'Swat: The Garden of Asoka', 45.

78. Swāti, 'Recent Discovery of Buddhist Sites in the Swāt Valley', 155.

79. Luca M. Olivieri, 'Behind the Buddhist Communities: Subalternity and Dominancy in Ancient Swat', *Journal of Asian Civilizations* (Islamabad), 34/1 (July 2011), 133–4.

80. Giuseppe Tucci, 'Oriental Notes: II An Image of a Devi Discovered in Swat and some Connected Problems', *East and West* (Rome), 14/3–4 (September–December 1963), 155 (Stable URL: http://www.jstor.org/stable/29754772; accessed: 30/10/2011).

81. Stein, *On Alexander's Track to the Indus*, 73.

82. Filigenzi, 'Wisdom and Compassion: Concept and Iconography of Avalokiteśvara/Padmapāṇi', 248.

83. Stein, *On Alexander's Track to the Indus*, 77.

84. Sarma, 'From Udyana, the Seat of Rig-Veda, to the Present Swat Valley in Pakistan under Taliban Control'.

85. Bellew, *A General Report on the Yusufzais*, 57–8.

86. Filigenzi, 'Wisdom and Compassion: Concept and Iconography of Avalokiteśvara/Padmapāṇi', 247–8.

87. Tucci, 'On Swāt. The Dards and Connected Problems', 68.

88. Tucci, 'Oriental Notes: II An Image of a Devi Discovered in Swat and some Connected Problems', 155.

89. Ibid., 180.

90. R.C. Agrawala, 'An Interesting Relief from the Swat Valley (I)', *East and West* (Rome), 16/1–2 (March–June 1966), 82.

91. Ibid.

92. Ibid.

93. Maurizio Taddei, 'An Interesting Relief from the Swat Valley, II', *East and West* (Rome), 16/1–2 (March–June 1966), 87.

94. Ibid., 88. For another example of the similar nature of a tray portraying Mithraic or Roman symbolism, see Maurizio Taddei, 'A Problematic Toilet-tray from Uḍegrām', ibid., 89–93.

95. A. Bagnera et al., 'Italian Archaeological Activities in Swat: An Introduction', *Journal of Asian Civilizations* (Islamabad), 34/1 (July 2011), 66. See also, Anna Filigenzi, 'Post-Gandharan Swat. Late Buddhist rock sculptures and Turki Śāhis' religious centres', ibid., 186–202.

96. Luca Colliva, 'The Excavation of the Archaeological Site of Barikot (Bīr-koṭ-ghwaṇḍai) and its Chronological Sequence', *Journal of Asian Civilizations*

(Islamabad), 34/1 (July 2011), 165. See also, Filigenzi, 'Post-Gandharan Swat. Late Buddhist rock sculptures and Turki Śāhis' religious centres', 196–9.

97. Filigenzi, 'Post-Gandharan Swat. Late Buddhist rock sculptures and Turki Śāhis' religious centres', 197–8; Anna Filigenzi, 'Sūrya, the Solar Kingship and the Turki Śāhis: New Acquisitions on the Cultural History of Swat', *East and West* (Rome), 56/1–3 (September 2006), 200 (Stable URL: http://jstor.org/stable/29757686; accessed: 30/10/2011).

98. Filigenzi, 'Post-Gandharan Swat: Late Buddhist rock sculptures and Turki Śāhis' religious centres', 199; Filigenzi, 'Sūrya, the Solar kingship and the Turki Śāhis: New Acquisitions on the Cultural History of Swat', 202.

99. Peirfrancesco Callieri et al., 'Bīr-koṭ-ghwaṇḍai, Swat, Pakistan. 1998–1999 Excavation Report', *East and West* (Rome), 50/1–4 (December 2000), 210 (Stable URL: http://www.jstor.org/stable/29757454; accessed: 30/10/2011).

100. Bellew, *A General Report on the Yusufzais*, 58.

101. Tucci, 'On Swāt. The Dards and Connected Problems', 69–70.

102. Ibid., 70.

103. Mohammad Habib, *Sultan Mahmud of Ghaznin* (2nd edn., Delhi: S. Chand & Co., n.d.), 46–7.

104. For examples of taking Nur and Qirat for Swat, see ibid.; Khan, *Tarikh-i Riyasat-i Swat wa Sawanih-i Hayat Baniy-i Riyasat-i Swat Hazrat Miangul Gul Shahzadah Abdul Wadud Khan Badshah Sahib*, 31.

105. See Muḥammad Nāẓim, *The Life and Times of Sulṭān Maḥmud of Ghazna*, with foreword by Thomas Arnold (Cambridge: At the University Press, 1931), 74–5, 74 n. 6. Nuristan, the province of Afghanistan, was also part of Kafiristan, which was named Nuristan by the Afghan Amir Abdur Rahman (who ruled from 1880 till 1905) after its occupation in late nineteenth century.

106. See Habib, *Sultan Mahmud of Ghaznin*, 47 n. *.

107. Sarma, 'From Udyana, the Seat of Rig-Veda, to the Present Swat Valley in Pakistan under Taliban Control'.

108. See Tucci, *Travels of Tibetan Pilgrims in the Swat Valley* in Tucci, *On Swāt. Historical and Archaeological Notes*, eds. P. Callieri and A. Filigenzi, 28–31, 41–4.

109. Ibid., 45.

110. Ibid., 44.

111. Ibid., 45.

112. See Pir Muazam Shah, *Tawarikh Hafiz Rahmat Khani*, with *dibachah* by Muhammad Nawaz Tair (Pashto/Persian) (2nd impression, Peshawar: Pukhtu Academy, 1987), 73.

113. See ibid., 78.

114. See Abdur Rahman, 'Arslān Jādhib, Governor of Ṭūs: the First Muslim Conqueror of Swat', *Ancient Pakistan* (Peshawar), 15 (2002), 11–14; Abdur Rehman, 'The Zalamkot Bilingual Inscription', *Lahore Museum Bulletin* (Lahore), 10–11/1–2 (1997–1998), 35–9.

115. Makhdum Tasadduq Ahmad, *Social Organization of Yusufzai Swat: A Study in Social Change* (Lahore: Panjab University Press, 1962), 8.

116. Also see Tucci, 'Oriental Notes, II: An Image of a Devi Discovered in Swat and some Connected Problems', in Tucci, *On Swāt. Historical and Archaeological*

Notes, with introduction by Domenico Faccenna, eds. P. Callieri and A. Filigenzi, 128–9.

117. For accounts of such *jihad*, see Sayyad Abdul Jabbar Shah Sithanawi, *Kitab al-Ibra: Subah Sarhad wa Afghanistan ki Char Sau Salah Tarikh; 1500 Iswi ta 1900 Iswi* (Urdu), Vol. 1 (Islamabad: Poorab Academy, 2011), 123–5.

118. Khushal Khan Khattak, *Kulyat-i Khushal Khan Khattak*, Vol. 2, *Qasaid, Rubaiyat, Qitat aw Mutafariqat* (Pashto) (Peshawar: Azeem Publishing House, n.d.), 349.

119. They should not be taken for the followers of Sayyad Ahmad Barailwi of Rayi Baraili. Both the schools of thought are poles apart.

6

PRE-YUSUFZI MUSLIM PERIOD

Arab Muslim armies made inroads into the territory of modern Afghanistan in the early years of the *khilafat* (caliphate) of Usman (RA), third caliph after the demise of Prophet Muhammad (SAW); but their advance came to a halt due to internal crisis in the Muslim Khilafat. During the Umayyad Khilafat, the advance was resumed and the Muslim forces collided with the Tibetan and Chinese powers. It has already been mentioned (in chapter 4) that the rulers of Swat sided with the Tibetans and Chinese against the Muslims in their struggle for supremacy in Central Asia. The Muslims succeeded to bring the territory of modern Afghanistan under their sway but Swat remained beyond their sphere of control until the time when the Turki Shahis annexed Swat to their dominion in about 745 CE and then till Mahmud of Ghazna's reign (998–1030 CE) in Afghanistan.

MUSLIM OCCUPATION

The precise date of Muslims occupation of Swat is not known. Dr Abdur Rahman, after detailing Mahmud of Ghazna's expedition against Jayapala (1001–2) has opined in his previous study that 'the fertile valley of Peshāwar was annexed and the districts of Swāt, Dīr and Bājaur were cut off from the main country and must have suffered a similar fate in a later expedition'.[1] He, however, in a later article, has suggested that the year might have been 1001–2 (November 1001 to April 1002), on the basis of the Zalamkut bilingual inscription; but only in respect of the then Lower Swat, which now falls in the Malakand Protected Area or the Malakand Agency or Malakand District.[2] Yogendra Mishra too supposes it to be the years 1001–2 CE.[3]

It is now clear that, when war ensued between the Hindu Shahis and the Muslims under Mahmud of Ghazna (998–1030 CE), Swat was also not spared. The Ghaznavid forces attacked Lower Swat (between

November 1001 and April 1002 CE) after Mahmud defeated the Hindu Shahi Raja Jaipal (Jayapala) in November 1001 CE. As Mahmud stayed in Peshawar till the spring of the next year (April 1002), he 'spent the winter months in reducing the adjoining territories'.[4] Dealing with Mahmud of Ghazna and his general Arsalan Jadhib's exploits and reduction of the 'adjoining territories', Dr Abdur Rahman has asserted, on the basis of the 'Zalamkot Bilingual Inscription', that it was due to the strategic location of Swat Valley that 'its reduction was considered necessary to mop up the remaining pocket of resistance'.[5] Hence, during the winter of 1001–2, Arsalan Jadhib 'was dispatched to lower Swat, with a view perhaps to effectively cutting the enemy retreat to the mountainous tract. Arsalān obviously captured lower Swat, if not more, of this area, but not without suffering serious casualties.'[6] Dr Abdur Rahman has further asserted, 'If our interpretation is correct, lower Swat was brought under the Ghaznavid sway towards the end of A.D. 1001 or early 1002, that is, before the month of April when the Ghaznavid army returned home.'[7]

The oral traditions and the books later written locally in Swat (secondary sources), however, state that the last Hindu Shahi ruler of Swat was Raja Gira (Gira Kafir: Gira the infidel), with his capital at Udigram.[8] But neither can Raja Gira be found among the Hindu Shahi *raja*s at the time of Mahmud's exploits, nor was Udigram a capital of the Hindu Shahi dynasty. It is likely that a 'local Hindu *rājā*'[9] ruled Swat at that time. Dr Abdur Rahman has asserted that Rajagira is not the name of the reigning *raja* (ruler) but is 'correctly Rājagṛha, i.e., [Rājagaṛha, i.e.] seat of government',[10] that was 'situated on the mountain top at Ūḍigrām'.[11]

In line with the oral history and due to the contention of the local writers, it is believed that Mahmud of Ghazna personally came to Swat during his campaigns and there are various traditions relating to his coming to Swat. Even Giuseppe Tucci has asserted that 'in the 10th [11th] century Swāt was plundered by Mahmud of Ghazni and then by his successors'.[12] And Prof. Mohammad Habib has contended, as also quoted in the previous chapter, that Mahmud of Ghazna started in 1021 CE

from Ghaznin with "a large number of carpenters, blacksmiths and stone-cutters" with the definite intention of establishing a regular government over the Punjab. The first objective were [was] the frontier tribes of Swat,

Bajaur [Bajawar] and Kafiristan, who had "not yet put the yoke of Islam round their necks" and worshipped the Buddha in the form of the lion (Sakya Sinha). The inhabitants were subdued and converted, and a fort was built in their territory.[13]

Prof. Habib has mentioned Swat in the account; but Dr Muhammad Nazim has, on the authority of Alberuni, identified the valleys of Nur (or Nardin) and Qirat (taken for Swat by some writers, e.g. Prof. Mohammad Habib, and Muhammad Asif Khan[14]) in 'Kāfiristān to the north of Lamaghān [Laghman]'.[15] Prof. Habib's note to the text and the sentence: 'Doubtless the frontier tribes are meant',[16] at no point testify and prove that this expedition of Mahmud of Ghazna led to Swat.

It is worth mentioning that the original Pashto version of *Tarikh-i Riyasat-i Swat wa Sawanih-i Hayat Baniy-i Riyasat-i Swat Hazrat Miangul Gul Shahzadah Abdul Wadud Khan Badshah Sahib* has clarified that history books make no mention of Mahmud of Ghazna personally coming to Swat. However, *Tarikh Farishtah* has mentioned that Sultan Mahmud made a *jihad* on Qirat Nardin, a locality of the *kufar* (infidels), and personally participated in this *jihad*. And it is said that Qirat and Nardin means Swat and Bajawar.[17]

Locating Nardin and Qirat, Muhammad Qasim Farishtah has stated that 'this country lies apparently' between Turkistan and Hindustan and that 'its climate is extremely cold'.[18] This definitely is not Swat as neither its climate is extremely cold nor can the previous statement of its lying between Turkistan and Hindustan aptly or properly be applied to it. While commenting about the ruler of Qirat, Farishtah has stated, in the account of the year 1021 CE, that unable to oppose Mahmud he not only 'submitted' to him but 'at the same time' embraced Islam[19] and that, after this, the Ghaznvid General Amir Ali, son of Arsalan Jadhib, was 'sent with a division of the army to reduce' Nardin, 'which he accomplished, pillaging the country and carrying away many of the people captives.... The King ordered a fort to be built in that place, and left it under the command of Amir Bin Kuddur Suljooky [Qadar Saljuqi].'[20] These assertions apparently do not apply to Swat as neither did the ruler of Swat surrender nor did he embrace Islam and nor was there any need of constructing a fort on the top of the mountain in Udigram that, it is said and believed, was taken. The fort was strong enough and situated at a strategic place because of which there was no need of constructing a new fort. Moreover, excavation of a mosque on the slope below that site testifies that the old fort of the local *raja*, on the mountain top, was not abandoned. The accounts about Qirat do not apply to Swat at least to the extent that the ruler of Swat neither surrendered nor became a Muslim, nor do the accounts of Nardin (Nur) apply Swat as already evaluated above. Even if accepted, for the sake of argument, they would negate Mahmud's personal coming Swat as it clearly states that he sent his general Amir Ali to reduce Nardin and hence did not come in person.

The valley of Nur (or Nardin) not being Swat but the territory of the Siyahpush Kafirs is also evident from the account of *Iqbal Namah-i Jahangiri* in which, according to H.G. Raverty, it has been stated that a deputation of them visited Emperor Jahangir in 1625 CE in Jalalabad when he was on his way to Kabul. Besides this, other details about them have also been recorded.[21] *Tuzuk-i Jahangiri*, also known as *Jahangir Namah*, and *Iqbal Namah-i Jahangiri*, however possess no mention of Siyahpush Kafirs but of *kufar* (infidels) only.[22]

Thus, the assertions that Mahmud of Ghazna personally came to Swat are not historically tested facts. Dr Abdur Rahman, too, has asserted: 'In the recorded accounts of Maḥmūd's Indian campaigns Swat is indeed nowhere mentioned expressly. The area was apparently still in the process of opening up. The Sulṭān personally, it seems, led no invasion of Swat, otherwise it would have been carefully recorded.'[23] And that:

> As indicated above history mentions no direct invasion of Swat in the time of the Ghaznavid Sulṭān Maḥmud. We must therefore necessarily assume that the invasion of Swat formed part of a larger campaign and was looked upon as an insignificant event not worth mentioning separately. The only time it could have happened was during Maḥmūd's first campaign against the Hindu Shahis of Udabhāṇḍapura [Hund].[24]

After evaluating the possible time of the Muslims' first invasion of Swat and the first general under whom they were sent, Dr Abdur Rahman has asserted that 'it seems therefore that Swat was conquered probably during an earlier campaign perhaps in A.D. 1001–2, when the Ghaznavid army attacked Peshawar and Hund successively' and 'whatever the case may be, the date of the inscription [i.e. the Zalamkut bilingual inscription] makes it absolutely clear that Arslān Jādhib, governor of Ṭūs, was the first Muslim conqueror of Swat'.[25]

Although the date when Muslims conquered Upper Swat is not known, it is certain now—after the inscription of the Ghaznavid period was 'discovered on the slopes of [Mount] Rāja Gīrā, near Uḍegrām' in

1984—that it was during the Ghaznavid rule, because this inscription has revealed the date of the foundation of the mosque, that is 440 AH (1048–1049 CE). The inscription also gives the name of the person on whose instructions it was constructed, that is al-Amir al-Hajib Abu Mansur Nushtegin al-Khairi.[26] Although 'this chance discovery on the slopes of [Mount] Rāja Gīrā is extremely important because it provides us with excellent proof of the Ghaznavid conquest of Swāt',[27] at the same time, it neither speaks of nor confirm that Udigram or Upper Swat were attacked and conquered by Mahmud of Ghazna in person or by his generals during his reign.

However, it confirms that Udigram, and to that effect part of Upper Swat, were conquered and occupied during the Ghaznavid rule, that of Mahmud and his successors, because without this the construction of the mosque was not possible. It is pertinent to mention here that Dr Alessandra Bagnera has contended: 'The original mosque foundation, smaller than the actual, has been possibly dated to Mahmūd's conquest times, maybe to the first decade of the 11th century.'[28] However, as is evident from the words 'possibly' and 'maybe', the contention is based on conjecture and not sound proof. For laying the foundation of the mosque, the presence of Muslims was required in the place, which was certainly not possible in the given times and circumstances without occupying the place. To prove the Muslim occupation of the place in 'the first decade of the 11th century', during Mahmud of Ghazna's reign, sound, authentic and tested proofs are lacking so far. Dr Alessandra Bagnera too has conceded:

> Although a *terminus ante quem* is therefore at our disposal in order to date the foundation of our mosque during Sultan Mahmūd's rule, we lack sufficient evidence so as to circumscribe this date to the first or the second decade of the 11th century. Thus, for the time being, the absence of other specific clues does not allow any further conclusions to be drawn in this regard.[29]

Significantly, the mosque discovered in the ruins on the slope of Gira or Mount Gira (as called locally: 'Gira' and 'Da Gira Ghar') Castle is not only the oldest one so far known in the province but, in the words of Muhammad Nazir Khan, the third 'oldest mosque to be dated so far in Pakistan, after those of Banbhore [8th century] and Mansura [9th century]'.[30] As mentioned earlier, Dr Abdur Rahman has asserted that Raja Gira is 'correctly Rājagṛha, i.e., [Rājagaṛha, i.e.] seat of government'.[31]

According to oral traditions, when the Muslims invaded Upper Swat to occupy its stronghold at Udigram, in the ensuing fighting, one of Mahmud's generals, Pir Khushal, fell. His grave on the spot of his fall has been venerated by the common masses and has been remembered as Pir Khushal Ghazi Baba.

The Ghaznavids took 'Rāja Girā's fortress' after a difficult and protracted siege of years.[32] Traditions and legend, however, have made a romance of the fall of the fortress by stating that the 'fortress, after resisting the vain and repeated assaults of Mahmud of Ghazni, was at last stormed because *the king's daughter, having fallen in love with one of Mahmud's generals* [my italics], revealed the place through which the water supplies passed'.[33] Consequently, the supply was cut down, which forced 'the garrison to fight'.[34]

It is interesting to note that a legend or myth is that water to the Garrison or Castle or the fortified settlement at the mount top in Udigram was provided through an underground pipeline from Manglawar or elsewhere above in the valley, made of baked mud. But it is worth noting that there existed 'a fine perennial spring gushes' a little above the fortification wall of Raja Gira's Castle about which Aurel Stein, in his report of his Swat visit in 1926, has asserted:

> It was the existence of this spring, the only source of water within the whole protected area, that rendered it capable of being used as a safe place of refuge. The importance attached to the spring is strikingly demonstrated by the special care taken to strengthen the defences intended to guard it. The walls on either side run in double lines down to the gully that holds this precious water.[35]

This nullifies the romance or at least the story of the supply of water to the Garrison or Castle or fortified settlement from the Swat River and of the supply being cut off by the invading Muslim forces.

For supplying water to the fortification at the mountain top from the Swat River in a pipeline, it was required that the pipeline be quite deep in the ground so that it would not to be damaged by the water of the numerous *nullah*s and streams traversing the area and the hills through which the pipeline passed for a long distance. This, certainly, was impossible and impracticable. Besides, the name of Pir Khushal, as a general of Mahmud of Ghazna, also is absent in the contemporary sources. The passage of a long period of one thousand years and the frequent demographic/population changes in Swat with the new comers brought by conquests and migrations have led to fantasies and romanticism.

The location of the Raja Gira Castle was so due to 'the peculiar hill formation that here had offered a natural stronghold in times when there were no fire-arms to interfere with safety in a place completely commanding its approaches'.[36]

As stated and evaluated above, and also in chapter 5, while it is told that Mahmud of Ghazna personally came to Swat during his campaigns, and various traditions relate with his coming to Swat, these are not historically tested facts.

SETTLEMENT OF THE AFGHANS AND ETYMOLOGY OF THE SWATI, AND THE ETHNOLOGY OF THE SWATIS

Muhammad Asif Khan has claimed:

> With the Sultan [Mahmud] was Yahya, the chief of the Dilazak [Dalazak] tribe of Pathans, [along] with his people, and a number of Swati Pathans. Sultan Mahmud granted the whole of the Valley of Swat to the Dilazaks and the…Swati Pathans, who settled down there for good…. The two tribes lived peacefully for some time. Mutual differences having developed between them, in 1024 A. D. the Swatis drove the Dilazaks out of Swat. The latter took refuge in the districts of Mardan and Peshawar.[37]

But Taj Muhammad Khan Zaibsar has asserted, on the authority of *Makhzan-i Afghani*, that it was Muhammad Ghauri who asked the Afghans, through Malak Azizuddin, to settle on the border of Hindustan (India) so as to maintain a hold on the country. Thus, the Afghans came and settled in the territory of 'Darwah' (درؤه). The mountainous stretch from Swat to Siwi (Sibi) in length and from Hassan Abdal to Kabul and Qandahar in breadth is known as 'Darwah'.[38] *Tarikh Khan Jahani wa Makhzan-i Afghani*, a book written in India by Khwajah Nimatullah Harwi in the early seventeenth century CE, supports Zaibsar's assertion.

According to *Tarikh Khan Jahani wa Makhzan-i Afghani*, Sultan Shahabuddin, namely Muhammad Ghauri, ordered that the Afghan tribes be settled in Kuhistan-i Ruh, Kuh-i Sulayman, Ashnaghar or Kashghar, in the surrounding of Bajawar, from Kabul to River Nilab (viz. River Indus), meaning in the area in the north of Attak, and from the suburb of Qandahar to the borders of Multan. Giving 20,000 men under the command of Malak Muizuddin Ghauri,[39] he assigned him the task of making arrangements for evacuation of the Afghan tribes from Kuhistan-i Ghaur and settling them in the aforesaid mountainous territories. The order was complied with and the task accomplished fully and completely; after which Malak Muizuddin attended the Sultan and apprised him that his order had been obeyed to the fullest and the task of the settlement of the Afghans had been completed. On hearing this, the Sultan showed great joy, because he considered the settlement of the Afghans in these areas the mean of or prelude to the conquest of India.[40]

It is to be mentioned that instead of Darwah, *Tarikh Khan Jahani wa Makhzan-i Afghani* has mentioned Ruh (روه), and Swat specifically has not been mentioned in the territory of Ruh (Roh), as it has stated that 'Ruh' is name of a specific mountainous range which stretches in length from Bajawar to the town of Siwi near Bhakar and in breadth from Hasan Abdal to Kabul and Qandahar.[41] However, Muhammad Qasim Farishtah has stated that Ruh extend from Swat and Bajawar, on the north, as far south as Siwi (Sibi) near Bhakar in Sindh; and from east to west from Hasan Abdal to Kabul and Qandahar.[42]

This speaks of a mass and planned Afghani settlement in Swat for the first time in the reign of Muhammad Ghauri. Muhammad Asif Khan's contention of the mass settlement of the Swatis and Dalazak in Swat during Mahmud's reign and of the expulsion of the Dalazak by the Swatis within Mahmud's reign does not seem accurate. Mass settlement of the Afghans/Pukhtuns in Swat certainly seems a later development.[43]

Why and how were they called 'Swati' before coming to and settling in Swat, or what was the etymology of the 'Swati' before their coming to Swat, is a question. There is no such name as 'Swati' in the genealogical tables or trees of the Afghan/Pukhtun/Pathan tribes.[44] If the Swati Pukhtuns/Afghans/Pathans (Swati Pukhtanah) were known by this name before their settlement in Swat, this name would certainly have been found among the genealogical tables or trees. Therefore, they became known with the name Swati Pukhtanah (Swati Pukhtuns/ Pathans) because of their settlement in Swat and we can conclude they got this name from Swat and not vice versa.

Sayyad Abdul Jabbar Shah has asserted that the old Swati nation was Bani Israel by ethnicity but their rulers were ancient Greeks.[45] As Abdul Jabbar Shah believed in the Bani Israelite theory about the ethnicity of the Afghans/Pukhtuns,[46] his assertion supports Taj Muhammad Khan Zaibsar's contention (mentioned above) about the settlement of the Afghans/Pukhtuns in the areas; and hence the old Swatis, residents of the Swat Valley proper from the thirteenth century till the attacks and occupation of the Yusufzi in the sixteenth century, were Afghan/Pukhtun by ethnicity.

As detailed in the previous chapter, although the Muslims occupied Swat and a foundation for the gradual spread of Islam here was laid, but the diaries of the Tibetan pilgrims O rgyan pa (1230–1293 CE), who visited Swat after 1260 CE, and sTag ts'an ras pa, also known as O rgyan pa Nag dban rgya mts'o, who came here about the middle of the seventeenth century, have evidence that Buddhists existed in the area as late as the seventeenth century.[47] *Tawarikh Hafiz Rahmat Khani* also testifies to the existence of the Dihgan non-Muslims in the Swat Valley.[48] 'It was with the Yusufzais's conquest' in the early sixteenth century CE that 'Islam became the dominant religion of Swat as it is these days'.[49] But then too, 'certain aspects of the traditional culture of Swat….retains interesting non-Islamic elements'.[50]

Swatis' Rule and the Related Issues

As illustrated above, people from different Afghan/Pukhtun tribes settled in Swat. They came to be known as Swati Pukhtanah (Swati Pukhtuns). They occupied the region and established their rule for three to four centuries. Information about their longstanding rule is scanty. They remained effectively independent and out of the sphere of influence of the neighbouring Muslim rulers of Afghanistan and India throughout their occupation. The *Gazetteer of the Peshawar District, 1897–98*, has recorded regarding Swat for the eleventh century CE: 'The hills to the north formed part of the Swat kingdom, which since the withdrawal of the Hindús from the Indus, had remained independent under a chief of its own with the title of Sultán.'[51]

As stated in chapter 1, according to Akhun Darwizah, Sultan Bahram and Sultan Fakhal were two brothers among the Sultans of Panj. When the line of rulers reached these brothers, Sultan Fakhal proceeded to the hills of Bajawar, Swat, and Kashmir, and brought the people of these areas under his suzerainty. After his death, his sons disputed in the State of Swat and fought a great war against each other. When the news of the war reached their mother, and she inquired about the affair, she cursed this state with the imprecation that the Almighty should not bring normalcy and peace to this state for long years. And this state was named 'Swat' in the meaning of 'one where cries or tumult are raised'.

This curse created a series of events and accidents in this place. One offshoot of this has been that if there is no outsider to fight with, the leaders/chiefs of this state create internal enmity and wrangle among themselves.[52]

It is interesting to note that, according to Muhammad Akhtar, Sultan Pakhal, accompanied by his sons and chiefs, invaded Swat. At the time, Raja Gira (Gira Kafir) was ruling Swat with a strong fort as his capital in the hills behind Udigram. Raja Gira came to fight the invaders, and the first battle was fought at Haibatgram near Tanra (also called Thana) in the present-day Malakand Protected Area or Malakand Agency or Malakand District. Defeated, Raja Gira fled and took abode in his fort at Udigram. Sultan Pakhal pursued and besieged him. Although strong, the fort was captured after hot fighting. Thus, the whole Swat Valley came into the possession of the Gabaris (Gibaris) and resultantly Bunair and Bajawar also subjugated. The rule over the territories of Bajawar was given to Sultan Shamur (also Shamhur) who was father-in-law of Sultan Bahram and Sultan Pakhal. The Tajak Swati rulers constructed the Manglawar Fort in Swat and Gabar Fort in Bajawar. These were strong forts. The Bajawar Fort was conquered by Babur in 1519 CE, using heavy artillery; whereas the Manglawar Fort was abandoned by the last Sultan Awais (Uwais) himself, which the Yusufzi demolished; hence, these two old historic forts faded away.[53]

It is to be noted that *Tawarikh Hafiz Rahmat Khani* has talked of the destruction of Manglawar city by the Yusufzi but has stated that the fort and palaces, which were strong, still (viz. in the eighteenth century CE) exist.[54] Besides, neither has Babur mentioned demolition of the fort of Bajawar, nor do *Tawarikh Hafiz Rahmat Khani*. Babur has talked of the inspection of the Fort and the palaces after the conquest and occupation of the Bajawar Fort; and *Tawarikh Hafiz Rahmat Khani* testifies that the fort of Manglawar was not demolished.[55] Muhammad Akhtar's book, entitled *Tajak Swati wa Mumlikat-i Gabar Tarikh kay Aayinah mayn*, contains a lot of contentions that do not hold ground.

Muhammad Akhtar's above mentioned contention contradicts the previous mentioned assertion of some writers in which it is contended that Raja Gira was the contemporary ruler of Swat during Mahmud of Ghazna's rule in Afghanistan; and that he was defeated by Mahmud's general.

Changiz Khan's Tatars (also Tartars) conquered the region up to the Indus, in 1242 CE, and beyond; but Swat remained independent.

According to Minhaj Siraj, defeating Sultan Jalaluddin on the bank of Indus, Changiz Khan personally went from there in pursuit of the Aghraq tribe, because the tribe was numerous and their forces were very large. Therefore, he proceeded towards Kiri, conquered the forts of Kiri and Kuh Payah, and martyred the Muslims. He stayed at Kiri for three months. Yet he did not march on to India as he received news of the rebellion of the Khans of Tamghaj and Tinkat; hence, he turned back from Kuh Payah and Kiri.[56] In the note to Kiri, it has been stated that the names of the place have been stated differently in different copies of the book *Tabaqat-i Nasari*, e.g. Kiri (کیری), Giri (گیری), Kabri (کبری : Kabari), Gabri (گبری : Gabari), Gibri (گیبری : Gibari).[57]

The text of *Tabaqat-i Nasari* never states clearly that Changiz Khan came and settled in Swat. But on the basis of this, and twisting some statements in Major Raverty's *Notes on Afghanistan and Baluchistan*, Muhammad Akhtar has taken the Kiri or Gabari for Swat,[58] which is unsound. Muhammad Akhtar himself has contended that the State of Gibar (Gabar) extended over a larger area, from Bajawar and Ashnaghar to Pakhli.[59] Therefore, *Tabaqat-i Nasari*'s statement does not testify to Changiz Khan's conquering Swat proper or that he stayed here for three months. He may have conquered some parts of the then State of Swat or of the Gabari Sultans and may have stayed there but not in Swat proper or the Swat Valley. It has also been mentioned in the previous chapter, on the authority of Alberuni, that Kiri may have had part of the Swat State of the time, as political geography never remains static or stagnant, but the signs shows that it was not the Swat Valley proper. Raverty has negated the contention of H.W. Bellew, in respect of Changiz Khan's return through Barughal Pass, etcetera, and has spoken of the stay of Changiz Khan in and leaving of 'the Gibari country near Parsháwar [Peshawar]'[60] and not Swat proper. As already explained, the Gibari (گباری) or Gibari (گبری) country comprised, not only Swat, but territories beyond it in the west, south and east were also included.

While dealing with the 'toponym Gīrī', 'referred to as a "region" or more frequently "a fortress" by several Muslim authors writing between the 11th and the 13th centuries....with reference to events involving the history first of the Ghaznavids, then of the Khwarizm Shahs and the Mongols', Dr Alessandra Bagnera has laboured to identify it as 'the site at Mt. [Mount] Rāja Gīrā' near Udigram.[61] She, moreover, has opined, on the basis of 'geographical and topographical clues... found in the texts narrating Chingiz [Changiz] Khan's expedition', of

Changiz Khan's travel in a south-north direction and his 'passage via one of the three major passes existing at the time…Karakar Pass, Cherat Pass, and Sha-kot Pass'.[62] To augment her contention, Dr Bagnera has stated that 'Jūzjānī made clear reference, in particular, to the region as a mountainous territory, suitable for hunting and where the peaks, in winter are covered with snow'.[63] But, as evaluated above in respect of *Tabaqat-i Nasari*'s narrative and Bellew's contention, it is conjecture, not tested by evidence, that Changiz Khan came to or passed through Swat.

Gazetteer of the Peshawar District, 1897–98, has stated, after Babur's occupation of the Kabul and Ghazni in 1504 CE,

> At this period, as has been before detailed, the plains and hills of Laghman, Kunar, Pesháwar, Swát, and Bajaur [Bajawar]….remained more or less independent under their hereditary native chieftains. Former Sultáns of Kábul and Ghazni had claimed them as subjects, but beyond the occasional compulsory payment of tribute, the subjection, both of these tribes and the Afgháns of the wilds and the mountains, had been little more than nominal.[64]

Before the advent of the Yusufzi from Afghanistan, the Shalmani[65] possessed Ashnaghar (also written as Hashtnagar) and they were subjects of Sultan Pakhal, the Sultan of Swat. The territory above Ashnaghar and from Swat to Bagyaray, from Hisar Bahlul to Shir Khanay and Murah to Swat and Tutai, Sarubai and Siwarai to the Malakand Pass and the entire Swat along with the neighbouring dependencies and entire Bunair were ruled by Sultan Pakhal. Besides, the territory inhabited by the Swati Dihgans was under him and paid taxes to him.[66]

Sultan Pakhal personally resided in the garrison at Manglawar which was the capital of the Sultans of Swat. The place greatly flourished during the reign of the Sultans of Swat. All the Sultans of Swat, including Sultan Pakhal, were from the line of Sultan Jahangir and hence were called the Jahangiri Sultans.[67] They ruled the State of Swat for many generations, the last of them being Sultan Awais (Uwais; Wais), son of Sultan Pakhal, whom the Yusufzi expelled from Swat after a number of great battles. After this the Yusufzi occupied the country, Sultan Awais fled to Niyag and constructed a strong fort there.[68] He was thus forced 'to retire to the Caufir [*kafir*] country, where he founded a new monarchy, which was enjoyed for some generations by his descendants'.[69]

According to Abul Fazal, the Swati rulers, scions of Sultan Jahangir and Sultan Pakhal, were 'claimed to be descended from a daughter of

Sultān Sikandar';[70] and the Yusufzi 'wrested' Swat 'from the Sultāns who affected to be descended from a daughter of Alexander Bicornutus. It is said that this monarch left some of his treasures in these parts with a few of his kindred and to this day the descendants of this band dwell in these mountains and affect to show their genealogical descent from Alexander.'[71] Whereas, the *Akbar Namah* has stated: 'In this land there was a tribe that had the title of Sultānī, and claimed to be descended from a daughter of Sultān Sikandar... The Yūsufzāīs....took possession of the choice lands [of them]. Up to the present day some of the former inhabitants spend their days in distress in the defiles, and from love for their native land are unable to leave.'[72]

It is evident from the accounts of Abul Fazal, that the Swati rulers, scions of Sultan Jahangir and Sultan Pakhal, were the descendants of Sultan Sikandar, taken generally for Alexander of Macedonia, as H. Beveridge has taken Sultan Sikandar to be 'Alexander the Great'.[73] Sayyad Abdul Jabbar Shah also has contended that they, the rulers of Swat, were ancient Greeks who had embraced Islam during Mahmud of Ghazna's reign and remained ruler over the country since then. Their offspring are now known with the title of Sahibzadahs.[74] But Muhammad Akhtar has asserted that Sultan Sikandar means not Alexander the Great but Kurush Azam (Cyrus the Great), the Iranian (Persian) ruler.[75]

A point to note is the contention of A.H. McMahon and A.D.G. Ramsay that Sultan Awais' power was said was 'extended over the Swat Valley, Hazara, and up to the borders of Kashmir'.[76] And Raverty has stated that the people between Swat and the Indus were of the Tajik stock like that of Sultan Awais' Swati subjects, and hence the Swatis migrated in that direction.[77] However, according to *Tawarikh Hafiz Rahmat Khani*, after leaving the fort at Manglawar, being compelled by the Yusufzi in the sixteenth century, as mentioned in the next chapter, Sultan Awais, along with his people and soldiers, crossed the Swat River, came to Tajkhilah, passed three-four nights in hills, reached Niyak (also Niyag) and stayed there. Niyak is between hills, a beautiful place with springs and abundance of water and surrounded by vast forests and grass. Around the country of Niyak were *kufar* (infidels) and till now all inhabitants are *kufar*. They constructed a strong high fort there which was named Lahur (Lahor). Around it were the villages of *kufar*, all of whom Awais brought under his suzerainty and became king as he was previously.[78]

If this was so and his power and domain extended to Hazarah and the border of Kashmir, then the territory between Swat and the border of Kashmir was part of his kingdom and the subject people also belonged to the same ethnic stock. Hence, his proceeding to, constructing a fort (named Lahur) and settling among the *kufar* there can be said was merely ending his rule over Swat and shifting his seat of government from Swat to Lahur, which is in the present-day Indus Kuhistan. As inhabitants of the Kuhistan have lately embraced Islam, they at that time would have been *kufar* (infidels). Moreover, it can be said that it was because of his rule over that area that the Swatis, or his people who left Swat, settled in the Hazarah region.

H.G. Raverty has stated that, abandoning Swat Valley, Sultan Awais 'took up his residence in the Nihák Darah [Nihak Valley]'. This valley is described as being 'about nine miles in length, at the present time also known as Láhor, and the village and small fort at its entrance is called Láhor, and Malik Láhor [Mulk-i Lahor?] likewise'.[79] At another place, too, he has written of Sultan Awais abandoning his kingdom and taking shelter 'farther north', 'in the Dara'h of Nihák, Níáka'h or Ní'ák'.[80] This Darah Nihak or Nihag or Niyak is in Dir. As far the presence of Lahur in Nihak or Niyag Darah is concerned, it was tried to ascertain it, but the people negate (in 2019 and 2020 CE) the presence of a place Lahur in Nihak/Niyag Darah.

It needs to be clarified that it never is Darah Nihak (دره نهاک) or Niyag (Valley Nihak or Niyag), as has been written and translated by Raverty and also by Roshan Khan in his book *Malikah-i Swat*,[81] as well as by Muhammad Akhtar in his book *Tajak Swati wa Mumlikat-i Gabar Tarikh kay Aayinah mayn*,[82] but it is *dar mulk-i Niyag* (در ملک نیاگ),[83] namely 'to the country or place of Nihak or Niyag'.

Raverty's *Notes on Afghanistan and Baluchistan* are not error free in locating or stating about places, an evident proof of which is that he has located 'Hazarah' (my, Sultan-i-Rome's, home village) away from Aligramah and on the left bank of the Swat River,[84] but it is the neighbouring village of Aligramah. Nowadays, it is difficult to separate the villages of Hazarah and Aligramah as residences of both have joined and overlapped each other. It is situated on the right bank of the Swat River and its landed limits are traversed by the stream of the Nikpi Khail which joins the Swat River, these days in 2020, in its limits.

According to *Tawarikh Hafiz Rahmat Khani*, at that time the language of the Sultans of Swat and other Jahangiri persons was Gabari (گبری)

and that of the subject people of Swat was Yadri (يادرى). And in those
times, the people of Swat conversed in these two languages;[85] according
to Raverty, the 'two languages or dialects' were 'Gibarí and Darí'.[86] If
this was so, and their language was not Pukhtu (Pashto) and they did
not converse with each other in Pukhtu, how and why do their offspring
know, speak and converse in pure Pukhtu even to this day (in 2020 CE)
in Mansihrah, Batgram (also Batagram), and other areas outside Swat,
where they settled after their expulsion or migration from Swat, some
four or five centuries back. As they went and settled in areas where the
language spoken was not Pukhtu hence it cannot be expected or was
not possible that there they learnt pure Pukhtu (which is the Yusufzi
language). Therefore, it appear sound to suggest that their language
was Pukhtu which their offspring uphold and have preserved till now.
Tawarikh Hafiz Rahmat Khani's aforementioned contention, however,
endorses or speaks of the rulers and the ruled being of different stock
or ethnicity.

During this time, Malak Hasan Mutrawi, the enemy of Sultan Awais,
ruled a separate area in Swat. The Mutrawi has been a large section of
the Swatis. They considered themselves superior to the Swatis both
in terms of ethnic stock and courage. They claimed themselves to be
Yusufzi. Their forefathers had migrated in earlier times from Garah
and Nushki, situated in the limits of Qandahar, and settled in Swat.[87]
It can be inferred from the account of *Tawarikh Hafiz Rahmat Khani*
that the Mutrawi were ruling the right bank Swat area above Swigalai.[88]
But the book also states that the territory from the Swigalai Pass till
the Khazarya and Manglawar was with Sultan Awais, whereas from
the Shamilai Pass till Landakay and Murah was under Malak Hasan
Mutrawi.[89] This point or issue needs investigation and clarification.

Anyhow, after conquering and occupying Sultan Awais' Swat areas,
the Yusufzi turned towards the Mutrawi, who strongly resisted but were
compelled by the situation to take shelter in the fort. However, because
of the hard pressed siege they fled at night from their seat and strong
hold of Baligram which the Yusufzi consequently occupied. The Yusufzi
obtained great wealth from the fort and also took all the country of the
Mutrawi. After living in distress and desperation for years, the Mutrawi
later gradually returned, settled in their villages and became subjects of
the Yusufzi. But Malak Hasan Mutrawi, along with his family, adopted
banishment and hard work in the hills because of shame and honour. At
his death his family requested the Yusufzi to allow them to return and

became their subjects.[90] Abul Fazal's account has also stated, 'Up to the present day some of the former inhabitants spend their days in distress in the defiles, and from love for their native land are unable to leave.'[91]

Thus the Swatis, both Mutrawi and the subjects of Sultan Awais who did not leave Swat after its conquest by the Yusufzi in the sixteenth century, became the *faqir*s or subjects of the Yusufzi.[92] However, some of them regained the status of Pukhtuns either by receiving a grant of *dawtar* from the Yusufzi or by purchasing shares in the *dawtar*.

Whereas, according to Abdul Jabbar Shah, those of the old Swatis who were ousted or left Swat as a result of the Yusufzi occupation, passed their life in distresses in the neighbouring areas for about one and a half to two centuries, when at last they accompanied Sayyad Jalal as a *lakhkar* (*lashkar*) in his assault on the northern parts of Hazarah. Resultantly, the old Turk inhabitants were expelled and the Swatis were made master of and owners of the land.[93]

Interestingly, it was the tradition of all the Sultans of Swat to wear two gold earrings as a mark of the Sultan's distinction or prerogative. However, others wore silver earrings. Even when the Yusufzi came to Swat, in line with the Swatis' aforesaid tradition, they wore gold earrings. This custom prevailed among the Akuzi Yusufzi.[94] Even in the early twentieth century Zarin Khan of Kuzah Bandai, Nikpi Khail, used to wear gold earrings called *diday* (ديدي).

No details about the life, customs, social institutions, administrative system, economy and so forth during the centuries' long period of the rulers who ruled since Sultan Pakhal are available in the sources consulted. Even material or sources about the political history of the period is scant. The sources have not mentioned the names of the long line of the Jahangiri Sultans who ruled Swat from Sultan Pakhal till Sultan Awais. The sources are also silent on the points that when the Mutrawi established their rule and what were the names of the line of their rulers. Only the names of the last two rulers of the Mutrawi, Sultan Jahangir and Malak Hasan Mutrawi, are mentioned.

Muhammad Akhtar has contended that Mumlikat-i Gabar came into existence in 1190 CE and remained strong till the attack by Amir Timur (1190–1399 CE). It is astonishing that no historian has presented such a vast empire as a separate empire, despite its strong existence for two hundred years, nor has compiled its comprehensive history. The centre of this state was Kunar, which later shifted to Papin and Swat. The Swati Sultans maintained their culture, internal system, and language till 1520 CE. When the Yusufzi occupied the plain areas of Swat, the languages of Swat were Gabari and Dari. Their government system too comprised of two classes: Sultan and Dihgan.[95]

But, although Muhammad Akhtar has worked hard on his book, and the title of the book suggests that it contain contents about the above mentioned dimensions and aspects, it provides no such information. Its sole purpose, it appears, is to prove the Swati Pukhtuns to be Tajiks and scions of Sultan Zulqarnain; and to show that they were fire-worshipers (Zoroastrians) before conversion to Islam. He has not even given any detail about the points he has mentioned: their culture, internal system, and the government system consisting of two classes.

Besides, Muhammad Akhtar's book and contentions suffers from contradictions and stark contrasts. To evaluate and analyse fully all the contentions of his book would needs another book. For instance, he has contended about the old Swatis that the word Swadi or Swati hints to their relation with Swat because of their settling in Swat. Whereas Tajik reveals their ethnic origin, and the word Gabari is reflective of their old residence and is equivalent to Zoroastrian.[96] However, later, he has asserted that calling the Gabari, Mumyali, and Mutrawi as Tajik is also incorrect.[97] Yet again he contends that the people of Badakhshan, Kunar etcetera, who terms themselves the offspring of Sikandar, are in fact Tajik of the same ethnicity as the Swati tribes, and that the Tajiks of Badakhshan, Wakhan, Kunar etcetera, in which the three branches of the Swati tribe—Gabari, Mutrawi, and Mumyali—are included, are from the race of Sikandar Zulqarnain (Kurush Kabir, viz. Cyrus the Great).[98]

After elaborating the background of Gabar and Gabari, Muhammad Akhtar has, moreover, contended that the Tajik Swati is a specific ruling family.[99] The question arises as to whether the rulers and Dihgans only—meaning the upper classes—were Tajik Swati or the masses and other peoples and the ruled too were Gabari and Tajak Swatis. If only the rulers and ruling class were Tajik Swati, and the Tajik Swati were different from the Afghans/Pukhtuns, the assertion of Nimatullah Harwi or *Tarikh Khan Jahani wa Makhzan-i Afghani* and Taj Muhammad Khan Zaibsar, as given earlier, that Muhammad Ghauri asked the Afghans to migrate and settle in Darwah or Ruh, which includes Swat, is correct and the common people of the main Swat Valley—before the advent of the Yusufzi in the sixteenth century—were Afghans/Pukhtuns by ethnicity.[100]

As stated earlier, 'both the history and the socio-economy of early Islamization of Swat' is 'a missing phase in the literary sources', which would expectedly be filled by 'an extraordinary amount of data' provided by the excavation of the 'Islamic Udegram project' of the IsIAO Italian Mission.[101]

The wooden objects, examined by the Italian Archaeological Mission, in Swat, 'provide an excellent, albeit limited, overview of the culture and traditions regarding life in the Swat Valley....during a period in which its society was undergoing great transformations'.[102] The examined objects are 'to be considered as the expression of a lesser folklore, the manifestation of local craftsmanship, while an in-depth analysis reveals that these...craftsmen achieved truly artistic forms representing the expression of the complex cultural past of this region'.[103]

NOTES

1. Abdur Rehman, *The Last Two Dynasties of the Śāhis: (An analysis of their history, archaeology, coinage and palaeography)* (Islamabad: Director, Centre for the Study of the Civilizations of Central Asia, Quaid-i-Azam University, 1979), 147.

2. See Abdur Rehman, 'The Zalamkot Bilingual Inscription', *Lahore Museum Bulletin* (Lahore), 10–11/1–2 (1997–1998), 37–8.

3. See Yogendra Mishra, *The Hindu Sahis of Afghanistan and the Punjab, A.D. 865–1026* (Patna: Vaishali Bhavan, 1972), 124.

4. Rehman, 'The Zalamkot Bilingual Inscription', 37.

5. Abdur Rahman, 'Arslān Jādhib, Governor of Ṭūs: the First Muslim Conqueror of Swat', *Ancient Pakistan* (Peshawar), 15 (2002), 14.

6. Rehman, 'The Zalamkot Bilingual Inscription', 37–8.

7. Ibid., 38.

8. For such contention in secondary sources, see Sayyed Abdul Ghafoor Qasmay, *Tarikh-i Riyasat-i Swat* (Pashto) (Printed by Hamidia Press, Peshawar, n.d.), 19; Sayyed Mohd. Abdul Ghafoor Qasmi, *The History of Swat* (Printed by D.C. Anand & Sons, Peshawar, 1940), 3; Muhammad Asif Khan, *Tarikh-i Riyasat-i Swat wa Sawanih-i Hayat Baniy-i Riyasat-i Swat Hazrat Miangul Gul Shahzadah Abdul Wadud Khan Badshah Sahib*, with *dibachah, hisah awal, saluramah hisah,* and *hisah pinzamah* by Muhammad Asif Khan (Pashto) (Printed by Ferozsons Ltd., Peshawar, [1958]), 30–1; Muhammad Asif Khan, *Tarikh Riyasat-i Swat wa Sawanih-i Hayat Bani Riyasat-i Swat Miangul Abdul Wadud* (Urdu) (2nd edn., Mingawarah, Swat: Shoaib Sons Publishers and Booksellers, 2001), 26; Muhammad Asif Khan, *The Story of Swat as told by the Founder Miangul Abdul Wadud Badshah Sahib to Muhammad Asif Khan*, with preface, introduction and appendices by Muhammad Asif Khan, trans. preface and trans. by Ashruf Altaf Husain (Printed by Ferozsons Ltd., Peshawar, 1963), xx; Saranzeb Swati, *Tarikh Riyasat-i Swat* (Pashto) (Peshawar: Azeem Publishing House, 1984), 29, 31. Also see Aurel Stein, *On Alexander's Track to the Indus: Personal Narrative of Explorations on the North-West Frontier of India* (repr., Karachi: Indus

Publications, 1995), 57–8. Muhammad Asif Khan (Urdu and English versions) and Saranzeb Swati, however, have mentioned him as the Buddhist Raja.

9. Muhammad Farooq Swāti, 'Recent Discovery of Buddhist Sites in the Swāt Valley', *Āthāriyyāt* (Peshawar), 1 (1997), 155.

10. Rehman, 'The Zalamkot Bilingual Inscription', 39 n. 11; Swāti, 'Recent Discovery of Buddhist Sites in the Swāt Valley', 155.

11. Swāti, 'Recent Discovery of Buddhist Sites in the Swāt Valley', 155.

12. Giuseppe Tucci, 'On Swāt. The Dards and Connected Problems', *East and West* (Rome), 27/1–4 (December 1977), 69–70.

13. Mohammad Habib, *Sultan Mahmud of Ghaznin* (2nd edn., Delhi: S. Chand & Co., n.d.), 46–7.

14. For examples of taking Nur (or Nardin) and Qirat for Swat, see ibid.; Khan, *Tarikh-i Riyasat-i Swat wa Sawanih-i Hayat Baniy-i Riyasat-i Swat Hazrat Miangul Gul Shahzadah Abdul Wadud Khan Badshah Sahib*, 31.

15. See Muḥammad Nāẓim, *The Life and Times of Sulṭān Maḥmūd of Ghazna*, with foreword by Thomas Arnold (Cambridge: At the University Press, 1931), 74–5, 74 n. 6. Nuristan, the province of Afghanistan, was also part of Kafiristan, which was named Nuristan by the Afghan Amir Abdur Rahman (who ruled from 1880 till 1905) after its occupation in late nineteenth century CE.

16. See Habib, *Sultan Mahmud of Ghaznin*, 47 n. *.

17. Khan, *Tarikh-i Riyasat-i Swat wa Sawanih-i Hayat Baniy-i Riyasat-i Swat Hazrat Miangul Gul Shahzadah Abdul Wadud Khan Badshah Sahib*, 31.

18. Mahomed Kasim [Muhammad Qasim] Ferishta, *History of the Rise of the Mahomedan* [Muhammadan] *Power in India till the year A.D. 1612*, trans. from the original Persian of Mahomed Kasim Ferishta by John Briggs, Vol. 1 (repr., Lahore: Sang-e-Meel Publications, 1977), 65.

19. Ibid.

20. Ibid.

21. See Henry George Raverty, *Notes on Afghanistan and Baluchistan*, Vol. 1 (2nd edn. in Pakistan, Quetta: Nisa Traders, 1982), 141–2.

22. See Jahangir, *Tuzuk-i Jahangiri*, Urdu trans. Salim Wahid Salim (Lahore: Majlis Taraqi Adab, 1960), 809.

23. Rehman, 'The Zalamkot Bilingual Inscription', 37. Also see Rahman, 'Arslān Jādhib, Governor of Ṭūs: the First Muslim Conqueror of Swat', 13–14.

24. Rehman, 'The Zalamkot Bilingual Inscription', 37.

25. Rahman, 'Arslān Jādhib, Governor of Ṭūs: the First Muslim Conqueror of Swat', 14.

26. Muhammad Nazir Khan, 'A Ghaznavid Historical Inscription from Uḍegrām, Swāt', *East and West*, 35/1–3 (September 1985), 153–60 (Stable URL: http://www.jstor.org/stable/29756717, Accessed: 30/10/2011).

27. Ibid., 166.

28. Alessandra Bagnera, 'Islamic Udegram. Activities and new perspectives', *Journal of Asian Civilizations* (Islamabad), 34/1 (July 2011), 227. Also see Alessandra Bagnera, *The Ghaznavid Mosque and the Islamic Settlement at Mt. Rāja Gīrā, Udegram*, with foreword A. Chiodi Cianfarani, note by L.M. Olivieri (Lahore: Sang-e-Meel Publications, 2015), 76, 88–9; Alessandra Bagnera, 'The site of Mount Rāja Gīrā, Udegram: Archaeological evidences and new Hypotheses', with note by Luca Maria Olivieri, *Frontier Archaeology* (Peshawar), 7 (2016), 141.

29. Bagnera, *The Ghaznavid Mosque and the Islamic Settlement at Mt. Rāja Gīrā, Udegram*, 89.

30. Khan, 'A Ghaznavid Historical Inscription from Uḍegrām, Swāt', 163. Also see Bagnera, 'Islamic Udegram. Activities and new perspectives', 227.

31. Rehman, 'The Zalamkot Bilingual Inscription', 39 n. 11; Swāti, 'Recent Discovery of Buddhist Sites in the Swāt Valley', 155.

32. Aurel Stein, *An Archaeological tour in Upper Swāt and Adjacent Hill Tracts* (Calcutta: Government of India, Central Publication Branch, 1930), 38.

33. Giuseppe Tucci, 'Preliminary report on an archaeological survey in Swat', *East and West* (Rome), 9/4 (1958), 291. Also see D.H. Muncherji, 'Swat: The Garden of Asoka', *Pakistan Quarterly* (Karachi), 9/3 (1959), 43.

34. Khan, *The Story of Swat as told by the Founder Miangul Abdul Wadud Badshah Sahib to Muhammad Asif Khan*, xxii–xxiii.

35. Stein, *An Archaeological tour in Upper Swāt and Adjacent Hill Tracts*, 36.

36. Stein, *On Alexander's Track to the Indus*, 53.

37. Khan, *The Story of Swat as told by the Founder Miangul Abdul Wadud Badshah Sahib to Muhammad Asif Khan*, xxiii.

38. See Taj Muhammad Khan Zaibsar, *Uruj-i Afghan* (Pashto, verse), Vol. 2 (Riyasat-i Swat, 1361 AH), 29–30.

39. Taj Muhammad Khan Zaibsar has given the name as Malak Azizuddin. Ibid., 29.

40. Khwajah Nimatullah Harwi, *Tarikh Khan Jahani wa Makhzan-i Afghani*, Urdu trans. Muhammad Bashir Husain (Lahore: Markazi Urdu Board, 1978), 123–4.

41. See ibid., 123.

42. Ferishta, *History of the Rise of the Mahomeden* [Muhammadan] *Power in India till the year A.D. 1612*, trans. John Briggs, Vol. 1, 8–9.

43. Also see Allah Bakhsh Yusufi, *Yusufzai* (Urdu) (Karachi: Muhammad Ali Educational Society, 1960), 211–12; Khan Roshan Khan, *Yusufzai Qaum ki Sarguzasht* (Urdu) (Karachi: Roshan Khan and Company, 1986), 80, 356–7.

44. See the genealogical tables given at the end of Khwajah Nimatullah Harwi's *Tarikh Khan Jahani wa Makhzan-i Afghani*, Urdu trans. Muhammad Bashir Husain.

45. See Sayyad Abdul Jabbar Shah Sithanawi, *Kitab al-Ibra: Subah Sarhad wa Afghanistan ki Char Sau Salah Tarikh; 1500 Iswi ta 1900 Iswi* (Urdu) Vol. 1 (Islamabad: Poorab Academy, 2011), 184–5.

46. See ibid., 132–66.

47. See G. Tucci, *Travels of Tibetan Pilgrims in the Swat Valley* (Calcutta: The Greater Indian Society), in G. Tucci, *On Swāt. Historical and Archaeological Notes*, eds. P. Callieri and A. Filigenzi (Rome: 1997), 28–31, 41–4.

48. See Pir Muazam Shah, *Tawarikh Hafiz Rahmat Khani*, with *dibachah* by Muhammad Nawaz Tair (Pashto/Persian) (2nd impression, Peshawar: Pukhtu Academy, 1987), 78.

49. Makhdum Tasadduq Ahmad, *Social Organization of Yusufzai Swat: A Study in Social Change* (Lahore: Panjab University Press, 1962), 8. Also see H.A. Deane, 'Note on Udyāna and Gandhāra', *Journal of the Royal Asiatic Society of Great Britain and Ireland* (October 1896), 662 (Stable URL: http://www.jstor.org/stable/25207806; accessed: 16/05/2011); Ilaria E. Scerrato, 'The ethnographic activity of the IsIAO Italian Archaeological Mission in Swat and Gilgit-Baltistan', *Journal of Asian Civilizations* (Islamabad), 34/1 (July 2011), 244.

50. Scerrato, 'The ethnographic activity of the IsIAO Italian Archaeological Mission in Swat and Gilgit-Baltistan', 244.

51. *Gazetteer of the Peshawar District, 1897–98* (repr., Lahore: Sang-e-Meel Publications, 1989), 53. Also see A.H. McMahon and A.D.G. Ramsay, *Report on the Tribes of the Malakand Political Agency (Exclusive of Chitral)*, revised by R.L. Kennion (Peshawar: Government Press, North-West Frontier Province, 1916), 28.

52. See Akhun Darwizah, *Tazkiratul Abrar-i wal Ashrar* (Persian) (Peshawar: Islami Kutub Khanah, n.d.), 107–8.

53. See Muhammad Akhtar, *Tajak Swati wa Mumlikat-i Gabar Tarikh kay Aayinah mayn* (Urdu) (Abbottabad: Sarhad Urdu Academy, 2002), 350–1.

54. See Shah, *Tawarikh Hafiz Rahmat Khani*, 64.

55. See Zahirud-din Muhammad Babur, *Babur-Nama*, trans. from the original Turki text by Annette S. Beveridge (repr., Lahore: Sang-e-Meel Publications, 1987), 367–70; Zahiruddin Babur, *Tuzuk-i Baburi*, Urdu trans. Rashid Akhtar Nadwi (Lahore: Sang-e-Meel Publications, n.d.), 147–8; Zahiruddin Muhammad Babur, *Waqay-i Babur*, Urdu trans. Yunus Jafri, from the Persian trans. of Abdur Rahim Khan-i Khanan, with notes and annotation by Hasan Beg (Krekardi, Scotland: Shahar Banu Publishers, 2007), 190–1; Shah, *Tawarikh Hafiz Rahmat Khani*, 91–2.

56. See Minhaj Siraj, *Tabaqat-i Nasari*, *tartib wa tahshiyah* by Abdul Hai Habibi, Urdu trans. *wa izafah* by Ghulam Rasul Mehr, revision by Sayyad Husam-ud-Din Rashidi, Vol. 2 (2nd impression, Lahore: Urdu Science Board, 1985), 154–5.

57. See ibid., 161 n. 6.

58. See Akhtar, *Tajak Swati wa Mumlikat-i Gabar Tarikh kay Aayinah mayn*, 114, 138, 175, 225, 345, 348.

59. See ibid., 177, 225.

60. See Raverty, *Notes on Afghanistan and Baluchistan*, Vol. 1, 156 n.

61. Bagnera, 'The site of Mount Rāja Gīrā, Udegram: Archaeological evidences and new Hypotheses', 139; Bagnera, *The Ghaznavid Mosque and the Islamic Settlement at Mt. Rāja Gīrā, Udegram*, 89.

62. Bagnera, 'The site of Mount Rāja Gīrā, Udegram: Archaeological evidences and new Hypotheses', 139–40.

63. Ibid., 140.

64. *Gazetteer of the Peshawar District, 1897–98*, 55. Also see Yusufi, *Yusufzai*, 212–13.

65. The Shalmani are Dihgan by ethnicity. Their original seat was Shalman and Karman, in the Kurram Valley, from where they migrated and settled in other areas; hence, they are named Shalmani after their original homeland. See Raverty, *Notes on Afghanistan and Baluchistan*, Vol. 1, 175–6; Shah, *Tawarikh Hafiz Rahmat Khani*, 31.

66. Shah, *Tawarikh Hafiz Rahmat Khani*, 31–2, 47–8. Also see Raverty, *Notes on Afghanistan and Baluchistan*, Vol. 1, 175–6.

67. Shah, *Tawarikh Hafiz Rahmat Khani*, 32, 64–5.

68. Ibid., 32.

69. Mountstuart Elphinstone, *An Account of the Kingdom of Caubul*, with new introduction by Olaf Caroe, Vol. 2 (repr., Karachi: Oxford University Press, 1972), 11. Also see Shah, *Tawarikh Hafiz Rahmat Khani*, 103–4.

70. Abu-l-Fazl, *The Akbar Nama of Abu-l-Fazl (History of the Reign of Akbar Including an Account of His Predecessors)*, trans. from the original Persian by H. Beveridge, Vol. 3 (repr., Lahore: Sang-e-Meel Publications, 2005), 561.

71. Abu 'l-Fazl 'Allāmī, *The Ā'īn-i Akbarī*, trans. from the original Persian by H. Blochmann, 2nd edn. rev. and ed. by D.C. Phillott, complete 3 Vols. (repr., Lahore: Sang-e-Meel Publications, 2004), 857.

72. Abu-l-Fazl, *The Akbar Nama of Abu-l-Fazl (History of the Reign of Akbar Including an Account of His Predecessors)*, trans. from the original Persian by H. Beveridge, Vol. 3, 561.

73. See ibid., n. 5.

74. See Sithanawi, *Kitab al-Ibra: Subah Sarhad wa Afghanistan ki Char Sau Salah Tarikh; 1500 Iswi ta 1900 Iswi*, Vol. 1, 185.

75. See Akhtar, *Tajak Swati wa Mumlikat-i Gabar Tarikh kay Aayinah mayn*, 220–319.

76. McMahon and A.D.G. Ramsay, *Report on the Tribes of the Malakand Political Agency (Exclusive of Chitral)*, revised by R.L. Kennion, 29.

77. See Raverty, *Notes on Afghanistan and Baluchistan*, Vol. 1, 277–8.

78. See Shah, *Tawarikh Hafiz Rahmat Khani*, 32, 103.

79. Raverty, *Notes on Afghanistan and Baluchistan*, Vol. 1, 231 n. *.

80. Ibid., 277.

81. See Roshan Khan, *Malikah-i Swat* (Karachi: Roshan Khan and Company, 1983), 45.

82. See Akhtar, *Tajak Swati wa Mumlikat-i Gabar Tarikh kay Aayinah mayn*, 97, 121, 351, 364–5, 376–7.

83. See Shah, *Tawarikh Hafiz Rahmat Khani*, 32, 103.

84. See Raverty, *Notes on Afghanistan and Baluchistan*, Vol. 1, 232, 242.

85. See Shah, *Tawarikh Hafiz Rahmat Khani*, 66.

86. Raverty, *Notes on Afghanistan and Baluchistan*, Vol. 1, 278.

87. See Shah, *Tawarikh Hafiz Rahmat Khani*, 72–3.

88. See ibid.

89. See ibid., 76–7.

90. See ibid., 104–7.

91. Abu-l-Fazl, *The Akbar Nama of Abu-l-Fazl (History of the Reign of Akbar Including an Account of His Predecessors)*, trans. from the original Persian by H. Beveridge, Vol. 3, 561.

92. Also see Elphinstone, *An Account of the Kingdom of Caubul,* Vol. 2, 14, 27.

93. Sithanawi, *Kitab al-Ibra: Subah Sarhad wa Afghanistan ki Char Sau Salah Tarikh; 1500 Iswi ta 1900 Iswi*, Vol. 1, 185.

94. See Shah, *Tawarikh Hafiz Rahmat Khani*, 74–5.

95. Akhtar, *Tajak Swati wa Mumlikat-i Gabar Tarikh kay Aayinah mayn*, 349.

96. See ibid., 164.

97. See ibid., 187.

98. See ibid., 197. Also see ibid., 217, 311, 314.

99. See ibid., 187–98.

100. Also see Sithanawi, *Kitab al-Ibra: Subah Sarhad wa Afghanistan ki Char Sau Salah Tarikh; 1500 Iswi ta 1900 Iswi*, Vol. 1, 132–66.

101. Bagnera, 'Islamic Udegram. Activities and new Perspectives', 236.
102. Scerrato, 'The ethnographic activity of the IsIAO Italian Archaeological Mission in Swat and Gilgit-Baltistan', 244.
103. Ibid.

7

YUSUFZI OCCUPATION, SOCIAL SYSTEM, AND MODE OF RULING

Yusufzi Migration and Occupation of Swat

The sixteenth century proved a turning point in the history of Swat as the Yusufzi (formerly pronounced as 'Isafzi' and 'Yusafzi' and now erroneously as 'Yusufzai') occupied the land. The advent of the Yusufzi (singular male: Yusufzay; female: Yusufzai) marks a mass migration and invasion by Muslims against their brethren in faith for the first time in the history of Swat.

The Yusufzi are a large and famous Afghan/Pukhtun tribe, scions of Shikhi (Khakhi), the son of Shirbun (Shirkbun). They received the area of Arghistan in the Qandahar region in the division of the land among the Afghans. As a result of wrangles and wars, they displaced, went to the Ghauri Khail (Ghaurya Khail) and were later displaced from there as a result of wars caused as a result of natural calamities and settled in Karu and Nushki (Garra and Nushki: also spelled as Noshki)[1] near Dasht-i Lut or the Great Salt Desert[2] (now part of Iran and Afghanistan with a minor portion in Pakistan's Baluchistan). According to Sayyad Abdul Jabbar Shah, Arghistan is also called Ghwarah Murghzi (also Ghwarah Murghah), the ancient name of which is Ghawar, or Ghaur.[3]

At the end of the thirteenth or beginning of the fourteenth century CE, the Yusufzi were compelled by circumstances or change of fortune to leave Garra and Nushki. They migrated and settled in the neighbourhood of Kabul and emerged strong there. They lent their support to Mirza Ulugh Beg, son of Mirza Abu Saeed, to make him ruler of Kabul. The relations remained cordial. Ulugh Beg was in need of the Yusufzi's support for his throne, so he treated them with distinction. The relations became strained in the last quarter of the fifteenth century CE. Ulugh Beg hatched a conspiracy, in collaboration with the Gigyani (also Gugyani; Gagyani), against the Yusufzi and seven hundred of their chiefs and leading men were treacherously killed. The Yusufzi were compelled to leave their homes. They migrated to Peshawar Valley. At first they sought shelter and assistance from the Dalazak. The Dalazak granted them the territory of Duabah (also Doaba) and the area up to Bajawar as well as Ashnaghar (also Hashtnagar). Later, they constantly fought against the Dalazak and occupied various of their territories. They continued their advance and gradually extended their limits and possessions.[4]

Akhun Darwizah and Abdul Jabbar Shah have given the name of Mirza Ulugh Beg as Mirza Quli Beg.[5] The sources do not agree on the number of the chiefs and leading men who were massacred on his order. Some have given the number as 'seven hundred'[6] and some have said that the delegation comprised 'eight hundred' men.[7] Although H.W. Bellew has given the number, on the authority of Akhun Darwizah, as 'over two hundred',[8] Akhun Darwizah's book *Tazkiratul Abrar-i wal Ashrar* has stated it at 'nine hundred'.[9] Abdul Jabbar Shah has stated about nine hundred.[10] *Gazetteer of the Peshawar District, 1897–98*, has stated it as 'seventy' only.[11] Taj Muhammad Khan Zaibsar has also stated that according to *Dur-i Mustatir* 'seventy' men were killed.[12] Although there is no concrete proof, the figure 'seventy' seems logically more sound.

The date of the massacre of the Yusufzi chiefs or leading figures is unknown. According to *Tawarikh Hafiz Rahmat Khani*, Malak Ahmad, whose life was spared at the request of Malak Shah Mansur, and who was elected or installed as *malak* of all the Yusufzi to replace Malak Sulaiman Shah,[13] who was killed by Ulugh Beg along with the other chiefs, was an inexperienced boy (خام هلک[14]) and youth (زلمے[15]). If his age presumed to have been fifteen years at the time, and his birth's year be reckoned as 1470 CE, as written on his picture,[16] the year becomes around 1485 CE.[17]

At that time, Swat was in the possession of the Swati Pukhtuns. When the Yusufzi occupied territory in the Peshawar Valley, Sultan Awais (Uwais; Wais) was the chief ruler of Swat (detailed in the previous chapter). As the Yusufzi were still in distress in the Samah and Ashnaghar areas, they would come to Swat for trade, bringing salt, etcetera. From the Yusufzi's trading excursions to Swat, Sultan Awais became acquainted with Malak Ahmad in absentia. Learning that Malak Ahmad has an unmarried sister, he asked for her betrothal. Malak Ahmad consented and she was married to the Sultan from Duabah.[18] H.G. Raverty has contended: 'It was with a view of getting a footing in Suwát [Swat] that Malik Aḥmad gave his sister in marriage to the Sulṭán.'[19] The Yusufzi were enticed by the richness of Swat, being a fertile, well irrigated, prosperous, and developed area. They extended their hold up to the boundaries of Swat and looked upon the Valley with covetous eyes.

Although the Yusufzi established matrimonial relations with Sultan Awais, they had their eyes set on the Valley. Not only may the fertile land and rich pastures of Swat have tempted them but, as expressed by Malak Ahmad, occupation of Swat was a must for being safe from the Mughals and the Dalazak.[20] After coming to the Peshawar Valley, the Yusufzi were constantly fighting against the Dalazak and were exposed to attacks and subjugation by the Mughal, i.e. Babur, the ruler of Kabul.

Interestingly, according to *Tawarikh Hafiz Rahmat Khani*, it was after the massacre of the Yusufzi chiefs that Shaikh Zangi ibn Mula Khalil Ranrizi Khwajah, who was a Yusufzi *stanadar* (the word or term *stanadar* has been explained hereinafter), told them, Go! Our country or place of abode is Swat, which the Almighty will give us.[21] This also impliedly means that the occupation of Swat was in their mind or plans even before or at the time of their departure from Kabul.

On the other hand, Sultan Awais feared the Yusufzi's covetous eyes on Swat and hence was anxious to foil their purposes. One of his steps, in this respect, was the murder of his wife, the sister of Malak Ahmad, so as to stop the Yusufzi coming into Swat and she being suspected of spying for them.[22] Interestingly, the sources do not mention the name of Malak Ahmad's sister married to Sultan Awais.

The murder of the Yusufzai lady, sister of Malak Ahmad and wife of Sultan Awais, strained relations between the two sides. The Yusufzi worked out their plan and strategy for taking Swat.[23] Abdul Jabbar Shah has asserted that, having made preparations for the assault on Swat, Malak Ahmad sent a message to Sultan Awais demanding to know why the latter had granted asylum to the fugitive Shalmani, who had not kept their word to the Yusufzi and hence were defeated and deprived of their seat in Hashtnagar (Ashnaghar in the present-day Charsadah District) and fled to Swat. It was demanded that he either had to surrender them to the Yusufzi or to be ready for combat. Combat was decided.[24]

As three passes—the Murah (Morah), Shahkut (Shahkot) and Malakand passes—were the main entrance routes from Samah to Swat, the Yusufzi moved up under the leadership of Shaikh Mali and Malak Ahmad and encamped opposite to the Shahkut Pass, 'which the Swatis accordingly occupied in strength'. Reconnaissance revealed that the Malakand Pass was undefended; therefore, a strategy was adopted by which the women and children were left in the 'camp to keep the camp fire burning, and to distract the enemy's attention by singing songs and beating drums, the fighting men under cover of darkness came round over the Malakand Pass and began to loot the villages in the valley behind'. Seeing 'their homes in flames behind them',[25] the Swatis left the pass and the Yusufzi entered the Swat Valley. Akhun Darwizah has mentioned Shaikh Mali by the title 'Malak Shaikh Mali'.[26]

After this, Sultan Awais and his forces fought for the defence of his strategic centre, namely Tanra (also Thana), in Lower Swat, but to no avail. The Yusufzi defeated the Sultan in the battle, called the battle of Tanra, and he fled from the battlefield.[27]

With this victory, the Yusufzi occupied two-thirds of Swat. Because of their good demeanour, people from different areas were coming and settling in their two part country. The remaining one-third beyond the Swigalai Pass, including Manglawar, was with Sultan Awais, and between Landakay and the Shamilai Pass were with the Mutrawi. After some time, despite the disagreement of the Yusufzi, the Mandanr, a sister tribe of the Yusufzi, besieged Manglawar, the capital of Sultan Awais, but the Sultan did not come out. Although the Mandanr-Yusufzi ravaged the vicinity, the capital was saved by the great fortification. After ravaging the surrounding villages, the Yusufzi went back to Tanra and the threat from the Sultan to them ended.[28] After occupying two-thirds of Swat, the Yusufzi went back to their homes in Samah.[29] Roshan Khan has spoken of the occupation of one-third of Swat, which is in contrast to the account of *Tawarikh Hafiz Rahmat Khani*, his source of information and the account of which he has rendered into Urdu.[30] *Tawarikh Hafiz Rahmat Khani*, however, speaks of the occupation of one-third of Swat with the occupation of Khar which is below Batkhilah.[31] Their advance came to a halt for a time.

Babur speaks of Sultan Alauddin and Sultan Awais (Wais/Uwais) of Swat as the two Sultans of Swat and their waiting on him at Bajawar at the time of his campaign. Sultan Awais was in agreement with Babur and served him. He himself was sent by Babur to collect the impost laid on the Kahraj people in agreement with him.[32] Babur not only treated Sultan Alauddin and Sultan Awais well at Bajawar[33] and gave honour to both, but he asked the Yusufzi in the final agreement, made with them in May 1519, that they should not advance into Swat above Abuhah

(Aboha) and that they should allow all the peasants or subject people of that area to leave the area.[34] It is to be noted that, at the occupation of the Lower Swat areas, the Yusufzi consoled and asked the Swatis not to abandon their villages.[35] They thus remained in the Yusufzi occupied areas, because of which Babur asked the Yusufzi to allow them to leave the area.

Interestingly, Rashid Akhtar Nadwi has mistranslated Babur's passage for 'above Abuhah' and hence has stated that no person from Aluhiyah Bala (الوہیہ بالا) may interfere in the affairs of Swat,[36] which has further been corrupted by Muhammad Akhtar as 'Alayi Bala'(الائ بالا),[37] namely 'Upper Alayi' in the cis-Indus Hazarah region.

McMahon and Ramsay have contended: 'It was a disputed point as to where the Yusufzai-Swati boundary was in the Swat Valley.' When the deputation of the Yusufzi's leading *malak*s, headed by Babur's father-in-law Malak Shah Mansur, waited on him at Kabul in May 1519 CE, 'at the request of the Jirga, Babur settled that as far as Abuha should be Yusafzai territory, and above that Swati'.[38] By stating that at the request of the delegation, Babur 'settled a long standing dispute as to the limit[s] of the Yusufzai territory, and decided that all the country up to Abua [Abuhah], in Swat, was Yusufzai land; with the country beyond they had no concern', H.W. Bellew, too, has made it clear that it is Abuhah.[39] Babur, however, has not mentioned that the agreement or settlement he made with the Yusufzi's delegation was at their request.[40] This puts a question mark on the aforementioned claim by A.H. McMahon and A.D.G. Ramsay as well as H.W. Bellew.

However, *Tawarikh Hafiz Rahmat Khani* speaks of Sultan Awais and Malak Hasan Mutrawi as the chiefs or rulers of Swat at the time of the Yusufzi inroads into Swat. As the Yusufzi occupation of Swat took place over a long period of seventeen years, Sultan Alauddin may have been the predecessor of Malak Hasan Mutrawi and Malak Hasan may have succeeded him during this period, sometime after Alauddin's waiting on Babur in Bajawar.

The Yusufzi resumed their advance during the reign of Humayun,[41] son and successor of Babur on the seat of Delhi. Their depredations, assaults and ravages at last compelled Sultan Awais to leave his possessions in Upper Swat and leave for Niyag.[42] At the departure of Sultan Awais from Manglawar, all Swat save the territory under the Mutrawi came into the possession of the Yusufzi. It is said that the Yusufzi occupied all the country of Sultan Awais over sixteen years and in the seventeenth year they raided the Mutrawi. The Mutrawi resisted: however, at last, compelled by the hard pressed siege of their seat, they fled. The seat and fort of their ruler Malak Hasan, Baligram, was captured by the Yusufzi. Malak Hasan and his people fled to the hills. The people later returned and became the subjects of the Yusufzi. It was in the seventeenth year that the Yusufzi occupied the whole of Swat. By this time, most of the leaders who had started the assaults on Swat have passed away. At the defeat of the Mutrawi, the Yusufzi distributed all Swat among themselves.[43] Muhammad Nawaz Tair has taken 'Baligram' as 'Balugram',[44] which is unsound. The account of *Tawarikh Hafiz Rahmat Khani* testifies it to be 'Baligram', situated in the precinct or proximity of the present-day Saidu Sharif. Although *Tawarikh Hafiz Rahmat Khani* has stated that it took the Yusufzi seventeen years to occupy all of Swat, according to Akhun Darwizah they occupied the entire Swat in twelve years.[45] Whereas, according to Abdul Jabbar Shah, the Yusufzi completely occupied entire Swat and Dir area in one-two years.[46]

Keeping in view the accounts and different aspects, such as taking Lower Swat first, the agreement with Babur in 1519 CE not to occupy the area beyond Abuhah, resumption of the advance after Babur's death in Humayun's reign, the period of seventeen years given in the *Tawarikh Hafiz Rahmat Khani* seems sound. Although the precise number of years of the Yusufzi occupation of Swat took is not easy to ascertain, keeping the different above-mentioned sources and accounts, it can be inferred that it took place in the period from 1515 to 1532 CE. Besides, as discussed hereinafter, the *waish* (*wesh*; detailed hereinafter) was effected by Shaikh Mali, who died in the year 1534 (see subsection *waish* hereinafter), so it was in his life time that all the Swat Valley proper was occupied, after which he got the opportunity and the time required for all the nitty-gritty of effecting the *waish* or land distribution.[47]

As a result of the Yusufzi's depredations and occupation of Swat, most of the old Swati Pukhtuns left Swat. They went to the cis-Indus territories, which falls in the present-day Mansihrah and Batgram (also Batagram) districts (in the Hazarah Division), where they still dwell. However, a number of them stayed, recognized the Yusufzi dominance, and became part and parcel of the new set-up in which they 'were reduced to the condition of....Fakeers [*faqir*s; subjects of the tribe]'.[48] The Yusufzi occupied Upper Swat Valley as far as Ayin, above Madyan, 'beyond which they have scarcely advanced' to date.[49]

However, the area from the villages Ayin and Satal Gharai till the limits of the villages of Piya and Landay, on the left and right sides of the Swat River, respectively, was granted to Akhun Khail Miangan and the Sayyads. It is to be noted that in the British official writings this area has been mentioned the Akhund Khail tract; and somewhere as part of Swat proper and somewhere of Swat Kuhistan.

For understanding the factors responsible for the stability of this ethnic border, Fredrik Barth, a Norwegian anthropologist, had examined, in 1950s, the specific requirements of the Pukhtun economy and organization. While stating that the 'Pathan territory extends to a critical ecologic threshold: the limits within which two crops can be raised each year',[50] he has claimed that 'the conclusion that the limits of double cropping constitute the effective check on further Pathan expansion seems unavoidable'.[51] John Biddulp, however, stated much early in the nineteenth century that the Turwali tract (see chapter 12) of Swat below Chudgram (now Balakut) comprises two cropping areas that yield 'two crops of great abundance yearly',[52] which is correct. However, the Yusufzi did not occupy this tract, and also the Chail Valley of this nature.

Although the Yusufzi did not advance towards the mountainous areas of the Swat Kuhistan beyond Ayin and Satal Gharai as well as to the Chail Valley, they continued their inroads into the other bordering areas. They not only occupied Swat Valley but extended their occupation to the territories of Ghwarband, Puran, Chakisar, and Kanra (part of Shanglahpar or present-day Shanglah District) as well.

Some sources have claimed that the original homeland of the Yusufzi was the country which is now under their occupation and that they had been compelled before the onslaughts of Central Asian invaders to migrate. After the consequent migration, they at last settled between Baluchistan and Afghanistan. Thus, their migration in the sixteenth century to the presently occupied territory was their return to their own country after about a thousand years.[53] A.H. Dani, however, has negated this contention by stating:

It is pertinent to dispel the commonly held notion that originally the Yusufzais lived in Gandhara and in about fifth century A.D. they migrated to Kandahar region as a result of Hun invasion. This suggestion was made by Dr. Bellew...to explain the origin of the city of Kandahar from the well-known regional name of Gandhara as a result of these migrant refugees. In Dr. Bellew's time of historical research this was acceptable, and it is also possible to agree with the author in the *Encyclopaedia of Islam* that the term *Kandahar* in modern Afghanistan is identical with Gandhara of ancient history. But....it has been earlier shown...that in the main valley of Gandhara and in the hill zone to its north the Afghan tribes had hardly any place in the remote ancient past. The coming of the Yusufzais and other allied tribes to this area must be traced to those political factors which led to the establishment of a branch of the Timurids in Herat. It was natural for them to seek shelter with another branch in Kabul under Ulugh Beg.[54]

Dani's contention seems sound, as concrete historical evidence in support of the contention put forth by H.W. Bellew and accepted by others does not exist.

The history of Swat after the Yusufzi occupation is replete with wars, turmoil, rivalries, fractions and faction feuds, exiles and banishments, and absence of state, government and ruling authority, all which disturbed the lives of the people and stunted progress and development on various counts. A bird eye-view of this state of affairs can be seen and observed in the succeeding chapters. Here, it is required to give a sketch of the Yusufzi's social system and mode of ruling.

YUSUFZI SOCIAL SYSTEM AND MODE OF RULING

In the tribal/social system that evolved in Swat after the Yusufzi's occupation, no single person was ever recognized as the ruler. There are, however, instances that the people have worked under a single leader or in unison at times of war and emergency, e.g. Malak Ahmad and Khan Kaju/Kachu. In the words of H.W. Bellew:

> Amongst themselves these several tribes had rival interests, that, continually producing feuds and jealousies, kept them estranged from, or opposed to, each other; but, in their relations with foreigners, putting aside their individual feuds and jealousies, the tribes all coalesced, and, for the time being, acted in unison under the guidance of the elders of their patriarchs or tribal chiefs.[55]

There having been no state, ruler, or formal governing body and machinery to govern and regulate the affairs of the people, the vacuum had to be filled by the social system or mode of ruling that evolved and which was based on certain cardinal norms, values, rules, and regulations.

The Yusufzi inhabiting the valley on either bank of the Swat River both belong to the Akuzi Yusufzi, but to different sub-branches. Those on the right bank belong to the Khwazuzi (also Khwajuzi, erroneously written as Khwazuzai) branch and those on the left bank to the Baizi (erroneously written as Baizai). In the system that evolved, they were divided into two opposing blocs or factions, called *dalay* (singular: *dalah*), with alliances on both the sides. Both the *dalay* had their own leaders/heads at *tal* (block) and village levels called *malakan* (also *malakanan*; singular *malak*); and at the *tapah* (segment) and valley levels called *khanan* (singular *khan*).

Among the Yusufzi, at first there had been no title of *khan* and the top leaders or heads too were called *malak*, e.g. Malak Sulaiman Shah, Malak Shah Mansur, and Malak Ahmad. As mentioned earlier, after the killing of the then chief or *malak* Sulaiman Shah by Ulugh Beg, the Yusufzi elected or installed Ahmad as their *malak*, as per the instruction of Malak Sulaiman Shah, and he became Malak Ahmad.[56] However, in course of time, the title of *khan* was also adopted. Thus, after the death of Malak Ahmad, Kaju was installed as their chief with the title of *khan*[57] and hence he became Khan Kaju.

The *khanan* and *malakan* were chiefs selected and designated by the people of the respective segments. These were in principle not hereditary posts or designations. Later, the *malakan* were, on the whole, lesser tribal chiefs compared to the *khanan* but it was in fact the personal power, influence, and say in the communal affairs and the size of the followers and adherents that denoted the parameters from which the status and position of a particular *khan* or *malak* was to be assessed.[58]

The *khanan* and *malakan* could be deposed or removed from the headship and replaced by their people. A person designated head or *khan* when the *pagrai* (turban) of headship has been tied onto his head by his people was called *da pagrai khan*: the *khan* designated by the people through the power of 'free choice and contract', a trait evaluated by the Norwegian anthropologist Fredrik Barth.[59]

This made the heads, i.e. *malakan* and *khanan*, dependent on the people as without their consent and support such leaders could not sustain their status and positions. To maintain their status they were therefore obliged to assist their *dalah* (bloc or faction) members on occasions of sorrow and joy (*gham-khadi*), to resolve disputes of their *dalah* members, and to protect their interests.[60] This trait of 'free choice and contract' also made them prone to machinations and rifts, because the potential rivals were always there to deprive the *khanan* and *malakan* of their supporters and to gain support for themselves.[61]

This created factionalism, wars and turmoil, enmity and rivalries, exiles and banishments, and financial stresses and strains. The *dalah*, or faction which had the upper hand was called *banday dalah* (*dalah* in power) and the one that suffered defeat and lost the upper hand was called *landay dalah* (*dalah* in opposition). It is noteworthy that the two *dalay* did not differ 'in their political ideas or modes of thought. Their object...to get into power' was 'to secure for themselves the profits of the position in fines' (*naghah*: explained hereinafter under the sub-topic *naghah*) etcetera. Such a system, of course led to frequent fighting, and a change of the *dalah* position never took place without a fight.[62] There was no mechanism, such as a *jargah* or the ratio of the *dawtar* held or possessed by the particular *dalah* members or adherents that worked as a parameter to effect a peaceful change in the *dalah* position.

In the words of Makhdum Tasadduq Ahmad, in the absence of a formal government, ruling authority and machinery, and frequent turmoil and fighting, 'They fought freely now and then and chased one another out of power. Perhaps this is the reason why Swat and its adjoining areas are commonly known as *yagistan* [*Yaghistan*], or the land of freedom and rebellion.'[63]

In this scenario, the lives of the people were regulated and governed by the unwritten code of conduct called Pukhtu (now also called Pukhtunwali). This is why this period of the history of Swat is generally referred to as *da Pukhtu dawar* (د پښتودور) and *da Pukhtu zamanah* (د پښتوزمانه), viz. 'the period of Pukhtu' and 'the age of Pukhtu', meaning the period and age in which Pukhtu was followed and it dictated and regulated the norms and life of the people.

In this system, power and authority remained in the hands of the minority land owning class, which included both *dawtar* and *sirai* (both terms are explained later) landowners. The majority of course consisted of the dependent non-landowners. The dependent non-land owners included the Gujar (also called Gujran: an ethnic group), *shpankyan* (also *shpunkyan*; an ethnic group: *bizugar* and *gadbanah*—shepherds), *brakhikhwarah* (tenants), *dihqanan* (ploughmen on crop-share; cultivators; peasants), and *kasabgar* (professionals) like *mulan/imaman* (prayers-leaders), *ingaran* (blacksmiths), *duruzgar* (carpenters), *nishanchyan* (standard-bearers), *jalawanan* (ferrymen), *julagan* (weavers), *nandafan* (cotton huskers; cotton dressers and cleaners), *parachkan* (also called *tataran*: shopkeepers; carriers; peddlers; owners of donkeys, mules and horses doing the job of transporting grain, manure etcetera for the landowners and receiving a share in the harvest; they are also an ethnic group like the Gujar), *shakhilan* (leather workers), *chamyaran* (cobblers; shoes-makers; tanners; curriers or workers in leathers), *ubahwari* (water-servers), *kulalan* (potters), *astazi* (messengers), *ghubanah* (village cattle graziers), *kakhyan* (village's fields-guards), *tilyan* (oil pressers; oil and soap makers), *sarkhamaran* (tailors), *baghwanan* (gardeners; fruiters), *dubyan* (dyers), *pansaryan* (druggist; perfumers), *zargaran* (gold and silver smiths; jewelers), *nazaran* (personal guards), *tayar-khwarah* (those who received cooked meals or food), *tangah-sari* (those who can be hired for a *tangah*, i.e. one-third of a rupee), *marayan* (slaves), *nayan* (barbers), *daman* (musicians; ballad-singers; pimps), and so forth. This majority had no voice in the *jargay* (singular *jargah*; for *jargay* see the sub-topic *jargah* hereinafter), in selecting or electing the heads (*malakan* and *khanan)* or other communal decision making. Their lot was to follow their respective heads or *naikan* (landowners/householders/employers).[64] Makhdum Tasadduq Ahmad has not included the *julagan, chamyaran*, and *tilyan* in the occupational groups attached to the groups of the Pukhtuns.[65]

Although theoretically, each *dawtari* (term explained later) held an equal vote in communal *jargay*, individuals by personal ability, sanctity, or prowess, or by means of intrigue, obtained greater influence and were given grants of *sirai* (*serai*) land for their services to the community.[66] In practice, the power and influence of *khanan* and *malakan* and individuals in the *jargay* rested upon their *dawtar* share, and also upon the strength of their followers and *dalah* (explained above). The greater the *dawtar* share, the greater their role, say, and respect. This is also evident from the proverb: *Jamruz warukay day khu Qambar yiy luy day*; (جمروز وروکے دے خو قمبر ئي لوئے دے) meaning: 'Although Jamruz, then a *khan* of Qambar, is small, his Qambar (the village or locality he represented) is big and thus he is big and has greater say and significance in the *jargah* and communal affairs.'

Besides, a person was considered Pukhtun (also Pukhtan) and had a say in the *jargay* as long as he retained his *dawtar* share.[67] When he lost his *dawtar*, he and his offspring lost the epithet of Pukhtun/ Pukhtan and their voice in the *jargay*, and gradually were ranked in the non-landowner categories.[68] Similarly, those who were not recognized members of the Pukhtan (Pukhtuns) class, obtained the status and epithet of Pukhtun/Pukhtan by gaining a share in the *dawtar* land and thenceforward not only held a vote and say in the communal *jargay* but their offspring too remained so categorized and empowered. 'Therefore', states Makhdum Tasadduq Ahmad, 'a *Pakhtun* [Pukhtun/Pukhtan] came to be defined as any person who had a share in the *dauter* [*dawtar*]'.[69]

Although there are instances where, despite having gained a share in the *dawtar*, the concerned persons, although having a voice and say in community *jargay*, were not generally considered or ranked as Pukhtuns, as in the case of the *sithan* (the wealthy traders) and *parachkan* (explained above among the *kasabgar*) of Mingawarah. Such persons' offspring have, with the passage of time, gained the status and epithet of Pukhtuns, the examples of which has also been noted and reported by Makhdum Tasadduq Ahmad.[70] Why the *sithan* and *parachkan* of Mingawarah did not get the epithet of Pukhtun was because of other factors, which, beside others, include the abolition of the *garzindah waish* (for the meaning and details, see the sub-topic *waish* further on), because of which they permanently remained settled in Mingawarah and did not shift to other places and also because they did not abandon their old profession as traders, shop-keepers, and contractors.

The *stanadar* (*astanadar*) were 'politically and socially the most significant class outside'. They were 'composed of the holy men or the descendants of the holy men', namely: *saydan* (Sayyads), *myagan* (Mians), *akhunzadgan* (Akhunzadahs), *sahibzadgan* (Sahibzadahs) and *mulan* (Mulas). The *mulan* 'who had a good following and were respected came into this category, otherwise a *Mulla* was occasionally treated as a *Kasabgar*, and was a member of [the] tul [*tal*]'.[71]

The *stanadar*'s 'social position and privileges' have been 'hereditary, and quite independent of individual merit'.[72] They played a significant role and exercised great prestige and power. They either lived in a separate section of a village (called *cham*, not *palau*) or in separate villages of their own, 'along with their tenants' and *kasabgar*, constructed on their *sirai* lands. The *stanadar* effected and performed social and political control. They not only mediated the disputes of the Pukhtun chiefs but living on and possessing mostly, but not necessarily, the intervening strips of the zones owned by the Pukhtuns, worked as a buffer zone because the lives and property of the *stanadar* 'were regarded as inviolable'. They also formed part of the *jargay* and used to go as *nanawatay* (see the sub-topic *nanawatay* hereinafter) for effecting conciliation between the Pukhtuns. The *stanadar* also 'were supposed to have powers to harm and to favour others because of their association with the supernatural'.[73]

At this point, it is pertinent to mention that the institution of the *stanadar* among the Yusufzi was an old one; a testament to this is that, according to *Tawarikh Hafiz Rahmat Khani*, after the massacre of their chiefs by Ulugh Beg, they went to their *stanadar* and asked to be told what their *mulk* (country or place of abode) was, where they were to proceed. Upon this, as stated earlier, Shaikh Zangi ibn Mula Khalil Ranrizi Khwajah told them, Go! Our country or place of abode is Swat, which the Almighty will give us.[74]

The system thus evolved had a democratic sense and appearance but was quite different in many aspects. A.H. McMahon and A.D.G. Ramsay have observed and asserted:

> It is necessary here to explain that the word "democratic" as applied to Pathan Government in these parts should only be used with an important reservation. The power is entirely in the hands of the land (*daftar*) owning Pathans (Pukhtana). The *fakir* [*faqir*] or artisan classes, cultivating tenants (*kashtkars*), soldiery (*mallatars* [*mlatar*]), musicians (*doms*), &c., are without the franchise, their position being practically that of serfs.[75]

This is not entirely correct. It needs to be asserted that, while power was indeed concentrated in the hands of the land owning classes, both *dawtar* and *sirai* land owners (the Pukhtanah and *stanadar* respectively), and the other segments and professionals were without franchise, the position of the non-land owners was never 'practically that of serfs' as stated by McMahon and Ramsay. This will become clear from the pages of this chapter that follow. McMahon and Ramsay themselves have explained:

> The autonomy which prevailed in the tribe as a whole extended not only to its sub-divisions and sub-sections, but also to individual villages. The management of all matters relating to a village rested with the village councilor [council or] jirga [*jargah*]. Each village was represented in the jirga of its *khel*, each khel in that of the sub-division, and each sub-division in the jirga of the whole tribe.[76]

The heads, namely *malakan* and *khanan*, acted as chiefs of their *talunah* (singular: *tal*), *tapay* (singular: *tapah*), and segments but seldom were

more than the leaders of their supporters and adherents in wars and their
agents in dealings with others. In a real sense, they possessed influence
rather than power and authority; the real power rested with the *jargay*.
Elphinstone's account, published in 1815, about the chief or head of the
Nikpi Khail also testify to this:

> His powers do not require a long enumeration; he commands in war,
> subject to the resolutions of a council of the Mulliks [*malak*s], who in
> their turn are influenced by the opinion of the members of their clans.
> He sometimes interferes in disputes between two clans, but his success
> in accommodating their difference, depends more on his arguments than
> his authority, and more on the caprice of the disputants than on either.
> Indeed the whole of his authority arises from his personal weight, and
> that is derived from his birth and his good conduct; he has no public
> revenue, and neither more wealth, more immediate clansmen, nor more
> hired servants than the head of any other clan. The heads of clans have
> not much more power; they are, however, referred to in disputes between
> individuals, particularly if they live in different villages; for each clan,
> instead of being assembled in one place, is scattered through different
> villages, which it shares with members of other clans, all, however, living
> in distinct quarters, and under separate chiefs.[77]

Furthermore, in cases of affray, the *malak* or chief 'interposes,
remonstrates, soothes, threatens, and entreats; but his instances are often
disregarded, and the quarrel continues till one party feels himself the
weakest, and leaves the village'.[78]

McMahon and Ramsay have contended that, judging as a whole, the
people of Swat, 'as compared with Pathan tribes elsewhere', 'appear to
differ materially from their neighbours' in one respect, namely 'in the
spirit of discipline which they possess'.[79]

The foundation of the set-up and social organization laid by the
Yusufzi and evolved in Swat, continued to function for four centuries,
until it was fundamentally altered by Miangul Abdul Wadud (ruler of
Swat State from 1917 to 1949), after his rise to power.[80] Makhdum
Tasadduq Ahmad has observed, in the 1950s,

> Perhaps to a casual observer the society would have seemed disorderly
> and lawless because of large number of *Pakhtun* chieftains strewn all
> over the land and subordinate to no single authority. They fought freely
> now and then and chased one another out of power.... But it appears
> to the investigator [Makhdum Tasadduq Ahmad] that the society was

well adjusted to the environment and had attained what is known as equilibrium. Actually it was very much of a self regulating system with periodical land distribution as a keystone. The system was sustained by the fighting role of the *Pakhtun* chiefs, the holiness of the saints, and the subordination of the lowly *Gujars*.[81]

Makhdum Tasadduq Ahmad has spoken of the subordination of the Gujars only, but, as stated above, all the tenants and professionals were subordinated within the system, which played a significant role in the maintenance of the system and of the social organization.

Interestingly, the professionals had to retain their position and services with a particular *khan* or *malak* or *tal*, called *naikan* (singular: *nayak*), only under the latter's sweet will. They were prone to be deprived or dismissed from service by the *naikan* and replaced by others. They, however, had the freedom to leave the service of one *nayak* or *naikan* and seek service with other(s) within the same or other village and locality.[82] Moreover, they were under no compulsion to go with their present *naikan* to the other or the newly allocated locality or village in the interchange of villages and localities in the periodical re-allocation under the *waish* (dealt with hereinafter) or to remain behind and join the service of the new comers.

Although dependent upon the *naikan*, or the concerned *khan* or *malak* or *tal*, for employment, these professionals played significant roles in many ways within the social organization. The *khanan*, *malakan*, and the landowners were in fact dependent upon them, and without them the system could not function and the machine of the social organization could not operate. Each professional group and segment played a key part in running and regulating the norms and values: the specifics cannot be elaborated adequately. For instance, although the *nayi* carried a low social status in the system, he at the same time enjoyed significance as a messenger who was trusted with secret messages of both the genders, sent through him and his wife. Besides, usually being vocal, he openly propagated against those who did not honour and respect him. This could cause defamation and loss of prestige for such persons, sometimes leading to loss of social status and seat of *khani* and *malaki* (*khan*- and *malak*-ship) as well.

Although the professionals were economically dependent, the landowning class could not run the affairs of every-day life without them, whether in war or peace. Thus, the professionals had a profound and significant role on and in the evolution, working, and modalities of the social system.

McMahon and Ramsay have noted at the beginning of the twentieth century that 'being an unwritten law' Pukhtu or Pukhtunwali 'is capable of extensive interpretation. It can be made to necessitate, justify or excuse most actions. It is regulated, however, by established local and tribal custom.'[83]

Some other ingredients of the Pukhtu or the Pukhtun social system will be briefly touched below. For others, i.e. *badragah/jalab*, *tur*, *tui*, *swarah*, *pighur*, *tigah*, *mirat/miratah*, *ghag*, *pat*, *shariat*, *amr-i bil maruf wa nahi anil munkar*, *bungah*, *bramatah* and *butah*, as well as for details of some of the following, see the author's book *The North-West Frontier (Khyber Pakhtunkhwa): Essays on History*.[84]

Waish (وِیش)

When the Yusufzi conquered and occupied their present-day held areas, including Swat, these were divided or distributed among and allocated to their various sections by their leader Shaikh Mali. Although the division or distribution was permanent, the allotment of the localities or zones was not permanent because the land differed in composition, fertility, location, availability of water, accessibility, and so forth. To ensure that all the shareholders could share the benefits and losses of the land, Shaikh Mali devised/adopted the system of land tenure called *waish* (*wesh*).

The precise time when the *waish* system was devised is not confirmed. However, if the account of the Swat occupation by the Yusufzi given earlier in this chapter be kept in view, and also that the Yusufzi resumed their advance into Upper Swat after Babur's death and occupied it during Humayun's reign, it would have been between the years 1532 and 1534 CE. Malak Ahmad died in the year 1535[85] and, according to *Tawarikh Hafiz Rahmat Khani*, he died one year after the death of Shaikh Mali.[86] As the *waish* was effected and completed by Shaikh Mali, it would fall between the years 1532 and 1534 CE, because for effecting the *waish* the survey and categorization of the vast occupied land, demarcating of zones, counting the Yusufzi among whom the land was to be distributed, preparing the records (it is stated that Shaikh Mali recorded all the particulars[87]) would certainly have taken at least a year or two.

Under this system, the land allotted to the major lineage segments of the tribe was further divided into sections and was re-allotted or interchanged or re-allocated every twenty, fifteen, ten, seven, or five years among the respective sub-sections. On every re-allotment or interchange or re-allocation all the shareholders in the land liable to re-allotment or interchange or re-allocation, moved and settled in the villages allotted to them for the next tenure, and allotted the houses and land of those villages among themselves according to their existing individual shares. As the land within the villages also had different categories, each category was divided among the shareholders so as to share the benefits and the losses. This *waish* system was called *garzindah waish* (moving distribution).[88]

Because of this *garzindah waish*, in the words of Makhdum Tasadduq Ahmad,

> In the first place the population became divided into those who had no permanent place to settle and the others who stayed behind. The former group consisted of the landowners, their artisans, and their mercenaries. The other part of the population consisted of the hereditary tenants, agricultural labourers, the *Stanadars*, or the saintly class. In the second place since there was no single recognized authority which could implement the *wesh*, every tenth or fifteenth year there was bloodshed and warfare, because sometimes the more fortunately placed *khails* refused to vacate their quarters. In the third place, even during the period when relative calm and peace prevailed, life and property were not safe.[89]

McMahon and Ramsay too have stated that this *waish* system was 'a fertile source of quarrel and strife' because those in 'possession of good lands and villages', which they 'considered better than those' of their neighbours, were 'in no hurry to exchange them for inferior ones' and hence used to argue numerous 'reasons for postponing the redistribution' or re-interchange. These arguments frequently were met by forcible measures and hence the drawing of lots was 'generally attended with fighting'.[90]

Although, there had been instances that support these assertions of McMahon and Ramsay, such arrangements have neither always been met by forcible measures nor was the drawing of lots generally attended by fighting. There was an inbuilt set of mechanisms that regulated such issues, the *jargah* being one of them, which is also evident from McMahon and Ramsay's following assertion.

The discipline which controls the members of a village community in Swat, and the effective control which thereby the jirgas [*jargah*s] wield in all matters of village or tribal interest, is remarkable. Their long standing system of communal government has doubtless inculcated this spirit, and so has the complicated system in vogue of periodically redistributing all tribal lands. Unless a very strong spirit of discipline was inborn in the people, it would be impossible to work either of these systems in the manner in which they are worked.[91]

Mountstuart Elphinstone's following account, recorded in the early nineteenth century, in respect of the Nikpi Khail, is also a testament to this inbuilt mechanism regulating the issues.

The two half Ooloosses [in Pashto: *ulasay* and *ulasunah*] meet every ten years to draw lots, at a village which lies on the borders of the two shares of lands. Vast numbers of people attend to witness the ceremony; but as the exultation of the victors, and the anger of the vanquished party, would produce tumults in such an assembly, the Mulliks [*malak*s, *malakan*] put off drawing the lots on various pretences, till the people get impatient, and return to their homes. When the crowd is dispersed, the chief of the whole Naikpeekhail [Nikpi Khail] draws the lots, and announces the result, which is received in the victorious party with public distributions of charity, firing of matchlocks, and all other marks of rejoicing. The change of lands is accomplished without much trouble or confusion; each clan of one half Oolooss [*ulas*] is paired with a clan of the other, and the two thus paired, cross over into each other's lands.[92]

And that:

It might also be expected, that there would be a civil war in the Oolooss [*ulas*], as often as the land was to be exchanged; and, in fact, at the expiration of the last term but one, the half of the Naikpeekhail [Nikpi Khail] which was in possession of the best lands, refused to submit to the usual custom of drawing lots. The Mulliks [*malak*s] of the other half complained loudly of this injustice, and called on all the other Accozyes [Akuzis] to prevent the subversion of the ancient custom of the tribe; so many Ooloosses [*ulasunah*] declared in their favour, that their opponents were forced to give way, and to draw lots as usual.[93]

Another aspect was that no grand and permanent residences or houses were constructed and to build anything other than temporary shanties of mud and thatch as dwelling-places was considered as folly. Even the mosques were mere roofs of mud or thatch, whichever came cheaper, resting on three sides on rough mud or stone walls that also included the courtyard on the forth side.[94]

Besides, there were often plots and machinations by powerful, ambitious, or crafty persons and groups to deprive the weaker and poorer of their *dawtar* or to squeeze more for themselves. In cases of exile of some persons, their opponents or even relatives could make common cause against the exiled (although the exiled ones may have been influential and powerful) to refuse granting their share in the *dawtar* at the time of the new *waish* by terming their share as *wrak* (ورک) or lost.

The land liable to re-allotment or interchange was called *dawtar* and its owner *dawtari* (plural: *dawtaryan*). Now, as mentioned earlier, a person was considered Pukhtun/Pukhtan and has had say in the *jargay* (*jargah*s) as long as he retained and possessed his *dawtar* share. Thus, when he lost his *dawtar*, he, as well as his offspring, lost the epithet of Pukhtun/Pukhtan and lost a voice in the *jargay*. Gradually, they came to be ranked in the non-landowners categories, depending on the specific profession adopted. Although a share in the *dawtar* could be purchased and thus a person could achieve the status of a *dawtari* and gain a voice and say in the concerned *jargay*, claiming *dawtar* was not easy a job as is evident from the proverbs: '*Raghay musafar, dawigir shah da dawtar*' (راغے مسافر، دعوي گیر شۀ د دوتر), meaning, 'Strangely enough, (he) came as a traveller/stranger and claimed ownership of *dawtar*'; and '*Raghlay musafar, dawigir shway da dawtar*' (راغلے مسافر، دعوي گیر شوې د دوتر), meaning, 'Strangely enough, you came as a traveller/stranger and became a claimant of *dawtar*.'

Despite its drawbacks, this system of interchange and re-allocation or re-allotment of the different localities, villages, and different categories of the land was one of the cardinal codes that shaped, guided, and regulated the system, lives, affairs, and events of the area held by the Yusufzi.[95]

Badal (بدل)

Although *badal* means revenge, it has other meanings and is used in other contexts as well. *Badal* is the term for reciprocating assistance rendered in any capacity or favour, but preferably reciprocated in a manner that is even better. *Badal* is regarded as the foremost obligation for one, and the greatest liability for the other, in all senses of its meaning and use.

In the case of revenge, *badal* is claimed as an obligation for all forms of criminal acts, and is intended to be carried out without any thought of potential consequences or costs. Not only the aggrieved person, but other family members and sometimes the sub-tribe and tribe too are also involved in the *badal*. Similarly, not only are the culprit(s) or aggressor(s) implicated but his family members and sometimes the sub-tribe and tribe too. The decision on how to react—take revenge, accept compensation, or to forgive—depends on the nature of the crime as well as the aggrieved. Generally, in cases of murder, the most influential and worthy person in the offender's family (called '*da sar saray*' د سر سرے: the leading figure) is killed in return, inflicting a greater loss on the offender's family. *Badal* is not time or space barred.

Badal is a restraining and deterrent force for maintaining and ensuring peace, order, and respect for human life and honour in a semi-acephalous tribal society in the absence of law-enforcing agencies and courts. It compels a person to think about potential consequences, not only for himself, but also for his family, tribe, and descendants, before committing a crime. Even if the crime is not detected at the time, should it be detected at a later date, *badal* would be obligatory. *Badal* is a restraining force and a surety that wrong-doings never go unpunished.

In its other forms and uses, such as providing assistance in some work, or granting a favour, *badal* promotes cooperation among people, and makes communal life easier through acknowledgement of help and favour.

Milmastya (ميلمستيا)

Milmastya, meaning hospitality, is not only meant to be offered to relatives, friends, and those known to the host, but also to strangers and those who invoke it. In *milmastya*, guests are served with food and offered boarding and lodging as required.

It is expected that today's guest shall be a host tomorrow. A Pukhtu saying, therefore, is '*Pukhtun khpalah dudai da bal pah kur khwri*' (پښتون خپله ډوډۍ د بل پۀ کور خوري), meaning 'A Pukhtun eats his own food at another's home.' Guests are mainly of two types: those who may be expected, one day, to be a host and reciprocate the hospitality received (preferably in a better way), and those unlikely to be ever a host. The stranger or wayfarer is called *Khudayi milmah* (خدائي ميلمه), meaning the guest to be served for the Almighty's sake.

A significant aspect of *milmastya* is the warmth with which a guest is meant to be received and served. A number of Pukhtu proverbs and sayings promote this concept, including '*Dudai tah mah gurah khu zama runr tandi tah gurah*' (دوډۍ ته مۀ ګوره خو زما رونر تندي ته ګوره), which means, 'Do not look at the foodstuff but into the warmness in my eyes (with which I serve you)'; and '*Kah da ghwaru gut wi khu chiy tanday but wi pah haghay bah sah kaway*' (كۀ د غوړو ګوټ وي خو چي تندي بوټ وي پۀ هغي به څۀ كوي), which means, 'To hell with the lavish food which is served with wrinkles on the host's forehead.'

Another aspect of *milmastya* is protection of the guest. If the guest has an enmity, or needs protection because of some other reason, his protection is regarded as the responsibility of the host as long as the guest remains within his house or territorial limits.

It was because of *milmastya* that the people, even in the absence of modern means of communication and hotels, did not worry for their food or boarding while travelling. They went to nearby settlements at meal times or at night, for their food and a place to stay, with no concern about their safety or protection.

Jargah (جَرګه)

Jargah (also spelled as *jarga*; and erroneously as *jirgah* and *jirga*) means: consultative assembly; forum; council; council of the tribal chiefs. *Jargah* is the forum and assembly where issues of common and communal interest are discussed and decided (see also the Glossary).

When there is a problem or issue of common interest, or a communal affair, the stakeholders assemble and discuss it. The attendants are free to express their viewpoints and put forward their opinions openly. Decisions are not majority-imposed, but are reached by consensus or unanimity after the deliberations.

Attendance depends on the nature of the problem and the issue being discussed but, generally, not everybody participates in the proceedings of the *jargay*. Only the elders or representatives of the families, members of religious families, religious figures of note and influence, and persons having some degree of influence participate in *jargay* at the ward and village levels; and, select representatives from among themselves to represent them in the *jargay* at the segment and tribe levels.

Jargah has different meanings, functions, composition, and uses in different contexts. These include to conciliate opposing and inimical parties, cool down tempers, strive for amity, effect settlements, mediate between parties, and bring normalcy in cases of tension and disputes. The meaning, formation, composition, and function of a particular *jargah* varies on a case-to-case basis.

The institution of the *jargah* provided a forum for solving common, communal, tribal, and inter-tribal problems, issues, and disputes, as well as personal and domestic problems, and problems between families.

Sharuntya (شرونتیا)

In the case of intentional or deliberate murder, the murderer and his family were liable to revenge (*badal*). However, another possible alternative was *sharuntya*, i.e. banishment or exile or expulsion of such a person or his family from his home or locality. The *sharuntya* lasted till the revenge remained pending or the parties' coming to terms and agreement[96] or for the stipulated period, if it was levied as a punishment by a *jargah* or third party arbiters. Sometimes the *sharuntya* was in turn. For a specific period one party to the dispute remained in exile and the other at home while for the next period it would be the other way round. There are instances of this practice in the Swat State period as well.[97]

Besides, as stated earlier, there had been continuous fighting between the adherents of the two *dalay*. In case of defeat, the defeated or *landay dalah* or their leaders were driven out of their homes and sought asylum with their friends, allies, or *dalah* members in other safer places. They had to strive and struggle, from there, to regain the lost position and possessions.[98] H.G. Raverty has, on the basis of the report of a Qandahari sent by him to Swat, in August 1858, recorded in this respect:

> Whenever two Maliks [*malaks*] or headmen of a village quarrel, the strongest, or the victorious one, if they come to blows, drives the other out of the village. After some time, the fugitive manages, by bribes and other means, to gain over to his side some of the friends and supporters of the successful party, and all the discontented flock to him. After a time he finds an opportunity, when his own party is strong and the other is weak, to enter the village and drive his rival out. This is enacted over and over again, now one is a fugitive, now another; and this it is that causes such contentions in these parts.[99]

The *sharunkay dalah*, or the exiled and banished party, was in some cases allowed to receive the produce of their lands cultivated by their *dihqanan* (ploughmen receiving share in the harvest usually one-fifth), *brakhikhwarah* (crop-sharers), or *faqiran* (those living in others quarters paying no rent but doing forced labour, etcetera, for the owners). In other cases, the land of the exiled was occupied by the *banday dalah*, or the other party, taking its produce.[100]

Raverty has recorded concerning another form, or type, of the *sharuntya*, or banishment, by stating that 'when two Maliks or Kháns chance to fall out, or to have any dispute, the people expel both parties from the place' and 'are then termed *sharúní* or, "the driven out, or expelled".' Elaborating on the point, he has further written:

> In this state, they are compelled to seek shelter in other villages, and are obliged to live on the charity of those who will take them in, for they lose all civil rights on such occasions, and have no claim to wife, or children, dwelling, cattle, or anything whatever. Some continue in this helpless state until they can come to an accommodation, or effect a reconciliation, which often does not take place for years. In Upper Suwát [Swat] they are even more severe than this, for there they expel the families also, and confiscate the property of the disputants altogether. One would imagine that such stringent rules as these would tend to keep the peace, if anything would, yet these people seem, notwithstanding, to be always at feud.[101]

As in *sharuntya*, the exiled or banished person, family, or party, was to seek asylum and support from others: mostly friends and allies, but sometimes also from adherents of the other or opposite *dalah*, the moral, material, and financial support was provided by those to whom the party in exile went and sought asylum and support. Although supported by others in this way, the life of *sharuntya* was at the mercy of others and hence vulnerable. The code of *sharuntya*, therefore, was not only a punishment but a restraining force in regulating society in the tribal environment.

Interestingly, while seeking to establish his view that Afghans, as a popular theory contends, were Bani Israel by ethnicity, Abdul Jabbar Shah has contended that, despite embracing Islam the Afghans had retained some of their old practices, which included banishment of others from their villages, even subduing near relatives, and banishing them from the village.[102]

Nang (ننگ)

Nang means honour, although the English word 'honour' does not depict the same meaning and sense. It is an important component of the code of life and has played a vital role in the social system of Pukhtu. Its primary importance, however, is in preserving national honour and independence. *Nang* has compelled the people to take-up arms in defence of the homeland and the protection of national honour when the occasion has demanded. *Nang* has also been honoured in cases of personal esteem as well as that of family, beloved, friends, dependants, sub-tribe, and tribe.[103]

Riwaj (رواج)

Riwaj means custom, prevalence, and customary law. Although Pukhtuns are mostly Muslims, *riwaj* governs the conduct, lives, and behaviour of the people to a large extent, and is followed more than Islamic law. Some examples are: common law marriage (court marriage) was not recognized; the eldest son received a greater share of a father's inheritance, called *da masharai hisah* (د مشری حصه) and *mashari* (مشري); daughters did not receive any inheritance in property; a widow was entitled to support only until her death or remarriage.

Panah (پناه)

Panah, meaning 'asylum' or 'sanctuary', is an important obligation of the social system. A person from whom *panah* is sought, must provide it. It cannot be denied, even to an arch-enemy. The person in *panah* is protected and defended at all costs, as long as he remains in the *panah* of the concerned person, tribe, etcetera.

An attempt on the life of the person in *panah* is regarded as an act against the provider of *panah*, and hence he has to fight those who do not respect his *panah*. There are instances where, in the absence of male members of a household, the female(s) have defended and protected the person(s) who sought *panah*. Even enemies or members of the opposite *dalah* have been entertained and protected when they have sought *panah*.

Nanawatay (ننواتے)

The negative aspect of *badal* was that it could lead to unending bloodshed, an unending cycle of revenge killings. However, there have been certain codes under which conciliation can be effected and potential bloodshed avoided. One of these codes is *nanawatay*.

When an offending person wishes to prevent or bring an end to the bloodshed and dispute in a peaceful manner, before *badal* is taken, he goes to the adversary, admits guilt, expresses contrition, and throws himself at the adversary's mercy. This has been called *nanawatay*, a type of repentance, and expression of regret of the wrong doing. The party resorting to *nanawatay* sometimes sends, or take with them, their women who are sometimes unveiled or bareheaded: called *sartur sar* (سرتور سر). They may also take the Holy Quran, and have a rope around their necks called '*Paray pah gharah tlal*' (پرے پۀ غاړه تلل), meaning 'Going with the rope in the neck.' The repentant party may also send members of religious families, or *stanadar*, as *nanawatay*.

If the aggrieved party accepts the repentance and agrees to renounce the right of *badal*, *nanawatay* is honoured, a *jargah* is held, conciliation effected, and the matter settled amicably and peacefully. The aggrieved party is required to honour the *nanawatay*; as to do otherwise would bring them a bad name.

Kalay Kalwighi (کلے کلویغي)

Kalay kalwighi is related to communal life. It lays down the guidelines for a multitude of circumstances: participation in betrothals, weddings, and other affairs related to happiness and joy; going to the house of a deceased to express sorrow, grief, and sympathy; visiting a sick person; providing assistance to fellow villagers in need. *Ashar ghubal* (اشرغویل) or cooperating with and assisting each other while harvesting, threshing, cutting grass, and such other jobs that cannot possibly be done individually, or by one family, are also part of *kalay kalwighi*. The society being tribal, and the people mainly living in villages, *kalay kalwighi* has remained an important code and commandment of the social system.

Gham-Khadi (غم ښادي)

To be with and assist others on occasions of sorrow, grief, and distress
(such as illness, accident, or death), as well as occasions of joy (such a
circumcisions, betrothals, or weddings) etcetera is called *gham-khadi*: a
major code and component of the Pukhtuns' life. It is through this code
that the people are not left alone in times of both grief and joy.

Hujrah (حجره)

Hujrah (plural: *hujray*) is not personal property, but communal property
of all the Pukhtuns of the corresponding block of the village, called
tal (تل), or of the whole village. They hold the proprietorial rights jointly
and are collectively responsible for its maintenance. *Hujray* play a vital
role in the social system, or organization, and lives of the people not
merely as men's houses, but also serves many other roles including guest
houses, focal points for community actions and opinions, and a places
for unmarried males to sleep. In this regard, Elphinstone has recorded,
in the early nineteenth century CE, that the *mashar* (head, chief) 'of
each Cundy [Kandi, *tal*] maintains a public apartment [i.e. *hujrah*],
where all councils are held; here also the men meet to converse and
amuse themselves; and here they receive guests, and transact all public
business, unmixed with the members of the other Cundies [Kandis;
talunah]'.[104] *Hujray* are multi-purpose community centres: 'It was from
here that the marriage processions started and the bier was carried to the
grave.'[105] It is to be mentioned that the marriage procession was called
janj (جنج) and its participants were called *janjyan* (جنجیان).

Tarburwali (تربورولي)

The term *tarbur* is used for both a paternal cousin and an enemy, and
tarburwali for both paternal cousinhood and for enmity. Although the
paternal cousins depend on and protect each other, and seek revenge in
case of loss or dishonour incurred on a *tarbur*, they consider each other
as enemies, being immediate rivals for family power and influence.
There is a proverb which means: 'When a cousin is little, rear him,
but when he grows up he is an enemy, make him fight with others.'
Another proverb translates as: 'A cousin starts biting his cousin first.'
Still another one says: 'Keep the cousin poor and use him against others.'

Whereas another one refers to the lack of trust among the cousins by stating that 'Tarbur kah di khar shi hum latai pray mah arawah artaw bah di kri' (تربور کۀ دې خر شي هم لتی پرې مۀ اړوه ارتاو به دې کړي), meaning: 'If the cousin becomes your ass still do not ride on him, he may throw you down.' Thus tarburwali has recognized itself in both roles.

Trabgani (تربګني)

Trabgani denote the ill will, unfriendly relations, and bitter feelings between paternal cousins. McMahon and Ramsay, in their writing about the Pukhtun Code of Life, have stated that 'a man should succour and help his own kith and kin, and yet may be at deadly feud with his own cousins'.[106] This certainly creates problems in tribal society because of its leading to machinations, factions and fractions. But in some respects, it works as a restraining force, keeping balance in the power between rivals or cousins.

Syali Kawal (سيالي کول)

Syali kawal, or to compete so as not to become or be considered low among equals is a trait of the code which works both in positive and negative ways. On the one side, it could induce and motivate worthy deeds, and on the other side create rivalries, ill-feelings, and efforts to bring others down.

Syali has been so engrained in the lives of the people of Swat that a proverb runs thus: 'Syali da Swat siri dah' (سيالي د سوات سيري ده), meaning, 'Syali in Swat is like the sirai land',[107] the status of which cannot be changed or ended. A saying goes: 'Syali da syal khayi' (سيالي د سيال ښائي), meaning: 'Competition sane with the equal.'

Jabah Kawal (ژبه کول)

Jabah kawal, or making a promise and giving assurance, has been one of the cardinal components of the code of life. A promise or assurance—whether of doing or not of an act, work, favour, disfavour, etcetera—is to be honoured and abided by. Those who do not keep their jabah, or word, are never trusted, are looked down upon and considered mean and unworthy: unless there has been some genuine and acceptable reason and ground for not behaving in the required manner.

'*Ma jabah karay dah*' (ما ژبه کړی ده), meaning, 'I have promised, or given my word', is the statement that justifies the relevant action and behaviour and which bars others (friends, family members, and so forth) from compelling the person to do the contrary.[108]

Yadah Kawal (یاده کول)

To make some rules or code or words enjoining, or the otherwise, some action, work, deed, behaviour etcetera is *yadah kawal*. This *yadah* is to be abided by all concerned and its violation is a violation of the code; the transgressor is subservient to the penalty, if any, or is to be considered worthless, and loses regard and respect in the eyes of the people.

Hadbandi (حد بندي)

In case of enmity between two families or parties, living in the same village or locality, and having the chance of confronting each other frequently, creating an unending chance of bloodshed, certain limits were to be marked for them, crossing or violating which was prohibited. This has been *hadbandi*, or drawing of boundaries. The violators were the guilty. Therefore, in case of retaliation, the offending side was not deemed wrong for the action. As is evident from the Swat State record, this code was also retained in the Swat State's time.[109]

Naghah (ناغه)

In cases of no fine having been fixed for a wrongdoing, a fine was to be fixed by consensus of the people concerned, or the *jargah*, and the violators were to pay the fine without any excuse. For instance, when required a ban on cutting some kind of trees or on herding cattle in a particular place or to compel the owners to properly look after their cattle so that not to cause damage to others' crops etcetera, fines were fixed in different proportions keeping in view the nature of the act and the damage incurred. This was *naghah*, which was honoured by all. This practice also continued in the Swat State era.[110]

Nagharah Kawal (نغاره کول)

At times of need or urgency or making an announcement, an alarm drum used to be beaten which was called *nagharah kawal*. For instance, to inform the people to gather and join an action against the invading enemy,[111] and for matter of *lakhkar* against opponents or for getting attention of the people for an announcement etcetera. The people were bound to act accordingly, otherwise they will be stigmatized. The proverb that *da nagharay da Sambat kwanay ta ghagigi* (دا نغارے د سمبت کوني ته غږيږي), meaning: 'The drums are beaten to alarm the people of Sambat and induce them to fight the enemy', is a testimony to it.

Pah Khardang Swarawal (پۀ خرډانگ سورول)

This was a sort of punishment for a wrongdoing. The culprit was carried by two strong men on a wooden beam, with his feet and legs dangling on either side, through the streets. They would stop at different places and announce to the people the particular offence committed by the culprit and warn them of the consequence and punishment which was before their eyes.[112] This was *pah khardang swarawal*, also *pah khardang kawal*, a degrading of a wrongdoer in the eyes of the people. It is no more practised.

Pah Khrah Swarawal (پۀ خره سورول)

A variant of the above, also now defunct, was to seat the culprit on a saddleless donkey facing the tail and take him through the streets, led by a drumbeater. Halting him at squares in such a state, the *aliman* (plural of *alim*) urged the people to abstain from such bad deeds.[113]

Makh Turawal (مخ تورول)

In cases of grave guilt, the face of the culprit was to be blackened with soot from a mosque's lamp (*turki* توركي). Sometimes, his trousers were wound around his head like a turban and the quill of a dead cock, or crow, or owl fitted in his turban. He might be garlanded with bones or old shoes; and the dung of cattle, horses, and donkeys thrown over him. Sometimes, a ride on a donkey was also resorted to (in the manner stated in the preceding sub-topic).[114] This was an amalgam of different punishments, which was adjusted to the nature of the crime for which the punishment was given in a particular case. This kind of thing is no more practised.

Sar Khrayal (سر خرئیل)

The punishment for a woman found to have a bad moral character was generally to shave her head.[115] To further intensify the penalty, sometimes mud from the latrine was applied to the shaved head. Sometimes, the punishment of both *sar khrayal* and *pah khrah swarawal* was also given. One penal punishment in such a case was divorce or banishing of the woman. Therefore, a proverb goes: '*Sar khrayalay khah dah, mirah sharalay nah*', (سر خرئیلے ښہ دہ، میرهٔ شرلے نهٔ), meaning: 'A head shaven woman is better than the one banished by the husband.' Such panel codes, however, are extinct now.

Puzah Prikawal (پوزه پری کول)

For some immoral acts, the nose of the culprit, or wrongdoer, was cut off which was called *puzah prikawal*. Mostly, the noses of women were cut off for allegedly immoral acts, which is also evident from the proverb which states, '*Mirah sharalay khah dah, puzah prikaray nah*' (میرهٔ شرلے ښہ دہ، پوزه پری کمے نهٔ), meaning that, 'The woman banished by her husband is better off than the one whose nose is cut off by her husband.'

Two decrees of the ruler of Swat State, issued in 1963, testify to this practice. In one of the decrees, it is ordained that whoever cut off his wife's nose would have to pay a fine of two thousand rupees or be jailed for seven years, and would have to divorce the wife.[116] The second decree is identical.[117]

According to another verdict given in a case of such a nature by the ruler of Swat State, the accused is first to divorce his wife and then give a bond that, on his release from jail, he will not live in Swat State, or else pay a fine of two thousand rupees.[118]

Las Warkawal (لاس ورکول)

To help and assist others at the times of need and emergencies was termed as *las warkawal*. This works well at the times of urgent needs and emergencies.

Prikrah Kawal (پریکره کول)

To end or close relationship, or not to deliberate more on or about an issue etcetera, was called *prikrah kawal*. Although on the one side it worked negatively, this had positive role in the sense that because of the fear or threat of closing a relationship it also worked as restraining force in not taking the issue to the extreme.

Tawanawal (تاوانول)

To put blame of, especially a monetary, loss or something over other and compelling him/her to pay the price, or the cost, or the monetary loss, or restitution is *tawanawal*. Although in some cases *tawanawal* is not regarded praiseworthy, especially when the other side's action is not intentional and wilful, or the loss is not incurred deliberately, its fear works as a restraining force in causing damages and losses to others and to remain alert, vigilant, and cautious in such matters.

Sayyad Abdul Jabbar Shah has contended that, aside from the *waish* system, Shaikh Mali specified punishments for all crimes and penalties in which a glimpse of the old Israelite Shariat can be found. More to the point, it has also been attempted to link them to the Islamic Shariat. Shaikh Mali termed the code *lar* (لار), which in English mean 'Path', the 'code of life', and the 'code of conduct'. Thus, the Arabic word *shara* and Pashto word *lar* have the same meaning. This law (Shaikh Mali's instituted law) is not written and recorded in any book but is known and memorised orally.[119]

Some people consider Pukhtu, the Pukhtun Code of Life, to be in conformity with Islamic teachings and codes and hence consider it their other form, while some have the opposite view. A Pukhtu saying is: '*Pukhtu pinzam mazhab day*'(پښتو پينځم مذهب دے), which means that, 'Pukhtu is the fifth of the Muslim schools of *fiqah*' (the first four being the Maliki, Hanafi, Shafi'i, and Hanbali *fiqah*s, or schools of thought, of Islamic jurisprudence); this implies that Pukhtu is different from the recognized Islamic codes but it is considered equally sacred.

As stated earlier, this state of affairs and mode of ruling worked, continued, and functioned for about four centuries. It was after the emergence of Swat State in 1915, and the rise to power, in 1917, of Miangul Abdul Wadud aka Bacha Sahib, that a sea change took place.[120] Also, as stated in note 80 of this chapter, changes in the system were effected in the parts of the Swat Valley, that were not the territory of Swat State, which went into the loose control or protectorate of the colonial British in 1895, and also those which went permanently under the rule of the Dir State in 1922.

NOTES

1. See Akhun Darwizah, *Tazkiratul Abrar-i wal Ashrar* (Persian) (Peshawar: Islami Kutub Khanah, n.d.), 86–91. Akhun Darwizah's book uses the name 'Bantaki' (see ibid., 91), whereas Abdul Jabbar Shah refers to 'Niki' (Sayyad Abdul Jabbar Shah Sithanawi, *Kitab al-Ibra: Subah Sarhad wa Afghanistan ki Char Sau Salah Tarikh; 1500 Iswi ta 1900 Iswi* (Urdu), Vol. 1 (Islamabad: Poorab Academy, 2011), 176), but it is generally called 'Nushki'. Also see Sithanawi, *Kitab al-Ibra: Subah Sarhad wa Afghanistan ki Char Sau Salah Tarikh; 1500 Iswi ta 1900 Iswi*, Vol. 1, 176.
2. Mountstuart Elphinstone, *An Account of the Kingdom of Caubul*, with new introduction by Olaf Caroe, Vol. 2 (repr., Karachi: Oxford University Press, 1972), 9.
3. Sithanawi, *Kitab al-Ibra: Subah Sarhad wa Afghanistan ki Char Sau Salah Tarikh; 1500 Iswi ta 1900 Iswi*, Vol. 1, 176.
4. For detail of the points mentioned, see Pir Muazam Shah, *Tawarikh Hafiz Rahmat Khani*, with *dibachah* by Muhammad Nawaz Tair (Pashto/Persian) (2nd impression, Peshawar: Pukhtu Academy, 1987), 5–62; Elphinstone, *An Account of the Kingdom of Caubul*, Vol. 2, 9–13; Henry George Raverty, *Notes on Afghanistan and Baluchistan*, Vol. 1 (2nd edn. in Pakistan, Quetta: Nisa Traders, 1982), 122–7; Khan Roshan Khan, *Yusufzai Qaum ki Sarguzasht* (Urdu) (Karachi: Roshan Khan and Company, 1986), 19–79; Darwizah, *Tazkiratul Abrar-i wal Ashrar*, 91–5; Sithanawi, *Kitab al-Ibra: Subah Sarhad wa Afghanistan ki Char Sau Salah Tarikh; 1500 Iswi ta 1900 Iswi*, Vol. 1, 177–83.
5. See Darwizah, *Tazkiratul Abrar-i wal Ashrar*, 91–2; Sithanawi, *Kitab al-Ibra: Subah Sarhad wa Afghanistan ki Char Sau Salah Tarikh; 1500 Iswi ta 1900 Iswi*, Vol. 1, 179–80.
6. See Shah, *Tawarikh Hafiz Rahmat Khani*, 17–26; Khan, *Yusufzai Qaum ki Sarguzasht*, 31–3; Olaf Caroe, *The Pathans: 550 B.C.–A.D. 1957* (repr., Karachi: Oxford University Press, 1976), 174.
7. See Sayyed Mohd. Abdul Ghafoor Qasmi, *The History of Swat* (Peshawar: Printed by D.C. Anand & Sons, 1940), 4; Taj Muhammad Khan Zaibsar, *Uruj-i Afghan*, Vol. 2 (Riyasat-i Swat, 1361 AH), 93.
8. See H.W. Bellew, *A General Report on the Yusufzais* (3rd edn., Lahore: Sang-e-Meel Publications, 1994), 162.
9. See Darwizah, *Tazkiratul Abrar-i wal Ashrar*, 93.
10. Sithanawi, *Kitab al-Ibra: Subah Sarhad wa Afghanistan ki Char Sau Salah Tarikh; 1500 Iswi ta 1900 Iswi*, Vol. 1, 180.
11. *Gazetteer of the Peshawar District, 1897–98* (repr., Lahore: Sang-e-Meel Publications, 1989), 54.
12. Zaibsar, *Uruj-i Afghan*, Vol. 2, 94.
13. Shah, *Tawarikh Hafiz Rahmat Khani*, 28–9.
14. Ibid., 22.
15. Ibid., 23.
16. See the year of birth given to the photo of Malak Ahmad, picture reproduced in Abasin Yusufzay, comp. and ed., *Da Pukhtunkhwa Bani: Malak Ahmad Baba*

(1470 Iswi–1535 Iswi) (Mingora, Swat: Shoaib Sons Publishers & Booksellers, 2016).

17. For Olaf Caroe's version in this respect, who take it between 1480 and 1490 CE, see Caroe, *The Pathans*, 174.

18. See Shah, *Tawarikh Hafiz Rahmat Khani*, 65.

19. Raverty, *Notes on Afghanistan and Baluchistan*, Vol. 1, 240.

20. See Shah, *Tawarikh Hafiz Rahmat Khani*, 62.

21. Ibid., 27–8.

22. See ibid., 63–5.

23. For detail, see ibid., 63–70.

24. See Sithanawi, *Kitab al-Ibra: Subah Sarhad wa Afghanistan ki Char Sau Salah Tarikh; 1500 Iswi ta 1900 Iswi*, Vol. 1, 182, 184.

25. A.H. McMahon and A.D.G. Ramsay, *Report on the Tribes of the Malakand Political Agency (Exclusive of Chitral)*, revised by R.L. Kennion (Peshawar: Government Press, North-West Frontier Province, 1916), 29. Also see Shah, *Tawarikh Hafiz Rahmat Khani*, 69–71. For Akhun Darwizah's version of this strategy, see Darwizah, *Tazkiratul Abrar-i wal Ashrar*, 95. Also see Raverty, *Notes on Afghanistan and Baluchistan*, Vol. 1, 240–1; Sithanawi, *Kitab al-Ibra: Subah Sarhad wa Afghanistan ki Char Sau Salah Tarikh; 1500 Iswi ta 1900 Iswi*, Vol. 1, 184.

26. See Darwizah, *Tazkiratul Abrar-i wal Ashrar*, 95, 106.

27. See Shah, *Tawarikh Hafiz Rahmat Khani*, 71–6. Also see Raverty, *Notes on Afghanistan and Baluchistan*, Vol. 1, 234.

28. Shah, *Tawarikh Hafiz Rahmat Khani*, 76–8.

29. Ibid., 81.

30. See Roshan Khan, *Malikah-i Swat* (Karachi: Roshan Khan and Company, 1983), 26.

31. See Shah, *Tawarikh Hafiz Rahmat Khani*, 71–2. Also see Khan, *Malikah-i Swat*, 21.

32. See Zahirud-din Muhammad Babur, *Babur-Nama*, trans. from the original Turki text by Annette S. Beveridge (repr., Lahore: Sang-e-Meel Publications, 1987), 372–4; Zahiruddin Muhammad Babur, *Waqay-i Babur*, Urdu trans. Yunus Jafri, from the Persian trans. of Abdur Rahim Khan-i Khanan, with notes and annotation by Hasan Beg (Krekardi, Scotland: Shahar Banu Publishers, 2007), 192.

33. Babur, *Babur-Nama*, 376; Babur, *Waqay-i Babur*, 193–4.

34. Babur, *Babur-Nama*, 400; Babur, *Waqay-i Babur*, 208. Also see William Erskine, *A History of India Under Baber* (repr., Karachi: Oxford University Press, 1974), 338; William Erskine, *A History of India under the Two First Sovereigns of the House of Taimur, Báber and Humáyun*, Vol. 1 (repr., Shannon: Irish University Press, 1972), 338.

35. See Shah, *Tawarikh Hafiz Rahmat Khani*, 72.

36. See Zahiruddin Babur, *Tuzuk-i Baburi*, Urdu trans. Rashid Akhtar Nadwi (Lahore: Sang-e-Meel Publications, n.d.), 163.

37. See Muhammad Akhtar, *Tajak Swati wa Mumlikat-i Gabar Tarikh kay Aayinah mayn* (Urdu) (Abbottabad: Sarhad Urdu Academy, 2002), 375.

38. McMahon and A.D.G. Ramsay, *Report on the Tribes of the Malakand Political Agency (Exclusive of Chitral)*, revised by R.L. Kennion, 29–30.

39. See Bellew, *A General Report on the Yusufzais*, 64.

40. For Babur's version, see Babur, *Babur-Nama*, 400; Babur, *Waqay-i Babur*, 208.
41. *Imperial Gazetteer of India: Provincial Series; North-West Frontier Province* (henceforward *Imperial Gazetteer of India, NWFP*) (repr., Lahore: Sang-e-Meel Publications, 1991), 217.
42. Shah, *Tawarikh Hafiz Rahmat Khani*, 103.
43. Ibid., 104–7.
44. See ibid., 105 n. *.
45. See Darwizah, *Tazkiratul Abrar-i wal Ashrar*, 95.
46. Sithanawi, *Kitab al-Ibra: Subah Sarhad wa Afghanistan ki Char Sau Salah Tarikh; 1500 Iswi ta 1900 Iswi*, Vol. 1, 184.
47. For Olaf Caroe's version in this respect, see Caroe, *The Pathans*, 181–3.
48. Elphinstone, *An Account of the Kingdom of Caubul*, Vol. 2, 14.
49. *Imperial Gazetteer of India, NWFP*, 217.
50. Fredrik Barth, 'Ecologic Relationships of Ethnic Groups in Swat, North Pakistan', *American Anthropologist*, 58/6 (December 1956), 1081.
51. Ibid.
52. John Biddulph, *Tribes of the Hindoo Koosh*, with preface to the 1971 edition by Karl Gratzl (repr., Lahore: Ali Kamran Publishers, 1986), 70.
53. See Allah Bakhsh Yusufi, *Yusufzai* (Urdu) (Karachi: Muhammad Ali Educational Society, 1960), 39–40, 455; Denzil Ibbetson, *Punjab Castes* (repr., Delhi: Low Price Publications, 1993), 62–3, 85–8; H.W. Bellew, *The Races of Afghanistan* (repr., Lahore: Sh. Mubarak Ali, n.d.), 67–71; H.W. Bellew, *An Inquiry into the Ethnography of Afghanistan* (repr., Karachi: Indus Publications, 1977), 75–6, 81; *A Glossary of the Tribes and Castes of the Punjab and North-West Frontier Province*, Vol. 3 (repr., Lahore: Aziz Publishers, 1978), 249–50.
54. Ahmad Hasan Dani, *Peshawar: Historic City of the Frontier* (2nd edn., Lahore: Sang-e-Meel Publications, 1995), 92–4.
55. Bellew, *A General Report on the Yusufzais*, 192.
56. See Shah, *Tawarikh Hafiz Rahmat Khani*, 28–9.
57. Ibid., 147.
    It is to be noted that the meaning of the word *khan* depends on the particular context in which it is used. It is used as a title for a chief; as a form of address and to show respect to a landowner or any other person and is also a personal name. On the other hand it can be used sarcastically for an unworthy person. In this book it is used to refer to a tribal chief.
58. After the emergence of Swat State in 1915, the situation gradually changed and the Swat State rulers started to designate whoever they wished as *khanan* and *malakan*, who besides other perks were also paid stipends or *muwajib* (locally *majab*) from the state exchequer, the amount of which represented the status of the *khan* or *malak* concerned. After the final merger of Swat State into the then Province of West Pakistan in 1969 and later into the then NWFP in 1970, this system came to an end, as neither did the people select the *khanan* and *malakan* nor did the government. Interestingly, all the families and offspring of the previous *khanan* and *malakan* continue to use these titles. But they have neither the role, as was in the pre- Swat State period nor that of the Swat State time.
59. For Barth's evaluation, see Fredrik Barth, *Political Leadership among Swat Pathans* (London: The Athlone Press, 1959).

60. Also see Sirajuddin Swati, *Sarguzasht-i Swat* (Urdu) (Lahore: Al-Hamra Academy, 1970), 8–9; Makhdum Tasadduq Ahmad, *Social Organization of Yusufzai Swat: A Study in Social Change* (Lahore: Panjab University Press, 1962), 21–4.

61. Also see Muhammad Asif Khan, *Tarikh-i Riyasat-i Swat wa Sawanih-i Hayat Baniy-i Riyasat-i Swat Hazrat Miangul Gul Shahzadah Abdul Wadud Khan Badshah Sahib,* with *dibachah, hisah awal, saluramah hisah,* and *hisah pinzamah* by Muhammad Asif Khan (Pashto) (Printed by Ferozsons Ltd., Peshawar [1958]), 176–9; Ahmad, *Social Organization of Yusufzai Swat: A Study in Social Change,* 32–3.

62. McMahon and A.D.G. Ramsay, *Report on the Tribes of the Malakand Political Agency (Exclusive of Chitral),* revised by R.L. Kennion, 67. Also see A.H. McMahon and A.D.G. Ramsay, *Report on the Tribes of Dir, Swat and Bajour together with the Utman-Khel and Sam Ranizai,* edited with introduction by R.O. Christensen (repr., Peshawar: Saeed Book Bank, 1981), 34.

63. Ahmad, *Social Organization of Yusufzai Swat: A Study in Social Change,* 8–9.

64. Also see Khan, *Tarikh-i Riyasat-i Swat wa Sawanih-i Hayat Baniy-i Riyasat-i Swat Hazrat Miangul Gul Shahzadah Abdul Wadud Khan Badshah Sahib,* 179; Elphinstone, *An Account of the Kingdom of Caubul,* Vol. 2, 27–30.

65. See Ahmad, *Social Organization of Yusufzai Swat: A Study in Social Change,* 14–15.

66. McMahon and A.D.G. Ramsay, *Report on the Tribes of the Malakand Political Agency (Exclusive of Chitral),* revised by R.L. Kennion, 68; McMahon and A.D.G. Ramsay, *Report on the Tribes of Dir, Swat and Bajour together with the Utman-Khel and Sam Ranizai,* 34.

67. Also see McMahon and A.D.G. Ramsay, *Report on the Tribes of the Malakand Political Agency (Exclusive of Chitral),* revised by R.L. Kennion, 67.

68. Also see ibid., 17.

69. Ahmad, *Social Organization of Yusufzai Swat: A Study in Social Change,* 14.

70. See ibid., 14, 31–2, 36.

71. Ibid., 17–18.

72. Bellew, *A General Report on the Yusufzais,* 187.

73. Ahmad, *Social Organization of Yusufzai Swat: A Study in Social Change,* 18, 38–9. For detail about the *stanadar,* their composition, status, and role, see ibid., 17–18, 36, 38–9; Bellew, *A General Report on the Yusufzais,* 184–90; Barth, *Political Leadership among Swat Pathans.*

74. Shah, *Tawarikh Hafiz Rahmat Khani,* 27–8.

75. McMahon and A.D.G. Ramsay, *Report on the Tribes of the Malakand Political Agency (Exclusive of Chitral),* revised by R.L. Kennion, 67; McMahon and A.D.G. Ramsay, *Report on the Tribes of Dir, Swat and Bajour together with the Utman-Khel and Sam Ranizai,* 33.

76. McMahon and A.D.G. Ramsay, *Report on the Tribes of the Malakand Political Agency (Exclusive of Chitral),* revised by R.L. Kennion, 67; McMahon and A.D.G. Ramsay, *Report on the Tribes of Dir, Swat and Bajour together with the Utman-Khel and Sam Ranizai,* 33.

77. Elphinstone, *An Account of the Kingdom of Caubul,* Vol. 2, 18–19.

78. Ibid., 21.

79. McMahon and A.D.G. Ramsay, *Report on the Tribes of the Malakand Political Agency (Exclusive of Chitral)*, revised by R.L. Kennion, 66.

80. Changes in the system were also effected in the parts of the Swat Valley which were not part of Swat State and went into loose control or protectorate of the colonial British in 1895, and also in those that went permanently under the rule of the Dir State in 1922.

81. Ahmad, *Social Organization of Yusufzai Swat: A Study in Social Change*, 8–9.

82. Also see Elphinstone, *An Account of the Kingdom of Caubul*, Vol. 2, 28.

83. McMahon and A.D.G. Ramsay, *Report on the Tribes of the Malakand Political Agency (Exclusive of Chitral)*, revised by R.L. Kennion, 11.

84. For the points and the detail, see Sultan-i-Rome, *The North-West Frontier (Khyber Pakhtunkhwa): Essays on History* (Karachi: Oxford University Press, 2013), chapter 3.

85. See the years of birth and death given to the photo of Malak Ahmad and the year given on the inscription of Malak Ahmad's tomb, pictures reproduced in Yusufzay, comp. and ed., *Da Pukhtunkhwa Bani: Malak Ahmad Baba (1470 Iswi–1535 Iswi)*.

86. Shah, *Tawarikh Hafiz Rahmat Khani*, 146. According to *Tawarikh Hafiz Rahmat Khani*, Shaikh Mali was a pious person and, under Malak Ahmad, leader of all the Yusufzi and Mandanr (ibid., 145); and Akhun Darwizah has twice mentioned him as Malak Shaikh Mali (see Darwizah, *Tazkiratul Abrar-i wal Ashrar*, 95, 106).

87. See Shah, *Tawarikh Hafiz Rahmat Khani*, 145; Darwizah, *Tazkiratul Abrar-i wal Ashrar*, 106.

88. For detail about the *waish* (*wesh*) system, its different aspects, and how it was abolished during 1925–1929 CE in the Swat State period, see Sultan-i-Rome, *Swat State (1915–1969): From Genesis to Merger; An Analysis of Political, Administrative, Socio-Political, and Economic Developments* (Karachi: Oxford University Press, 2008), 229–37; Sultan-i-Rome, *Forestry in the Princely State of Swat and Kalam (North-West Pakistan): A Historical Perspective on Norms and Practices*, IP6 Working Paper No.6 (Zurich: Swiss National Centre of Competence in Research (NCCR) North-South, 2005), 31–44; Sultan-i-Rome, *Land and Forest Governance in Swat: Transition from Tribal System to State to Pakistan* (Karachi: Oxford University Press, 2016), chapter 2. Also see Sithanawi, *Kitab al-Ibra: Subah Sarhad wa Afghanistan ki Char Sau Salah Tarikh; 1500 Iswi ta 1900 Iswi*, Vol. 1, 105, 171–2, 185–7.

89. Ahmad, *Social Organization of Yusufzai Swat: A Study in Social Change*, 12–13.

90. McMahon and A.D.G. Ramsay, *Report on the Tribes of the Malakand Political Agency (Exclusive of Chitral)*, revised by R.L. Kennion, 18.

91. Ibid., 66.

92. Elphinstone, *An Account of the Kingdom of Caubul*, Vol. 2, 15–16.

93. Ibid., 16.

94. McMahon and A.D.G. Ramsay, *Report on the Tribes of the Malakand Political Agency (Exclusive of Chitral)*, revised by R.L. Kennion, 19.

95. For detail about how, and to what extent the *waish* system affected the system and the lives of the people, see Ahmad, *Social Organization of Yusufzai Swat: A Study in Social Change*, 12–13; McMahon and A.D.G. Ramsay, *Report on the Tribes of the Malakand Political Agency (Exclusive of Chitral)*, revised by R.L. Kennion, 17–19, 66–8.

96. For such instance, also see Elphinstone, *An Account of the Kingdom of Caubul*, Vol. 2, 21–2.

97. See for instances, *Kitab No. 6: Munsifan Riyasat-i Swat, az Ibtida-i Safhah 1/6-10-61 Lighayat-i Safhah 373/23-9-67 (Purana: No. 2, Register Daftar Munsifan)*, Faisalah No. 211, dated 18 October 1966; *Riwaj Namah-i Swat* (Urdu), comp. Ghulam Habib Khan, Superintendent, Deputy Commissioner Office, Swat (n.p., n.d.), 62–5, 69–70. According to Muhammad Asif Khan, it is not *Riwaj Namah* (customary law book) but *Mizaj Namah* (temperament law book) as it contains the decisions/verdicts/orders that the Wali Sahib (Miangul Jahanzeb, ruler of Swat State, who ruled from 12 December 1949 till 15 August 1969) made according to his temperament. (Muhammad Asif Khan, interview by the author, at Saidu Sharif, Swat, 24 May 1998).

98. Also see Swati, *Sarguzasht-i Swat*, 7–8; McMahon and A.D.G. Ramsay, *Report on the Tribes of the Malakand Political Agency (Exclusive of Chitral)*, revised by R.L. Kennion, 67.

99. H.G. Raverty, 'An account of Upper and Lower Suwát, and the Kohistán, to the source of the Suwát River; with an account of the tribes inhabiting those valleys', *Journal of the Asiatic Society* (Calcutta), 31/3 (1862), 273. Also see Raverty, *Notes on Afghanistan and Baluchistan*, Vol. 1, 211.

100. McMahon and A.D.G. Ramsay, *Report on the Tribes of the Malakand Political Agency (Exclusive of Chitral)*, revised by R.L. Kennion, 67.

101. Raverty, *Notes on Afghanistan and Baluchistan*, Vol. 1, 211. Also see Raverty, 'An account of Upper and Lower Suwát, and the Kohistán, to the source of the Suwát River; with an account of the tribes inhabiting those valleys', 272–3.

102. See Sithanawi, *Kitab al-Ibra: Subah Sarhad wa Afghanistan ki Char Sau Salah Tarikh; 1500 Iswi ta 1900 Iswi*, Vol. 1, 161.

103. For the instance of a war fought, in Swat, for three years ensued because of *nang* for a dependent's cause, see Elphinstone, *An Account of the Kingdom of Caubul*, Vol. 2, 23–5.

104. Elphinstone, *An Account of the Kingdom of Caubul*, Vol. 2, 20.

105. Ahmad, *Social Organization of Yusufzai Swat: A Study in Social Change*, 27.

106. McMahon and A.D.G. Ramsay, *Report on the Tribes of the Malakand Political Agency (Exclusive of Chitral)*, revised by R.L. Kennion, p. 11. Also see Ahmad, *Social Organization of Yusufzai Swat: A Study in Social Change*, 13, 22, 32–3.

107. For detail about the *sirai* (*serai*) land and its status, see Sultan-i-Rome, *Swat State (1915–1969): From Genesis to Merger*, 234–5; Sultan-i-Rome, *Forestry in the Princely State of Swat and Kalam (North-West Pakistan): A Historical Perspective on Norms and Practices*, 33; Sultan-i-Rome, *Land and Forest Governance in Swat: Transition from Tribal System to State to Pakistan*, chapter 2.

108. Also see Swati, *Sarguzasht-i Swat*, 8–9.

109. For instances, see *Riwaj Namah-i Swat*, 57–64.

110. For instances, see ibid., 138–9, 141.

111. Also see Bellew, *A General Report on the Yusufzais*, 227.

112. See Muhammad Nawaz Tair, *dibachah* to Shah, *Tawarikh Hafiz Rahmat Khani*, 29.

113. See ibid.

114. See ibid., 29–30.

115. See ibid., 30.

116. See decree of Hukamran Riyasat-i Swat (printed), No. 46, 25 November 1963, File No. nil, in *District Record Room, Gulkadah, Swat*; Copy also in *Personal Collection of the Author, Hazarah, Swat*. Both the number and date had been given by hand most probably after the merger of the state. Also see Sultan-i-Rome, *Swat State (1915–1969): From Genesis to Merger*, 200; *Riwaj Namah-i Swat*, 120.

117. See decree of Hukamran Riyasat-i Swat (printed), No. 49, 25 November 1963, File No. nil, in *District Record Room, Gulkadah, Swat*; Copy also in *Personal Collection of the Author, Hazarah, Swat*. Both the number and date had been given by hand most probably after the merger of the state. Also see Sultan-i-Rome, *Swat State (1915–1969): From Genesis to Merger*, 200.

118. See *Riwaj Namah-i Swat*, 121.

119. See Sithanawi, *Kitab al-Ibra: Subah Sarhad wa Afghanistan ki Char Sau Salah Tarikh; 1500 Iswi ta 1900 Iswi*, Vol. 1, 186.

120. For detail of the changes brought, see Sultan-i-Rome, *Swat State (1915–1969): From Genesis to Merger*.

1. Ramachandara's *ashnan* pit on the top of Ilam Mountain
(courtesy: Dr Mohammad Usman FRCS).

2. A view of Ilam top
(courtesy: Dr Mohammad Usman FRCS).

3. View of Ilam Mountain from Barikut side
(photo by Sultan-i-Rome, 19 June 2013).

4. Seated Buddha and Cave at Ghaligay
(photo by Sultan-i-Rome, 18 December 2011).

5. Seated Buddha at Shakhurai (wrongly called Jahanabad)
(photo by Sultan-i-Rome, 1 July 2019).

6. The Shingardar Stupa near Ghaligay
(photo by Sultan-i-Rome, 18 December 2011).

7. Stupa at archaeological site Butkara I
(photo by Sultan-i-Rome, 2 July 2019).

8. Stupa at archaeological site Butkara I, with three different statues in front (photo by Sultan-i-Rome, 2 July 2019).

9. Chapels at archaeological site Saidu Sharif (photo by Sultan-i-Rome, 2 July 2019).

10. Votive stupa at archaeological site Saidu Sharif (photo by Sultan-i-Rome, 2 July 2019).

11. A stupa at Gumbatunah in Shamuzi
(photo by Sultan-i-Rome, 5 July 2019).

12. View of Bazira (Barikut Ghwandai) from the side
of the Swat River (photo by Sultan-i-Rome, 5 July 2019).

13. A view of archaeological site Barikut Ghwandai 4–5:
the quarter at the southwest corner of the city (*ca.* 270 CE)
(photo by Sultan-i-Rome, 5 July 2019).

14. A view of archaeological site Barikut Ghwandai 11:
Block B, one of the rooms of the monastic quarter
(*ca.* 200 CE)(photo by Sultan-i-Rome, 5 July 2019).

15. A view of archaeological site Barikut Ghwandai 2: the
pillared temple of the Shahi dynasty (*ca.* 870 CE)
(photo by Sultan-i-Rome, 5 July 2019).

16. A view of Aba Sayb (Saib; Sahib)
China site near Najigram
(photo by Sultan-i-Rome, 5 July 2019).

17. A stupa at the Aba Sayb (Saib; Sahib) China site near Najigram (photo by Sultan-i-Rome, 5 July 2019).

18. Stupa called Masum Shahid Stupa, now in a graveyard at Jrandu Dag near Najigram (photo by Sultan-i-Rome, 5 July 2019).

19. Buddhist shrine at Balu Kalay in Kandak side-valley, at some distance from Barikut (photo by Sultan-i-Rome, 5 July 2019).

20. A cell at archaeological site Butkara III
(photo by Sultan-i-Rome, 30 July 2019).

21. A votive stupa at archaeological site Butkara III
(photo by Sultan-i-Rome, 30 July 2019).

22. Buddha's footprints at Swat Museum
(photo by Sultan-i-Rome, 6 July 2019).

23. The site of the rock/boulder (opposite village Jaray) at which Buddha dried his clothes, now submerged in the Swat River after the 2010 floods (photo by Sultan-i-Rome, 21 July 2019)

24. Buddhists remains adjacent to the Ghaznavid Mosque at Udigram (photo by Sultan-i-Rome, 6 July 2019).

25. Outer wall of Raja Gira's Castle at Udigram
(photo by Sultan-i-Rome, 6 July 2019).

26. View of Raja Gira's Castle at Udigram
(photo by Sultan-i-Rome, 6 July 2019).

27. A view of the Swat Valley from Raja
Gira's Castle at Udigram
(photo by Sultan-i-Rome, 6 July 2019).

28. The Ghaznavid Mosque, in the slope of Mount Gira, at Udigram (photo by Sultan-i-Rome, 6 July 2019).

29. An old hujrah in village Khazanah (Shamuzi) called Da Zarif Khilu Hujrah (Photo by Sultan-i-Rome, 20 July 2019).

30. Outer wall of an old hujrah in village Garhai (Shamuzi) called Da Arya Khilu Barah Hujrah (photo by Sultan-i-Rome, 20 July 2019).

31. Inner view of an old *hujrah* in village Garhai
(Shamuzi) called Da Arya Khilu Barah Hujrah
(photo by Sultan-i-Rome, 20 July 2019).

32. An old mosque in Bar Aba Khail in Nikpi Khail
(courtesy: Dr Mohammad Usman FRCS,
1 November 2006).

33. An old mosque at Bar Kalay Saidu Sharif
(photo by Sultan-i-Rome, 6 August 2019).

8

THE MUGHALS AND SWAT

As is evident from the previous chapters, the Yusufzi left Kabul in consequence of the then ruler of Kabul, Ulugh Beg, massacring their chiefs. Eventually, they occupied Swat. While they were struggling for Swat, Ulugh Beg had passed away and his nephew Zahiruddin Babur had occupied and taken charge of Kabul in 1504 CE.

BABUR AND SWAT

Babur, the founder of Mughal dynastic rule in India, came from Farghanah (now in the present-day State of Uzbekistan in Central Asia). While he occupied Kabul, the Yusufzi gained their foothold in Swat. Collision between the two sides was unavoidable as one of Babur's routes to India fell within the domain of the Yusufzi. With the intention of attacking the Yusufzi, Babur marched on Swat and dismounted between the water of Panjkurah (Panjkora) and the united waters of Jandul and Bajawar.[1]

Tawarikh Hafiz Rahmat Khani has claimed that the Dalazak bribed or gave seventy thousand rupees to Babur to kill Malak Ahmad, the Yusufzi chief.[2] To carry out the deed, Babur summoned Malak Ahmad to Kabul. The Yusufzi collected presents for Babur; and Malak Ahmad left Swat for Kabul, along with some other leading figures. The plot, however, failed as Babur's attempt of hitting Malak Ahmad with an arrow did not succeed because Malak Ahmad opened his clothes and bared his chest so that Babur's shot did not fail to strike correctly. For Malak Ahmad's act, Babur honoured him and bestowed robes of honour and gold earrings upon the delegation members and bade him farewell with all honours.[3]

The next year, Babur re-summoned Malak Ahmad to Kabul for consultation regarding certain matters. Malak Ahmad summoned the Yusufzi's gathering, and apprised them of the call from Kabul and of his apprehensions about going to Kabul. As a result of the deliberations, it was decided that this time Malak Shah Mansur would go to Kabul. Presents for Babur were collected, and Shah Mansur left. He met Babur, who showed his displeasure over Shah Mansur's coming instead of Malak Ahmad. At the conclusion of Shah Mansur's considerable stay in Kabul, Babur said farewell to him with a robe of honour. Back in Swat, Shah Mansur apprised his people of the Kabul story. As Malak Ahmad had refused to go to Kabul and had sent Shah Mansur instead, he feared that Babur would come after Malak Ahmad in person or would send his forces but would leave no stone unturned to destroy the Yusufzi. So, as a precautionary measure, he advised them to take refuge in the Murah (Morah) Hill.[4]

On the other side, after Shah Mansur's leaving for home, Babur left Kabul for Swat via Bajawar, at the head of a large armed force. After dealing with Mir Haidar Ali Gabari and his people in Bajawar, Babur turned towards Swat. He wrote to Malak Ahmad to come to him, solemnly promising that he would not be harmed but would be honoured and rewarded. But Malak Ahmad could not be trapped and ignored the summons. Annoyed at Malak Ahmad's not attending him, Babur resolved to invade in the hope that because of this fear he may come and request. His forces left for Manglawar, crossed the Swat River, reached Manglawar, and plundered all that were outside the fort. Those that were in the fort with Sultan Awais (Uwais; Wais) remained safe as the fort was strong. After this, Babur retired from Manglawar to Diyarun.[5]

After camping at Diyarun, Babur appointed spies to investigate the route to Murah (Mahurah) in order to attack it. Malak Ahmad, however, had secured all the routes. Finding no other way, Babur resolved to go in person in the guise of a mendicant. In this way, he succeeded in reaching the Yusufzi houses on the top of Murah. By chance, he saw, from the outside through the door of the house, Shah Mansur's daughter Bibi Mubarakah and fell in love with her. He kept the evidence of his subterfuge, which was the meat of a cow sacrificed on the eve of Eid-ul-Azha and given him by Bibi Mubarakah, thinking him a beggar. Babur enquired about the girl and was told she was the daughter of Shah Mansur. He asked Shah Mansur for her hand in marriage but the latter denied he had any daughter. At Babur's showing the signs and proofs, and requesting in a somewhat humble manner, Malak Ahmad at last agreed to accept the match. This was also because of the Yusufzi wishing him to honour Babur's request. Consequently, Bibi Mubarakah was married to Babur with pomp and splendour when he was still in Bajawar. After this, Babur went back to Kabul.[6]

The account of *Tawarikh Hafiz Rahmat Khani* is silent on the point of the rival rulers of Swat, Sultan Awais and Sultan Alauddin, waiting on Babur in Bajawar, serving him there, and his bestowing robes of honour upon them. It is surprising that Babur came in pursuit of the Yusufzi, as is also evident from the account of *Tawarikh Hafiz Rahmat Khani*, but, instead of first invading and dealing with them in the nearby Lower Swat, he invaded the far-off Manglawar in Upper Swat, the seat of Sultan Awais, who was not only the Yusufzi's enemy, but had served Babur in Bajawar for which Babur had honoured him with a robe of honour.

The account of eleven years is missing in Babur's *Tuzuk*. He has resumed his account from 1 Muharram 925 AH (2 January 1519 CE). Hence, his *Tuzuk* has neither provided the specifics about the causes and other details of his expedition[7] nor does he reveal the details about his relations and communication with the Yusufzi in the preceding days and years. It has nevertheless provided clear information about the succeeding events, the two more significant of which are the point as to whether he in fact entered Swat Valley and invaded Manglawar, and about his marriage to Malak Shah Mansur's daughter Bibi Mubarakah.

The lack of soundness in the assertion of Babur's invasion of Manglawar is also evident from the point, already dealt in some detail in the previous chapter, that Babur safeguarded the interest of Sultan Awais by asking the Yusufzi in the final agreement made with them in Kabul in May 1519 that they should not advance into Swat beyond Abuhah and that they should allow all the people who were the subjects of Sultan Awais to leave the area they have occupied in Swat.[8]

The account of *Tawarikh Hafiz Rahmat Khani,* and also of those which have reproduced its version of events without critical evaluation, sees and speaks of elements of fantasy and romance in the story of the marriage of Babur with Bibi Mubarakah. They, moreover, state that Babur wrote to Malak Ahmad asking that they had only to marry Bibi Mubarakah to him and he thereby would make no intrusion upon them and would bestow great benefits upon them.[9] Babur's account, however, neither gives any clue to the legends and fantasies nor does his statement corroborate these. The marriage was arranged for political and diplomatic gains rather than Babur's love for the lady, which Babur had clarified by stating: 'In order to conciliate the Yūsuf-zāī horde, I had asked for a daughter of one of my well-wishers, Malik Sulaimān Shāh's son Malik Shāh Manṣūr, at the time he came to me as envoy from the Yūsuf-zāī Afghāns.'[10] Thus, it was when Malak Shah Mansur came to Babur 'as envoy' from the Yusufzi that he asked for the marriage, the purpose of which was 'to conciliate' them.

Basically, he 'sought to conciliate [the] men whom it was not always easy to chastise or to reach, by asking in marriage the daughter of Malek-shah Mansúr, one of their chiefs'.[11] Babur thus used diplomacy and tactics instead of arms. 'This union….gave him a strong and intimate connection with the tribe, assisted in checking the customary *raids* and outrages of several of its branches.'[12] According to Akhun Darwizah, proceeding to and visiting the Mughal rulers of Kabul was not banned for the Yusufzi chiefs and *malakan* so that Malak Ahmad could come from Swat to Kabul to pay homage.[13]

Babur has stated that in the final agreement with the Yusufzi's delegation, concluded in May 1519 in Kabul, it was also included that the Afghan cultivators of Bajawar and Swat 'should cast into the revenue 6000 ass-loads of rice'.[14] On the basis of this statement, it is believed that Babur levied and received annual revenue from the Swat Yusufzi. There, however, is no sound proof that Babur ever received this tribute from Swat. *Tawarikh Hafiz Rahmat Khani* has stated that though the Yusufzi were obedient to the king (Babur) at that time, but not in the sense that a *hakim,* or *shiqdar*, was appointed over them or that they paid any tax or tribute to him. They ignored such stipulations and Malak Ahmad refused to go to Kabul.[15] Akhun Darwizah's account also has clarified that, save his marriage to Malak Shah Mansur's daughter, Babur took nothing from the Yusufzi.[16] In light of the aforesaid, the assertion by Annette S. Beveridge that Babur 'had held…Swat since 1519'[17] is not sound.

As mentioned above, *Tawarikh Hafiz Rahmat Khani* has stated, as also reproduced by others, that Babur had come to Upper Swat, crossed the river to Manglawar, and ravaged the vicinity thereof.[18] H.W. Bellew has, on the authority of Akhun Darwizah, described Babur's route from Kabul to Swat, his affairs and settlement with the Swat Yusufzi, and his passage through Swat.[19] But Akhun Darwizah's books *Tazkiratul Abrar-i wal Ashrar* and *Makhzan* are silent on these points.[20]

Babur neither entered Swat nor went up to Manglawar against Sultan Awais. He achieved his principal purpose with the establishment of a matrimonial alliance with the Yusufzi. As has also been stated in the previous chapter, the Swati rulers Sultan Alauddin and Sultan Awais

waited on Babur and were present in his camp at Bajawar at the time
of his intending attack on the Yusufzi. Sultan Awais was even sent to
collect the impost from the Kahraj people. Both of them were honoured
with robes and horses and were allowed, with the accomplishment
of their tasks, to go back. Babur has stated, in this respect, that 'we
bestowed horses and robes on Sl. [Sultan] Wais and Sl. 'Alā'u'u-din
of Sawād [Swat], gave them leave to go'.[21] There was, therefore, no
need, or question, of action and marching up to Manglawar. A glance
on *Tuzuk-i Baburi* reveals the facts.[22]

Babur 'refrained from advancing into the Yusufzai area of Swat',
asserts A.H. Dani, because the Yusufzi 'were coming into greater
importance'[23] at the time; and he had also found, asserts William Erskine,
from experience 'the difficulty of subduing them by open force in the
rugged country which they occupied'.[24]

While writing about his not proceeding to Swat and leaving for the
Samah (plain) in the southwest of Swat, Babur has stated:

On Tuesday the 7th of the month the begs [Begs] and the Dilazāk Afghān
headmen were summoned, and, after consultation, matters were left at
this:—"The year is at its end,... only a few days of the Fish are left; the
plainsmen have carried in all their corn; if we went now into Sawād
[Swat], the army would dwindle through getting no corn. The thing to
do is to march along the Aṃbahar and Pānī-mānī road, cross the Sawād-
water above Hash-nagar, and surprise the Yūsuf-zāī and Muḥammadī
[Muhammadzi] Afghāns who are located in the plain over against the
Yūsuf-zāī *sangur* of Māhūrā. Another year, coming earlier in the harvest-
time, the Afghāns of this place must be our first thought." So the matter
was left.[25]

After this, Babur has stated about his bestowing horses and robes on
Sultan Awais and Sultan Alauddin of Swat and giving them leave to
go, and leaving Bibi Mubarakah at Bajawar till his arrival back; and
then has narrated his march down to the plains of Hindustan. All these
narrations also negate this assertion of Muhammad Qasim Farishtah that
Babur defeated the Swat Yusufzi and carried 'some thousands of them
away with him'.[26]

The text of the above block quote from Babur's account reveals that
the main objective of his projected Swat campaign was plunder. As the
people had safely taken the corn or harvest to their homes, the adventure
was abandoned.

Sayyad Abdul Jabbar Shah has asserted that Malak Ahmad had great courage and was farsighted. Despite conquering the territories now held by the Yusufzi and Mandanr, he went to Kabul so that the Mughals may have no hint of the extent of the conquests of the Yusufzi-Mandanr, as well as to retain relationships with the tribes of Afghanistan.[27]

AKBAR AND SWAT

The Swat Yusufzi retained their independent position during Babur, Kamran (son of Babur and brother of Humayun; at first Governor of Kabul and later the ruler at Kabul after his brother Humayun's flight to Persia till Humayun's return and reoccupation of Kabul) and Humayun's reigns. The region remained un-penetrated by the Mughals till Akbar's time. Akbar ascended the throne in 1556, but he did not manage to rule Swat, nor 'any territories west of the Indus until 1581, and not absolutely until his brother Hakim's death in 1585'.[28]

The real issue between the Swat Yusufzi and the Mughals started after the death of Mirza Hakim. On 20 December 1585 Akbar dispatched an army to Kashmir and on the same day Zain Khan Koka 'was sent off to guide aright the Yūsufzāīs, and to conquer Swād (Swat) and Bajaur [Bajawar]'.[29] Whereas, according to Nizamuddin Ahmad it was 'on the *next day* [my italics]' that Akbar sent Zain Khan Koka 'with a well-equipped army against the Afghāns of Sawād (Swat) and Bajaur [Bajawar], for the extirpation of those turbulent tribes'.[30]

The contention and belief that Akbar's forces proceeded to Swat against the Rushniyas[31] (Roshniyas; Rukhanyan: followers of Bayazid Ansari,[32] also called Tarikyan—Tarikis) seems to have no relevance. Akhun Darwizah[33] has also mentioned in his book *Tazkiratul Abrar-i wal Ashrar* that the Rushniyas later reached Swat and obtained a foothold here and hence the Mughal forces entered in their pursuit. When the Rushniyas lost power over their entire state, Akbar's army laid the foundations of a fort at Damghar and plundered the Yusufzi from all sides.[34]

Akhun Darwizah speaks of the Mughal-Yusufzi pitched battles and of the Mughals' attempt to hold Swat by founding a fort here, but he neither testifies to the hold of the Mughals over Swat nor to that of the followers of Bayazid Ansari, although some of the latter may have had fled Swat to take shelter and be safe from the Mughal forces.

Nizamuddin Ahmad Bakhshi has clarified that the campaign against the Rushniyas was separate from that of Swat by stating, in this regard, 'His Majesty, the Khalifa-i-Ilahī, deputed Kunar [Kunwar] Mān Singh to extirpate and destroy the *Raushnāis*, who were really Tārīkīs, and in future would be called by that name, and conferred Kabul on him as his *jāgīr*';[35] and that Man Singh 'met that sect in the Khaibar pass'.[36] H.G. Raverty has made it clear that it was later in 1587 that Zain Khan was sent to operate against some of the Tarikis, who had taken themselves away 'to the difficult tract of country in and around' Bajawar.[37]

At the time of the Mughal forces' advance into Swat, Bayazid Ansari had died and the Rushniya influence had begun to fade away as the tribal tide turned against them in the Yusufzi Samah (plain) because of strong opposition by Akhun Darwizah. Strangely enough, Muhammad Abdul Ghafoor Qasmi had not only brought Bayazid Ansari to Swat and Akhun Darwizah in pursuit, but has also recorded the fiction about Bayazid's challenge to Akhun Darwizah to show his *kiramat* (miracle); consequently the Katilai (now Amankut) spring ensued due to Akhun Darwizah's prayers and Bayazid's trick failed.[38] It is noteworthy that this story has been omitted in the English rendering of Qasmi's book *The History of Swat*.[39]

Besides the insubordination of the people of Swat, it was the Kashmir issue which caused the march of Akbar's forces into Swat. Akbar considered Kashmir to be in the sphere of influence of his empire. He asked the ruler of Kashmir to acknowledge his supremacy by either attending his court in person or sending his son. The demand was not honoured. Therefore, in 1585, Akbar sent Mirza Shah Rukh and Raja Bhagwan Das with an army to Kashmir to enforce his authority.[40] It was a strategic necessity, as it had been in the case of Alexander of Macedonia at the time of his march upon Punjab, and also the case with Babur before his forays into India, to prevent any possible help from the people of Swat to the Kashmiris, as well as the need 'to maintain the line of communications for this expedition [that] a force was sent under Zain Khan against the Yusufzais in the Swat Valley'.[41] Another viewpoint about the strategic significance of Swat and Bajawar is that the Yusufzi 'were the most powerful and the strongest tribe among all Afghans, and their contiguity to the Uzbeg territory was a potential danger to the Mughuls'.[42]

Anyway, Akbar's imperialism led to fighting. The Mughal forces sent under the command of Zain Khan faced stiff resistance and suffered great hardships. In Olaf Caroe's words, 'Zain Khan reported that, while he had been able to force an entry into Bajaur [Bajawar], he was powerless to proceed to the heart of the trouble in Swat until reinforcements reached him. These reinforcements must also harry and devastate the Mandanr settlements in the Samah to prevent their aiding their brethren in the hills.'[43] Akbar, therefore, 'despatched two forces, one under his Brahmin favourite, Raja Birbal (Birbar, or the very courageous)…and the other under another of his cronies, Hakim Abul Fateh'.[44]

In the meantime, Akbar also arrived at Attak-Banaras in person on 23 December 1585, 'after travelling 305 *kos*[45] and a little more in 4 months and 1 day and in sixty-five marches'.[46] The Mughal forces entered Swat in 1586 with great difficulty. Chakdarah was made the base and the foundation of a fort laid there. The reinforcements also joined Zain Khan. However, the three generals, Zain Khan, Birbal, and the Hakim, did not agree on the strategy and course of action. Disagreeing with Zain Khan's wise counsel, Raja Birbal, and Hakim Abul Fatah prevailed and hence withdrawal to Akbar at Attak was decided. Again, the advice of Zain Khan, to withdraw through the Malakand Pass, was not honoured; and retirement through the Karakar and Malandarai (Mlandarai) passes was chosen.[47]

The tribesmen greatly harassed the Mughal forces at the Karakar Pass. According to Khwajah Nizamuddin Ahmad:

> When they arrived at the pass of…Karākar, a man came to Rāja Bīr Bar, and said "The Afghāns intend to make a night attack, this night, and the breadth of the mountain defile is not more than three or four *karohs*.[48] If you pass through this defile, you may be free from all anxiety about the night attacks." Rāja Bīr Bar started with the intention of passing through the defile, without acting in concert with Zain Khān, and the whole army started behind him. At the close of the day, when the sun was setting, they came to the narrowest path. The Afghāns from the different sides, having climbed to the top [tops] of the hills, attacked them with arrows and stones. The men lost their way in the narrow defiles, in the darkness of the night, and were killed in the holes and caverns… There was a terrible defeat, and a great disaster. About eight thousand men met their death. Rāja Bīr Bar who for fear of death had attempted to take flight, was killed…Hasan Behti,…Raja Dharmkand, Khwaja 'Arab, who was the *bakhshi* of the army, and…Mulla Shīrī the poet, and a large number of chief men were killed that night.[49]

Akbar was so grieved at the loss of Birbal and his body not being brought that he did not eat for two days and nights, nor did he permit Zain Khan and Hakim Abul Fatah to meet him for several days.[50]

Abul Fazal, H.G. Raverty, and V.A. Smith, and those who had followed them, have mentioned the disaster that befell the Mughal forces at the Malandarai (also Mlandarai) defile.[51] Abul Fazal's narrative of the retreat from Chakdarah through the Karakar and Malandarai passes is somewhat detailed, compared to Khwajah Nizamuddin Ahmad's, but is ambiguous and somewhat unclear regarding the Mughal forces passage through and losses in the Karakar defile.[52]

Khwajah Nizamuddin Ahmad, however, had stated, after the afore-quoted passage about the disaster of the Mughal forces in Karakar, that 'Zain Khān Koka and Hakīm Abul Fath sustained another defeat on the 5th Rabī'-ul-āwwal of the year; and reached the…fort of Atak with much hardship'.[53] He has hence clarified that Raja Birbal, along with other prominent figures and about eight thousands soldiers, perished in the Karakar Pass (two days prior) and the Malandarai defile's defeat was later sustained by the remaining retreating Mughal forces led by Zain Khan and Hakim Abul Fatah in which, according to Abul Fazal, 'as many as 500' of the Mughal army 'lost their lives'.[54]

Thus, the first campaign not only 'resulted in failure insofar as the Yusufzis in Swat and Buner could not be brought under control',[55] but it 'created a terror of Afghan prowess and aversion to hill fighting throughout the imperial dominions'.[56] Moreover, the defeat of the Mughal forces not only 'left a very demoralising effect on the imperial army',[57] but also proved a final blow for the Mughal forces sent into Kashmir under the command of Mirza Shah Rukh and Raja Bagwan Das. They yielded 'before the dispirited' forces of the ruler of Kashmir and concluded 'a peace treaty' with him on such terms that 'did not satisfy Akbar'.[58]

The Mughals made further bids by sending forces under the command of Raja Todar Mal, Muhammad Sadiq Khan, Zain Khan, and Asaf Khan, in turn or from time to time, who fought in Bajawar and Swat from 1586 to 1593,[59] 'but without any real or lasting success'.[60] Mughal historians have exaggerated the exploits of the Mughal forces. Their accounts portray the Yusufzi of Swat as being crushed and reduced to great straits.[61] Muhammad Asif Khan, too, has asserted, as stated earlier, that after the death of Bayazid Ansari 'Swat and Buner were annexed

to the Mughal Empire without much ado'.[62] But according to Ahmad
Hasan Dani,

> A battle of game started between the Yusufzais and the Mughals in which
> hill forts played a dominant role.... The Mughals learnt the tactics of
> hill fighting from the Yusufzais and as long as they held the forts they
> managed to keep the passage open. However, except for this passage
> over Malakand to Chakdara and beyond to Bajaur, the Mughals never
> attempted to enter the main home of the Yusufzais in Swat and Buner.[63]

After dealing in some detail with the accounts and assertions of
Abul Fazal, some other historians of Akbar's reign, and Akhun
Darwizah, Raverty has asserted that these 'assertions are contrary to
fact'.[64] He further has asserted:

> In reality, as is clearly proved by events, the Afghàns were never really
> subdued by the Mughals at any time, not even the Yúsufzís and Mandaṛs
> and others around the Pes'háwar district; and the Mughals were unable to
> hold an inch of ground in their difficult country without overwhelming
> forces, and even then their communications were continually interrupted.[65]

Besides other things, H.W. Bellew had contended that the Mughal
General Zain Khan Kukah 'built the fort of Damghar[66] in the midst of...
[the] valley, and, leaving a garrison in it, scoured the country around,
and severely punished the Yusufzais for their insolence'.[67] Bellew did
not mention the source of his contention in respect of the construction of
the fort at Damghar by the Mughal general. Although, as stated earlier,
Akhun Darwizah has stated that Akbar's army laid the foundations
of the Damghar fort and plundered the Yusufzi from all sides,[68] it is
never established that the fort was actually constructed and a garrison
stationed therein.

Abul Fazal's account of the forts constructed by Zain Khan in the
region does not tally with or testify to the construction of a fort in
Damghar in the middle of the Swat Valley plain. He has talked of 'the
Afghans of Damghār' coming 'off to the hill of Mahra [Murah] with
the idea that something might be done'; and that the Yusufzi 'were
much disturbed by the fort which had been founded on the top of the
ravine, and were lying in wait to attack it. Now they united with the
men of Mahra and attacked it. There was a hot engagement from dawn
till evening. The broken nature of the ground and the height of the hill
made the contest a long one.'[69]

Olaf Caroe's assertion endorses Dani's earlier quoted contention, as it states:

> There is other, and even better, evidence as regards Swat, Buner and Bajaur, the hill tracts, showing that they never came under imperial control. In his *Ain-i-Akbari*, Abul Fazl includes these areas in the Sarkar of Swat under the Kabul Province. Throughout the *Ain* there are ruled columns for particulars respecting the names of places, people and number of men available for service, and the amount of assessment. These, for the parts in question, are all blank. "The fact is," says Raverty, "the Mughal rulers never obtained a permanent footing in these parts, notwithstanding the slaughter of the people and the devastation of their lands. They were never in a position for obtaining the particulars for the said columns to be filled up, and no copy of the *Ain-i-Akbari* will be found complete in this respect."[70]

Even Abul Fazal, Akbar's favourite and a historian, has admitted insubordination of the people of the Sarkar of Swat by recording: 'Under the present ever-during [sic] Imperial sway, of the lawless inhabitants of this country, some have been put to death, others imprisoned, *while some happily dwell under their tribal rule* [my italics].'[71]

Interestingly, Sayyad Abdul Jabbar Shah has asserted that the Swat Yusufzi did surrender to the Mughals; that, in the disaster befell the Mughal forces at the time of their retreat from Swat, thirty-forty thousand of the Mughals were killed; and that, in the retaliatory invasion, afterwards, they were subdued and their chiefs were taken to Delhi-Agra, to be released after a long period.[72] It, however, is evident from the detailed analysis above that Abdul Jabbar Shah's assertions are rootless.

AKBAR'S SUCCESSORS AND SWAT

The failure of Akbar's forces and might in Swat proved decisive. Although his son and successor Jahangir has stated in his *Memoir* that he bestowed the title of Khan-i Duran upon Shah Beg Khan, on 3 Rajab 1016 AH (Thursday, 15 October 1607 CE), and entrusted him with the task of suppressing the turmoil of the Afghans of Kabul, Tirah, Bangash, and Walayat-i Swat Bajawar,[73] no intrusion of the Mughal forces into Swat during his reign is on record. Thus, Jahangir and his son and successor Shah Jahan did not make a significant bid for Swat. In Aurangzeb's reign the Swat Yusufzi came to the help of their brethren in the plains[74] who, in 1667, were fighting the Mughals. In reprisal, the Mughal commander-in-chief entered the Swat Valley and destroyed a village but returned in haste.[75]

Strangely enough, the English translation of Muhammad Asif Khan's book has asserted, 'In short, Swat and Buner remained a part of the Mughal Empire throughout Aurangzeb's reign.'[76] But, to the contrary, Olaf Caroe has recorded a 1947 statement of Miangul Abdul Wadud, aka Bacha Sahib, 'Never in all history…not even in the time of Akbar or Aurangzeb, much less under the Durranis, were the Yusufzais of this country the subjects of any empire.'[77] Caroe has endorsed this claim by writing: 'The claim can be made good. The people of Dir, Swat and Buner have never paid taxes to Delhi or Kabul. They have never had to yield obedience to any foreign law or administrative system.'[78]

Khushal Khan Khattak, who visited Swat for the purpose of rallying the Yusufzi of Swat against Aurangzeb, has also endorsed their freedom by stating, 'Neither are they the subjects of anyone nor they give away anything to anybody.'[79]

NOTES

1. See Zahirud-din Muhammad Babur, *Babur-Nama*, trans. from the original Turki text by Annette S. Beveridge (repr., Lahore: Sang-e-Meel Publications, 1987), 373; Zahiruddin Babur, *Tuzuk-i Baburi*, Urdu trans. Rashid Akhtar Nadwi (Lahore: Sang-e-Meel Publications, n.d.), 149.

2. See Pir Muazam Shah, *Tawarikh Hafiz Rahmat Khani*, with *dibachah* by Muhammad Nawaz Tair (Pashto/Persian) (2nd impression, Peshawar: Pukhtu Academy, 1987), 83.

3. See ibid., 82–9.

4. See ibid., 89–91. Also see Henry George Raverty, *Notes on Afghanistan and Baluchistan*, Vol. 1 (2nd edn. in Pakistan, Quetta: Nisa Traders, 1982), 128.

5. See Shah, *Tawarikh Hafiz Rahmat Khani*, 91–5. Also see Raverty, *Notes on Afghanistan and Baluchistan*, Vol. 1, 234–5.

6. For detail, see Shah, *Tawarikh Hafiz Rahmat Khani*, 95–102. Also see Raverty, *Notes on Afghanistan and Baluchistan*, Vol. 1, 234–5.

7. Raverty, *Notes on Afghanistan and Baluchistan*, Vol. 1, 128.

8. See Babur, *Babur-Nama*, 400; Zahiruddin Muhammad Babur, *Waqay-i Babur*, Urdu trans. Yunus Jafri, from the Persian trans. of Abdur Rahim Khan-i Khanan, with notes and annotation by Hasan Beg (Krekardi, Scotland: Shahar Banu Publishers, 2007), 208. Also see William Erskine, *A History of India Under Baber* (repr., Karachi: Oxford University Press, 1974), 338; William Erskine, *A History of India Under the Two First Sovereigns of the House of Taimur, Báber and Humáyun*, Vol. 1 (2nd edn., Shannon: Irish University Press, 1972), 338.

9. See Shah, *Tawarikh Hafiz Rahmat Khani*, 95–102. Also see Roshan Khan, *Malikah-i Swat* (Karachi: Roshan Khan and Company, 1983), 34–42; Khan Roshan Khan, *Yusufzai Qaum ki Sarguzasht* (Karachi: Roshan Khan and Company, 1986), 111–18.

10. Babur, *Babur-Nama*, 375. Also see Babur, *Tuzuk-i Baburi*, 149; Babur, *Waqay-i Babur*, 193.

11. Erskine, *A History of India Under Baber*, 338; Erskine, *A History of India Under the Two First Sovereigns of the House of Taimur, Báber and Humáyun*, Vol. 1, 338.

12. Erskine, *A History of India Under Baber*, 338; Erskine, *A History of India Under the Two First Sovereigns of the House of Taimur, Báber and Humáyun*, Vol. 1, 338.

13. See Akhun Darwizah, *Tazkiratul Abrar-i wal Ashrar* (Persian) (Peshawar: Islami Kutub Khanah, n.d.), 96.

14. Babur, *Babur-Nama*, 400. Also see Babur, *Waqay-i Babur*, 208; Babur, *Tuzuk-i Baburi*, 163.

15. See Shah, *Tawarikh Hafiz Rahmat Khani*, 91.

16. See Darwizah, *Tazkiratul Abrar-i wal Ashrar*, 104.

17. Annette S. Beveridge, introduction to Gul-Badan Begam, *The History of Humāyūn (Humāyūn-Nāma)*, trans. with introduction, notes, illustration and bibliographical appendix and reproduced in the Persian from the only known MS. of the British Museum by Annette S. Beveridge (repr., Delhi: Low Price Publications, 1994), 1.

18. See Shah, *Tawarikh Hafiz Rahmat Khani*, 93–4; Khan, *Yusufzai Qaum ki Sarguzasht*, 111; Fazle Rabbi Rahi, *Swat Tarikh kay Aayinay mayn* (Urdu) (2nd edn., Mingawarah, Swat: Shoaib Sons Publishers, Booksellers, 1997), 35.

19. See H.W. Bellew, *A General Report on the Yusufzais* (3rd edn., Lahore: Sang-e-Meel Publications, 1994), 61–4.

20. See Darwizah, *Tazkiratul Abrar-i wal Ashrar*; Akhun Darwizah, *Makhzan* (Pashto/ Persian), with *muqadimah* by Sayyad Muhammad Taqwim-ul-Haq Kaka Khail, *pishlafz* by Muhammad Nawaz Tair (2nd impression, Peshawar: Pukhtu Academy, 1987).

21. Babur, *Babur-Nama*, 376. Also see Babur, *Tuzuk-i Baburi*, 150; Babur, *Waqay-i Babur*, 192–4.

22. See Babur, *Babur-Nama*, 372–6; Babur, *Tuzuk-i Baburi*, 148–50; Babur, *Waqay-i Babur*, 191–5.

23. Ahmad Hasan Dani, *Peshawar: Historic City of the Frontier* (2nd edn., Lahore: Sang-e-Meel Publications, 1995), 96–8.

24. Erskine, *A History of India Under Baber*, 338; Erskine, *A History of India Under the Two First Sovereigns of the House of Taimur, Báber and Humáyun*, Vol. 1, 338.

25. Babur, *Babur-Nama*, 376. Also see Babur, *Waqay-i Babur*, 193; Babur, *Tuzuk-i Baburi*, 150.

26. Mahomed Kasim [Muhammad Qasim] Ferishta, *History of the Rise of the Mahomedan [Muhammadan] Power in India till the year A.D. 1612*, trans. from the original Persian of Mahomed Kasim Ferishta by John Briggs, Vol. 2 (repr., Lahore: Sang-e-Meel Publications, 1977), 35.

27. Sayyad Abdul Jabbar Shah Sithanawi, *Kitab al-Ibra: Subah Sarhad wa Afghanistan ki Char Sau Salah Tarikh; 1500 Iswi ta 1900 Iswi* (Urdu), Vol. 1 (Islamabad: Poorab Academy, 2011), 185.

28. Olaf Caroe, *The Pathans: 550 B.C.–A.D. 1957* (repr., Karachi: Oxford University Press, 1976), 196–7.

29. Abu-l-Fazl, *The Akbar Nama of Abu-l-Fazl (History of the Reign of Akbar Including an Account of His Predecessors)*, trans. from the original Persian by H. Beveridge, Vol. 3 (repr., Lahore: Sang-e-Meel Publications, 2005), 561.

30. Khwājah Niẓāmuddin Aḥmad, *The Ṭabaqāt-i-Akbarī of Khwājah Niẓāmuddin Aḥmad: (A History of India from the Early Musalmān Invasions to the Thirty-eight Year of the Reign of Akbar)*, Vol. 2, trans. Brajendra Nath De, rev. and ed. by Baini Prashad (Delhi: Low Price Publications, 1992), 607.

31. For such a contention, see Muhammad Asif Khan, *The Story of Swat as told by the Founder Miangul Abdul Wadud Badshah Sahib to Muhammad Asif Khan*, with preface, introduction and appendices by Muhammad Asif Khan, and trans. preface and trans. by Ashruf Altaf Husain (Printed by Ferozsons Ltd., Peshawar, 1963), xxix–xxxv; Muhammad Asif Khan, *Tarikh-i Riyasat-i Swat wa Sawanih-i Hayat Baniy-i Riyasat-i Swat Hazrat Miangul Gul Shahzadah Abdul Wadud Khan Badshah Sahib*, with *dibachah, hisah awal, saluramah hisah,* and *hisah pinzamah* by Muhammad Asif Khan (Pashto) (Printed by Ferozsons Ltd., Peshawar [1958]), 46–54; Saranzeb Swati, *Tarikh Riyasat-i Swat* (Peshawar: Azeem Publishing House, 1984), 64–8; Rahi, *Swat Tarikh kay Aayinay mayn*, 37; Muhammad Parwaish Shaheen, *Da Swat Gwalunah* (Pashto) (Mingawarah, Swat: Shoaib Sons Publishers, Booksellers, 1988), 116–25; Rahim Shah Rahim, 'Malakand da Tarikh pah Ranra kay', *Pukhtu* (Peshawar), 20/4 (May 1988), 39; Sayed Abid Bokhari, ed. and comp., *Through the Centuries: North-West Frontier Province* (Quetta: Mr. Reprints, 1993), 146. Abid Bukhari's (page 146) statement about the Bayazid rising in Dir and the claim made, according to *The Story of Swat as told by the Founder Miangul Abdul Wadud Badshah Sahib to Muhammad Asif Khan*, that after the death of Bayazid Ansari: 'Swat and Buner were annexed to the Mughal Empire without much ado' (English version, page xxxv; and Pashto version, book page 54) are also surprising.

32. For Bayazid Ansari, his doctrines and beliefs, see Sulṭān-ī-Rome, 'Bāyazīd Anṣarī and his *Khairul Bayān*', *Hamdard Islamicus* (Karachi), 20/3 (July–September 1997), 87–95.

33. Akhun Darwizah was a disciple of Sayyad Ali Tarmizi aka Pir Baba and a staunch opponent of Bayazid Ansari and his teachings and beliefs. His fame is also because of his books *Makhzan* (Pashto/Persian) and *Tazkiratul Abrar-i wal Ashrar* (Persian).

34. See Darwizah, *Tazkiratul Abrar-i wal Ashrar*, 101–2.

35. Aḥmad, *The Ṭabaqāt-i-Akbarī*, Vol. 2, 608. Also see Nizam-ud Din Ahmad Bakhshi, *Tabakat-i Akbari*, trans. and eds. H.M. Elliot and John Dowson (repr., Lahore: Sang-e-Meel Publications, 2006), 285; Abu-l-Fazl, *The Akbar Nama of Abu-l-Fazl*, Vol. 3, 562.

36. Aḥmad, *The Ṭabaqāt-i-Akbarī*, Vol. 2, 611. Also see Bakhshi, *Tabakat-i Akbari*, 286; Ferishta, *History of the Rise of the Mahomedan* [Muhammadan] *Power*

in India till the year A.D. 1612, Vol. 2, 260; Abu-l-Fazl, *The Akbar Nama of Abu-l-Fazl*, Vol. 3, 577.

37. See Raverty, *Notes on Afghanistan and Baluchistan*, Vol. 1, 112, 169. Also see Aḥmad, *The Ṭabaqāt-i-Akbarī*, Vol. 2, 619, 637–8; Bakhshi, *Tabakat-i Akbari*, 297, 302; Abu-l-Fazl, *The Akbar Nama of Abu-l-Fazl*, Vol. 3, 746.

38. For the story, see Sayyed Abdul Ghafoor Qasmay, *Tarikh Riyasat-i Swaṭ* (Pashto) (Printed by Hamidia Press, Peshawar, n.d.), 33–4.

39. See Sayyed Mohd. Abdul Ghafoor Qasmi, *The History of Swat* (Printed by D.C. Anand & Sons, Peshawar, 1940), 6.

40. See Abu-l-Fazl, *The Akbar Nama of Abu-l-Fazl*, Vol. 3, 554–61.

41. J.C. Powell-Price, *A History of India* (London: Thomas Nelson and Sons Ltd., 1955), 269. Also see G.B. Malleson, *Rulers of India: Akbar and the Rise of the Mughal Empire* (Pakistan repr., Lahore: Islamic Book Service, 1979), 131–2.

42. Arif Ali Ansari, 'The North-West Frontier Policy of the Mughuls under Akbar', *Journal of the Pakistan Historical Society* (Karachi), 4/1 (January 1956), 48.

43. Caroe, *The Pathans*, 214. For some detail, see Raverty, *Notes on Afghanistan and Baluchistan*, Vol. 1, 258. Also see Ferishta, *History of the Rise of the Mahomedan* [Muhammadan] *Power in India till the year A.D. 1612*, Vol. 2, 259; Abu-l-Fazl, *The Akbar Nama of Abu-l-Fazl*, Vol. 3, 570.

44. Caroe, *The Pathans*, 214. For some detail, see Raverty, *Notes on Afghanistan and Baluchistan*, Vol. 1, 258. Also see Abu-l-Fazl, *The Akbar Nama of Abu-l-Fazl*, Vol. 3, 564–5, 570; Ferishta, *History of the Rise of the Mahomedan* [Muhammadan] *Power in India till the year A.D. 1612*, Vol. 2, 259; Muhammad Hussain Azad, *Darbar-i Akbari* (Urdu) (Facts of publication have been torn out), 372–3.

45. For *kos*, see note 48 below.

46. Abu-l-Fazl, *The Akbar Nama of Abu-l-Fazl*, Vol. 3, 562.

47. Vincent A. Smith, *Akbar: The Great Mogul [Mughul], 1542–1605*, 2nd edn. revised (Indian repr., Delhi: S. Chand & Co., 1958), 168. For some detail, see Raverty, *Notes on Afghanistan and Baluchistan*, Vol. 1, 257–61; Caroe, *The Pathans*, 214–16; Abu-l-Fazl, *The Akbar Nama of Abu-l-Fazl*, Vol. 3, 570–2; Azad, *Darbar-i Akbari*, 373–5.

48. 'The kuroh [*kuruh/karoh*] is the third part of a farsakh of 12,000 gaz, each kuroh consisting of 3,000 gaz of 32 angusht or fingers' breadth, or 4,000 gaz of 24 fingers' breadth, equal to six fists, or the hand with the fingers doubled up, each angusht being computed as equal in breadth to six barley corns laid side by side, and each barley corn as equal in breadth to six hairs from the mane of a Turkī horse or the tail of a camel. It varies, however, in different localities, and is, on the average, something less than two miles. In Hindústán, the Panjáb, and the Derah-ját, the kuroh is termed kos, in length 4,000 gaz, as above described. This is also called the gau kos, which means the distance at which the lowing of a cow can be heard at midnight on a calm night.' Raverty, *Notes on Afghanistan and Baluchistan*, Vol. 1, 1 n. *. For detail about the *kuruh* and *kos/kus* and its length in different localities and as mentioned by different sources, see ibid. Also see Abu 'l-Faẓl 'Allāmī, *The Ā'īn-i Akbarī*, trans. from the original Persian by H. Blochmann, 2nd edn. revised and edited by D.C. Phillott, complete 3 Vols. (repr., Lahore: Sang-e-Meel Publications, 2004), 866–7.

49. Aḥmad, *The Ṭabaqāt-i-Akbarī*, Vol. 2, 609–10. Also see Bakhshi, *Tabakat-i Akbari*, 285–6; Ferishta, *History of the Rise of the Mahomedan* [Muhammadan] *Power in India till the year A.D. 1612*, Vol. 2, 259; Dani, *Peshawar: Historic City of the Frontier*, 102.

50. Raverty, *Notes on Afghanistan and Baluchistan*, Vol. 1, 265. Also see *Akbar: The Great Mogul*, 170; Caroe, *The Pathans*, 218; Abu-l-Fazl, *The Akbar Nama of Abu-l-Fazl*, Vol. 3, 574.

51. For such a contention, see Abu-l-Fazl, *The Akbar Nama of Abu-l-Fazl*, Vol. 3, 573–4; Raverty, *Notes on Afghanistan and Baluchistan*, Vol. 1, 263–4; Smith, *Akbar: The Great Mogul*, 168; Caroe, *The Pathans*, 217–8; Sayyad Bahadar Shah Zafar Kaka Khail, *Pukhtanah da Tarikh pah Ranra kay* (Pashto) (Peshawar: University Book Agency, n.d.), 553; Swati, *Tarikh Riyasat-i Swat*, 68; Himayatullah Yaqubi, *Mughal-Afghan Relations in South Asia: History and Developments* (Islamabad: National Institute of Historical and Cultural Research, 2015), 132.

52. See Abu-l-Fazl, *The Akbar Nama of Abu-l-Fazl*, Vol. 3, 572–3. Also see Azad, *Darbar-i Akbari*, 375–80.

53. Aḥmad, *The Ṭabaqāt-i-Akbarī*, Vol. 2, 610. Also Bakhshi, *Tabakat-i Akbari*, 286.

54. Abu-l-Fazl, *The Akbar Nama of Abu-l-Fazl*, Vol. 3, 574.

55. Dani, *Peshawar: Historic City of the Frontier*, 102.

56. Jadunath Sarkar, *History of Aurangzeb*, Vol. 3, *Northern India, 1658–1681* (new edn., repr., Karachi: South Asian Publishers, 1981), 146.

57. Ansari, 'The North-West Frontier Policy of the Mughuls under Akbar', 50.

58. Ibid., 54–5. Also see Aḥmad, *The Ṭabaqāt-i-Akbarī*, Vol. 2, 613; Bakhshi, *Tabakat-i Akbari*, 287.

59. See Aḥmad, *The Ṭabaqāt-i-Akbarī*, Vol. 2, 610, 614, 622, 637–8, 649; Bakhshi, *Tabakat-i Akbari*, 286, 291, 297, 302; Abu-l-Fazl, *The Akbar Nama of Abu-l-Fazl*, Vol. 3, 574–5, 625–6, 629, 632–4, 646, 663, 676, 730, 745–6, 765.

60. Caroe, *The Pathans*, 218.

61. For such a contention, see Aḥmad, *The Ṭabaqāt-i-Akbarī*, Vol. 2, 610–11, 649; Bakhshi, *Tabakat-i Akbari*, 286, 302; Abu-l-Fazl, *The Akbar Nama of Abu-l-Fazl*, Vol. 3, 575–7, 579, 625–6, 632–4, 663, 787.

62. Khan, *The Story of Swat as told by the Founder Miangul Abdul Wadud Badshah Sahib to Muhammad Asif Khan*, xxxv.

63. Dani, *Peshawar: Historic City of the Frontier*, 103. Also see Raverty, *Notes on Afghanistan and Baluchistan*, Vol. 1, 169–72.

64. Raverty, *Notes on Afghanistan and Baluchistan*, Vol. 1, 172.

65. Ibid.

66. The village of Damghar lies in Nikpi Khail or present-day Kabal *tahsil* areas in-between the present-day Saidu Sharif (Swat) Airport and the Swat River.

67. Bellew, *A General Report on the Yusufzais*, 72.

68. See Darwizah, *Tazkiratul Abrar-i wal Ashrar*, 102.

69. Abu-l-Fazl, *The Akbar Nama of Abu-l-Fazl*, Vol. 3, 633–4.

70. Caroe, *The Pathans*, 218–19. Also see Raverty, *Notes on Afghanistan and Baluchistan*, Vol. 1, note on pages 203–4; Abū 'l-Fazl ʿAllāmī, *The Āʿīn-i Akbarī*, trans. H.S. Jarrett, 2nd edn. corrected and further annotated by Jadunath Sarkar, Vol. 2, *A Gazetteer and Administrative Manual of Akbar's Empire and Past*

History of India (3rd edn., repr., from 2nd edn. of 1949, New Delhi: Oriental Books Reprint Corporation, 1978), 397–9; 'Allāmī, *The Ā'īn-i Akbarī*, trans. H. Blochmann, complete 3 Vols., 856–7.

71. ʿAllāmī, *The Ā·īn-i Akbarī*, trans. H.S. Jarrett, Vol. 2, 399; 'Allāmī, *The Ā'īn-i Akbarī*, trans. H. Blochmann, 857.

72. See Sithanawi, *Kitab al-Ibra: Subah Sarhad wa Afghanistan ki Char Sau Salah Tarikh; 1500 Iswi ta 1900 Iswi*, Vol. 1, 38.

73. Jahangir, *Tuzuk-i Jahangiri*, Urdu trans. Salim Wahid Salim (Lahore: Majlis Taraqi Adab, 1960), 150.

74. See Sarkar, *History of Aurangzeb*, Vol. 3, 148.

75. See ibid., 149.

76. Khan, *The Story of Swat as told by the Founder Miangul Abdul Wadud Badshah Sahib to Muhammad Asif Khan*, xxxviii. It is to be noted that the Pashto version of the book have no such contention. For the Pashto version, see Khan, *Tarikh-i Riyasat-i Swat wa Sawanih-i Hayat Baniy-i Riyasat-i Swat Hazrat Miangul Gul Shahzadah Abdul Wadud Khan Badshah Sahib*, 60–3.

77. Caroe, *The Pathans*, 205.

78. Ibid.

79. Khushal Khan Khattak, *Swat Nama of Khushal Khan Khattak*, edited and trans. in to English by Shakeel Ahmad, with preface by Raj Wali Shah Khattak (Peshawar: Pashto Academy, n.d.), 22.

9

KHUSHAL KHAN KHATTAK
AND SWAT

Khushal Khan Khattak (Khushhal Khan Khattak) was a renowned and versatile poet and prose writer. He is considered also a swordsman and a warrior. Since his great-grandfather Malak Akur's time, his family had been loyal to the Mughal rulers of India and fought for them against other Afghan/Pukhtun tribes. This created grudges, hatred, and enmity between the Khattak and the Yusufzi-Mandanr.[1]

Khushal Khan succeeded his father as the chief of his tribe in 1641 CE. He too continued to loyally serve the Mughals to the best of his abilities against other Afghan/Pukhtun tribes, a fact he has accepted in his poetry. He has said in this regard:

زۀ د يُوسـفزئ پـه خَـان زهـر وُم قاتـل

بل مقصود مے نه وُه په خدمت کښے د مغل

ډيـر شـاهان خُوانـان مـے يَـو ذ بلـه وُوَژل

تير ساعت ارمان دے پښيماني نښته حاصل 2

> *Meaning: I was a deadly poison for the Yusufzi and wished nothing else in serving the Mughals but to kill and destroy them. I have killed numerous kingly youths that I regret now.*

Interestingly, when Emperor Shah Jahan asked him as to why he continuously fought the Yusufzi, his reply was: Because they (the Yusufzi) are insubordinate and are rebels against the Mughal government, while he (Khushal Khan) is its well-wisher.[3]

And that:

د مغــل د پـاره مـا تـوري وهلـي

پښتنو بـه راتـه کړي ډيـري کنځلـي

کۀ ورکزي دي کۀ بنګښ او کۀ يوسف دي

ديـو همـه زمـا د تبـغ پـه تأسف دي

پښتانۀ مـي پـه زرګونو دي وژلـي

پـه سرونو بـه ئـي خرۀ غوايۀ وولشلـي

لا تـر اوسـه د سـرونو ئـي انبـار دے

پـه اټـک پـه پېښـور کښـي ئـي مينـار دے ۴

Meaning: I was fighting for the Mughals and the Pukhtuns
were cursing me for this. Whether Urakzi, or the Bangakh (Bangash),
or Yusufzi, all are aggrieved in respect of my sword. I have killed
thousands of Pukhtuns, so many that the animals would walk over
their dead bodies. Even now there are heaps of their skulls,
and in Attak and Peshawar their skull-towers still exist.

He recognized Aurangzeb's rule and continued to serve him and hence
fought not only the Yusufzi-Mandanr but also joined the Mughal forces
against the Afridi and Urakzi in the battle of Tirah in 1659. However,
later differences developed between Khushal Khan and the Mughal
court, which led to his imprisonment in January 1664. During this time
of trial and tribulation, despite his previous anti-Yusufzi role, the Yusufzi
provided protection to his family against the Mughals.

Khushal Khan did not revolt against the Mughals even after his
imprisonment and remained loyal thereafter too. It happened only when
he was pushed to the wall and was left with no option but either to
surrender or to fight for his personal survival. His own son became his
rival for the chieftainship and thus his tribe also became divided. He
then took up arms for the first time against the Mughals. His fighting
against the Mughals, therefore, was not for the Afghan *nang* (Afghan
honour/cause), as he has claimed in the following couplet:

د افغـان پـه ننـګ مے وتړلـه تُوره

ننګيالے د زمانے خوشحال ختـک یم ۵

Meaning: I raised up my sword (against the Mughals) for the
sake of the Afghan nang (honour). I, Khushal Khattak, am the
esteemed of the age.

It should be noted that, when the Yusufzi had been fighting against the Mughals, Khushal Khan had been serving the Mughals wholeheartedly against the Afghans/Pukhtuns.[6]

KHUSHAL KHAN'S ACCOUNT OF SWAT

In the aforesaid scenario, after his fall from the favour of the Mughal Emperor Aurangzeb, and his endeavours for his survival, Khushal Khan tried to instigate the Afghan/Pukhtun tribes against Aurangzeb and personally visited Swat to seek and enlist support of the Swat Yusufzi against the Mughals.

During his seven months stay in Swat,[7] he toured and observed its every aspect and later wrote a book entitled *Swat Namah*. He has praised its meadows, natural riches, scenic beauty, fertility, fragrant breezes, low prices, rich past, and so forth. For instance, comparing Swat with Kabul and Kashmir, he has said that the air of Swat is better than that of Kabul in summer and its pleasant climate is like that of Kashmir; but the pity is that, compared to Kashmir, Swat is narrower.[8] Referring to its springs, snow, and climate, he has asserted that Swat is blessed with springs and rivulets of cold water as well as snow, that there are no hot winds in Swat nor dust and other impurities, and that small rivulets flow from house to house in every village.[9]

While referring to the abundance of the crop-yield and low prices, he has asserted that the people of Swat had no activity other than indulging in agriculture and that they reaped a rich harvest, due to which the prices of the commodities could fall so low that, in the paltry sum of two *turah* (a copper coin) twenty guests can be served.[10]

Praising the rich archaeological past of Swat, he has stated that it has great ancient minarets, viz. Buddhist *stupa*s or topes, and monasteries, and remains of palatial houses and forts of great antiquity.[11]

While discussing different birds that were trapped and hunted, Khushal Khan has said that every year two to three hundred falcons were trapped. And, while other types of game are limited, francolins are most common. Wild ducks are abundant in the Swat River, which are shot at mercilessly by amateurs. Although abundant previously, the wild sheep, goats and deer etcetera are now reduced to the level of extinction by the gunmen.[12] Besides, flies and fleas are common in Swat, not to mention the *mangwanr* (bed-bugs) and *barurah* (a species of wood-louse; swallow-bugs).[13] Referring to the dogs and fowls, Khushal Khan has asserted that in every house there are as many dogs as household members and hundreds of fowls walk in their courtyards.[14]

Khushal Khan has acknowledged the freedom of the Swat Yusufzi by stating that they are neither subjects of any ruler nor do they pay taxes to anybody.[15] However, he is critical of them for his own reasons. In the course of speaking and praising the natural beauty and rich natural resources of Swat as well as its destruction by the Yusufzi, he has contended that 'the natural beauty of Swat renders it suitable for the enjoyment of kings and monarchs' but the Yusufzi has turned it 'into a ruined inn;'[16] and that: 'Every place in Swat is worthy of kings and Knights. But as there is no Sardar or chieftain in the region, it is just a country of crude mountain dwellings.'[17] He, moreover, has asserted that Swat is suitable for the gardens of fruits and flowers, and befitting for kings during summer time, and natural fountain-springs and waterfalls and cascade are everywhere over here as well as good cities and decent inns and markets but such a beautiful and praiseworthy country has been turned into mere meadows and grazing grounds by the Yusufzi.[18]

Khushal Khan has said that he 'studied the people of Swat in full depth' and has 'analysed every group and individual thoroughly'.[19] Referring to the frequent shifting of the population from one place to another, under the *waish*[20] system, he has stated that 'they lose their properties due to "hisk" [drawing lots] year to year, and invade themselves without using forces'.[21] He has lamented that their men alone inherit property from their fathers, and as soon as a person is buried his brother takes his sister-in-law in wedlock by obligation. In taking revenge, they kill the person more valued and influential than the real murderer; and that all the *mulan* favour these injustices and evil acts.[22]

Putting a question mark on the religious bona fides and *nang* of the people of Swat, Khushal Khan has asserted that, although they claim they are Muslims, in practice they care little for religion.[23] He had believed that Swat was inhabited by Muslims but, as he now discovered, they were all heathens.[24] They have no concept of the 'Afghan *nang*'. As they are cowards and lack courage, they avoid going to the battlefield and fighting bravely. Although they are not any good at warfare, yet they boast of their bravery.[25]

Khushal Khan has observed the absence of a government or leading head or chief; and the consequent dismal situation and ruinous state of Swat. In condemnation of the people, he has further stated that, although there were once rulers here, the present occupants have no men of the calibre for ruling.[26] He, also contended that though the Yusufzi were numerous, they were like a herd of animals, so their numbers were useless.[27] They lived in dirty, stinking houses like some unclean and foul-smelling inn.[28] They kept a number of grain-bins in their houses and were thus worse than the Hindus in hording grain. The Baizi (the section of the Yusufzi who inhabits the left side of the Swat Valley) among them could socially mix with the nobler people but the Khwajuzi (also Khwazuzi, the section of the Yusufzi who inhabits the right side of the Swat Valley) were just money-minded.[29]

Khushal Khan reviled the people of Swat because (in his estimation) they did not abide by their word. They went after small gains, minor benefits, and insignificant purposes; and for minor reasons they were either pleased or displeased. They made friends just for personal gain and did not appreciate the value of honour and grace. And all of them were hen-pecked money-mongers. Moreover, they tolerated the vanity and undue expectations of their wives and obeyed whatever they commanded of them. They did not spend their wealth themselves but either the *shaikh* and *mula* profited from it with his cunning and deception, or it was spent by their wives. They betrothed their daughters in return for money and cared little for the breed of the man.[30]

Khushal Khan has asserted that the people of Swat had superficial friendships, and were capable of causing great damage to others for minor personal gains. They even caused themselves great losses for small immediate benefits. They may be rich but ate tasteless food and lacked manners. The entire population was like some wild flock; and all of them were malicious, extremely self-centred, and ego-centric.[31] Their 'yes' was not trustworthy, but their 'no' was. They made promises which they did not abide by and which they turned their backs on easily.[32]

They performed work all the year round and never sat quietly. Money was their faith and idol, and they always longed for gold and silver. They tried to turn each *paisah* (the lowest unit of the *rupai*: rupee) into two by whatever means they could, and all of them—male and female, young and old—were completely absorbed in this process. They neither welcomed a guest with open heart nor did they have any courtesy of words and deeds.[33] If an aggrieved person sought justice from a *malak*, the other party could manipulate the *malak* with a rupee to turn the poor innocent one into the guilty party.[34]

Condemning some other alleged traits of the people of Swat, Khushal Khan asserted that they did not use common sense and wisdom but believed in hearsay. They were engulfed by wrong manners and deeds, and the wicked among them went unpunished. If someone fraudulently claimed to be a doctor, no one would expose his falsehood. And, if someone cunningly pretended to be an *alim* or *darwaish* (scholar or hermit), no one would be concerned about his bona fides.[35] Besides, all their *malakan* and *khanan* were as stupid as donkeys and all their religious *ulama* and *shaikhan* (scholars and holy persons) were ignorant.[36] The *malakan* fought with their brothers over the landed property and the estates of their fathers became divided into small bits and pieces.[37] Although the *ulama* and *shaikhan* should do their work and the *khanan* theirs', the Yusufzi mixed them up.[38] Their *ulama* were quite ignorant, as were their scholars. Their jurists were not educated, their knowledge being limited to only the basic books of *fiqah* (*Kanz* and *Quduri*), and even this knowledge was superficial and lacking in depth. They exploited their religious status and position for worldly gains caring not for what was fair or unfair.[39]

While condemning and reviling Mian Nur[40] especially, Khushal Khan put question mark on his knowledge and beliefs.[41] He contended that it was Mian Nur who caused the failure of his mission of collecting *lakhkaray* (plural of *lakhkar*) from Swat against the Mughals.[42] He stated about Swat:

دوه کاره دی په سوات کنبے کہ خفی دی کہ جلی

مخـزن د درویـزه دے یـا دفتـر د شیخ ملـی

دا دوه نشتـه په سوات کنبے څوک چه وائی یا علی

اَلصّالحُــــوْنَ لِلّهِ وَالطّالحُـــوْنَ لِـــئَ 43

Meaning: Two works are reputed in Swat, in public and in private: the Makhzan of (Akhun) Darwizah or the Daftar of Shaikh Mali. And two are non-existent in Swat: those who invoke Ali (i.e. Shias) and those who attribute all the good things to Allah and the bad to themselves (probably referring to some sect or religion).

Whereas, at another place he has stated:

مخـزن د درویـزه د میـاںنـور شـیخی پیـری

الثَّالثُ بالخیـر د حمـزه خانـی میـری

دا درے توکه ڈیر قدر ڈیر عزت لَری په سوات کښے

وَخدائے وتـه ښکاره دی وَئیل نشی پـه خَیـری ٤٤

*Meaning: The Makhzan of Darwizah and shaikhi and piri (priesthood
and sainthood) of Mian Nur, and the third one is the khan-ship and
chieftainship of Hamzah. All the three carry great value and respect in
Swat. This I am not saying due to a grudge but
Allah knows it is so.*

ANALYSIS OF SOME POINTS OF KHUSHAL KHAN

As is evident from the aforesaid, Khushal Khan Khattak has praised
some aspects of Swat such as the meadows, natural riches, scenic beauty,
fertility, fragrant breezes, low prices, and rich past. At the same time,
he has criticized some of its aspects, and has accused the people of not
honouring the blessings and not acting in a manner required of them
such as Swat deserves. He has also criticized the social and religious
evils, the *khanan*, *malakan*, *piran*, *faqiran*, and *mulan*, alike, for their
behaviour, misconduct, unworthiness, and abuse of their status, power,
and prestige for worldly gains. He condemns the ignorance, incorrect
religious beliefs, and violations of Islamic laws, as well failing to honour
'Afghan *nang*' through not forming a *lakhkar* and taking up arms on his
side against the Mughals.

Some of Khushal Khan's contentions are sound. For instance, his
analysis of the drawbacks of the *waish* system (although doubtless, it was
instituted in good faith and was ideal in its own time and circumstances);
giving no share in inheritance to the female heirs; wedlock with the
in-laws by brothers or other near male agnates of the deceased; and
killing not the real murderer in revenge but a person of his family more
influential or valued. His condemnation of the role of the *malakan* and
khanan (e.g. bribery and exploitation of their status for personal gain)
and of religious persons (e.g. exploiting their status for worldly gain)
is also justifiable.

However, all Khushal Khan's contentions and assertions are not
sound. For instance, most of the vices he enumerates are not specific to
Swat only. They could be claimed as being prevalent in other Pukhtun

and the neighbouring areas as well to a degree greater than in Swat. For instance taking money by the bride's family from the bridegroom's family was prevalent in other areas with greater frequency. In any case, this money was mostly spent on the bride's marriage arrangements and other paraphernalia and therefore a daughter's marriage was not a burden for her family (as it is these days, as in this way all the marriage expenses were borne by the bridegroom's family).

Khushal Khan's condemnation of the people of Swat for not looking into the breed of the person to whom they marry their daughters and sisters is justified by their establishing matrimonial relation with Khushal Khan himself, as Malak Malu Khan's daughter (Malak Hamzah Khan's sister) was married to Khushal Khan in total disregard of Khushal Khan and his family's past anti-Yusufzi and pro-Mughal role, and hence his breed. Khwajah Muhammad Sayal has questioned, in his book *Khushalyat aw Haqayaq (Intiqadi Jaaj)*, whether Khushal Khan was in fact ethnically an Afghan or Pukhtun.[45]

Khushal Khan has condemned the people of Swat for hard work, which is not a condemnable but a praiseworthy trait. As far his condemnation of the division of land among the brothers is concerned, it was due to their being the real owners of the land. The practice was perhaps strange for Khushal Khan because the land in his country was under the ownership of the rulers,[46] which they granted in *jagir*s (fiefs) to whom they wished and which could be resumed at their free will from whom they wished. There is a significant difference between an owner and a fief-holder (he himself was a fief-holder and not an owner).

Khushal Khan's reviling the people of Swat for not being hospitable is also not justifiable. His misconception is perhaps due to his long stay of seven months in Swat. A person who stays for a long period is not considered a guest and so is treated or served like a family members in routine. And a Pashto saying about a guest who stays for long is:

ميلمه چې د درېو ورځونه زيات شي نو شيطان شي

Meaning: When a guest's stay exceeds three days,
he becomes as unwanted as Satan.

More important, a guest like Khushal Khan, who remained pro-Mughal and anti-Yusufzi for most of his life, would have been entertained as guest as an obligation of the Pukhtun code of life but certainly not very warmly. The Qandahai, sent by H.G. Raverty to Swat in 1858, has reported:

> The Afgháns of Suwát, like others of their countrymen, are very hospitable. When strangers enter a village, and it be the residence of a Khán or Chief, he entertains the whole party; but if there be no great man resident in the place, each stranger of the party is taken by some villager to his house, and is entertained as his guest.[47]

As regards the religious bona fides of the people of Swat, which are questioned by Khushal Khan, the same would be the case with other Pukhtuns. His condemnation of some other traits of the people of Swat, e.g. the lack of manners, superficial friendship, causing great losses to others for minor self-interest, tolerating vanity and obeying orders of their wives, and so forth, also do not withstand hundred per cent scrutiny. These are remarks and contentions of a person who left Swat in anger and as a failed person.

Similarly, Khushal Khan has asserted:

هـر مغـل چپي پـه سـوات راشـي شـهزاده شـي

هـر سمے ئي و   منصب تـه امـاده شـي 48

Meaning: Any stray Mughal who enters Swat, turns to become a prince and everyone from amongst the people of Swat long for rank and status from him.

And that:

د هغـو چپي زړۀ د چرګ پـه مرګ ریـږدي

مصلحت د سپینو تـورو ورتـه پلیـژدي 49

Meaning: Those who tremble at the sight of a dying chicken, cannot be expected to enter the field with drawn swords.

And that:

د بی بی پـه کور ئے ووری کټ کټ کاڼری

چـه د سـوات خلمی بیلیـبری لـه پالنگـه 50

Meaning: As if a storm of stones will hit his wife if a youth of Swat leaves the bed (meaning: goes out of Swat).

These verses are clear testament of Khushal Khan's unfounded allegations and absurd contentions, as neither Swat remained under Mughal suzerainty, despite Akbar's attempts, nor did any Mughal come to Swat, nor did the people of Swat seek Mughal service. The people of Swat gallantly fought the Mughal forces for years during Emperor Akbar's reign, and not only made a failure of that Mughal attempt but continually sustained their independence, as detailed in the previous chapter.[51] They did not serve the Mughals like Khushal Khan and his family, nor long for rank and status from them. He himself also has asserted at another place:

كه د سمے كه د غرهٔ دى يوسف زئ
همگى مزرى دى مهٔ ئے وى زوال [52]

Meaning: Long live the Yusufzi—lions of both plains and hills.

Khushal Khan has condemned the people of Swat and has written what came into his heart, which he himself has admitted. He has condemned the rituals of the area and has made undue allegations. However, his own writings speak of his prejudices and absurdities and the contradictions are visible. One can find the true picture in his writings about Swat.[53] Rahim Shah Rahim has aptly asserted:

هر بيان ئى د نفرت او حقارت دى
په لهجه كښى ئى بى كچه ډير شدت دى
د سوات خلق ئى ويستلى ټول د دين نه
خارج كړى ئى د شرعى د آئين نه
د جهان واړه عېبونه ئى شمېرلي
هغه ټول ئى په سواتيانو ورتپلي
كار روزگار دى كه مذهب دى كه رواج دى
خوشحال خان وائي بى دينه ټول سماج دى [54]

Meaning: All what he has said is hate and sarcasm, and the tone is greatly harsh. In his estimation he has ousted all the people of Swat from Islam. He has counted all the vices of the world and has linked them with the people of Swat. All, whether it is the profession or the religion or the customary law, prevalent in Swat have been condemned and reviled by Khushal Khan.

And that:

وروستو بیا پسې تحریر ئې سواتنامه کړه
پـه کنځلو ئـې داغـي ورلـه جامـه کـړه 55

Meaning: And subsequently he wrote Swat Namah,
all stained by abuses.

The main reason of Khushal Khan grudges against and reviling of the
Swat Yusufzi was their not taking up arms at his behest to fight the
Mughals, although some did. But, in this respect, he had excessive
expectations, which is evident from his following verse.

چـه د ننـگ تـوره دِ واخیسـته خوشـحاله!
درومـه سـوات تـه خُـهٔ ختـک خُهٔ ئـې لښکـرِ 56

Meaning: If you Khushal ought to fight for the nang, you have to look
to Swat, for Khattaks and their lakhkaray are of no worth.

The Swat Yusufzi have their own grounds for such a course of action
and policy. They could not side with Khushal Khan because relations
between Aurangzeb and their brethren, the Yusufzi of the plains area,
had already become cordial. Mian Nur's role, because of divergence in
his and Khushal Khan's viewpoint and beliefs, also contributed to the
failure of Khushal Khan's mission in Swat, for which he has reviled both
Mian Nur and the people of Swat.[57] But, he is himself to be blamed for it.
He visited Swat for making the Yusufzi his allies but instead he caused
unnecessary controversies and debates by objecting to and criticizing
Akhun Darwizah's beliefs, stature, and also his book *Makhzan* as well as
Mian Nur's.[58] Surprisingly enough, a time which Khushal Khan should
have spent on the battlefield or swiftly convening the Swat Yusufzi to
fight for a cause, was instead wasted (a long seven months) in touring,
hunting, debates, creating controversies, and nurturing unwanted grudges
against the people and leaders (both religious and secular) of Swat.

KHUSHAL KHAN'S PITFALLS

Khushal Khan uses his own yard stick of love and hate. While
condemning Mian Nur, he says that it was not he, but his heart, that
spoke out against Mian Nur; when his heart judged someone as good,

he can never be called bad, and those whom his heart rejected, must stand rejected.[59] That was why the Mughals were good as far as he was in their good books and the Pukhtuns (including Yusufzi), who opposed the Mughals, were bad and hence deserved to be beheaded, effaced from the surface of the earth, and have mounds made of their skulls. And, when he turned against the Mughals, the Mughals became the lot to be beheaded, destroyed, and effaced from the surface of the earth, and the Yusufzi to be made allies and befriended in self-interest. Rahim Shah Rahim has negated Khushal Khan's contention about Mian Nur's stature and education and has asserted that Mian Nur acquired his education in Lahore, Sultanpur, and Delhi, stayed in Makkah and Madinah for years, and had done great services for the cause of Islam.[60]

On the one hand, Khushal Khan has proudly contended:

هر پښتون چه د مغلو نوکری کا

که دِ زده د هغو واړو بهترکؽ یَم [61]

Meaning: I am better than any Pukhtun who is in the service of the Mughal, should you have any wisdom.

He, however, already foresaw his future and fortune in Mughal services as he has admitted:

ما وے زۀ به د مغل په نوکرئ کښے

رکیبونه کړم د سرو، د سپینو نال [62]

Meaning: I believed that in Mughal service I would make the saddles of my horses of gold and their shoes of silver.

And later when things went wrong, he cursed all those Pukhtuns who served with the Mughals. He, moreover, has admitted poetically that he has killed thousands of Pukhtuns (Urakzi, Bangash, and Yusufzi) for the Mughals, so much so that the animals walked over their dead bodies and that there were heaps of their skulls; and in Attak and Peshawar one could still see those skull-towers in existence.[63] He has said himself, And then suddenly Pukhtuns rose against the Mughals once again; and this turmoil reminded me of my revenge against the Mughals.[64] He has admitted that it was not he but Emperor Aurangzeb who severed their relations.[65] However, as said earlier, all his sons and the Khattak did not side with him, and hence his assertion that:

شکایت لـه نـورو مـه کـوه خوشحاله!

چه خپل څویه هم په ننگ لـه تا ویزار دی 66

*Meaning: O Khushal! Do not make complaints against others, when
your own sons are disgusted with you and do not side with you in nang.*

Khushal Khan has spoken of the support that the Yusufzi promised[67] but
has also condemned them, terming them lazy in the cause of *nang*.[68] His
condemnation is not justified. A person who not only served himself
the Mughals, but whose ancestors had done so against the same
fellow Pukhtun Yusufzi, could not be trusted by the Yusufzi without
reservations. He personally has admitted:

لکه زۀ وُم په راستئ په درستئ کښے

د مغُل پـه خدمـت نـه وُه بـل افغـان 69

Meaning: No Afghan was ever so loyal to the Mughals as I was.

And that:

زۀ نوکر ووم یوسفزي ئي روگردان وو

څکه ورغلـۀ تـر سـواتـه زمـا کران وو 70

*Meaning: I was loyal to the Mughals whereas the Yusufzi were rebels.
That made my going to Swat difficult.*

Khushal Khan, therefore, should not have expected unquestioned support
and alliance from his former enemies.

But, despite all this, when he came to Swat, a *jargah*, or a meeting,
was held in Damghar. The Swat Yusufzi pardoned his past deeds and
promised to take up arms and form *lakhkaray* in his support against the
Mughals.[71] It was his reviling of, and sarcastic remarks about, a copy
of Akhun Darwizah's book *Makhzan* that turned the tide,[72] and the core
issue of forming *lakhkaray* and fighting the Mughals went into the
background. Basically, he was not a good politician and stumbled at
each and every step. He, moreover, did not know the politics of Swat.[73]
His undiplomatic and unwise behaviour and stand even divided the
khanan and *malakan* into two blocs, one siding with Mian Nur and the
other with him.[74] Instead of having been diplomatic and courteous and
accepting the counsels of his friends and well-wishers, he was taken over
by emotions which ruined all his previous efforts and the main purpose
for which he was in Swat.[75]

Hamesh Khalil has evaluated Khushal Khan's pitfalls and shortcomings in this regard and has contended that, for obtaining the alliance of the Swat Yusufzi, Khushal Khan needed to concentrate all his efforts on the completion of his mission rather than indulging in activities that would be counterproductive. Instead of controlling his temper, he went beyond moderation which directly resulted in his failure.[76] Bahadar Shah Zafar Kaka Khail has said that Khushal Khan was an extremist by nature.[77]

While dealing with Khushal Khan's approach to the Yusufzi for an alliance against the Mughals, Olaf Caroe has stated, 'With the Yusufzais he failed, and failed completely'. He has asserted that this 'failure was more or less inevitable; it was rooted in history'.[78] Because,

> The Khataks had basked in Mughal smiles when the empire was fighting the Yusufzais; they had taken advantage of the imperial aid to occupy large slices of Yusufzai territory. Now that the Khataks were out of favour, the Yusufzais saw no reason to help them—very much the reverse. Khushhal himself seemed unable to see this; he merely scorned the Yusufzais as cowards and opportunists. Some of the verses he wrote about them are amusing, but their colour has to be corrected with this in view. In Khushhal's eyes they were double-dyed villains, first because they were hereditary foes and secondly because, when he approached them, they would not play.[79]

Interestingly, the people of Swat had no conflict of interest with Aurangzeb. They were neither his subjects nor neighbours. Neither had Aurangzeb made any attempt against Swat, like his great-grandfather Emperor Akbar, nor did he usurp their independence. There was no ground or logic for the people of Swat to take up arms against Aurangzeb at the instigation and behest of a person who had not only been loyal to the Mughals but served them to his best against the interests of the Pukhtuns and who had remained anti-Yusufzi in his past career, and 'whose father, grandfather and great grandfather have died fighting the Yusufzais',[80] basically for the cause of the Mughals.

While evaluating the causes of why the Yusufzi did not take up arms and side with Khushal Khan against the Mughals, Bahadar Shah Zafar Kaka Khail has stated that one of the reasons was that the enmity between the Yusufzi and the Khattaks was quite old and, despite the relations becoming somewhat friendly after Khushal Khan's imprisonment, its roots had spread.[81] Besides, Khushal Khan himself has openly admitted his personal and of his father and grandfathers' loyalty and services to the Mughals and was proud of them.[82]

Significantly, despite all the above-said, the Swat Yusufzi ignored the past grudges and grievances, but Khushal Khan turned the tide by causing fresh controversies and debates. Therefore, the people of Swat seem justified in not joining him against the Mughals. It was his past history and his behaviour in Swat that caused his failure to win over the Swat Yusufzi (although some formed a *lakhkar* and attacked a Mughal fort).

A MISS

It is pertinent to state that writers and researchers generally make no difference between the Swat Yusufzi, or the Yusufzi that inhabit Swat (and also Bunair, Dir, and Shanglahpar), and those of the Samah, Mardan and Swabi areas who are mainly basically Mandanr, a sister tribe of the Yusufzi but commonly counted as Yusufzi. Hence, while writing about the history and affairs of the Yusufzi or Mandanr of the Samah, Mardan and Swabi regions, they also include and take for granted the Swat Yusufzi. This is unsound and unrealistic, as the history and affairs of Swat are different to those other areas because of its geographical location.

A case of this nature is of Dr Himayatullah Yaqubi. While negating my contention, although he has not given the source from which he had taken the assertion, it has been made in my article 'Khushal Khan Khattak and Swat': a major part of which forms this chapter, 'that the people of Swat had no conflict of interest with Aurangzeb. They were neither his subject[s] nor neighbors. Neither Aurangzeb has made attempt against Swat like his grand-grandfather Emperor Akbar nor did he usurp their independence',[83] Dr Himayatullah has asserted:

> In fact, Aurangzeb dispatched several expeditions against the Yusufzais for their suppression. In the year 1667, Afghan borderland witnessed the uprising of the Yusufzais under the leadership of Bhaku Khan. They also defeated Kamil Khan, the *faujdar* of Attock. An expedition of the Mughal was routed in 1667 in which two thousand Mughal soldiers were killed while fighting against the Yusufzais... Aurangzeb personally came to Hasan Abdal in June 1675. As stated somewhere else, Mukaram Khan was sent *en route* to Bajaur to restore imperial sway in the areas. In one of his battles against the Yusufzais considerable numbers of Mughals were slain.[84]

Dr Himayatullah has failed to comprehend my assertion. My contention is solely about Swat, and not the Samah, Mardan and Swabi Yusufzi-Mandanr. Whereas Dr Himayatullah's contentions has no relations to Swat.

While dealing with Khushal Khan's Swat visit and its nature, viz. whether he failed in achieving the objective of his Swat visit, in negating this assertion of Olaf Caroe, also quoted by me, that 'with the Yusufzais he failed, and failed completely',[85] Dr Himayatullah has asserted:

> Unlike Olaf Caore and Sultan-i-Rome's claims, Khushal Khan did not fail completely rather the timing of his effort was not quite appropriate. The Yusufzais had already established their writ in their areas under Bhaku Khan after inflicted so many defeats upon the Mughals. At that moment there was no need of fresh mobilization of *lashkar* in Swat. At the end, he mobilized a section of the Yusufzai tribe but it was not of so much use as they had already defeated Mughal several times under Bhaku Khan. In fact, Bhaku Khan at that time was the virtual ruler of the entire area from Bajaur to the Indus and there are no evidences to support the claim whether he needed the support of Khushal Khan at that time.[86]

Dr Himayatullah's assertion negates his own contention and reveals his failure in negating Olaf Caroe's contention with sound evidence. His own assertion that 'in fact, the timing of Khushal Khan's struggle for a united action against the Mughals was such that it could not motivate all the Afghans for such adventurism';[87] that 'therefore, Khushal Khan's struggle for reinforcement did not held much ground at that time';[88] and that 'rather the timing of his effort was not quite appropriate.... In fact, Bhaku Khan at that time was the virtual ruler of the entire area'[89] are sufficient to negate his refutation of Olaf Caroe's assertions.

It needs to be mentioned (as I have also recorded that 'although some formed a *lakhkar* and attacked a Mughal fort'[90]) that the taking up arms of a small band of the Yusufzi against the Mughals on Khushal's behest and attacking a Mughal fort do not imply that he did not fail. He certainly failed in enlisting support of the Yusufzi for the reasons already detailed, which the contentions of Dr Himayatullah have fully endorsed, perhaps inadvertently, by repeatedly stating that the timing of Khushal's struggle for a united action against the Mughals was inappropriate, that Bhaku Khan had established his authority in the areas contested for by the Mughals, and that Aurangzeb had made a 'truce with the Afghans and the Yusufzai of the *samah* areas'.[91]

Dr Himayatullah has stated: 'Sultan-i-Rome is of the view that the Swat Yusufzais have their own grounds for such a course of action and policy. They could not side with him, because relations between Aurangzeb and their brethren—the Yusufzais of the plain area—had already become cordial.'[92] Refuting this view, he has asserted:

> In fact, the timing of Khushal Khan's struggle for a united action against the Mughals was such that it could not motivate all the Afghans for such adventurism. The relations of the Yusufzais and Aurangzeb were not cordial as claimed by Sultan-i-Rome. Emperor Aurangzeb several times sent punitive expeditions against the Yusufzai Afghans. The fact was that Bhaku Khan had firmly resisted their entry to the Afghan mainland and established his rule over the entire areas. In quelling his uprising Aurangzeb even personally came to Hasan Abdal but gained no success. At last, he was compelled to make truce with the Afghans and the Yusufzai of the *samah* areas. However, the truce between the Mughal and Yusufzais can not be called the end of their rivalry. The ascendency of Bhaku Khan was due to the failure of several Mughal expeditions in the areas. Therefore, Khushal Khan's struggle for reinforcement did not held much ground at that time.[93]

As is evident from Dr Himayatullah's above quoted view, I have talked of only relations between the Swat Yusufzi and Aurangzeb, not the Yusufzi in general. Nor have I claimed that the relations between the Yusufzi in general and Aurangzeb were cordial, as is evident from my words, also quoted by Dr Himayatullah: 'because relations between Aurangzeb and their brethren—the Yusufzais of the plain area had already become cordial'. Dr Himayatullah has endorsed my contention and contradicted his own by asserting, 'In fact, the timing of Khushal Khan's struggle for a united action against the Mughals was such that it could not motivate all the Afghans for such adventurism'; and also by his assertion, 'At last, he [Aurangzeb] was compelled to make truce with the Afghans and the Yusufzai of *samah* areas.' Dr Himayatullah's further assertion, 'However, the truce between the Mughal and Yusufzai can not be called the end of their rivalry', is unneeded and out of context as neither have I said that rivalry between the Yusufzi and the Mughals ended, nor do relations becoming cordial imply an end to rivalry.

NOTES

1. See Dost Muhammad Khan Kamil Mohmand, *Khushal Khan Khattak: Sawanih Hayat aur Adabi Aasar par Tabsirah* (Urdu) (2nd edn., Peshawar: Shaheen Books, 2006) [henceforward Mohmand, *Khushal Khan Khattak*], 161–270; Sultan-i-Rome, 'Khushḥāl Khān Khattak: An Afghan Nationalist or a Mughul Loyalist?', *Journal of the Pakistan Historical Society* (Karachi), 64/3 (July–September 2016), 61–94; Afzal Khan Khattak, *Tarikh Murasa: Muqabilah, Tashih aw Nutunah lah* Dost Muhammad Khan Kamil Momand (Peshawar: University Book Agency, 2006), 316–22; Olaf Caroe, *The Pathans: 550 B.C.–A.D. 1957* (repr., Karachi: Oxford University Press, 1976), 231; Allah Bakhsh Yusufi, *Yusufzai* (Karachi: Muhammad Ali Educational Society, 1960), 277. For the causes and factors responsible for and the enmity, and the wars between the Khattak and Yusufzi-Mandarn, see Hamesh Khalil, *sarizah* to Khushal Khan Khattak, *Swat Namah da Khushal Khan Khattak*, with *muqadimah, tahqiq aw samun* by Hamesh Khalil (Akurah Khattak: Markazi Khushal Adabi wa Saqafati Jargah (Regd.), 1986) [henceforward Khattak, *Swat Namah da Khushal Khan Khattak*], 32–3; Sayyad Bahadar Shah Zafar Kaka Khail, *Pukhtanah da Tarikh pah Ranra kay* (Pashto) (Peshawar: University Book Agency, n.d.), 551, 557, 634–5; Khushal Khan Khattak, *Kulyat-i Khushal Khan Khattak*, Vol. 2, *Qasaid, Rubaiyat, Qitat aw Mutafariqat* (Pashto) (Peshawar: Azeem Publishing House, n.d.) [henceforward Khattak, *Kulyat-i Khushal Khan Khattak*, Vol. 2], 45–7, 53, 283; Sher Shah Tarkhawi, *da Khushal pah Haqlah* to Khushal Khan Khattak, *Kulyat-i Khushal Khan Khattak*, Vol. 1, *Ghazliyat* (Pashto) (Peshawar: Azeem Publishing House, n.d.) [henceforward Khattak, *Kulyat-i Khushal Khan Khattak*, Vol. 1], شپږ-اووه (*shpag-uwah*); Caroe, *The Pathans*, 241; Yusufi, *Yusufzai*, 267–9; Khan Roshan Khan, *Yusufzai Qaum ki Sarguzasht* (Karachi: Roshan Khan and Company, 1986), 235–56.
2. Khattak, *Kulyat-i Khushal Khan Khattak*, Vol. 2, 366. Also see Muhammad Nawaz Tair, *dibachah* to Pir Muazam Shah, *Tawarikh Hafiz Rahmat Khani*, with *dibachah* by Muhammad Nawaz Tair (Pashto/Persian) (2nd impression, Peshawar: Pukhtu Academy, 1987), 20. See also Khattak, *Kulyat-i Khushal Khan Khattak*, Vol. 2, 369.
3. Mohmand, *Khushal Khan Khattak*, 95.
4. Khushal Khan Khattak, *Swat Nama of Khushal Khan Khattak*, edited and trans. in to English by Shakeel Ahmad, with preface by Raj Wali Shah Khattak (Peshawar: Pashto Academy, n.d.) (henceforward Khattak, *Swat Nama of Khushal Khan Khattak*), 8.
5. Khattak, *Kulyat-i Khushal Khan Khattak*, Vol. 2, 52.
6. For some details of Khushal Khan's loyalty to and services for the Mughals, see Sultan-i-Rome, 'Khushḥāl Khān Khattak: An Afghan Nationalist or a Mughul Loyalist?', 61–94.
7. See Khattak, *Swat Nama of Khushal Khan Khattak*, 13; Khattak, *Swat Namah da Khushal Khan Khattak*, 56; Khattak, *Tarikh Murasa*, 380.
8. See Khattak, *Swat Nama of Khushal Khan Khattak*, 2; Khattak, *Swat Namah da Khushal Khan Khattak*, 48; Khattak, *Tarikh Murasa*, 377.
9. See Khattak, *Swat Nama of Khushal Khan Khattak*, 3; Khattak, *Swat Namah da Khushal Khan Khattak*, 48–9; Khattak, *Tarikh Murasa*, 378.

10. See Khattak, *Swat Nama of Khushal Khan Khattak*, 3; Khattak, *Swat Namah da Khushal Khan Khattak*, 48–9; Khattak, *Tarikh Murasa*, 378.

11. See Khattak, *Swat Nama of Khushal Khan Khattak*, 4; Khattak, *Swat Namah da Khushal Khan Khattak*, 49; Khattak, *Tarikh Murasa*, 378.

12. See Khattak, *Swat Nama of Khushal Khan Khattak*, 6; Khattak, *Swat Namah da Khushal Khan Khattak*, 51; Khattak, *Tarikh Murasa*, 378.

13. See Khattak, *Swat Nama of Khushal Khan Khattak*, 5; Khattak, *Swat Namah da Khushal Khan Khattak*, 50; Khattak, *Tarikh Murasa*, 378.

14. See Khattak, *Swat Nama of Khushal Khan Khattak*, 5; Khattak, *Swat Namah da Khushal Khan Khattak*, 50; Khattak, *Tarikh Murasa*, 378.

15. See Khattak, *Swat Nama of Khushal Khan Khattak*, 22; Khattak, *Swat Namah da Khushal Khan Khattak*, 64; Khattak, *Tarikh Murasa*, 382.

16. Khattak, *Swat Nama of Khushal Khan Khattak*, 2. Also see Khattak, *Swat Namah da Khushal Khan Khattak*, 48; Khattak, *Tarikh Murasa*, 377.

17. Khattak, *Swat Nama of Khushal Khan Khattak*, 3. Also see Khattak, *Swat Namah da Khushal Khan Khattak*, 49; Khattak, *Tarikh Murasa*, 378.

18. See Khattak, *Swat Nama of Khushal Khan Khattak*, 4; Khattak, *Swat Namah da Khushal Khan Khattak*, 49–50; Khattak, *Tarikh Murasa*, 378.

19. Khattak, *Swat Nama of Khushal Khan Khattak*, 16. Also see Khattak, *Swat Namah da Khushal Khan Khattak*, 59; Khattak, *Tarikh Murasa*, 381.

20. Under the landownership and tenure system devised, or adopted, by Shaikh Mali, after the occupation of the land by the Yusufzi in the sixteenth century, the land and villages were interchanged among the owners after every few years. For the *waish* see chapter 8. For details about the *waish* (*wesh*) system, see Sultan-i-Rome, *Land and Forest Governance in Swat: Transition from Tribal System to State to Pakistan* (Karachi: Oxford University Press, 2016), 43–65; Sultan-i-Rome, *Forestry in the Princely State of Swat and Kalam (North-West Pakistan): A Historical Perspective on Norms and Practices*, IP6 Working Paper No.6 (Zurich: Swiss National Centre of Competence in Research (NCCR) North-South, 2005), 31–44; Sultan-i-Rome, *Swat State (1915–1969): From Genesis to Merger; An Analysis of Political, Administrative, Socio-Political, and Economic Developments* (Karachi: Oxford University Press, 2008), 229–37.

21. Khattak, *Swat Nama of Khushal Khan Khattak*, 5. Also see Khattak, *Swat Namah da Khushal Khan Khattak*, 50; Khattak, *Tarikh Murasa*, 378.

22. See Khattak, *Swat Nama of Khushal Khan Khattak*, 23; Khattak, *Swat Namah da Khushal Khan Khattak*, 64; Khattak, *Tarikh Murasa*, 383.

23. See Khattak, *Swat Nama of Khushal Khan Khattak*, 21; Khattak, *Swat Namah da Khushal Khan Khattak*, 62; Khattak, *Tarikh Murasa*, 382.

24. See Khattak, *Swat Nama of Khushal Khan Khattak*, 60; Khattak, *Swat Namah da Khushal Khan Khattak*, 92.

25. See Khattak, *Swat Nama of Khushal Khan Khattak*, 25; Khattak, *Swat Namah da Khushal Khan Khattak*, 66; Khattak, *Tarikh Murasa*, 383. Also see Khattak, *Kulyat-i Khushal Khan Khattak*, Vol. 2, 286–7. For his further contention that the Yusufzi have no concern for *nang*, see Khattak, *Swat Nama of Khushal Khan Khattak*, 52, 57; Khattak, *Swat Namah da Khushal Khan Khattak*, 86, 90; Khattak, *Tarikh Murasa*, 390; Khattak, *Kulyat-i Khushal Khan Khattak*, Vol. 2, 334–5.

26. See Khattak, *Swat Nama of Khushal Khan Khattak*, 3; Khattak, *Swat Namah da Khushal Khan Khattak*, 49; Khattak, *Tarikh Murasa*, 378.

27. See Khattak, *Swat Nama of Khushal Khan Khattak*, 7; Khattak, *Swat Namah da Khushal Khan Khattak*, 52; Khattak, *Tarikh Murasa*, 379. Also see Khattak, *Kulyat-i Khushal Khan Khattak*, Vol. 1, 82.

28. See Khattak, *Swat Nama of Khushal Khan Khattak*, 5; Khattak, *Swat Namah da Khushal Khan Khattak*, 50; Khattak, *Tarikh Murasa*, 378.

29. See Khattak, *Swat Nama of Khushal Khan Khattak*, 5; Khattak, *Swat Namah da Khushal Khan Khattak*, 50; Khattak, *Tarikh Murasa*, 378.

30. See Khattak, *Swat Nama of Khushal Khan Khattak*, 16–17, 22, 68; Khattak, *Swat Namah da Khushal Khan Khattak*, 59–60, 63, 98; Khattak, *Tarikh Murasa*, 381–2, 390. Also see Khattak, *Kulyat-i Khushal Khan Khattak*, Vol. 1, 82.

31. See Khattak, *Swat Nama of Khushal Khan Khattak*, 18; Khattak, *Swat Namah da Khushal Khan Khattak*, 60–1; Khattak, *Tarikh Murasa*, 381–2.

32. See Khattak, *Swat Nama of Khushal Khan Khattak*, 19; Khattak, *Swat Namah da Khushal Khan Khattak*, 61; Khattak, *Tarikh Murasa*, 382; Khattak, *Kulyat-i Khushal Khan Khattak*, Vol. 1, 82.

33. See Khattak, *Swat Nama of Khushal Khan Khattak*, 20, 25–6; Khattak, *Swat Namah da Khushal Khan Khattak*, 62, 66; Khattak, *Tarikh Murasa*, 382–3. Also see Khattak, *Kulyat-i Khushal Khan Khattak*, Vol. 2, 263.

34. See Khattak, *Swat Nama of Khushal Khan Khattak*, 21; Khattak, *Swat Namah da Khushal Khan Khattak*, 62; Khattak, *Tarikh Murasa*, 382. Also see Khattak, *Kulyat-i Khushal Khan Khattak*, Vol. 1, 82.

35. See Khattak, *Swat Nama of Khushal Khan Khattak*, 24–5; Khattak, *Swat Namah da Khushal Khan Khattak*, 65; Khattak, *Tarikh Murasa*, 383.

36. See Khattak, *Swat Nama of Khushal Khan Khattak*, 27, 36–7, 41–2, 54; Khattak, *Swat Namah da Khushal Khan Khattak*, 67, 77–8, 88; Khattak, *Tarikh Murasa*, 383, 386–7. Also see Khattak, *Kulyat-i Khushal Khan Khattak*, Vol. 1, 82; Khattak, *Kulyat-i Khushal Khan Khattak*, Vol. 2, 286–7.

37. See Khattak, *Swat Nama of Khushal Khan Khattak*, 28; Khattak, *Swat Namah da Khushal Khan Khattak*, 68; Khattak, *Tarikh Murasa*, 384.

38. See Khattak, *Swat Nama of Khushal Khan Khattak*, 59; Khattak, *Swat Namah da Khushal Khan Khattak*, 92.

39. See Khattak, *Swat Nama of Khushal Khan Khattak*, 28–30; Khattak, *Swat Namah da Khushal Khan Khattak*, 68–70; Khattak, *Tarikh Murasa*, 384.

40. Mian Nur was the grandson of Akhun Darwizah and a revered religious person in Swat at that time. He had differences with Khushal Khan over his views about Akhun Darwizah's religious stature and the criticism of his book *Makhzan*. Khushal Khan alleges that he was a Mughal agent. For details about Mian Nur, his family and influence, Khushal Khan's allegations against him, and Rahim Shah Rahim's rebuke of Khushal Khan's contention, see Khattak, *Swat Nama of Khushal Khan Khattak*; Khattak, *Swat Namah da Khushal Khan Khattak*; Rahim Shah Rahim, *Swat Namah Jawab Namah* (Pashto verse) (Mingawarah, Swat: Shoaib Sons Publishers and Booksellers, 2006), 106–10, 113.

41. See Khattak, *Swat Nama of Khushal Khan Khattak*, 31–33; Khattak, *Swat Namah da Khushal Khan Khattak*, 70–2; Khattak, *Tarikh Murasa*, 385.

42. See Khattak, *Swat Nama of Khushal Khan Khattak*, 52; Khattak, *Swat Namah da Khushal Khan Khattak*, 86; Khattak, *Tarikh Murasa*, 390.

43. Khattak, *Kulyat-i Khushal Khan Khattak*, Vol. 2, 349.

44. Ibid., 281.

45. For detail, see Khwajah Muhammad Sayal, *Khushalyat aw Haqayaq (Intiqadi Jaaj)* (Pashto) (n.p.: By the Author, 2006).

46. Also see Sayyad Abdul Jabbar Shah Sithanawi, *Kitab al-Ibra: Subah Sarhad wa Afghanistan ki Char Sau Salah Tarikh; 1500 Iswi ta 1900 Iswi* (Urdu), Vol. 1 (Islamabad: Poorab Academy, 2011), 129.

47. H.G. Raverty, 'An account of Upper and Lower Suwát, and the Kohistán, to the source of the Suwát River; with an account of the tribes inhabiting those valleys', *Journal of the Asiatic Society* (Calcutta), 31/3 (1862), 274.

48. Khattak, *Swat Nama of Khushal Khan Khattak*, 25; Khattak, *Swat Namah da Khushal Khan Khattak*, 66; Khattak, *Tarikh Murasa*, 383.

49. Khattak, *Swat Nama of Khushal Khan Khattak*, 25; Khattak, *Swat Namah da Khushal Khan Khattak*, 66; Khattak, *Tarikh Murasa*, 383.

50. Khattak, *Kulyat-i Khushal Khan Khattak*, Vol. 2, 287.

51. For detail, also see Sultan-i-Rome, 'Mughuls and Swat', *Journal of the Pakistan Historical Society* (Karachi), 50/4 (October–December 2002), 39–50.

52. Khattak, *Kulyat-i Khushal Khan Khattak*, Vol. 2, 38.

53. Rahim, *Swat Namah Jawab Namah*, 153–4. For a judicious analysis of Khushal Khan's condemnations and allegations against the people of Swat, also see ibid., 155–8.

54. Ibid., 155.

55. Ibid., 72.

56. Khattak, *Kulyat-i Khushal Khan Khattak*, Vol. 1, 59.

57. See Khattak, *Swat Nama of Khushal Khan Khattak*, passim; Khattak, *Swat Namah da Khushal Khan Khattak*, passim; Khattak, *Tarikh Murasa*, 385–91.

58. See Khattak, *Swat Nama of Khushal Khan Khattak*, 34–70; Khattak, *Swat Namah da Khushal Khan Khattak*, 72–100; Khattak, *Tarikh Murasa*, 385–91.

59. See Khattak, *Swat Nama of Khushal Khan Khattak*, 64; Khattak, *Swat Namah da Khushal Khan Khattak*, 95–6.

60. See Rahim, *Swat Namah Jawab Namah*, 92–8.

61. Khattak, *Kulyat-i Khushal Khan Khattak*, Vol. 2, 51.

62. Ibid., 40.

63. See Khattak, *Swat Nama of Khushal Khan Khattak*, 8; Khattak, *Swat Namah da Khushal Khan Khattak*, 52–3; Khattak, *Tarikh Murasa*, 379.

64. See Khattak, *Swat Nama of Khushal Khan Khattak*, 9; Khattak, *Swat Namah da Khushal Khan Khattak*, 53; Khattak, *Tarikh Murasa*, 379.

65. See Khattak, *Swat Nama of Khushal Khan Khattak*, 10; Khattak, *Swat Namah da Khushal Khan Khattak*, 54; Khattak, *Tarikh Murasa*, 379; Khattak, *Kulyat-i Khushal Khan Khattak*, Vol. 2, 50, 367. Also see Khattak, *Kulyat-i Khushal Khan Khattak*, Vol. 1, 190; Khattak, *Kulyat-i Khushal Khan Khattak*, Vol. 2, 37, 39–40, 50, 54–5, 62, 149, 268–9, 287. See also Caroe, *The Pathans*, 239–40.

66. Khattak, *Kulyat-i Khushal Khan Khattak*, Vol. 1, 295.

67. See Khattak, *Swat Nama of Khushal Khan Khattak*, 13, 15; Khattak, *Swat Namah da Khushal Khan Khattak*, 56, 58; Khattak, *Tarikh Murasa*, 380–1. Also see Khattak, *Kulyat-i Khushal Khan Khattak*, Vol. 2, 201.

68. See Khattak, *Swat Nama of Khushal Khan Khattak*, 25, 52, 57; Khattak, *Swat Namah da Khushal Khan Khattak*, 66, 86, 90; Khattak, *Tarikh Murasa*, 383, 390. Also see Khattak, *Kulyat-i Khushal Khan Khattak*, Vol. 2, 24–5, 286–7, 317, 324.

69. Khattak, *Kulyat-i Khushal Khan Khattak*, Vol. 2, 62.

70. Khattak, *Swat Nama of Khushal Khan Khattak*, 1; Khattak, *Swat Namah da Khushal Khan Khattak*, 47; Khattak, *Tarikh Murasa*, 377. Also see Khattak, *Swat Nama of Khushal Khan Khattak*, 8–9.

71. See Rahim, *Swat Namah Jawab Namah*, 115–21.

72. See ibid., 121–30.

73. Ibid., 153.

74. Ibid., 132.

75. Ibid., 139–41.

76. Khalil, *sarizah* to Khattak, *Swat Namah da Khushal Khan Khattak*, 39–42, 45–6.

77. Kaka Khail, *Pukhtanah da Tarikh pah Ranra kay*, 639.

78. Caroe, *The Pathans*, 241.

79. Ibid., 241–2.

80. Munawwar Khan, 'Swat in History', *Peshawar University Review* (Peshawar), 1/1 (1973), 62. Also see Kaka Khail, *Pukhtanah da Tarikh pah Ranra kay*, 634; Caroe, *The Pathans*, 231, 240.

81. See Kaka Khail, *Pukhtanah da Tarikh pah Ranra kay*, 619. For some other would be causes due to which the Yusufzi did not take arms against the Mughals at this stage, see ibid.

82. Ibid., 635. Also see Khattak, *Kulyat-i Khushal Khan Khattak*, Vol. 2, 36–7, 40, 45–7, 50, 53–5, 366–7, 369; Yusufi, *Yusufzai*, 277.

83. See Himayatullah Yaqubi, *Mughal-Afghan Relations in South Asia: History and Developments* (Islamabad: National Institute of Historical and Cultural Research, 2015), 209.

84. Ibid., 209–10.

85. Caroe, *The Pathans*, 241; Sultan-i-Rome, 'Khushal Khan Khattak and Swat', *Journal of the Research Society of Pakistan* (Lahore), 51/1 (January–June 2014), 128.

86. Yaqubi, *Mughal-Afghan Relations in South Asia: History and Developments*, 210.

87. Ibid., 206.

88. Ibid., 207.

89. Ibid., 210.

90. Sultan-i-Rome, 'Khushal Khan Khattak and Swat', 129.

91. Yaqubi, *Mughal-Afghan Relations in South Asia: History and Developments*, 207.

92. Ibid., 206.

93. Ibid., 206–7.

10

1707–1857 CE

With the death of the Emperor Aurangzeb in 1707 CE, the disintegration of the Mughal Empire began and Mughal power shrank slowly. During this period in 1747 CE, Ahmad Shah Abdali, also known as Ahmad Shah Durrani, was installed as the ruler of Afghanistan. He crossed the Indus eight times; and extended his dominion to all of the Punjab and Kashmir. He ravaged the country as far as Delhi and defeated and shattered the powerful army of the Maratha Confederacy in 1761, at the historic battlefield of Panipat.[1]

The plains of the Peshawar Valley were incorporated into the Durrani domain, but Swat remained independent. In 1812–1814 CE, Mountstuart Elphinstone noted the independence of the Swat Yusufzi by stating, 'It is hardly necessary to say that the Eusofzyes [Yusufzis] set the King at defiance; they boast of their independence of him, and scarcely consider the tribes under his government as Afghauns [Afghans].'[2]

When the Durranis weakened, Ranjit Singh, leader of the Sukercharia Sikh *Misl* rose to power and assumed sovereign status. The Sikhs not only established their rule in the cis-Indus area, but extended it to the trans-Indus Pukhtun territory as well.[3] They, however, never occupied Swat.

SAYYAD AHMAD BRAILWI AND SWAT

Sayyad Ahmad of Rayi Baraili, who came to fight the Sikhs and to reform some of the social and religious norms and practices of the Pukhtuns, toured parts of Swat as well. He had two purposes in view, viz. to convince the people 'through preaching to join him and finding a new, secure centre'.[4] He left Chinglai in Ramazan 1242 AH (April 1827)[5] and, after touring different villages of Bunair, entered Swat via Karakar.[6] He stayed in Barikut for some days and then left for Tanra (also written

200

as Thanra). After visiting Tanra, Chakdarah, Uch, and Kutigram, he left for Upper Swat, where he visited and halted at Bandai, Mingawarah, Manglawar, Charbagh, Gulibagh, Khwaza Khilah, Khunay (Khunah),[7] Asalah, Durush Khilah, Shakardarah, Barah Bandai, and Udigram.[8] He 'exhorted the people to join his mission and to shun off the social and religious "innovations" prevailing in the area'.[9]

It has been claimed that all segments of the society, including the religious segment, welcomed him, that his tour was a success as he enlisted the support of the people of the area, and that his verdicts adjudicating disputes of the people were obeyed and acquiesced to.[10] However, the overall impact was not positive, as the people failed to demonstrate any enthusiasm to join his mission or endeavours. Only one, Anbalay Khan of Sakhrah,[11] later joined his followers at the battle of Utmanzi. For the rest, his tour produced no major lasting results.[12] He, however, has termed the people of Swat as kind-hearted and having more potential as compared to the people of Bunair.[13] The reason for the overall more or less passive attitude of the people of Swat was that they had not been subservient to any imperialism nor suffered any aggression in the near past. Besides, they were neither affected by nor had any stake in the contemporary political developments in India and Afghanistan.

Sayyad Ahmad Barailwi came to the Swat Valley the second time in December 1827 and stayed at Khar, in Lower Swat near Malakand, for about a year until December 1828/January 1829.[14] During this second stay of Sayyad Ahmad and his associates, known as the Mujahidin, at Khar, physical exercises and training in warfare were started.[15] The influential figures of the area attended and took *bi'at* at his hands, of following him; and he visited some nearby villages.[16] While in Khar, he tried to resolve the disputes of the locals, which were mainly over land issues, but having no ruling authority in and over the area he merely tried to convince the people to resolve their disputes in accordance to the *shariat* and played only a mediator's role. At times, the locals did not accept his suggested solutions.[17]

Although the stay at Khar linked Sayyad Ahmad Barailwi and his Mujahidin to Swat, he abandoned the place after the battle of Utmanzi, fought against the Barakzi *sardar*s (chiefs),[18] for the obvious reasons of its location not being really suitable for a centre and an offensive, as well as the ill feelings developing towards the Mujahidin among the local people, and the consequent defections among the latter.[19] Later, when Ghazan Khan of Dir requested the Sayyad to send a mission to his domain, the local people would not allow the mission, sent by Sayyad Ahmad Barailwi under Shah Ismail, to pass through their area to Dir.[20]

THE BRITONS[21] AND SWAT

As stated earlier, although the Yusufzi Afghan tribe occupied Swat in the sixteenth century CE and emerged as the dominant group, they did not establish a state and government. In the meantime, the Britons came to the subcontinent in the seventeenth century CE for trade purposes but, with the passage of time, emerged strong enough to establish their rule here. In the process of expansion of their power in India, the territories of the Frontier plains, the then prospective districts of Hazarah, Peshawar, Kuhat, Bannu, and Dera (Dirah) Ismail Khan, virtually came under the Britons' control by1846 as a result of the first Anglo-Sikh war (1845–1846) but directly fell into their hands in 1849 'as the successors of the Sikhs'[22] in the upshot of the second Anglo-Sikh war (1848–1849), and became part of the Britons' Indian possession.

With the annexation of the Punjab and the occupation of Peshawar by the Britons, a new phase in the history of Swat began. While remaining independent, the region became 'a harbour of refuge for outlaws' and for refugees and opponents of the colonial rulers from the Briton-occupied territories.[23] It also became a centre of anti-British sentiments. The Pukhtuns under the Britons' control constantly received inspiration from Swat to rise against the foreigners. The *Confidential, Gazetteer of the North-West Frontier* has recorded:

> After the annexation of the Pesháwar district in 1849, the Swátís [the people of Swat] uniformly proved themselves bad neighbours to the British....Again the Swátís harboured renegades, refugee criminals, internal malcontents, and external enemies, the names of whom might be specified, were not the list too long. For years the valley was a rendezvous for any and every person hostile to the British government; and among them were several persons who had been dismissed from British service....Not only did Swát receive and support enemies of the British, but it encouraged them to commit depredations in British territory. Further, the Swátís [the people of Swat] took every opportunity of inciting British villages to set authority at nought. They invited their fellow Patháns to throw off British yoke, and acknowledge a nominal allegiance to Swát.[24]

FORMATION OF GOVERNMENT (1849/1850)

Although the Swat Yusufzi did not recognize any person as their ruler or head and remained divided into two opposite factions called *dalay* (singular: *dalah*) headed by their own *khanan*, they put behind them their factional infighting, 'mutual rivalries and hostilities…in cases of national emergencies'.[25] This trait of their character and social set-up once more worked, when the Britons occupied Peshawar in 1849 and led punitive expeditions into Sam Baizi on the border of Swat in December 1849 under Colonel Bradshaw, attacking the villages of Palai, Zurmandai and Shair Khanah.[26]

Positively responding to this threat to their independence, the people of Swat agreed to make common cause for defence under one responsible chief and to nominate a king for Swat. They held *jargay* and consulted the Akhund of Swat: Abdul Ghafur, later commonly called by the people, in Swat, Saidu Baba.[27] The Akhund

> advised that the only chance of making a stand would be by appointing one chief to command the whole disposable forces, and all others sworn on the Kurán [Quran] to implicitly obey him, and that the land-tax of one-tenth produce authorized by the Mahamadan [Muhammadan] law should be at once collected to provide the sinews of war.
>
> This proposal being agreed to, the chiefs commenced a scramble for the command, which threatened to involve the whole of the troops in a general mélée. Gházan Khán of Dír left the council, declaring that he could never obey any man save the Akhúnd.[28]

The Akhund was reluctant to assume temporal power himself. Although there were many claimants to the seat, the matter was settled amicably by the Akhund as he proposed that a person hitherto unconnected with Swat should be chosen as the chief. Besides, he pointed out, Sayyad Akbar Shah of Sithanah, a man of energy, intelligence, and a follower of true Islamic principles, with the additional advantage of being a Sayyad, qualified for the post. Sayyad Akbar Shah of Sithanah was accordingly invited and installed as the 'king of Swāt'.[29] As far the Akhund himself was concerned, 'during his lifetime there was no question of his assuming any degree of temporal power'.[30]

Sayyad Akbar Shah was a descendant of Sayyad Ali Tarmizi, aka Pir Baba,[31] and an associate of Sayyad Ahmad Barailwi. According to T.J.C. Plowden, Sayyad Akbar Shah was 'both Treasurer and Prime Minister' to Sayyad Ahmad Barailwi.[32] Dr Altaf Qadir, however, has refuted this contention by asserting:

> During Sayyid Ahmad's visit to Hazara, he [Sayyid Akbar Shah] personally visited Sayyid Ahmad in Kabal and asked to accompany the former to his abode. This was their first meeting. We did not find any reliable source stating that Sayyid Akbar Shah remained treasurer and prime minister of Sayyid Ahmad as has been claimed by few writers including Plowden, T.J.C. 1932....; Caroe, Olaf. 1995....; Sultan-i-Rome. 2008.... These sources have referred to his premiership and treasurership during Sayyid Ahmad's possession of Peshawar but we did not find any reliable source about his holding these portfolios. Peshawar was managed for few days by Arbab Juma Khan, brother of Arbab Bahram Khan, and was restored to Sultan Muhammad Khan when Sayyid Ahmad was leaving the city for Panjtar.[33]

If T.J.C. Plowden's report is not a 'reliable source' on this point, as contended by Dr Altaf Qadir, and if he was not 'Treasurer and Prime Minister' to Sayyad Ahmad Barailwi, Sayyad Akbar Shah, according to Ghulam Rasul Mehr, remained a member of his *majlas-i shurah* (consultative council), with whom he consulted in matters of *jihad* and general administration.[34] And, as also stated by Dr Altaf Qadir, he 'was amongst the most trusted associates of Sayyid Ahmad'.[35] Besides, in the colonial British writings, Peshawar is not used in the narrow sense of the Peshawar city, as taken by Dr Altaf Qadir, but for the whole Peshawar Valley and the Samah area as well; and hence in T.J.C. Plowden's report it refers to Sayyad Ahmad's rule in the Pukhtun areas and not strictly the Peshawar city or Peshawar proper.

Anyway, Sayyad Akbar Shah formed a friendship with Sayyad Ahmad's Hindustani followers. At the death of Sayyad Ahmad at Balakut in 1831, while fighting the Sikhs, he gave Sayyad Ahmad's surviving followers asylum in Sithanah,[36] the place that 'defied Hari Singh and later Ranjit [Singh] himself in 1824',[37] where he himself resided. He was in close and constant contact with the followers of Sayyad Ahmad Barailwi, who had settled in the Pukhtun regions and turned anti-Britons.

The sources do not agree on the year of Sayyad Akbar Shah's installation as the King of Swat. W.J. Keen has given the year as 1849.[38] T.J.C. Plowden has given it once as 1849, and twice as 1850.[39] And W.R. Hay has given it as 1850.[40] Hay's *Monograph on Swat State*, suffers from errors in respects of dates, however.

If it was the activities of the colonial forces under Colonel Bradshaw, in December 1849 in the Sam Baizi area against the villages of Palai, Zurmandai and Shair Khanah that prompted the chiefs of Swat to appoint a ruler as a defensive measure, it can be deduced that Sayyad Akbar Shah was installed the ruler of Swat in late December 1849 or early 1850.

On assuming charge as the King of Swat, Sayyad Akbar Shah made Ghaligay his capital. Taking advantage of his experience of administration and revenue collection, as evolved by Sayyad Ahmad Barailwi in these regions, he developed a machinery of administration in its crude form. He started to collect the revenue, i.e. *ushar*, as agreed upon before his installation as the king, to meet the expenditures and 'the sinews of war'.[41] When his authority was a somewhat established, he set about creating 'a standing army, and eventually managed to collect a force of 800 mounted men, 3000 footmen and five or six guns',[42] 'all receiving pay in grain directly from himself'.[43]

Interestingly, H.G. Raverty and A.H. McMahon and A.D.G. Ramsay did not recognize Sayyad Akbar Shah as the ruler or King of Swat, in the true sense of the term.[44] Negating C.M. MacGregor's and others' accounts, Raverty has tried to refute the contention that Sayyad Akbar Shah was the king or ruler of Swat and has applied the word '*bacha*' (*badshah*) to denote, not a king, but a *sayyad*. Dr Robert Nichols has also asserted that Raverty has 'analysed the complex secular and religious connotations of the title "Badshah" conferred by the Akhund upon Sayyid Akbar Shah before the Sayyid's death in 1857'; and that:

Any later knowledgeable disagreement about the level of secular and spiritual authority actually possessed by the Akhund or by Sayyid Akbar Shah came long after reductive colonial annals that, for the rest of the nineteenth century, characterized clan resistance as springing from an outdated, irrational religion.[45]

The following excerpts from Raverty's *Notes on Afghanistan and Baluchistan* are imperative to be reproduced so as to examine the point in its proper perspective.

Some years before the rebellion of 1857, the Akhúnd of Suwát [Swat], as the spiritual guide of Afgháns of that part, was requested by some of his most orthodox followers to appoint a Bádsháh, that is to say, a Sayyid, *not a king*—and the word also means a great lord, noble, or headman—but as a sort of high-priest, or rather a legate, to whom the *zakát* and *'ushr* [*'ushar*], certain alms and a tithe sanctioned by the Ḳur'án [Quran], might be legally paid...., and who must be a Sayyid, which the Ākhúnd himself was not. As the Sayyid, Akbar Sháh, of Sathánah [Sithanah] on the Indus, was the head of the most influential family of Sayyids in those parts, the Ākhúnd named him as the most proper person to whom these alms and tithe might be legally paid, as being a descendant of the prophet, Muḥammad [SAW]. He died *some months after* the Díhlí massacre, on which his son, the Sayyid, Mubárak Sháh, desired to be nominated to the same office, but, as the Suwátís [Swatis, the people of Swat] were no longer inclined to pay the tithe, the Ākhúnd declined to do so.

These are the facts concerning the "King of Swat," so called. All appear to have forgotten that there were several powerful independent chiefs in Suwát, and that the most powerful chief of all the parts around was Ghazan Khán of Panj-Korah, and that his ancestors, and the ancestors of the other chiefs, never tolerated a king, not even Aḥmád Sháh, Durrání, in the height of his power, and never have done so.[46]

He, moreover, has elaborated:

The crude idea that the word Bádsháh applies to a king alone has caused a deal of nonsense to be written. If Bádsháh stood alone for king, there must have been a king of Buner between three and four centuries ago, for the Sayyid 'Alí's village is called "The Bádsháh's Village." There must have been a great number of dynasties unknown to history, according to the same logic. I find also that the Hindústání Waḥábí, the Sayyid, Aḥmad, who gave such trouble to the Sikhs and Bárakzís, and who was killed at Bálá-Koṭ, in Hazárah, in 1831, has also been dubbed a king, "to whom," says one, 'Futteh Khan Mundur' [sic] "may be said *to have given* "*the crown*." He was not even styled Bádsháh, however, but Khalífah, and the writer might have said "given the Khiláfat," and so had a "Caliph," as well as a "King."

With all the discoveries, notwithstanding, respecting the "king of Swat *succeeding to the throne*," "which "*entailed the kingdom on the heirs for ever*," and such like nonsense, the writers do not appear to have discovered to what family the "Syad king," Akbar Bádsháh, referred to in the previous note, belonged. He was a lineal descendant of no other than the Sayyid, 'Ali, the Tirmiẕi, the Pír Bábá...and after whom the above-mentioned village is called "The Bádsháh's Village." There were, a few years ago, and probably are still, three principal branches of this family, the head being two brothers, the Sayyid, 'Azim Sháh, and the Sayyid, Mían Sháh. The former, who was of an easy good-natured disposition, left his more active-minded and energetic brother to exercise his spiritual authority. They resided a good deal at Takhta'h-band....

The head of the second branch was the Sayyid, Akbar Shâh, of Sathánah [Sithanah], the same who has been made "king of "Swát" by English writers. The head of the third branch was the Sayyid, Rasúl Sháh, of Chamla'h. All these were both Sháhs and Bádsháhs, but not kings, and Akbar Bádsháh was no more "king of Swat" than "king" of "Sama," or "king" of "Búnér," or, indeed, "king" of "Yághistán." How numerous the "king" family was is proved from the fact that, at the attack of Sathánah, in May, 1857, among the "fanatics" killed were "four leaders, one of whom was known as 'the Badshah'." Thus, by these accounts, in May, 1857, there were "two Richmonds in the field" at the same time, the Bádsháh of Suwát and the Bádsháh of Sathánah, and, it may be added, scores of others in the same locality, namely, all the Sayyids of the family referred to. Kings must have been, and must be, very numerous in the parts north of Landaey Sín, for esides [besides] all these Bádsháhs, if it meant king only, there is the Bádsháh of the Spín Káfirís, mentioned in these surveys, the Bádsháh of Kanjút, and the Bádsháhs of Káshkár, etc. With regard to these latter, Bádsháh means Chief. *See* also page 172, where the Ākhúnd, Darwezah, says the Yúsufzís made Ghází Khán their Bádsháh, or Chief.[47]

Raverty has considered and taken into account only one meaning and aspect of the Pashto (Pukhtu) word *bacha*, namely what is one called *badshah* in Urdu and *padshah* in Persian, the synonym of which in English is 'king' and 'ruler'. Since in Pukhtun society, the *sayyad*s/ *saidan* are commonly addressed as *bacha* and *pacha* out of courtesy, he has merely evaluated Sayyad Akbar Shah's status, even after his being designated and installed as King of Swat from that perspective. However, his contention is flawed.

If Raverty's contention be accepted as sound, Sayyad Akbar Shah was a *bacha* by birth, being a *sayyad*. Hence, before becoming ruler of Swat in 1849/1850, he was already a *bacha*. Although he was called *bacha*, like the other *sayyad*s/*saidan*, before his nomination and installation as the King of Swat, he was neither considered nor recognized as a ruler by anyone till then. In 1849/1850, he was designated *bacha* of Swat in the meaning and connotation of the word as 'king' and 'ruler', and assumed the authority that went with that capacity. In the common use of the word *bacha* for *saidan*, they do not possess ruling authority; and the same was the case with Sayyad Akbar Shah before 1849/1850. His status, however, changed after he was designated as *bacha* or King of Swat. He chose a capital and created a standing army, requisites of a ruler. Therefore, he, like the other *saidan*, remained a *bacha* outside

Swat (even in his home place Sithanah) in the sense of being *sayyad*, not a ruler, but in Swat and for those who installed and recognized him as the ruler, he was *bacha* in both the meanings and senses of the word, viz. a *sayyad* as well as a ruler.

Besides, although there were a number of local Afghan or Pukhtun chiefs as stated by Raverty, the prominent one being Ghazan Khan, it was these very chiefs who needed a head and authority to guard their collective interest. For this purpose, they brought Sayyad Akbar Shah from Sithanah and recognized him as the King of Swat. Another important evidence of Sayyad Akbar Shah being *bacha* of Swat, in its meaning, connotation and status of king and ruler, was that he was now paid *ushar*. Significantly, *ushar* is a source of the state revenue, paid to a Muslim ruler. Although, according to Hanafi *fiqah* (Hanafi jurisprudence or Hanafi School of thought) *ushar* can be given to poor individuals personally, and hence not paid to the state and ruler, it can never be given to a *sayyad* individual or to his person because a *sayyad*, being a descendant of the Prophet Muhammad (saw), is *ghani* (rich and wealthy by descent), even if not in fact well off financially. Hence, he cannot receive *ushar* and *zakat* at all, although, being poor financially, he can receive other kinds of alms.

The *ushar* paid to Sayyad Akbar Shah did not go into his pocket and it was not a source of his personal income but was paid to him as the ruler and therefore went into the state exchequer and was expended on the state affairs. That was why Sayyad Akbar Shah was a ruler and king for all practical purposes, after his installation in that capacity in 1849/1850, till his death. Thus, Raverty's contention does not stand up to scrutiny.

It was in this sense, i.e. of being a ruler, that Sayyad Akbar Shah's son Sayyad Mubarak Shah tried to occupy his father's seat after him. However, he failed to maintain his position and status as the ruler of Swat. Although no one disputed his status of a *bacha*, as used for a *sayyad*, Mubarak Shah was not recognized as a successor to his father in the capacity of ruler of Swat. And as the rule of the family collapsed shortly after the death of Sayyad Akbar Shah, it did not take the form of dynastic rule or monarchy in which sense and context Raverty has tried to evaluate and analyse Sayyad Akbar Shah's status. Raverty's evaluation and analysis of Sayyad Akbar Shah's status as a ruler is largely out of context and does not keep the local dynamics in view.

As the Britons' rule had been established in the Peshawar Valley, Swat State came into being with Sayyad Akbar Shah as its king.

Sayyad Akbar Shah, a staunchly anti-Britons follower of Sayyad
Ahmad Barailwi, pursued vehement anti-Britons policies. H.C. Wylly
has asserted that, when Peshawar Valley was annexed by the Britons,
'then and thereafter' the people of Swat 'proved themselves bad
neighbours'. 'Plunderers and marauders, mounted and on foot, issued
from Swat, passed through Ranizai, and raided into' the Britons-held
'territory'. 'They kidnapped almost all classes except Pathans; and Swat
became an Alsatia where evilly-disposed persons' and 'criminals of all
shades', from the Britons perspective, and 'people hostile to the British
Government were readily granted help, asylum and countenance'.[48]

In December 1849, when Colonel Bradshaw lead a punitive
expedition against the villages of Palai, Zurmandai and Shair Khanah
in Sam Baizi, 5000 to 6000 people from Swat came to the assistance
of their fellow tribesmen, but to no avail.[49] The people of Swat
even 'invited their fellow Pathans to throw off the British yoke and
acknowledge a nominal allegiance to Swat'. For this purpose they were
ready to 'assemble troops' on the border and to 'send horsemen' into
villages under the colonial control 'partly as emissaries, and partly as
representatives of [their] authority'.[50] In 1852, the colonial authorities
sent 'a conciliatory letter' to Sayyad Akbar Shah, 'but [it] was very
rudely received and never answered'.[51] In fact, 'it was reported that the
killing of the messenger' was debated 'to mark the King's determination
not to hold any intercourse with the infidels'.[52] And when the colonial
authorities imposed a fine of 5000 rupees on the people of Sam Ranizi
for their insolence, the Akhund of Swat urged the payment thereof but
Sayyad Akbar Shah opposed him and urged the people not to pay.[53]

Even in May 1852, 'some 4,000 foot and 500 horse from the
Swat Valley' assisted the people of Sam, the plain to the south and
southwest of Swat, against the Britons' forces, which were under Colin
Campbell, with Colonel Mackeson as political officer.[54] The British
colonial authorities have complained in the *Mutiny Reports* that it is well
known that 'in the first years' of the Britons' rule in the Peshawar Valley,
'the border was chiefly disturbed by the hostility of the neighbouring
country of Swat';[55] and that 'the King, to justify his own existence, made
himself as bad a neighbour to the English as he could do without actually
drawing down an expedition on his head'.[56] Swat was the fountainhead
of offences against the colonial Britons.[57]

Although the people of Swat made frequent inroads into the territory
under the colonial Britons' control in Ashnaghar (Hashtnagar) for

plundering in the forms of bands and in twos and threes and on foot and mounted, they usually refrained from molesting the Pukhtuns, while not sparing persons of all other origins.[58] The British officials, while discussing offences and other acts on the part of the people of Swat, have complained:

> The rulers [ruler] and people of Swát had been the head and front of all this offending was evident. We had never interfered with them, but they had chosen to make war upon us. Our chief fault in their eyes was, that we were infidels by religion, and that we were the lords of a fair and fertile valley within reach of plunder.[59]

The sources evidently show that the political head and the spiritual leader of the people of Swat—their King, and their Saint, Sayyad Akbar Shah and the Akhund, respectively—having contrasting viewpoints, both politically and religiously, were not unanimous on the course of action against and the policy towards the colonial Britons. When the people of Palai committed raids on the Britons-occupied territory, the Akhund advised them, both in 1847 and 1849, not to interfere or oppose the Britons.[60] When a fine of 5,000 rupees was levied in 1852 upon the people of Sam Ranizi by the colonial Britons, Sayyad Akbar Shah opposed it and urged the people to refuse payment; but 'the Akhund urged the payment thereof'.[61] In the autumn of 1849, immediately after the annexation of the Peshawar plain, the people of Swat incited the people of Lundkhwar not to pay the revenue to the colonialists. They took up arms against the troops when an expedition marched into their area towards the end of 1851 and placed the bodies of the Britons' soldiers in Ranizi and at the foot of the Murah Mountain, to create consternation along the Britons' border.[62]

In March 1852, the Britons' detachment 'of the Guide Corps stationed' at Gujar Garhi 'as an escort to a party of the Great Trigonometrical Survey' was attacked. The nephew of Sayyad Akbar Shah (the King of Swat) accompanied by a company of his own men, was with the party who led the attack on 'the detachment of the Guides'.[63] The Ranizi were fined 5,000 rupees for the act and a force was dispatched against them, which was withdrawn when the Ranizi paid the fine. The colonialists government then sent a message of conciliation to the King of Swat, but received no reply.[64] Arjan Khan, also known as Aujun Khan and Ajun Khan, of Tangi who had murdered a *tahsildar* of the Britons tract of Ashnaghar in his bed (on 20 April 1852), was well received and given awards in Swat. An official British statement in this regard is: 'It was ascertained that this man was well received' by the people of Swat, and 'had been presented with a fief; and, in short, that the Swát government, if it had not instigated him to the deed, had encouraged and abetted him after its commission'.[65]

At this point, it must be mentioned that no details about Sayyad Akbar Shah's rule, administrative apparatus, and internal policies, etcetera, are available in the sources consulted, other than that, although he was himself brave, able, and judicious, he brought in administrative personnel from outside Swat who were arrogant and did not honour the local traditions. Hence, he created resentment and grudges against himself which led to trouble for him and proved the cause of his failure as a ruler in Swat.[66]

As evidence of failure to respect local traditions, it has been alleged that some of his soldiers violated the integrity of a house in Khwaza Khilah thus: 'The house contained a vine-tree [grapevine]. The troopers cared little for the exposure of the ladies of the house and forcibly entering the house began to enjoy the grapes. This fanned to flame the smouldering ashes of Afghan hostility. The Azi Khel tribe assembled and finished off the troopers.'[67] To punish the Azi Khail, Sayyad Akbar Shah 'sent some cavalry' but to no avail because of the strong resistance. Although reconciliation was effected, the situation did not improve when Sayyad Akbar Shah's followers 'committed some more excesses which inflamed all the Swat tribes'.[68]

To bring normalcy to the volatile situation, efforts for reconciliation between Sayyad Akbar Shah and the Yusufzi were made, but he died 'before any settlement could be effected'.[69] Reputedly, 'the cruelties perpetrated' by his servants 'exhausted the patience' of the people. 'The atrocities committed by them were talked of everywhere.'[70]

Such allegations, about the violation of the integrity of a house in Khwaza Khilah and the cruelties committed by the soldiers and servants of Sayyad Akbar Shah, have been made by the Swat State's court writers and are not confirmed from other authentic sources. As there was a clash of interests between Sayyad Akbar Shah and the Akhund of Swat, aka Saidu Baba, the ancestor of the Swat State rulers (who ruled from 1917 till 1969), and who rose to power at the deposition of Sayyad Abdul Jabbar Shah, a scion of Sayyad Akbar Shah's family, these allegations are not to be taken at face value. In the book quoted, the role of the Akhund of Swat in matters between the people of Swat and Sayyad Akbar Shah has been depicted in an exaggeratedly positive manner that does not correlate with what has been analysed in the pages above and the pages that follow.

THE WAR OF INDEPENDENCE (1857) AND SWAT

In the backdrop of the aforesaid strained relations between the colonial rulers of India and the people and King of Swat, and Sayyad Akbar Shah's anti-Britons background, the War of Independence of 1857 against the colonial rulers flared up in regions of India, distant from Swat.

As already noted, Sayyad Akbar Shah, a staunchly anti-Britons follower of Sayyad Ahmad Barailwi, was installed as King of Swat owing to the fear of possible Britons occupation of the valley. Although not a part of the territories over which the Britons held sway in the subcontinent, Swat had a significant position in relation to the War of Independence. Swat, being a centre of anti-Britons sentiment, became a refuge for rebels and its king was in league with the rebel elements in the Britons-held parts of the subcontinent. Sayyad Akbar Shah and Swat were considered dangerous enemies and a source of trouble, not only in the Frontier but elsewhere in India as well.

Swat and Sayyad Akbar Shah's connections with those who planned and executed the uprising against the colonialists came to the surface later. 'It appeared afterwards', states a British official report, that there had 'long been intrigues going on between the 55th and 64th Native Infantry and the 10th Irregular Cavalry' and the Hindustani 'fanatics in Swat and the neighbouring hills'; and that two Hindustani Mawlwis 'in the collectorate' of Mardan 'were the hosts of the emissaries who passed to and fro'.[71] Besides, there had been 'the most rancorous and seditious letters', intercepted from the Muslims of Patna and Thanisar, 'to soldiers of the 64th Native Infantry', speaking of the atrocities committed to the Muslims in India and arousing the sepoys to revenge. 'These letters also alluded to a long series of correspondence that had been going on, through the 64th Native Infantry, with the fanatics[72] in Swát and Sitana.'[73] A note in the *Mutiny Reports* speaks of the correspondence between the Indian revolutionaries and Swat by stating that 'this is farther confirmed by Mahomedan [Muslims] correspondence; for a rabid letter from a "Kuleefa Nathoo" at Thaneysur [Thanisar] to friends in Swat, through a Naik of 64th Native Infantry'.[74]

The pitch of communication from Swat with those planning rebellion in the Britons held territories are also evident from this assertion of John Nicholson, made on 30 May 1857:

I am strongly inclined to believe that we should not merely disarm but disband that corps [i.e. 64th Native Infantry] and the 10th Irregular Cavalry. There is no doubt that they have both been in communication with the Akhund of Swât.... I believe we did not pitch into the 55th one day too soon. That corps and the 64th were all planning to go over to the Akhund together. I have got a man who taunted my police on the line of march with siding with infidels in a religious war. May I hang him?[75]

This piece confirms that, not only were Sayyad Akbar Shah and other anti-colonialists elements in Swat in league and in active communication with the Indian revolutionaries, but so was the Akhund of Swat as well. However, the Qandahari—resident of Qandahar sent to Swat by H.G. Raverty—has asserted about the Akhund:

He has been said, at Peshâwar, to possess the most despotic power over a most fanatical tribe; and even the old miscreant who lately set himself up at Delhí, had it proclaimed, that the poor old Akhúnd was coming to assist him with from 12,000, to 18,000 Ghâzís at his back. I need scarcely add, that the whole is a mass of falsehood got up by interested parties. I will now endeavour to give a sketch of the Akhúnd as he appeared to us.[76]

After giving his own sketch of the Akhund, the Qandahari has stated: 'Such is the true history, and such the faithful portrait of the terrible, fanatic, plotting Akhúnd of Suwát, the bugbear of Peshâwar.'[77] Keeping aside the issue of determining the truthfulness or otherwise of the news of the coming of the Akhund to the assistance of the Indian revolutionaries, this was no minor a thing as the news certainly generated enthusiasm and added fuel to the rising fire against the colonialists in those distant parts; hence, using the Akhund's name in the affair could not be underestimated. However, the role-played by him later, when sepoys of the 55th Native Infantry reached Swat, and the course adopted by him thenceforward needs scrutiny and analysis, done herein later.

According to Dr Ansar Zahid Khan, while 'working on Katwal's [Kotwal's] Diary'[78] he 'repeatedly found references that the Jihadis of Muslim Revolutionaries [in India] were repeatedly told that Wali [King] of Swat and Amir of Rabil were coming to their help'.[79] Keeping his past

career and role in view, and his association, relations and communication
with the anti-colonialists elements and the Indian revolutionaries,
Sayyad Akbar Shah would have certainly come to the freedom fighters'
help and joined the war with might and main. However, to the benefit of
the colonialists, he died on 11 May 1857, the day when the news of the
uprising in India reached Peshawar.[80] It is believed among some that he
was poisoned to death, probably at the colonialists instigation or due to
the alleged strained relations with the people, referred to at the end of
the previous sub-section.

Whatever the cause of his death, Sayyad Akbar Shah's demise barred
him from taking part in the cherished war against the colonialists. This
development and the state of affairs in Swat, moreover, 'prevented from
making those aggressions' on the Britons' occupied territories, records
Gazetteer of the Peshawar District, 1897–98, 'which might otherwise
have been looked for'.[81] The observations and remarks of Herbert
Edwardes, Commissioner Peshawar Division, are also revealing. He
has stated that 'the King, to justify his own existence, made himself as
bad a neighbour to the English as he could do without actually drawing
down an expedition on his head'.[82] Hence,

> It might naturally have been expected therefore that this Padshah [King]
> of Swat would be at the head of all mischief when the troubles of 1857
> overtook us [viz. the Britons]. It is a remarkable fact, however, that he
> died on 11th May, the very day that the first news of the mutiny reached
> Peshawur [Peshawar], so that Swat itself was simultaneously plunged
> into civil war and entirely pre-occupied with its own affairs.[83]

This, however, was not an end of the fears and troubles from Swat for
the colonialists, as defections occurred in the Frontier in the course of
which sepoys of 'the 55th Native Infantry at Nowshera broke across
the river, on 21st May', so as to join the main body of their regiment
at Mardan. And, on 23 May, the 55th Native Infantry, having been in
a state of rebellion at Mardan, was reported to the colonial authorities.
Action against them was, therefore, deemed necessary and hence
forces were sent under the command of Colonel Chute, accompanied
by Colonel John Nicholson as political officer. On the colonial forces'
nearing Mardan 'the 55th Native Infantry, with the exception of about
120 men…broke from the fort and fled'.[84]

The sepoys of the 55th Native Infantry, after their defection, asserts
Lionel J. Trotter, the biographer of John Nicholson, 'marched off with

drums beating and colours flying towards the hills of Swât'.[85] Although it seemed inadvisable and unfeasible, Colonel Nicholson followed in pursuit of the rebel sepoys who, as Nicholson 'himself admitted in a private note to Edwardes', 'fought stubbornly "as men always do who have no chance of escape but by their own exertions".'[86]

On the other side, as stated earlier, Sayyad Akbar Shah died the day the first news of the war reached Peshawar, which proved a great setback. As a result, on the one hand, the intended moves from Swat against the colonialists could not be made and, on the other, the part of the plan related to Swat could not materialize as intended. Besides, the power game in Swat between Sayyad Mubarak Shah, son of Sayyad Akbar Shah, and the Akhund of Swat, commenced. Although Sayyad Akbar Shah 'was succeeded by his son, Mir Mubarak Ali Shah, or more commonly Mubarak Shah' the people of Swat detested being under firm control for long and so were reluctant to be under Mubarak Shah's rule.[87] Already grown tired of the tithes they had paid to Sayyad Akbar Shah, the people of Swat were reluctant to recognize Mubarak Shah as his successor, i.e. as King of Swat, and hence called on the Akhund of Swat to excommunicate him.[88] The Akhund was also inclined to make a failure of Mubarak Shah for his own reasons, hence 'after debate the people, under the Akhund's influence, rejected Mubarik'.[89] Therefore, 'both sides'—Mubarak Shah and his followers and the Akhund of Swat and his followers—'called in their friends and allies and prepared to settle' the issue 'by arms'.[90]

In such a situation of strife and disorder, 500 of the rebel sepoys of the 55th Native Infantry[91] 'succeeded in crossing the border' and reaching Swat 'with their arms, ammunition and plundered treasure'.[92] The sources are not agreed upon the number of the sepoys that made good their escape to Swat. The *Military Report and Gazetteer on Buner and Adjacent Independent Territory* has given the number that reached Swat as 600[93] and the *Mutiny Reports* has stated the number to have been 500,[94] as also quoted above, 'upwards of 600' as they reached Swat,[95] and as 600 and 700 when crossing the Indus after their expulsion from Swat.[96]

Whether five, six, or seven hundred in number, the sepoys, on reaching Swat, gave a new dimension to the power struggle there, as, to the chagrin of the Akhund, they went over to Mubarak Shah, the young king, and he at once took them into his service. At this, despite Sayyad Akbar Shah's death at a critical juncture, Swat would have become again a centre of anti-colonialists activity with the advent of trained rebel soldiers, but certain factors worked to the benefit of the colonialists. Mubarak Shah, having been refused allegiance and *ushar* by a large segment of the people of Swat, was short of armed local supporters and finances. This made his position vulnerable and he had to struggle for maintaining his own in Swat. To pay the sepoys of the 55th Native Infantry, who had sided with and fought for him one battle, Mubarak Shah borrowed 1000 rupees from their leader, a grey-haired *jamadar*, but the sum was soon exhausted and he was unable to pay further, without which the sepoys were not ready to fight for him.[97] Moreover, for the sepoys in question, 'most of whom were high-caste Hindoos [Hindus]', remaining in a strange land among tribal Muslims became difficult, not only due to the lack of funds with Mubarak Shah for paying them as salaries, but also because they did not understand the language of the people among whom they had come.[98]

Despite these unfavourable factors, the sepoys sided with Mubarak Shah who was not only struggling to secure his power in Swat, despite his not hailing from the land and being disliked by the people, but to the chagrin of the Akhund of Swat as well. The Akhund, who saw a threat to his own influence in Swat if Mubarak Shah were to gain a firm footing, exerted his influence both against Mubarak Shah and the sepoys. He thus 'sided with the popular party' and caused the expulsion of both Mubarak Shah and the sepoys from Swat,[99] thus bringing an end to 'the first Islamic State of Swat'.[100] The Hindu faith of the sepoys might, it is probable, also have worked in turning the people against them and Mubarak Shah.

In this way, the War of Independence of 1857 played great role and left its mark on the politics of Swat as well, as resultantly the rule of members of an influential religious family, descendants of Pir Baba, was brought to an end. This in turn secured and strengthened the Akhund's own status and position since, if the Sayyads had remained in power for long, the Akhund's own status and influence would have been overshadowed by theirs.

The policy and course of action adopted by the Akhund of Swat at this juncture, not only left its effects and impacts on the course of events, politics and history of Swat, but also on that of India. His refusal to side with the anti-colonialists rebels, despite his having previously been in contact and communication with them, as has also been quoted above, and his not declaring war against the colonialists, rescued them from a general and mass uprising and war, at least on the Frontier, which has also been assessed by H.B. Edwardes, Commissioner Peshawar Division, by stating:

Had the Akhoond [Akhund] of Swat at this time, standing *forward* [my italic] as the champion of the faith, preached a crescentade against us, and hushing intestine strife moved across the passes and descended into Peshawur [Peshawar] Valley, with all the prestige of the 55th Sepoys in his favour, I do not doubt that he would have excited among our subjects that spirit of religious zeal which may be overlaid for a while, but never extinguished by material prosperity. Instead of this he suddenly sided with the popular party, dismissed the 55th Sepoys with guides to conduct them across the Indus and expelled the young King [Sayyad Mubarak Shah] from Swat.[101]

'This conclusion', asserts Edwardes, 'assured the peace of our northern frontiers, and Colonel Nicholson with Colonel Chute's Moveable Column returned to cantonments in the second week of June'.[102]

Terming Edwardes' assertion as 'a correct assessment of the situation', S. Moinul Haq has contended that 'there can be no doubt that with the departure of the sepoys of the 55th from Swat, the course of the Revolution was changed in that region'.[103] Ghulam Rasul Mehr has contended that the rebel sepoys of the 55th Native Infantry reached Swat with the intention of taking the Muslims of that place with them in order to attack the colonialists with greater force and better organization and thus assist in the *jihad* for independence of the country by expelling the Britons from the Frontier.[104] Lamenting the attitude of the Akhund of Swat and the people of Swat, adopted towards the sepoys due to the petty local affair of the payment of *ushar* and to the succession or otherwise of Mubarak Shah, Ghulam Rasul Mehr has said that, had the people of Swat or the Akhund Sahib thought over the end result of the issue and comprehended that the people who had sacrificed their prestigious service for the sake of independence of the country, as they believed, and had sustained injuries and laid down lives, certainly deserved better treatment. Their sacrifices were not warranted to be linked with the limited personal issues of a land. But such is the case when the hearts and minds, and ideas and thoughts of the people in those days were confined to such limited thinking, and were not ever prepared to reflect on major issues and affairs.[105]

After discussing Sayyad Akbar Shah's death, the people's general attitude towards Mubarak Shah, the coming of the sepoys, and their expulsion by the Akhund, S. Moinul Haq has asserted, 'This decision of the Akhund Ṣāḥib about Swat's attitude towards the Revolution was solely prompted by the local conditions which were uncertain.'[106]

What it was that prompted the Akhund of Swat towards the adoption of such a course needs to be examined. Referring to the apathy of the tribes in not taking up arms against the Britons, the course adopted towards Mubarak Shah and the sepoys, and the attitude of the Akhund of Swat, Dr Munawwar Khan has contended: 'The tribes followed their tribal interests. Relegious [religious] doctors could unite the tribes for some purpose but unfortunately, the Akhund Sahib had been so impressed by British superiority in war, and so concerned with the independence of Swat and Buner, that he on this occasion decided to keep quiet.'[107] However, after his this assertion and citing the above quoted analysis of Edwardes, Dr Munawwar Khan has stated, in perhaps a rejoinder or rebuke to Ghulam Rasul Mehr,

> It is bad logic in history to judge people and individuals according to one's own standards. The people of Swat had no knowledge of the Mughul ruler in whose name the rising took place. Swat had never been an integral part of the Mughul Empire, and anyway that empire had long ceased to exist. It would be too much to expect the tribes of Swat to be imbued with the spirit of nationalism and patriotism which did not exist ever in the rest of India. How else can one explain the few British crushing the whole of India with the help of Indian mercenaries? The one force which could be effective was tribal loyalty and religious appeal. The same Swatis *when properly led by religious leaders* [my italics] put up a stubborn resistence [resistance] to the British arms in 1863, 1895 and 1897.
>
> The policy of the Akhund Sahib of Swat was to protect the independence of Swat and Buner. He induced the tribesmen that the invasion was imminent, but was careful not to offend the [colonial] Government to such an extent that an expedition would become inevitable. At the same time he would not create the impression that he was lagging behind in a religious rising against the infidels.[108]

Dr Munawwar Khan's assertion itself, however, confirms that, had the Akhund of Swat called upon the people and come out to lead them against the colonialists, or at least enjoined upon them if he himself was not ready to lead them, they would have certainly taken up arms and fought the colonialists outside Swat, whether or not Swat remained part of Mughal Empire and whether that Empire existed or not. There were prior links and communications between the Indian revolutionaries and at least the religious leaders of Swat in connection with the projected uprising in India, and the Akhund of Swat was one of those leaders, as stated and quoted earlier. Swat, despite not being a part of the Mughal Empire, had been a source of trouble for the colonialists since their occupation of Peshawar, as they themselves have endorsed and complained in their reports and writings. Even, previously, 'one letter from the *Akhund* [himself] authorised…one Ajun Khan, to destroy all Europeans and Hindus in the Peshawar valley, and all Muhammadans in the British service; but enjoined him to spare all other Muhammadans'.[109] Dr Munawwar Khan himself has stated about Aujun [Ajun] Khan, who used to raid the Britons-held territories, that he 'went to Kabul via Jalalabad. Letters from the Akhund Sahib and Sayed Akbar were discovered among his papers.'[110]

As stated earlier, H.G. Raverty has contended that Sayyad Akbar Shah died in August 1857 and that, when the rebel sepoys fled into Swat, they remained as the Akhund's guests for a few days, 'as travellers generally do'. He, however, has asserted that the Akhund then advised them to leave Swat, although Sayyad Akbar Shah 'wished them to remain', and that 'in this case the Akhúnd indeed persisted that they should not be permitted to remain in Suwát [Swat]'.[111] Raverty has further stated: 'Other mutineers also came from Murree, all of whom he [the Akhund] dismissed as quickly as possible to Kábul.'[112]

'The whole tendency' of the Akhund's 'policy at the time was distinctly peaceful', as the *Gazetteer of the Peshawar District, 1897–98*, has asserted,[113] and also 'to protect the independence of Swat and Buner' and hence 'was careful not to offend the [colonial] Government to such an extent that an expedition would become inevitable', as asserts Dr Munawwar Khan.[114] But there is 'no doubt' that in expulsion of both Mubarak Shah and the sepoys from Swat, in 1857, 'he was partly actuated by motives of fear, lest [Mubarak Shah] the son of the late king of Swát, with the assistance of the sepoys, might be able to gain firm power in Swát and overshadow his, the Akhund's, authority'.[115]

This assertion and conclusion of the Akhund's apprehensions about the people of Swat and also averting the colonialist invasion of the valley gains support from this report of the Deputy Commissioner Hazarah as well that despite their being expelled from Swat, the sepoys were not only guided across the Indus but the Akhund's 'confidential messengers' accompanied them with 'letters calling on all good Mussulmans [Muslims] to aid and escort them, and excommunicating and denouncing as unbelievers all who should oppose them'.[116] And that when, on 5–6 July 1857, a combination of the natives took action against the sepoys 'below the village Guddarh' on the edge of the Blue River in consequence of which 'many of the sepoys were killed or wounded, or drowned in the rapid stream', a *mula* from Palas had forbidden 'their further molestation', 'to whom' the Akhund 'had commended them'.[117] The *mula*, moreover, then 'conveyed them to Kote Gullee, on the border of Chilass' from where 'they made for Durawah'.[118]

Thus, partly driven by motives of the fear that Mubarak Shah, with the assistance of the sepoys, might be able to gain firm power in Swat and overshadow his authority, and partly by not wishing to offend the colonialists into leading an expedition to Swat, the Akhund exerted his influence and caused the expulsion from Swat of Mubarak Shah— after his rising to the seat of power—and of the sepoys of the 55th Native Infantry. Consequently, Swat remained aloof from the War of Independence of 1857. It, thus, greatly benefited and indirectly assisted the Britons colonialists in the War, as they were relieved from worries from this quarter. H.B. Edwardes has stated, and quoted earlier as well, that 'this conclusion assured the peace of our northern frontier, and Colonel Nicholson with Colonel Chute's Moveable Column returned to cantonments in the second week of June'.[119] Olaf Caroe has also asserted: 'That there was not more disturbance in that critical year was due mainly to the refusal of the Akhund to permit the Swat Yusufzais to be implicated.'[120] H.C. Wylly has opined that the Akhund supported the colonial government so far as was 'in his power during the anxious days of the Mutiny'.[121] The remarks of the *Imperial Gazetteer of India*, however, are also worth mentioning, which states that 'the year of the Mutiny (1857) passed off without disturbance', in Swat and the adjoining territories, because 'a refuge in Swāt' was 'actually denied to the mutineers of the 55th Native Infantry by the Akhund, who, however, adopted this course for reasons of local policy, not from love of the British Government'.[122]

Had Sayyad Akbar Shah not died at this juncture, or Mubarak Shah and the sepoys not been expelled from Swat, the course of events of the War of 1857 could have been quite different. Sayyad Akbar Shah was vehemently anti-Britons colonialists and not only roused and assisted people against them but was in collaboration and had links with the Indian revolutionaries. Mubarak Shah also took up the mission of his father and hence, after his expulsion from Swat, he 'in a huff went off to Panjtar, just across the border from Swabi, and from that centre, reinforced as related by mutineers from the district, raised the Chamla tribes against the British'.[123]

In such a scenario, it really was, as H.C. Wylly has opined, 'strangely enough' for the colonial rulers, that 'the troubles of the Mutiny year were not taken advantage of by the leaders in Swat'. Because 'the King died on the very day that the first news of the outbreak at Meerut reached Peshawar, and the Akhund took no action inimical to British authority— on the contrary….he deported' the rebel sepoys 'who sought an asylum in Swat'.[124]

The policy and course of the Akhund of Swat, at this time, although mainly adopted for local and personal reasons, was favourable to the colonial government[125] and benefited them in this crucial time. The course the events took in Swat after the coming of the sepoys of the 55th Native Infantry and their siding with Mubarak Shah, to the chagrin of the Akhund of Swat, and his consequent policy and course of action, and his not permitting 'the Swat Yusufzais to be implicated'[126] brought an end to the then Swat State (1849/1850–1857). The people of Swat regressed to their former tribal welter; with many consequences on the subsequent course of events and history of Swat and the region.

THE AKHUND OF SWAT (1794–1877 CE)

A note about the Akhund of Swat,[127] who, although negated by H.G. Raverty, was considered a great religious person in Swat at that time and who played crucial role, as is evident from the preceding pages and also from the next chapter, is required.

Akhund Abdul Ghafur, in Swat commonly called Saidu Baba, was born in Jabrai in Upper Swat in the year 1794.[128] Starting life as a herd boy, he at last resolved, at the age of eighteen, to 'devote himself to a religious life'.[129] In pursuit of religious education and spiritual attainment, he visited and stayed at Brangulah, Gujar Garhai, Turdhair and various other places. At last, he settled on the bank of River Indus near Bika (Beka), and dwelt there for twelve years in a *zuzkhanah* (camel's thorn hut)[130] following 'the *Nakshbandia* [Naqshbandiyah] form of religious devotion—sitting silent and motionless, his head bowed on his chest, and his eyes fixed on the ground....His fame as a saint dates from his sojourn at Beka'.[131] Muhammad Asif Khan has stated that, according to Dr Bellew, he taught the people the lesson of Qadriyah *tariqah* of mysticism at Baiki (Bika),[132] but Bellew has stated that he adopted '*Nakashbandia*' (Naqshbandiyah) *tariqah*.[133]

He was still in Bika when 'his sanctity and holiness began to attract universal attention, and he got the title of Akhund'.[134] From Bika he went to Ghulaman, and from there to Salim Khan. Being involved in the murder of Khadi Khan of Hund, at the hands of the followers of Sayyad Ahmad Barailwi with the Sayyad's consent, he left Salim Khan and stayed at different places. During this period, his fame spread far and wide. In 1835, Amir Dost Muhammad Khan of Afghanistan sought his cooperation against the Sikhs. He joined the Amir's camp at Shaikhan near Barah along with his followers. The Sikhs emerged victorious and the Akhund fled to Bajawar.[135] Deserted by his few adherents, he resumed his early wandering habit and at last settled at Kaldarah in the Ranizi hills. From there he moved to Batkhilah and thence to Upper Swat. Moving from place to place, he at last permanently settled at Saidu in the year 1845. In Saidu, 'the people gave him a portion of land for his own and his disciples' support'.[136] Here, he became a prominent figure, attended by his devotees. It was his residence in Saidu that it was given the epithet of Sharif, i.e. it became Saidu Sharif, or 'noble Saidu', and he obtained the title of Saidu Baba.

The *Imperial Gazetteer of India: Provincial Series; North-West Frontier Province*, has claimed that the Akhund 'exercised an irresistible influence over the Yusufzais and their neighbours'.[137] Olaf Caroe, however, has asserted that 'his authority was not absolute'.[138] The Qandahari, a resident of Qandahar in Afghanistan, sent by Raverty on a mission to search out a copy of Shaikh Mali's *daftar*, in August 1858, has reported:

> The Akhúnd is high priest or rather a devotee, whom the people regard as a saint, and who is looked upon, by the people of those extensive regions around, as the head of their religion; but he is without the slightest real power, either temporal or spiritual; his influence being solely through the respect in which he is held.[139]

He has further stated: 'The Suwátí [Swati] Afgháns are so tyrannical, so prejudiced, and so fanatical, that even the admonitions, and the expostulations of the Akhúnd are unpalatable to them. Whatever they do not like, or whatever may be against the custom of their Afghán nature from time immemorial, they will neither listen, nor attend to.'[140]

To endorse his contention, the Qandahari had narrated an event.[141] Further illustrating the routine and position of the Akhund, he has reported about his conduct and position in respect of public affairs thus: 'If two parties chance to have a dispute, and they both agree that it shall be settled according to the *shara* or orthodox law of Muhammad [SAW], he explains to them the particular precept bearing on the case, from the Arabic law-books. Save this, he has no connection in the matter.'[142]

The Akhund's policy towards the colonial Imperial Power has been exaggerated and painted by the Swat State court writers. It has been claimed that 'he had a few set aims before him for which he strove throughout his life'. 'Some of them' were: 'revival of the true faith in Islam'; 'reformation of the Pathans; eradication of corrupt practices and uninformed innovations from amongst them'; 'establishment of an Islamic State in Swat and Buner'; 'defending Swat and Buner against the British'; and 'emancipation of the Frontier region from the British domination'. 'He succeeded in the first four, and was engaged in paving the way for the fifth when the inevitable hour arrived.'[143]

It is difficult to agree with these contentions, save the fourth one in partial. Although detailed analysis of these contentions is beyond the scope of this study,[144] some points, however, are clear from the preceding pages and certain other will become clear and illustrated in the succeeding pages/next chapter. Analysis of the colonial British authorities is, however, valid and meets the mark of objectivity, as below:

> With regard to the real feelings of the Akhúnd towards ourselves [the colonial British], conflicting accounts are given; but if he be judged by the actions and the sentiments expressed by him on certain important occasions, he will be found to have, as a rule, used his influence more to support than to frustrate or hamper our action, so long as we refrained from aggressive measures against any of the tribes in his neighbourhood, who looked up to him as their spiritual guide. The best proof of the Akhúnd's wise restraint of the evil spirit of Swát and Búnér is the almost total immunity, for many years previous to his death, of that portion of our border from raids and other serious offences.[145]

'The three main objects of the Akhúnd's policy', 'in his later years', 'seems to have been': 'to preserve the independence of Swát for at least his own life time'; 'to silence all his religious rivals'; and 'to bring about the election of his eldest son' Miangul Abdul Hanan 'to the kingship of Swát'. 'In the first two he was successful; in the last he was not.'[146]

The Akhund's policy towards the colonial Imperial Power was conciliatory and submissive. Some of the British official's writings, however, have attributed this course and policy, on his part, to his attempts and endeavours to retain the independence of Swat from the British occupation.[147]

NOTES

1. For the Durranis and their rule of the area, see Olaf Caroe, *The Pathans: 550 B.C.– A.D. 1957* (repr., Karachi: Oxford University Press, 1976), 249–326; Ganda Singh, *Ahmad Shah Durrani: Father of Modern Afghanistan* (Bombay: Asia Publishing House, 1959).
2. Mountstuart Elphinstone, *An Account of the Kingdom of Caubul*, with new introduction by Olaf Caroe, Vol. 2 (repr., Karachi: Oxford University Press, 1972), 19.
3. For the Sikh rule, see Caroe, *The Pathans*, 286–326.
4. Altaf Qadir, *Sayyid Ahmad Barailvi: His Movement and Legacy from the Pukhtun Perspective* (New Delhi: SAGE Publications India Pvt Ltd, 2015), 81.
5. Ibid.
6. See *Waqay-i Sayyad Ahmad Shahid, jama wa tartib hasb-i irshad*, Nawab Muhammad Wazir Khan Bahadar, with *muqadimah* by Muhammad Rabi Hasni Nadwi (Lahore: Sayyad Ahmad Shahid Academy, 2007), 1146–50. Also see Ghulam Rasul Mehr, *Sayyad Ahmad Shahid* (3rd edn., Lahore: Shaikh Ghulam Ali and Sons, 1981), 392–94.
7. According to Dr Altaf Qadir: 'We could not find Khonay or Khoni in the vicinity of Khwaza Khela though there are villages or Muhallahs with similar names in Swat. Some of them are either new developments or were never visited by Sayyid Ahmad.' (Qadir, *Sayyid Ahmad Barailvi: His Movement and Legacy from the Pukhtun Perspective*, 100 n. 29). However, according to H.G. Raverty, 'Khúna'h, also called Khúna'h Khela'h'/'Khunah' is situated, opposite Durush Khilah, up Shinr and below Fatihpur. See Henry George Raverty, *Notes on Afghanistan and Baluchistan*, Vol. 1 (2nd edn. in Pakistan, Quetta: Nisa Traders, 1982), 233, 235; H.G. Raverty, 'An account of Upper and Lower Suwát, and the Kohistán, to the source of the Suwát River; with an account of the tribes inhabiting those valleys', *Journal of the Asiatic Society* (Calcutta), 31/3 (1862), 249. In fact, Khunah or Khunah *kalay* (Khunah village) is situated up village Kutanai and below Shinr, on the Khwaza Khilah–Fatihpur Road, opposite to it on the other side of the Swat River is village Durush Khilah. As the village was destroyed and ruined by the people because of some immoral act of a *pir* who lived there, the place became known as *kandaray* (ruins); and hence is now commonly known as Kandaray; but it is also called Khunah and a portion of it as Mya Dhirai.

8. For details, see *Waqay-i Sayyad Ahmad Shahid*, 1150–73. Also see Mehr, *Sayyad Ahmad Shahid*, 394–400.

9. Qeyamuddin Ahmad, *The Wahabi Movement in India* (repr., Islamabad: National Book Foundation, n.d.), 50; Qeyamuddin Ahmad, *Hindustan mayn Wahabi Tahrik*, Urdu trans. Muhammad Muslim Azeemabadi (2nd edn., Karachi: Nafees Academy, 1976), 86. Also see Mehr, *Sayyad Ahmad Shahid*, 401–2.

10. See *Waqay-i Sayyad Ahmad Shahid*, 1146–73. Also see Qadir, *Sayyid Ahmad Barailvi: His Movement and Legacy from the Pukhtun Perspective*, 82–4.

11. *Waqay-i Sayyad Ahmad Shahid*, 1169.

12. Qadir, *Sayyid Ahmad Barailvi: His Movement and Legacy from the Pukhtun Perspective*, 82–4. For Anbalay Khan's joining him in the war, see *Waqay-i Sayyad Ahmad Shahid*, 1284.

13. See *Waqay-i Sayyad Ahmad Shahid*, 1177; Qadir, *Sayyid Ahmad Barailvi: His Movement and Legacy from the Pukhtun Perspective*, 85.

14. Qadir, *Sayyid Ahmad Barailvi: His Movement and Legacy from the Pukhtun Perspective*, 94.

15. See *Waqay-i Sayyad Ahmad Shahid*, 1266–8.

16. See ibid., 1255–7.

17. See ibid., 1309–16, 1318.

18. For the battle, see ibid., 1281–1306.

19. Qadir, *Sayyid Ahmad Barailvi: His Movement and Legacy from the Pukhtun Perspective*, 95–8.

20. For the request from Ghazan Khan of Dir, Sayyad Ahmad's sending his men, and the refusal of the Lower Swat *khan*s to allow them to pass through their area, because of the local politics and their own interest, and the consequent return of the mission from Khar, see *Waqay-i Sayyad Ahmad Shahid*, 2004–8.

21. In this book, the term or the word 'Britons' has neither been used in racist sense nor is it referring to the primitive ethnicity. The term or the word 'Briton'also means and is used for the native or citizen of Great Britain, person from Britain, and British person. In her rare televised address to the nation, on 5 April 2020, in connection with the coronavirus (Covid 19) pandemic, Queen Elizabeth II also used the word 'Britons', which testified that this is neither racist nor unsound. It was the East India Company not the British Government or British Crown that came to India and gradually occupied territories and emerged a ruling power. The Queen Proclamation of 1858 divested the Company of its ruling power in India and took over control of its occupied territories. This is why, to differentiate between the Imperial British Government or British Crown and the East India Company, 'Britons' has been used for those from Great Britain who were working in India under the East India Company until the Queen Proclamation of 1858. Used in the given context and sense, the term or word 'Britons' is more correct and relevant than the commonly used term or word 'English'.

22. Caroe, *The Pathans*, 324.

23. A.H. McMahon and A.D.G. Ramsay, *Report on the Tribes of Dir, Swat and Bajour* [Bajawar] *together with the Utman-Khel and Sam Ranizai*, edited with introduction by R.O. Christensen (repr., Peshawar: Saeed Book Bank, 1981), 69–70.

24. *Confidential, Gazetteer of the North-West Frontier: From Bajaur and the Indus Kohistán on the North to the Mari Hills on the South* [henceforward *Confidential*,

Gazetteer of the North-West Frontier], Vol. 4, Compiled for Political and Military Reference in the Intelligence Branch of the Quarter Master General's Department in India, completed and edited by A.L'e. Holmes (Simla: Printed at the Government Central Branch Press, 1887), 1850. Also *(Confidential), Central Asia*, Part I, *A Contribution towards the Better Knowledge of the Topography, Ethnography, Statistics, & History of the North-West Frontier of British India* [henceforward *(Confidential), Central Asia*], compiled for military and political reference by C.M. MacGregor, Vol. 3 (Calcutta: Office of the Superintendent of Government Printing, 1873), 155; *Frontier and Overseas Expeditions from India*, Vol. 1, *Tribes North of the Kabul River* [henceforward *Frontier and Overseas Expeditions from India*, Vol. 1] (2nd edn. in Pakistan, Quetta: Nisa Traders, 1982), 333–4.

25. Makhdum Tasadduq Ahmad, *Social Organization of Yusufzai Swat: A Study in Social Change* (Lahore: Panjab University Press, 1962), 33.

26. See T.J.C. Plowden, Assistant Commissioner in charge of Yúsafzai, to Deputy Commissioner Pesháwar, 8 February 1876, 'Report on the Leading Men and State of Factions in Swat', *Files of Tribal Affairs Research Cell, Home Department, Govt. of NWFP* [henceforward *TARC*], Serial No. (henceforward SN) 71/Swat, File No. (henceforward FN) 17-States I, 1932, 6; T.J.C. Plowden, *Report on the Leading Persons and State of Factions in Swat* (repr., Simla: Government of India Press, 1932), 9.

27. Some parts of his role are mentioned and referred to in the succeeding pages, and for a sketch of his life and role see the section 'The Akhund of Swat (1794–1877)' at the end of this chapter.

28. *Confidential, Gazetteer of the North-West Frontier*, Vol. 4, 1849; *Frontier and Overseas Expeditions from India*, Vol. 1, 343. Also see H.C. Wylly, *The Borderland: The Country of the Pathans* (repr., Karachi: Indus Publications, 1998), 124.

29. *(Confidential), Central Asia*, Vol. 3, 155; *Confidential, Gazetteer of the North-West Frontier*, Vol. 4, 1849; T.J.C. Plowden, Assistant Commissioner in charge of Yúsafzai, to Deputy Commissioner Pesháwar, 8 February 1876, 'Report on the Leading Men and State of Factions in Swat', *TARC*, SN 71/Swat, FN 17-States I, 1932, 6; Plowden, *Report on the Leading Persons and State of Factions in Swat*, 10. Also see Caroe, *The Pathans*, 363; W.W. Hunter, *The Indian Musalmans*, repr., with introduction by Bimal Prasad (New Delhi: Rupa & Co, 2002), 11.

30. Caroe, *The Pathans*, 363.

31. For Pir Baba, see Sher Afzal Khan Barikuti, *Pir Baba* (Mingawarah, Swat: Shoaib Sons Publishers and Booksellers, 1999; Abdur Rashid, *Islami Tasawuf aur Sufyayi Sarhad: Daswayn Sadi Hijri mayn Ilmi aur Adabi Khidmat* (Islamabad: Tasawuf Foundation, 1988); Hamesh Khalil, 'Hazrat Syed Ali Ghawas Tirmizi (Pir Baba)', in *Muslim Celebrities of Central Asia* (Peshawar: Area Study Centre (Central Asia), n.d.).

32. See T.J.C. Plowden, Assistant Commissioner in charge of Yúsafzai, to Deputy Commissioner Pesháwar, 8 February 1876, 'Report on the Leading Men and State of Factions in Swat', *TARC*, SN 71/Swat, FN 17-States I, 1932, 6; Plowden, *Report on the Leading Persons and State of Factions in Swat*, 10.

33. Qadir, *Sayyid Ahmad Barailvi: His Movement and Legacy from the Pukhtun Perspective*, 132 n. 89.

34. See Ghulam Rasul Mehr, *Jamat-i Mujahidin* (Lahore: Shaikh Ghulam Ali and Sons Limited, n.d.), 41–2.

35. Qadir, *Sayyid Ahmad Barailvi: His Movement and Legacy from the Pukhtun Perspective*, 132 n. 89.

36. T.J.C. Plowden, Assistant Commissioner in charge of Yúsafzai, to Deputy Commissioner Peshāwar, 8 February 1876, 'Report on the Leading Men and State of Factions in Swat', *TARC*, SN 71/Swat, FN 17-States I, 1932, 6; Plowden, *Report on the Leading Persons and State of Factions in Swat*, 10.

37. Caroe, *The Pathans*, 361.

38. See W.J. Keen, Political Agent, Dir, Swat and Chitral, to Secretary to the Chief Commissioner, North-West Frontier Province, No. 1690, 7 July 1915, and No. 2848, 22 October 1915, *Files of the Chief Commissioner Office, Peshawar, at Provincial Archives at Peshawar*, BN 5, SN 64.

39. See T.J.C. Plowden, Assistant Commissioner in charge of Yúsafzai, to Deputy Commissioner Peshāwar, 8 February 1876, 'Report on the Leading Men and State of Factions in Swat', *TARC*, SN 71/Swat, FN 17-States I, 1932, 6, 14; Plowden, *Report on the Leading Persons and State of Factions in Swat*, 9–10, 22.

40. See W.R. Hay, *Monograph on Swat State* (Simla: Government of India Press, 1934), 4.

41. *Confidential, Gazetteer of the North-West Frontier*, Vol. 4, 1849; *(Confidential), Central Asia*, Vol. 3, 154; *Frontier and Overseas Expeditions from India*, Vol. 1, 343. Also see *Mutiny Reports from Punjab & N.W.F.P.*, Vol. 2 (repr., Lahore: Al-Biruni, n.d.), 159–60; *Gazetteer of the Peshawar District, 1897–98* (repr., Lahore: Sang-e-Meel Publications, 1989), 84.

42. Wylly, *The Borderland: The Country of the Pathans*, 125; *Confidential, Gazetteer of the North-West Frontier*, Vol. 4, 1850; *(Confidential), Central Asia*, Vol. 3, 155; *Frontier and Overseas Expeditions from India*, Vol. 1, 344.

43. *Confidential, Gazetteer of the North-West Frontier*, Vol. 4, 1850; *(Confidential), Central Asia*, Vol. 3, 155.

44. For A.H. McMahon and A.D.G. Ramay's contention, see A.H. McMahon and A.D.G. Ramsay, *Report on the Tribes of the Malakand Political Agency (Exclusive of Chitral)*, revised by R.L. Kennion (Peshawar: Government Press, North-West Frontier Province, 1916), 33.

45. Robert Nichols, *Settling the Frontier: Land, Law, and Society in the Peshawar Valley, 1500–1900* (Karachi: Oxford University Press, 2001), 180. Although detailed analysis of Dr Robert Nichols' contention, made in the block quoted text, is out of place in this study and is also impossible because the required details could not be adjusted here, his words: 'characterized clan resistance as springing *from an outdated, irrational religion* [my italics]', are in itself 'irrational'.

46. Raverty, *Notes on Afghanistan and Baluchistan*, Vol. 1, 251 n. §§.

47. Ibid., 252–3 n. ‡. Also see Raverty, 'An account of Upper and Lower Suwát, and the Kohistán, to the source of the Suwát River; with an account of the tribes inhabiting those valleys', 246–7.

48. Wylly, *The Borderland: The Country of the Pathans*, 120–1. Also see *Frontier and Overseas Expeditions from India*, Vol. 1, 333–4; *Confidential, Gazetteer of the North-West Frontier*, Vol. 4, 1850; *(Confidential), Central Asia*, Vol. 3, 155.

49. See Wylly, *The Borderland: The Country of the Pathans*, 122–3; *Frontier and Overseas Expeditions from India*, Vol. 1, 337–8.

50. *Frontier and Overseas Expeditions from India*, Vol. 1, 334; *Confidential, Gazetteer of the North-West Frontier*, Vol. 4, 1850; *(Confidential), Central Asia*, Vol. 3, 155.

51. McMahon and A.D.G. Ramsay, *Report on the Tribes of the Malakand Political Agency (Exclusive of Chitral)*, revised by R.L. Kennion, 34; McMahon and A.D.G. Ramsay, *Report on the Tribes of Dir, Swat and Bajour together with the Utman-Khel and Sam Ranizai*, 71–2; *Confidential, Gazetteer of the North-West Frontier*, Vol. 4, 1851; *Frontier and Overseas Expeditions from India*, Vol. 1, 348.

52. *Frontier and Overseas Expeditions from India*, Vol. 1, 348.

53. McMahon and A.D.G. Ramsay, *Report on the Tribes of the Malakand Political Agency (Exclusive of Chitral)*, revised by R.L. Kennion, 34; McMahon and A.D.G. Ramsay, *Report on the Tribes of Dir, Swat and Bajour together with the Utman-Khel and Sam Ranizai*, 72; *Frontier and Overseas Expeditions from India*, Vol. 1, 349.

54. McMahon and A.D.G. Ramsay, *Report on the Tribes of the Malakand Political Agency (Exclusive of Chitral)*, revised by R.L. Kennion, 34; McMahon and A.D.G. Ramsay, *Report on the Tribes of Dir, Swat and Bajour together with the Utman-Khel and Sam Ranizai*, 72; *Frontier and Overseas Expeditions from India*, Vol. 1, 350.

55. *Mutiny Reports from Punjab & N.W.F.P.*, Vol. 2, 159.

56. Ibid., 160.

57. *Frontier and Overseas Expeditions from India*, Vol. 1, 352–3; *Confidential, Gazetteer of the North-West Frontier*, Vol. 4, 1851.

58. *Confidential, Gazetteer of the North-West Frontier*, Vol. 4, 1850; *(Confidential), Central Asia*, Vol. 3, 155; Wylly, *The Borderland: The Country of the Pathans*, 120–1.

59. *Confidential, Gazetteer of the North-West Frontier*, Vol. 4, 1851.

60. McMahon and A.D.G. Ramsay, *Report on the Tribes of Dir, Swat and Bajour together with the Utman-Khel and Sam Ranizai*, 70.

61. Ibid., 72.

62. *Confidential, Gazetteer of the North-West Frontier*, Vol. 4, 1850; *(Confidential), Central Asia*, Vol. 3, 155–6.

63. *Frontier and Overseas Expeditions from India*, Vol. 1, 344–5.

64. *Confidential, Gazetteer of the North-West Frontier*, Vol. 4, 1850–1; *(Confidential), Central Asia*, Vol. 3, 156; *Frontier and Overseas Expeditions from India*, Vol. 1, 348.

65. *Confidential, Gazetteer of the North-West Frontier*, Vol. 4, 1851; *(Confidential), Central Asia*, Vol. 3, 156.

66. For such point of view and allegation, see Sayyed Abdul Ghafoor Qasmay, *Tarikh Riyasat-i Swat* (Pashto) (Printed by Hamidia Press, Peshawar, n.d.), 55–7; Sayyed Mohd. Abdul Ghafoor Qasmi, *The History of Swat* (Printed by D.C. Anand & Sons, Peshawar, 1940), 15–16; Muhammad Asif Khan, *Tarikh-i Riyasat-i Swat wa Sawanih-i Hayat Baniy-i Riyasat-i Swat Hazrat Miangul Gul Shahzadah Abdul Wadud Khan Badshah Sahib*, with *dibachah, hisah awal, saluramah hisah*, and *hisah pinzamah* by Muhammad Asif Khan (Pashto) (Printed by Ferozsons Ltd., Peshawar [1958]), 91; Muhammad Asif Khan, *Tarikh Riyasat-i Swat wa Sawanih*

Hayat Bani Riyasat-i Swat Miangul Abdul Wadud (Urdu) (2nd edn., Mingawarah, Swat: Shoaib Sons Publishers and Booksellers, 2001), 64; Muhammad Asif Khan, *The Story of Swat as told by the Founder Miangul Abdul Wadud Badshah Sahib to Muhammad Asif Khan*, with preface, introduction and appendices by Muhammad Asif Khan, trans. preface and trans. by Ashruf Altaf Husain (Printed by Ferozsons Ltd., Peshawar, 1963), xlvii–xlviii.

67. Qasmi, *The History of Swat*, 15.
68. Ibid., 15–16.
69. Ibid., 16.
70. Ibid., 15.
71. *Mutiny Reports from Punjab & N.W.F.P.*, Vol. 2, 152.
72. Dr Munawwar Khan rightly points to the 'chivalry and bravery' of the tribesmen and local people as 'fanaticism to the British historians'. (Munawwar Khan, 'Swat: Second Instalment', *Peshawar University Review* (Peshawar), 1/1 (1974–75), 67). H.G. Raverty has also remarked sardonically, that 'all are "fanatics", "rebels["], or "dacoits", who fight against us [viz. the Britons] according to some people' (Raverty, *Notes on Afghanistan and Baluchistan*, Vol. 1, 251 n. §§).
73. *Gazetteer of the Peshawar District, 1897–98*, 80; *Mutiny Reports from Punjab & N.W.F.P.*, Vol. 2, 141.
74. *Mutiny Reports from Punjab & N.W.F.P.*, Vol. 2, 143 n. 2.
75. Lionel J. Trotter, *The Life of John Nicholson: Soldier and Administrator based on Private and Hitherto Unpublished Documents* (first edition in Pakistan, Karachi: Karimsons, Jamshed Road, 1978), 217.
76. Raverty, 'An account of Upper and Lower Suwát, and the Kohistán, to the source of the Suwát River; with an account of the tribes inhabiting those valleys', 241.
77. Ibid., 246.
78. For the *Kotwal's Diary*, see Sayyid Mubarak Shah (Kotwal of Delhi), *The Kotwal's Diary: (An account of Delhi during the War of Independence 1857)*, Eng. trans. R.M. Edwards, ed. Ansar Zahid Khan (Karachi: Pakistan Historical Society, 1994).
79. Ansar Zahid Khan (General Secretary and Director of Research, Pakistan Historical Society, and Editor, *Journal of the Pakistan Historical Society*) to Sultan-i-Rome (the present author), 6 October 1996, *Personal Collection of the Author*, Village Hazarah, Swat.
80. For Sayyad Akbar Shah's death on 11 May 1857, the day when the news of the uprising in India reached Peshawar, see *Confidential, Gazetteer of the North-West Frontier*, Vol. 4, 1851; *Frontier and Overseas Expeditions from India*, Vol. 1, 353; *Mutiny Reports from Punjab & N.W.F.P.*, Vol. 2, 160; Whylly, *The Borderland: The Country of the Pathans*, 129; *Gazetteer of the Peshawar District, 1897–98*, 84. All other sources have stated that he died on 11 May 1857, but H.G. Raverty has contended that he died in August 1857. For Raverty's contention, see Raverty, 'An account of Upper and Lower Suwát, and the Kohistán, to the source of the Suwát River; with an account of the tribes inhabiting those valleys', 246 n. *. Also see Raverty, *Notes on Afghanistan and Baluchistan*, Vol. 1, 251 n. §§.
81. *Gazetteer of the Peshawar District, 1897–98*, 84.
82. *Mutiny Reports from Punjab & N.W.F.P.*, Vol. 2, 160.
83. Ibid. Also see T.J.C. Plowden, Assistant Commissioner in charge of Yúsafzai, to Deputy Commissioner Peshawar, 8 February 1876, 'Report on the Leading

Men and State of Factions in Swat', *TARC*, SN 71/Swat, FN 17-States I, 1932, 6; Plowden, *Report on the Leading Persons and State of Factions in Swat*, 10; *Frontier and Overseas Expeditions from India*, Vol. 1, 353; *Confidential, Gazetteer of the North-West Frontier*, Vol. 4, 1851.

84. *Mutiny Reports from Punjab & N.W.F.P.*, Vol. 2, 149–51.
85. Trotter, *The Life of John Nicholson*, 215.
86. Ibid.; *Mutiny Reports from Punjab & N.W.F.P.*, Vol. 2, 151.
87. H.W. Bellew, *A General Report on the Yusufzais* (3rd edn., Lahore: Sang-e-Meel Publications, 1994), 97.
88. *Mutiny Reports from Punjab & N.W.F.P.*, Vol. 2, 160; *Frontier and Overseas Expeditions from India*, Vol. 1, 353; T.J.C. Plowden, Assistant Commissioner in charge of Yúsafzai, to Deputy Commissioner Pesháwar, 8 February 1876, 'Report on the Leading Men and State of Factions in Swat', *TARC*, SN 71/Swat, FN 17-States I, 1932, 6–7; Plowden, *Report on the Leading Persons and State of Factions in Swat*, 10.
89. Caroe, *The Pathans*, 364.
90. *Mutiny Reports from Punjab & N.W.F.P.*, Vol. 2, 160; T.J.C. Plowden, Assistant Commissioner in charge of Yúsafzai, to Deputy Commissioner Pesháwar, 8 February 1876, 'Report on the Leading Men and State of Factions in Swat', *TARC*, SN 71/Swat, FN 17-States I, 1932, 7; Plowden, *Report on the Leading Persons and State of Factions in Swat*, 10.
91. *Mutiny Reports from Punjab & N.W.F.P.*, Vol. 2, 160.
92. Ibid., 114.
93. See *Military Report and Gazetteer on Buner and Adjacent Independent Territory* (2nd edn., Delhi: Government of India Press, 1926), 7.
94. *Mutiny Reports from Punjab & N.W.F.P.*, Vol. 2, 160. Also see *Frontier and Overseas Expeditions from India*, Vol. 1, 353; McMahon and A.D.G. Ramsay, *Report on the Tribes of the Malakand Political Agency (Exclusive of Chitral)*, revised by R.L. Kennion, 34; McMahon and A.D.G. Ramsay, *Report on the Tribes of Dir*, Swat and Bajour together with the Utman-Khel and Sam Ranizai, 74.
95. *Mutiny Reports from Punjab & N.W.F.P.*, Vol. 2, 152.
96. See ibid., 114.
97. The *Mutiny Reports* and T.J.C. Plowden have stated the amount borrowed by Mubarak Shah from the *jamadar* of the sepoys as rupees 100 (one hundred), but *Gazetteer of Peshawar District, 1897–98*, has stated it as rupees 1000 (one thousand) which seems correct, because rupees one hundred were not sufficient for the one month pay of 500, 600, or 700 sepoys. See *Mutiny Reports from Punjab & N.W.F.P.*, Vol. 2, 160; T.J.C. Plowden, Assistant Commissioner in charge of Yúsafzai, to Deputy Commissioner Pesháwar, 8 February 1876, 'Report on the Leading Men and State of Factions in Swat', *TARC*, SN 71/Swat, FN 17-States I, 1932, 7; Plowden, *Report on the Leading Persons and State of Factions in Swat*, 10 cf. *Gazetteer of the Peshawar District, 1897–98*, 84.
98. *Mutiny Reports from Punjab & N.W.F.P.*, Vol. 2, 114.
99. *Gazetteer of the Peshawar District, 1897–98*, 84.
100. Khan, *The Story of Swat as told by the Founder Miangul Abdul Wadud Badshah Sahib to Muhammad Asif Khan*, xlviii.

101. *Mutiny Reports from Punjab & N.W.F.P.*, Vol. 2, 160–1. Also see T.J.C. Plowden, Assistant Commissioner in charge of Yúsafzai, to Deputy Commissioner Pesháwar, 8 February 1876, 'Report on the Leading Men and State of Factions in Swat', *TARC*, SN 71/Swat, FN 17-States I, 1932, 7; Plowden, *Report on the Leading Persons and State of Factions in Swat*, 11; Khan, 'Swat: Second Instalment', 64; *Frontier and Overseas Expeditions from India*, Vol. 1, 353–4; *Confidential Gazetteer of the North-West Frontier*, Vol. 4, 1852.

102. *Mutiny Reports from Punjab & N.W.F.P.*, Vol. 2, 161.

103. Syed Moinul Haq, *The Great Revolution of 1857* (Karachi: Pakistan Historical Society, 1968), 262.

104. Ghulam Rasul Mehr, *1857 Iswi: Pak wa Hind ki Pihli Jang-i Azadi* (Urdu) (Lahore: Shaikh Ghulam Ali and Sons (Private) Limited, Publishers, n.d.), 418.

105. Ibid., 420.

106. Haq, *The Great Revolution of 1857*, 261.

107. Khan, 'Swat: Second Instalment', 64.

108. Ibid., 64–5.

109. *Frontier and Overseas Expeditions from India*, Vol. 1, 348.

110. Khan, 'Swat: Second Instalment', 63.

111. Raverty, 'An account of Upper and Lower Suwát, and the Kohistán, to the source of the Suwát River; with an account of the tribes inhabiting those valleys', 246.

112. Ibid.

113. *Gazetteer of the Peshawar District, 1897–98*, 273.

114. Khan, 'Swat: Second Instalment', 65.

115. *Gazetteer of the Peshawar District, 1897–98*, 273.

116. *Mutiny Reports from Punjab & N.W.F.P.*, Vol. 2, 116.

117. Ibid., 118–19.

118. Ibid., 120.

119. Ibid., 161.

120. Caroe, *The Pathans*, 364.

121. Wylly, *The Borderland: The Country of the Pathans*, 115.

122. *Imperial Gazetteer of India: Provincial Series; North-West Frontier Province* [henceforward *Imperial Gazetteer of India, NWFP*] (repr., Lahore: Sang-e-Meel Publications, 1991), 218.

123. Caroe, *The Pathans*, 364. Also see Bellew, *A General Report on the Yusufzais*, 97.

124. Wylly, *The Borderland: The Country of the Pathans*, 129.

125. *Gazetteer of the Peshawar District, 1897–98*, 273.

126. Caroe, *The Pathans*, 364.

127. For some detail about the Akhund of Swat, see Sultan-i-Rome, 'Abdul Ghaffūr (Akhūnd): Saidū Bābā of Swāt; Life, Career and Role', *Journal of the Pakistan Historical Society* (Karachi), 40/3 (July 1992), 299–308; Sultan-i-Rome, ''Abd al-Ghafūr, the Akhūnd of Swāt' in *The Encyclopaedia of Islam*, 3rd edn., Kate Fleet et al., eds., Vol. 1 (Leiden: Brill, 2015), 4–6.

128. Accounts differ regarding the ethnicity as well as place and year of the Akhund's birth. See *Imperial Gazetteer of India, NWFP*, 221; Caroe, *The Pathans*, 362; Allah Bakhsh Yusufi, *Yusufzai* (Karachi: Muhammad Ali Educational Society, 1960), 460; McMahon and A.D.G. Ramsay, *Report on the Tribes of Dir, Swat and Bajour together with the Utman-Khel and Sam Ranizai*, 24; Akbar

S. Ahmed, *Millennium and Charisma among Pathans: A Critical Essay in Social Anthropology* (London: Routledge & Kegan Paul, 1976), 93–4; and Umar Mahiyuddin, 'Saidu Baba of Swat', *The Frontier Post* (daily), *Weekend Post*, 19 February 1988, 6. Nevertheless, the correct place and year are Jabrai and 1894, respectively.

129. Bellew, *A General Report on the Yusufzais*, 102–3.
130. Ibid., 103–4.
131. Wylly, *The Borderland: The Country of the Pathans*, 112–13.
132. See Khan, *Tarikh-i Riyasat-i Swat wa Sawanih-i Hayat Baniy-i Riyasat-i Swat Hazrat Miangul Gul Shahzadah Abdul Wadud Khan Badshah Sahib*, 80.
133. See Bellew, *A General Report on the Yusufzais*, 103–4.
134. McMahon and A.D.G. Ramsay, *Report on the Tribes of Dir, Swat and Bajour together with the Utman-Khel and Sam Ranizai*, 25.
135. Ibid. Also *Frontier and Overseas Expeditions from India*, Vol. 1, 329–30.
136. Bellew, *A General Report on the Yusufzais*, 105.
137. *Imperial Gazetteer of India*, NWFP, 221.
138. Caroe, *The Pathans*, 363.
139. Raverty, 'An account of Upper and Lower Suwát, and the Kohistán, to the source of the Suwát River; with an account of the tribes inhabiting those valleys', 243.
140. Ibid.
141. For the event, see ibid.
142. Ibid., 244.
143. Khan, *The Story of Swat as told by the Founder Miangul Abdul Wadud Badshah Sahib to Muhammad Asif Khan*, lvii–lviii. Also see Khan, *Tarikh-i Riyasat-i Swat wa Sawanih-i Hayat Baniy-i Riyasat-i Swat Hazrat Miangul Gul Shahzadah Abdul Wadud Khan Badshah Sahib*, 109.
144. For some detailed analysis, see Sultan-i-Rome, 'Saidu Baba and the Spread of Islam', *The Frontier Post* (Daily), *Weekend Post*, Peshawar, 15 July 1988, 4–5; and Sultan-i-Rome, 'Abdul Ghaffūr (Akhūnd): Saidū Bābā of Swāt; Life, Career and Role', 299–308; Sultan-i-Rome, ' 'Abd al-Ghafūr, the Akhūnd of Swāt', 4–6.
145. *Confidential, Gazetteer of the North-West Frontier*, Vol. 4, 1854; *Frontier and Overseas Expeditions from India*, Vol. 1, 356.
146. *Confidential, Gazetteer of the North-West Frontier*, Vol. 4, 1854; *Frontier and Overseas Expeditions from India*, Vol. 1, 357.
147. For example of such British official writings, see Caroe, *The Pathans*, 368; *Confidential, Gazetteer of the North-West Frontier*, Vol. 4, 1854; *Frontier and Overseas Expeditions from India*, Vol. 1, 357; *Imperial Gazetteer of India*, NWFP, 218.

11

1857–1915 CE

As stated in the previous chapter, the course of action adopted by the Akhund of Swat, Abdul Ghafur aka Saidu Baba, not only benefited the British but brought an end to the then Swat State. The region reverted to its former tribal welter.

SWAT AND THE BRITISH

After 1857, the people of Swat had no significant collision with the British until the Ambilah (Ambela) campaign in 1863, when 'relying in part on the Akhund's promise to restrain the Pathans',[1] the British forces made their advance to pass from Bunair (Bunir; Buner) through the Ambilah Pass in October 1863 in order to attack the followers of Sayyad Ahmad Barailwi in their colony, at Malka.

As mentioned in the previous chapter, some of the remnants of the followers of Sayyad Ahmad Barailwi, commonly called Hindustani Mujahidin, were provided shelter and asylum by Sayyad Akbar Shah in Sithanah. Some of them later shifted to Malka in the Bunair hills and established a colony there. In the course of time, the Hindustani Mujahidin turned anti-British and conducted attacks into the neighbouring British-controlled areas. This led to a number of British expeditions against their colonies and the Pukhtun tribes supporting them.

One such British expedition was the well-known Ambilah campaign of 1863, which was meant to punish and crush the colony of the Hindustani Mujahidin at Malka in the Bunair hills. The intended passage of the British forces from Bunair was considered an action in opposition to Pukhtu, or the tenets of the Pukhtun code of life, by the tribes of Bunair. They therefore resolved to oppose the British forces' advance. The British advance was blocked at the Ambilah Pass, situated in the Ambilah hills between Bunair and the Samah area.

The advance of the British forces was blocked by the tribes of Bunair. They also sought the assistance of the tribes of Swat and other areas, which was positively responded to. As the tribes of Bunair and Swat 'rose *en masse*',[2] the Akhund of Swat, who, according to James W. Spain (quoted above) had made a promise to the British that he will prevent the tribes from rising against them, 'was no longer able to stem the tide',[3] because 'the Swat Yusufzai paid no attention to' his 'remonstrances'.[4]

Although the Akhund of Swat had no desire to be drawn into direct opposition to the British, the circumstances were beyond his control and he was left with no other option but to join the war, in person, along with his followers as not responding to the call of the people would have been to risk the chance that Sayyad Mubarak Shah, whom he had expelled from Swat in 1857, 'might usurp a large amount of the influence which the Akhund then held over' the Yusufzi.[5]

The British Imperial government ordered that the operation against Malka 'should be completed by the 15th November' 1863,[6] but, because of the stiff resistance from the coalition of the tribes, it received 'telegram after telegram…from the Frontier, begging for more and yet more troops'.[7] The combined tribes staunchly resisted the mighty British forces and gave them a tough time for about two months. British military power failed. However, their diplomacy worked. W.W. Hunter has aptly remarked: 'But a coalition of mountain tribes is always capricious; and what our arms had failed to accomplish, dissentions and diplomacy began to effect.'[8]

A truce was concluded, and the tribes dispersed. Nevertheless, the British government admitted failure of the campaign by recording that 'it "had come to a close without our having been able either to drive out the Hindustání fanatics, or to induce them to surrender and to return to their homes in Hindustán [India]".'[9] 'The Campaign of 1863', moreover, taught the British that an expedition against the base of the Mujahidin 'may mean a War with a coalition of 53,000 fighting men… of the bravest races in the world'.[10] 'The actual number in the field' against the British, in 1863, 'rose at one time to 60,000'.[11] Losses to the British troops were also remarkable: 'amounted to no less than 847 men killed and wounded, or close on one-tenth of the total strength of the army when it was eventually raised to 9000 Regular troops. This was in the [Ambilah] Pass alone', and does not include 'men invalided from exposure or who died of disease'.[12]

The inhabitants of Swat remained peaceful, after the Ambilah war. They made no real attempt against the British government up till the death of the Akhund of Swat, on 12 January 1877, because the Akhund prevailed over the situation despite great pressure on him.[13] The British authorities had recorded that the Akhund of Swat 'advised the people of Swát and Bunér and other independent tracts to behave towards us [viz. the British] as good neighbours, and if they offended the British Government, to meet such demands as it might make, and to comply with such terms as might be imposed'.[14]

After the death of the Akhund of Swat, his sons 'endeavoured to create a *jahád* [*jihad*]' but the attempt failed due to internal developments in Swat.[15] The attempts from outside Swat in 1880, in the course of the second Anglo-Afghan war (1878–80), 'to incite the tribes of Dír and Swát to commence a crusade by an attack on the British line of communications near Jalálabad'[16] did not succeed.

The Malakand War, 1895

As the leading figures of Swat, Dir, and Bajawar were busy in conspiracies and internecine struggle for their personal supremacy and authority in the area, no heed was paid towards creating trouble for the neighbouring colonial[17] British government, so no significant collision had been reported since the Ambilah war of 1863.

The internal developments, however, did result in a collision and stiff fighting took place between the people of Swat and the British forces in 1895, when the Swat residents resolved to block the passage of the British forces from their country to Chitral and against Umara Khan of Jandul (Jandol). A brief reference to the Chitral crisis and to Umara Khan of Jandul is necessary before the account of the fighting at Malakand in 1895.

The Chitral Crisis (1892–1895)

Bounded by the Hindu Kush range on the north, Badakhshan and Kafiristan on the west, Dir on the south, and Gilgit Agency, Mastuj and Yasin on the east, Chitral State was an approximately 600 years old princedom. The last ruling dynasty had maintained themselves for more than 300 years at the time of the crisis. During the greater part of this period 'Chitrāl, with or without Mastūj', had been 'constantly at war with her neighbours—Gilgit, Yāsīn, the Sikh governor of Kashmīr, the Chilāsis, and the Pathān tribes to the south'.[18]

Being a seasoned politician, Amanul Mulk, the Mihtar (Mehtar: ruler) of Chitral, was well aware of the intentions of his neighbouring rulers. He established friendly relations with the powerful British so as to consolidate his state and rule.[19] The British also needed friendly relations and influence in the region to safeguard their interests in the context of the menace of Russia and its expansion from the north. The first negotiations, in this respect, took place between the British authorities and the Chitral State in 1877 and friendly relations were established. Amanul Mulk 'did all he could to maintain [the] friendly relations' with the British government.[20]

At his death in August 1892, Amanul Mulk was succeeded by his son Afzalul Mulk, but the other sons of Amanul Mulk wrangled for the succession. Fishing in the troubled water, Amanul Mulk's brother, Sher (Shir) Afzal, made his bid for the seat of ruler-ship. Afzalul Mulk was removed from the seat and killed by Sher Afzal, after which Sher Afzal was accepted as ruler; but Afzalul Mulk's brother Nizamul Mulk made 'his bid' for the seat after 'securing the concurrence of the British authorities at Gilgit' and emerged as the ruler.[21] He, however, was killed by his brother Amirul Mulk. Finding himself in trouble after the murder of his brother, Amirul Mulk asked Umara Khan of Jandul for assistance. Umara Khan proceeded to assist him, but suddenly Amirul Mulk repudiated his invitation and asked Umara Khan to go back.[22] Umara Khan did not heed either the Mihtar or the British authorities, who asked him to refrain from advancing. He continued his advance and occupied the fort of Drush (Drosh), where Sher Afzal, who reappeared from Afghanistan, joined him.[23]

In the meantime, a British column had reached Chitral from Gilgit under Surgeon-Major Robertson. Umara Khan asked Robertson to return to Mastuj, but he reproved Umara Khan for the manner in which he made the demand and informed him that 'he had applied to the Government of India for instructions' in the matter. Robertson occupied the fort of Chitral, with the forces he had with him. He deposed Amirul Mulk and replaced him with Shujaul Mulk, a boy of ten years age, as Mihtar.[24]

UMARA KHAN OF JANDUL (1860–1904 CE)

Umara Khan of Jandul was the younger son of the Khan of Jandul. 'He quarrelled with his father' and so 'was expelled from the country'.[25] As ambitious as he was, he tried to make himself master of Jandul, but did not succeed at the time. He did so two years later, after his return from *haj*, when 'he murdered his brother'. He annexed valley after valley to his dominion and established his rule on a firm footing. 'His, indeed, was one of those uncontrollable spirits which feed upon high adventure, and tire of nought but rest.'[26] He faced, courageously, a confederacy of the surrounding tribes. This collective attempt was ignited by Makrani Mula sent by the Afghan Amir Abdur Rahman.[27]

Umara Khan occupied all of Dir; the Khan of Dir, Sharif Khan, was exiled and took asylum in Swat. Seriously worried with regard to the ambitions of the Amir of Afghanistan for Bajawar, Dir, and Swat, upon which he himself had his eyes, Umara Khan made overtures to the colonial British government. In a letter, in September 1890, after his occupation of Dir, addressed to the commissioner at Peshawar, he wrote:

> My rulers, having once entered into communication and friendship with you, God willing, I shall not care for any other person. I have finished my work in Dír, and operations against Swát, which in my opinion are not so difficult, will be carried out. When the curtain now existing between me and the [colonial British] Government is lifted, by the grace of God I am prepared in every way to realize success for the [colonial British] Government, and to the best of my ability I shall not fail in any way.[28]

It was with the cooperation of Umara Khan and the *khanan* of Lower Swat that postal services were opened in 1891 between Peshawar and Chitral, 150 miles beyond the British frontier, by means of a direct route through those areas.[29] The relations, however, became strained, after the Durand Line Agreement, when the Amir of Afghanistan renounced his claim, besides others, over the territories of Bajawar, Dir, and Swat. Umara Khan's invasion of Chitral in 1895 and his refusal to comply with the advice and instructions of the British officials, caused him to face their forces (as is evident from the text below). Failing against the British, he fled to Afghanistan.[30] Umara Khan died on 10 September 1904.[31]

The War (1895)

Although Umara Khan was warned by the British colonial government
to refrain from advancing and was asked to go back, he continued his
advance into Chitral, along with Sher Afzal—brother of the former
Mihtar Amanul Mulk, and now contending for the seat of Chitral—and
ignored the warnings and advice of the British officials at Chitral, Gilgit,
Peshawar,[32] or those with the Asmar boundary mission. He was warned
to withdraw from Chitral before April 1895. To implement the order,
the colonial British authorities ordered mobilization, at Peshawar, of the
First Division of the field army, under Major-General Sir Robert Low,
as the Chitral Relief Force of some 15,000 men.[33]

A proclamation informed the tribes about the causes for the passage
of the British colonial forces through their territory. They were assured
that if they remained neutral and did not try to 'molest the passage of
the troops no harm would be done to them or their property, and that
[the colonial British] Government had no intention of annexing their
country'.[34] As the tribes 'really desired to retain their independence'[35]—
and, as they were not only 'anxious to retain their independence of the
Kabul Government' but 'to obtain a recognition of such independence
by the British Government' as well,[36] they were not ready to allow the
passage of the imperialist forces through their country. Their sentiments
and feelings about the Chitral Relief Force, and its passage through their
country, can be judged from the *tapah*:

چرته لندن چرته چترال دے
بې ننگي زور شوه فرنگيان چترال ته ځينه

*Meaning: London and Chitral are poles apart, but the British try to grab
Chitral due to the lack of patriotism and self-respect in the Pukhtuns.*

Disregarding the British proclamation, the people of Swat held all the
three passes from which the British troops could enter Swat *en route*
to Chitral.

The Chitral Relief Force left Nowshera (Nawshihrah; in Pashto
Nawkhar) on 1 April 1895, under the command of Sir Robert Low. To
keep the enemy divided, it was decided that the Murah and Shahkut
passes be threatened and that the main attack should be made on the
Malakand,[37] the strategy adopted some four centuries earlier by the
Yusufzi against the then defenders of Swat. The attack was carried out

on 3 April. The tribesmen, most of whom were unarmed, defended themselves with great gallantry against the well-trained, well-equipped, and well-organized British forces. However, finding themselves pressed hard, by the resolute British advance from the front, they felt compelled to give way and retreat 'towards the Swat River'.[38] They continued their resistance and halted the advance of the colonial British until 7 April 1895. H.C. Thomson has admitted: 'It was impossible not to admire the courage displayed by the enemy, who exposed themselves most recklessly'.[39] And H.C. Whylly has admitted that the main reason for the heavy losses of the tribesmen was 'their holding the position to the last'.[40]

The Ranizi and other clans of Swat 'stoutly opposed' the passage of the British forces from the Malakand Pass and their advance to the Swat River,[41] but their determined design was foiled. The British colonialists succeeded in making their advance and 'for the first time since the days of Zain Khan, leader of Akbar's armies, a host from the south entered the green belt of the Swat Valley'.[42] Thus, Swat—which 'up to 1895', 'remained an untrodden land of Erewhon, its beauties a legend and unseen by any European',[43] was opened to the British colonialists.

The Swat Valley, as far as the town of Tanra, almost up to Jalalah on the border with Landakay, was brought under a loose British 'administrative control that had already proved effective in Baluchistan and Kurram'.[44] This safeguarded the strategic Peshawar-Chitral route, *via* Lower Swat, and secured the safe passage and communications of the relief forces with Chitral. The valley 'beyond Tanra' remained for the time being 'in its chronic condition of tribal welter'.[45]

It is pertinent to mention that, in his poem '*Charbaytah*', Yasin has described and recorded the role played by the eminent local figures in the Malakand war, both for and against the British imperial power. Those who played a role on behalf of the British and were reviled by Yasin are: the Manki Mula (Pir of Manki), Sharif Khan (the *khan* of Alahdand), Ghulam Haidar (of Dargai), Khadi [Khan] (of Lund Khwar), Baz [Muhammad Khan] (of Shairgarh), Suhbat (of Skhakut), Sharif Khan (the exiled *khan* of Dir), Mian Rahim Shah (Kaka Khail), Nasray Malak (of Uch, Dir), Aslam [Khan] and Inayat [Khan] (*khanan* of Tanra), the *khanan* of Alahdand, and Safdar (of Nawagai, Bajawar). On the other hand, he has praised and appreciated the roles played by Mir Azam (of Batkhilah), Sadullah (of village Dhiri), Haji Pir (of Batkhilah), Saadat Khan (of Batkhilah), Ms Masumah (of village Dhiri),

Qadar [Khan] (of village Dhiri), a youth from Gugdarah (Upper Swat), Muhammad Shah Khan (brother of Umara Khan of Jandul), Hadah Mula, and Shahzadah [Sultan Ibrahim Jan] (extra assistant commissioner Peshawar).[46]

The colonial British government did not honour its words and set about establishing garrisons at Malakand and Chakdarah after their success against Umara Khan. The Political Agency of Dir and Swat was instituted with headquarter at Malakand and placed under the direct control of the central government at Delhi due to its strategic significance.[47] The territory of Ranizi and Khan Khail, on the left bank of the Swat River, from the limits of Landakay in the east to that of Qalangai (Qulangai) in the west, were brought under the loose control of the colonial government.

At the time of its formation, the Agency was named as the Agency of Dir and Swat, but Chitral (formerly linked with Gilgit Agency) was also added to this Agency in March 1897 and it was renamed as the Agency of Dir, Swat and Chitral. There was a single political agent for the whole Agency. At first, he was agent and representative of the central government because, at the creation of the Agency, it was not under the provincial government of Punjab but was placed under the direct orders of the central government of British India. After the formation of the North-West Frontier Province (the present-day Khyber Pukhtunkhwa), it was transferred from the foreign department of the Government of India to the chief commissioner of the Frontier Province. The political agent was posted at Malakand. It was through him that the correspondences took place between the central government and the princely states and tribes of these areas, and their affairs were conducted through him. He, moreover, was in-charge of the administration for those areas of the Agency that were under the direct loose-control of the colonial government, viz. the Malakand Protected Area, later also commonly called Malakand Agency and now Malakand District.

THE MALAKAND WAR, 1897

At the defeat and flight of Umara Khan of Jandul, the colonial British reinstalled Sharif Khan, the exiled Khan of Dir, in 1895 as the Khan of Dir. He had been in exile in Swat since 1890 and had sided with and assisted the colonial British in the grave situation in 1895. All the territories previously occupied by Umara Khan were bestowed upon him and he was elevated to the status of Nawab of Dir in 1897. His southern boundary was now the Swat River and he claimed as his subjects the Abazi, Khadakzi, Adinzi, Shamuzi, Nikpi Khail, Sibujni, and Shamizi sections, on the right bank of the Swat River.

The colonial government and authorities seemed satisfied with the new arrangements, and recorded: 'The new arrangements appeared to be entirely satisfactory, trade increased rapidly, and all signs of hostility on the part of the people quickly disappeared.'[48]

It, however, was not easy to win the hearts of the people; as they considered the very presence of the British as a common danger. Emotions ran high and, within the passage of barely two years of the establishment of garrisons at Malakand and Chakdarah, started 'the most formidable' revolt against the British arms that was ever witnessed even on the North-West Frontier of India.[49]

There was great unrest not only in Swat but throughout the tribal belt on the North-West border of the British Indian Empire. In such a time the Sartur (Sartor) Faqir[50] appeared in Upper Swat in July 1897. Taking abode at Landakay, he announced that 'someone' had sent him and that four other (mythical) *faqiran* were also to join him. About the 20 July, besides other claims of magical powers and unseen support, he claimed that 'his mission was to turn the British off the Malakand and out of Peshawar'.[51] In spite of all the prevailing excitements and developments, he was regarded as a madman by the authorities at Malakand and their allies.[52] The Mianguls (Pashto: *myagwalan*), the grandsons of Abdul Ghafur, the Akhund of Swat aka Saidu Baba, communicated to the Political Agent, H.A. Deane, that they would expel him 'should he continue to cause any trouble'.[53] However, a folk verse has illustrated:

پهٔ لنډاکي ورته ديره سرتور فقير دے
ديـن فبرنګے د خان پهٔ ويـر دے

Meaning: The Sartur Faqir has taken his abode at Landakay,
against the British; hence Deane, the English, (the political agent)
is perturbed for his/their safety/defence.

The colonialists gave little importance to the new movement at first, but 'the gravity of the situation could no longer be ignored' towards the end of July. The troops stationed in the neighbourhood were alerted and were asked to be ready for action at the shortest notice. On the 26th of

July 1897, the Guides, a separate contingent of the British forces, were summoned from Mardan.[54]

The Sartur Faqir started his march from Landakay on the 26th of July, for Malakand and Chakdarah. He announced that he would sweep away the British forces from both the places within eight days.[55] He was followed by a few boys, 'one of whom he proclaimed king of Delhi'.[56] The response to his appeals was enthusiastic and the people joined him as he proceeded. All the headmen, with a solitary exception, were carried away by the popular enthusiasm, and by nightfall a resolute body of the people of Swat was on the move to attack Malakand, while another party turned its attention to Chakdarah.[57]

The Sartur Faqir's standard 'became the rallying point for thousands of fighting-men from Upper Swat, Buner, the Utman Khel country, and even more distant parts'.[58] The tribesmen, who barely exceeded one thousand men on the first night, rapidly increased in number to some twelve thousands or more at Malakand and to upwards of eight thousand at Chakdarah.[59] On the British side, the Guides arrived from Mardan at Malakand on the next day, after their famous quick march. By the 28th, the mobilization of more troops in India was ordered and some of them were even then on their way. On 30th of July, the 35th Sikhs and 38th Dogras arrived and the 31st was marked by the arrival of more troops from India.[60] Heavy fighting continued at both the places, which never actually ceased until Malakand was relieved on the 1st and Chakdarah on the 2nd of August 1897.[61]

Realizing the severe nature of the uprising, the governor-general in council sanctioned the dispatch of the Malakand Field Force on the 30th of July 1897,[62] for holding Malakand and the adjacent posts and for the punishment of the tribes involved. For the support of the Field Force, the immediate formation of a reserve brigade was also decided early in August 1897.[63] The first punitive expedition in the Swat Valley was led, because it was observed that 'the wave of fanatical feeling which travelled from north to south along the western border of British India had its origin in the Swat Valley'.[64]

The forces reached Mingawarah on 19 August 1897, after facing stiff resistance at various places up the valley and after bearing heavy losses in men, especially of H.L.S. MacLean and Lt. R.T. Greaves. Reconnaissances were made, from here up the valley as far as Gulibagh and the Ghwarband Pass. After a stay of four days at Mingawarah, the forces went back. Similar punitive expeditions were sent against all those tribes who had joined the people of Swat in the Malakand Jihad.[65]

The severity of the fighting at Kutah (Kotah) and Naway Kalay, near Landakay, in 1897, at the time of the punitive expedition up the valley, and its significance to the British, can be judged from the fact that the British government awarded their highest award, the Victoria Cross, to Lt. Col. Adams and Viscount Fincastle, whereas, Lt. MacLean remained deprived due to his death in the course of fighting, near Naway Kalay. Five persons were awarded the 'Order of Merit'.[66]

It is pertinent to dispel the commonly held belief that Winston S. Churchill, later the renowned prime minister of Britain, was present in the Malakand war. At the time of the Malakand war, Mr Churchill was not in India. He came to India later, to join the Malakand Field Force, but not as a member of the Force; because there was no vacancy on the staff of Bindon Blood, commander of the Malakand Field Force, so he was advised, by Bindon, to come to the Frontier as a correspondent. Consequently, Churchill approached the editor of the *Allahabad Pioneer*, who showed a willingness to use his articles about the Malakand Field Force and 'would pay for them, too, though not a princely sum'. He also asked his mother, Lady Randolph Churchill, to make arrangements with a London newspaper, upon which she 'arranged with the editor of the *Daily Telegraph* to use his work and to pay for it at the rate of £5 a column'.[67] He thus came to India and accompanied the Malakand Field Force later as a war correspondent. He was not with the Malakand Field Force at the time of the punitive expedition to Swat, even as a correspondent of the *Daily Telegraph* or the *Pioneer*. He only accompanied the Malakand Field Force in its operation in Bajawar and against the Utman Khails (Khels). His account of the Malakand war and the punitive expedition to Swat was not an eye-witness account but one written on the basis of what he later heard from others.[68]

T.H. Holdich has admitted the gallantry of the people, in 1897, in these words: 'So fierce was the fanatical fervour of that half-armed mob that General Meiklejohn has told me that he saw unarmed boys and men actually turning on the cavalry and attacking them with sticks and stones.'[69] He has further stated:

It would not be difficult to quote writers who brand our transfrontier neighbours—Swatis, Mohmands, Afridis, and Waziris alike—as cowards. They must know now that in calling them cowards they erred. It is perhaps one of the most useful lessons that we learnt from this boundary war—the lesson of respect for the people who fought well for their independence.[70]

Whereas, H.C. Whylly has written about the people of Swat: 'At one time their courage was not held in very high esteem, but the fighting in 1895 and 1897 seems to prove that in this respect they have been by us and others curiously misjudged.'[71]

The people of Swat, in their uprising of 1897, not only compelled the mighty British army for a full week to fight 'against untold odds',[72] but turned 'the year of the Diamond Jubilee'[73] of the Britons' successful emergence from the Indian War of Independence, 1857, into 'surely one of the most troublous years in all Indian history'.[74] The tribesmen failed to achieve their objective due to a combination of factors, which included lack of planning for a long drawn war, the Sartur Faqir's false claims, no proper discipline and organization in their ranks, their non-acquaintance with a long drawn war, false promises of help from the Afghan commander-in-chief at Asmar, lack of proper arrangements for the provision and supply of ammunition and foodstuffs to the fighters, and the Sartur Faqir's precipitation of matters. The British supremacy in arms and ammunition, communication system, and a regular, trained and disciplined army made their success certain.[75] Their action, however, opened the flood gate of simultaneous tribal risings on the North-West Frontier, resulting in far reaching consequences for the administrative set up of the region and in the formulation of the policy of containment.

POST-MALAKAND WAR YEARS

In the years following the Malakand war, no significant armed tussle with nor outbreak against the colonial British government in Swat was noted.

The Sartur Faqir, however, again tried to make his bid towards the end of 1898. It caused trouble for the colonialists, who sent the movable column towards Landakay, but the Faqir's attempt failed due to the opposition of Abdullah Khan of Rabat, Dir.[76] The colonial British concluded agreements with the Nawab of Dir, the tribes of Swat, and the Mianguls—the grandsons of the Akhund of Swat, or Saidu Baba—to prevent further attempts on the part of Sartur Faqir.[77] In April 1905, the Mianguls and the chief men from Upper Swat attended a *darbar*, held by the chief commissioner of the province. In May 1905, the political agent at Malakand accepted an invitation from the Upper Swat *jargay* to visit their country. The political agent made a successful visit to Upper Swat and proceeded up to Charbagh. The discipline and attitude of the people during this visit have been praised.[78]

Thus despite some attempts by the Sartur Faqir, due to the intermittent internecine struggles and factional fights within Swat and against the Nawab of Dir, and the role of some of those who were influential but were ambitious for the ruler-ship and were on good terms with the colonial British, notable collisions did not occur between the people of Swat and the Imperial British government. It was in 1915 that once more a bid was made, after the formation of Swat State. An attack on Chakdarah was made, but with no success. This attack on the British garrison at Chakdarah proved to be one of the factors that contributed to the fall of Abdul Jabbar Shah, the then ruler of Swat State, and led to his replacement by Miangul Abdul Wadud, the second ruler of Swat State.

THE POWER GAME AND THE POLITICAL DIMENSION

On the internal side, although the Akhund of Swat had influence in Swat, factional feelings and feuds did not subside completely and wrangles for local power continued. Hence, although more cautious in establishing temporal power himself, the Akhund of Swat tried twice, in May 1871 and June 1875, to have Miangul Abdul Hanan, his eldest son, elected as the King of Swat, but to no avail. There were other influential and powerful figures with ambitions for their own rule. A British official report, for the year 1875–76, has given an insight to the issue:

> The great age of the Akhund and the disputes regarding his succession have given rise to some disturbances in the country itself. The most prominent claimants to the succession are Mian Gul, son of the Akhund, and Sher Dil Khan, chief of the Ránazai [Ranizai; Ranizi], one of the most powerful of the Swat clans, whose claims are supported by a large number of the people.[79]

In the post-Akhund, or post 12 January 1877, days there were constant wrangles for power in Swat. Rahmatullah Khan of Dir, Shir (Sher) Dil Khan of Alahdand, and Miangul Abdul Hanan, the eldest son of the Akhund, were all claimants to power.[80] Rahmatullah Khan of Dir, son and successor of Ghazan Khan, supported Shir Dil Khan. There were two great *dalay* in Swat, one headed by Shir Dil Khan, the chief of the Ranizi (now in the Malakand Protected Area or Malakand Agency or Malakand District) and the other by the eldest son of the Akhund (the Saidu Baba). All the principal figures of Swat and the surrounding areas, sided with one or the other of these factions.[81]

Miangul Abdul Hanan was generally successful in his contests with the Babuzi and with the partisans of Rahmatullah Khan of Dir.

> But the excesses committed by his rabble followers on women of captured villages brought his cause into discredit and increased the popularity of the Dír Khan, who invaded Swát in October [1879], but was soon after compelled to retire owing to disturbances in Bajour [Bajawar], leaving an agent to uphold his authority in the Adinzai tappah [Adinzi *tapah*] of Swát.[82]

Shir Dil Khan died in April 1880, and 'the chief political power in Swat passed into the hands of Rahmatullah Khan, the Khan of Dir'.[83] Early in 1881, the agents of Rahmatullah Khan were driven out of the Adinzi *tapah* of Swat,[84] which was occupied by the Dir's Khan in 1879. His influence, however, 'remained undisputed and undisturbed' in that part of the valley which lies north of the Swat River.[85] Rahmatullah Khan, favoured by faction disputes/affairs in Swat for many years, became the virtual ruler of the right bank in Upper Swat by the end of 1881. He would have attained the object of his ambition and 'conquered the whole valley', had he not met with difficulties as a result of his quarrels with the Khan of Bajawar and with his own sons.[86]

Miangul Abdul Hanan tried to play a prominent role in the party politics,

> But his efforts to gain a leading political position in Swát were met by the passive resistance of the people, who view[ed] with concealed jealousy and dislike[d] his attempts to efface the local tribal chiefs, and apprehend[ed] that the consequences of his rule, if established, will take the shape of taxation. This feeling...[was] naturally...fostered by the Khans themselves.[87]

The Miangul's influence, which had been 'on the wane' for some time,[88] suddenly increased and, by the end of 1882, his position was stronger than that of any other chief in Swat. He was, however, personally unpopular and the people of Swat had 'a rooted aversion to seeing any one man in a position of power, which may be expected to be permanent' and thus 'lead to the imposition of taxes or a demand for land revenue'.[89]

At this time, Umara Khan acquired power in Bajawar and entered the contest for power in Swat. A desultory contest for supremacy in Swat was carried on between the Miangul and the Khan of Dir in 1883, but they came to terms in March 1884. The Miangul acknowledged the authority of Dir over Malizi and Rahmatullah Khan, the Khan of Dir, promised that he would not 'interfere unasked in the affairs of Swát Proper'.[90]

The Swat Valley was a hotbed of intrigues and factional feuds between the years 1884 and 1890, due to the ambitious actions of Umara Khan of Jandul. Miangul Abdul Hanan sided sometimes with Muhammad Sharif Khan, the Khan of Dir, who had succeeded his father Rahmatullah Khan, and at other times with the chief of Jandul.[91]

It was very probable that Abdul Hanan's claim to power would eventually have been 'acknowledged by the people', although he did not 'possess the character of his father'.[92] 'At one time it appeared' that he would have 'undisputed supremacy in Swát', but his natural indolence and carelessness, coupled with a failure 'to consolidate his power', 'conciliate his subjects', and restrict 'the predatory habits of his followers', resulted in reverses for him on more than one occasion.[93] He died in September 1887.[94]

THE BRITISH JOIN THE POWER GAME (1888)

Miangul Abdul Hanan was succeeded by his brother, Miangul Abdul Khaliq, who had no interest in mundane affairs. The struggle for the overlord-ship of Swat now became a contest between Umara Khan of Jandul and Sharif Khan of Dir, neither of whom hailed from Swat. In order to safeguard their interest in the region, the British, the third foreign power, also joined the power game. Furthermore, since the early 1880s, the people of Swat had been apprehensive of the Kabul government's designs and attempts on their area.[95] In 1888, owing to the unrest in Swat caused by the actions of the Amir of Afghanistan, the British government, which had hitherto refrained from interfering in the internal affairs of Bajawar, Dir, and Swat, decided to intervene for their own interests. After a protest by the British government, the Amir of Afghanistan 'at once acknowledged that Swat was outside his sphere of influence, though he asserted [his] claim to the other countries',[96] i.e. Bajawar, and Dir. Nevertheless, the Afghan intrigues continued till the Durand Line Agreement, signed on 12 November 1893 by Amir

Abdur Rahman, the Amir of Afghanistan, and Mortimer Durand, the British envoy. Section 3 of the Agreement stated:

> The British Government thus agrees to His Highness the Amir retaining Asmar and the valley above it, as far as Chanak. His Highness agrees, on the other hand, that he will at no time exercise interference in Swat, Bajaur, or Chitral, including the Arnawai or Bashgal valley.[97]

Amir Abdur Rahman has himself stated that he renounced his claims over 'Bajaur, Swat, Buner, Dir, Chilas, and Chitral'.[98] The Durand Line Agreement brought an end, for the time being, to Afghanistan's claim over Swat and any future attempts at annexation. On the other hand, it paved the way for British influence in the affairs of Swat, by placing it firmly in the territories lying beyond the Durand Line on the Indian side.[99]

The internal situation during this time remained unsettled with factional fighting continuing as usual. Umara Khan, on one occasion, succeeded in taking Alahdand and other villages but was repelled and forced to negotiate terms.[100] When a number of Afghani refugees, headed by General Faiz Muhammad Khan Ghilzay, settled in Swat in 1889, the people of Swat

> became divided on the question of the administration of their country—some advocated the intervention of the Government of India, others wished to call in the headmen of the Hindustani fanatics at Palosi [Palusai], and a third party suggested making the Afghan General Faiz Muhammad Khan their chief. All seemed to be agreed as to the necessity of opposing Umra [Umara] Khan, who had threatened to attack Thana [Tanra] and might attempt to overrun all Swat.[101]

It is noteworthy that no party had suggested the Akhund's surviving son, Miangul Abdul Khaliq.

The prophecy of the British authorities, that the death of the Akhund of Swat, whom they considered the most powerful and influential pillar of peace and order, would contribute to their interests, came true. They believed:

> In one way the death of the Akhund was an advantage to the [colonial British] Government, seeing that Swát being now divided by hostile and almost equal factions, there will be always found one ready to join the

[colonial British] Government in the hope of, with its help, crushing its rivals.[102]

Some of the *khanan* had made prior overtures to the colonial British government, but only in their personal capacities. In 1889, for the first time, a segment of the people of Swat advocated the direct intervention of the colonial British in the affairs of Swat. During this uncertainty, and before the formation of a government in Swat, Umara Khan of Jandul succeeded in ousting Sharif Khan from Dir; he took refuge in Upper Swat. Umara Khan gained more power with his occupation of Dir and had already made overtures to the colonial British for an agreement to incorporate Swat into his dominion. Hoping to signify his loyalty and usefulness to the British government, the third of his three petitions, of October 1888, runs thus:

> By my exertions all the Chiefs of Bajaur [Bajawar] and Swat will wait on the British Government, and it is advisable that all such Chiefs should be placed under me and my authority. Those who may be well disposed towards me should be honored by the [colonial] Government, and those who incur my displeasure should be considered as if they had incurred the displeasure of the [colonial] Government.[103]

Umara Khan frankly expressed his motives and ambitions in a letter to the commissioner at Peshawar in September 1890.[104] He wanted a free hand, with no interference from the British Indian government. The *malakan* and *khanan* of Swat contacted the British authorities themselves to seek support against Umara Khan's incursions and encroachments into Swat. In December 1892, they even threatened to turn for help either to the Indian Mujahidin or to the Amir of Afghanistan, in the event of Umara Khan's advancing onto Swat.[105]

The colonial British, however, had no love for Umara Khan or the people of Swat, but were concerned only with their own interests. Writing about the latter, H.A. Deane observed:

> Having once lost the confidence of the Kháns of Swat, which we should do if Umra [Umara] Khán took the country, there would be small chance of our regaining it. The attitude of Swat is this. It desires to be left independent, it fears Umra Khán and it fears the Amír of Kabul....there is nothing to be gained by Umra Khán's interference in Swat and that its independence should be maintained.[106]

On the other hand, he stated that 'there would probably be no necessity for any communication with Umra Khán on the subject until such time as he may commence to make a move against Swat'.[107] The Lt. Governor of the Punjab's view, on the letter from the *khanan* of Swat, was that they 'write merely in order to deter us from supporting Umra Khán against them, or to lead us to insist on his leaving Swat alone'.[108] The commissioner Peshawar Division, while discussing the proposed agreement with Umara Khan, stated:

> So far as Swat is concerned, I think it was a mistake to make such a promise [with Umara Khan], because *we may find it desirable some day to establish our own influence in that valley* [my italics], unless meanwhile it has been conquered by Umra Khán and we are able to gain our end through his instrumentality.[109]

Referring to the letter of the *khanan* of Tanra he stated:

> I did not consider it necessary to take any notice. I do not suppose that [the colonial] Government are prepared at present to assume a protectorate over Swat on their own account, and it is quite certain that Umra Khán would bitterly resent any requisition from us to hold his hand in that quarter. If therefore we desire to maintain our friendship with him, no attention can be paid to communications of this kind, and the parties must be left to fight it out.[110]

The governor-general in council agreed that Deane's proposal was impracticable, but stated that 'it would be better not to give Umra Khan the proposed warning against interference with Swat'. In his opinion, 'such a warning would not necessarily have the desired effect, and it would not improbably make Umra Khan more than ever sore' against the colonial British. He did, however, make it clear:

> Unless [the colonial] Government interference is absolutely forced on us, it is very desirable to avoid becoming entangled in the rivalries and intrigues which are always rife on that part of the frontier. The Government of India were at one time inclined to give Umra Khan encouragement, in order to prevent the Amir [of Afghanistan] from overrunning the whole country, but that is a very different thing from coming in between Umra Khan and the Swatis [viz. the people of Swat].[111]

In 1893, Umara Khan made some headway into Swat and factional fighting continued in Swat for the next two years. Umara Khan had not yet succeeded in overrunning Swat when he made his advance on Chitral, resulting in his flight to Afghanistan and also the passage of the British forces from Lower Swat (detailed earlier).

In 1895, Sharif Khan,[112] who had been in exile in Swat since 1890 and had sided with the colonial British against Umara Khan, was reinstalled as the Khan of Dir after the defeat and flight of Umara Khan of Jandul. He thus regained possession of the territories he had lost five years previously, and also took over Umara Khan's other ruled areas. His southern boundary was now the Swat River and he claimed as his subjects the Abazi, Khadakzi, Adinzi, Shamuzi, Nikpi Khail (Khel), Sibujni and Shamizi sections, on the right bank of the Swat River, whose people, excluding the Abazi and Khadakzi, belonged to the Khwazuzi branch of Akuzi Yusufzi to which Sharif Khan and his clan also belonged. In 1896, however, fighting resumed in Upper Swat and Sharif Khan's interference with the subject clans on the right bank of the Swat River, caused unrest amongst the people.[113]

Umara Khan had not been in the struggle for supremacy over Swat for long and the left bank Lower Swat, up to certain limits, came under British protectorate, but Sharif Khan of Dir could not establish absolute and unchallenged authority in Upper Swat, nor did he remain the sole contender. At no single *khan*'s exercising unchallenged power in Swat, the region's politics were characterised by the *dalah* system, i.e. opposition between the two rival *dalay*, each under the leadership of its *khan*.[114]

In 1897, the Mianguls, the grandsons of Saidu Baba, joined the power-game in Swat. In June, the rivalry between the Mianguls and the Khan of Dir was causing friction. The Khan of Dir was permitted by the colonial British authorities 'to put a stop to the intrigues of the fanatical faction by coercing the tribes on the right bank of the river over whom he claimed authority'.[115] The Upper Swat *jargay*, representing the four Khwazuzi clans on the right bank and the Musa Khail, Babuzi, and Jinki Khail on the left bank of the Swat River collectively met Major Deane, the political agent, at Chakdarah and requested him to settle the matters between them and the Khan of Dir.[116] The *jargay* assured the colonial government of their loyalty and support. On the British side, Major Deane explained:

[The colonial] Government had no desire to interfere with their internal administration, but would assist them in settling their disputes if they brought them before the Political Agent; that [the colonial] Government did not intend to impose revenue on them, and that all that [the colonial] Government wanted was to secure peace and order in Upper Swat, as had been done in Lower Swat and Ranizai [Ranizi].[117]

On 30 October 1897, an important meeting was held between the colonial British and six hundred *malakan* and representatives from Upper Swat, brought by the Mianguls (the grandsons of Saidu Baba).

The *jirga* [*jargah*] raised the question of the future administration of their country, and a large majority of the tribesmen expressed themselves in favour of direct control by the [colonial] Government of India, stating that by no other means could they obtain justice or *settle their interminable disputes* [my italics].[118]

In Major Deane's words: 'The visit was an important one as completing submission on the part of the religious, as well as the tribal leaders of Upper Swat, and it gave a further opportunity of allaying hostile feelings to [the imperialist] Government.'[119]

The imperialist government, not interested in direct control, did not ask the Khan of Dir, Sharif Khan, to refrain from interfering in Swat. Incensed by Sharif Khan's various acts of intrusion into their affairs, in November 1898, the clans on the right bank of the Swat River appealed to the Sartur Faqir. He crossed the river and took up their cause against the Nawab, but without success because he turned against the British.[120] The imperialist government, which had elevated Sharif Khan to the status of Nawab, acknowledged the suzerainty of the Nawab of Dir 'over the tribes on the right bank' of the Swat River,[121] although the tribes were only 'nominally subject' to his rule.[122]

The Nawab of Dir was so ambitious to gain complete control over Swat that he became extremely annoyed by the colonial British government's 'direct settlement' with the people of Upper Swat in Mingawarah, in August 1897. He even sent his own faction to Mingawarah 'to induce them to join him' and 'only settle up with' the colonial British 'Government through him'.[123] The people of Swat, who were tired of the infighting and of the Nawab of Dir's depredations, were anxious for an organized government of their own. Major Deane, the political agent at Malakand, reported, in November 1897, after his meeting with the Upper Swat *jargay*:

> The feeling on the present want of government in Upper Swat is so strong, that I understand the jirga [*jargah*] have lately sent some of their leading Maliks [*malakan*] to Peshawar with a blank paper, bearing all their seals, inviting Amir Shah, a brother of Mian Rahim Shah, to go to Swat as their "Badshah," and saying they will accept any conditions he enters on the document containing their seals. This is the fourth time to my knowledge they have made this request to him.[124]

The political situation in the left bank Upper Swat,[125] in 1901, has been summarized in the Annual Administration Report thus:

> There was the usual factional quarrelling, and the country is internally in a state of hopeless anarchy. The Mianguls' attempts to acquire secular power have failed, The Mad Fakir [the Sartur Faqir] has sunk to insignificance, and the Babuzai Maliks [Babuzi *malakan*] have lost what combined influence they might have, by their inveterate enemity [enmity] to one another.[126]

On the right bank of the Swat River, the exactions of the Nawab's revenue collectors caused great resentment which 'led to their being replaced by a better class' of men. There was general discontent throughout the Swati territories—that were under the Nawab of Dir—'owing to this and [to] his own apathy regarding the interests of the people'.[127] In 1904, the same clans once more 'became greatly incensed at the tyranny and oppression of the Nawab of Dir', but before their call for help to the Sartur Faqir and 'their kinsmen on the other side of the valley', Major Deane, Political Agent at Malakand, effected a settlement,[128] mainly to avoid unrest and problems for the colonial British government.

Sharif Khan died in December 1904, and was succeeded by his son, Aurangzeb Khan, commonly known as Badshah Khan (also Bacha Khan, and Chara Nawab). Badshah Khan's relations with his brother Miangul Jan, even during their father's lifetime, had not been good. Their conflict continued through the succeeding years, which caused shifting alliances and intrigues throughout Dir, Bajawar, and Swat. Badshah Khan was hot tempered and he managed not only to annoy the tribes of Swat under his jurisdiction, but also alienated 'the sympathies of his subjects by high-handed and avaricious conduct'.[129] In 1907, a change of parties in power in Swat led to the cessation of *ushar* and the overthrow of the allegiance to the Nawab of Dir. For the time being, the Nawab of Dir's control over the right bank Swat came to an end.[130]

Relations between the Nawab of Dir and the tribes on the right bank of the Swat River remained strained. On the pretext of escorting the *jargay* of Shamuzi and Nikpi Khail, to their home, he made an attack on Nikpi Khail in August 1909, which resulted in considerable losses. The British official report has stated: 'The Nawab, however, withdrew his men at the instance of the Political Agent. The quarrel is one eminently suited for mediation; and efforts will be made to establish a *modus vivendi* acceptable to both the parties concerned.'[131]

After the loss of the Swati territories, the Nawab of Dir continually urged the colonial British to settle his claim over the area. When they insisted that they 'would not interfere, he boldly invaded the country', reoccupied it in 1910, and started 'building forts' to consolidate 'his position'. The tribes held the colonial British responsible, to some extent, for the Nawab's action as he was their *protégé*.[132] This view was endorsed by the report of the following year, where the Nawab of Dir's strong position was seen as an advantage for the colonial British. The report has stated:

> In the Malakand the Nawab of Dir has strengthened his position. Various coalitions of the Bajaur [Bajawar] Chiefs have been formed against him, but he has held his own. He has extended his power in the Swat Kohistan, though the tribes on the left bank of the Swat river have prevented extension in that direction. He is a difficult man to deal with....but he seems anxious loyally to abide by his agreements with [the colonial] Government, *and the fact that he has strengthened his position is to our advantage* [my italics].[133]

The Nawab of Dir also succeeded in taking the Shamuzi area, in January 1911. He was thus able to make himself master of the entire right bank Swat above Chakdarah up to Kuhistan (Kohistan), owing to factional disputes among the tribes. He was keen to profit further from the feuds and the enmity between the Mianguls. He started to build a fort in the Azi Khail limits, on the left bank in Upper Swat, but the tribes there resisted and the work was abandoned. The Aba Khail and Musa Khail asked the British to bring them under their protection and to be treated like the Khan Khail.[134] The Nawab of Dir's rule was unpopular, as he was 'badly served by many of his agents', and it was feared that his 'tyranny may lead to a demonstration with the object of compelling [the colonial] Government to interfere'.[135]

Badshah Khan, the Nawab of Dir, seemed 'bent on emulating the deeds' of Umara Khan of Jandul, but his administration of the area was such that it estranged him from many of the chiefs and the people from whom he was to seek support.[136] The clans of Upper Swat were tired of the strains of constant fighting, and of the Nawab of Dir's depredations and the high-handedness of his agents—who did not even spare the Nawab of Dir's supporters.[137] They did not even send the Nawab of Dir the total revenue realized. For instance, the Nawab of Dir's general, Syed Badshah, although he realized Rs. 46,000 from the Sibujni and Shamizi area, had sent only Rs. 22,000 to Dir.[138]

Having no authority to dispense justice and settle cases and disputes, the clans of Upper Swat, periodically, made overtures to the political agent at Malakand in the hope that the colonial British would provide protection to them; but in vain.

The Nawab of Dir asked the clans of the right bank to send a *lakhkar* for his action against Jandul.[139] He fined the Nikpi Khail area three rupees per holding for the delay in sending *lakhkar* to Maidan.[140] The Nawab of Dir's occupation and tyranny even brought the Hindustani Mujahidin into action. They approached the Sartur Faqir to acquire land in the Jinki Khail country, on the left bank in Upper Swat to construct a fort as a base against the Nawab.[141] They visited the Bunair *jargah* and Ghwarband. The Sartur Faqir promised that 'the question of a war with [the British] Government would be discussed after the Nawab had been crushed'.[142]

The Nawab of Dir, however, sent eight hundred rupees to the Sartur Faqir with the message that it was to purchase arms. The Faqir refused the money but on being assured that the Nawab was now the British government's enemy, he accepted. The Nawab of Dir also promised four hundred maunds of grain annually to the Sartur Faqir.[143] Although the Sartur Faqir had remained relatively quiet, according to reports, 'he should not be neglected as a factor in the politics of these parts'.[144]

The people of Swat, once more, refused to pay *ushar* to the Nawab of Dir, so he sent Syed Badshah Khan to collect it. Miangul Abdul Wadud, grandson of Saidu Baba, also urged the people to pay the *ushar* to the Nawab of Dir.[145] The Nawab of Dir succeeded in obtaining the *ushar* from the right bank clans by force of arms, but too late.[146] The tribes, who were weary of the factional fighting, the Nawab of Dir's agents' excesses and tyrannies, and 'heartily weary of the Mianguls and their constant feuds',[147] had already made an attempt, at the close of 1913, to install a ruler of a state of their own. In 1913, they made overtures to the cousins of Abdul Jabbar Shah, scions of the family of Sayyad Akbar Shah, who had ruled in Swat from 1849/1850 till 1857, who were in Bunair and Malka, and offered them the throne.[148]

After consultations amongst themselves, Abdul Jabbar Shah's cousins proposed Abdul Jabbar Shah's name. He, however, sent the *jargah* back having 'thought over the matter and thinking that the difficulties likely to occur were more than the probable advantages'.[149]

The people of Swat also made a secret deal within Dir and Bajawar. The Nawab of Dir's brother, Miangul Jan, was in conflict with him and there were constant alliances, moves and counter moves in Bajawar. Miangul Jan was killed at the Nawab's instigation, and he proceeded to Bajawar as the head of his forces against Miangul Jan's supporters. The affectees in Dir and Bajawar also tried to make common cause with the people of Swat against the Nawab of Dir and afterwards joined Sayyad Abdul Jabbar Shah as well.[150]

Abdul Jabbar Shah again refused the invitation, which the *jargah* renewed after a few months. He was urged by his kinsmen not to decline the throne. In the case of his refusal, Hazrat Jamal of Nawagai, Chamlah, his kinsman, consented to accept.[151] Hence, this time, Abdul Jabbar Shah accepted the offer and the *jargah* waited with him for two months. A large number of letters were also sent to him by the people of Swat, Dir, and Bajawar.[152] Abdul Jabbar Shah called upon the chief commissioner, of the Frontier Province, on 25 June 1914, consulted him on the subject, and assured him of his loyalty.[153] Abdul Jabbar Shah's loyalty to the British government had also been endorsed by W.J. Keen, DC Hazarah, in 1908.[154]

Abdul Jabbar Shah prepared to oust the Nawab of Dir from the Swati territories and to make arrangements for his own installation as the ruler of Swat. The Sartur Faqir, the Hindustani Mujahidin, and the people of Bunair pledged their support to him.[155] The Nawab of Dir's mother agreed to replace the present Nawab with his brother, Muhammad Isa Khan, as ruler of Dir. All arrangements were in place for the move against the Nawab of Dir and for the future arrangements in Dir and Swat, even the border between Dir and Swat had been agreed upon. The date, 8 September 1914, was fixed for Abdul Jabbar Shah's entry into Swat along with the Bunair forces. The people of Swat and Bajawar undertook to 'fulfil their part of the agreement at the same time'.[156]

Before the plan could materialize, Assistant Commissioner Mardan, Mr Bruce, came to know of the move. He at once called Abdul Jabbar Shah and his relatives and inquired into the affair. He asked him to abandon the project and to visit the political agent in Malakand.[157] The First World War had started, and rumours were rife. 'Absolutely idiotic most of them but then the trans-frontier' did not know much about the war, or what it was, or what it meant. Moreover, 'had these Lashkars [*lakhkars*] moved even with the ostensible object of a sort of family quarrel', Mr Bruce thought that their energies might easily be 'used for other purposes', and the movements of such large bodies of men were unwise. Bruce further considered that Abdul Jabbar Shah and his relatives could be 'used as tools in some Political intrigue'.[158]

Abdul Jabbar Shah abandoned the project for the time being. On Bruce's instruction, he visited the political agent, who warned him that if he 'did not give up the idea' of his 'entry into' Swati territory 'as a ruler, the [colonial British] Government would help the Nawab of Dir'. Consequently, he went back and informed his family members and the people that 'it was not proper' for them 'to make any move in the matter in opposition to the wishes of the British Government'.[159] Thus, the attempt of the people of Swat, to form a state and a government, was foiled by the colonial British for their own reasons and interests.

The people, although divided by factions, at last created a united front against the Nawab of Dir's occupation. The Sandakai Baba[160] was largely instrumental in effecting the alliance against the Nawab of Dir. Although the Nawab's position was strong, after the death of his brother and rival, an insurrection against him started in the Nikpi Khail, Sibujni and Shamizi sections of Upper Swat at the beginning of 1915. The insurgents inflicted heavy losses on the Nawab's forces, and took possession of the forts in their areas. The Nawab dispatched Syed Badshah, of Kumbar, against the people of Swat but, although he used both force and diplomacy, he failed.[161] The Nawab sent reinforcements,[162] and the people of Swat asked the people of Kuhistan and Bunair as well as the Hindustani Mujahidin and Abdul Jabbar Shah for help.[163] The political agent at Malakand tried to persuade the left bank people of Swat not to help those of the right bank, against the Nawab of Dir,[164] but the right bank people of Swat, belonging to Nikpi Khail, Sibujni and Shamizi areas, emerged victorious.

Instead of siding with the people of Swat, the Mianguls went to see the political agent.[165] Miangul Abdul Wadud later met with the Nawab's general while his brother was prevented by illness from visiting him. The people of Swat of the aforesaid areas of Nikpi Khail, Sibujni and Shamizi, even then, 'offered to pay *Ushar* to the Mianguls, and to substitute their rule for that of the Nawab. Gulshazada [Miangul Abdul Wadud], however, replied that his brother would not make common cause with him, and that therefore the idea was impracticable.'[166]

The Nawab of Dir's forces were, at last, completely defeated and driven out of Upper Swat to Adinzi area. 'The losses on both sides were heavy both in numbers and in the importance of men killed.'[167] The victors endeavoured 'to organize an independent state', and the Sandakai Baba arbitrated over their differences. A council of five men—Zarin Khan, Amir Sultan, and Jafar Khan (from Nikpi Khail), Taj Muhammad Khan (from Sibujni), and Masam Khan (from Shamizi)—was appointed to act as the government.[168] All the real power, however, was in the hands of the Sandakai Baba.[169]

The Nawab of Dir's authority over the right bank Upper Swat territories ended completely, at the end of March 1915.[170] The council, tried to persuade Miangul Abdul Wadud to take on the leadership.

> They…told him that they are grieved that he has not yet helped them, but they are prepared to overlook his past lukewarmness if only he will place himself at their head now and definitely throw in his lot with them. They…[said] that otherwise they will be obliged to call in some outsider to help them, and this would probably be Sayyad Abdul Jabbar Shah of Sitana [Sithanah].[171]

Miangul Abdul Wadud, however, said that 'the step which they propose is a very important one and not to be lightly undertaken. *He…added he cannot give a definite answer till he has seen and consulted the Political Agent* [my italics].'[172]

The council tried to strengthen the forts taken from the Nawab of Dir's forces, and negotiated an alliance with the Khan of Barwa (now Samar Bagh), against the Nawab.[173] The people 'agreed to present 20,000 logs' to the Sandakai Baba 'in return for his assistance during the crisis with the Nawab'. They, moreover, 'urged him to stay in Swat and be their leader but he…declined the honour'.[174]

After the refusal of both Miangul Abdul Wadud and Sandakai Baba, the people again turned to Abdul Jabbar Shah, who accepted the invitation and came to Swat at the end of April 1915.[175] He was installed as the King of Swat, on 24 April 1915,[176] when the Swat State era proper (1915–1969 CE) begins.[177]

During all the period, covered in this chapter (1857–1915 CE), and also in the previous chapters since the occupation of Swat by the Yusufzi, Pukhtu or the Pukhtun code of conduct, detailed in chapter 7, was the law of the land and governed the affairs of the people of Swat, as also stated in chapter 7, despite the right bank areas occupied by the Dir rulers and the left bank Lower Swat or the Ranizi and Khan Khail areas being brought under the loose control of the British.

NOTES

1. James W. Spain, *Pathans of the Latter Day* (Karachi: Oxford University Press, 1995), 99.
2. *Imperial Gazetteer of India: Provincial Series; North-West Frontier Province* [henceforward *Imperial Gazetteer of India, NWFP*] (repr., Lahore: Sang-e-Meel Publications, 1991), 225.
3. Ibid., 21.
4. Spain, *Pathans of the Latter Day*, 99.
5. A.H. McMahon and A.D.G. Ramsay, *Report on the Tribes of Dir, Swat and Bajour* [Bajawar] *together with the Utman-Khel and Sam Ranizai*, edited with introduction by R.O. Christensen (repr., Peshawar: Saeed Book Bank, 1981), 74. Also *Confidential, Gazetteer of the North-West Frontier: From Bajaur and the Indus Kohistán on the North to the Mari Hills on the South* [henceforward *Confidential, Gazetteer of the North-West Frontier*], Vol. 4, Compiled for Political and Military Reference in the Intelligence Branch of the Quarter Master General's Department in India, completed and edited by A.L'e. Holmes (Simla: Printed at the Government Central Branch Press, 1887), 1852; *Frontier and Overseas Expeditions from India*, Vol. 1, *Tribes North of the Kabul River* [henceforward *Frontier and Overseas Expeditions from India*, Vol. 1] (2nd edn. in Pakistan, Quetta: Nisa Traders, 1982), 251.
6. W.W. Hunter, *The Indian Musalmans*, with introduction by Bimal Prasad (repr., New Delhi: Rupa & Co, 2002), 26. Also see W.W. Hunter, *Hamaray Hindustani Musalman*, Urdu trans. Sadiq Hussain (repr., Lahore: Makki Darul Kutub, 1997), 35.
7. Hunter, *The Indian Musalmans*, 23. Also see Hunter, *Hamaray Hindustani Musalman*, 32.
8. Hunter, *The Indian Musalmans*, 29. Also see Hunter, *Hamaray Hindustani Musalman*, 37. For detail, see Hunter, *The Indian Musalmans*, 29; Hunter, *Hamaray Hindustani Musalman*, 37; H.C. Wylly, *The Borderland: The Country of the Pathans* (repr., Karachi: Indus Publications, 1998), 97–8.
9. Hunter, *The Indian Musalmans*, 33. Also see Hunter, *Hamaray Hindustani Musalman*, 40.

10. Hunter, *The Indian Musalmans*, 21–2. Also see Hunter, *Hamaray Hindustani Musalman*, 30.

11. Hunter, *The Indian Musalmans*, 22 n. 1. Also see Hunter, *Hamaray Hindustani Musalman*, 30–1 n. 3.

12. Hunter, *The Indian Musalmans*, 30. Also see Hunter, *Hamaray Hindustani Musalman*, 38. For the native versions of the Ambilah war, expressed in Pashto *charbaytay*, see Raza Hamdani, comp. and trans., *Razmiyah Dastanayn*, Pashto with Urdu trans. by Raza Hamdani (Islamabad: Lok Virsay ka Qaumi Idarah, 1981), 179–85; 237–41; Hamesh Khalil, comp., *Da Charbaytay Pakhwani Shairan* (Pashto) (Peshawar: Pukhtu Academy, 2008), 15–18, 47–8, 58–60, 126–7, 290–1, 340–5, 506–9, 733–6, 749–52; Hamesh Khalil, comp. and trans., *Jangi Charbaytay*, Pashto with Urdu trans. by Hamesh Khalil (Peshawar: Pashto Academy, 2008), 87–118. Also Muhammad Nawaz Khan, *Tarikhi Tapay* (Pashto) (Peshawar: University Book Agency, 2004), 26–7.

13. *Report on the Administration of the Punjab and its Dependencies for the Year 1876–77* (Lahore: Printed at the Government Civil Secretariat Press, 1877), 11. Also see Fredrik Barth, *The Last Wali of Swat: An Autobiography as told to Fredrik Barth* (repr., Bangkok: White Orchid Press, 1995), 21.

14. *Gazetteer of the Peshawar District, 1897–98* (repr., Lahore: Sang-e-Meel Publications, 1989), 273. Also see *Confidential, Gazetteer of the North-West Frontier*, Vol. 4, 1853; *Frontier and Overseas Expeditions from India*, Vol. 1, 354; Barth, *The Last Wali of Swat*, 21 cf. John Keay, *The Gilgit Game: The Explorers of the Western Himalayas, 1865–95* (repr., Karachi: Oxford University Press, 1993), 47; Hilary Adamson and Isobel Shaw, *A Traveller's Guide to Pakistan* (Islamabad: The Asian Study Group, 1981), 143.

15. *Report on the Administration of the Punjab and its Dependencies for 1878–79* (Lahore: Printed at the Punjab Government Civil Secretariat Press, 1879), 35–6; *Confidential Gazetteer of the North-West Frontier*, Vol. 4, 1855; *Frontier and Overseas Expeditions from India*, Vol. 1, 359–60.

16. *Report on the Administration of the Punjab and its Dependencies for 1880–81* (Lahore: Printed at the Punjab Government Civil Secretariat Press, 1881), 13; *Confidential, Gazetteer of the North-West Frontier*, Vol. 4, 1855; *Frontier and Overseas Expeditions from India*, Vol. 1, 360.

17. With the Queen's Proclamation in 1858, the entire subcontinent was not taken over to become British India or part of the British Empire or Imperial British. It was only the territory occupied by the colonialist East India Company that was taken over and became British India or part of British Empire. As the Indian or Princely states and the tribal areas were not taken over they were not part of British India or British Empire or Imperial British. That was why the British government executed agreements and entered into treaty relations with the Indian states and the tribes of the tribal areas. Besides, the Pukhtun land occupied by the colonialists as part of the then Sikh kingdom, later separated from the Province of Punjab as the North-West Frontier Province in 1901, was denied, till 1932, the reforms granted to and the laws introduced in British India. Even when granting the status of a full-fledged province in 1932 and extending the reforms introduced under the Government of India Act, 1919, and later the Government of India Act, 1935, the repressive and infamous Frontier Crimes Regulation, 1901, was not repealed.

This still operated even in the settled districts of the Province. Therefore, the Pukhtun land made part of British India was neither brought on a par with the British territory in Europe nor with other areas of British India, and was ruled on colonial lines. The Pukhtun tribal areas were neither part of British India nor were they ruled under the laws in vogue in Britain or British India. Moreover, although the head of British India was now called 'Viceroy', being representative of the British Crown, the title and the post of 'Governor-General' was not abolished. The Viceroy also acted and governed British India in the capacity of governor-general, which testifies to the colonial tinge of the British rule in India. The post of governor-general was retained till the last day of the British rule in India. In this backdrop, the adjective 'colonial' or the term 'colonialists' used for the British in this book at the time of their campaigns or communications, etcetera, in the Pukhtun lands are historically correct and appropriate.

18. *Imperial Gazetteer of India*, *NWFP*, 210–11.
19. Mirza Muhammad Ghufran and Mirza Ghulam Murtaza, *Nayi Tarikh-i Chitral*, Urdu trans. Wazir Ali Shah (Printers: Public Art Press, Peshawar, 1962), 128–9.
20. H.C. Thomson, *The Chitral Campaign: A Narrative of Events in Chitral, Swat, and Bajour* (repr., Lahore: Sang-e-Meel Publications, 1981), 2.
21. H.L. Nevill, *Campaigns on the North-West Frontier* (repr., Lahore: Sang-e-Meel Publications, 2003), 164–5.
22. McMahon and A.D.G. Ramsay, *Report on the Tribes of Dir, Swat and Bajour together with the Utman-Khel and Sam Ranizai*, 95.
23. Nevill, *Campaigns on the North-West Frontier*, 166. Also see Sultan-i-Rome, 'The Malakand Jihad (1897): An Unsuccessful Attempt to Oust the British from Malakand and Chakdara', *Journal of the Pakistan Historical Society* (Karachi), 43/2 (April 1995), 171–3.
24. Nevill, *Campaigns on the North-West Frontier*, 166.
25. H.C. Wylly, *The Borderland: The Country of the Pathans* (repr., (Karachi: Indus Publications, 1998), 161.
26. G.J. Younghusband and Francis Younghusband, *The Relief of Chitral* (repr., Rawalpindi: English Book House, 1976), 17–8.
27. M. Hasan Kakar, *Afghanistan: A Study in International Political Development, 1880–1896* (Kabul, 1971), 104; Allah Bakhsh Yusufi, *Yusufzai* (Urdu) (Karachi: Muhammad Ali Educational Society, 1960), 401; Syed Abid Bokhari, ed. and comp., *Through the Centuries: North-West Frontier Province* (Quetta: Mr Reprints, 1993), 148.
28. C.L. Tupper, Chief Secretary [henceforward CS], to Government [henceforward Govt.], Punjab and its Dependencies [henceforward PD], to Secretary [henceforward Secy.] to Government of India [henceforward GI], Foreign Department [henceforward FD], No. 154, Lahore 13 March 1893, *Files of the Commissioner Office Peshawar*, at the Provincial Archives at Peshawar [henceforward COP], Bundle No. [henceforward BN] 34, Serial No. [henceforward SN] 952-B.
29. *Report on the Administration of the Punjab and its Dependencies for 1892–93* (Lahore: Printed at the Punjab Government Press, MDCCCXCIV), 44.
30. According to Allah Bakhsh Yusufi, some English writers have referred to Umara Khan of Jandul as the Afghan Napoleon (see Yusufi, *Yusufzai*, 400). This was

because of his rise to power, rapid conquests and military exploits. Both Napoleon (Napoleon Bonaparte: the French general and ruler) and Umara Khan were ultimately defeated by the British. Napoleon was imprisoned but Umara Khan escaped and fled to Afghanistan. While Napoleon died as a prisoner, Umara Khan died in exile in Afghanistan.

Umara Khan did make overtures to the British Indian government and asked for a personal interview with the viceroy or other official to prove he was not concerned with the disturbances in Chitral and Bajawar (see Secretary to Government of India, Foreign Department, to Umra [Umara] Khan, Quetta, No. 52 P.O., 5 August 1896, *COP*, BN 906, SN 33). The colonial government not only refused a personal interview but finally declined to reconsider the question of his share in the disturbances in Chitral and Bajawar and to allow him to return to Jandul (see Secretary to Government of India, Foreign Department, to Agent to Governor General in Baluchistan, Simla, No. 2104 F., 5 August 1896, ibid.). He was addressed: 'No evidence that you can bring forward can disprove the facts that you disregarded the orders of [the colonial British] Government in interfering with Chitral; that you did not withdraw when you were told to do so; and that you opposed the British troops both in Chitral and in Bajaur. For these reasons, the Government of India must decline finally to entertain your wish to be allowed to return to Jandol' (Secretary to Government of India, Foreign Department, to Umra [Umara] Khan, Quetta, No. 52 P.O., 5 August 1896, ibid.). However, a suitable provision for his maintenance was offered if he elected to reside in Baluchistan, for his honourable treatment of the British officers when they were his prisoners (ibid).

31. Abdul Halim Dirvi, *The Life and Achievements of Ghazi Umra Khan* (Unpublished MA Thesis, Pakistan Study Centre, University of Peshawar, 1989), 92.

32. McMahon and A.D.G. Ramsay, *Report on the Tribes of Dir, Swat and Bajour together with the Utman-Khel and Sam Ranizai*, 95.

33. Nevill, *Campaigns on the North-West Frontier*, 166, 189.

34. McMahon and A.D.G. Ramsay, *Report on the Tribes of Dir, Swat and Bajour together with the Utman-Khel and Sam Ranizai*, 96. For full text of the Proclamation, see Nevill, *Campaigns on the North-West Frontier*, 166–7.

35. *Report on the Administration of the Punjab and its Dependencies for 1883–84* (Lahore: Printed at the Punjab Government Press, MDCCCLXXXV), 2.

36. *Report on the Administration of the Punjab and its Dependencies for 1884–85* (Lahore: Printed by W. Ball & Co., MDCCCLXXXVI), 6.

37. Nevill, *Campaigns on the North-West Frontier*, 189.

38. Ibid., 191–2.

39. Thomson, *The Chitral Campaign: A Narrative of Events in Chitral, Swat, and Bajour*, 173.

40. Wylly, *The Borderland: The Country of the Pathans*, 167.

41. *Punjab Frontier Administration Report for the Year 1894–95* (Simla: Punjab Government Branch Press, 1895), 3.

42. Olaf Caroe, *The Pathans: 550 B.C.–A.D. 1957* (repr., Karachi: Oxford University Press, 1976), 385.

43. Ibid., 370.

44. Ibid., 386.

45. Ibid.
46. For details, see a copy of the manuscript of the *charbaytah* in my (Sultan-i-Rome's) personal collection. Also see Khalil, comp., *Da Charbaytay Pakhwani Shairan*, 788–99; Khalil, comp. and trans., *Jangi Charbaytay*, 123–47. According to Muhammad Asif Khan, Yasin was *mali* (gardener) in the Company Bagh Mardan. Nawab Akbar Khan (of Huti, Mardan) called Yasin and had him recite the *charbaytah* before Shah Jahan Khan: the Nawab of Dir and grandson of Sharif Khan of Dir. Shah Jahan rewarded Yasin with five hundred rupees but remarked that it would have been better had he used decent/polite language. (Muhammad Asif Khan, interview by the author, at Saidu Sharif, Swat, 24 May and 14 June 1998). It is to be mentioned that the manuscript of the *charbaytah*, whose copy is in my (Sultan-i-Rome's) personal collection, bears the date '1.8.1901' (1 August 1901) and the caption '*charbaytah da* Yasin, *umar panzus kalah, pah lik nah puhigi, pah* Mardan *kay chaprasi di, da* Mardan *di*', which means: Yasin's *charbaytah*, who hails from Mardan, is fifty years of age, is unlettered and is peon in Mardan.

    For other Pashto accounts about the Malakand war of 1895, see Hamdani, comp. and trans., *Razmiyah Dastanayn*, 210–14; Khalil, comp., *Da Charbaytay Pakhwani Shairan*, 120–2; Khalil, comp. and trans., *Jangi Charbaytay*, 72–9. For the role of Mian Rahim Shah Kaka Khail, also see Hamdani, comp. and trans., *Razmiyah Dastanayn*, 206–9; Sultan-i-Rome, *Land and Forest Governance in Swat: Transition from Tribal System to State to Pakistan* (Karachi: Oxford University Press, 2016), 148.

47. Caroe, *The Pathans*, 386; Sayyad Bahadar Shah Zafar Kaka Khail, *Pukhtanah da Tarikh pah Ranra kay* (Pashto) (Peshawar: University Book Agency, n.d.), 909; Diwan Chand Obhrai, *The Evolution of North-West Frontier Province: Being a Survey of the History and Constitutional Development of N.-W. F. Province in India* (repr., Peshawar: Saeed Book Bank, n.d.), 68; Lal Baha, *N.-W.F.P. Administration under British Rule, 1901–1919* (Islamabad: National Commission on Historical and Cultural Research, 1978), 8.

    Imperial Gazetteer of India, NWFP, and also Dr Lal Baha—on the authority of C. Collin Davies—has spoken of the formation of the Agency in 1896, but it was created in 1895. (See *Imperial Gazetteer of India, NWFP*, 210; Baha, *N.-W.F.P. Administration under British Rule, 1901–1919*, 7. cf. Caroe, *The Pathans*, 383, 414.) In *Files of the Commissioner Office Peshawar, in Record Section of the Provincial Archives at Peshawar*, Bundle No. 33, Serial No. 947, there are Diaries of the Political Officer, Dir and Swat, which are related to the year 1895, and hence are testimony to the formation of the Agency in 1895.

48. *Frontier and Overseas Expeditions from India*, Vol. 1, 364.
49. Nevill, *Campaigns on the North-West Frontier*, 209.
50. Hailing from village Riga (in Bunair, Bunir, Buner) and son of a *malak*, Hamidullah, Sartur Faqir's original name was Sadullah Khan. He visited and stayed in India and Afghanistan. He returned Bunair in 1895 and tried to stir up a *jihad*, but did not succeed. In 1897 he re-appeared, but this time in Swat; he subsequently played significant role against the colonial British power and emerged a prominent figure in the area. He at last settled in Fatihpur (in Swat); died at the age of ninety in January 1917; and was buried in Fatihpur. For more

details about the Sartur Faqir, see Sultan-i-Rome, 'The Sartōr Faqīr: Life and Struggle against British Imperialism', *Journal of the Pakistan Historical Society* (Karachi), 42/1 (January 1994), 93–105. Also see Sultan-i-Rome, *Swat State (1915–1969): From Genesis to Merger; An Analysis of Political, Administrative, Socio-Political, and Economic Developments* (Karachi: Oxford University Press, 2008), chapters 2–4; Sultan-i-Rome, *The North-West Frontier (Khyber Pakhtunkhwa): Essays on History* (Karachi: Oxford University Press, 2013), chapter 6.

51. PP Encl. 28, dated 8 August 1897, quoted in Akbar S. Ahmed, *Millennium and Charisma among Pathans: A Critical Essay in Social Anthropology* (London: Routledge & Kegan Paul, 1976), 108.

52. See *Frontier and Overseas Expeditions from India*, Vol. 1, 366.

53. Ibid. Also see McMahon and A.D.G. Ramsay, *Report on the Tribes of Dir, Swat and Bajour together with the Utman-Khel and Sam Ranizai*, 110.

54. Nevill, *Campaigns on the North-West Frontier*, 223, 225; *Frontier and Overseas Expeditions from India*, Vol. 1, 367.

55. H. Woosnam Mills, *The Pathan Revolts in North West India* (repr., Lahore: Sang-e-Meel Publications, 1996), 35.

56. *Imperial Gazetteer of India*, NWFP, 23.

57. Mills, *The Pathan Revolts in North West India*, 35.

58. Ibid.

59. McMahon and A.D.G. Ramsay, *Report on the Tribes of Dir, Swat and Bajour together with the Utman-Khel and Sam Ranizai*, 111.

60. Ibid.

61. *Imperial Gazetteer of India*, NWFP, 23.

62. Mills, *The Pathan Revolts in North-West India*, 64–5.

63. Ibid., 71.

64. Nevill, *Campaigns on the North-West Frontier*, 249.

65. For detail, see Mills, *The Pathan Revolts in North-West India*, 64 ff.; *Frontier and Overseas Expeditions from India*, Vol. 1, 381 ff.; Wylly, *The Borderland: The Country of the Pathans*, passim.

66. *Frontier and Overseas Expeditions from India*, Vol. 1, 386. Also see Winston S. Churchill, *The Story of the Malakand Field Force: An Episode of Frontier War* (repr., London: Leo Cooper, 2002), 81.

   Fazli Zaman Shalman has contended that three persons were rewarded with 'Victoria Cross' due to the significance of the Malakand war in the sight of the British government (see Fazli Zaman Shalman, 'Da Pakistan da Juridu Panzus Kalanah aw da Qabayalu da Ghazaganu Sal Kalanah', *Pukhtu* (Peshawar), 30/9–10, (September–October1998), 49–50).

   In fact, only two persons received the award, but that, too, was not for their gallantry in the Malakand war but for the gallantry displayed during an encounter with the tribesmen, near Kutah and Naway Kalay (above Landakay), at the time of the punitive expedition of the Malakand Field Force up the Swat Valley (see *Frontier and Overseas Expeditions from India*, Vol. 1, 386; Churchill, *The Story of the Malakand Field Force*, 81; George Macmunn, *The Romance of the Indian Frontiers* (1st edn. published in Pakistan, Quetta: Nisa Traders, 1978), 205). A later 'announcement (1907) in the *London Gazette*', however, stated that

'Lieutenant Maclean would also have received Victoria Cross had he survived, and the decoration' was 'handed to his relatives' (*Frontier and Overseas Expeditions from India*, Vol. 1, 386 n. 1). Although Fazli Zaman Shalman has talked of three army officers but he has given four names. Besides, three of the names, given by Fazli Zaman Shalman, also do not tally with the names given by the cited sources.

67. John Marsh, *The Young Winston Churchill* (London: World Distributors, 1962), 47–8. For details, see ibid., 44–50. Also see J.G. Elliott, *The Frontier, 1839–1947: The Story of the North-West Frontier of India*, with preface by Olaf Caroe (London: Cassell & Company Ltd, 1968), 159; Charles Miller, *Khyber: British India's North West Frontier; The Story of an Imperial Migraine* (London: Macdonald and Jane's Publishers Limited, 1977), 268.

68. His accounts and reporting of that time were later published in a book form, entitled *The Story of the Malakand Field Force: An Episode of Frontier War*, with utilizing and incorporating information from other sources as well. Churchill's account and narration, moreover, consisted of fancies and fantasies, and has suffered from factual errors and absurdities. For instance, about the Pukhtuns, he has written: 'Their wives and their womankind generally have no position but that of animals. They are freely bought and sold and are not infrequently bartered for rifles' (Churchill, *The Story of the Malakand Field Force*, 6). And, about the men hailing from the religious segment, besides other things he has stated that 'no man's wife or daughter is safe from them' (ibid., 7). Churchill's contentions of this kind are far from the truth, and are unsound.

69. T.H. Holdich, *The Indian Borderland, 1880–1900* (repr., Delhi: Gian Publishing House, 1987), 344.

70. Ibid., 350.

71. Wylly, *The Borderland: The Country of the Pathans*, 110. Also see Nevill, *Campaigns on the North-West Frontier*, 249–50.

72. Mills, *The Pathan Revolts in North-West India*, 35.

73. Holdich, *The Indian Borderland, 1880–1900*, 338.

74. Ibid.

75. For some details about the Malakand and Chakdarah war, its causes, and causes of its failure, see Sultan-i-Rome, 'The Malakand Jihad (1897): An Unsuccessful Attempt to Oust the British from Malakand and Chakdara', 171–86. Also see Sultan-i-Rome, *The North-West Frontier (Khyber Pakhtunkhwa): Essays on History*, chapter 6.

76. See *Frontier and Overseas Expeditions from India*, Vol. 1, 390–1; McMahon and A.D.G. Ramsay, *Report on the Tribes of Dir, Swat and Bajour together with the Utman-Khel and Sam Ranizai*, 28, 120–1.

77. See *Frontier and Overseas Expeditions from India*, Vol. 1, 387–90; McMahon and A.D.G. Ramsay, *Report on the Tribes of Dir, Swat and Bajour together with the Utman-Khel and Sam Ranizai*, 122.

78. See *Frontier and Overseas Expeditions from India*, Vol. 1, 391–2.

79. *Report on the Administration of the Punjab and its Dependencies for the Year 1875–76* (Lahore: Printed at the Government Civil Secretariat Press, 1876), 6.

80. *Report on the Administration of the Punjab and its Dependencies for the Year 1877–78*, 'Summary' (Lahore: Printed at the Punjab Government Civil Secretariat Press, 1878), 8.

81. *Frontier and Overseas Expeditions from India*, Vol. 1, 357; *Confidential, Gazetteer of the North-West Frontier*, Vol. 4, 1854. Also see *Report on the Administration of the Punjab and its Dependencies for the Year 1877–78*, 12.

82. *Report on the Administration of the Punjab and its Dependencies for 1879–80* (Lahore: Printed at the Punjab Government Civil Secretariat Press, 1880), 12–13.

83. *Frontier and Overseas Expeditions from India*, Vol. 1, 360.

84. *Report on the Administration of the Punjab and its Dependencies for 1880–81*, 13.

85. *Report on the Administration of the Punjab and its Dependencies for 1881–82* (Lahore: Printed at the Punjab Government Civil Secretariat Press, 1882), 10.

86. *Report on the Administration of the Punjab and its Dependencies for 1882–83* (n.p., n.d.), 72.

87. *Report on the Administration of the Punjab and its Dependencies for 1881–82*, 10–11.

88. *Report on the Administration of the Punjab and its Dependencies for 1879–80* (Lahore: Printed at the Punjab Government Civil Secretariat Press, 1880), 13.

89. *Report on the Administration of the Punjab and its Dependencies for 1882–83*, 72; *Confidential, Gazetteer of the North-West Frontier*, Vol. 4, 1855.

90. *Report on the Administration of the Punjab and its Dependencies for 1883–84*, 7–8. Also see *Frontier and Overseas Expeditions from India*, Vol. 1, 360; *Confidential, Gazetteer of the North-West Frontier*, Vol. 4, 1855.

91. *Frontier and Overseas Expeditions from India*, Vol. 1, 361. Also see *Report on the Administration of the Punjab and its Dependencies for 1883–84*, 7–8; *Report on the Administration of the Punjab and its Dependencies for 1884–85*, 5.

92. *Report on the Administration of the Punjab and its Dependencies for the Year 1877–78*, 8.

93. *Report on the Administration of the Punjab and its Dependencies for 1883–84*, 7.

94. *Report on the Administration of the Punjab and its Dependencies for 1887–88* (Lahore: Printed at the Punjab Government Press, MDCCCLXXXIX), 8. Date of his death given in the genealogical table in the *Gazetteer of the Peshawar District, 1897–98*, on page 274, is 1890, which is incorrect.

95. See *Report on the Administration of the Punjab and its Dependencies for 1883–84*, 2; *Report on the Administration of the Punjab and its Dependencies for 1884–85*, 6; *Report on the Administration of the Punjab and its Dependencies for 1886–87*, 'General Summary' (Lahore: Printed by W. Ball & Co., 1888), 2.

96. *Frontier and Overseas Expeditions from India*, Vol. 1, 361.

97. Kakar, *Afghanistan: A Study in International Political Developments, 1880–1896*, 286; Ludwig W. Adamec, *Afghanistan, 1900–1923: A Diplomatic History* (Berkeley: University of California Press, 1967), 176.

98. Sultan Mahomed Khan, ed., *The Life of Abdur Rahman: Amir of Afghanistan*, with new introduction by M.E. Yapp, Vol. 2 (repr. in Pakistan, Karachi: Oxford University Press, 1980), 161.

99. See section 2 of the agreement. Full text of the first three sections of the agreement between Amir Abdur Rahman and Henry Mortimer Durand, known as the Durand Line Agreement, are as follows:
    (1) The eastern and southern frontier of his [His] Highness's dominions, from Wakhan to the Persian border, shall follow the line shown in the map attached to this agreement.

(2) The Government of India will at no time exercise interference in the territories lying beyond this line on the side of Afghanistan, and His Highness the Amir will at no time exercise interference in the territories lying beyond this line on the side of India.

(3) The British Government thus agrees to His Highness the Amir retaining Asmar and the valley above it, as far as Chanak. His Highness agrees, on the other hand, that he will at no time exercise interference in Swat, Bajaur, or Chitral, including the Arnawai or Bashgal valley. The British Government also agrees to leave to His Highness the Birmal tract as shown in the detailed map already given to His Highness, who relinquishes his claim to the rest of the Waziri country and Dawar. His Highness also relinquishes his claim to Chageh. [Kakar, *Afghanistan: A Study in International Political Developments, 1880–1896*, 286; Adamec, *Afghanistan, 1900–1923: A Diplomatic History*, 176].

100. See *Report on the Administration of the Punjab and its Dependencies for 1886–87*, 6; *Report on the Administration of the Punjab and its Dependencies for 1887–88*, 8.

101. *Frontier and Overseas Expeditions from India*, Vol. 1, 361–2.

102. *Report on the Administration of the Punjab and its Dependencies for the Year 1877–78*, 8.

103. Translation [henceforward trans.] of a letter, dated 21 Saffar 1306=28 October 1888, from Umra [Umara] Khan, Khán of Jandol, to Commissioner and Superintendent, Peshawar Division [henceforward CSPD], *COP*, BN 2, FN 23.

104. See C.L. Tupper, CS to Govt., PD, to Secy. to GI, FD, No. 154, Lahore 13 March 1893, ibid., BN 34, SN 952-B.

105. Trans. of a letter from Muhammad Aslam Khan and Inayatullah Khan, Khans of Thanra in Swat, to Deane, Deputy Commissioner [henceforward DC], Pesháwar, 27 December 1892, ibid.

106. H.A. Deane, DC, Pesháwar, to CSPD, No. 1 C., 5 January 1893, ibid.

107. Ibid.

108. C.L. Tupper, CS to Govt., PD, to Secy. to GI, FD, No. 154, Lahore 13 March 1893, ibid.

109. R. Udny, CSPD, to CS to Govt. of Punjab, No. 65 C., 2 March 1893, ibid.

110. Ibid.

111. Deputy Secretary [henceforward DS] to GI, to CS to Govt. of Punjab, No. 1845 F., Shimla, 28 July 1893, ibid.

112. Both Sharif Khan and his father were loyal to the British but the British did not come to his rescue against Umara Khan in 1890, because of the factors mentioned in the governor-general in council's statement, in spite of the fact that he (Sharif Khan) proposed to the colonial British at the end of 1889 that the colonial British 'should appoint him as an "Amír in the Yusafzai territory (meaning Dir and Bajaur)", and give him' their 'protection and support, and that he would establish his authority in Swat and elsewhere.' See C.L. Tupper, CS to Govt., PD, to Secy. to GI, FD, No. 154., Lahore, 13 March 1893, *COP*, BN 34, SN 952-B.

113. *Frontier and Overseas Expeditions from India*, Vol. 1, 363–4.

114. Christensen, introduction to *Report on the Tribes of Dir, Swat and Bajour together with the Utman-Khel and Sam Ranizai*, by A.H. McMahon and A.D.G. Ramsay, 17.

115. *Frontier and Overseas Expeditions from India*, Vol. 1, 364.

116. Ibid.

117. Ibid., 365.

118. Ibid., 390. Also see H.A. Deane, Political Agent [henceforward PA], Dir, Swat and Chitral [henceforward DSC], to Secy. to GI, FD, No. 1991 F., 18 November 1897, *COP*, BN 33, SN 923.

119. H.A. Deane, PA, DSC, to Secy. to GI, FD, No. 1991 F., 18 November 1897, ibid.

120. McMahon and A.D.G. Ramsay, *Report on the Tribes of Dir, Swat and Bajour together with the Utman-Khel and Sam Ranizai*, 120–1.

121. *Frontier and Overseas Expeditions from India*, Vol. 1, 365.

122. Ibid., 383.

123. H.A. Deane, PA, DSC, to Secy. to GI, FD, No. 1991 F., 18 November 1897, *COP*, BN 33, SN 923.

124. Ibid.

125. The then Upper Swat was the Swat Valley beyond the south-western limits of Landakay and Shamuzi on the left and right banks of the Swat River, respectively.

126. *Report on the Administration of the Border of the North-West Frontier Province for the year 1901–1902*, 'General' (Peshawar: Printed at the "Commercial" Press, 1902), 3.

127. *Report on the Administration of the Border of the North-West Frontier Province for the year 1902–03*, 'General' (Peshawar: Printed at the N.W.F. Province Government Press, 1903), 3.

128. *Frontier and Overseas Expeditions from India*, Vol. 1, 391.

129. *Report on the Administration of the Border of the North-West Frontier Province for the year 1906–07*, 'General' (Peshawar: Government Press, North-West Frontier Province, 1907), 2.

130. *Report on the Administration of the Border of the North-West Frontier Province for the year 1910–11*, Part II (Peshawar: Government Press, North-West Frontier Province, 1911), 5.

131. *Report on the Administration of the Border of the North-West Frontier Province for the year 1909–10*, Part II (Peshawar: Government Press, North-West Frontier Province, 1910), 5.

132. *Report on the Administration of the Border of the North-West Frontier Province for the year 1910–11*, Part II, 5.

133. *Report on the Administration of the Border of the North-West Frontier Province for the year 1911–12*, Part I (Peshawar: Government Press, North-West Frontier Province, 1912), 3.

134. Ibid., Part II, 9.

135. *Report on the Administration of the Border of the North-West Frontier Province for the year 1910–11*, Part II, 5.

136. *Report on the Administration of the Border of the North-West Frontier Province for the year 1911–12*, Part II, 9.

137. See Confidential, North-West Frontier Provincial Diary (Political) [henceforward CNWFPD] No. 12 for week ending 23 March 1912; and CNWFPD No. 15 for week ending 13 April 1912, *Files of the Deputy Commissioner Office Peshawar*, *at the Provincial Archives at Peshawar* [henceforward DCOP], BN 4, SN 47.

138. CNWFPD No. 13 for the week ending 28 March 1914, ibid., SN 48.

139. CNWFPD No. 24 for the week ending 15 June 1912, ibid., SN 47.

140. CNWFPD No. 25 for the week ending 22 June 1912, ibid.

141. CNWFPD No. 15 for the week ending 13 April 1912, ibid.

142. CNWFPD No. 16 for the week ending 20 April 1912 cf. CNWFPD No. 44 for the week ending 2 November 1912, and CNWFPD No. 49 for the week ending 7 December 1912, ibid.

143. CNWFPD No. 19 for the week ending 11 May 1912, ibid. cf. Habibur Rahman's statement in Sultan-i-Rome, 'The Sartōr Faqīr: Life and Struggle against British Imperialism', 99–100.

144. *Report on the Administration of the Border of the North-West Frontier Province for the year 1911–12*, Part II, 10. Also see CNWFPD No. 15 for the week ending 13 April 1912 and CNWFPD No. 16 for the week ending 20 April 1912, *DCOP*, BN 4, SN 47.

145. CNWFPD No. 8 for the week ending 21 February 1914, ibid., SN 48.

146. CNWFPD No. 9 for the week ending 28 February 1914; CNWFPD No. 11 for the week ending 14 March 1914; and CNWFPD No. 13 for the week ending 28 March 1914, ibid.

147. CNWFPD No. 31 for the week ending 1 August 1914, ibid.

148. See Sayyad Abdul Jabbar Shah [henceforward A.J. Shah] to DC, Hazara, 26 June 1914, *Files of the Tribal Research Cell Agencies, at the Provincial Archives at Peshawar* [*TRCA*], BN 37, SN 1028; A.J. Shah to Chief Commissioner [henceforward CC], North-West Frontier Province [NWFP], 2 October 1914, ibid.

149. A.J. Shah to DC, Hazara, 26 June 1914, ibid.

150. A.J. Shah to CC, NWFP, 2 October 1914, ibid.; Bruce, Assistant Commissioner [henceforward AC], Mardan, to Secy. to CC, 7 September 1914, ibid.

151. A.J. Shah to DC, Hazara, 26 June 1914, ibid.

152. A.J. Shah to CC, NWFP, 2 October 1914, ibid.; Bruce, AC, Mardan, to Secy. to CC, NWFP, 7 September 1914, ibid.

153. A.J. Shah to DC, Hazara, 26 June 1914, ibid.; A.J. Shah to CC, NWFP, 2 October 1914, ibid.

154. See W.J. Keen, DC, Hazara, to Secy. to the CC, NWFP, No. 1797, 6 August 1908, ibid., SN 1018.

155. Bruce, AC, Mardan, to Secy. to CC, 7 September 1914, ibid., SN 1028.

156. A.J. Shah to CC, NWFP, 2 October 1914, ibid.

157. Bruce, AC, Mardan, to Secy. to CC, NWFP, 7 September 1914, ibid.; A.J. Shah to CC, NWFP, 2 October 1914, ibid.

158. Bruce, AC, Mardan, to Secy. to CC, NWFP, 7 September 1914, ibid.

159. A.J. Shah to CC, NWFP, 2 October 1914, ibid.

160. Sandakai Baba's original name has been stated variously as Wali Ahmad and Ahmad Jan by different writers. He hailed from Sandakai—a place on the right bank of the Indus, in Shanglahpar, in Khyber Pukhtunkhwa—and hence got the epithet of Sandakai Baba and Sandakai Mula. He played a key role in the emergence of Swat State and the politics of Swat from 1915 to 1925 CE. In 1925, Miangul Abdul Wadud (the then Swat State ruler: who first needed and got the blessing and support of the Sandakai Baba in rising to power and securing his position as ruler), caused his flight to Dir, from where he did his utmost to work against Miangul Abdul Wadud but in vain. He died in Kuhan, in Dir, on 6 February

1927; and was buried there. For detail about the Sandakai Baba and his role, see Sultan-i-Rome, *Swat State (1915–1969): From Genesis to Merger; An Analysis of Political, Administrative, Socio-Political, and Economic Developments*, chapters 3–5; Khurshid, 'Sandākai Mullah: Career and Role in the Formation of Swat State, Pakistan', *Journal of the Pakistan Historical Society* (Karachi), 47/2 (April–June 1999), 77–81; *Pandrah Ruzah Rah-i Wafa* (Urdu) (Karachi), 4/13 (16–31 July 2004).

161. CNWFPD No. 8 for the week ending 20 February 1915; and CNWFPD No. 9 for the week ending 27 February 1915, *DCOP*, BN 4, SN 49.

162. *Report on the Administration of the Border of the North-West Frontier Province for the year 1914–15*, Part II (Peshawar: North-West Frontier Province Government Press, 1915), 9. Also CNWFPD No. 10 for the week ending 6 March 1915, *DCOP*, BN 4, SN 49.

163. CNWFPD No. 11 for the week ending 13 March 1915, ibid.

164. CNWFPD No. 10 for the week ending 6 March 1915, ibid.

165. CNWFPD No. 9 for the week ending 27 February 1915, ibid.

166. CNWFPD No. 11 for the week ending 13 March 1915, ibid.

167. CNWFPD No. 14 for the week ending 3 April 1915, ibid.; *Report on the Administration of the Border of the North-West Frontier Province for the year 1914–15*, Part II, 9.

168. CNWFPD No. 15 for the week ending 10 April 1915, *DCOP*, BN 4, SN 49. Also see *Report on the Administration of the Border of the North-West Frontier Province for the year 1914–15*, Part II, 9.

169. *Report on the Administration of the Border of the North-West Frontier Province for the year 1915–16*, Part II (Peshawar: North-West Frontier Province Government Press, 1916), 15.

170. Also see A.H. McMahon and A.D.G. Ramsay, *Report on the Tribes of the Malakand Political Agency (Exclusive of Chitral)*, revised by R.L. Kennion (Peshawar: Government Press, North-West Frontier Province, 1916), 65.

171. CNWFPD No. 15 for the week ending 10 April 1915, *DCOP*, BN 4, SN 49. Also see *Report on the Administration of the Border of the North-West Frontier Province for the year 1915–16*, Part II, 15.

172. CNWFPD No. 15 for the week ending 10 April 1915, *DCOP*, BN 4, SN 49.

173. Ibid.

174. CNWFPD No. 16 for the week ending 17 April 1915, ibid.

175. *Report on the Administration of the Border of North-West Frontier Province for the year 1915–16*, Part II, 15.

176. Ghulam Rasul Mehr, *Sarguzasht-i Mujahidin* (Urdu) (Lahore: Shaikh Ghulam Ali and Sons Publishers, n.d.), 525.

177. Swat State era proper (1915–1969 CE) has been dealt in detail in the author's (Sultan-i-Rome's) book: *Swat State (1915–1969): From Genesis to Merger; An Analysis of Political, Administrative, Socio-Political, and Economic Developments* (Karachi: Oxford University Press, 2008).

12

KUHISTAN

Swat Valley is divided into two main parts: Swat proper and Swat Kuhistan (Kohistan), the mountainous parts in the northeast of the Valley. The contents of the previous chapters mainly deal with and are related to Swat proper. The Kuhistan area is dealt with in this chapter.

Swat Kuhistan, too, is divided into two main parts, namely the Turwali (Torwali) and Gawri tracts. The Turwali tract is adjacent to and bounds the Swat Valley proper, whereas the Gawri tract is situated beyond Pishmal (Peshmal). Being a remote area, the inhabitants of Kuhistan have remained independent for most of known history and lived in a tribal fashion under their own code of life.

A.H. McMahon and A.D.G. Ramsay stated in 1901 that 'little is as yet known' about the inhabitants of Swat Kuhistan, the Turwali and Gawri. 'They would appear to be remnants of the races who, prior to the invasion of Swat by the Yusafzai [Yusufzi] Pathans in the sixteenth century, occupied both Lower and Upper Swat. They are practically independent, but pay at irregular intervals a small nominal tribute to the Kushwakht [Khushwakht] ruling family in Yasin and Mastuj.'[1] The revised edition of McMahon and Ramsay's Report, however, has stated: 'They would appear to be remnants of the races who, prior to the arrival *of the Swatis* [my italics; for the Swatis, see chapter 6], occupied both Lower and Upper Swat.'[2]

John Biddulph, however, has stated about the Turwalis that their 'large number..., as compared with most of the other Dard tribes, indicates that they must have once occupied some extensive valley like Boneyr [Bunair; Buner], from whence they, like the rest, have been expelled and thrust up into the more mountainous tracts by the aggressive Afghans'.[3] Unlike McMahon and Ramsay, Biddulph has spoken of the payment of tribute to Yasin only by 'three villages in the Swat Valley'[4] or Swat Kuhistan, which seems more sound.

Nawshirawan Kiwhur has disagreed with Biddulph's theory of the Turwalis coming from Bunair by stating that, despite great endeavour, he did not find proof of any link of the Turwalis with Bunair.[5] He has contended, after some analysis, that it would be right to claim on this basis that all the tribes of Turwal, save a few, have their roots among the Kafir tribes of the Siyahpush.[6] He, however, has reproduced the claim of two of the sections of the area that they have migrated from Bunair,[7] which endorses, to some extent, Biddulph's thesis.

Commonly called Kuhistani, the inhabitants of both the Turwali and Gawri tracts are 'distinct ethnic groups' but all are 'being what has been called Dardic (Linguistic Survey of India), i.e. old Indo-Aryan speaking peoples'.[8] Sayyad Abdul Jabbar Shah has termed the Kuhistanis as Aryan by ethnicity.[9] Whereas, according to Aurel Stein, they 'are of the same Dard race that inhabited the whole of Swāt down to the Pathān invasion'.[10] Although Nawshirawan Kiwhur has claimed that John Biddulph has concluded, after thorough research, that the Turwali, Kalami, Gawri and Bishkari belong to the same race and all their languages are Dardi or of the Dardic group,[11] Biddulph's assertion about the Dard and Dardistan theory, while dealing with the different tribes of the Hindu Kush area, including Swat Kuhistan, is as under:

> Dr. Leitner was the first to bring into prominent notice the existence of an Aryan race of great ethnological interest in these remote valleys. His scanty opportunities, however, have caused him to fall into the error of believing that the tribes which he has classed under the name of Dard are all of the same race, and he has applied the term of Dardistan, a name founded on a misconception, to a tract of country inhabited by several races, speaking distinct languages, who differ considerably amongst themselves.[12]

Biddulph has retained 'the names of Dard and Dardistan', only because, according to him: 'As, however, there is no one name which will properly apply to the peoples and countries in question, it will be perhaps convenient to retain the names of Dard and Dardistan when speaking collectively of the tribes in question and the countries they inhabit.'[13]

Some earlier sources have mentioned the Turwali tract with the name 'Torwal' (Turwal).[14] H.G. Raverty, however, has contended that 'the most correct way of writing this is Torú Āl, or Torw Āl, not Torwál'.[15] He, on the basis of the report of the Qandahari, sent by him to Swat, has mentioned the inhabitants as 'Tor-wáls',[16] whereas, Biddulph has called them 'Torwalik'.[17] Stein, however, has mentioned the language and the inhabitants of 'Torwal' (Turwal) as 'Tōrwālī' (Turwali),[18] the name which is now in general applied to both the language and inhabitants by outsiders and the inhabitants themselves. Situated between the 'Yūsūfzai clans of Upper Swāt' and the Gawri tract, 'the Tōrwālīs remained a small independent community',[19] some until 1921 and some until 1922. Stein has noted, in 1926, the 'complete absence of ancient remains' in the Turwali area.[20]

Fredrik Barth has recoded, in the 1950s, regarding the Turwalis, that they 'are a linguistic and political group inhabiting the Swat valley from Laikot [Laikut] down to, and including, Bahrein [Bahrain], called by the Torwális Baraniál'.[21] They, however, also inhabit some area below Bahrain and the Chail Valley; as has also been mentioned by Biddulph much earlier, 'The more considerable…are the Torwalik [Turwali] in the Swat Valley, who occupy the main valley for about 60 miles from Araneh [Aryanai] to Chiroleh [Churrai, now Madyan], and the Chahil Durrah [Chail Darah], the habitable part of which is about 20 miles long.'[22]

According to Barth, 'The Torwáli as a unit do not appear to claim a common ancestor peculiar to them as a tribe; the four major groups have different histories.'[23] Although the Turwali resemble the Gawri in their political organization and social system in some respects, their system is more similar to that of the neighbouring Pathans or the Yusufzi in respect of the division in *khail*s (*khel*s), land ownership, not giving daughters in marriage to the craftsmen or professionals (*kasabgar*), tenancy, inheritance, village council or *jargah*, adultery and murder.[24] However, in respect of landownership in inheritance, in contrast, Biddulph has much earlier stated that 'in Torwal, women inherit the father's land in equal shares with the sons',[25] which is in contrast to the ground reality.

Barth has recorded, in 1950s, about the Gawri area:

The area lacks any resemblance of recorded history, and does not appear to be mentioned in available historical sources. I was further unable to find traditions of stories relating to outside contacts in the past which might be fixed in time. The time and circumstances of conversion to Islam were unknown.[26]

In 1968, the Archaeological Survey unearthed some remains between the villages of Kalam and Utrur (Utror), 'where there is evidence of phases of frequentation that have equivalents in the middle Swāt Valley and that can be dated to the protohistorical period'.[27] These remains include those in the terrain near the village of Utrur, an ancient cemetery near the village of Ushoram (Ushuran), and a cemetery in the Rashnel (Rashnil) area.[28] Giorgio Stacul has inferred:

> Settlement of the valleys around Kālām in protohistorical times might easily be explained by the abundant pasturage the region offers in the summer season, within the framework of those periodic transfers of the flocks from the valleys to the heights that are even today practiced by the nomadic and semi-nomadic peoples of Hindukush, Pamir and Karakorum [Qaraquram].[29]

As per oral traditions, a significant portion of the inhabitants of the Gawri tract, however, claim to be the descendants of Raja Gira (for Raja Gira see chapter 6) and his ethnic brethren, who fled from Udigram, owing to defeat by the Ghaznavid army, and settled in Dir; after which their descendants came and settled in the area. There, however, also found Gujar and Pukhtuns (as well as Chitralis, also called Qashqari, and other people), all of whom speak their own languages[30] but are influenced by Gawri, the language of the majority inhabitants. The details of the theory, as transmitted orally, regarding Raja Gira's being Arab by ethnicity, his defeat, and escape to Dir and the other details, have loopholes and it is hard for the story to withstand scrutiny.

The political organization and social system of the Gawri tract, however, is different from the Yusufzi of Swat to the extent that 'no distinction is made in Gáwri organization between descent unit and political faction, a distinction particularly important among the neighboring Pathans'.[31] In other major issues or points, like the division in *khail*s, village council or *jargah*, ownership of property, adultery, murder, widow's re-marriage, death ceremony, and the beating of the drum or *nagharah*, their system bears resemblance to that of the Yusufzi in Swat.[32] Like the Swat Yusufzi, 'only owners of land are qualified to sit in the council [*jargah*]' and 'beating of the drum is specifically the signal of an impending attack, and serves to mobilize the whole village'.[33]

Unlike the Yusufzi-dominated Swat Valley, the Gujar in the Kuhistan, found in both the Turwali and Gawri areas, were a settled community and owned land.[34] 'The Gujar population' in the Kuhistan, however, 'is made up of a number of local, mutually unrelated patrilineal descent groups', who 'are not found [in] any other place, are not localized in wards in the village, and their relevance to internal organization appears to be limited'.[35]

As per oral tradition, the Kuhistanis were Buddhists before their conversion to Islam. Sayyad Abdul Jabbar Shah, however, has asserted that their religion and belief were non-ascertainable.[36] They did not embrace Islam until the occupation of the Swat Valley proper by the Yusufzi, after which the invasion of Kuhistan was undertaken, as also stated in chapter 5, by the Muslims under the command of the descendants of Akhun Darwizah and Pir Baba.[37] Resultantly, although Kuhistan was not occupied, the inhabitants gradually embraced Islam and Islam became the dominant religion in the area. John Biddulph, however, has asserted about the Turwalis that they 'have been too long converted to Islam and exposed to the preaching of Swat Moollahs [*mulas*] to have retained any customs connected with other religions'.[38]

Although it has been reported in 1858, by the Qandahari, sent by Raverty to Swat, that beyond Churrai (now Madyan) 'the Pushto [Pukhtu, Pashto] or Afghán language ceases to be spoken, and the Kohistání language is used',[39] the Kuhistanis, as a whole, have become bilingual, speaking their own and the Pashto languages.

NOTES

1. A.H. McMahon and A.D.G. Ramsay, *Report on the Tribes of Dir, Swat and Bajour* [Bajawar] *together with the Utman-Khel and Sam Ranizai*, edited with introduction by R.O. Christensen (repr., Peshawar: Saeed Book Bank, 1981), 4.
2. A.H. McMahon and A.D.G. Ramsay, *Report on the Tribes of the Malakand Political Agency (Exclusive of Chitral)*, revised by R.L. Kennion (Peshawar: Government Press, North-West Frontier Province, 1916), 2.
3. John Biddulph, *Tribes of the Hindoo Koosh*, with preface to the 1971 edition by Karl Gratzl (repr., Lahore: Ali Kamran Publishers, 1986), 69.
4. Ibid., 70.
5. Nawshirawan Kiwhur, *Turwal kay Qabail* (Urdu) (Peshawar: Gandhara Hindku Academy, 2017), 180.
6. Ibid., 181.
7. Ibid., 234.
8. Fredrik Barth, *Indus and Swat Kohistan: An Ethnographic Survey* (Oslo: Forenede Trykkerier, 1956), 12.
9. Sayyad Abdul Jabbar Shah Sithanawi, *Kitab al-Ibra: Subah Sarhad wa Afghanistan ki Char Sau Salah Tarikh; 1500 Iswi ta 1900 Iswi* (Urdu), Vol. 1 (Islamabad: Poorab Academy, 2011), 122.
10. Aurel Stein, *On Alexander's Track to the Indus: Personal Narrative of Explorations on the North-West Frontier of India* (repr., Karachi: Indus Publications, 1995), 83.

11. Kiwhur, *Turwal kay Qabail*, 22–3.
12. Biddulph, *Tribes of the Hindoo Koosh*, 8–9.
13. Ibid., 9.
14. See ibid., 69–70; Stein, *On Alexander's Track to the Indus*, 89, 94, 96, 98; Aurel Stein, *An Archaeological tour in Upper Swāt and Adjacent Hill Tracts* (Calcutta: Government of India, Central Publication Branch, 1930), 61, 63–5.
15. Henry George Raverty, *Notes on Afghanistan and Baluchistan*, Vol. 1 (2nd edn. in Pakistan, Quetta: Nisa Traders, 1982), 237 n. §.
16. H.G. Raverty, 'An account of Upper and Lower Suwát, and the Kohistán, to the source of the Suwát River; with an account of the tribes inhabiting those valleys', *Journal of the Asiatic Society* (Calcutta), 31/3 (1862), 252. Also see McMahon and A.D.G. Ramsay, *Report on the Tribes of Dir, Swat and Bajour together with the Utman-Khel and Sam Ranizai*, 4; McMahon and A.D.G. Ramsay, *Report on the Tribes of the Malakand Political Agency (Exclusive of Chitral)*, revised by R.L. Kennion, 2.
17. Biddulph, *Tribes of the Hindoo Koosh*, 69–71.
18. See Stein, *On Alexander's Track to the Indus*, 90–2, 95.
19. Stein, *An Archaeological tour in Upper Swāt and Adjacent Hill Tracts*, 63.
20. Ibid.
21. Barth, *Indus and Swat Kohistan: An Ethnographic Survey*, 69.
22. Biddulph, *Tribes of the Hindoo Koosh*, 69.
23. Barth, *Indus and Swat Kohistan: An Ethnographic Survey*, 72.
24. For detail, see ibid., 69–76.
25. Biddulph, *Tribes of the Hindoo Koosh*, 82.
26. Barth, *Indus and Swat Kohistan: An Ethnographic Survey*, 53.
27. Giorgio Stacul, 'An Archaeological Survey near Kālām (Swāt Kohistān)', *East and West* (Rome), 20/1–2, (March–June 1970), 87.
28. Ibid., 87–90.
29. Ibid., 90.
30. See Muhammad Zaman Sagar, *Kalam Kuhistan ki Riwayati Tarikh: Gawri Qabail aur un ka Nizam-i Muashirat (Hisah Awal–Kalam Khas)* (Urdu) (Peshawar: Frontier Language Institute, 2007), 25–74.
31. Barth, *Indus and Swat Kohistan: An Ethnographic Survey*, 61.
32. For detail, see 56–66.
33. Ibid., 63.
34. Also see Raverty, *Notes on Afghanistan and Baluchistan*, Vol. 1, 237; Raverty, 'An account of Upper and Lower Suwát, and the Kohistán, to the source of the Suwát River; with an account of the tribes inhabiting those valleys', 252–3.
35. Barth, *Indus and Swat Kohistan: An Ethnographic Survey*, 77.
36. Sithanawi, *Kitab al-Ibra: Subah Sarhad wa Afghanistan ki Char Sau Salah Tarikh; 1500 Iswi ta 1900 Iswi*, Vol. 1, 122.
37. Ibid., 122–5.
38. Biddulph, *Tribes of the Hindoo Koosh*, 70.
39. Raverty, 'An account of Upper and Lower Suwát, and the Kohistán, to the source of the Suwát River; with an account of the tribes inhabiting those valleys', 252.

GLOSSARY

14C data: A scientific method of dating old things, societies, cultures and archaeological sites. Samples of organic material, such as small amounts of charcoal, wood, shell, skin, burnt bone, hair etcetera, are used for the purpose. The sample is first physically examined. Then, through elaborate laboratory work, radiocarbon years are obtained. These are converted into calendar years through a process called calibration. The radiocarbon dates are considered as absolute, unlike other traditional methods, such as dating through comparison, etcetera.

Alim (plural: *ulama*; **in Pashto also** *aliman*): Scholar; commonly used in the meaning of a Muslim scholar of Islamic theology.

Ashnan: ablution; bathing; washing.

Ayudhapurusa (Ayudha-puruṣa): In Hindu mythology, anthropomorphic weapon of a deity.

Bi'at: The act of swearing allegiance to a *pir*, ruler etcetera; homage; fealty.

Bhaisajyavastu (Bhaiṣajya-vastu): A chapter of the Buddhist *Vinaya* text, also of the *Vinaya* of the Mula Sarvastivada school (*Mūlasarvāstivāda-vinaya*).

Bakhshi: A high-ranking officer in the Mughal administrative apparatus/hierarchy in India.

Bhikshu (Bhikṣu): A Buddhist monk or a religious mendicant.

Bodhisattva: The concept of a Bodhisattva in Mahayana Buddhism relates to a person who, although has achieved *nirvana*, refrains from entering that state out of love and compassion for others who still face the sufferings of this world. He is distinct from an Arhat. An Arhat is a perfected person who would be no more reborn. A Bodhisattva declines to enter Buddhahood and *nirvana*, in order to serve and guide other human beings towards enlightenment and final emancipation.

Buddha Sakyamuni (Buddha Śākyamuni [Gautama]): The historical Buddha, Gautama of the Sakya (*Śākya*) clan ('a sage of *Śākya*). The term is usually used in China and Japan.

Caitya/Chaitya: In Buddhism: any object of veneration, especially a sacred grove, a sanctuary or a prayer hall with a *stupa* (*stūpa*: reliquary mound). It also embodies the 'Buddhist Universe'. Commonly, it refers to a sanctuary, shrine, temple or prayer hall in South Asian religions.

Cakrapurusa (Cakra-puruṣa): This figure appears along with the various representations of Vishnu (Viṣṇu). It is generally a male figure with round eyes and a drooping belly embellished with various ornaments. Normally, Cakrapurus appears with Visnu's lower left hand placed on the head of Cakrapurusa.

Charbaytah: The genre of Pashto poetry in which historical and love stories are narrated. Continuity in its verses is required; and the rhyme is repeated after each verse or stanza.

Dalazak: Dalazak or Dalazak tribe were Afghan/Pukhtun and the inhabitants and in possession of the Peshawar Valley when the Yusufzi migrated from Afghanistan. When the Yusufzi migrated to and occupied their areas in the trans-Indus tract they migrated to the cis-Indus area. Due to their insubordination and depredations, Mughal Emperor Jahangir demolished one lakh of their houses and exiled them to remote parts of India. Therefore, as a whole, they are extinct now as a separate entity.

Darbar: A court; reception; shrine of a *pir*.

Devipurana (Devi-purāṇa): Mahapuranas are Hindu Texts which comprise eighteen volumes and the Devipurana (also known as the Devi Bhagavatam/Shrimad Devi)belongs among them. It consists of 12 chapters containing 18000 verses.

277

Dharmagupta/Dharmaguptaka: A school in Buddhism branching off from the Mahisasakas (Mahīśāsaka) school which derived from Sarvastivada (Sarvāstivāda) school. It has also been considered as one of the 18 early Buddhist schools.

Diadem: A kind of crown which symbolized sovereignty.

Drachm/drachma: An ancient silver coin and unit for weight, used in Greece. Its weight is equal to 60 grains. Drachm is perhaps of late Middle English origin and its etymology may be found in the drachma of ancient Greece.

Faqir (plural: *faqiran*): Religious mendicant without status; resident in someone's quarter free of rent but liable to do some manual work for the proprietor; subject person.

Gadadevi (*Gadā-devī*): The Kaumodaki is considered a *gada* (*gadā*: mace) of Vishnu (Viṣṇu), the god. Occasionally, it seems to be a woman known as Gadadevi or Gadanari (Gadādevī or Gadānarī). In pictorial depictions, Vishnu (Viṣṇu) rests his hands on her head and she holds the *gada* (*gadā*).

Haj: Pilgrimage; one of the main pillars of Islam, obligatory subject to certain conditions, performed in Makkah in the last month of the Islamic/Hijrah calendar.

Hakim: An administrative official. It also means a sage; a wise person; one who practices *unani* or Eastern medicine.

Hinayana (*Hinayāna*): ('lesser vehicle') a pejorative term, coined by the Mahayanists (Mahāyānists), for their opponents who were considered as more conservative in their religious views. There are some points of agreement between Mahayanists (Mahāyānists) and Hinayanists (Hinayānists); however, fundamental differences in terms of worship and emancipation are also found. Neutral non-derogatory terms: Nikaya (Nikāya) Buddhism, or the early Buddhism. The term refers to the tradition of early Buddhism and its schools ('sects'). (See *Mahayana/ Mahāyāna*).

Jargah (plural: *jargay*): The traditional consultative assembly; forum; council of the tribal chiefs or elders where matters of common interest and communal affairs are discussed and decided. It has other meanings, compositions, functions, and uses in different contexts. In a *jargah*, all the stakeholders are represented; all the attendants express their viewpoints and present their arguments freely; and the decisions are made by consensus or unanimously, after the deliberations. Therefore, the decisions, made in such a manner, are abided by all and the violators become liable to a fine or punishment. Also see the sub-topic *Jargah* in chapter 7.

Jataka (*Jātaka*): *Jataka*s (*Jātaka*s) are the stories of the former lives of the Buddha. Some Buddhist collections describe about 550 previous life stories of Buddha. Beside the *Jataka*s (*Jātaka*s), a separate category is that of *Avadana* (*Avadāna*); *Avadana*s (*Avadāna*s) recount the previous lives of other Bodhisattvas than the Buddha.

Kambala: A *siddha* who contested a magic with Kukkuripa, another *siddha*, at Mountain Murunda: both the *siddha*s were connected with Indrabhuti. It also refers to an annual buffalo race held at Karnataka, a south-western Indian state, and to an upper garment, with special significance at marriage ceremonies.

Kasyapiya (*Kāśyapīya*): One of the schools of early Buddhism. The name derives from Kasyapiya (Kāśyapa).

Kramasampradaya (*Krama-sampradaya* or *sampradaya*): 'Tradition/succession in sequence' or 'tradition/succession'. The term can be used in various contexts, e.g. *Brahma-sampradaya*, in Hinduism, denotes a succession of gurus starting with Brahma. Mostly, it refers to the beliefs and teachings of Madhvacharya and his Dvaita philosophy.

Kukkuripa (*Kukkuripā*): Mahasiddha, a tantric Buddhist practitioner, who lived in India and selected the path of renunciation to resolve the problems of life. He kept a dog with him in his cave while meditating, that is why he is called as Kukkuripa, meaning 'dog lover'. Mahasiddhas and Kukkuripas are the old advocators of the textual tradition of Vajrayana Buddhism.

Lakhkar (plural: *lakhkaray*): A tribal force taking the field under the tribal banner when required. They do not take payment and also fight at their own cost, with their own arms and ammunition. It neither is nor has the role of a permanent standing army.

Mahasanghika (*Mahāsāṇghika*): An important and influential school of early Buddhism. Its followers are known to have been forerunners of the concept of the Bodhisattva (of the Mahāyāna school).

Mahayana (*Mahāyāna*): ('Greater vehicle'). A tradition of later Buddhism, which gradually formed around the first century CE. The concept of the Bodhisattva is the kernel to Mahayanists (Mahāyānists). Personal emancipation is highly desired in the Hinayana (Hināyāna) tradition. But the Bodhisattva's ideal is to help others gain salvation, and for this he avoids personal *nirvana*.

Mahisasakas (*Mahīśāsaka*): A school of early Buddhism.

Manichaeism: Manichaeism was a major religious movement initiated by the Iranian prophet, Mani, in the Sassanian Empire. Manichaeism taught an elaborate dualistic cosmology elaborating the struggle between a good, spiritual world of light, and an evil, material world of darkness. Mani is believed by his followers to have been crucified by the Sassanian rulers.

Meru: A mountain in Hindu, Buddhist, and Jain mythologies, believed to be located at the centre of the world.

Miangul/Mianguls: *Mian/mya* (plural: *miangan/myagan*) are the descendants of saints and spiritual leaders of the past who have acquired widespread fame and reputation among many tribes. The descendants of Abdul Ghafur, aka Saidu Baba of Swat, were not yet ranked in that segment, so they were given the courtesy title of Miangul (plural: *miangwalan/myagwalan*—Mianguls). In a sense it is a lesser title than *Mian*. It is also a term used for addressing the minors of the Mians.

Mihira Kula/Mahiragula (*Mihirakula*): A ruler of the White/Alchon Huns (Hūṇa), notorious, according to traditional understanding, for the annihilation of Buddhist monasteries and monks.

Mulasarvastivadins (*Mūla-sarvāstivāda*): A school of early Buddhism.

Nang: *Nang* means honour, although the English word 'honour' does not have the same meaning and sense. It compels one to take-up arms in defence of the homeland and the protection of national honour when occasion demands; also for retaining personal esteem as well as that of family, one's beloved, friends, the sub-tribe, and the tribe. Also see the sub-topic *Nang* in chapter 7.

Nestorianism: A Christian theological doctrine.

Nirvana: In Buddhism, it means release from the cycle of reincarnation.

Pir (plural: *piran*): A spiritual guide; a saint; a holy man.

Political agent: A representative and administrative official of the British colonial government posted and working in the areas designated as Agencies by the British imperial power in India.

Protected area: A tribal area the colonial British took under their protectorate during their rule in India.

Raja: ruler; king; monarch; prince.

Saiva school (*Śaiva school*): An Indian School of Mystical Thought. Saiva (Śaiva) is an adjective of Siva (Śiva), the Hindu god, and Saiva (Śaiva) can refer to anything. In fact, there is no particular Saiva school, rather there are plenty of Saiva schools, each having their own names.

Sarkar: An administrative unit, in Mughal India, interposed between the *parganah* and the province.

Sarvastivada (*Sarvāstivāda*): A school of early Buddhism.

Sarvastivadins: Members of the Sarvastivada School of Buddhism. It was established during the reign of Ashoka (Aṣoka).

Sayyad (plural: *saidan/saydan*): Descendants commonly believed to be of the line of Prophet Muhammad (SAW) from his daughter Fatimah (RA) and son-in-law Ali (RA).

Shaikh (plural: *shaikhan*): Persons not well versed in Islamic learning but who have dedicated their lives to saintliness and passing a religious life.

Shara: Islamic law and customs.

Shiqdar: During the Sultanate and Mughal periods, the *shiqdar* was the administrator of a **shiq/ parganah**: a part of a *sarkar*/province.

Siddha: Siddha may simply be called a saint. Its concept is found in Indian religions, e.g. Hinduism, Buddhism, and Jainism. Siddha literally means 'one who is accomplished'. The accomplishment is expressed in Sanskrit by the idea of Siddhi. Siddhi may be interpreted as 'psychic abilities and powers' and it is achieved through rigorous spiritual labour. Dedication, meditation, mantras, control of senses and even respectable birth may help one realize Siddhi.

Tahsil: The smallest administrative unit in the North-West Frontier during and after the colonial British rule in India; and also in Swat State.

Tahsildar: The *tahsil*'s officer.

Tapah (تپه): A segment among the Yusufzi Afghans/Pukhtuns; the area held/owned by the segment.

Tapah (ٹپه): A genre of Pashto verse. Its formation is not attributed to anyone; it is believed that, in general, it originates from women, but not necessarily.

Turah: a copper coin.

Uddiyana-pitha (*Uḍḍiyāna-pīṭha*)/Tantric commentaries: Traditionally speaking, Indrabhuti, the King of Swat, wrote many Tantric commentaries in Swat which are called Uddiyana-pitha.

Ushar/ushr: According to Islamic law the Muslims are required to pay a portion of their lands' produce to the Islamic state—according to one viewpoint at the rate of 10 or 5 per cent, depending upon the nature of the water given to the fields, but according to another view point one-fifth or at the rate of 20 per cent—which is called *ushar* (also spelled as *ushr*). However, the heads under which the *ushar* is utilized and disbursed have also been specified.

Vajrayana (*Vajrayāna*)/Tantric Buddhism: ('Diamond vehicle'). A name for the *Tantric* tradition of Buddhism which emphasizes mystical practices and concepts to attain enlightenment.

Vajrapani (*Vajrapāṇi*): One of the eight main Bodhisattvas of Mahayana (Mahāyāna) Buddhism. He is the guard or protector of the meditating Buddha. Usually, he holds a thunderbolt (*vajra*) in his hand (*pani/pāṇi*).

Vinaya: One part, or 'basket', of the Tripitaka (*Tri-piṭaka*), the 'three baskets' of the Buddhist Canon, beside Sutta Pitaka and Abhidhamma Pitaka (*Sūtra-piṭaka* and *Abhidharma-piṭaka*). *Vinaya-piṭaka* is the 'Basket of Monastic Discipline'.

Yaghi/Yaghistan: Yaghi means rebel, and unruly. The area of Bunair, Swat, Dir, and Bajawar (and also some other parts of the then tribal areas, e.g. Waziristan)—having not been ruled by the British and having not recognized the sovereignty of any external power—was termed and called Yaghistan, i.e. the land of the rebels, the land of the unruly. The very word and nomenclature, Yaghistan, explains and speaks volume of the areas' remaining independent and insubordinate to the mighty powers who ruled the Peshawar Valley, India, and Afghanistan.

Yaksha **(feminine Yakshi or Yakshini):** In Indian mythology Yakshas belong to a class of nature spirit. They are generally benevolent beings but sometimes can be malignant and cruel. Their responsibility is to take care of nature's treasures. Yakshas also act as tutelary deities of lakes, wells, cities etcetera. They have been worshiped from very earlier times and it is also said that their representation in art precedes depictions of the Bodhisattva and some Hindu deities. In Buddhism, Yakshas protect the dharma and they have received benevolence through Buddhist teachings.

SELECTED BIBLIOGRAPHY

Manuscripts

MS No. ڧ [Qaaf]-569, *Swat Namah da Khushal Khan Khattak*. Library of Pashto Academy, University of Peshawar.

Jang Namah (Persian, verse), Scribed by Mirza Abdul Haq, Date Torn, *Personal Collection of Ziaullah Khan, Gulkadah, Swat*. (Photo-state copy, personal collection of Sultan-i-Rome, Hazarah, Swat).

Unpublished Official Record

Provincial Archives Khyber Pukhtunkhwa, Peshawar

Files of Chief Commissioner Office, Peshawar
Files of Commissioner Office, Peshawar
Files of Deputy Commissioner Office, Peshawar
Files of Foreign Department
Files of Special Branch Police NWFP
Files of Tribal Research Cell (Agencies)

District Record Room, at Gulkadah, Swat

Record of Swat State/District Swat

Personal Collection of Bahadar Khan, Fatihpur, Swat

Miscellaneous.

Personal Collection of Sultan-i-Rome, Hazarah, Swat

Miscellaneous.

Tribal Affairs Research Cell of the Home Department, Khyber Pukhtunkhwa, at Peshawar

Miscellaneous record/reports
Swat Files

Personal Communication/Interviews

Note: Age and other particulars given for those personally interviewed by the author are at the time of the first interview of each one of them. However, the year of death has been given for the one who has passed away since then.

Muhammad Asif Khan: 72 years old; hails from Saidu Sharif, Swat; died 2002. Writer of the autobiography of Miangul Abdul Wadud (ruler of Swat State, 1917–1949), with *dibachah, hisah awal, saluramah hisah*, and *hisah pinzamah* by him. A learned person with analytical ability and critical perception but fell prey to distorting facts being court writer, a fact he admitted in the course of his interview, 24 May and 14 June 1998.

Muhammad Farooq Swati: 44 years old; hails from Peshawar; Associate Professor, Department of Archaeology, University of Peshawar, 8 February 1999, 20 November 2000.

Rafiullah Khan: 38 years old; hails from Sair, Tahsil Charbagh, Swat; Assistant Professor, Taxila Institute of Asian Civilizations, Quaid-i-Azam University, Islamabad, August 2016.

UNPUBLISHED WORKS

Dirvi, Abdul Halim, *The Life and Achievements of Ghazi Umra Khan* (MA Thesis, Pakistan Study Centre, University of Peshawar, 1989).

Jadoon, Muhammad Mushtaq, *Note on Durand Line Issues*, June 2003 (Tribal Affairs Research Cell, Home & Tribal Affairs Department, Government of North-West Frontier Province, Peshawar, Book No. 988).

Hay, W.R., *History of the Descendants of the Akhund of Swat and of the Formation and Development of Swat State* (n.d.).

Khan, Rafiullah, *Begininng [Beginning] of Archaeology in Malakand-Swat (1896–1926): Protagonists, Fieldwork and the Legal Framework* (PhD Dissertation, Taxila Institute of Asian Civilizations, Quaid-i-Azam University, Islamabad, 2014).

Swati, Muhammad Farooq, *Gandhara Art in the Swat Valley, Pakistan: A Study Based on the Peshawar University Collection*, Vol. 1, *Text* (PhD Dissertation, Faculty of Oriental Studies, University of Cambridge, 1996).

Sultan-i-Rome, *Swat State under the Walis (1917–69)* (PhD Dissertation, Department of History, University of Peshawar, 2000).

Zada, Rahim, *The Battle of Ambela [1863] Against the British in N-W.F.P.* (MA Thesis, Pakistan Study Centre, University of Peshawar, 1995).

Tribal Areas: Status, Border Control and Policy: Governor's Committee Report (Government of North-West Frontier Province, Home and Tribal Affairs Department, September–October 1997).

Charbaytah da Yasin, Umar Panzus Kalah, Pah Lik nah Puhigi, Pah Mardan kay Chaprasi di, Da Mardan di, 1.9.1901.

Confidential Official Reports

Administration Reports of the North-West Frontier Province

Administration Report of the North-West Frontier Province from 9th November 1901 to 31st March 1903.

Punjab Frontier Administration Reports

Punjab Frontier Administration Reports for the Years 1893–94, 1894–95.

Reports on the Administration of the Border of the North-West Frontier Province

Reports on the Administration of the Border of the North-West Frontier Province for the Years: 1901–2, 1902–3, 1906–7, 1907–8, 1909–10, 1910–11, 1911–12, 1912–13, 1913–14, 1914–15, 1915–16.

Reports on the Administration of the Punjab and its Dependencies

Reports on the Administration of the Punjab and its Dependencies for the Years: 1875–6, 1876–7, 1877–8, 1878–9, 1879–80, 1880–1, 1881–2, 1882–3, 1883–4, 1884–5, 1886–7, 1887–8, 1888–9, 1889–90, 1890–1, 1891–2, 1892–3, 1893–4, 1895–6, 1896–7, 1897–8, 1898–9.

Census Reports

Census of India, 1941, Vol. 10–Appendix, *Trans-Border Areas: Report and Tables*, By I.D. Scott (Delhi: Manager of Publications, 1942).

Census of Pakistan, 1951, Vol. 4, *North-West Frontier Province, Report & Tables*, By Sheikh Abdul Hamid (Karachi: Manager of Publications, Government of Pakistan, n.d.).

Population Census of Pakistan 1961: Census Report of Tribal Agencies, Part 1–3, *General Description, Population Tables and Village Statistics* (Karachi: Manager of Publications, Government of Pakistan, n.d.).

Population Census of Pakistan 1972: District Census Report, Swat (Karachi: Manager of Publications, Government of Pakistan, 1975).

Official/Semi Official Works

Hay, W.R., *Monograph on Swat State* (Simla: Government of India Press, 1934).

McMahon, A.H., and A.D.G. Ramsay, *Report on the Tribes of the Malakand Political Agency (Exclusive of Chitral)*, revised by R.L. Kennion (Peshawar: Government Press, North-West Frontier Province, 1916).

Plowden, T.J.C., *Report on the Leading Persons and State of Factions in Swat*, repr. (Simla: Government of India Press, 1932).

Stein, Aurel, *An Archaeological tour in Upper Swāt and Adjacent Hill Tracts* (Calcutta: Government of India, Central Publication Branch, 1930).

(Confidential), Central Asia, Part I, *A Contribution towards the Better Knowledge of the Topography, Ethnography, Statistics, & History of the North-West Frontier of British India*, Vol. 3, Compiled for Military and Political Reference by C.M. MacGregor (Calcutta: Office of the Superintendent of Government Printing, 1873).

Confidential, Gazetteer of the North-West Frontier: From Bajaur and the Indus Kohistán on the North to the Mari Hills on the South, Vols. 1 & 4, Compiled for Political and Military Reference in the Intelligence Branch of the Quarter Master General's Department in India, Completed and edited by A.L'e. Holmes (Simla: Printed at the Government Central Branch Press, 1887).

'Extract from Civil and Mily: Gaz: dated 6 March 1898, "The Rising in Swat State [sic]".' *Civil & Military Gazette*, 1898.

Military Report and Gazetteer on Buner and Adjacent Independent Territory, 2nd edn. (Delhi: Government of India Press, 1926).

Military Report and Gazetteer on Dir, Swat and Bajaur, Part II, *Military Report*, 2nd edn. (Calcutta: Government of India Press, 1928).

Riwaj Namah-i Swat, comp. Ghulam Habib Khan, Superintendent, Deputy Commissioner Office, Swat (n.p., n.d.).

Official Works Privately Published

A Glossary of the Tribes and Castes of the Punjab and North-West Frontier Province, Vol. 3, repr. (Lahore: Aziz Publishers, 1978).

Frontier and Overseas Expeditions from India, Vol. 1, *Tribes North of the Kabul River*, 2nd edn. published in Pakistan (Quetta: Nisa Traders, 1982).

Gazetteer of the Peshawar District, 1897–98, repr. (Lahore: Sang-e-Meel Publications, 1989).

Imperial Gazetteer of India: Provincial Series; North-West Frontier Province, repr. (Lahore: Sang-e-Meel Publications, 1991).

Malakand, 1958–68: A Decade of Progress, with Foreword by Mohammad Humayun Khan (n.p., n.d.).

Mutiny Reports from Punjab & N.W.F.P., Vol. 2, repr. (Lahore: Al-Biruni, n.d.).

Religious Scriptures

The Hymns of the Rigveda, Eng. trans. Ralph T.H. Griffith, 2nd edn. (Kotagiri (Nilgiri), 1896), downloaded in pdf form from http://www.sanskritweb.net; accessed also on http://www.hinduwebsite.com/sacredscripts/rigintro.htm on 20/8/2019.

Walmiki Urdu Ramayan ba Taswir wa Mukammal, Urdu trans. Babu Munawwar Sahib, Khalf-ur-Rashid Munshi Dwarka Prashad Sahib, Ufaq Lakhnawi, Hasb-i Farmaish J.S. Sanat Singh and Sons, Publishers wa Tajiran-i Kutub, Chawak Mati Lahore (Lahore: Printed by Hindustan Press, Haspatal Road, n.d.).

Books
English

Abu-l-Fazl, *The Akbar Nama of Abu-l-Fazl (History of the Reign of Akbar Including an Account of His Predecessors)*, trans. from the original Persian by H. Beveridge, Vol. 3, repr. (Lahore: Sang-e-Meel Publications, 2005).

Adamec, Ludwig W., *Afghanistan, 1900–1923: A Diplomatic History* (Berkeley: University of California Press, 1967).

Adamson, Hilary and Isobel Shaw, *A Traveller's Guide to Pakistan* (Islamabad: The Asian Study Group, 1981).

Adye, John, *Sitana: A Mountain Campaign on the Borders of Afghanistan in 1863*, repr. (East Sussex: The Naval & Military Press Ltd, 2004).

Ahmad, Khwājah Niẓāmuddīn, *The Ṭabaqāt-i-Akbarī of Khwājah Niẓāmuddīn Ahmad: (A History of India from the Early Musalmān Invasions to the Thirty-eight year of the Reign of Akbar)*, Vol. 2., trans. Brajendra Nath De, rev. and ed. by Baini Prashad (Delhi: Low Price Publications, 1992).

Ahmad, Makhdum Tasadduq, *Social Organization of Yusufzai Swat: A Study in Social Change* (Lahore: Panjab University Press, 1962).

Ahmad, Qeyamuddin, *The Wahabi Movement in India*, repr. (Islamabad: National Book Foundation, n.d.).

Ahmed, Akbar S., *Millennium and Charisma among Pathans: A Critical Essay in Social Anthropology* (London: Routhledge & Kegan Paul, 1976).

Ahmed, Sameeta, ed., *Cherishing Poetry in Wood & Stone: The Conservation of a Traditional Swat Valley Mosque* (Saidu Sharif, Swat: Swat Participatory Council, 2015).

Alberuni, Abu Rehan, *Alberuni's India: An Account of the Religion, Philosophy, Literature, Geography, Chronology, Astronomy, Customs, Laws and Astrology of India about A.D. 1030*, ed. with Notes and Indices by Edward C. Sachau, two vols. in one, Popular edn., 1st Indian repr. (Delhi: S. Chand & Co., 1964).

'Allāmī, Abū 'l-Fazl, *The Ā'īn-i Akbarī*, trans. from the original Persian by H.S. Jarrett, 2nd edn. corrected and further annotated by Jadunath Sarkar, Vol. 2, *A Gazetteer and Administrative Manual of Akbar's Empire and Past History of India*, 3rd edn., repr. from 2nd edn. of 1949 (New Delhi: Oriental Books Reprint Corporation, 1978).

'Allāmī, Abu 'l-Faẓl, *The Ā'īn-i Akbarī*, trans. from the original Persian by H. Blochmann, 2nd edn. rev. and ed. by D.C. Phillott, complete 3 Vols., repr. (Lahore: Sang-e-Meel Publications, 2004).

Antonini, C. Silvi and G. Stacul, *The Proto–Historic Graveyards of Swāt (Pakistan), Part 1: Description of Graves and Finds, Text* (Rome: Istituto Italiano per il Medio ed Estremo Oriente, 1972).

Babur, Zahirud-din Muhammad, *Babur-Nama*, trans. from the original Turki text by Annette S. Beveridge, repr. (Lahore: Sang-e-Meel Publications, 1987).

Baha, Lal, *N.-W.F.P. Administration Under British Rule, 1901–1919* (Islamabad: National Commission on Historical and Cultural Research, 1978).

Balala, Abdul Qayum, *The Charming Swat* (Lahore: Maqsood Publishers, [2000]).

Bakhshi, Nizam-ud Din Ahmad, *Tabakat-i Akbari*, trans. and eds. by H.M. Elliot and John Dowson, repr. (Lahore: Sang-e-Meel Publications, 2006).

Bagnera, Alessandra, *The Ghaznavid Mosque and the Islamic Settlement at Mt. Rāja Gīrā, Udegram*, with Foreword by A. Chiodi Cianfarani, Note by L.M. Olivieri (Lahore: Sang-e-Meel Publications, 2015).

Barger, Evert and Philip Wright, *Excavations in Swat and Explorations in the Oxus Territories of Afghanistan*, repr. (Delhi: Sri Satguru Publications, 1985).

Barth, Fredrik, *Indus and Swat Kohistan: An Ethnographic Survey* (Oslo: Forenede Trykkerier, 1956).

————, *Political Leadership among Swat Pathans* (London: The Athlone Press, 1959).

————, *The Last Wali of Swat: An Autobiography as told to Fredrik Barth*, repr. (Bangkok: White Orchid Press, 1995).

Barua, Beni Madhab, *Asoka and His Inscriptions*, 2nd edn. (Calcutta: New Age Publishers Ltd., 1955).

Basham, A.L., *The Wonder that Was India: A survey of the history and culture of the Indian sub-continent before the coming of the Muslims*, 3rd rev. edn., 1st paperback edn. (London: Sidgwick & Jackson, 1985).

Begam, Gul-Badan, *The History of Humāyūn (Humāyūn-Nāma)*, trans. with Introduction, Notes, Illustration and Bibliographical Appendix and Reproduced in the Persian from the only known MS. of the British Museum by Annette S. Beveridge, repr. (Delhi: Low Price Publications, 1994).

Bellew, H.W., *An Inquiry into the Ethnography of Afghanistan*, repr. (Karachi: Indus Publications, 1977).

————, *A General Report on the Yusufzais*, 3rd edn. (Lahore: Sang-e-Meel Publications, 1994).

————, *The Races of Afghanistan*, repr. (Lahore: Sh. Mubarak Ali, n.d.).

Bhattacharyya, Benoytosh, *The Indian Buddhist Iconography: Mainly Based on the Sādhanamālā and Other Cognate Tāntric Texts of Rituals*, with 283 Illustations (Humphrey Milford: Oxford University Press, 1924).

Biddulph, John, *Tribes of the Hindoo Koosh*, with Preface to the 1971 edition by Karl Gratzl, repr. (Lahore: Ali Kamran Publishers, 1986).

Bridget and Raymond Allchin, *The Rise of Civilization in India and Pakistan*, repr. (New Delhi: Cambridge University Press India Pvt. Ltd., 2008).

Bruce, Richard Isaac, *The Forward Policy and Its Results or Thirty-Five Years Work Amongst the Tribes on Our North-Western Frontier of India*, 2nd edn. in Pakistan (Quetta: M/S Nisa Traders, 1979).

Bokhari, Syed Abid, ed. and comp., *Through the Centuries: North-West Frontier Province* (Quetta: Mr. Reprints, 1993).

Burn, A.R., *Alexander the Great and the Hellenistic Empire*, 2nd edn. (London: English Universities Press, Ltd., 1951).

Callieri, Pierfrancesco, Luca Colliva, Marco Galli, Roberto Micheli, Emanuele Morigi, and Luca Maria Olivieri, eds., *Valleys of Memory: Ancient People, Sites and Images from Swat; 50 Years of the IsIAO Italian Archaeological Mission in Pakistan* (Rome: Istituto Italiano per l'Africa e l'Oriente, 2006).

Caroe, Olaf, *The Pathans, 550 B.C.–A.D. 1957*, repr. (Karachi: Oxford University Press, 1976).

Chandra, Moti, *Trade and Trade Routes in Ancient India* (New Delhi: Abhinav Publications, 1977).

Churchill, Winston S., *The Story of the Malakand Field Force: An Episode of Frontier War*, repr. (London: Leo Cooper, 2002).

[Cunningham, Alexander], *Cunningham's Ancient Geography of India*, ed. with Introduction and Notes by Surendranath Majumdar Sastri (Calcutta: Chuckervertty, Chatterjee & Co., Ltd., 1924).

Dani, Ahmad Hasan, *Peshawar: Historic City of the Frontier*, 2nd edn. (Lahore: Sang-e-Meel Publications, 1995).

Deambi, B.K. Koul, *History and Culture of Ancient Gandhāra and Western Himalayas from Sāradā Epigraphic Sources* (New Delhi: Ariana Publishing House, 1985).

Dupree, Louis, *Afghanistan* (Princeton: Princeton University Press, 1973).

Eade, Charles, ed., *Churchill: By his Contemporaries*, repr. (London: Hutchinson & Co. (Publisher) Ltd., 1954).

Elliott, J.G., *The Frontier, 1839–1947: The Story of the North-West Frontier of India*, with Preface by Olaf Caroe (London: Cassell & Company Ltd, 1968).

Elphinstone, Mountstuart, *An Account of the Kingdom of Caubul*, with New Introduction by Olaf Caroe, 2 Vols., repr. (Karachi: Oxford University Press, 1972).

Erskine, William, *A History of India Under Baber*, repr. (Karachi: Oxford University Press, 1974).

————, *A History of India under the Two First Sovereigns of the House of Taimur, Báber and Humáyun*, Vol. 1, repr. (Shannon: Irish University Press, 1972).

Faccenna, Domenico, *A Guide to the Excavations in Swat (Pakistan), 1956–1962* (Roma: Department of Archaeology of Pakistan and Istituto Italiano per il Medio ed Estremo Oriente, 1964).

_____, *Butkara I (Swāt, Pakistan), 1956–1962*, Part 1, *Text* (Rome: Istituto Italiano per il Medio ed Estremo Oriente, 1980).

_____, *Butkara I (Swāt, Pakistan), 1956–1962*, Part 2, *Text* (Rome: Istituto Italiano per il Medio ed Estremo Oriente, 1980).

_____, *Butkara I (Swāt, Pakistan), 1956–1962*, Part 3, *Text* (Rome: Istituto Italiano per il Medio ed Estremo Oriente, 1980).

_____, *Butkara I (Swāt, Pakistan), 1956–1962*, Part 4, *Text* (Rome: Istituto Italiano per il Medio ed Estremo Oriente, 1981).

_____, *Butkara I (Swāt, Pakistan), 1956–1962,* Part 5.1, *Plates* (Rome: Istituto Italiano per il Medio ed Estremo Oriente, 1981).

_____, *Butkara I (Swāt, Pakistan), 1956–1962*, Part 5.2, *General Plans* (Rome: Istituto Italiano per il Medio ed Estremo Oriente, 1981).

Faccenna, Domenico and Giorgio Gullini, *Reports on the Campaigns 1956–1958 in Swat (Pakistan)* (Roma: Istituto Italiano per il Medio ed Estremo Oriente, 1962).

Fagan, Brian M., *Archaeology: A Brief Introduction*, 4th edn. (New York: HarperCollins Publishers, 1991).

Fa Hian, *The Pilgrimage of Fa Hian: From the French Edition of the Foe Koue Ki of MM. Remusat, Klaproth, and Landresse with Additional Notes and Illustrations*, trans. and ed. by anonymous (Calcutta: The 'Bangabasi' Office, 1912).

Fa-Hein, *A Record of Buddhistic Kingdoms*, trans. and annotated by James Legge, repr. (New Delhi: Munshiram Manoharlal Publishers Pvt. Ltd., 1991).

Ferishta, Mohamed Kasim [Muhammad Qasim], *History of the Rise of the Mahomedan* [Muhammadan] *Power in India till the year A.D. 1612*, trans. from the original Persian of Mahomed Kasim Ferishta by John Briggs, 2 Vols., repr. (Lahore: Sang-e-Meel Publications, 1977).

Filigenzi, Anna, 'A Vajrayanic Theme in the Rock Sculpture of Swat', in Giovanni Verardi and Silvio Vita, eds., *Buddhist Asia 1: Papers from the First Conference of Buddhist Studies Held in Naples in May 2001* (Kyoto: Italian School of East Asian Studies, 2003).

Foucher, A., *Notes on the Ancient Geography of Gandhara (A Commentary on a Chapter of Hiuan Tsang)*, trans. by H. Hargreaves (Calcutta: Superintendent Government Printing, India, 1915).

Getty, Alice, *The Gods of Northern Buddhism: Their History, Iconography and Progressive Evolution through the Northern Buddhist Countries*, with A General Introduction on Buddhism, trans. from the French of J. Deniker, Illustrations from the Collection of Henry H. Getty (Oxford: At the Clarendon Press, 1928).

Gökalp, Zia, *Turkish Nationalism and Western Civilization: Selected Essays of Zia Gökalp*, trans. and ed. with Introduction by Niyazi Berkes (London: George Allen and Unwin Ltd., 1959).

Gokhale, B.G., *Ancient India: History and Culture*, 4th edn. (Bombay: Asia Publishing House, 1959).

Habib, Mohammad, *Sultan Mahmud of Ghaznin*, 2nd edn. (Delhi: S. Chand & Co., n.d.).

Haq, Syed Moinul, *The Great Revolution of 1857* (Karachi: Pakistan Historical Society, 1968).

Holdich, Thomas, *The Gates of India: Being an Historical Narrative*, 1st edn. published in Pakistan (Quetta: Gosha-e-Adab, 1977).

Holdich, T.H., *The Indian Borderland, 1880–1900*, repr. (Delhi: Gian Publishing House, 1987).

Hunter, W.W., *The Indian Musalmans*, 2nd edn. (London: Trübner and Company, 1872).

_____, *The Indian Musalmans*, repr. with Introduction by Bimal Prasad (New Delhi: Rupa & Co, 2002).

Ibbetson, Denzil, *Punjab Castes*, repr. (Delhi: Low Price Publications, 1993).

Jahangir, *Wakiat-i Jahangiri or Dwazda Sala Jahangiri (Twelve Years of Jahangir's Reign)*, trans. and ed. by H.M. Elliot and John Dowson, repr. (Lahore: Sang-e-Meel Publications, 2006).

Jairazbhoy, R.A., *Foreign Influence in Ancient India* (Bombay: Asia Publishing House, 1963).

Kakar, M. Hasan, *Afghanistan: A Study in International Political Development, 1880–1896* (Kabul, 1971).

Keay, John, *The Gilgit Game: The Explorers of the Western Himalayas, 1865–95*, repr. (Karachi: Oxford University Press, 1993).

Khalil, Hamesh, 'Hazrat Syed Ali Ghawas Tirmizi (Pir Baba)', in *Muslim Celebrities of Central Asia* (Peshawar: Area Study Centre (Central Asia), n.d.).

Khaliq, Fazal, *The Uddiyana Kingdom: The Forgotten Holy Land of Swat* (Mingora, Swat: Shoaib Sons Publishers & Booksellers, 2014).

Khan, Ahmad Nabi, *Buddhist Art and Architecture in Pakistan* (Islamabad: Ministry of Information and Broadcasting, Directorate of Research, Reference and Publication, Government of Pakistan, n.d.).

Khan, Ghani, *The Pathans: A Sketch*, repr. (Islamabad: Pushto Adabi Society (Regd), 1990).

Khan, M. Ashraf, *Buddhist Shrines in Swat* (Saidu Sharif: By the Author, Archaeological Museum, Saidu Sharif, Swat, 1993).

————, *Gandhara Sculptures in the Swat Museum* (Saidu Sharif: By the Author, Archaeological Museum, Saidu Sharif, Swat, 1993).

Khan, Makin, *Archaeological Museum Saidu Sharif, Swat: A Guide*, with Forward [Foreword] by Farzand Ali Durrani (Saidu Sharif: By the Author, Archaeological Museum, Saidu Sharif, Swat, 1997).

Khan, Muhammad Asif, *The Story of Swat as told by the Founder Miangul Abdul Wadud Badshah Sahib to Muhammad Asif Khan*, with Preface, Introduction and Appendices by Muhammad Asif Khan, and trans. Preface and trans. by Ashruf Altaf Husain (Printed by Ferozsons Ltd., Peshawar, 1963).

Khan, Munawwar, *Anglo-Afghan Relations, 1798–1878: A Chapter in the Great Game in Central Asia* (Peshawar: University Book Agency, n.d.).

Khan, Sāqi Mustʿad, *Maāsir-i-ʿĀlamgiri: A History of the Emperor Aurangzeb-ʿĀlamgir (reign 1658–1707 A.D.)*, trans. into English and annotated by Jadu-Nath Sarkar, repr. (Lahore: Suhail Academy, 1981).

Khan, Sultan Mahomed, ed., *The Life of Abdur Rahman: Amir of Afghanistan*, with New Introduction by M.E. Yapp, 2 Vols., repr. in Pakistan (Karachi: Oxford University Press, 1980).

Khattak, Khushal Khan, *Swat Nama of Khushal Khan Khattak*, edited and trans. in to English by Shakeel Ahmad, with Preface by Raj Wali Shah Khattak (Peshawar: Pashto Academy, n.d.).

Khattak, Muhammad Habibullah Khan, *Buner: The Forgotten Part of Ancient Uddiyana* (Karachi: By the Author, Department of Archaeology and Museums, Government of Pakistan, 1997).

Macmunn, George, *Afghanistan: From Darius to Amanullah* (London: G. Bell & Sons Ltd, 1929).

————, *The Romance of the Indian Frontiers*, 1st edn. published in Pakistan (Quetta: Nisa Traders, 1978).

Malleson, G.B., *Rulers of India: Akbar and the Rise of the Mughal Empire*, Pakistan repr. (Lahore: Islamic Book Service, 1979).

Majumdar, R.C., H.C. Raychaudhuri and Kalikinkar Datta, *An Advanced History of India*, repr. (Lahore: Famous Books, 1992).

Marsh, John, *The Young Winston Churchill* (London: World Distributors, 1962).

Marshall, John, *The Buddhist Art of Gandhāra: The Story of the Early School, Its Birth, Growth and Decline* (Cambridge: At the University Press, 1960).

McMahon, A.H. and A.D.G. Ramsay, *Report on the Tribes of Dir, Swat and Bajour* [Bajawar] *together with the Utman-Khel and Sam Ranizai*, repr., edited with Introduction by R.O. Christensen (Peshawar: Saeed Book Bank, 1981).

Mʿcrindle, J.W., *The Invasion of India by Alexander the Great: As Described by Arrian, Q Curtius, Diodoros, Plutarch and Justin*, with Introduction by J.W. Mʿcrindle, repr. (Karachi: Indus Publications, 1992).

Miller, Charles, *Khyber: British India's North West Frontier; The Story of an Imperial Migraine* (London: Macdonald and Jane's Publishers Limited, 1977).

Mills, H. Woosnam, *The Pathan Revolts in North West India*, repr. (Lahore: Sang-e-Meel Publications, 1996).

Mishra, Yogendra, *The Hindu Sahis of Afghanistan and the Punjab, A.D. 865–1026* (Patna: Vaishali Bhavan, 1972).

Mookerji, Radhakumud, *Chandragupta Maurya and His Times*. Facts of publication have been torn out.

————, *Asoka*, repr. (Delhi: Motilal Banarsidass, 1986).

Narain, A.K., *The Indo-Greeks*, repr. (Oxford: At the Clarendon Press, 1962).

Nāzim, Muḥammad, *The Life and Times of Sulṭān Maḥmud of Ghazna*, with Foreword by Thomas Arnold (Cambridge: At the University Press, 1931).

Nevill, H.L., *Campaigns on the North-West Frontier*, repr. (Lahore: Sang-e-Meel Publications, 2003).

Nichols, Robert, *Settling the Frontier: Land, Law, and Society in the Peshawar Valley, 1500–1900* (Karachi: Oxford University Press, 2001).

Obhrai, Diwan Chand, *The Evolution of North-West Frontier Province: Being a Survey of the History and Constitutional Development of N.-W. F. Province, in India*, repr. (Peshawar: Saeed Book Bank, n.d.).

Olivieri, Luca M. and Elisa Iori, 'Early-historic Data from the 2016 Excavation Campaigns at the Urban Site of Barikot, Swat (Pakistan): A Shifting Perspective', in A. Hardy and L. Greaves, eds., *South Asian Art and Archaeology* (New Delhi: Dev Publishers & Distributers, 2016), 19–43.

Powell-Price, J.C., *A History of India* (London: Thomas Nelson and Sons Ltd, 1955).

Qadir, Altaf, *Sayyid Ahmad Barailvi: His Movement and Legacy from the Pukhtun Perspective* (New Delhi: SAGE Publications India Pvt Ltd, 2015).

Qasmi, Sayyed Mohammad Abdul Ghafoor, *The History of Swat* (Printed by D.C. Anand & Sons, Peshawar, 1940).

Qureshi, I.H., ed., *A Short History of Pakistan*, 2nd edn. (Karachi: University of Karachi, 1984).

Raverty, Henry George, *Notes on Afghanistan and Baluchistan*, 2 Vols., 2nd edn. in Pakistan (Quetta: Nisa Traders, 1982).

Rehman, Abdur, *The Last Two Dynasties of the Śāhis (An analysis of their history, archaeology, coinage and palaeography)* (Islamabad: Director Centre for the Study of the Civilizations of Central Asia, Quaid-i-Azam University, 1979).

Richards, D.S., *The Savage Frontier: A History of the Anglo-Afghan Wars* (London: Macmillan London Limited, 1990).

Rhys-Davids, T.W., *Buddhist India*, 3rd Indian edn. (Calcutta: Susil Gupta (India) Ltd., 1957).

Roberts, Lord, *Forty-One Years in India: From Subaltern to Commander-in-Chief*, New edition in One Volume, with Forty-Four Illustrations (London: Macmillan and Co. Limited, 1898).

Saeed-ur-Rahman, ed., *Archaeological Reconnaissance in Gandhara* (Karachi: Department of Archaeology and Museums, Pakistan, 1996).

Sardar, Badshah, *Buddhist Rock Carvings in the Swāt Valley* (Islamabad: By the Author, 2005).

Sarkar, Jadunath, *History of Aurangzeb*, Vol. 3, *Northern India, 1658–1681*, new edn., repr. (Karachi: South Asian Publishers, 1981).

Sastri, K.A. Nilakanta, ed., *A Comprehensive History of India*, Vol. 2, *The Mauryas & Satavahanas, 325 B.C.–A.D. 300* (Bombay: Orient Longmans, 1957).

Savill, Agnes, *Alexander the Great and His Time*, 3rd edn. (London: Barrie and Rockliff, 1959).

Scott, George B., *Afghanistan and Pathan: A Sketch* (London: The Mitre Press, 1929).

Shah, Sayyid Mubarak, (Kotwal of Delhi), *The Kotwal's Diary (An account of Delhi during the War of Independence 1857)*, English trans. R.M. Edwards, ed. by Ansar Zahid Khan (Karachi: Pakistan Historical Society, 1994).

[Shui-ching-chu], *Northern India According to the Shui-ching-chu*, English trans. L. Petech, Rome Oriental Series 2 (Roma: Istituto Italiano per il Medio ed Estremo Oriente, 1950).

Smith, Vincent A., *The Early History of India: From 600 B.C. to the Muhammadan Conquest, Including the Invasion of Alexander the Great*, 4th edn., rev. by S.M. Edwardes, repr. (Oxford: At the Clarendon Press, 1957).

———, *Asoka: The Buddhist Emperor of India*, repr. (Delhi: S. Chand & Co., 1957).

———, *Akbar: The Great Mogul [Mughul], 1542–1605*, 2nd edn., revised Indian repr. (Delhi: S. Chand & Co., 1958).

———, *The Oxford History of India*, 3rd edn., ed. Percival Spear, Part I revised by Mortimer Wheeler and A.L. Basham, Part II revised by J.B. Harrison, and Part III rewritten by Percival Spear (Oxford: At the Clarendon Press, 1958).

Singh, Ganda, *Ahmad Shah Durrani: Father of Modern Afghanistan* (Bombay: Asia Publishing House, 1959).

Spain, James W., *Pathans of the Latter Day* (Karachi: Oxford University Press, 1995).

Stacul, Giorgio, *Prehistoric and Protohistoric Swāt, Pakistan (c. 3000–1400 B.C.)*, with Foreword by Karl Jettmar, and Contributions by Bruno Compagnoni and Lorenzo Costantini (Rome: Istituto Italiano per il Medio ed Estremo Oriente, 1987).

Stein, Aurel, *On Alexander's Track to the Indus: Personal Narrative of Explorations on the North-West Frontier of India*, repr. (Karachi: Indus Publications, 1995).

Sultan-i-Rome, 'Merger of Swat State with Pakistan: Causes and Effects', *MARC Occasional Papers No. 14* (Geneva: Modern Asia Research Centre, 1999).

————, *Forestry in the Princely State of Swat and Kalam (North-West Pakistan): A Historical Perspective on Norms and Practices*, IP6 Working Paper No.6 (Zurich: Swiss National Centre of Competence in Research (NCCR) North-South, 2005).

————, *Swat State (1915–1969): From Genesis to Merger: An Analysis of Political, Administrative, Socio-Political, and Economic Developments* (Karachi: Oxford University Press, 2008).

————, 'The War of Independence and Swat' in *Proceedings of the Two-Day International Conference on 150th Anniversary of the War of Independence 1857* (Peshawar: Department of History, University of Peshawar, 2008). Also in *Mutiny at the Margins: New Perspectives on the Indian Uprising of 1857*, Vol. 1, *Anticipations and Experiences in the Locality*, ed. Crispin Bates (New Delhi: SAGE Publications India Pvt. Ltd, 2013).

————, *The North-West Frontier (Khyber Pakhtunkhwa): Essays on History* (Karachi: Oxford University Press, 2013).

————, ''Abd al-Ghafūr, the Akhūnd of Swāt', in *The Encyclopaedia of Islam*, 3rd edn., Kate Fleet et al., eds., Vol. 1 (Leiden: Brill, 2015).

————, *Land and Forest Governance in Swat: Transition from Tribal System to State to Pakistan* (Karachi: Oxford University Press, 2016).

Tarn, W.W., *The Greeks in Bactria & India*, repr. (Cambridge: At the University Press, 1966).

Thapar, Romila, *Aśoka and the Decline of the Mauryas*, 2nd edn., 6th impression (Delhi: Oxford University Press, 1985).

Thomson, H.C., *The Chitral Campaign: A Narrative of Events in Chitral, Swat, and Bajour*, repr. (Lahore: Sang-e-Meel Publications, 1981).

Trotter, Lionel J., *The Life of John Nicholson: Soldier and Administrator based on Private and Hitherto Unpublished Documents*, 1st edn. in Pakistan (Karachi: Karimsons, Jamshed Road, 1978).

[Tsiang, Hiuen], *Chinese Accounts of India: Translated from the Chinese of Hiuen Tsiang*, trans. and annotated by Samuel Beal, Vol. 2, new edn. (Calcutta: Susil Gupta (India) Limited, 1958).

Tucci, Giuseppe, *On Swat. Historical and Archaeological Notes*, eds. P. Callieri and A. Filigenzi (Rome, 1997).

————, *Travels of Tibetan Pilgrims in the Swat Valley* (Calcutta: The Greater Indian Society, 1940).

————, *On Swāt. Historical and Archaeological Notes*, with Introduction by Domenico Faccenna, eds. P. Callieri and A. Filigenzi, repr. of the original 1997 edn. with Preface by M. Ashraf Khan (Islamabad: Taxila Institute of Asian Civilizations, 2013).

Vidale, Massimo, Roberto Micheli and Luca M. Olivieri, eds., *Excavations at the Protohistoric Graveyards of Gogdara and Udegram* (Lahore: Sang-e-Meel Publications, 2016).

Warburton, Robert, *Eighteen Years in the Khyber, 1879–1898*, repr., 3rd impression (Karachi: Oxford University Press, 1975).

Wheeler, J. Talboys, *A Short History of India and of the Frontier States of Afghanistan, Nipal, and Burma*, with Maps and Tables (London: Macmillan and Co., 1884).

Woodcock, George, *The Greeks in India* (London: Faber and Faber Ltd, 1966).

Wylly, H.C., *The Borderland: The Country of the Pathans*, repr. (Karachi: Indus Publications, 1998).

————, *From the Black Mountain to Waziristan*, with Introduction by Horace L. Smith Dorrien, repr. (Lahore: Sang-e-Meel Publications, 2003).

Yaqubi, Himayatullah, *Mughal-Afghan Relations in South Asia: History and Developments* (Islamabad: National Institute of Historical and Cultural Research, 2015).

Younghusband, G.J. and Francis Younghusband, *The Relief of Chitral*, repr. (Rawalpindi: English Book House, 1976).

Yunus, Mohammad, *Frontier Speaks*, with Foreword by Jawahar Lal [Jawaharlal] Nehru, Preface by Khan Abdul Ghaffar Khan, and Maps by Sardar Abdur Rauf (Lahore: Minerva Book Shop, Anarkali, n.d.).

Italian Archaeological Mission, (IsMEO) Pakistan, Swāt, 1956–1981: Documentary Exhibition (Rome: Istituto Italiano per il Medio ed Estremo Oriente, 1982).

The Cambridge History of India, Vol. 1, *Ancient India*, ed. E.J. Rapson, 1st Indian repr. (Delhi: S. Chand & Co., 1955).

The Risings on the North-West Frontier, Compiled from the Special Correspondence of the "Pioneer" (Allahabad: The Pioneer Press, 1898).

Pashto

Asar, Abdul Halim, *Swat da Tarikh pah Ranra kay* (Bajawar: Darul Ishaat Bajawar, n.d.).

Barq, Sadullah Jan, *Da Pukhtanu Asal Nasal*, Vol. 3 (Peshawar: University Book Agency, 2010).

Darwizah, Akhun, *Makhzan* (Pashto/Persian), with *Muqadimah* by Sayyad Muhammad Taqwimul Haq Kaka Khail, *Pishlafz* by Muhammad Nawaz Tair, 2nd Impression (Peshawar: Pukhtu Academy, 1987).

Hamdani, Raza, comp. and trans., *Razmiyah Dastanayn*, Pashto with Urdu trans. Raza Hamdani (Islamabad: Lok Virsay ka Qaumi Idarah, 1981).

Jan, Nur Muhammad Shah Ghubah, *Manzum Tarikh-i Swat* (verse) (Printed by Ahmad Printing Press, Mingawarah, Swat, n.d.).

Kaka Khail, Sayyad Bahadar Shah Zafar, *Pukhtanah da Tarikh pah Ranra kay* (Peshawar: University Book Agency, n.d.).

Khalil, Hamesh, comp., *Da Charbaytay Pakhwani Shairan* (Peshawar: Pukhtu Academy, 2008).

————, comp. and trans., *Jangi Charbaytay*, Pashto with Urdu trans. Hamesh Khalil (Peshawar: Pashto Academy, 2008).

Khan, Muhammad Asif, *Tarikh-i Riyasat-i Swat wa Sawanih-i Hayat Baniy-i Riyasat-i Swat Hazrat Miangul Gul Shahzadah Abdul Wadud Khan Badshah Sahib*, with *Dibachah, Hisah Awal, Saluramah Hisah,* and *Hisah Pinzamah* by Muhammad Asif Khan (Printed by Ferozsons Ltd., Peshawar [1958]).

Khan, Muhammad Nawaz, *Tarikhi Tapay* (Peshawar: University Book Agency, 2004).

Khattak, Afzal Khan, *Tarikh Murasa: Muqabilah, Tashih aw Nutunah lah* Dost Muhammad Khan Kamil Momand (Peshawar: University Book Agency, 2006).

Khattak, Khushal Khan, *Swat Namah da Khushal Khan Khattak*, with *Muqadimah, Tahqiq aw Samun* by Hamesh Khalil (Akurah Khattak: Markazi Khushal Adabi wa Saqafati Jargah Regd., 1986).

————, *Kulyat-i Khushal Khan Khattak*, with *Da Khushal pah Haqlah* by Sher Shah Tarkhawi, Vol. 1, *Ghazliyat* (Peshawar: Azeem Publishing House, n.d.).

————, *Kulyat-i Khushal Khan Khattak*, Vol. 2, *Qasaid, Rubaiyat, Qitat aw Mutafariqat* (Peshawar: Azeem Publishing House, n.d.).

Nasar, Nasrullah Khan, *Swat* (Peshawar: Azeem Publishing House, 1963).

————, *Akhund Sahib Swat*, 2nd edn. (Peshawar: Dar-ul-Tasnif, 1964).

Qasmay, Sayyed Abdul Ghafoor, *Tarikh-i Riyasat-i Swat* (Printed by Hamidia Press, Peshawar, n.d.).

Rahim, Rahim Shah, *Swat Namah Jawab Namah* (Mingawarah, Swat: Shoaib Sons Publishers and Booksellers, 2006).

Sayal, Khwajah Muhammad, *Khushalyat aw Haqayaq (Intiqadi Jaaj)* (n.p.: By the Author, 2006).

Shah, Pir Muazam, *Tawarikh Hafiz Rahmat Khani*, with *Dibachah* by Muhammad Nawaz Tair, 2nd impression (Peshawar: Pukhtu Academy, 1987).

Shaheen, Muhammad Parwaish, *Da Swat Gwalunah* (Mingawarah, Swat: Shoaib Sons Publishers, Booksellers, 1988).

Sultan-i-Rome, *Tapay* (Mingawarah, Swat: Shoaib Sons Publishers and Booksellers, 2018).

Swati, Saranzeb, *Tarikh Riyasat-i Swat* (Peshawar: Azeem Publishing House, 1984).

Yusufzay, Abasin, comp. and ed., *Da Pukhtunkhwa Bani: Malak Ahmad Baba (1470 Iswi–1535 Iswi)* (Mingawarah, Swat: Shoaib Sons Publishers & Booksellers, 2016).

Zaibsar, Taj Muhammad Khan, *Uruj-i Afghan* (verse), 2 Vols. (Riyasat-i Swat, 1360 AH/1361 AH).

Persian

Darwizah, Akhun, *Tazkiratul Abrar-i wal Ashrar* (Peshawar: Islami Kutub Khanah, n.d.).

Urdu

Ahmad, Qeyamuddin, *Hindustan mayn Wahabi Tahrik*, Urdu trans. Muhammad Muslim Azeemabadi, 2nd edn. (Karachi: Nafees Academy, 1976).

Akhtar, Muhammad, *Tajak Swati wa Mumlikat-i Gabar Tarikh kay Aayinah mayn* (Abbottabad: Sarhad Urdu Academy, 2002).

Alberuni, Abu Rehan, *Hindu Dharam, Hazar Bars Pihlay* (Lahore: Nigarishat, 2000).

————, *Kitabul Hind*, Urdu trans. Sayyad Asghar Ali, rev. by Sayyad Atta Hussain (Lahore: Al-Faisal Nashran, 2008).

Azad, Muhammad Hussain, *Darbar-i Akbari*. Facts of publication have been torn out.

Babur, Zahiruddin, *Tuzuk-i Baburi*, Urdu trans. Rashid Akhtar Nadwi (Lahore: Sang-e-Meel Publications, n.d.).

Babur, Zahiruddin Muhammad, *Waqay-i Babur*, Urdu trans. Yunus Jafri, from the Persian trans. of Abdur Rahim Khan-i Khanan, with Notes and Annotation by Hasan Beg (Krekardi, Scotland: Shahar Banu Publishers, 2007).

Balala, Abdul Qayum, *Dastan-i Swat* (Kabal, Swat: Jan Kitab Koor, 2010).

Barikuti, Sher Afzal Khan, *Pir Baba* (Mingawarah, Swat: Shoaib Sons Publishers and Booksellers, 1999).

Danishwar, Mahmud, *Kafiristan aur Chitral-Dir-Swat ki Sayahat*, Urdu trans. Khalil Ahmad, 2nd revised edn. (Lahore: West Pak Publishing Company Limited, 1953).

Ghufran, Mirza Muhammad and Mirza Ghulam Murtaza, *Nayi Tarikh-i Chitral*, Urdu trans. Wazir Ali Shah (Printers: Public Art Press, Peshawar, 1962).

Harwi, Khwajah Nimatullah, *Tarikh Khan Jahani wa Makhzan-i Afghani*, Urdu trans. Muhammad Bashir Husain (Lahore: Markazi Urdu Board, 1978).

Hazrawi, Muhammad Yusuf, *Sir-i Swat: Hisah Awal* (Calcutta: Manager Aksirat-i Hind Dawa Khanah, [1945]).

Hunter, W.W., *Hamaray Hindustani Musalman*, Urdu trans. Sadiq Hussain, repr. (Lahore: Makki Darul Kutub, 1997).

————, *Hamaray Hindustani Musalman*, Urdu trans. Sadiq Hussain (Lahore: Qaumi Kutub Khanah, n.d.).

Jahangir, *Tuzuk-i Jahangiri*, Urdu trans. Salim Wahid Salim (Lahore: Majlis Taraqi Adab, 1960).

Kanbuh, Muhammad Salih, *Shahjahan Namah (Amal-i Salih)*, Urdu trans. Nazir Hassan Zaidi, Vols. 2 and 3 (Lahore: Markazi Urdu Board, 1974).

Khaliq, Fazal, *Udhyana: Swat ki Jannat-i Gumgushtah*, 2nd edn. (Mingawarah, Swat: Shoaib Sons Publishers & Booksellers, 2018).

Khan, Muhammad Asif, *Tarikh Riyasat-i Swat wa Sawanih-i Hayat Bani Riyasat-i Swat Miangul Abdul Wadud*, 2nd edn. (Mingawarah, Swat: Shoaib Sons Publishers and Booksellers, 2001).

Khan, Muhammad Irshad, *Tarikh-i Hazarah: Turku ka Ahad* (Lahore: Tufail Art Printers, 1976).

Khan, Roshan, *Malikah-i Swat* (Karachi: Roshan Khan and Company, 1983).

Khan, Khan Roshan, *Yusufzai Qaum ki Sarguzasht* (Karachi: Roshan Khan and Company, 1986).

Khan, Muhammad Saqi Mustaid, *Maasir-i Alamgiri*, Urdu trans. Muhammad Fida Ali Talib (Karachi: Nafees Academy, 1962).

Kiwhur, Nawshirawan, *Turwal kay Qabail* (Peshawar: Gandhara Hindku Academy, 2017).

Mehr, Ghulam Rasul, *Sayyad Ahmad Shahid*, 3rd edn. (Lahore: Shaikh Ghulam Ali and Sons, 1981).

————, *Sarguzasht-i Mujahidin* (Lahore: Shaikh Ghulam Ali and Sons Publishers, n.d.).

————, *Jamat-i Mujahidin* (Lahore: Shaikh Ghulam Ali and Sons Limited, n.d.).

————, *1857 Iswi: Pak wa Hind ki Pihli Jang-i Azadi* (Lahore: Shaikh Ghulam Ali and Sons (Private) Limited, Publishers, n.d.).

Mohmand, Dost Muhammad Khan Kamil, *Khushal Khan Khattak: Sawanih Hayat aur Adabi Aasar par Tabsirah*, 2nd edn. (Peshawar: Shaheen Books, 2006).

Qadiri, Muhammad Amir Shah, *Tazkirah Ulama wa Mashaikh-i Sarhad*, Vol. 1 (Peshawar: Maktabah al-Hasan, n.d.).

Qasmi, Sayyed Abdul Ghafoor, *Hidyah Wadudiyah yani Sawanih Hayat Ala Hazrat Badshah Abdul Wadud Khan Khuldullah Mulkahu Hukamran Riyasat-i Yusufzai Swat wa Mutaliqat* (Printed by Sawdagar Press Baraili, n.d.).

Qasuri, Muhammad Ali, *Mushahidat-i Kabul wa Yaghistan* (Karachi: Anjuman Taraqi Urdu, n.d.).

Rahi, Fazle Rabbi, *Swat Tarikh kay Ayinay mayn*, 2nd edn. (Mingawarah, Swat: Shoaib Sons Publishers, Booksellers, 1997).

————, *Riyasat-i Swat: Tarikh ka Aik Warq* (Mingawarah, Swat: Shoaib Sons Publishers and Booksellers, 2000).

————, *Swat: Sayahu ki Jannat* (Mingawarah, Swat: Shoaib Sons Publishers and Booksellers, 2000).

Rashid, Abdur, *Islami Tasawuf aur Sufyay-i Sarhad: Daswayn Sadi Hijri mayn Ilmi aur Adabi Khidmat* (Islamabad: Tasawuf Foundation, 1988).

Sabir, Muhammad Shafi, *Tarikh Subah Sarhad* (Peshawar: University Book Agency, 1986).

Sagar, Muhammad Zaman, *Kalam Kuhistan ki Riwayati Tarikh: Gawri Qabail aur un ka Nizam-i Muashirat (Hisah Awal–Kalam Khas)* (Peshawar: Frontier Language Institute, 2007).

Siraj, Minhaj, *Tabaqat-i Nasari, Tartib wa Tahshiyah* by Abdul Hai Habibi, Urdu trans. *wa Izafah* by Ghulam Rasul Mehr, revised by Sayyad Husam-ud-Din Rashidi, Vol. 2, 2nd impression (Lahore: Urdu Science Board, 1985).

Sithanawi, Sayyad Abdul Jabbar Shah, *Kitab al-Ibra: Subah Sarhad wa Afghanistan ki Char Sau Salah Tarikh; 1500 Iswi ta 1900 Iswi*, Vol. 1 (Islamabad: Poorab Academy, 2011).

Swati, Sirajuddin, *Sarguzasht-i Swat* (Lahore: Al-Hamra Academy, 1970).

Yusufi, Allah Bakhsh, *Yusufzai* (Karachi: Muhammad Ali Educational Society, 1960).

Waqay-i Sayyad Ahmad Shahid, Jama wa Tartib Hasb-i Irshad Nawab Muhammad Wazir Khan Bahadar, with *Muqadimah* by Muhammad Rabi Hasni Nadwi (Lahore: Sayyad Ahmad Shahid Academy, 2007).

JOURNAL ARTICLES

English

Agrawala, R.C., 'An Interesting Relief from the Swat Valley (I)', *East and West* (Rome), 16/1–2 (March–June 1966), 82–3.

Agrawala, R.C. and Maurizio Taddei, 'An Interesting Relief from the Swat Valley', *East and West* (Rome), 16/1–2 (March–June 1966), 82–8, Stable URL: http://www.jstor.org/stable/29754986, accessed: 30/10/2011.

Ansari, Arif Ali, 'The North-West Frontier Policy of the Mughuls under Akbar', *Journal of the Pakistan Historical Society* (Karachi), 4/1 (January 1956), 36–63.

Antonini, Chiara Silvi, 'Swāt and Central Asia', *East and West* (Rome), 19/1–2 (March–June 1969), 100–15.

————, 'More about Swāt and Central Asia', *East and West* (Rome), 23/3–4 (September–December 1973), 235–44, Stable URL: http://www.jstor.org/stable/29755885, accessed: 30/10/2011.

Azzaroli, Augusto, 'Two Proto-historic Horse Skeletons from Swāt, Pakistan', *East and West* (Rome), 25/3–4 (September–December 1975), 353–7, Stable URL: http://www.jstor.org/stable/29756092, accessed: 30/10/2011.

Bagnera, Alessandra, 'Preliminary Note on the Islamic Settlement of Udegram, Swat: The Islamic Graveyard (11th–13th century A.D.)', *East and West* (Rome), 56/1–3 (September 2006), 205–28, Stable URL: http://www.jstor.org/stable/29757687, accessed: 30/10/2011.

————, 'Islamic Udegram. Activities and new perspectives', *Journal of Asian Civilizations* (Islamabad), 34/1 (July 2011), 224–41.

————, 'The site of Mount Rāja Gīrā, Udegram: Archaeological evidences and new Hypotheses', with Note by Luca Maria Olivieri, *Frontier Archaeology* (Peshawar), 7 (2016), 137–61.

Bagnera, A., P. Callieri, L. Colliva, A. Filigenzi, M. Galli, R. Micheli, F. Noci, L.M. Olivieri, I.E. Scerrato, P. Spagnesi, and M. Vidale, 'Italian Archaeological Activities in Swat: An Introduction', *Journal of Asian Civilizations* (Islamabad), 34/1 (July 2011), 48–80.

Banerjee, Anukul Chandra, 'Expansion of Buddhism in Tibet', *Journal of the Asiatic Society of Pakistan* (Dacca), 10/2 (1965), 17–28.

Barth, Fredrik, 'Ecologic Relationships of Ethnic Groups in Swat, North Pakistan', *American Anthropologist*, 58/6 (December 1956), 1079–89.

Bernard, Paul, 'Hellenistic Arachosia: A Greek Melting Pot in Action', *East and West* (Rome), 55/1–4 (December 2005), 13–34, Stable URL:http://www.jstor.org/stable/29757633; accessed: 04/11/2013.

Burton-Page, John, 'Muslim Graves of the "Lesser Tradition": Gilgit, Puniāl, Swāt, Yūsufzai', *Journal of the Royal Asiatic Society of Great Britain and Ireland* (London), No. 2 (1986), 248–54, Stable URL: http://www.jstor.org/stable/25211996, accessed: 30/10/2011.

Callieri, Peirfrancesco, Luca Colliva, Roberto Micheli, Abdul Nasir, Luca Maria Olivieri, and Maurizio Taddei, 'Bīr-koṭ-ghwaṇḍai, Swat, Pakistan. 1998–1999 Excavation Report', *East and West* (Rome), 50/1–4 (2000), 191–226, Stable URL: http://www.jstor.org/stable/29757454, accessed: 30/10/2011.

Caloi, Lucia and Bruno Compagnoni, 'Bone Remains from Loebanr III (Swāt, Pakistan)', *East and West* (Rome), 26/1–2 (March–June 1976), 31–43, Stable URL: http://www.jstor.org/stable/29756225, accessed: 30/10/2011.

Colliva, Luca, 'The Excavation of the Archaeological Site of Barikot (Bīr-koṭ-ghwaṇḍai) and its Chronological Sequence', *Journal of Asian Civilizations* (Islamabad), 34/1 (July 2011), 152–85.

Court, M., 'Conjectures on the March of Alexander', *The Asiatic Journal and Monthly Register for British and Foreign India, China, and Australia* (London), New Series, 23/89 (May–August 1937), 46–51.

Dani, Ahmad Hasan, 'The Pathan Society: A Case Study of a Traditional Society, Its Disintegration and the Process of Modernization', *Journal of Central Asia*, 1/2 (December 1978), 47–67.

Deane, H.A., 'Note on Udyāna and Gandhāra', *Journal of the Royal Asiatic Society of Great Britain and Ireland* (October 1896), 655–75, Stable URL: http://www.jstor.org/stable/25207806, accessed: 16/05/2011.

Faccena, Claudio, Sergio Lorenzoni, Luca M. Olivieri, and Eleonora Zanettin Lorenzoni, 'Geo-Archaeology of the Swāt Valley (NWFP, Pakistan) in the Chārbāgh-Barikoṭ Stretch: Preliminary Note', *East and West* (Rome), 43/1–4 (December 1993), 257–70, Stable URL: http://www.jstor.org/stable/29757095, accessed: 30/10/2011.

Faccena, Domenico, 'At the Origin of Gandharan Art. The Contribution of the IsIAO Italian Archaeological Mission in the Swat Valley Pakistan…; *The Butkara I Complex: Origins and Development*', *Ancient Civilizations from Scythia to Siberia* (Leiden), 9/3–4 (2003), 277–86.

Faccena, Domenico, Pierfrancesco Callieri, and Anna Filigenzi, 'Pakistan–1: Excavations and Researches in the Swat Valley', *East and West* (Rome), 34/4 (December 1984), 483–500, Stable URL: http://www.jstor.org/stable/29758164, accessed: 30/10/2011.

Faccena, Domenico, Robert Göbl, and Mohammad Ashraf Khan, 'A Report on the Recent Discovery of a Deposit of Coins in the Sacred Area of Butkara I (Swat, Pakistan)', *East and West* (Rome), 43/1–4 (December 1993), 95–114, Stable URL: http://www.jstor.org/stable/29757085, accessed: 30/10/2011.

Filigenzi, Anna, 'Wisdom and Compassion: Concept and Iconography of Avalokiteśvara/ Padmapāṇi', *Annali* (Napoli), 60–61 (2000–2001), 247–64.

————, 'Sūrya, the Solar Kingship and the Turki Śāhis: New Acquisitions on the Cultural History of Swat', *East and West* (Rome), 56/1–3 (September 2006), 195–203, Stable URL: http://www.jstor.org/stable/29757686, accessed: 30/10/2011.

————, 'Post-Gandharan Swat. Late Buddhist rock sculptures and Turki Śāhis' religious centres', *Journal of Asian Civilizations* (Islamabad), 34/1 (July 2011), 186–202.

Fussman, Gérard, 'Southern Bactria and Northern India before Islam: A Review of Archaeological Reports', *Journal of the American Oriental Society*, 116/2 (April–June, 1996), 243–59, Stable URL: http://www.jstor.org/stable/605700, accessed: 30/10/2011.

Genna, Giuseppe, 'First Anthropological Investigations of the Skeletal Remains of the Necropolis of Butkara II (Swat, West Pakistan)', *East and West* (Rome), 15/3–4 (September–December 1965), 161–7, Stable URL: http://www.jstor.org/stable/29754918, accessed: 30/10/2011.

Giunta, Roberta, 'A Selection of Islamic Coins from the Excavations of Udegram, Swat', *East and West* (Rome), 56/1–3 (September 2006), 237–62, Stable URL: http://www.jstor.org/stable/29757689, accessed: 30/10/2011.

Gnoli, Gherardo, 'The Tyche and the Dioscuri in Ancient Sculptures from the Valley of Swat (New Documents for the Study of the Art of Gandhāra)', *East and West* (Rome), 14/1–2 (March–June 1963), 29–37, Stable URL: http://www.jstor.org/stable/29754698, accessed: 30/10/2011.

Gullini, Giorgio, 'Marginal note on the excavations at the Castle of Udegram: restoration problems', *East and West* (Rome), 9/4 (December 1958), 329–48.

Gupta, Chāru Chandra Dāsa, 'A Short Note on the Swat Relic Vase Inscription', *Journal of the Royal Asiatic Society of Great Britain and Ireland*, 2 (April 1933), 403–5, Stable URL: http://www.jstor.org/stable/25194776, accessed: 30/10/2011.

Iori, Elisa, 'The Early-Historic Urban Area at Mingora in the light of Domenico Faccenna's Excavations at Barama – I (Swat)', With Note by Luca M. Olivieri, *Frontier Archaeology* (Peshawar), 7 (2016), 99–112.

Iori, Elisa, Luca M. Olivieri, and Amanullah Afridi, 'Urban Defenses at Bīr-koṭ-ghwaṇḍai, Swat (Pakistan). The Saka-Partian Phases: Data from the 2015 Excavation Campaign', *Pakistan Heritage* (Mansehra), 7 (2015), 73–94.

Khan, A. Nazir, Abdul Nisar [Nasir], Luca M. Olivieri, and Matteo Vitali, 'The Recent Discovery of Cave Paintings in Swat: A Preliminary Note', *East and West* (Rome), 45/1–4 (December 1995), 333–53, Stable URL: http://www.jstor.org/stable/29757220, accessed: 30/10/2011.

Khan, M. Ashraf and Tahira Saeed, 'A Newly Discovered Stone Relic-Casket from Shnaisha-Gumbat in Swat', *Lahore Museum Bulletin* (Lahore), 12/2 (1999), 43–8.

Khan, Muhammad Nazir, 'A Ghaznavid Historical Inscription from Udegrām, Swāt', *East and West* (Rome), 35/1–3 (September 1985), 153–66, Stable URL: http://www.jstor.org/stable/29756717, accessed: 30/10/2011.

Khan, Munawwar, 'Swat in History', *Peshawar University Review* (Peshawar), 1/1 (1973), 51–63.

———, 'Swat: Second Instalment', *Peshawar University Review* (Peshawar), 1/1 (1974–75), 57–77.

Khan, Rafiullah, 'Pre-Buddhism Swat: A Historical Description', *Journal of Asian Civilizations* (Islamabad), 27/2 (December 2004), 1–12.

———, 'Visual iconicity along the ancient routes: Buddhist heritage of the Malam-jabba valley (Swat)', *Journal of Asian Civilizations* (Islamabad), 34/1 (July 2011), 203–23.

Khurshid, 'Sandākai Mullah: Career and Role in the Formation of Swat State, Pakistan', *Journal of the Pakistan Historical Society* (Karachi), 47/2 (April–June 1999), 77–81.

Krishan, Y., 'Was Gandhāra Art a Product of Mahāyāna Buddhism?', *Journal of the Royal Asiatic Society of Great Britain and Ireland*, 3–4 (October 1964), 104–19, Stable URL: http://www.jstor.org/stable/25202761, accessed: 31/10/2011.

Law, Bimala Churn, 'Śākala: an Ancient Indian City', *East and West* (Rome), 19/3–4 (September–December 1969), 401–9, Stable URL: http://www.jstor.org/stable/29755450; accessed: 08/11/2013.

Lewis, C.G., 'Records of the Survey of India. Vol. XXV. Surveys in Swat, Chitral, and Gilgit, and Neighbouring Territories. 1925 to 1931', Review by K.M. *The Geographical Journal*, 84/5 (November 1943), 447–9, Stable URL: http://www.jstor.org/stable/1786943, accessed: 30/10/2011.

Lüders, H., 'A Buddhist Inscription in Swat', *Journal of the Royal Asiatic Society of Great Britain and Ireland*, (July 1901), 575–6, Stable URL: http://www.jstor.org/stable/25208332, accessed: 30/10/2011.

Manna, Gabriella, 'Some Observations on the Pottery from the Islamic Settlement of Udegram, Swat', *East and West* (Rome), 56/1–3 (September 2006), 229–36, Stable URL: http://www.jstor.org/stable/29757688, accessed: 30/10/2011.

Morant, G.M., 'A Contribution to the Physical Anthropology of the Swat and Hunza Valleys Based on Records Collected by Sir Aurel Stein', *The Journal of the Royal Anthropological Institute of Great Britain and Ireland*, 66 (January–June 1963), 19–42, Stable URL: http://www.jstor.org/stable/2844114, accessed: 30/10/2011.

Muncherji, D.H., 'Swat: The Garden of Asoka', *Pakistan Quarterly* (Karachi), 9/3 (1959), 40–5.

Olivieri, Luca M., 'Recent Discoveries of Rock-Carving in Buner and Puran (NWFP, Pakistan)', *East and West* (Rome), 44/2–4 (December 1994), 467–80, Stable URL: http://www.jstor.org/stable/29757167, accessed: 31/10/2011.

———, 'Notes on the Problematical Sequence of Alexander's Itinerary in Swat: A Geo-Historical Approach', *East and West* (Rome), 46/1–2 (June 1996), 45–78, Stable URL: http://www.jstor.org/stable/29757254; accessed: 30/10/2011.

———, 'Behind the Buddhist Communities: Subalternity and Dominancy in Ancient Swat', *Journal of Asian Civilizations* (Islamabad), 34/1 (July 2011), 123–51.

Cults and Preliminary Chronology: Data from the 2012 Excavation Campaign in Swat', *Journal of Inner Asian Art and Archaeology* (New York), 6/2011, 7–40, 217–20.

————, 'When and why the ancient town of Barikot was abandoned?: A preliminary note based on the last archaeological data', *Pakistan Heritage* (Mansehra), 4 (2012), 157–69.

————, 'Urban Defenses at Bīr-koṭ-ghwaṇḍai, Swat (Pakistan): New Data from the 2014 Excavation Campaign', *Ancient Civilizations from Scythia to Siberia* (Leiden), 21 (2015), 183–99.

————, '"Frontier Archaeology": Sir Aurel Stein, Swat, and the Indian Aornos', *South Asian Studies* (London), 31/1 (2015), 58–70.

————, 'The Graveyard and the Buddhist Shrine at Saidu Sharif I (Swat, Pakistan): Fresh Chronological and Stratigraphic Evidence' with Contributions by Filippo Terrasi, Fabio Marzaioli, Isabella Passariello, and Manuela Capano, and Notes by Aatif Iqbal, *Journal of Ancient History* (Moscow), 76/3 (2016), 559–78.

————, 'Guru Padmasambhava in Context: Archaeological and Historical·Evidence from Swat/ Uddiyana (c. 8th century CE)', *Journal of Bhutan Studies* (Thimphu), 34 (Summer 2016), 20–42.

Olivieri, Luca M., Massimo Vidale, Abdul Nasir Khan, Tahir Saeed, Luca Colliva, Riccardo Garbini, Leonardo Langella, Roberto Micheli, and Emanuele Morigi, 'Archaeology and Settlement History in a Test Area of the Swat Valley: Preliminary Report on the AMSV Project (1st Phase)', *East and West* (Rome), 56/1–3 (September 2006), 73–150, Stable URL: http:// www.jstor.org/stable/29757683, accessed: 30/10/2011.

Oman, Giovanni, 'On Eight Coins of Akbar Found in a Rock-Shelter near Ghālīgai, Swāt', *East and West* (Rome), 20/1–2 (March–June 1970), 105–7.

Pardini, Edoardo, 'The Human Remains from Aligrāma Settlement (Swāt, Pakistan)', *East and West* (Rome), 27/1–4 (December 1977), 207–26.

Petech, Luciano, 'A Kharoṣṭhī Inscription from Butkara I (Swat)', *East and West* (Rome), 16/1–2 (March–June 1966), 80–1.

Petrie, Cameron A. and Peter Magee, 'Histories, Epigraphy and Authority: Achaemenid and Indigenous Control in Pakistan in the 1st millennium BC', *Gandhāran Studies*, 1 (2007), 3–22.

Pincott, Frederic, 'The Route by which Alexander entered India', *Journal of the Royal Asiatic Society of Great Britain and Ireland* (October 1894), 677–89, Stable URL: http://www.jstor. org/stable/25197226; accessed: 30/10/2011.

Qamar, Mian Said, 'A Prelimenary Report on the Excavation of a Buddhist Site at Nawagai Tehsil Barikot, Swat', *East and West* (Rome), 54/1–4 (December 2004), 181–221, Stable URL: http:// www.jstor.org/stable/29757610, accessed: 30/10/2011.

Rahman, Abdur, 'Arslān Jādhib, Governor of Ṭūs: the First Muslim Conqueror of Swat', *Ancient Pakistan* (Peshawar), 15 (2002), 11–14.

————, 'Ethnicity of the Hindu Shāhīs', *Journal of the Pakistan Historical Society* (Karachi), 51/3 (July–September 2003), 3–10.

Rahman, Abdur and Shah Nazar Khan, 'Alexander's Route and Stein: Massaga to Ora', *Ancient Pakistan* (Peshawar), 19 (2008), 49–54.

Rapson, E.J., 'Impressions of Inscriptions Received from Captain A.H. McMahon, Political Agent for Swat, Dir, and Chitral', *Journal of the Royal Asiatic Society of Great Britain and Ireland* (April, 1901), 291–4, Stable URL: http://www.jstor.org/stable/25208296, accessed: 30/10/2011.

Raverty, H.G., 'An account of Upper and Lower Suwát, and the Kohistán, to the source of the Suwát River; with an account of the tribes inhabiting those valleys', *Journal of the Asiatic Society* (Calcutta), 31/3 (1862), 227–81.

————, 'The Discovery of the Very Important Lundai Sin, or Swat River', *The Geographic Journal*, 8/5 (November 1896), 525–6, Stable URL: http://www.jstor.org/stable/1774094, accessed: 30/10/2011.

Rehman, Abdur, 'The Zalamkot Bilingual Inscription', *Lahore Museum Bulletin* (Lahore), 10–11 (1997–1998), 35–40.

Salvatori, Sandro, 'Analysis of the Association of Types in the Protohistoric Graveyards of the Swāt Valley (Loebanr I, Kātelai, Butkara II)', *East and West* (Rome), 25/3–4 (September–December 1975), 333–51, Stable URL: http://www.jstor.org/stable/29756091, accessed: 30/10/2011.

Scerrato, Ilaria E., 'Wood Carvers in Swat Valley: Fieldwork Documentation and Preliminary Analysis', *East and West* (Rome), 56/1–3 (September 2006), 275–99, Stable URL: http://www.jstor.org/stable/29757691, accessed: 30/10/2011.

————, 'The ethnographic activity of the IsIAO Italian Archaeological Mission in Swat and Gilgit-Baltistan', *Journal of Asian Civilizations* (Islamabad), 34/1 (July 2011), 242–76.

Scerrato, Umberto, 'Pakistan – 2: The Wooden Architecture of Swat and the Northern Areas of Pakistan: a Report on the Research carried out in 1884', *East and West* (Rome), 34/4 (December 1984), 501–15, Stable URL: http://www.jstor.org/stable/29758165, accessed: 30/10/2011.

Sinha, Nirmal C., 'Gilgit (and Swat)', 47–55, URL: http://himalaya.socanth.cam.ac.uk.collections/journals/bot/pdf_08_01_03.pdf, accessed: 03/05/2010.

Stacul, Giorgio, 'Preliminary Report on the Pre-Buddhist Necropolises in Swat (W. Pakistan)', *East and West* (Rome), 16/1–2 (March–June 1966), 37–79.

————, 'Notes on the Discovery of a Necropolis near Kherai in the Ghorband Valley (Swāt-West Pakistan', *East and West* (Rome), 16/3–4 (September–December 1966), 261–74.

————, 'Excavations in a Rock Shelter near Ghālīgai (Swāt, W. Pakistan). Preliminary Report', *East and West* (Rome), 17/3–4 (September–December 1967), 185–219.

————, 'Discovery of Four Pre-Buddhist Cemeteries near Pācha in Buner (Swāt W. Pakistan)', *East and West* (Rome), 17/3–4 (September–December 1967), 220–32.

————, 'Excavation near Ghālīgai (1968) and Chronological Sequence of Protohistorical Cultures in the Swāt Valley', *East and West* (Rome), 19/1–2 (March–June 1969), 44–91.

————, 'An Archaeological Survey near Kālām (Swāt Kohistān)', *East and West* (Rome), 20/1–2 (March–June 1970), 87–91.

————, 'The Gray Pottery in the Swāt Valley and the Indo-Iranian Connections (ca. 1500–300 B.C.)', *East and West* (Rome), 20/1–2 (March–June 1970), 92–102.

————, 'A Decorated Vase from Gogdara (Swāt, Pakistan)', *East and West* (Rome), 23/3–4 (September–December 1973), 245–8, Stable URL: http://www.jstor.org/stable/29755886, accessed: 30/10/2011.

————, 'The Fractional Burial Custom in the Swāt Valley and Some Connected Problems', *East and West* (Rome), 25/3–4 (September–December 1975), 323–32, Stable URL: http://www.jstor.org/stable/29756090, accessed: 30/10/2011.

————, 'Excavations at Loebanr III (Swāt, Pakistan)', *East and West* (Rome), 26/1–2 (March–June 1976), 13–30, Stable URL: http://www.jstor.org/stable/29756224, accessed: 30/10/2011.

————, 'Dwelling-and Storage-Pits at Loebanr III (Swāt, Pakistan), 1976 Excavation Report', *East and West* (Rome), 27/1–4 (December 1977), 227–53.

————, 'Kalako-ḍeray, Swāt: 1994 and 1996 Excavation Reports', *East and West* (Rome), 47/1–4 (December 1997), 363–78, Stable URL: http://www.jstor.org/stable/29757329, accessed: 30/10/2011.

Stacul, Giorgio and Sebastiano Tusa, 'Report on the Excavations at Aligrāma (Swāt, Pakistan) 1966, 1972', *East and West* (Rome), 25/3–4 (September–December 1975), 291–321, Stable URL: http://www.jstor.org/stable/29756089, accessed: 30/10/2011.

————, 'Report on the Excavations at Aligrāma (Swāt, Pakistan) 1974', *East and West* (Rome), 27/1–4 (December 1977), 151–205.

Stein, Aurel, 'Notes on Inscriptions from Udyāna, Presented by Major Deane', *Journal of the Royal Asiatic Society of Great Britain and Ireland* (October 1899), 895–903, Stable URL: http://www.jstor.org/stable/25208156, accessed: 31/10/2011.

————, 'Alexander's Campaign on the Indian North-West Frontier: Notes from Explorations between Upper Swāt and the Indus', *The Geographical Journal* (London), 70/5 (November 1927), 417–40, Stable URL: http://www.jstor.org/stable/1783476; accessed: 30/10/2011.

————, 'Alexander's Campaign on the Indian North-West Frontier: Notes from Explorations between Upper Swāt and the Indus', *The Geographical Journal* (London), 70/6 (December 1927), 515–40, Stable URL: http://www.jstor.org/stable/1782915; accessed: 30/10/2011.

————, 'From Swat to the Gorges of the Indus', *The Geographical Journal* (London), 100/2 (August 1942), 49–56.

Sultan-i-Rome, 'Abdul Ghaffūr (Akhūnd): Saidū Bābā of Swāt; Life, Career and Role', *Journal of the Pakistan Historical Society* (Karachi), 40/3 (July 1992), 299–308.

————, 'The Sartōr Faqīr: Life and Struggle against British Imperialism', *Journal of the Pakistan Historical Society* (Karachi), 42/1 (January 1994), 93–105.

————, 'The Malakand Jihad (1897): An Unsuccessful Attempt to Oust the British from Malakand and Chakdara', *Journal of the Pakistan Historical Society* (Karachi), 43/2 (April 1995), 171–86.

————, 'Bāyazīd Anṣārī and his *Khairul Bayān*', *Hamdard Islamicus* (Karachi), 20/3 (July–September 1997), 87–95.

————, 'Merger of Swat State with Pakistan: Causes and Effects', *Journal of the Pakistan Historical Society* (Karachi), 47/3 (July–September 1999), 53–64.

————, 'Mughuls and Swat', *Journal of the Pakistan Historical Society* (Karachi), 50/4 (October–December 2002), 39–50.

————, 'Lord Roberts' Forty One Years in India: An Overview', *Pakistan Journal of History & Culture* (Islamabad), 27/1 (January-June 2006), 165–73.

————, 'Pukhtu: The Pukhtun Code of Life', *Pakistan Vision* (Lahore), 7/2 (December 2006), 1–30.

————, 'Religious Perspective of Pre Muslims Swat, Pakistan', *Journal of Asian Civilizations* (Islamabad), 35/2 (December 2012), 117–42.

————, 'Alexander the Great and Swat', *Journal of the Pakistan Historical Society* (Karachi), 61/1 (January–March 2013), 35–56.

————, 'Khushal Khan Khattak and Swat', *Journal of the Research Society of Pakistan* (Lahore), 51/1 (January–June 2014), 109–38.

————, 'Khushḥāl Khān Khattak: An Afghan Nationalist or a Mughul Loyalist?', *Journal of the Pakistan Historical Society* (Karachi), 64/3 (July–September 2016), 61–94.

————, 'Social System of the Swat Yūsufzī', *Hamdard Islamicus* (Karachi), 40/2 (April–June 2017), 81–110.

Swāti, Muhammad Farooq, 'Recent Discovery of Buddhist Sites in the Swāt Valley', *Āthāriyyāt* (Peshawar), 1 (1997), 151–84.

————, 'Pre-Kuṣāṇa Reliquaries from Pātaka, Swāt', *Journal of the Royal Asiatic Society*, 7/2 (July 1997), 249–55, Stable URL: http://www.jstor.org/stable/25183351, accessed: 30/10/2011.

————, 'Special Features of the Buddhist Art in the Swāt Valley', *Ancient Pakistan* (Peshawar), 18 (2007), 105–57.

Taddei, Maurizio, 'On a Hellenistic Model Used in Some Gandharan Reliefs in Swat', *East and West* (Rome), 15/3–4 (September–December 1965), 174–8, Stable URL: http://www.jstor.org/stable/29754920, accessed: 30/10/2011.

————, 'An Interesting Relief from the Swat Valley (II)', *East and West* (Rome), 16/1–2 (March–June 1966), 84–8.

————, 'A Problematical Toilet-tray from Uḍegrām', *East and West* (Rome), 16/1–2 (March–June 1966), 89–93.

————, 'Some Remarks on the Preliminary Reports Published on the Shnaisha Excavations, Swat)', *East and West* (Rome), 48/1–2 (June 1998), 171–88, Stable URL: http://www.jstor.org/stable/29757373, accessed: 30/10/2011.

Tribulato, Olga and Luca Maria Olivieri, 'Writing Greek in the Swat Region: A New Graffito from Barikot (Pakistan)', *Zeitschrift für Papyrologie und Epigraphik* (Köln) 204 (2017), 128–35.

Tucci, Giuseppe, 'Preliminary report on an archaeological survey in Swat', *East and West* (Rome), 9/4 (December 1958), 279–328.

————, 'Oriental Notes: II An Image of a Devi Discovered in Swat and some Connected Problems', *East and West* (Rome), 14/3–4 (1963), 146–82, Stable URL: http://www.jstor.org/stable/29754772, accessed: 30/10/2011.

————, 'Oriental Notes V: Preliminary Account of an Inscription from North-Western Pakistan', *East and West* (Rome), 20/1–2 (March–June 1970), 103–4.

————, 'On Swāt. The Dards and Connected Problems', *East and West* (Rome), 27/1–4 (December 1977), 9–103.

Tusa, Sebastiano, 'Notes on Some Protohistoric Finds in the Swāt Valley (Pakistan)', *East and West* (Rome), 31/1–4 (December 1981), 99–120, Stable URL: http://www.jstor.org/stable/29756585, accessed: 30/10/2011.

Vidale, Massimo, 'Entering the Jambil Valley: Two Enigmatic Stones from Panr', *East and West* (Rome), 56/1–3 (September 2006), 63–71, Stable URL: http://www.jstor.org/stable/29757682, accessed: 31/10/2011.

Vidale, Massimo, and Luca M. Olivieri, 'Painted Rock Shelters of the Swat Valley: Further Discoveries and New Hypotheses', *East and West* (Rome), 52/1–4 (December 2002), 173–223, Stable URL: http://www.jstor.org/stable/29757544, accessed: 30/10/2011.

————, 'Analytical Recognition or Visual "maya"?: A Cup-Marked Megalith in the Kandak Valley (Swat, Pakistan)', *East and West* (Rome), 55/1–4 (December 2005), 445–63, Stable URL: http://www.jstor.org/stable/29757658, accessed: 30/10/2011.

Vidale, Massimo and Roberto Micheli, 'Protohistoric graveyards of the Swat Valley, Pakistan: new light on funerary practices and absolute chronology', *Antiquity* (Cambridge), 91/356 (2017), 389–405.

Vidale, Massimo, Roberto Micheli, and Luca Olivieri, 'Iconography of Protohistoric Swat and the Agricultural Intensification of Period IV (2nd Millennium BCE)', *Journal of Asian Civilizations* (Islamabad), 34/1 (July 2011), 94–122.

Vinogradova, Natalja, 'Towards the Question of the Relative Chronology for Protohistoric Swat Sequence (on the Basis of the Swat Graveyards)', *East and West* (Rome), 51/1–2 (June 2001), 9–36, Stable URL: http://www.jstor.org/stable/29757493, accessed: 30/10/2011.

Widemann, François, 'Maues King of Taxila: An Indo-Greek Kingdom with a Saka King', *East and West* (Rome), 53/1–4 (December 2003), 95–125, Stable URL:http://www.jstor.org/stable/29757574; accessed: 12/11/2013.

'Italian Archaeological Activities in Swat: An Introduction', *Journal of Asian Civilizations* (Islamabad), 34/1 (July 2011), 48–80.

Pashto

Rahim, Rahim Shah, 'Malakand da Tarikh pah Ranra kay', *Pukhtu* (Peshawar) 20/4 (May 1988), 28–43.

Shalman, Fazli Zaman, 'Da Pakistan da Juridu Panzus Kalanah aw da Qabayalu da Ghazaganu Sal Kalanah', *Pukhtu* (Peshawar), 30/9–10 (September–October 1998), 41–51.

Sultan-i-Rome, ' "Da Saidu Babaji nah tar Wali Swat Puray": Yawah Tanqidi Jaizah', *Pukhtu* (Peshawar), 29/11–12 (November–December 1997), 12–23.

————, 'Bayazid Ansari, Khairul Bayan aw da Qalandar Momand Muqadimah', *Pukhtu* (Peshawar), 30/3–4 (March–April 1998), 26–52.

————, ' "Da Swat Ghrunah aw kah da Azadai da Tarikh Babunah": Yawah Tajziyah', *Pukhtu* (Peshawar), 30/11–12 (November–December 1998), 44–57.

Urdu

Pandrah Ruzah Rah-i Wafa (Karachi), 4/13 (16–31 July 2004).

NEWSPAPER ARTICLES

Mahiyuddin, Umar, 'Saidu Baba of Swat', *The Frontier Post* (daily), *Weekend Post*, 19 February 1988.

Sultan-i-Rome, 'Saidu Baba and the Spread of Islam', *The Frontier Post* (daily), *Weekend Post*, Peshawar, 15 July 1988.

WEBSITE ARTICLES

Hussain, Naveed, 'Sawan Sangran', n.d., Stable URL: http://www.valleyswat.net, accessed: 20/09/2010.

Sarma, V.V.S., 'From Udyana, the Seat of Rig-Veda, to the Present Swat Valley in Pakistan under Taliban Control', *Hindu Heritage of Swat Valley*, 3 May 2009, 11:07 am, Website: http://indianrealist.wordpress.com/2009/05/03/hindu-heritage-of-swat-valley, accessed: 10/06/2010.

INDEX

10th Irregular Cavalry, 212, 213
14C data, 52, 277
35th Sikhs, 242
38th Dogras, 242
55th Native Infantry, 212, 213, 214, 215, 216, 217, 220, 221
64th Native Infantry, 212, 213

A

Aba Khail, 254
Abazi, 241, 251
Abbott, James, 38
Abdali, Ahmad Shah, 200; installed ruler of Afghanistan 200, *see also* Durrani, Ahmad Shah
Abhidhamma Pitaka (Abhidhamma-pitaka), 281
Abhisara country, 33, 39
Abisares, 27
Aboha/Abua/Abuha/Abuhah, 9, 90, 126, 127, 128, 163, *see also* Ambuh
Acadira, 36, *see also* Azara; Hazara/Hazarah (village)
Accozyes, 140, *see also* Akuzi/Akuzis; Akuzi Yusufzi
Achaemenian, 17; administration, 17, 57, *see also* Achaemenidian
Achaemenians of Iran, 17
Achaemenid, 16; domination, 17; Empire, 16
Achaemenidian, 17, *see also* Achaemenian
Adams, Lieutenant-Colonel, 243
Adinzai tapah, 246, *see also* Adinzi *tapah*
Adinzi, 90, 241, 251, 258
Adinzi *tapah*, 246, *see also* Adinzai tapah
Afghan, 108, 185, 190, 277, *see also* Pakhtun; Pathan; Pukhtan; Pukhtun
Afghan Amir (Abdur Rahman), 98 n., 118 n., 237, *see also* Rahman, Abdur (Afghan Amir)
Afghan borderland, 192; chiefs (local), 208; commander-in-chief, 244; cultivators of Bajawar and Swat, 164; general, 248; hostility, 211; intrigues, 247; language, 275; mainland, 194; *nang*, 179, 181, 184; Napoleon, 261 n.; nature, 223; prowess, 169; territory/territories, 24; tribe(s), 106, 107, 108, 123, 130, 178, 180

Afghani refugees, 248; settlement in Swat, 107
Afghanistan, 3, 4, 24, 49, 55, 57, 98 n., 100, 108, 109, 111, 118 n., 123, 129, 130, 166, 200, 201, 222, 236, 237, 248, 251, 262 n., 263 n., 267 n., 277, 281
Afghans, 106, 107, 111, 116, 123, 145, 165, 167, 168, 170, 180, 193, 194, 200, 205, 271; of Damghār, 170; of Kabul, 171; of Sawād and Bajaur, 166; of Suwat, 186, *see also* Afghauns; Pathans; Pukhtanah
Afghauns, 200, *see also* Afghans; Pathans; Pukhtanah
Afridi(s), 179, 243
Afzal, Sher (Shir), 236, 238
Agathocleia, 53
Agathocles, 53
Agency of Dir and Swat, 240
Agency of Dir, Swat and Chitral, 240
Aghraq tribe, 110
Agrawala, A.G., 87
Agrawala, R.C., 87
Ahmad, Khwajah Nizamuddin, 166, 168, 169; narrative, 169, *see also* Bakhshi, Nizamuddin Ahmad
Ahmad, Makhdum Tasadduq, 132, 133, 134, 136, 137, 139
Ahmad, Malak/Malik, 124, 125, 130, 131, 138, 154 n., 158 n., 161, 162, 163, 164, 166
Ahmad, Sayyad/Sayyid (of Rayi Baraili), 200, 201, 204, 206, 224 n., 225 n.; Sayyad Ahmad's Hindustani followers, 204; rule, 204; surviving followers, 204; visit, 204, *see also* Barailwi, Sayyad Ahmad
Ahmad, Wali, 269 n., *see also* Jan, Ahmad; Sandakai Baba
Ain-i-Akbari (book), 171
Akbar (Mughal Emperor), 166, 167, 168, 169, 172, 191, 192; Akbar's army, 166, 170; armies, 239; attempt(s), 187; Brahmin favourite, 168; forces, 166, 167, 171; imperialism, 167; reign, 170, 187; time, 166
Akbar Namah (book), 112
Akbar, Sayed, 219, *see also* Shah, Sayyad/ Sayyid Akbar (of Sithanah)
Akhoond of Swat, 217, *see also* Akhund; Akhund of Suwat/Swat; Akhund Sahib; Ghafur, Abdul; Ghafur, Akhund Abdul; Saidu Baba

Akhtar, Muhammad, 109, 110, 112, 113, 115, 116, 127

Akhun Khail Miangan, 129; tract, 129

Akhund, 203, 205, 206, 210, 213, 215, 216, 218, 219, 220, 221, 222, 223, 235, 245, 246, 248; Akhund's apprehensions, 219; authority, 219; birth, 231 n.; confidential messengers, 220; ethnicity, 231 n.; feelings, 223; guests, 219; influence, 215, 234; joined the Amir's camp, 222; name, 213; own status, 216; policy, 219, 223, 224; promise, 233; wise restrant, 223; post-Akhund, 245, see also Akhoond of Swat; Akhund of Suwat/Swat; Ghafur, Abdul; Ghafur, Akhund Abdul; Saidu Baba

Akhund of Suwat/Swat, xx, 203, 205, 209, 211, 212, 213, 215, 216, 217, 218, 219, 221, 231 n., 233, 234, 235, 241, 244, 245, 248, see also Akhoond of Swat; Akhund; Akhund Sahib; Ghafur, Abdul; Ghafur, Akhund Abdul; Saidu Baba

Akhund Sahib, 217, 218, see also Akhoond of Swat; Akhund; Akhund of Swat; Ghafur, Abdul; Ghafur, Akhund Abdul; Saidu Baba

Akhunzadahs/Akhunzadgan, 134

Akur, Malak, 178

Akuzi/Akuzis, 140, see also Accozyes; Akuzi Yusufzi

Akuzi Yusufzi, 115, 131, 251, see also Accozyes; Akuzi/Akuzis

Alahdand, 248

Alauddin, Sultan, 126, 127, 163, 164, 165, see also 'Alā'u'u-din, Sl.

'Alā'u'u-din, Sl., 165, see also Alauddin, Sultan

Alayi Bala, 127, see also Aluhiyah Bala; Upper Alayi

Alberuni, 76, 89 n., 93 n., 102, 110

Alchon Huns, 279, see also Ephtalites/ Ephthalites; Hūṇa; White Huns

Alexander/Alexander of Macedonia/Alexander the Great, 2, 17, 18, 24, 25, 26, 27, 28, 29, 30, 31, 32, 33, 34, 35, 36, 38, 39, 40, 41 n., 42 n., 44 n., 47 n., 112, 167; campaign, 24, 38, 40, 42 n.; descent from Alexander, 112; Alexander's arrival, 17; attack, 18; departure, 40; expedition, 25; exploits, 25; historians, 2, 8, 38; intelligence, 30; invasion, xx, xxi, 25, 65, 76; post-Alexander, 40; pre and post-Alexander period in Swat, 64; route(s), 36, 38, 46 n.; strategy, 42 n.; time, 41 n., 64, see also Bicornutus, Alexander

al-Khairi, al-Amīr al-Hajib Abu Mansur Nushtegin, 104

Ali (RA), 91, 183, 280

Ali, Amir (Ghaznavid general), 102, 103

Ali, Sayyid, 206 see also Pir Baba; Tarmizi, Sayyad Ali

Aligrama/Aligramah (village), 14, 15, 35, 36, 113; Hill, 36

Alim, 151, 183, 277

Aliman, 151, 277

Alketas, 27

Allah, 91, 183, 184

Allahabad Pioneer, 243

Almighty, 3, 108, 125, 135; Almighty's sake, 143

Alsatia, 209

Aluhiyah Bala, 127, see also Alayi Bala; Upper Alayi

Amar Nath Cave, 75

Ambahar, 165

Ambilah (Ambela) campaign, 233; hills, 233; Pass, 233, 234; war, 235, 260 n.

Ambuh (Abuhah; Aboha?), 90, see also Aboha/ Abua/Abuha/Abuhah

Amir of Afghanistan, 237, 247, 248, 249, 250, see also Afghan Amir; Amir of Kabul

Amir of Kabul, 249, see also Afghan Amir; Amir of Afghanistan

Amir of Rabil, 213

Amīr in the Yusafzai territory, 267 n.

Amr-i bil maruf wa nahi anil munkar, 138

Anabasis (book), 42 n.

Ancient civilizations, xxi

Ancient Greece, 278

Ancient Greeks, 107, 112

Angusht, 175 n.

Annual Administration Report (official report), 253

Ansari, Bayazid, 166, 167, 169, 174 n.; Bayazid's challenge, 167; rising in Dir, 174 n.; trick, 167

Antialcidas, 53

Antimachus II, 51, 52, 53

Antiochos (King of Syria), 49

Aornos, 9, 18, 25, 29, 34, 36, 37, 38, 40, 45 n., 46 n.

Apalala ('O-po-lo-lo), 83

Apollodotus, 51, 53, 54

Apollodotus I, 52

Arab, Khwaja, 168

Arab (by ethnicity), 274; Muslim armies, 100

Arabic etymology, 3; language, 3; law-books, 223; name, 3; word, 3, 153

Arabs, 3, 65, 66

Arachoshia/Arachosia, 52, 53, 69 n.; (around Ghazni), 53

Araneh, 273, see also Aryanai

Archaeological data, 16, 55; discoveries, 66; evidence(s), 54, 55, 80; excavation(s), 14, 15, 19, 20 n., 50, 54 n.; finds, 18; materials,

14; missions, 14; remains, 58; site(s), 77, 78, 277; sources, xx; survey, 273; unit, 20 n.

Archaeologists, xx

Archaeology, xxi, 20 n., 21 n.; folk, 20; popular, 20; popular folk, 20

Arghistan, 123

Arhat, 277

Arnawai, 248, 267 n.

Arrian (Greek historian), 1, 2, 5, 8, 25, 28, 29, 32, 34, 35, 36, 37, 38, 42 n., 47 n.

Aryan, 18, 272; migration, 16; race, 272; settlement, 16; theory, 22 n.

Aryanai, 273, *see also* Araneh

Asalah, 201

Asar, Abdul Halim, 4

Ashar ghubal, 147

Ashnaghar, 106, 110, 111, 124, 125, 209, 211, *see also* Hash-nagar/Hashtnagar

Ashnan, 277

Ashoka, 49, 50, 76, 77, 280 *see also* Ashoka the Great; Ashoka-raja; Asoka

Ashoka the Great, 77, *see also* Ashoka; Ashoka-raja; Asoka

Ashoka's Empire, 49, 50; authority, 49; park, 50; period, 50, *see also* Asoka's Empire; Asokan Empire

Ashoka-raja, 49, 76, *see also* Ashoka; Ashoka the Great; Asoka

Ashokan Empire, 7, 49, 50, *see also* Asoka's Empire; Asokan Empire

Aslam (Khan) (of Tanra), 239

Asmar, 244, 248, 267 n.; boundary mission, 238

Aśoka, 49, 50, 77, 280, *see also* Ashoka; Ashoka the Great; Ashoka-raja

Asoka: The Buddhist Emperor of India (book), 7

Asoka's Empire, 49, 50; passion for building, 49; time, 50, *see also* Ashokan Empire; Asokan Empire

Asokan Empire, 7; topes, 49, *see also* Ashokan Empire; Asoka's Empire

Aspasians, 33, 35

Assacános, 26, *see also* Assacanus; Assakenos

Assacanus, 26, 28, *see also* Assacanos; Assakenos

Assacenian rebels, 40

Assakenians, 25, 33, 35, *see also* Assakenoi

Assakenoi, 2, 8, 16, 18, 24, 25, 32, 38, *see also* Assakenians

Assakenois, 33, 39

Assakênos, 26, 28, *see also* Assacanos; Assacenus

Assistant commissioner Mardan, 257

Astanadar, 134, *see also* stanadar(s)

Astazi, 133

Aśvakas, 35

Āśvakāyana, 18

Aswad, 3

At, 4

Atak/Attak, 106, 168, 169, 179, 189, *see also* Attak-Banaras; Attock

Athens, 44 n.

Attak-Banaras, 168, *see also* Atak/Attak; Attock

Attalos, 27

Attock, 192, *see also* Atak/Attak; Attak-Banaras

Audriyana, 2

Aurangzeb (Mughal Emperor), 172, 180, 188, 189, 191, 192, 193, 194, 200; Aurangzeb's reign, 171, 172; rule, 179; time, xx

Aurdāyana, 18

Aurddi, 2

Aurdi, 8

Aurdiyana, 2

Avadana(s), 278

Avalokiteśvara, 86, *see also* Padmapāṇi

Awais, Sultan (Wais/Uwais), 109, 111, 112, 113, 114, 115, 124, 125, 126, 127, 162, 163, 164, 165; Awais's power, 112; Swat areas, 114; Swati subjects, 112, 115, *see also* Uwais; Wais, Sl. (Sultan)

Ayin (village), 128, 129

Ayudhapurusa (*Ayudha-puruṣa*), 87, 277

Azam, Kurush (the Iranian/Persian ruler), 112, *see also* Cyrus the Great; Kabir, Kurush; Zulqarnain, Sikandar; Zulqarnain, Sultan

Azam, Mir (of Batkhilah), 239

Azara, 36, *see also* Acadira; Hazara/Hazarah (village)

Azes, 54

Azi Khail/Khel, 211, 254

Azilises, 54

Azizuddin, Malak, 106, 119 n.

B

Babur, xx, 3, 109, 111, 125, 126, 127, 128, 138, 161, 162, 163, 164, 165, 166, 167; Babur's account, 163, 165; attempt of hitting, 161; founder of Mughal dynastic rule in India, 161; invasion of Manglawar, 163; love for the lady, 163; request, 162; route Kabul to Swat, 164; route to India, 161; shot, 161; *Tuzuk*, 163; version, 156 n., *see also* Babur, Zahiruddin

Babur, Zahiruddin, 161, *see also* Babur

Babuzai Maliks, 253, *see also* Babuzi *malakan*

Babuzi, 246, 251

Babuzi *malakan*, 253, *see also* Babuzai Maliks

Bacha, 205, 207, 208, *see also* Badshah; *Padshah*

Bacha of Swat, 207, 208

Bacha Sahib, 153, 172, *see also* Gulshazada; Wadud, Miangul Abdul

Bactria, 55
Bactrian, 52
Bactrian Greeks, 50; chiefs, 53
Badakhshan, 116, 235
Badal, 141, 144, 147
Badragah, 138, *see also jalab*
Badshah, 205, 206, 207, 253, *see also Bacha*; Padshah
Badshah, Akbar, 206, 207; *see also* Shah, Sayyad/Sayyid Akbar
Badshah, Syed (the Nawab of Dir's general), 255, 257, *see also* Khan, Syed Badshah
Bádsháh of Kanjút, 207
Bádsháh of Sathánah, 207
Bádsháh of Suwát, 207
Bádsháh of the Spin Kafiris, 207
Bádsháh's Village, 206
Bádsháhs, 207
Bádsháhs of Káshkár, 207
Baghwanan, 133
Bagnera, Dr Alessandra, 104, 110, 111
Bagyaray, 111
Baha, Dr Lal, 263 n.
Bahrain, 273, *see also* Bahrein; Baranial; Branial
Bahram, Sultan, 2, 108, 109
Bahrein, 273, *see also* Bahrain; Baranial; Branial
Baiki, 222, *see also* Beka; Bika
Baizi (erroneously written as Baizai), 131, 182
Bajaur, 24, 35, 50, 51, 52, 89, 100, 102, 111, 166, 168, 170, 171, 192, 193, 246, 248, 162 n.; 267 n.; Agency, 4; Chiefs, 254, *see also* Bajawar; Bajour
Bajawar, 2, 24, 34, 35, 45 n.; 50, 51, 102, 106, 107, 108, 109, 110, 111, 124, 126, 127, 161, 162, 163, 165, 166, 167, 168, 169, 222, 235, 237, 243, 246, 247, 253, 254, 256, 262 n., 281; casket inscription, 51; Fort, 109, *see also* Bajaur; Bajour
Bajour, 246, *see also* Bajaur; Bajawar
Bakhshi, 168, 277
Bakhshi, Nizamuddin Ahmad, 167, *see also* Ahmad, Khwajah Nizamuddin
Bálá-Kot, 206, *see also* Balakut
Balakut, 204, *see also* Bálá-Kot
Baligram, 114, 128
Baltistan, 66
Baluchistan, 49, 129, 239, 262 n.; Pakistan's Baluchistan, 123
Balugram, 128
Ban-bas, 74, 75, *see also Vanavasa*
Banbhore, 104
Bandai, 201
Banday dalah (*dalah* in power), 132, 145
Bangakh, 179
Bangash, 171, 179, 189

Bani Israel, 107, 145
Bani Israelite theory, 107
Bannu (district), 202
Bantaki, 154 n.
Barah (place), 222
Barah Bandai (village), 201
Barailwi, Ahmad Raza Khan (of Bans Baraili), 92
Barailwi, Sayyad Ahmad (of Rayi Baraili), xx, 99 n., 200, 201, 202, 203, 204, 205, 209, 212, 222, 233, *see also* Ahmad, Sayyad/ Sayyid (of Rayi Baraili)
Barailwi school of thought, 92
Barakzi *sardar*s (chiefs), 201
Bárakzís, 206
Barama I/Barama-I, 9
Baraniál, 273, *see also* Bahrain; Bahrein; Branial
Barger, Evert, 20 n.
Bari Kot inscription, 57, 58
Barikot/Bari-kot, 34, 35, 37, 52, 75, 85, 87, 88, *see also* Barikut; Bazira; Bir-kot; Bir-Kut
Barikut, 15, 20, 34, 37, 46 n., 52, 54, 57, 58, 61, 87, 200; early-historic (now protohistoric), 16, *see also* Barikot/Bari-kot; Bazira; Bir-kot; Bir-Kut
Barikut Ghwandai, 35, 51, 52, 54, 55, 56, 61, 88
Barth, Fredrik (Norwegian anthropologist), 129, 131, 273
Barua, Beni Madhab, 50
Barughal Pass, 110
Barurah, 180
Bashgal valley, 248, 267 n.
Basket of Monastic Discipline, 281
Batagram/Batgram, 114; District, 128
Batkhilah, 126, 222
Baz (Muhammad Khan) (of Shairgarh), 239
Bazar, 45 n.
Bazdara/Bazdarah, 45 n., *see also* Bazdira
Bazdira, 45 n., *see also* Bazdara/Bazdarah
Bazira, 8, 25, 27, 28, 32, 33, 34, 35, 37, 39, 40, 45 n., 46 n., 55, *see also* Barikot/Bari-kot; Barikut; Bir-kot; Bir-Kut
Bazirians, 27, 37, 39
Beal, Samuel, 1, 2
Beas River, 58
Beg, Mirza Quli, 124, *see also* Beg, Mirza Ulugh
Beg, Mirza Ulugh, 123, 124, 130, 131, 135, 161, *see also* Beg, Mirza Quli
Begs, 165
Behti, Hasan, 168
Beka, 221, 222, *see also* Baiki; Bika
Bellew, H.W., 76, 86, 88, 90, 91, 110, 111, 124, 127, 129, 130, 164, 170, 220
Benares (Banaras), 55
Beveridge, Annette S., 164

Beveridge, H., 112
Bhâdrupadâ (Bhadu), 76
Bhaisajyavastu (Bhaiṣajya-vastu), 77, 277
Bhakar, 107
Bhikshu(s), 78, 277
Bi'at, 201, 277
Bicornutus, Alexander, 112, *see also* Alexander/ Alexander of Macedonia/Alexander the Great
Biddulph, John, 129, 271, 272, 273, 275; Biddulph's assertion, 272; theory, 272; thesis, 272
Bika, 221, 222, *see also* Baiki; Beka
Bindusara, 49
Bīr Bar, Rāja, 168, *see also* Birbal; Birbal, Raja
Birbal, 168, 169, *see also* Bir Bar, Raja; Birbal, Raja
Birbal, Raja, 168, 169, *see also* Bir Bar, Raja; Birbal
Bir-kot, 37, 39, *see also* Barikot/Bari-kot; Barikut; Bazira; Bir-Kut
Bir-Kut, 34, *see also* Barikot/Bari-Kot; Barikut; Bazira; Bir-kot
Birmal tract, 267 n.
Bishkari, 272
Bizugar, 132, *see also* shpankyan/shpunkyan
Blood, Bindon, 243
Blue River, 220
Bodhisattva, 76, 86, 277, 279, 281
Bodhisattvas, 86, 278, 281; Bodhisattvas' statues, 90
Boneyr, 271, *see also* Bunair; Buner; Bunir
Bradshaw, Colonel, 203, 205, 209
Brahma, 279
Brahma-sampradaya, 279
Brahmanism, 85, 88, *see also* Hinduism
Brahmin, 168
Brakhikhwarah, 132, 145
Bramatah, 138
Brangulah, 221
Branial, 52, *see also* Baraniál; Bahrain; Bahrein
Britain, 225 n., 261 n.; prime minister of, 243
British, xx, 202, 218, 221, 223, 233, 234, 235, 236, 237, 238, 239, 241, 243, 247, 252, 254, 261 n., 262 n., 267 n., 281; advance(s), 233, 239; arms, 218, 241; army, 244; authority, 221; authorities, 235, 236, 248, 249; colonial authorities, 209; colonial forces, 238; colonial government, 238, 280; political agent, 34; colonialists, 239; column, 236; controlled areas, 233; Crown, 225 n., 261 n.; domination, 223; Empire, 260 n.; envoy, 248; expeditions, 233; forces, 233, 234, 235, 239, 242, 251; frontier, 237; garrison, 245; government, 202, 209, 220, 225 n., 234, 235, 236, 238, 243, 247, 248, 249, 255, 256, 257, 260 n.,

264 n., 267 n.; historians, 229 n.; Imperial government, 234; imperial power, 239, 280; India, 242, 260 n., 261 n.; Indian Empire, 241; Indian government, 249, 262 n.; influence, 248; line of communication, 235; loose administrative control, 239, 240, 259; military power, 234; occupation, 224; officers, 262 n.; official report, 212, 245, 254; official statement, 211; official's writings, 129, 224, 232 n.; officials, 210, 237, 238; person, 225 n.; proclamation, 238; protectorate, 153, 251; Regular troops, 234; rule in India, 261 n.; service(s), 202, 219; side, 242, 251; superiority, 218; supremacy, 244; territory, 202; territory in Europe, 261 n.; troops, 234, 238, 262 n.; villages, 202; yoke, 202, 209
Briton, 225 n.; held territory, 219; occupied territories, 202
Britons, 202, 203, 209, 210, 214, 217, 218, 225 n.; 229 n.; colonial, xx, 210; colonialists, 220; held parts/territories, 209, 212, 213, 219; held sway, 212; occupation, 212; occupied territory, 210; perspective, 209; tract, 210; turned anti-Britons, 204
Britons' border, 210; control, 202, 209; detachment, 210; forces, 209; Indian possession, 202; occupied territories, 214; rule, 208, 209; soldiers, 210; successful emergence, 244
Bruce, Mr, 257; Bruce's instruction, 257
Buddha, 52, 63, 75, 76, 77, 78, 79, 82, 83, 84, 89, 102, 277, 278, 281; Buddhahood, 277; image of a seated Buddah, 86; the Law of, 64, 78; Buddha's foot-prints, 78, 83, 84; garments, 95 n.; law, 79; own command, 84; relics of body, 84; statues, 90; visit to Swat, 84; wishes, 84, *see also* Buddha, Gautama; Foe; Tathagata
Buddha, Gautama, 78 *see also* Buddha; Foe; Tathagata
Buddhism, 60, 61, 76, 77, 78, 79, 80, 81, 82, 83, 84, 85, 86, 87, 88, 89, 90, 91, 94 n., 96 n., 277, 278, 280, 281; in Swat, 76, 79, 83; early Buddhism, 278, 279, 280; later Buddhism, 279, *see also* Budhism
Buddhist, 60, 77, 87, 92, 275; art and beliefs, 81, 91; calendar, 90; Canon, 281; collections, 278; cults, 61; culture, 85; dominance, 88; early schools, 278; establishments, 80; foundations, 62; Gandhara, 87; ilands, 89; learning and piety, 78; monk, 277; monasteries, 279; monuments, 77; mythology, 279; pantheon, 60, 86; pattern, 61; period, 57; philosophy and metaphysics, 83; pilgrim, 78; practitioner, 279; raja, 118 n.; relieves, 86; sanctuaries, 78; schools,

278; *stupa*s, 180; teachings, 281; times, 64; Universe, 277; *Vinaya* text, 277; non-Buddhist beliefs, 77; non-Buddhist cults, 88; pre-Buddhist beliefs, 91; prebuddhistic (pre-Buddhistic) cults, 86

Buddhists, 75, 81, 83, 85, 90, 92, 108, 275

Budhism, 76, *see also* Buddhism

Bukhari's, Abid, statement, 174 n.

Bunair, 32, 37, 109, 111, 192, 200, 233, 256, 263 n., 271, 272, 281; forces, 256; hills, 233; *jargah*, 255; people of, 201, 256, 257; tribes of, 233, 234, *see also* Boneyr; Buner; Bunir

Bunbury, 16

Buner, 5, 18, 24, 32, 38, 51, 80, 169, 170, 171, 172, 174 n., 206, 218, 219, 223, 233, 235, 242, 248, 263 n., 271, *see also* Boneyr; Bunair; Bunir

Bungah, 138

Bunir, 233, 263 n., *see also* Boneyr; Buner; Bunair

Burn, Prof. A.R., 76

Burton-Page, John, 54

Burzahom (Kashmir), 14

But Bat (place), 90

Butah, 138

Butkara, 79, 81

Butkara I/Butkara-I, 9, 79, 95 n., *see also* T'a lo; T'o-lo

C

Caitya, 88, 277

Cakrapurus, 277, 278

Cakrapuruṣa, 87, 277

Cakravartin Raja, 50, *see also* Chakravarti raja

Caliph, 100, 206, *see also* Khalifah

Caliphate, 100, *see also* Khilafat

Campbell, Colin, 209

Caroe, Olaf, 37, 172, 191, 193, 204, 220, 222; Careo's assertion(s), 171, 193; claim, 193; contention, 193; version, 153; words, 168

Caspian Sea, 15, 16

Caufir (*kafir*) country, 111

Central Asia, 4, 15, 19, 55, 65, 66, 81, 83, 100, 161

Central Asian, 18; groups, 60; invaders, 129; peoples, 15

Central government, 240; at Delhi, 240; of British India, 240

Central India (language of), 62; people of, 62

Chageh, 267 n.

Chahil Durrah, 273, *see also* Chail Darah; Chail Valley

Chail Darah, 273, *see also* Chahil Durrah; Chail Valley

Chail Valley, 129, 273, *see also* Chahil Durrah; Chail Darah

Chaitya, 277

Chakdara/Chakdarah/Chakdarra, 18, 24, 168, 169, 170, 201, 240, 241, 242, 245, 251, 254, 265 n.

Chakisar, 37, 129

Chakravarti raja, 1, *see also* Cakravartin Raja

Cham, 134

Chamla/Chamlah, 207, 221

Chamyaran, 133

Chanak, 248, 267 n.

Chandar Ji, Ram, 74, *see also* Ram, Sri; Rama; Ramachandara

Chandra, Moti, 58

Chara Nawab, 253, *see also* Khan, Aurangzeb; Khan, Bacha; Khan, Badshah

Charbagh, 201, 345

Charbaytah, 239, 260 n., 263 n., 277

Charsada, 42 n.

Charsadah District, 125

Cherat Pass, 111

Chief commissioner, 240, 244, 256

Chiefs of Bajaur (Bajawar) and Swat, 249

Chilas/Chilass, 220, 248

Chilāsis, 236

China, 19, 55, 61, 65, 66, 277

Chīnapati, 50

Chinese, 1, 65, 66, 100; I-lo, 75; interpreter, 66; monk, 19; pilgrim(s), 5, 9, 62, 63, 64, 78, 79, 95 n.; power, 100; sources, 57, 58; transcription, 8; travellers, 79; visitor, 81

Chinese-Tibetan collision, 65; quarrels, 66

Chinglai, 200

Chiroleh, 273, *see also* Churrai; Madyan

Chitral, 4, 6, 18, 65, 235, 236, 237, 238, 239, 240, 248, 251, 262 n., 267 n.; crisis, xx, 235; Relief Force, 238; fort of, 236; State, 235, 236; Upper Chitral, 61

Chitralis, 274

Christ, 79

Christian theological doctrine, 280

Chudgram (now Balakut), 129

Churchill, Lady Randolph, 243

Churchill, Winston S., 243, 265 n.

Churrai, 273, 275, *see also* Chiroleh; Madyan

Chute, Colonel, 214; Colonel Chute's Moveable Column, 217, 220

Chwang, Yuan, 8, 49, 59, 74, *see also* Hiouan thsang; Hsüan-tsang; Thsang, Hwen; Tsang, Hsüan; Tsiang, Hiuen; Xuanzang; Zang, Xuan

Cleophis, 26, 28

Coenus, 27, 39, *see also* Koinos

Colonial (adjective), 261 n.; authorities, 209, 214, 241; British, 153, 158 n., 223, 239, 240, 244, 245, 249, 250, 251, 252, 254, 255,

257, 267 n., 280; British authorities, 223, 238, 251; British government, 237, 238, 240, 244, 248, 249, 252, 253, 257, 262 n.; British power, 263 n.; British rule in India, 280; British writings, 204; government, 218, 219, 220, 221, 240, 241, 249, 250, 251, 252, 254, 255, 262 n.; government of India, 252; Imperial Power, 223, 224; lines, 260 n.; rulers (of India), 202, 212

Colonial Britons, xx, 209, 210

Colonialists, 210, 212, 214, 215, 216, 217, 218, 219, 220, 241, 244, 260 n.; term, 261 n.; government, 210; anti-colonialists activity, 215; elements, 213; rebels, 216

Commissioner, 237, 249; Peshawar Division, 214, 217, 250

Common Era, 55

Company Bagh Mardan, 263 n.

Confidential, Gazetteer of the North-West Frontier (book), 202

Court, M., 45 n.

Covid 19 (virus), 225 n., *see also* Pandemic

Cultural material, 14; patterns, 14; phases, 14; tradition, 14, 21 n.; waves, 15

Cundies, 148, *see also* Kandis; *talunah*

Cundy, 148, *see also* Kandi; *tal*; Tul

Cunningham, Alexander, 5, 7, 38

Curtius, 29, 34, 36, *see also* Rufus, Q. Curtius

Cutch, 49, *see also* Kachh

Cyrus the Great, 112, 116, *see also* Azam, Kurush; Kabir, Kurush; Zulqarnain, Sikandar; Zulqarnain, Sultan

D

Da masharai hisah, 146

Da nagharay da Sambat kwanay tah ghagigi, 151

Da pagrai khan, 131

Da Pukhtu dawar (the period of Pukhtu), 132

Da Pukhtu zamanah (the age of Pukhtu), 132

Da sar saray, 142

Dadíkai, 17

Daedala/Daiolai/Deolai/Diwlai, 36

Daedalae, 36

Daedali mountains, 29

Daftar, 135, *see also dauter*; *dawtar*

Daftar of Shaikh Mali (book/register), 183, 222

Daily Telegraph (London newspaper), 243

Daiyals, 87

Daka, 92 n.

Dakas, 87, 91

Dakinis, 82, 87, 91, 92 n.

Dalah, 131, 132, 133, 145, 146, 203, 251; members, 132

Dalay, 131, 132, 144, 203, 245, 251

Dalazak, 106, 107, 124, 125, 161, 277; tribe, 277, *see also* Dilazak Afghan/tribe; Dilazaks

Daman, 133, *see also doms*

Damghar (village), 176 n., 190; fort, 166, 170

Dani, Ahmad Hasan, 32, 129, 130, 165, 170, 171

Dar mulk-i Niyag (country or place of Nihak or Niyag), 113

Daradas, 36, *see also* Dards; Daraddesa

Daraddesa, 16, *see also* Daradas; Dards

Darah Nihak or Nihag or Niyak, 113, *see also* Dara'h of Nihák or Níáka'h or Ní'ák; Nihag or Nihak or Niyak Darah; Nihag or Niyag or Niyak Valley; Nihak (Valley); Niyag (Valley); Valley Nihak or Niyag

Dara'h of Nihák or Níáka'h or Ní'ák, 113, *see also* Darah Nihak or Nihag or Niyak; Nihag or Nihak or Niyak Darah; Nihag or Niyag or Niyak Valley; Nihak (Valley); Niyag (Valley); Valley Nihak or Niyag

Darbar, 244, 278

Dard country, 4, 6; name, 272; race, 272; theory, 272; tribes, 271

Dardi (languages), 272

Dardic, 17, 272; form, 62; group, 18; group (languages of), 272; tribes, 18

Dardistan (name), 272; term, 272; theory, 272

Dards, 16, 17, 36, *see also* Daradas; Darradesa

Darel, 5, 7, 8, 18

Darí, 114, 116

Daritæ, 16

Darius I, 17

Darwah, 106, 107, 116

Darwaish, 183

Darwezah, Ākhúnd, 207, *see also* Darwizah, Akhun

Darwizah, Akhun, 2, 62, 108, 124, 126, 128, 154 n., 158 n., 164, 166, 167, 170, 174 n., 183, 188, 190, 197 n., 275, *see also* Darwezah, Ākhúnd

Das, Raja Bhagwan, 167, 169

Dasht-i Lut, 123, *see also* Great Salt Desert

Datia, 52

Dauter, 134, *see also daftar*; *dawtar*

Davies, C. Collin, 263 n.

Dawar, 267 n.

Dawtar, 115, 132, 133, 134, 135, 141, *see also daftar*; *dauter*

Dawtari, 133, 141

Dawtaryan, 141

DC/Deputy Commissioner Hazarah, 219, 256

Deambi, 51

Deane, Herold/Deane, H.A. (Political Agent), 5, 7, 66, 74, 83, 84, 241, 249, 251, 252, 253; Dean's proposal, 250

Delhi, 127, 172, 189, 200, 213, *see also* Dihli

Delhi-Agra, 171
Dêmêtrios, 27
Demetrius I, 53
Department of Archaeology, University of
	Peshawar, 60
Dera (Dirah) Ismail Khan, 202
Derah-jat, 175 n.
Deva temple, 74
Devas, 74, 80; great assembly of, 84
Devī, 76
Devi Bhagavatam, 278, see also Shrimad Devi
Devīpurāṇa, 76, 278
Dhanakosha lake, 82
Dharmaguptaka, 83, 278
Dharmagupta(s), 80, 278
Dharmarajika (Taxila) (stupa), 50
Dharmkand, Raja, 168
Diadem, 51, 278
Diamond Jubilee, 244
Diamond vehicle, 281
Diday, 115
Dihgan (by ethnicity), 116, 120 n.; kafirs, 90;
	non-Muslims, 108
Dihgans, 116
Díhlí, 206, see also Delhi
Dihqanan,132, 145
Dilazāk Afghān/tribe, 106, 165, see also
	Dalazak; Dilazaks
Dilazaks, 106, see also Dalazak; Dilazak
	Afghan/tribe
Diodotus, 53
Dionysos/Dionysus, 25
Dīr, 4, 80, 100, 113, 128, 172, 192, 202, 235,
	237, 247, 248, 249, 251, 253, 256, 267 n.,
	269 n., 274, 281; Khan, 245, 246; ruler(s)
	of, 256, 259; State, 153, 158 n.
Diyarun, 162
Doaba/Duabah, 124
Doms, 135, see also daman
Drachm/drachma, 51, 278
Dubyan, 133
Dudai tah mah gurah khu zama runr tandi tah
	gurah (proverb), 143
Durand Line, 248; Agreement, 237, 247, 248,
	266 n.
Durand, Henry Mortimer, 247, 266 n.
Durawah, 220
Dur-i Mustatir (book), 124
Durrani, Ahmad Shah, 200, 206, see also
	Abdali, Ahmad Shah
Durrani, Dr Farzand Ali, 95 n.
Durrani domain, 200
Durranis, 172, 200, 224 n.
Durush Khilah, 201, 224 n.
Duruzgar, 132
Dvaita philosophy, 279

E

East, 15, 24, 62
East India Company, 225 n., 260 n.
Ecbolima, 38, see also Embolima
Edwardes, Herbert/Edwardes, H.B., 214, 215,
	217, 218, 220
Eid-ul-Azha, 162
Elphinstone, Mountstuart, 136, 140, 148, 200
Embolima, 38, see also Ecbolima
Emperor of China, 65
Encyclopaedia of Islam (book), 130
English (language), 153, 207; persons/rulers,
	209, 214, 241; term or word, 146, 225 n.,
	278, 279; writers, 207, 261 n.
Ephtalites/Ephthalites, 56, 80, 81, see also
	Alcon Huns; Huna; White Huns
Erewhon, 239
Erskine, William, 165
Eudamos (Macedonian general), 40
European, 239
Europeans, 219
Eusofzyes, 200, see also Isafzi; Yusafzi;
	Yusufzai; Yusufzais; Yusuf-zai; Yusufzi;
	Yusufzis
Extra assistant commissioner Peshawar, 240
Ex Qriente, 51

F

Fa-Hein, 5, 62, 63, 65, 78, 80, 82, 83, 95 n., see
	also Fa hian; Fa-hian; Fa-Hian; Fa Hiun;
	Faxian; Xian, Fa
Fa hian, 1, see also Fa-Hein; Fa-hian; Fa-Hian;
	Fa Hiun; Faxian; Xian, Fa
Fa-hian, 1, see also Fa-Hein; Fa hian; Fa-Hian;
	Fa Hiun; Faxian; Xian, Fa
Fa-Hian, 5, see also Fa-Hein; Fa hian; Fa-hian;
	Fa Hiun; Faxian; Xian, Fa
Fa Hiun, 95 n., see also Fa-Hein; Fa hian; Fa-
	hian; Fa-Hian; Faxian; Xian, Fa
Faccenna, Dr, 56
Fakeers, 128, see also faqiran; faqirs
Fakhal, Sultan, 2, 108, 109, 111, 112, see also
	Pakhal, Sultan
Fakir/faqir, 135, 278
Fakir, Mad, 253, see also Faqir, Sartur (Sartor);
	Khan, Sadullah
Faqir, Sartur (Sartor), 241, 242, 244, 245, 252,
	253, 255, 256, 263 n., 264 n., see also Fakir,
	Mad; Khan, Sadullah
Faqiran, 184, 241, 278
Faqiran, 145, see also Fakeers; faqirs
Faqirs, 115, 128, see also Fakeers; faqiran
Farghanah, 161
Farishtah, Muhammad Qasim, 102, 107, 165

Fatah, Hakim Abul, 168, 169, *see also* Fateh, Hakim Abul; Fath, Hakim Abul; Hakim
Fateh, Hakim Abul, 168, *see also* Fatah, Hakim Abul; Fath, Hakim Abul; Hakim
Fath, Hakim Abul, 169, *see also* Fatah, Hakim Abul; Fateh, Hakim Abul; Hakim
Fatihpur, 224 n., 263 n.
Fatimah (RA), 280
Faxian, 5, 62, 63, 65, 78, 80, 82, 83, *see also* Fa-Hein; Fa hian; Fa-hian; Fa-Hian; Fa Hiun; Xian, Fa
Fazal, Abul/Fazl, Abul, 111, 112, 115, 169, 170, 171; Abul Fazal's account, 170; Akbar's favourite and a historian, 171; narrative, 169
Filigenzi, Dr Anna, 72 n., 81, 86
Fincastle, Viscount, 243
Fiqah(s), 153, 183
First Anglo-Sikh war (1845–1846), 202
First Division of the field army, 238
First punitive expedition in the Swat Valley, 242
First World War, 257
Fish (month), 165
Fleet, J.F., 54
Foe, 63, 79, *see also* Buddha; Buddha, Gautama; Tathagata
Foreign department, 240
Fort of Drush (Drosh), 236
French general and ruler, 262 n.
Frontier, 212, 214, 217, 234, 243; plains, 202; Province, 240, 256; region, 223; tribes, 89, 101
Frontier Crimes Regulation, 1901, 260 n.

G

Gabar, 116
Gabar Fort in Bajawar, 109
Gabari, 110, 113, 114, 116, 162, *see also* Gabri; Gibari; Gibri; Kabri
Gabari, Mir Haidar Ali, 162
Gabari Sultans, 110
Gabaris, 109, *see also* Gibaris
Gabri, 110, *see also* Gabari; Gibari; Gibri; Kabri
Gada, 278
Gadādevī, 87, 278
Gadanari, 278
Gadara, 17, *see also* Gandhara
Gadbanah, 132, *see also* shpankyan/shpunkyan
Gagyani/Gigyani/Gugyani, 123
Gandhara, xx, 2, 4, 5, 6, 7, 8, 16, 17, 51, 52, 53, 56, 57, 58, 65, 66, 81, 84, 129, 130; ancient, 4; art, 7; civilization, xix, 7, 61; civilization (of Swat), xix, xxi; country, 7; kingdom, 51; satrapy of, 16, 17, *see also* Gadara

Gandharan art, 87; art images, 87; culture, 57; genius, 79; images, 87
Gāndhāras, 50
Ganesha, 87
Ganges, 55
Garah, 114, *see also* Garra
Garra, 123, *see also* Garah
Garrisons at Malakand and Chakdarah, 240, 241
Garzindah waish, 134, 139
Gau kos, 175 n.
Gauraians, 33
Gautama of the Sakya, 277
Gawri, 271, 272, 273; area, 273, 274; language, 274; organization, 274; tract, 271, 272, 273, 274
Gaz, 175 n.
Gazetteer of the Peshawar District, 1897–98 (book), 108, 111, 124, 214, 219, 230 n.
Ghafur, Abdul, 203, 233, 241, 279, *see also* Akhoond of Swat; Akhund; Akhund of Swat; Akhund Sahib; Ghafur, Akhund Abdul; Saidu Baba
Ghafur, Akhund Abdul, 221, 241, *see also* Akhoond of Swat; Akhund; Akhund of Swat; Akhund Sahib; Ghafur, Abdul; Saidu Baba
Ghag, 138
Ghaligay, 9, 14, 15, 19, 74, 84, 205; cave, 14
Gham-khadi, 131, 148
Ghani, 208
Ghaur, 123, *see also* Ghawar
Ghauri, Malak Muizuddin, 106, *see also* Muizuddin, Malak
Ghauri, Muhammad, 106, 107, 116, *see also* Shahabuddin, Sultan
Ghauri Khail/Ghaurya Khail, 123
Ghawar, 123, *see also* Ghaur
Ghazi Baba, 105, *see also* Pir Khushal
Ghazis, 213
Ghaznavid, 103; army, 101, 103, 274; conquest of Swat, 104; forces, 100; period, 103; rule, 104; sway, 101
Ghaznavides, 89, *see also* Ghaznavids
Ghaznavids, 89, 105, 110, *see also* Ghaznavides
Ghazni, 53, 111
Ghaznin, 89, 101
Ghilzay, General Faiz Muhammad Khan, 248
Ghubanah, 133
Ghulaman (place), 222
Ghwarah Murghah, 123, *see also* Ghwarah Murghzi
Ghwarah Murghzi, 123, *see also* Ghwarah Murghah
Ghwarband, 129, 255; Pass, 242
Gibari, 110, 114; country, 110, *see also* Gabari; Gabri; Gibri; Kabri

Gibaris, 109, *see also* Gabris
Gibri, 110, *see also* Gabari; Gabri; Gibari; Kabri
Gilgit, 66, 81, 236, 238; Agency, 235, 240
Gilgit-India routes, 65
Gira or Mount Gira (as called locally: 'Gira' and 'Da Gira Ghar'), 104, *see also* Mt. (Mount) Raja Gira
Giri (toponym), 110
Gnoli, G., 87
God, 237
Gogdara, 15, *see also* Gugdarah
Goruaia (Bajaur), 51, 52
Gould, B.J., 34
Government of India, 236, 240, 248, 250, 262 n., 267 n.
Government of India Act, 1919, 260 n.
Government of India Act, 1935, 260 n.
Governor-General, 261 n.
Governor-general in council, 242, 250, 267 n.
Graeco-Buddhist art, 52; art of Gandhara, 61
Gram, 2
Grāma, 2
Great Britain, 225 n.
Great Salt Desert, 123, *see also* Dasht-i Lut
Great Trigonometrical Survey, 210
Great/Greater Vehicle, 63, 80, 279
Greaves, Lieutenant R.T., 242
Greece, 16, 32, 278
Greek, 2, 25; historians, 2; inscriptions, 52; literature, 1, 3; pattern, 61; power, 51; provinces, 52; rendering, 2; rule, 51; rulers, 50; seaman, 16; writers, 25, 27, 28, 29, 30, 31, 32, 38
Greeks, xx, 6, 24, 25, 44 n., 45 n., 51, 52, 60, 76, 107, 112
Groups of kings (groups I, II and III; IV and V groups), 51
Guddarh (village), 220
Gugdarah, 15, 20, *see also* Gogdara
Gugdarah (a youth from), 240
Guide Corps, 210, 242
Gujar/Gujran/Gujars/Gurjars (an ethnic group), 85, 93 n., 132, 133, 137, 274; population in the Kuhistan, 274
Gujar Garhai/Gujar Garhi, 210, 221
Gulibagh, 201, 242
Gullini, Giorgio, 59
Gulshazada, 258, *see also* Bacha Sahib; Wadud, Miangul Abdul
Gumbatūna, 34
Guraeans, 35

H

Habib, Prof. Mohammad, 89, 90, 91, 101, 102

Hadbandi, 150
Haibatgram, 109
Haidar, Ghulam (of Dargai), 239
Haj, 237, 278
Hakim, (administrative officer), 164, 278
Hakim (Abul Fatah), 168, *see also* Fatah, Hakim Abul; Fateh, Hakim Abul; Fath, Hakim Abul
Hakim, Mirza, (Mughal Emperor Akbar's brother), 166
Hamdani, Mir Sayyad Ali, 62
Hamidullah, 263 n.
Hamzah, 184, *see also* Khan, Malak Hamzah
Hanafi *fiqah*, 153, 208; jurisprudence, 208; School of *fiqah*, 91; School of thought, 208
Hanan, Miangul Abdul, 224, 245, 246, 247
Hanbali (*fiqah*), 153
Hanging Pass, 53
Hapiḍei, 87
Haq, S. Moinul, 217, 218
Harwi, Khwajah Nimatullah, 106, 116
Hasan, Malak, 127, 128, *see also* Mutrawi, Malak Hasan
Hasan Abdal/Hassan Abdal, 106, 107, 192, 194
Hash-nagar/Hashtnagar, 111, 124, 125, 165, 209, *see also* Ashnaghar
Hay, W.R., 204
Hazara/Hazarah (area/district/region), 54, 89, 112, 113, 115, 202, 204, 206; Division, 128
Hazara/Hazarah (village), 36, 113, *see also* Acadira; Azara
Hellas, 51
Hellenistic pottery, 52; traditions, 53
Heracles, 53
Herodotus, 16
Hilo mountain of the Chinese, 75
Himalayas, 82; trans-Himalayan territories, 19
Himayatullah, Dr, 192, 193, 194, *see also* Yaqubi, Dr Himayatullah
Hinayana school, 77, 78, 80, 82, 278; tradition, 279
Hinayanists, 278
Hindoos, 216, *see also* Hindus
Hindu, 86, 92; belief, 75; communities, 87; deities, 281; faith, 216; god, 280; ilands, 89; mythology, 277, 279; pilgrims, 75; principalities, 90; *raja*, 59, 101; sacred place, 75; temple(s), 74, 77, 87, 88; Texts, 278
Hindu Kush/Hindu-Kush/Hindukush (mountain range), 4, 6, 24, 49, 79, 235, 274; area(s), 88, 272
Hindu Sahi/Hindu Shahi dynasty, 56, 57, 59, 101; kingdom, 58; period, xx, xxi, 58, 87; *rajas*, 58, 101; reign, 57; ruler, 58, 101
Hindu Šāhis/Hindu Shahis, xxi, 57, 58, 86, 100, 103; coins of, 54; period, 88

Hinduism, 74, 77, 86, 87, 88, 89, 90, 91, 279, 280; in Swāt, 74, 86, *see also* Brahmanism

Hindus, 74, 75, 76, 80, 92 n., 93 n., 108, 182, 216, 219, *see also* Hindoos

Hindustan, 102, 106, 165, 175 n., 234

Hindustani fanatics, 212, 234, 248; Mawlwis, 212; Mujahidin, 233, 255, 256, 257; turned anti-British, 233; Waḥābī, 206

Hiouan thsang, 1, *see also* Chwang, Yuan; Hsüan-tsang; Thsang, Hwen; Tsang, Hsüan; Tsiang, Hiuen; Xuanzang; Zang, Xuan

His Highness/His Highness the Amir (Amir of Afghanistan), 248, 266 n., 267 n.

Hisar Bahlul, 111

Hisk, 181

Holdich, Thomas, 5, 16, 29, 33, 45 n.

Holdich, T.H., 243

Holy Quran, 147, *see also* Kuran; Quran

Hsüan-tsang, 63, 77, 79, 80, 81, *see also* Chwang, Yuan; Hiouan thsang; Tsang, Hsüan; Thsang, Hwen; Tsiang, Hiuen; Xuanzang; Zang, Xuan

Hujrah, 148

Hujray, 148

Humayun (Mughal ruler), 127, 166; flight to Persia, 166; reign, 128, 138, 166; reoccupation of Kabul, 166; return, 166

Hun invasion, 129

Hūṇa, 279, *see also* Alchon Huns; Ephtalites/Ephthalites; White Huns

Hund, 57, 58, 103, 222, *see also* Udabhāṇḍapura

Hunter, W.W., 234

Hystaspes, Darius, 16

I

Ilam (Chinese I-lo, Tibetan Hilo), 37, 75, 93 n.; of today, 75, *see also* Mount Ilam

Ilo parvata of the Tibetans, 75

Imaman, 132, *see also* mulan

Imperial aid, 191; army, 169; sway, 171; system, 40

Imperial British, 260 n.; government, 225 n., 245

Imperial Court of China, 65

Imperial Gazetteer of India: Provincial Series; North-West Frontier Province (book), 16, 76, 220, 222, 263 n.

Imperialist government, 252

Inayat (Khan) (of Tanra), 239

India, 16, 17, 21 n., 24, 25, 33, 41 n., 54, 55, 57, 60, 63, 79, 82, 83, 106, 107, 108, 110, 161, 167, 201, 202, 212, 214, 216, 218, 219, 225 n., 229 n., 234, 242, 243, 263 n., 267 n., 277, 278, 279, 280, 281; more troops from, 242

Indian borderland, 40; empire, 49; explanation, 87; history, 61, 244; king, 29; mercenaries, 25, 26, 28, 30, 218; Mujahidin, 249; mythology, 281; origin, 51; ports, 55; religions, 280; revolutionaries, 212, 213, 214, 219, 221; scholars, 12 n.; school of Mystical Thought, 280; side, 248; soldiers, 25, 28, 30, 31, 32, 33; trans-frontier, 16; War of Independence, 244; words, 1

Indian states, 260 n., *see also* Princely states

Indians, 16, 26, 29, 30, 32, 39, 41 n.

Indica (book), 42 n.

Indo-Aryan, 272

Indo-Aryans, 16

Indo-Greek, 50; coins (of), 50, 52, 54; kingdom(s), 51; period, xx; reign, 53; rulers, 53, 54

Indo-Greeks, 16, 50, 51, 52, 54, 59, 60

Indo-Parthians (coins of), 54

Indo-Scythian coins, 50; kings, 54; period, xx

Indo-Scythians (coins of), 54

Indra, 87

Indrabhuti (Buddhist King), 57, 82, 83, 278, 280

Indus, 4, 5, 6, 16, 32, 33, 36, 37, 38, 39, 40, 42 n., 51, 55, 108, 109, 110, 112, 193, 200, 205, 215, 217, 220, 269 n.; country/territories west of, 40, 166; cis-Indus area(s)/territories, 28, 33, 128, 278; Hazarah region, 127; people, 32; plain, 19; territories, 128; hinter-Indus territory, 50; territory/territories west of, 40, 166; trans-Indus country, 40; territory, 50; tract, 278; trans-Indus Pukhtun territory, 200, *see also* River Indus

Indus character, 14; period, 14; Valley, 16

Indus *kōhistān*/Indus Kuhistan, 4, 113

Ingaran, 132

Iori, Elisa, 17

Iqbal Namah-i Jahangiri (book), 103, *see also* *Jahangir Namah* (book); *Tuzuk-i Jahangiri* (book)

Iran, 15, 19, 123

Iranian cemeteries of Iron-Age Period I, 15; prophet, 279; ruler, 112

Isafzi, 123, *see also* Eusofzyes; Yusafzi; Yusufzai; Yusufzais; Yusuf-zai; Yusufzi; Yusufzis

Islam, xix, 88, 89, 90, 91, 102, 108, 112, 113, 116, 145, 187, 189, 223, 275, 278

Islamic calendar, 278; codes, 153; jurisprudence, 153; law(s), 184, 280; learning, 280; principles, 223; Shariat, 153; State, 223, 280; teachings and code, 153; theology, 277; non-Islamic elements, 108

Islamic State of Swat, 216

Islamic Udegram project, 117

Islamization of Swat, 116
Islamized, 90
Ismail, Shah, 202
Israelite Shariat, 153
Italian Archaeological Mission, 15, 20, 52, 67,
    77, 117

J

Jabah, 149; *kawal*, 149
Jabrai, 221
Jadhib, Arsalan/Jādhib, Arslān, 102; general,
    101; governor of Ṭūs, 103
Jāgīr, 167
*Jagir*s, 185
Jahád, 235, *see also jihad*
Jahan, Emperor Shah, 171, 178
Jahangir, Mughal Emperor, 103, 171, 278
Jahangir, Sultan, 111, 112, 115
Jahangir Namah (book), 103, *see also Iqbal
    Namah-i Jahangiri* (book); *Tuzuk-i
    Jahangiri* (book)
Jahangiri persons, 113; Sultans, 111, 115
Jahanzeb, Miangul, 159 n.
Jain mythology, 279
Jainism, 280
Jaipal (Hindu Shahi Raja), 101; Jaipal's
    (Jayapala's) reign, 57, *see also* Jayapala;
    Jayapaladeva; Raja Jaipal; Sri-Jayapaladeva
Jairazbhoy, 52
Jalab, 138, *see also badragah*
Jalal, Sayyad, 115
Jalalabad, 57, 103, 219, 235, *see also* Jelalabad;
    Nagar
Jalalah, 239
Jalaluddin, Sultan, 110
Jalawanan, 133
Jalendra, 57
Jamadar (a grey-haired), 216, 230 n.
Jamal, Hazrat (of Nawagai, Chamlah), 256
Jambil river/stream, 36
Jamruz (a *khan* of village Qambar), 133
Jamruz warukay day khu Qambar yiy luy day
    (proverb), 133
Jan, Ahmad, 269 n., *see also* Ahmad, Wali;
    Sandakai Baba
Jan, Miangul, 253, 256
Jandol, 262 n., *see also* Jandul
Jandul, 161, 235, 236, 237, 240, 247, 251, 255,
    261 n., 262 n.; chief of, 247, *see also* Jandol
Janj, 148
Janjyan, 148
Japan, 277
Jaray (village), 78
Jarga, 143, *see also Jargah*; *Jirga*; *Jirgah*

Jargah, 132, 133, 135, 139, 143, 144, 147, 150,
    190, 252, 253, 256, 273, 274, 278, *see also
    Jarga*; *Jirga*; *Jirgah*
*Jargah*s, 140, 141, *see also Jargay*; *Jirgas*
Jargay, 133, 134, 136, 141, 143, 144, 203, 251,
    254, 278, *see also Jargah*s; *Jirgas*
Jataka(s), 278; stories, 78, 278
Jayapala (Hindu Shahi Raja), 58, 100,
    101; kingdom of, 58, *see also* Jaipal;
    Jayapaladeva; Raja Jaipal; Sri-Jayapaladeva
Jayapaladeva (Hindu Shahi Raja), 58; reign,
    57, *see also* Jaipal; Jayapala; Raja Jaipal;
    Sri-Jayapaladeva
Jelalabad, 49, *see also* Jalalabad; Nagar
Jesus, 24
Jihad, 91, 99 n., 102, 204, 217, 235, 263 n.,
    see also Jahád
Jihadis, 213
Jinki Khail, 251, 255
Jirga, 127, 135, 143, 252, 253, *see also Jarga*;
    Jargah; *Jirgah*
Jirgah, 143, *see also Jarga*; *Jargah*; *Jirga*
Jirgas, 140, *see also Jargah*s; *Jargay*
Jîvaśarman, 76
Jugyanu Sar, 75, *see also* Yogis' Peak
Julagan, 133
Jupiter, 26
Justin, 25, 29, 47 n.
Jūzjānī, 111

K

Kabal (place in Hazarah region), 204
Kabal *tahsil*, 36, 37, 176 n.
Kabari, 110
Kabir, Kurush, 116, *see also* Azam, Kurush;
    Cyrus the Great; Zulqarnain, Sikandar;
    Zulqarnain, Sultan
Kabri, 110, *see also* Gabari; Gabri; Gibari;
    Gibri
Kabul, 33, 103, 106, 107, 111, 123, 125, 127,
    130, 161, 162, 163, 164, 166, 167, 172, 180,
    219; Government, 238, 247; Province, 171;
    ruler of, 123, 124, 125
Kabul River, 16, 32, 33, 40, 51, 52, 55, *see also*
    River Kabul
Kabul Valley, 33, 50, 55
Kachh, 49, *see also* Cutch
Kadphises I, 55
Kafir culture, 61, 62; tribes, 272; tribesmen,
    25; villages, 61
"Kafir"-Dardic cultures, 62; environment, 62
Kafiristan, 49, 89, 98 n., 102, 118 n., 235, *see
    also* Kapis
*Kah da ghwaru gut wi khu chiy tanday but wi
    pah haghay bah sah kaway* (proverb), 143

Kahraj people, 126, 165
Kaju, Khan/Kachu, 130, 131
Kaka Khail, Sayyad Bahadar Shah Zafar, 191
Kakhyan, 133
Kalam, 65, 273, 274
Kalami, 272
Kalay kalwighi, 147
Kaldarah, 222
Kaliraja, 84
Kambala, 75, 278
Kampala, 57, *see also* Sambola
Kamran (son of Babur and brother of Humayun), 166; governor of Kabul, 166; ruler at Kabul, 166
Kandahar, 129, 130, *see also* Qandahar
Kandaray (ruins), 224 n.
Kandi, 148, *see also* Cundy; *tal*; Tul
Kandis, 148, *see also* Cundies; *talunah*
Kanishka, 55; Kanishka's reign, 55; time, 77
Kanra, 129
Kanz (book), 183
Kapis, 49, *see also* Kafiristan
Kapiśa, 57, 65
Karakar, 169, 200; defile, 169; Pass, 32, 38, 111, 168, 169
Karakorum (Qaraquram), 274
Karman, 120 n.
Karnataka, 279
Karoh, 175 n.
Karohs, 168
Karu, 123
Kasabgar, 132, 134, 273
Kashghar, 106
Kashmir, 3, 14, 16, 19, 58, 62, 66, 75, 108, 112, 113, 166, 167, 169, 180, 200; issue, 167; ruler of, 167, 169
Kashmiris, 167
Kashtkars, 135
Kasmira, 16, *see also* Kaspira
Kaspioi, 16
Kaspira, 16, *see also* Kasmira
Kasyapa, 279
Kasyapiya(s), 80, 83, 279
Katilai (now Amankut), 36, 167
Katwal's (Kotwal's) Diary (book), 213, *see also* Kotwal's Diary, 229 n.
Kaumodaki, 278
Keen, W.J., 204, 256
Khadakzi, 241, 251
Khadi (Khan) (of Lund Khwar), 239
Khagendra, 92 n.
Khaibar pass, 167; route, 33
Khails, 139, 273, 274
Khakhi, 123, *see also* Shikhi
Khalífah, 206, *see also* Caliph
Khalifa-i-Ilahī (His Majisty), 167
Khalil, Hamesh, 191

Khaliq, Miangul Abdul, 247, 248
Khan, 131, 133, 137, 156 n., 186, 251
Khan, Abdullah (of Rabat, Dir), 244
Khan, Ahmad Nabi, 56
Khan, Ajun, 210, 219, *see also* Khan, Arjan/ Khan, Aujun
Khan, Amir Dost Muhammad (Amir of Afghanistan), 222
Khan, Anbalay, 201
Khan, Arbab Bahram, 204
Khan, Arbab Juma, 204
Khan, Arjan, 210, *see also* Khan, Ajun; Khan, Aujun
Khan, Asaf, 169
Khan, Aujun, 210, 219, *see also* Khan, Ajun; Khan, Arjan
Khan, Aurangzeb, 253, *see also* Chara Nawab; Khan, Bacha; Khan, Badshah
Khan, Bacha, 253, *see also* Chara Nawab; Khan, Aurangzeb; Khan, Badshah
Khan, Badshah, 253, 255, *see also* Chara Nawab; Khan, Aurangzeb; Khan, Bacha
Khan, Bahram, 179
Khan, Bhaku, 192, 193, 194
Khan, Changiz, 109, 110, 111
Khan, Dr Ansar Zahid, 213
Khan, Dr M. Ashraf, 80, 95 n., 96 n.
Khan, Dr Munawwar, 218, 219, 229 n.
Khan, Dr Rafiullah, 20, 22 n., 44 n., 50, 60, 67 n., 72 n.
Khan, Ghazan (Khan of Dir), 201, 203, 206, 208, 225 n., 245
Khan, Ghazi, 207
Khan, Jafar, 258
Khan, Kamil (*faujdar* of Attock), 192
Khan, Khadi (of Hund), 222
Khan, Khushal, 178, 179, 180, 181, 182, 183, 184, 185, 186, 187, 188, 189, 190, 191, 192, 193, 194, 197 n.; Khushal Khan's allegation(s), 187, 197 n.; anti-Yusufzi role, 179, 185, 191; approach, 191; behaviour in Swat, 192; behest, 193; condemnation, 185, 186, 187; contentions, xx, 184, 187, 189, 197 n.; ethnicity, 185; eyes, 191; imprisonment, 179, 191; mission in Swat, 188; past history, 192; pitfalls, 188, 191; pro-Mughal role, 185; reviling, 185, 188, 190; struggle, 193, 194; Swat visit, 193; viewpoint and beliefs, 188; visit to Swat, xx; writing about Swat, 187, *see also* Khattak, Khushal/Khattak, Khushal Khan/ Khattak, Khushhal Khan
Khan, Malak Hamzah, 185, *see also* Hamzah
Khan, Malak Malu, 185
Khan, Masam, 258
Khan, Muhammad Asif, 102, 106, 107, 118 n., 159 n., 169, 172, 222, 263 n.

Khan, Muhammad Isa, 256
Khan, Muhammad Nazir, 104
Khan, Muhammad Sadiq, 169
Khan, Muhammad Shah (brother of Umara Khan of Jandul), 240
Khan, Muhammad Sharif, 247, *see also* Khan, Sharif (Khan/Nawab of Dir)
Khan, Mukaram, 192
Khan, Nawab Akbar (of Huti, Mardan), 263 n.
Khan, President Ayub, 78
Khan, Rahmatullah (Khan of Dir), 245, 246, 247
Khan, Roshan, 113, 126
Khan, Saadat (of Batkhilah), 239
Khan, Sadullah, 263 n., *see also* Faqir, Mad; Faqir, Sartur (Sartor)
Khan, Shah Beg, 171
Khan, Shah Jahan (Nawab of Dir), 263 n.
Khan, Shah Nazar, 27, 34, 35, 37
Khan, Sharif, 237, 239, 240, 247, 249, 251, 252, 253, 263 n., 267 n., *see also* Khan, Muhammad Sharif (Khan/Nawab of Dir)
Khan, Sharif (of Alahdand), 239
Khan, Sher Dil/Khan, Shir Dil (of Alahdand), 245, 246
Khan, Sultan Muhammad, 204
Khan, Syed Badshah (Nawab of Dir's general), 255, *see also* Badshah, Syed
Khan, Taj Muhammad, 258
Khan, Umara (of Jandul)/Khan, Umra (of Jandol), xx, 235, 236, 237, 238, 240, 247, 248, 249, 250, 251, 255, 261 n., 262 n., 267 n.; invasion of Chitral, 237
Khan, Zain, 167, 168, 169, 170, 239, *see also* Koka, Zain Khan; Kukah, Zain Khan
Khan, Zarin (of Kuzah Bandai, Nikpi Khail), 115, 258
Khan Khail, 240, 254, 259
Khan-i Duran, 171
Khan of Bajawar, 246
Khan of Barwa (now Samar Bagh), 258
Khan of Dir, 237, 240, 246, 247, 251, 252
Khan of Jandul, 237
Khanan, 131, 132, 133, 135, 137, 156 n., 183, 184, 190, 203, 237, 249, *see also* Khans
Khanan of Alahdand, 239
Khanan of Swát, 250, *see also* Khans of Swat
Khanan of Tanra, 239, 250
Khani, 137
Khans, 145, 225 n., 246, *see also* khanan
Kháns of Swat, 249, *see also* Khanan of Swat
Khans of Tamghaj and Tinkat, 110
Khapirai/khapiray/khapiri, 91
Khar, 126, 201, 225 n.
Khari-dron-lda-btsan (Tibetan King), 83
Kharoshṭhī inscription, 52
Khataks, 191, *see also* Khattaks

Khattak (tribe), 178, 189, 195 n.
Khattak, Khushal/Khattak, Khushal Khan/ Khattak, Khushhal Khan, xx, xxi, 3, 60, 91, 172, 178, 179, 184, 191, 192, *see also* Khan, Khushal
Khattak, Muhammad Habibullah Khan, 45 n., 58, 76
Khattaks, 188, 191, *see also* Khataks
Khazarya, 114
Khel(s), 135, 273
Khilafat, 100, 206, *see also* Caliphate
Khonay, 224 n., *see also* Khoni; Khunah; Khunah *kalay* (Khunah village); Khúna'h; Khúna'h Khela'h'; Khunay
Khoni, 224 n., *see also* Khonay; Khunah; Khunah *kalay* (Khunah village); Khúna'h; Khúna'h Khela'h'; Khunay
Khudayi milmah, 143
Khunah, 201, 224 n., *see also* Khonay; Khoni; Khunah *kalay* (Khunah village); Khúna'h; Khúna'h Khela'h'; Khunay
Khunah *kalay* (Khunah village), 224 n., *see also* Khonay; Khoni; Khunah; Khúna'h; Khúna'h Khela'h'; Khunay
Khúna'h, 224 n., *see also* Khonay; Khoni; Khunah; Khunah *kalay* (Khunah village); Khúna'h Khela'h'; Khunay
Khúna'h Khela'h', 224 n., *see also* Khonay; Khoni; Khunah; Khunah *kalay* (Khunah village); Khúna'h; Khunay
Khunay, 201, *see also* Khonay; Khoni; Khunah; Khunah *kalay* (Khunah village); Khúna'h; Khúna'h Khela'h'
Khushal Khan Khattak and Swat (article), 192
Khushalyat aw Haqayaq (Intiqadi Jaaj) (book), 185
Khushwakht, 271, *see also* Kushwakht
Khyber Pukhtunkhwa, 240, 269 n.
Khwajah, Shaikh Zangi ibn Mula Khalil Ranrizi, 125, 135
Khwajuzi, 131, 182, *see also* Khwazuzai; Khwazuzi
Khwarizm Shahs, 110
Khwaza Khela/Khwaza Khilah, 201, 211, 224 n.
Khwaza Khilah–Fatihpur Road, 224 n.
Khwazuzai, 131, *see also* Khwajuzi; Khwazuzi
Khwazuzi, 131, 182, 251; clans, 251, *see also* Khwazuzai; Khwajuzi
King, 102, 200, 205, 206, 207, 209, 210, 214, 215, 217, 221
King family, 207; king's determination, 209
King Girã's Castle, 59
King Milinda, 54
King of Buner, 207
King of Delhi, 242
King of great kings, 58

King of Ki-pin, 65
King of "Ki-pin and Uḍḍiyāna", 65
King of Sama, 207
King of Swat, 82, 83, 84, 203, 204, 205, 206, 207, 208, 210, 212, 215, 219, 245, 258, 280
King of Yaghistan, 207
Kingdom, 206
Kingdom of Ouchhang, 1
Kingdom of Swat, 82
Kingdom of Uddiyana, 5, 6, 7, 65
Kings, 84, 181, 207
Kings of kings, 17
Kings and Knights, 181
Kingship of Swát, 224
Kiramat (miracle), 167
Kiri, 76, 110
Kiwhur, Nawshirawan, 271
Kleophis, 30, *see also* Queen Cleophis/Kleophis
Kohistan, 254, *see also* Kuhistan
Kohistání language, 275
Koinos, 27, *see also* Coenus
Koka, Zain Khan (Mughal general), 166, 169, *see also* Khan, Zain; Kukah, Zain Khan
Kos, 168, 175 n.
Kot, 61
Kote Gullee, 220
Kotwal's Diary (book), 229 n., *see also* Katwal's Diary (book)
K*ouan, Chhing*, 65
Kramasaṃpradāya, 74, 279
Kshanti-rishi, 84
Kufar (infidels), 90, 102, 103, 112, 113
Kuh Payah, 110
Kuhan, 269 n.
Kuhat (district), 202
Kuh-i Sulayman, 106
Kuhistan, xx, xxi, 91, 113, 254, 257, 271, 274, 275; area, 91, 271, *see also* Kohistan
Kuhistan-i Ghaur, 107
Kuhistan-i Ruh, 106
Kuhistani, 106, 272; language, 275
Kuhistanis, 272, 275
Kukah, Zain Khan (Mughal general), 170, *see also* Khan, Zain; Koka, Zain Khan
Kukkuripā, 76, 278, 279
Kukkuripas, 279
Kula, Mihira, 81, 279, *see also* Mahiragula; Mihirakula
Kulalan, 133
Kuluta, 50
Kumbar, 257
Kunar, 35, 111, 115, 116
Kunar river, 51
Kung, Wu, 81
Kurán, 203, 205, *see also* Holy Quran; Quran
Kuroh/kuruh, 175 n.
Kurram, 239; Valley, 120 n.

Kus, 175 n.
Kuṣāṇa, 55; Early Kuṣāṇa dynasty, 55; Empire, 55; period, 55, 56, 87, *see also* Kushana
Kusanas, 57, *see also* Kushanas; Kushans
Kushan power, 55; sub-Kushan coins, 56; times, 54; vassal chiefs, 55
Kushana, 55; dynasty, 55, 56, 96 n.; Empire, 55; Emperors, 54; period, xx, *see also* Kusana
Kushanas, 55, 57; coins of, 54, *see also* Kusanas; Kushans
Kushans, 56, 59, 60, *see also* Kusanas; Kushanas
Kushwakht, 271, *see also* Khushwakht
Kutah (village), 9, 84, 243, 264 n.
Kutanai (village), 224 n.
Kutigram (village), 201

L

Laghman, 58, 89, 102, 111; area, 57, *see also* Lamaghān
Lahor, 112, 113, *see also* Lahur
Lahore, 189
Lahore Museum, 58
Lahur, 112, 113 *see also* Lahor
Laikot/Laikut, 273
Lais, Yaqub bin, 57
Lake of Aral, 15
Lakhkar, 115, 151, 183, 184, 192, 193, 255, 279, *see also lashkar*
Lakhkaray, 183, 188, 190, 279, *see also lakhkar*s; Lashkars
*Lakhkar*s, 257, *see also Lakhkaray*/Lashkars
Lamaghān, 89, 102, *see also* Laghman
Laṇḍaey Sín, 207
Landakay, 84, 114, 126, 239, 240, 241, 242, 243, 244, 264 n., 268 n.
Landay (village), 129
Landay dalah (*dalah* in opposition), 132, 144
Lankapuri, 57
Lar, 153
Las warkawal, 152
Lashkar, 115, 193, *see also lakhkar*
Lashkars, 257, *see also lakhkaray*; *lakhkar*s
Late Middle English origin, 278
Latin historian, 35
Layers 19 and 18 of the rock-shelter near Ghaligay, 19
Legge, James, 1
Leitner, Dr, 272
Lesser Traditions, 54
Linguistic Survey of India (book), 272
Local Hindu *raja*, 59
Loebanr, 14, 15
London, 238; newspaper, 243
London Gazette, 264 n.
Low, Major-General Sir Robert, 238

Lower Talash, 90
Lt. Governor of the Punjab's views, 250
Luca, Dr, 35, 36, 61, 62, 85, *see also* Olivieri, Dr Luca M.
Lu-hi-ta-kia (*stupa*), 49, 76, *see also* Rohitaka
Lundkhwar (people of), 210

M

Ma jabah karay dah, 150
Macedonian, 40; control, 40; forces, 39; garrison, 40; posts, 40; power, 44, 49; rule, 40; satrap(s), 40; yoke, 40
Macedonians, 25, 26, 27, 28, 31, 37, 39, 40; posts, 32
MacGregor, C.M., 205
Mackeson, Colonel, 209
MacLean, H.L.S., 242, 243, 265 n.
Madhvacharya, 279
Madinah, 189
Madyan, 128, 273, 275, *see also* Chiroleh; Churrai
Mahaban, 38
Mahâdeva, 76
Mahak (torrent), 35
Mahamadan (Muhammadan) law, 203, *see also* Islamic Shariat; Shariat
Mahapuranas, 278
Maharajadhiraja, 58
Mahasanghika(s), 80, 83, 279
Mahasiddha(s), 279
Mahayana, 80, 278, 279; Buddhism, 277, 281; School, 82, 279
Mahayanists, 278, 279
Mahiragula, 279, *see also* Kula, Mihira; Mihirakula
Mahisasaka(s), 80, 83, 278, 279
Mahmud (of Ghazna/Ghazni), 59, 86, 88, 89, 91, 100, 101, 102, 104, 105; personally coming to Swat, 102, 103, 106; Mahmud of Ghazna's assaults of, 105; conquest times, 104; expedition, 89, 100, 102; exploits, 58, 59, 101; generals, 105, 109; Indian campaigns, 103; invasion of Swat, 103; *jihad* on, 102; reign, 58, 100, 104, 107, 112; rule, 91, 104, 109; soldiery, 88, 90, 91, *see also* Mahmud, Sultan
Mahmud, Sultan, 102, 103, 106, *see also* Mahmud (of Ghazna/Ghazni)
Mahomedan, 212, *see also* Muhammadans; Muslims; Mussulmans
Mahra, 170, *see also* Mahura; Mahurah; Mora/ Morah; Murah
Mahura, 165, *see also* Mahra; Mahurah; Mora/ Morah; Murah

Mahurah, 162, *see also* Mahrah; Mahura; Mora/ Morah; Murah
Maidan, 255
Majab, 156 n., *see also* muwajib
Majlas-i shurah (consultative council), 204
Makh turawal, 151
Makhzan (Akhun Darwizah's book), 164, 174 n., 183, 184, 188, 190, 197 n.
Makhzan-i Afghani (Khwajah Nimatullah Harwi's book), 106
Makkah, 82, 189, 278
Makran, 49
Mal, Raja Todar, 169
Malak, 124, 131, 136, 137, 156 n., 182, 263 n.
Malak, Nasray (of Uch, Dir), 239
Malakan, 131, 132, 133, 135, 137, 140, 156 n., 183, 184, 190, 249, 252, 253, *see also* malakanan; *malak*s; Maliks; Mulliks
Malakanan, 131, *see also* malakan; *malak*s; Maliks; Mulliks
Malakand (place), 34, 170, 201, 235, 240, 241, 242, 245, 253, 255, 256; Agency, 4, 45 n., 100, 109, 240, 246, 254, 263 n.; District, 100, 109, 240, 246; Division, 4; Field Force, 242, 243, 264 n.; Jihad, 243; mountains, 5; Pass, 34, 45 n., 111, 125, 126, 168, 238, 239; Protected Area, 100, 109, 240, 246; war, 239, 243, 244, 264 n., 265 n.; war of 1895, xx, 235, 263 n.; war of 1897, xx, 240
Malaki, 137
*Malak*s, 127, 136, 140, 144, *see also* malakan; *malakanan*; Maliks; Mulliks
Malandarai (Mlandarai) defile, 169; Pass, 168, 169
Mali (gardener), 263 n.
Mali, Malak Shaikh, 126, 158 n., 196 n., *see also* Mali, Shaikh
Mali, Shaikh, 125, 126, 128, 138, 153, 158 n., 183, *see also* Mali, Malak Shaikh
Malik Láhor [Mulk-i Lahor?], 113
Malikah-i Swat (book), 113
Maliki (*fiqah*, school of thought), 153
Maliks, 144, 145, 253, *see also* malakan; *malakanan*; *malak*s; Mulliks
Malizi, 247
Malka, 233, 234, 256
Mallatars, 135, *see also* mlatar
Malwa, 55
Mandanr, 126, 158 n., 166, 168, 192
Mandanr-Yusufzi, 126
Mandaṛs, 170
Mangalaor, 8, *see also* Manglawar; Minglaur; *Manglora* of General Court's map; *Mangora* of Wilford's surveyor
Mangalor, 8, 9
Mang-chi-li, 8

Manglawar, 7, 8, 9, 32, 44 n., 86, 105, 111, 112, 114, 126, 127, 162, 163, 164, 165, 201; city, 109; Fort, 109, 112, 162, *see also* Mangalaor; Minglaur; *Manglora* of General Court's map; *Mangora* of Wilford's surveyor

Manglora of General Court's map, 7, *see also* Mangalaor; Manglawar; *Mangora* of Wilford's surveyor; Minglaur

Mangora of Wilford's surveyor, 7, *see also* Mangalaor; Manglawar; *Manglora* of General Court's map; Minglaur

Mangwanr, 180

Mani, 279

Manichaenism (Manichaeism), 83, 279, 280

Mankyāl, 54

Mansehra/Mansihrah, 50, 114; District, 128

Mansur, Malak Shah/Mansúr, Malek-shah/ Manṣūr, Malik Shāh, 124, 127, 131, 162, 163, 164

Mansura, 104

Maratha Confederacy, 200

Marayan, 133

Mardan, 192, 193, 212, 214, 242, 263 n.; District, 106

Marshall, John, 80

Martin, V. de St./Martin, Vivien de Saint, 7, 8

Mashar, 148

Mashari, 146

Massaga, 2, 18, 24, 25, 26, 27, 28, 29, 30, 31, 32, 33, 34, 35, 36, 39, 40, 42 n., 44 n., 45 n., 46 n., *see also* Massaka

Massagan defence, 31

Massagans, 28

Massaka, 35, *see also* Massaga

Mastuj, 235, 236, 271

Masumah, Ms (of village Dhiri), 239

Matkanai, 45 n.

Matta *tahsil*, 37

Maues (Śaka king in India), 53, 54, 69 n.

Maurya, 49; period, xx, xxi, 49

Maurya, Chandragupta, 49

Mauryan empire, 50; period, 50

Mauryas, xx, xxi, 49, 50, 67, 67 n.; heyday, 77

McMahon, A.H., 112, 127, 135, 136, 138, 139, 149, 205, 271

M'crindle, J.W., 28

Mecca (Makkah), 82

Meerut, 221

Mehr, Ghulam Rasul, 204, 217, 218

Mehtar, 236, *see also* Mihtar

Meiklejohn, General, 243

Memoir, 171, 280

Menander, 7, 51, 52; Menander's kingdom, 52; realm, 51; reign, 51; sub-kings, 52

Meng-chi-li, 8, 9, *see also* Mêng-ch'ieh-li; Mêng chie li; Mingaur; Mingawarah;

Mingora/Mingora of Wilford's Surveyor; Mung Kie-li

Mêng-ch'ieh-li, 9, *see also* Meng-chi-li; Mêng chie li; Mingaur; Mingawarah; Mingora/ Mingora of Wilford's Surveyor; Mung Kie-li

Mêng chie li, 7, 8, 9, *see also* Meng-chi-li; Mêng-ch'ieh-li; Mingaur; Mingawarah; Mingora/Mingora of Wilford's Surveyor; Mung Kie-li

Meru, 279; of Indian cosmology, 75; of Swāt, 75

Mian, 279, *see also* mya

Mian Gul (Abdul Hanan), 245, 246, 247

Miangan, 279, *see also* Mians; *myagan*

Miangul, 279

Mianguls, 241, 244, 251, 252, 253, 254, 255, 257, 258, 279, *see also* Miangwalan; *myagwalan*

Miangwalan, 279, *see also* Mianguls; *myagwalan*

Mians, 134, 279, *see also* Miangan; *myagan*

Mihirakula, 279, *see also* Kula, Mihira; Mahiragula

Mihtar, 236, 238, *see also* Mehtar

Milinda (king), 54

Military Report and Gazetteer on Buner and Adjacent Independent Territory (book), 215

Milmastya, 142, 143

Mingaur, 7, *see also* Meng-chi-li; Mêng chie li; Mêng-ch'ieh-li; Mingawarah; Mingora/ Mingora of Wilford's Surveyor; Mung Kie-li

Mingawarah, 7, 8, 9, 20, 79, 93 n., 134, 201, 242, 252, *see also* Meng-chi-li; Mêng chie li; Mêng-ch'ieh-li; Mingaur; Mingora/ Mingora of Wilford's Surveyor; Mung Kie-li

Mingawarah-Amankut, 36

Minglaur, 7, *see also* Mangalaor; Manglawar; *Manglora* of General Court's map; *Mangora* of Wilford's surveyor

Mingora/Mingora of Wilford's Surveyor, 7, 9, 66, *see also* Meng-chi-li; Mêng chie li; Mêng-ch'ieh-li; Mingaur; Mingawarah; Mung Kie-li

Mir Zakah Treasure, 53

Mirah sharalay khah dah, puzah prikaray nah (proverb), 152

Mirat/miratah, 138

Mishra, Yogendra, 58, 100

Mithraic or Roman symbolism, 97 n.

Mizaj Namah (temperament law book), 159 n., *see also Riwaj Namah* (customary law book)

Mk'a'agro ma (sky flying), 82

Mlatar, 135, *see also mallatars*

Mogal Beg, 7
Mohmand area, 35; country, 64, *see also* Muhmand area
Mohmands, 243
Mongols, 110
Monograph on Swat State (book), 204
Mookerji, Radhakumud, 49
Mora/Morah, 67 n., 162, *see also* Mahra; Mahura; Mahurah; Murah
Mount Ilam, 37, 38, 75, 93 n., *see also* Ilam
Mount Mora (Murah), 49, *see also* Murah Hill/ Mountain
Mountain Murunda, 278
Movable Column, 217, 220
Mt. (Mount) Rāja Gīrā, 104, 110, *see also* Gira or Mount Gira (as called locally 'Gira' and 'Da Gira Ghar')
mts'o, O rgyan pa Nag dban rgya (Tibetan pilgrim), 90, 108, *see also* pa, sTag ts'an ra (Tibetan pilgrim)
Mubarakah, Bibi, 162, 163, 165
Mughal, 125, 186, 187, 189, 193, 194; administrative apparatus/hierarchy, 277; agent, 197 n.; army, 169; attempt, 187; commander-in-chief, 172; court, 179; dynastic rule in India, 161; Empire, 170, 172, 174 n., 200, 219; expeditions, 192, 194; forces, 166, 167, 168, 169, 171, 179, 187; fort, 192, 193; general, 170; government, 178; historians, 3, 169; India, 280; period, 3, 280; power, 200; ruler(s), xx, 171, 218; rulers of India, 178; rulers of Kabul, 164; service(s), 187, 189; smile, 191; soldiers, 192; suzerainty, 187
Mughal-Yusufzi pitch battles, 166
Mughals, xx, xxi, 125, 161, 166, 167, 169, 170, 171, 172, 178, 179, 180, 183, 184, 187, 188, 189, 190, 191, 192, 193, 194, 199 n.; attempt, 166
Mughul Empire, 218; ruler, 218
Mughuls, 167
Muhallahs, 224 n.
Muhammad, Prophet (SAW), 100, 206, 208, 223, 280
Muhammadans, 219; pre-Muhammadan times, 93 n., *see also* Mahomedan; Muslims; Mussulmans
Muḥammadī (Muhammadzi) Afghāns, 165
Muharram, 163
Muhmand area, 35, *see also* Mohmand area
Muizuddin, Malak, 107, *see also* Ghauri, Malak Muizuddin
Mujahidin, 201, 234
Mula, 182, 220, *see also mulla*
Mula, Hadah, 240
Mula, Makrani, 237
Mula, Manki (Pir of Manki), 239

Mula, Sandakai, 269 n.
Mula Sarvastivada school (*Mūlasarvāstivāda-vinaya*), 277
Mulan, 132, 134, 181, 184, *see also imaman*; Mulas
Mulas, 134, 275, *see also mulan*
Mūlasarvāstivādins, 77, 279
Mulk, 135
Mulk, Afzalul, 236
Mulk, Amanul, 236, 238
Mulk, Amirul, 236
Mulk, Nizamul, 236
Mulk, Shujaul, 236
Mulla, 134, *see also mula*
Mulliks, 136, 140, *see also malakan*; *malakanan*; *malak*s; Maliks
Multan, 58, 106
Mumlikat-i Gabar, 115
Mumyali, 116
Muncherji, D.H., 8, 56, 59, 60, 64, 83, 84
Mundur, Futteh Khan, 206
Mung Kie-li, 7, *see also* Meng-chi-li; Mêng chie li; Mêng-ch'ieh-li; Mingaur; Mingawarah; Mingora/Mingora of Wilford's Surveyor
Mungali (Mung-kie-li), 7, 8, 9, 49, 76, 84
Munkir (angel), 20
Murah, 111, 114, 162, 170, *see also* Mahra; Mahura; Mahurah; Mora/Morah
Murah Hill, 162; Mountain, 210; Pass, 125, 238, *see also* Mount Mora (Murah)
Murree, 219
Murundaka, 76
Musa Khail, 251, 254
Muslim, 90, 92, 103; authors, 110; conquerer, 103; first Muslim conquerer of Swat, 103; forces, 100, 105; graves (of the Lesser Traditions), 54; invaders, 3; invasion of Swat, 58, 103; Khilafat, 100; occupation of the place, 104; occupation of Swat, 108; occupied Swat, xix; revolutionaries (in India), 213; rule, xix; ruler, 208; rulers of Afghanistan, 108; rulers of India, 108; scholar, 277; schools of *fiqah*, 153; pre-Muslim Swat, 74; pre-Yusufzi Muslim Period, xx, xxi, 100
Muslim, Qutaybah bin, 65
Muslims, xix, xx, xxi, 75, 91, 92, 100, 103, 104, 105, 108, 110, 123, 146, 181, 212, 216, 217, 220, 275, 280; non-Muslims, xix, 91, 92, *see also* Mahomedan; Muhammadans; Mussulmans
Mussulmans, 220, *see also* Mahomedan; Muhammadans; Muslims
Mutiny, 220, 221
Mutiny Reports (book), 209, 212, 215, 230 n.
Mutrawi, 114, 115, 116, 126, 127, 128; section of the Swatis, 114

Mutrawi, Malak Hasan, 114, 115, 127, 128, *see also* Hasan, Malak
Muwajib, 156 n., *see also majab*
Mya, 279, *see also Mian*
Mya Dhirai, 224 n.
Myagan, 134, 279, *see also Miangan*; Mians
Myagwalan, 241, 279, *see also* Mianguls; *Miangwalan*

N

Nadwi, Rashid Akhtar, 127
Nāga Apalāla, 77
Nagar, 49, *see also* Jalalabad; Jelalabad
Nagaraja, 83
Nagas, 82
Naghah, 132, 150
Nagharah, 274
Nagharah kawal, 150
Naik (of the 64th Native Infantry), 212
Naikan, 133, 137
Naikpeekhail (Nikpi Khail), 140, *see also* Nikpi Khail; Nikpi Khel; Nipkhi-Khel
Nakir (angel), 20
Nakshbandia tariqah, 221, 222, *see also* Naqshbandiyah
Nanawatay, 135, 147
Nandafan, 133
Nang, 146, 159 n., 181, 188, 190, 279, 280
Napoleon (Napoleon Bonaparte), 262 n.
Naqshbandiyah, 221, 222, *see also Nakshbandia tariqah*
Narain, A.K., 7, 51, 52, 53, 54
Nardin (place), 102, 103, 118 n., *see also* Nur
Nathoo, Kuleefa, 212
Nawab of Dir, 241, 244, 245, 252, 253, 254, 255, 256, 257, 258, 263 n.; Nawab's action, 254; agents, 254, 255; authority, 258; brother, 256; depredations, 252, 255; forces, 257, 258; general, 255, 258; instigation, 256; mother, 256; occupation, 257; occupation and tyranny, 255; position, 254, 257; revenue collectors, 253; rule, 254
Naway Kalay (village near Kutah), 9, 84, 243, 264 n.
Nawkhar, 238, *see also* Nawshihrah; Nowshera
Nawshihrah, 238, *see also* Nawkhar; Nowshera
Nayak, 137
Nayan, 133
Nayi, 137
Nazaran, 133
Nazim, Dr Muhammad, 89, 102
Nestorianism, 83, 280
Nicanor, 40
Nichols, Dr Robert, 205, 227 n.

Nicholson, Colonel John, 213, 214, 215, 217, 220
Nihag or Nihak or Niyak Darah, 113, *see also* Darah Nihak or Nihag or Niyak; Dara'h of Nihák or Niáka'h or Ní'ák; Nihag or Nihak or Niyak Valley; Nihak (Valley); Niyag (Valley); Valley Nihak or Niyag
Nihag or Nihak or Niyak Valley, 113, *see also* Darah Nihak or Nihag or Niyak; Dara'h of Nihák or Niáka'h or Ní'ák; Nihag or Nihak or Niyak Darah; Nihak (Valley); Niyag (Valley); Valley Nihak or Niyag
Nihak (Valley), 112, 113, *see also* Darah Nihak or Nihag or Niyak; Dara'h of Nihák or Niáka'h or Ní'ák; Nihag or Nihak or Niyak Darah; Nihag or Nihak or Niyak Valley; Niyag (Valley); Valley Nihak or Niyag
Nikaya (Nikāya) Buddhism, 278
Nikepheros (the Victorious), 52
Niki, 154 n.
Nikpi Khail, 35, 36, 37, 113, 136, 140, 176 n., 241, 251, 254, 255, 257, 258, *see also* Naikpeekhail; Nikpi Khel; Nipkhi-khel
Nikpi Khel, 35, *see also* Naikpeekhail; Nikpi Khail; Nipkhi-khel
Nipkhi-khel, 35, *see also* Naikpeekhail; Nikpi Khail; Nikpi Khel
Nirvana, 84, 277, 279, 280
Nishanchyan, 133
Niyag (Valley), 111, 112, 113, 127, *see also* Darah Nihak or Nihag or Niyak; Dara'h of Nihák or Niáka'h or Ní'ák; Nihag or Nihak or Niyak Darah; Nihag or Nihak or Niyak Valley; Nihak (Valley); Valley Nihak or Niyag
Nora of Curtius Rufus, 18, *see also* Ora of Arrian
North India, 83
North West/North-West, 77
North-West border, 241
North-West Frontier, 39, 57, 244, 280
North-West Frontier of India, 241
North-West Frontier Province, 240, 260 n. *see also* NWFP
Northern India, 66
Northern India and Adjacent countries, 7
Northern Neolithic, 14
Noshki, 123, *see also* Nushki
Notes on Afghanistan and Baluchistan (book), 110, 113, 205
Nowshera, 214, 238, *see also* Nawkhar; Nawshihrah
*Nullah*s, 105
Nur (place), 89, 98 n., 102, 103, 118 n., *see also* Nardin

Nur, Mian, 183, 184, 188, 189, 190, 197 n.;
    Mian Nur's beliefs, 188; role, 188; stature,
    188, 189
Nuristan, 98 n., 118 n.
Nushki, 114, 123, 154 n., *see also* Noshki
NWFP, 156 n., *see also* North-West Frontier
    Province
Nysa, 24, 25, 45 n.; location of, 25; people of,
    25; story of, 25
Nysan affairs, 25
Nysans, 24

O

O rgyan (Swat), 90
Oddiyana/Odiyana, 2, 5, 7, 50, *see also*
    Oudyana; Uddiyana; Udiyana; Udyana
Odi, 18
Oḍigrām, 2, 8, *see also* Udegram; Uḍigrām
Oḍis, 2, 8; the land of, 2, 8, *see also* Udis
Ohind (kings of), 6
Olivieri, Dr Luca M., 9, 16, 20, 29, 33, 34, 35,
    36, 38, 40, 42 n., 56, 60, 61, 85, *see also*
    Luca, Dr
On Alexander's track to the Indus (book), 52
Oolooss, 140, *see also* ulas
Ooloosses, 140, *see also* ulasay; ulasunah
Ora, 2, 8, 18, 25, 27, 28, 32, 33, 34, 35, 36, 37,
    39, 40, 45 n., 46 n.
Ora of Arrian, 18, *see also* Nora of Curtius
    Rufus
Order of Merit, 243
Oriental Note II, 86
Orrissa, 12 n.
Ou chang/Ou chang na/Ou chha/Ou chhang, 1,
    see also Ou san chhang; U-chang; U-chang-
    na; Woo-chang; Wu ch'a; Wuchung
Ou san chhang, 1, *see also* Ou chang/Ou chang
    na/Ou chha/Ou chhang; U-chang; U-chang-
    na; Woo-chang; Wu ch'a; Wuchung
Oudyana, 1, *see also* Oddiyana/Odiyana;
    Uddiyana; Udiyana; Udyana
Oxus (river), 55

P

pa, O rgyan (pilgrim), 64, 84, 89, 90, 108
pa, sTag ts'an ra (Tibetan pilgrim), 62, 64, 84,
    89, 90, 108, *see also* mts'o, O rgyan pa Nag
    dban rgya (Tibetan pilgrim)
Pacha, 207
Padmapāṇi, 86, *see also* Avalokiteśvara
Padmasambhava, Guru Rimpoche, 82
Padshah, 207, *see also Bacha/Badshah*
Padshah (King) of Swat,˙214
Pagrai (turban), 131

Pah khardang kawal, 151
Pah khardang swarawal, 151
Pah khrah swarawal, 151, 152
Pahlavas, 54
Paisah, 182
Pakhal, Sultan, 2, 108, 109, 111, 112, 115, *see
    also* Fakhal, Sultan
Pakhli, 110
Pakhtun, 134; chiefs, 136, 137, *see also* Afghan;
    Pathan; Pukhtan; Pukhtun
Pakistan, 21 n., 24, 66, 104; Pakistan's
    Baluchistan, 123
Pakistani archaeologists, 67; armed forces, xix
Palai, 203, 205, 209, 210
Palas, 220
Palau, 134
Pali (language), 5, 69 n., 77
Palosi, 248, *see also* Palusai
Palusai, 248, *see also* Palosi
Pamir, 66, 166, 274; area, 65
Panah, 146
Pandemic, 225 n., *see also* Covid 19
Pani, 281
Pānī-mānī road, 165
Panini, 1
Panipat (battlefield of), 200
Panjab, 175 n.
Panjkhora/Panjkora/Panj-Korah/Panjkurah, 35,
    206; River, 25, 161
Panjtar, 204, 221
Pansaryan, 133
Papin (place), 115
Parachkan, 133, 134, *see also tataran*
Paramabhattaraka, 58
Paramesvara, 58
Paray pah gharah tlal, 147
Parganah, 280
Parsháwar, 110, *see also* Peshawar/Peshawur
Parthians, 59, 60
Parvata, 50
Pashto/Pashtu/Pukhtu/Pushto accounts, 263 n.;
    language, 114, 140, 238, 241, 275; poetry,
    277; populations, 18; version, 102; word,
    153, 207, 277, *see also* Pukhtu language
Pat, 138
Pathan expansion, 129; government, 135;
    invasion, 272; population, 64; successors,
    40; territory, 129; tribes, 39, 64, 107, 136,
    236, *see also* Afghan; Pakhtun; Pukhtan;
    Pukhtun
Pathans, 93 n., 106, 107, 135, 202, 209, 223,
    233, 273, 274, *see also* Afghans; Afghauns;
    Pukhtanah
Patna, 212
Pax kushanica, 56
Peri, 87

Period I and II (of the rock shelter near Ghaligay), 15
Period III (at Ghaligay cave), 14
Period IV of the Barikut Ghwandai (Barikut, Swat), 52
Period V, (cultural, in the Swat Valley), 15
Peristan better than "Greater Kafiristan", 61
Persia, 24, 56, 65, 83, 166
Persian, 16; border, 266 n.; domination, 16; Empire, 17, 33, 44 n.; king/ruler, 24, 112; language, 207; satrapy, 16; side, 44 n.
Persians, 16, 24, 32, 60
Peshawar/Peshawur, 4, 51, 101, 103, 110, 111, 179, 189, 202, 203, 204, 213, 214, 215, 219, 221, 229 n., 237, 238, 241, 249, 253; city, 204; district, 33, 106, 170, 202; plain, 210; plains, 80; proper, 204
Peshawar/Peshawur Valley, 7, 32, 33, 35, 40, 100, 124, 125, 200, 204, 208, 209, 217, 219, 277, 281
Peshawar-Chitral route, 239
Peshmal, 271, see also Pishmal
Peucolaitis, 52
Peukelāoitis, 32
Peukelaotis, 40; Plain, 33
Phase (in archaeology), 20 n.
Philoxenus, 54
Pighur, 138
Pincott, Frederic, 29, 36, 45 n.
Pir, 224 n., 277, 278, 280
Pir, Haji (of Batkhilah), 239
Pir Baba, 174 n., 203, 206, 216, 226 n., 275, see also Ali, Sayyid; Tarmizi, Sayyad Ali
Pir Khushal, 105, see also Ghazi Baba
Pirai/piray/piryan, 91
Piran, 184, 280
Piri, 184
Pir-sar, 9, 34, 37, 38
Pishmal, 271, see also Peshmal
Pithas, 82
Piya (village), 129
Plowden, T.J.C., 203, 204, 230 n.
Plutarch, 25, 29, 32, 47 n.
po sse, Tha mo in tho (king), 65
Political Agency of Dir and Swat, 240
Political Agency of Dir, Swat and Chitral, 240
Political agent, 240, 241, 244, 245, 251, 252, 253, 254, 255, 257, 258, 280
Political intrigue, 257
Political officer, Dir and Swat, 263 n.
Porus, 40
Powell-Price, 33
Prakrit (language), 1, 6
Prashad (blessed confectionary), 93 n.
Prehistoric, xx, 74; graveyards, 15; period, xx, 15; time(s), 76, 21 n.

Preliminary Reports and Studies on the Italian Excavations in Swat (Pakistan), 86, 87
Prikrah kawal, 152
Princely states, 240, 260 n., see also Indian states
Protected area, 280
Protohistoric, xx, 16, 20, 74; cultures, 19; graveyards, 15; times, 15
Protohistorical period, 274; time(s), 19, 274
Proto-Indo-Aryans, 75
Province of Punjab, 260 n.
Province of West Pakistan, 156 n.
Provincial government of Punjab, 240,
Przyluski, (Jean), (a French linguist and scholar of Buddhism), 77, 94 n.
Ptolemy, 51, 52
Pukhtan, 133, 134, 141, see also Afghan; Pathan; Pakhtun; Pukhtun
Pukhtana/Pukhtanah, 135, see also Afghans; Afghauns; Pathans
Pukhtu (code of conduct/code of life), 132, 138, 145, 146, 153, 233, 259, see also Pukhtunwali
Pukhtu (language), 114, 275; proverb(s), 143, 148, 152; saying, 142, 153; word, 207, see also Pashto/Pashtu/Pushto (language)
Pukhtu pinzam mazhab day (saying), 153
Pukhtun, 108, 133, 134, 141, 142, 184, 185, 189, 277; areas, 184, 185, 204; chiefs, 134, 208; code of conduct, 259; code of life, 149, 153, 185; economy and organization, 129; land(s), 260 n., 261 n.; regions, 204; social system, 138, 146; society, 207; trans-Indus territory, 200; tribal areas, 261 n.; tribe(s), 107, 108, 123, 178, 180, 223, 233; Yusufzi, 190, see also Afghan; Pakhtun; Pathan; Pukhtan
Pukhtun khpalah dudai da bal pah kur khwri (saying), 142
Pukhtunkhwa, 32
Pukhtuns, 107, 115, 116, 133, 134, 135, 146, 148, 179, 180, 186, 189, 191, 200, 202, 210, 238, 265 n., 274; Pukhtuns' life, 148
Pukhtunwali, 132, 138, see also Pukhtu (code of conduct/code of life)
Pundit, 93 n.
Punjab, 5, 76, 89, 101, 167, 200, 202; Northern Punjab, 57; rivers of, 40; Upper Punjab, 5; West Punjab, 51
Puran, 129
Pushkalavati/Puskālavatī, 32, 42 n.
Pushto (language), 275, see also Pashto/Pashtu/Pushto; Pukhtu (language)
Puzah prikawal, 152

Q

Qadar (Khan) (of village Dhiri), 240
Qadir, Dr Altaf, 204, 224 n.
Qadriyah *tariqah*, 222
Qalangai/Qulangai, 240
Qambar (village), 133
Qandahar, 106, 107, 114, 123, 213, 222; region, 123, *see also* Kandahar
Qandahari (sent by Raverty to Swat), 144, 186, 213, 222, 223, 272, 275
Qasmi, Muhammad Abdul Ghafoor, 167; Qasmi's book, 167
Qashqari, 274
Qirat (place), 89, 98 n., 102, 103, 118 n.
Qirat Nardin (place), 102
Quduri (book), 183
Queen (of Massaga), 29
Queen Cleophis/Kleophis, 29, *see also* Kleophis
Queen Elizabeth II, 225 n.
Queen Proclamation of 1858, 225 n., 260 n.
Quran, 203, 206, *see also* Holy Quran; Kuran

R

Rabī'-ul-āwwal, 169
Radiocarbon dates, 14, 277
Raghay musafar, dawigir shah da dawtar (proverb), 141
Raghlay musafar, dawigir shway da dawtar (proverb), 141
Rahim, Rahim Shah, 187, 189; Rahim Shah Rahim's rebuke, 197 n.
Rahman, Abdur (Afghan Amir), 98 n., 118 n., 237, 247, 248, 266 n., *see also* Afghan Amir (Abdur Rahman)
Rahman, Dr Abdur, 1, 2, 8, 27, 34, 35, 37, 59, 81, 100, 101, 103, 104
Raja, 59, 84, 101, 103, 280
Raja Arans, 32
Raja Gira (Gira Kafir), 58, 59, 101, 103, 104, 109, 274; Raja Gira's Castle, 59, 105, 106; fortress, 59, 105
Raja Jaipal (Hindu Shahi Raja), 101; reign, 57, *see also* Jaipal; Jayapal; Jayapaladeva; Sri-Jayapaladeva
Rajab, 171
Rājagaṛha, 101, 104, *see also* Rājagṛha
Rajagira, 59, 101
Rājagṛha, 59, 101, 104, *see also* Rājagaṛha
Rām, Śrī, 75, *see also* Chandar Ji; Ram; Rama; Ramachandara
Ram Takht (Ram Throne), 75, 92 n., 93 n.
Rama, 74, 75, 92 n., *see also* Chandar Ji; Ram; Ramachandara; Ram, Sri

Ramachandara, 74, *see also* Chandar Ji; Ram; Ram, Sri; Rama
Ramayan/Ramayana (book), 75; Ramayana's text, 75
Ramazan, 200
Ramsay, A.D.G., 112, 127, 135, 136, 138, 139, 149, 205, 271
Ránazai, 245, *see also* Ranizai; Ranizi
Ranigat, 38
Ranizai, 209, 245, 252, *see also* Ranazai; Ranizi
Ranizi, 210, 239, 240, 245, 246, 252, 259, *see also* Ranazai; Ranizai
Ranizi hills, 222
Rashnel/Rashnil, 274
Raushnāis, 167, *see also* Roshniyas; Rukhanyan; Rushniyas; Tarikis; Tarikyan
Raverty, H.G., 103, 110, 112, 113, 114, 124, 144, 145, 167, 169, 170, 171, 186, 205, 207, 208, 213, 219, 221, 222, 224 n., 229 n., 272, 275
Revolution (of 1857), 217, 218
Richmonds, 207
Riga (village), 263 n.
Rigveda (book), 10 n., 16
Rishi, 84
River Indus, 106, 221, *see also* Indus
River Kabul, 33, *see also* Kabul River
River Nilab, 106
River Swat, 35, *see also* Swat River
Riwaj, 146
Riwaj Namah (customary law book), 159 n., *see also* Mizaj Namah (temperament law book)
Robertson, Surgeon-Major, 236
Roh, 107, *see also* Ruh
Rohitaka (*stupa*), 49, 76, *see also* Lu-hi-ta-kia
Roman age, 87
Roshniyas, 166, *see also* Raushnāis; Rukhanyan; Rushniyas; Tarikis; Tarikyan
Rufus, Q. Curtius, 25, 26, 28, 29, 35, 36, 38, 47 n., *see also* Curtius
Ruh, 107, 116, *see also* Roh
Rū-ï, 87
Rukh, Mirza Shah, 167, 169
Rukhanyan, 166, *see also* Raushnāis; Roshniyas; Rushniyas; Tarikis; Tarikyan
Rupai, 182
Rushniya influence, 167
Rushniyas, 166, 167, *see also* Raushnāis; Roshniyas; Rukhanyan; Tarikis; Tarikyan
Russia, 236
Rustam (place), 45 n.

S

Sacred Building, 88
Sadullah (of village Dhiri), 239

Saeed, Mirza Abu, 123

Safdar (of Nawagai, Bajawar), 239

Sāgala, 54, 69 n.

Śāhi, 57, 88, *see also* Shahi

Sahibzadahs/*Sahibzadgan*, 112, 134

Sahis, 58

Sai of the Upper Ili, 53

Saidan, 207, 280, *see also Saydan*; Sayyads/
Sayyids

Saidgai Lake, 83

Saidu/Saidu Sharif, 15, 128, 222

Saidu Baba, 203, 211, 221, 222, 233, 241, 244,
246, 251, 252, 255, 279, *see also* Akhoond
of Swat; Akhund; Akhund of Swat; Akhund
Sahib; Ghafur, Abdul; Ghafur, Akhund
Abdul

Saidu river/stream/Marghuzar river/stream, 36

Saidu Sharif (Swat) Airport, 176 n.

Saint, 210

Saiva, 280

Saiva school(s) (Indian School of Mystical
Thought), 74, 280

Saka, 60

Saka-Parthian times, 54

Sākala, 50, 69 n.

Śakas, 54, 59

Sakhrah (village), 201

Sakya clan, 277

Sakya Sinha, 89, 102

Sakyamuni, Buddha, 82, 277

Salim Khan (village), 222

Sam (people of), 209

Sam Baizi, 203, 205, 209

Sam Ranizi, 209, 210

Samah, 124, 125, 126, 165, 168, 192, 193; area,
204, 233

Sambat (village), 151

Sambola, 57, *see also* Kampala

Sampradaya, 279

Sandakai (place), 269 n.

Sandakai Baba, 257, 258, 269 n., 270 n., *see
also* Ahmad, Wali; Jan, Ahmad

Sandracottus, 40, *see also* Sisicottus

Sangharamas (monasteries), 78, 79

Sanskrit, 1, 2, 5, 6, 79, 280; literature, 1, 3

Sar khrayal, 152

Sar khrayalay khah dah, mirah sharalay nah
(proverb), 152

Sarai Khola I (Taxila), 14

Sardar, 181

Sarkar, 280; of Swat, 171

Sarkhamaran, 133

Sarma, V.V.S., 86, 89, 90

Sartur sar, 147

Sarubai, 111

Sarvastivada (School of Buddhism), 278, 280

Sarvastivadin(s), 80, 83, 280

Sasanian/Sassanian, 56; Empire, 279;
governors, 56; ruler(s), 56, 279

Sasanians/Sassanians, 56, 80; governors, 56

Sastri, S.M., 34

Śatadru, 50

Satal Gharai (village), 129

Satan, 185

Sathánah, 206, 207, *see also* Sitana; Sithanah

Satrapy (special/of Gadara/Gandhara), 16, 17;
eleventh, 16

Satrapies, 17, 57

Savill, Agnes, 25, 26, 30

Sawad, 3, 165, 166, *see also* Souastene; Suat;
Suwát; Svat; Swat

Sawād-water, 165

Sawan, 75, 93 n.

Sawan Sangran, 75, 92 n.

Sawt, 3

Sayal, Khwajah Muhammad, 185

Saydan, 134, 280, *see also* Saidan; Sayyads/
Sayyids

Sayyad/Sayyid, 203, 205, 206, 208, 280

Sayyads/Sayyids, 129, 134, 206, 207, 216, *see
also* Saidan; *Saydan*

Scythian origin, 54; tribe, 53

Scythians, 50; of the Jaxartes valley, 53

Second Anglo-Afghan war (1878–80), 235

Second Anglo-Sikh war (1848–1849), 202

see, Tha mo in tho po (king), 65

Sepoys, 212, 213, 214, 215, 216, 217, 218, 219,
220, 221, 230 n.

Serai, 133, 159 n., *see also sirai*

Settled districts of the province, 261 n.

Shafi'i (*fiqah*, school of thought), 153

Shah, Abdul Jabbar, 124, 125, 128, 145, 171,
245, 256, 257, 258, *see also* Shah, Sayyad
Abdul Jabbar

Shah, Amir, 253

Shah, Malak Sulaiman, 124, 131, 164

Shah, Mian Rahim (Kaka Khail), 239, 253, 263

Shah, Mir Mubarak Ali, 208, 215, *see also*
Shah, Mubarak; Shah, Sayyad Mubarak

Shah, Mubarak, 208, 215, 216, 217, 218,
219, 220, 221, 230 n., *see also* Shah, Mir
Mubarak Ali; Shah, Sayyad Mubarak

Shah, Sayyad Abdul Jabbar, 107, 112, 115, 123,
124, 153, 154 n., 166, 171, 211, 245, 256,
258, 272, 275, *see also* Shah, Abdul Jabbar

Shah, Sayyad/Sayyid Akbar (of Sithanah),
203, 204, 205, 206, 207, 208, 209, 210,
211, 212, 213, 214, 215, 219, 220, 233,
256; Sayyad Akbar Shah's anti-British/
Briton(s) background, 212; connections,
212; colonialists, 220; death, 205, 208, 215,
218, 229 n.; demise, 214; died, 211, 214,
215, 219, 220, 221; family, 211; follower,
209, 211, 212; installation, 204, 205, 207,

208; installed, 203, 205, 207, 212; policies, 209; rulership and rule, xx, 211; status, 207, 208, *see also* Akbar, Sayed

Shah, Sayyad/Sayyid Mubarak, 206, 208; ruler of Swat, 208, 215, 217, 234, *see also* Shah, Mir Mubarak Ali; Shah, Mubarak

Sháh, Sayyid 'Azim, 206

Sháh, Sayyid Mían, 206

Sháh, Sayyid Rasúl, 207

Shahabuddin, Sultan, 106, *see also* Ghauri, Muhammad

Shahbazgarhi, 50

Shaheen, Muhammad Parwaish, 44 n.

Shahi, 65, *see also* Sahi

Shahis, xx, 67; of Kabul, 6

Shahkot/Shahkut Pass, 62, 125, 238, *see also* Sha-kot Pass

Shahs, 207

Shahzadah (Sultan Ibrahim Jan), 240

Shaikh, 182, 280

Shaikh Mali's *daftar*, 222

Shaikhan (place), 222

Shaikhan, 183, 280

Shaikhi, 184

Shair Khanah, 203, 205, 209

Shakardarah (village), 201

Shakhilan, 133

Sha-kot Pass, 111, *see also* Shahkot/Shahkut Pass

Shalman, 120 n.

Shalman, Fazli Zaman, 264 n., 265 n.

Shalmani, 111, 120 n., 125

Shamhur, Sultan, 109, *see also* Shamur, Sultan

Shamilai Pass, 114, 126

Shamizi, 241, 251, 255, 257, 258

Shamur, Sultan, 109, *see also* Shamhur, Sultan

Shamuzi, 241, 251, 254, 268 n.

Shanglah District, 129

Shanglahpar, 37, 129, 192, 269 n.

Shapur I (Sassanian ruler of Persia), 56

Shara, 153, 223, 280

Shariat, 138, 201, *see also* Islamic Shariat; Mahamadan (Muhammadan) law

Sharif, 222

Sharuni, 145

Sharunkay dalah, 145

Sharuntya, 144, 145

Shia(s), 91, 183

Shikhi, 123, *see also* Khakhi

Shingardar/Shinkardar, 74

Shinr (village), 224 n.

Shiq, 280

Shiqdar, 164, 280

Shir Khanay, 111

Shirbun, 123, *see also* Shirkbun

Shírí, Mulla, 168

Shirkbun, 123, *see also* Shirbun

Shisha, 87

Shishakah, 91

Shiva, 87

Shpankyan/shpunkyan, 132, *see also* bizugar; gadbanah

Shrimad Devi, 278, *see also* Devi Bhagavatam

Sialkot, 54, 69 n.

Sibi, 106, 107, *see also* Siwi

Sibujni, 241, 251, 255, 257, 258

Siculus, Diodoros, 29, 31, 47 n.

Siddha, 278, 280

*Siddha*s, 278

Siddhi, 280

Sikandar, 116

Sikandar, Sultán, 112

Sikh, 92; governor of Kashmír, 236; kingdom, 260 n.

Sikhs, 75, 93 n., 200, 202, 204, 206, 222

Simhapura, 50

Sind/Sindh, 49, 107

Singh, Hari, 204

Singh, Kunar (Kunwar) Mán, 167

Singh, Ranjit, 200, 204

Sin-ho-to, 5

Sino-American-Central Asian scene, 66

Sirai, 132, 133, 134, 135, 159 n., *see also* serai

Siraj, Minhaj, 110

Sisicottus, 40, *see also* Sandracottus

Sistan, 57

Sita, 75

Sitana, 212, 258, *see also* Sathana; Sithanah

Sithan, 134

Sithanah, 203, 204, 206, 207, 208, 233, 258, *see also* Sathánah; Sitana

Siva, 86, 87, 280

Siwarai, 111

Siwi, 106, 107, *see also* Sibi

Siyahpush Kafirs, 103, 272

Skylax (Greek seaman), 16

Smith, V.A., 7, 30, 32, 49, 50, 169

Soastos (river), 1, 6, *see also* River Swat; Souastene; Souastos; Suastus; Subhavastu; Suvastu; Su-po-fa-su-tu; Swat River

Souastene (land), 51, 52, *see also* Sawad; Suat; Suwát; Svât; Swat

Souastene (river), 6, *see also* River Swat; Soastos; Souastos; Suastus; Subhavastu; Suvastu; Su-po-fa-su-tu; Swat River

Souastos (river), 6, *see also* River Swat; Soastos; Souastene; Suastus; Subhavastu; Suvastu; Su-po-fa-su-tu; Swat River

South Asia, 65

South Asian religions, 277

South Asian subcontinent, 4, 49, *see also* Subcontinent/sub-continent

South-western Indian state, 279

Spain, James W., 234
Special Features of the Buddhist Art in the Swāt Valley (article), 60
Spín Káfirís (Badshah of), 207
Sri-Jayapaladeva (Hindu Shahi Raja), 58, *see also* Jaipal; Jayapala; Jayapaladeva; Raja Jaipal
Stacul, Giorgio, 15, 274
Stanadar(s), 125, 134, 135, 139, 147, 157 n., *see also astanadar*
Stanza of the Doctrine, 75
State of Gibar (Gabar), 110
State of Swat, 3, 108, 110, 111
Stein, Aurel, 2, 5, 7, 8, 9, 28, 29, 32, 33, 34, 35, 37, 38, 39, 42 n., 45 n., 52, 53, 54, 59, 64, 78, 84, 86, 93 n., 105, 272, 273
Steuer–Berzirke, 17
Strato I, 53
Stupa, 9, 49, 50, 74, 76, 78, 84, 277
*Stupa*s, 50, 55, 60, 90; of Asoka, 50
Su, 4
Suadat, 3
Suastus (river), 3, 5, 6, *see also* River Swat; Soastos; Souastene; Souastos; Subhavastu; Suvastu; Su-po-fa-su-tu; Swat River
Suat, 4, *see also* Sawad; Souastene; Suwat; Svat; Swat
Suat (river), 5
Subcontinent/sub-continent, 15, 19, 92, 202, 212, 260 n., *see also* South Asian subcontinent
Subhavastu (river), 1, 5, 6, *see also* River Swat; Soastos; Souastene; Souastos; Suastus; Suvastu; Su-po-fa-su-tu; Swat River
Subhavastu (Swat), 5
Suhbat (of Skhakut), 239
Sukercharia Sikh *Misl*, 200
Suljooky, Amir Bin Kuddur (Qadar Saljuqi), 102
Sultan, 103, 107; title of, 108, 116, 124, 125, 126; Sultan's distinction, 115
Sultan, Amir, 258
Sultanate period, 280
Sultan-i-Rome, 113, 193, 194, 204
Sultānī (title), 112
Sultanpur, 189
Sultans of Kabul and Ghazni, 111
Sultans of Panj, 2, 108
Sultan(s) of Swat, 111, 112, 113, 115, 126
Su-po-fa-su-tu (river), 1, 5, 6, 79, *see also* Swat River; Soastos; Souastene; Souastos; Suastus; Subhavastu; Suvastu; Swat River
Sun, 4
Sun god, 4
Sung-yun, 5
Sunni sect, 91
Sunnis, 91, 92

Surya, 87
Sutta Pitaka (*Sūtra-piṭaka*), 281
Suvastu (Swat), 1, 4, 6, 16
Suvastu (river), 3, 5, 6, 10 n., *see also* River Swat; Soastos; Souastene; Souastos; Suastus; Subhavastu; Su-po-fa-su-tu; Swat River
Suvastus, 5
Suwát, 50, 125, 206, 219, *see also* Sawad; Souastene; Suat; Svat; Swat
Suwátí (Swati) Afgháns, 222
Suwátís, 206
Svât, 76, *see also* Sawad; Souastene; Suat; Suwát; Swat
Swabi, 192, 193, 221
Swad (Swat), 166
Swadi, 116
Swarah, 138
Swat, xix, xx, xxi, 1, 2, 3, 4, 5, 6, 7, 8, 12 n., 14, 15, 16, 17, 18, 19, 20, 24, 25, 28, 32, 33, 34, 35, 36, 38, 39, 40, 44 n., 49, 50, 51, 52, 53, 55, 56, 57, 58, 59, 60, 61, 62, 63, 64, 65, 66, 67, 74, 75, 76, 77, 78, 79, 80, 81, 82, 83, 84, 85, 86, 87, 89, 90, 91, 92, 93 n., 95 n., 96 n., 98 n., 100, 101, 102, 103, 104, 105, 106, 107, 108, 109, 110, 111, 112, 113, 114, 115, 116, 117, 118 n., 123, 124, 125, 126, 127, 128, 129, 130, 132, 135, 136, 138, 140, 144, 159 n., 161, 162, 163, 164, 165, 166, 167, 168, 169, 170, 171, 172, 174 n., 178, 180, 181, 183, 184, 185, 186, 187, 188, 190, 191, 192, 193, 197 n., 200, 201, 202, 203, 205, 208, 209, 211, 212, 213, 214, 215, 216, 217, 218, 219, 220, 221, 224, 234, 235, 237, 238, 239, 240, 241, 243, 244, 245, 246, 247, 248, 249, 250, 251, 252, 253, 254, 256, 258, 259, 263 n., 267 n., 269 n., 271, 272, 274, 275, 279, 280, 281; ancient, 20; ancient history, 14, 72 n.; ancient times, 60; clans of, 239, 245; campaign, 165; centre of anti-British sentiments, 202, 212; crisis in, 55, 66; District, 4; early historic period, 20; early sites of, 14; Eastern (part of), 77; first Muslim ruler of, 89, 90; government, 211; history of, 14, 67, 88, 123, 130, 132, 202, 216, 221; inhabitants of, 16, 39, 40, 87, 91, 235; *khan*s, 225 n.; kingdom, 108; location, 15; people of, 16, 38, 40, 62, 114, 136, 167, 172, 180, 181, 182, 183, 185, 186, 187, 188, 191, 192, 201, 202, 203, 206, 209, 210, 211, 212, 215, 216, 217, 218, 219, 221, 233, 235, 238, 242, 243, 244, 245, 246, 247, 248, 249, 250, 252, 255, 256, 257, 258, 259; power game in, 215; prehistoric people/ residents, 17, 74; prehistoric period, 14, 15; prehistory (period), xix, xxi; pre-Muslim, 74; pre-state history, xix; pre-Swat State

period, xix, 156 n.; proper, 38, 110, 129, 247, 271; protohistoric people/residents, 17, 74; protohistoric period, xxi, 14, 20; region, 53, 87; ruler(s) of, 100, 109, 112, 127, 163, 205, 207, 208, 256; rulers in, 211; tour, 54; tribes, 89, 101, 211, 218, 234, 235, 244, 253; Sultan(s) of, 111; Western (part of), 77; Yusufzi, 164, 165, 166, 171, 172, 180, 181, 188, 190, 191, 192, 194, 200, 203, 274; Yusufzais, 194, 220, 221, 234; Lower Swat, 32, 34, 51, 90, 100, 101, 126, 127, 128, 163, 201, 237, 239, 251, 252, 259, 271; Middle Swat, 51, 52, 62; Upper Swat/Suwat, 5, 27, 57, 58, 62, 103, 104, 105, 127, 128, 138, 145, 163, 164, 201, 221, 222, 225 n., 241, 242, 244, 245, 246, 249, 251, 252, 253, 254, 255, 257, 258, 268 n., 271, 273; *jargay*, 245, 251, 253, *see also* Sawad; Souastene; Suat; Svat; Suwát

Swat Kohistan, 4, 254, 271, *see also* Swat Kuhistan

Swat Kuhistan, xx, 53, 129, 271, 272, *see also* Swat Kohistan

Swat Moollahs (*mula*s), 275

Swat Museum, 78; inauguration, 78; staff, 78

Swat Namah (book), 180, 188

Swat River, 1, 3, 4, 5, 6, 10 n., 36, 52, 62, 77, 78, 105, 112, 113, 129, 131, 162, 176 n., 180, 224 n., 238, 239, 240, 241, 246, 251, 252, 253, 254, 268 n., *see also* River Swat; Soastos; Souastene; Souastos; Suastus; Subhavastu; Suvastu; Su-po-fa-su-tu

Swat State, xix, xx, 3, 5, 75, 93 n., 110, 136, 152, 153, 156 n., 158 n., 208, 221, 233, 245, 280; area, 4; court writers, 211, 223; emergence of, 153, 156 n., 269 n.; era, 150, 259, 270 n.; merger, 156 n., 160 n.; period, 144, 158 n.; pre-Swat State period, 156 n.; record, 150; ruler(s), 34, 152, 156 n., 159 n., 211, 245, 269 n.; time, 150, 156 n.

Swat State (1915—1969): From Genesis to Merger; An Analysis of Political, Administrative, Socio-Political, and Economic Developments (book), 270 n.

Swat Valley, xix, xx, 3, 4, 5, 6, 7, 14, 15, 17, 19, 24, 32, 35, 37, 40, 45 n., 49, 51, 52, 53, 54, 56, 58, 60, 77, 85, 87, 91, 93 n., 101, 106, 108, 109, 110, 112, 113, 116, 117, 125, 126, 127, 128, 129, 153, 158 n., 163, 167, 170, 172, 182, 201, 209, 239, 242, 247, 264 n., 268 n., 271, 273, 274, 275

Swati, 106, 107; Dihgans; 111; forces, 44 n.; monks, 81; nation, 107; Prince, 56; rulers, 111, 112, 164; subjects, 112; Sultans 115; territory/territories, 127, 253, 254, 256, 257; tribe, 116; word, 116

Swati, Dr Muhammad Farooq, 4, 8, 10 n., 17, 58, 60, 77, 85

Swati, Saranzeb, 118 n.

Swati Afghans, 107, 222, *see also* Swati Pathans; Swati Pukhtanah; Swati Pukhtuns

Swati Pathans, 106, 107, *see also* Swati Afghans; Swati Pukhtanah; Swati Pukhtuns

Swati Pukhtanah, 107, 108, *see also* Swati Afghans; Swati Pathans; Swati Pukhtuns

Swati Pukhtuns, 107, 108, 116, 124, 128, *see also* Swati Afghans; Swati Pathans; Swati Pukhtanah

Swatis, 106, 107, 108, 112, 113, 114, 115, 116, 125, 126, 127, 202, 206, 218, 243, 250, 271; ancient, 74

Sweta, 3

Swigalai (place), 114; Pass, 114, 126

Syad king, 206

Syali, 149

Syali da Swat siri dah (proverb), 149

Syali da syal khayi (saying), 149

Syali kawal, 149

Syriac, 4

Syrian (empire), 49

T

Tabaqat-i Nasari (book), 110, 111

Taddei, Maurizio, 87

Tahsil, 280

Tahsildar, 210, 280

Tair, Muhammad Nawaz, 128

Tajak Swati wa Mumlikat-i Gabar Tarikh kay Aayinah mayn (book), 109, 113

Tajik, 116; stock, 112; Swati(s), 116; Swati rulers, 109

Tajiks, 116

Tajkhilah, 112

Takhta'h-band, 206

Tal (block), 131, 134, 135, 137, 148, *see also* Cundy; Kandi; Tul

Talash Valley, 34

T'a lo (most probably Butkara), 79, *see also* Butkara I/Butkara-I; T'o-lo

Talunah, 135, 148, *see also* Cundies; Kandis

Tangah, 133

Tangah-sari, 133

Tangi, 210

Tanra, 109, 126, 200, 201, 239, 248; the battle of, 126, *see also* Thana; Thanra

Tantric Buddhism, 82, 281; books, 82; centres, 82; commentaries, 82, 280; doctrines, 82; places, 82; tradition, 281

Tantrism, 82

Tapah (genre of Pashto verse), 238, 280

Tapah (segment), 131, 135, 280

Tapay (segments), 135

Tarbur, 148

Tarbur kah di khar shi hum latai pray mah arawah artaw bah di kri (proverb), 149

Tarburwali, 148, 149

Tarikh Farishtah (book), 102

Tarikh Khan Jahani wa Makhzan-i Afghani (book), 106, 107, 116

Tarikh-i Riyasat-i Swat wa Sawanih-i Hayat Baniy-i Riyasat-i Swat Hazrat Miangul Gul Shahzadah Abdul Wadud Khan Badshah Sahib (book), 102

Tarikis, 166, 167, *see also* Raushnāis; Roshniyas; Rukhanyan; Rushniyas; Tarikyan

Tarikyan, 166, *see also* Raushnāis; Roshniyas; Rukhanyan; Rushniyas; Tarikis

Tarmizi, Sayyad Ali, 174 n., 203, 206, *see also* Ali, Sayyid; Pir Baba

Tarn, W.W., 51, 52

Tartars, 109, *see also* Tatars

Tataran, 133, *see also* Parachkan

Tatars, 110, *see also* Tartars

Tathagata, 76, *see also* Buddha; Buddha, Gautama; Foe

Tawanawal, 153

Tawarikh Hafiz Rahmat Khani (book), 90, 108, 109, 112, 113, 114, 124, 125, 126, 127, 128, 135, 138, 158 n., 161, 163, 164

Taxila, 14, 50, 54, 69 n., 72 n.

Tayar-khwarah, 133

Tazkiratul Abrar-i wal Ashrar (book), 124, 164, 166, 174 n.

Thana, 109, 126, 248, *see also* Tanra; Thanra

Thaneysur/Thanisar, 212

Thanra, 201, *see also* Thana; Tanra

The History of Swat (book), 167

The Indo-Greeks (book), 7

The North-West Frontier (Khyber Pakhtunkhwa): Essays on History (book), 138

The Problem of Aornos, 38

The Story of the Malakand Field Force: An Episode of Frontier War (book), 265 n.

The Story of Swat as told by the Founder Miangul Abdul Wadud Badshah Sahib to Muhammad Asif Khan (book) 174, n.

Theodorus (the Meridarch), 52

Thomson, H.C., 239

Thsang, Hwen, 5, *see also* Chwang, Yuan; Hiouan thsang; Hsüan-tsang; Tsang, Hsüan; Tsiang, Hiuen; Xuanzang; Zang, Xuan

Tibet, 16, 61, 82, 83

Tibetan, 82; Hilo, 75; king, 83; pilgrim(s), 62, 90, 108; power, 100; sources, 57; traditions, 82

Tibetans, 65, 66, 82, 100

Tigah, 138

Tilyan, 133

Timur, Amir, 115

Timurids in Herat, 130

Tindo Dag (village), 88

Tindo Dag-Manyar, 88

Tirah, 171; battle of, 179

Tirat (village), 77

Tod, 54

Todar Mal, Raja, 169

T'o-lo, 9, *see also* Butkara I/Butkara-I; T'a lo

Torú Āl, 272, *see also* Torw Āl; Torwal; Turwal

Torw Āl, 272, *see also* Torú Āl; Torwal; Turwal

Torwal, 272, 273, *see also* Torú Āl; Torw Āl; Turwal

Torwali (tract), 271, 273, *see also* Turwali tract

Torwalik, 273, *see also* Turwali

Tōrwālīs, 273, *see also* Tor-wáls; Turwalis

Tor-wáls, 272, *see also* Tōrwālīs; Turwalis

Trabgani, 149

Tranjâi, 76, *see also* trêvanjâha (Sindhi)

Treasurer and Prime Minister, 203, 204

Trêvanjâha (Sindhi), 76, *see also* Tranjâi

Tribal area(s), 260 n., 261 n., 280, 281; banner, 279; belt, 241; chiefs, 246; force, 279; interest, 218; leaders, 252; loyalty, 218; Muslims, 216; risings, 244; rule, 171; settlements, 33; tide, 167; units, 60; welter, xix, 221, 233, 239

Tribulato, Olga, 40

Tripitaka (*Tri-piṭaka*), 281

Trotter, Lionel J., 214

Tsang, Hsüan, 8, 19, *see also* Chwang, Yuan; Hiouan thsang; Hsüan-tsang; Thsang, Hwen; Tsiang, Hiuen; Xuanzang; Zang, Xuan

Tsiang, Hiuen, 1, 4, 5, 6, 7, 11 n., 49, 50, 63, 74, 76, 79, 80, 81, 83, 84, *see also* Chwang, Yuan; Hiouan thsang; Hsüan-tsang; Thsang, Hwen; Tsang, Hsüan; Xuanzang; Zang, Xuan

Tucci, Giuseppe, 2, 6, 7, 8, 9, 17, 18, 19, 24, 25, 26, 29, 32, 35, 36, 37, 50, 55, 56, 57, 60, 62, 66, 74, 75, 76, 77, 80, 81, 83, 84, 85, 86, 89, 90, 91, 93 n., 101

Tui, 138

Tul, 134, *see also* Cundy; Kandi; *tal*

Tur, 138

Turah (a copper coin), 180; 280

Turdhair, 221

Turk (inhabitants), 115

Turk Sahis, 81

Turki, 151

Turki horse, 175 n.

Turki Śāhi/Turki Shahi, 57, 88; kingdom of Kabul, 57; period, xx, 87

Turki Sahis/Turki Shahis, 57, 81, 100

Turkistan, 102

Turwal, 272, 273, *see also* Torú Āl; Torw Āl; Torwal

Turwali, 271, 272, 273; area, 273, 274; tract, 129, 271, 272, *see also* Turwali tract; Torwalik

Turwalis, 271, 272, 273, 275, *see also* Tor-wáls; Tŏrwālīs

Tutai, 111

Tuzuk/Tuzuk-i Baburi (book), 163, 165

Tuzuk-i Jahangiri (book), 103, *see also Iqbal Namah-i Jahangiri* (book); *Jahangir Namah* (book)

U

Ubahwari, 133

Uch, 201

U-chang, 1, 5, *see also* Ou chang/Ou chang na/Ou chha/Ou chhang; Ou san chhang; U-chang-na; Woo-chang; Wu ch'a; Wuchung

U-chang-na, 1, 5, *see also* Ou chang/Ou chang na/Ou chha/Ou chhang; Ou san chhang; U-chang; Woo-chang; Wu ch'a; Wuchung

Udabhāṇḍapura, 103, *see also* Hund

Uḍḍi, 2, *see also* Uḍe; *Uḍe-*; Uḍi; *Uḍi-*; Udri; Urdi

Uddiyan (place or land of), 10 n.

Uddiyana, xx, 1, 2, 4, 5, 6, 7, 8, 10 n., 12 n., 17, 18, 49, 50, 51, 55, 59, 64, 65, 66, 76, 77, 79, 80, 82, 87, 90; *see also* Oddiyana/Odiyana; Oudyana; Uḍiyana; Udyana

Uḍḍiyāna-Swāt, 57

Uddiyanapitha/Uddiyana-pitha, 82, 280

Uddiyanian (genius), 79

Uḍe/Udi/Udri/Urḍi (tribe), 2

Uḍe, 2, *see also* Uḍḍi; *Uḍe-*; Uḍi; *Uḍi-*; Udri; Urdi

Uḍe-, 2, *see also* Uḍḍi; Uḍe; Uḍi; *Uḍi-*; Udri; Urdi

Udegram, 2, 8, 18, 34, 103, *see also* Odigram; Udigram

Uḍi, 2, 8, 18, *see also* Uḍḍi; Uḍe; *Uḍe-*; *Uḍi-*; Udri; Urdi

Uḍi-, 2, *see also* Uḍḍi; Uḍe; *Uḍe-*; Uḍi; Udri; Urdi

Uḍigrām, 2, 8, 15, 20, 32, 34, 36, 58, 59, 61, 90, 101, 102, 104, 105, 109, 110, 201, 274, *see also* Odigram; Udegram

Udis, 2, *see also* Oḍis

Uḍiyana, 2, 8, *see also* Oḍḍiyāna/Odiyana; Oudyana; Uddiyana; Udyana

Udri, 2, 18, *see also* Uḍḍi; Uḍe; *Uḍe-*; Uḍi; *Uḍi-*; Urdi

Udyana, 1, 2, 5, 6, 7, 9, 49, 50, 51, 54, 59, 64, 79, 83, 84, 85, *see also* Oddiyana/Odiyana; Oudyana; Uddiyana; Uḍiyana

Ujjana, 1, 5, 6

Ulama, 183, 277

Ulas, 140, *see also* Oolooss

Ulasay, 140, *see also* Ooloosses; *ulasunah*

Ulasunah, 140, *see also* Ooloosses; *ulasay*

Umayyad Khilafat, 100

Una or Unra, 37

Una-sar, 37

Unani or Eastern medicine, 278

Upper Alayi, 127, *see also* Alayi Bala; Aluhiyah Bala

Urakzi, 179, 189, *see also* Orakzi

Urdi, 2, 8, 18, *see also* Uḍḍi; Uḍe; *Uḍe-*; Uḍi; *Uḍi-*; Udri

Urdu, 126, 207

Urgyan, 82

Ushar/Ushr, 205, 206, 208, 216, 217, 254, 255, 258, 280, 281

Ushoram/Ushuran, 274

Usman (RA), 100

Utman Khails (Khels), 243

Utman Khel country, 242

Utmanzi (battle of), 201

Utror/Utrur, 273, 274

Uttarāpatha division, 50

Uttarasena (King of Swat), 84, *see also* Uttarasena-raja

Uttarasena-raja, 84, *see also* Uttarasena (King of Swat)

Uwais, 109, 111, 124, 126, 162, *see also* Awais, Sultan; Wais, Sl. (Sultan)

Uzbeg territory, 167

Uzbekistan (State of), 161

V

Vajirasthana, 55

Vajra, 281

Vajrapāṇi, 77, 82, 281

Vajrayāna, 81, 82, 87, 281; Buddhism, 279; schools, 81

Vajrayanic presence, 82; themes, 81

Valley Nihak or Niyag, 113, *see also* Darah Nihak or Nihag or Niyak; Dara'h of Nihák or Niáka'h or Ni'ák; Nihag or Nihak or Niyak Darah; Nihag or Nihak or Niyak Valley; Nihak (Valley); Niyag (Valley)

Valmiki's *Ramayana* (book), 75, *see also* Walmiki's *Ramayan* (book)

Vanavasa, 74, *see also Ban-bas*

Varamudrā, 86

Vedas (books), 1

Verma, K.M., 7

Viceroy, 261 n., 262 n.
Victoria Cross, 243, 264 n., 265 n.
Vinaya(s), 77, 80, 277, 281
Vinaya-pitaka, 281
Visnu/Vishnu, 75, 87, 277, 278
Viyakamitra, 51

W

Waddell, Laurence A., 67 n.
Wadud, Miangul Abdul (ruler of Swat State), 75, 136, 153, 172, 245, 255, 257, 258, 269 n., *see also* Bacha Sahib; Gulshazada
Wais, Sl. (Sultan), 111, 124, 126, 162, 165 *see also* Awais, Sultan; Uwais
Waish, 128, 134, 137, 141, 153, 158 n., 196 n.; system, 138, 139, 181, 184; system of land tenure, 138, *see also* wesh
Wakhan, 116, 266 n.
Walayat-i Swat Bajawar, 171
Wali (King) of Swat, 213
Wali Sahib (Miangul Jahanzeb, ruler of Swat State), 159 n.
Wali's (Swat State's ruler), 34
Walmiki's *Ramayan* (book), 75, *see also* Valmiki's *Ramayana* (book)
War of Independence 1857, xx, 212, 216, 220, 244
Waziri country, 267 n.
Waziris, 243
Waziristan, 58, 64, 281
Wesh, 128, 138, 139, 158 n., *see also* waish
West, 15, 24, 62
White Huns, 56, 65, 80, 279, *see also* Alchon Huns; Ephtalites/Ephthalites; Hūṇa
Wilford's Surveyor, 7
Woo-chang, 1, 5, *see also* Ou chang/Ou chang na/Ou chha/Ou chhang; Ou san chhang; U-chang; U-chang-na; Wu ch'a; Wuchung
Woodcock, George, 24, 25
Wrak, 141
Wright, Philip, 20 n.
Wu ch'a, 2, *see also* Ou chang/Ou chang na/Ou chha/Ou chhang; Ou san chhang; U-chang; U-chang-na; Woo-chang; Wuchung
Wuchung, 5, *see also* Ou chang/Ou chang na/Ou chha/Ou chhang; Ou san chhang; U-chang; U-chang-na; Woo-chang; Wu ch'a; Wuchung
Wylly, H.C., 209, 220, 221, 239, 244

X

Xerxes, 16
Xerxes II, 17

Xian, Fa, 5, 62, *see also* Fa-Hein; Fa hian; Fa-hian; Fa-Hian; Fa Hiun; Faxian
Xuanzang, 1, 5, 6, 7, 11 n., 49, 50, 63, 74, 76, 79, 80, 81, 82, 83, 84, *see also* Chwang, Yuan; Hiouan thsang; Hsüan-tsang; Thsang, Hwen; Tsiang, Hiuen; Tsang, Hsüan; Zang, Xuan

Y

Yadah, 150
Yadah kawal, 150
Yadri, 114
Yaghi, 281
Yaghistan, 132, 281, *see also* Yagistan
Yagistan, 132, *see also* Yaghistan
Yahya (chief of the Dalazak tribe), 106
Yaksha(s), 76, 281
Yakshi, 281, *see also* Yakshini
Yakshini, 281, *see also* Yakshi
Yaqubi, Dr Himayatullah, 192, *see also* Himayatullah, Dr
Yasin (place), 235, 236, 271
Yasin (poet), 239, 263 n.
Yogis' Peak, 75, *see also* Jugyanu Sar
Yü ti yen, 2
Yun, Soung, 1, *see also* Yun, Sung
Yun, Sung, 63, 66, 79, 80, 81, *see also* Yun, Soung
Yunus, Mohammad, 49
Yusafzai territory, 127
Yusafzi, 123, *see also* Eusofzyes; Isafzi; Yusufzai; Yusufzais; Yūsuf-zāī; Yusufzi; Yusufzis
Yusufi, Allah Bakhsh, 261 n.
Yusufzai (female), 123
Yusufzai (Yusufzi), 123, 194; Afghans, 164, 194; area of Swat, 165; clans, 273; country, 51; land 127; of the Samah area, 193, 194; Pathans, 271; territory, 127, 191; tribe, 193, *see also* Eusofzyes; Isafzi; Yusafzi; Yūsuf-zāī; Yusufzais; Yusufzi; Yusufzis
Yusufzai lady (sister of Malak Ahmad and wife of Sultan Awais), 125
Yusufzai-Swati boundary, 127
Yūsuf-zāī, 165; Afghāns, 164; horde, 163; *sangur*, 165, *see also* Eusofzyes; Isafzi; Yusafzi; Yusufzai; Yusufzais; Yusufzi; Yusufzis
Yusufzais, 112, 129, 130, 166, 167, 170, 172, 191, 192, 193, 194, 222, *see also* Eusofzyes; Isafzi; Yusafzi; Yusufzai; Yūsuf-zāī; Yusufzi; Yusufzis
Yusufzais's, 91; conquest, 108
Yusufzay (male), 123

Yusufzi, xix, xx, 90, 108, 109, 111, 112, 114, 115, 116, 123, 124, 125, 126, 127, 128, 129, 130, 131, 135, 136, 138, 141, 158 n., 161, 162, 163, 164, 165, 166, 167, 170, 178, 179, 180, 181, 182, 183, 187, 188, 189, 190, 191, 192, 193, 194, 196 n., 199 n., 211, 234, 238, 259, 273, 274, 275, 277, 278; Afghan(s), xix, 202, 280; chief(s), 123, 124, 125, 161, 164; houses, 162; in general, 194; language, 114; leading *malaks*/men, 124, 127; of Swat, xx, 169, 172, 274; occupation, xix, xxi, 90, 108, 111, 127, 128, 130; occupation of Swat, xx, 91, 127, 128; Pukhtuns, 280; *malakan*, 164; Samah, 167; Yusufzi's covetous eyes on Swat, 125; delegation, 127, 164; enemy, 163; gathering, 161; migration, 123; social system and mode of ruling, xx, 123, 130; support to Ulugh Beg, 123; trading excursions, 124, *see also* Eusofzyes; Isafzi; Yusafzi; Yusufzai; Yūsuf-zāī; Yusufzais; Yusufzis

Yusufzi-Mandanr, 166, 178, 179, 193, 195 n.

Yusufzis, 169, 170, 200, 207, *see also* Eusofzyes; Isafzi; Yusafzi; Yusufzai; Yūsuf-zāī; Yusufzais; Yusufzi

Z

Zaibsar, Taj Muhammad Khan, 106, 107, 116, 124

Zakat, 205, 208

Zalamkut bilingual inscription, 100, 101, 103

Zang, Xuan, 1, 49, 74, *see also* Chwang, Yuan; Hiouan thsang; Hsüan-tsang; Thsang, Hwen; Tsiang, Hiuen; Tsang, Hsüan; Xuanzang

Zargaran, 133

Zeus, 26

Zoilus I (king of the Swat Valley), 51; sub-king of Arachosia, 53; sub-king of the Swat valley, 53

Zoroastrian(s), 116

Zulqarnain, Sikandar, 116, *see also* Azam, Kurush; Cyrus the Great; Kabir, Kurush; Zulqarnain, Sultan

Zulqarnain, Sultan, 116, *see also* Azam, Kurush; Cyrus the Great; Kabir, Kurush; Zulqarnain, Sikandar

Zurmandai, 203, 205, 209

Zuzkhanah, 221